CLASSICS OF ANALYTIC PHILOSOPHY

ISBN 0-87220-101-5 paperback
0-87220-102-3 cloth
(formerly 07-0-01580-5)

CLASSICS OF ANALYTIC PHILOSOPHY

Edited by ROBERT R. AMMERMAN
Emeritus Professor
University of Wisconsin

Hackett Publishing Company, Inc.

Indianapolis / Cambridge

Cover design by Dan Kirklin

For further information, please contact

Hackett Publishing Company, Inc.
P.O. Box 44937
Indianapolis, Indiana 46244-0937

Library of Congress Cataloging in Publication Data

Classics of analytic philosophy / edited by Robert R. Ammerman.
      p.   cm.
  Reprint. Originally published: New York: McGraw-Hill, 1965.
  Includes bibliographical references and index.
  ISBN 0-87220-102-3   ISBN 0-87220-101-5 (pbk.)
  1. Analysis (Philosophy) I. Ammerman, Robert R.
B808.5.A4 1990
146'.4—dc20   90-38344
                                       CIP

TO MY MOTHER

PREFACE

The writings collected together in this book are intended to be representative of the main stream of analytic philosophy since 1900. An attempt has been made to include as many "classics" of analytic philosophy as would lend themselves to inclusion in an anthology of this size. The editor is nevertheless aware that in a subject as recent and controversial as contemporary analytic philosophy, there can be honest disagreement regarding what is to count as a classic. This much at least can be said for the selections contained herein: They are all well known to persons familiar with contemporary philosophy, and most of them have exerted influence of one sort or another upon philosophers writing in the analytic tradition today. There are no doubt many other equally important selections by other philosophers which could have been included in this collection. Their exclusion is not to be interpreted as any commentary on their worth or influence, but rather as a fact necessitated by spatial limitations.

There is one prominent omission which must be explained. Despite the unrivaled importance of Ludwig Wittgenstein in the history of analytic thought, he is not represented by any of his own writings in this collection. Repeated appeals were made to the executors of his literary estate, but permission could not be secured to reproduce any of his writings. The editor deeply regrets the omission of Wittgenstein's work from this volume, especially because it is most important that the writings of the most stimulating philosopher of our age should have the widest possible dissemination. Fortunately, permission was granted from other sources to include Moore's excellent set of notes on Wittgenstein's 1930–1933 lectures (selection 11). Although these are not an adequate substitute for Wittgenstein's own writings, they will perhaps allow the reader to gain some familiarity with Wittgenstein's distinctive approach to philosophy.

The selections included in this book have been restricted primarily to important works in the philosophy of language, the philosophy of mind, and metaphysics. Because of the nature of the volume, it was not deemed advisable to attempt to include selections from other important areas of analytic thought, e.g., ethics or the problems of perception. References to some important works of analytic philosophy in other areas are to be found in the Bibliography.

Many of the selections have been chosen to exemplify differing approaches to important problems of analytic philosophy. The problems concerning the nature of mind, for example, are discussed, directly or indirectly, by Russell (selection 3), Moore (4), Broad (6), Ryle (13), Wittgenstein's lectures (11), and Austin (17). Because these authors approach the same family of questions in different ways, the reader can gain some appreciation of the changing techniques of analytic philosophy. Other topics dealt with in more than one selection are the nature of philosophy, Russell (2), Ayer (7), Hempel (10), Wittgenstein's lectures (11), Wisdom (12), and Austin (18), and the problem of meaning, Ayer (7), Carnap (8), Hempel (10), and Wittgenstein's lectures (11). The reader will also find other problems discussed by several different philosophers.

It should also be noted that several of the selections are "paired" in the sense that one of them was written as a direct reply to another. Strawson's "On Referring" (14) is an obvious example, directed as it was against Russell's "Theory of Descriptions" (1). Russell's recent reply to Strawson is included (15) to increase the richness of the encounter. In a similar manner, Strawson and Grice wrote "In Defence of a Dogma" (16) to reply to Quine's "Two Dogmas of Empiricism" (9). Again, Hempel's discussion of the empiricist criterion (10) can be read quite profitably as a continuation of Ayer's discussion (7) of the verifiability criterion.

Each selection is preceded by a brief introduction, intended to acquaint the reader with some of the background of the selection and give some guidance for reading it with understanding. The introductions will be most meaningful if they are read after having read the history of analytic philosophy which opens the volume.

Brief biographies of the authors are included at the end of the book.

It is the belief of the editor that the selections included in this volume are both sufficiently varied and sufficiently related to allow for a variety of classroom uses.

The editor wishes to thank Professors Herbert Feigl and Michael Scriven for their assistance in reviewing an early outline of the book. A special debt of gratitude is due to Professor Kai Neilson, whose thorough and penetrating criticisms undoubtedly have made the book better than it would otherwise have been. Professor Marcus G. Singer also was greatly helpful in eliminating error. The idea for such a book as this was originally suggested by Professor William H. Hay, to whom the editor is greatly indebted.

Permission to reprint their work was obtained from all living authors represented herein. The editor wishes to thank them for their kindness in granting such permission. He wishes to thank especially Lord Russell and Professor John Wisdom for their thoughtfulness in taking the time to suggest ways in which the book could be improved. Mrs. Dorothy Moore also was kind enough to help the editor secure permission for the use of some of her late husband's writings.

Robert R. Ammerman

CONTENTS

part iii LINGUISTIC ANALYSIS

A SHORT HISTORY

OF ANALYTIC PHILOSOPHY

The twentieth century has been a time of rapid change. Science has progressed at a rate barely conceivable to most people prior to our century; new nations have arisen, and the map of the world has had to be redrawn. Every decade brings new and important changes in technology, art, and even manners and morals. Philosophy has not been an exception to this general characteristic of our age. Around the turn of the century a revolution began in philosophy which is not yet over. Like all revolutions, it has its roots deep in the past. Nevertheless, it is fair to say that within our century a fundamental shift in philosophical perspective has occurred. Standing as close to these changes as we do, it is often difficult to see clearly what has happened. Yet, some understanding of the development and growth of analytic thought is essential if one is to understand the state of philosophy today. This introduction, brief and incomplete as it must be, is intended to give the reader some grasp of the main directions of philosophic thought in England and America since 1900. The interested reader will find fuller accounts of the history of analysis in any of the several books cited in the bibliography.

It is not uncommon to characterize our time as the "Age of Analysis" in philosophy. This is not to say that analytic philosophy began with the early writings of Bertrand Russell or the beginnings of this century. On the contrary, few great philosophers from Plato to the present day have failed to employ analytic tools as a philosophic technique at least some of the time in their writings. It is only in the present century, however, that analytic techniques have come to dominate the thinking of a majority of English-speaking philosophers and are considered by them to be the most fruitful approach to philosophical questions.

This is not to say, however, that all contemporary philosophers agree about the value of analysis for resolving philosophical problems. It is primarily in England (and the Commonwealth), America, and Scandinavia that analysis is dominant. It has few adherents in France, Germany, Russia, or the Far East, although interest in it has grown rapidly even there in recent years. Neo-

Thomism, Existentialism, Marxism, and a host of other isms are the predominant philosophies in many parts of the world; even among English-speaking philosophers there are many who espouse an approach to philosophizing quite different from the analytic approaches.

Indeed, it is misleading to speak of "analytic philosophy" as if it were homogeneous and monolithic. There is no single philosophy of analysis. There is no analytic "party line," no heresies, no pontifical authorities. The word "analysis" is used here as a way of grouping together a number of heterogeneous philosophers who share certain interests and procedures. It is this common core of agreement which must be isolated before we proceed.

We must first try to clarify what analysis is in general; this is not an easy thing to do. The word "analysis" when used in philosophy bears obvious affinities to the word's use in a science such as chemistry. To analyze, we may say roughly, is to take apart in order to gain a better understanding of what is being analyzed. The chemist is concerned with the analysis of complex physical substances into their constituent parts. The philosopher, on the other hand, is interested in analyzing linguistic or conceptual units. He is concerned, in general, with coming to understand the structure of language by a careful study of its elements and their interrelations.

We will use the word "analysis" (or "analytic philosophy"), then, to refer to any philosophy which places its greatest emphasis upon the study of language and its complexities. We will contrast the *analytic* with the *speculative* philosopher, who, if he studies language at all, does so only in order to facilitate the achievement of his main goal: speculation about the metaphysical foundations of the universe. Of course, there are philosophers who have been both analytic and speculative in their writings, but this fact does not destroy the value of the broad distinction.

Philosophical analysis is essentially the study of language, but it must not be confused with other important studies of language. Linguists, philologists, grammarians, lexicographers, etc., are also involved in a study of language. Their interest, however, is primarily in empirical investigation. They are interested in discovering facts about how our language is used; what meanings words have; how languages begin, change, and die, etc. These are *scientific* questions about language which can only be answered through use of the scientific method. The analytic philosopher studies language not in order to formulate scientific hypotheses about it, but rather because he believes that such a study is an invaluable tool to help him achieve his primary goal of settling philosophical questions.

Although all analytic philosophers would agree that the study of language is of the greatest importance, there is no general agreement about *which* language can most fruitfully be studied by the philosopher. Indeed, it is just at this point that a fundamental cleavage has occurred between the various philosophers who practice analysis. Some of them have concluded that philosophical analysis ought to consist primarily in the construction of new, artificial language systems (sometimes called calculi, because of their affinity to mathematical systems). The rules of these artificially constructed languages are intended to be clearer, more complete, and more precise than the rules that govern our use of language in ordinary discourse. Just as science had to create its own technical vocabulary and introduce concepts (e.g., force, mass, atom) that are more precise than those supplied by common sense, so also, these philosophers argue, philosophy must develop its own vocabulary and set of concepts in order to resolve its problems.

Other analysts have disagreed with this argument. They contend that such artificial languages are of little help in resolving philosophical problems. It is their view that philosophical problems can best be approached by a careful analysis of the ordinary, natural language we all use to communicate with each other. For this reason, these philosophers are sometimes (but not accurately) referred to as "ordinary language" philosophers. A more accurate way of distinguishing these two main "schools" of analysis is to refer to the proponents of artificial language analysis as Logical Positivists and the philosophers interested in analyzing ordinary language as Linguistic Analysts. There are many analysts who do not fit neatly into either of these categories, but the majority of analytic philosophers can, without too much injustice, be put in one category or another. The important differences between Logical Positivism and Linguistic Analysis will perhaps become clearer if we now discuss the historical development of analysis.

Most contemporary Anglo-American philosophers are quick to acknowledge a permanent debt to the two early pioneers of contemporary analysis: Bertrand Russell and G. E. Moore. Although there were several outstanding philosophers in the nineteenth century whose writings foreshadowed analysis as we know it, it was Russell and Moore primarily, around the turn of the century, who challenged decisively the predominant philosophical views of the period and took the first giant steps toward a new conception of philosophy.

When Russell and Moore were fellow students at Cambridge University in the 1890s, the predominant philosophic tradition in England (and America) was Neo-Hegelianism. With few exceptions, the men they studied under were in the tradition of G. F. Hegel (1770–1831), espousing a form of Idealism derived from Hegel's famous philosophical system. Neo-Hegelian Idealism is speculative metaphysics in the grand style. It attempted to present a complete world-view which would describe the nature of Reality, insofar as it can be known by man, and the ultimate relation of Man and his Values to that Reality. Idealism, as it flourished in the late nineteenth century, was the culmination of the centuries of metaphysical thought which began so long ago with the speculations of Thales (sixth century B.C.).

The most brilliant and famous of the British Idealists of that time was F. H. Bradley (1846–1924), whom both Moore and Russell studied as students and by whom they were initially much influenced. Their early commitment to Idealism did not last long, however, for they soon became disillusioned with the Neo-Hegelian approach to philosophical questions and began to raise questions about the basic tenets of idealistic thought which ultimately led them to reject it completely.

This is not to say, however, that Moore and Russell were in complete agreement about what was wrong with Idealism or how best to expose the error contained in it. On the contrary, their differing interests soon led them in diverging directions, although they remained united always in their rejection of Neo-Hegelianism.

Moore expressed his dissatisfaction with Idealism in a series of brilliant papers which attacked that view from a uniquely original standpoint. Idealism, of course, had had many critics prior to Russell and Moore, but no one before Moore had concentrated his critical attack with such intensity upon the *meanings* of the metaphysical propositions advanced by the Idealists. Moore refused even to consider the truth or falsity of those propositions until he had first satisfied himself that he understood exactly what they asserted. "In all . . . philosophical studies," he wrote, "the difficulties and disagreements, of which its history is full, are mainly due to a very simple cause: namely to the attempt to answer questions, without first discovering precisely what question it is which you desire to answer." In the course of his painstaking examination of the possible meanings of philosophical questions and the solutions which the Idealists advanced for them, Moore came repeatedly to the conclusion that when the philosopher's abstract thesis was clearly understood, it could be seen to be patently mistaken.

Two of Moore's most valuable tools in his attack upon Idealism were his acceptance of Common Sense and his repeated appeal to the ordinary meanings of words. It is instructive to see how Moore attacked one of the most basic of the Idealist's principles: the doctrine of the Internality of Relations. For many reasons, too complex to present in detail here, the major Idealists had held that all relations are internal, i.e., that a thing is what it is in part because of its relations and that if its relations change, it becomes a different thing. For example, owning a dog as I do, I would be a different person if I gave the dog away, for one of my relations would have been altered. No relation, in other words, is a mere "accidental" or external relation of an individual: The way a person relates to all other things in the world determines necessarily who he is.

Moore rejected this doctrine, and one of his famous arguments against it illustrates the kind of original approach he introduced into philosophy. After painstakingly attempting to discover exactly how the Idealist is using his words when he says "All relations are internal," Moore concludes that this must be false because it "flies in the face of Common Sense." It is often a matter of fact that a certain person owns a dog, but Common Sense would not admit that that person becomes a different person merely because he gives the dog away. Common Sense (and ordinary speech) allows that although I may in fact be related to certain things in certain ways, I *might not have been* so related, and yet the "I" in each case has the same reference. Moore concludes, on the basis of his appeal to Common Sense, that some relations are internal, some are external, and that the Idealist principle is quite mistaken.

Needless to say, metaphysicians, whose primary interest was in propounding sweeping theses about the Nature of Reality, found Moore's approach trivial and irritating. Moore's insistence upon detailed analysis of the meanings of words as they occur in philosophical sentences, his refusal to speculate before clarity was gained, his repeated adherence to Common Sense and the way language is commonly used—these philosophical techniques were viewed sympathetically by few metaphysicians, although their importance was not lost upon certain other philosophers, who came to respect Moore's distinctive approach to philosophical questions even when they disagreed with his conclusions. By helping to turn philosophers' attention to the meanings of the questions they were asking and by discouraging speculation prior to clarification, Moore exerted an influence upon the history of analytic thought which is unparalleled.

Moore's writings were influential in other ways also. His early writings in ethics, for example, introduced into that subject a thesis which had far-reaching influence on later moral philosophers. Nor did Moore restrict himself to attacking Idealism. Although many of his early papers have not been published until recently, it is clear that he had always been interested in a range of philosophical questions, always bringing to them the skillful tools of analysis which he was in the process of forging.

Russell rejected Idealism for somewhat different reasons. This was partly due to interests which he had that were not shared by Moore. Russell's earliest writings were in the areas of logic and foundations of mathematics. Together with A. N. Whitehead (1861–1947) he published in 1910 the first volume of a monumental treatise on logic and mathematics, entitled *Principia Mathematica*. In addition to the great logical and mathematical advance which it represented, the *Principia* was also of the greatest interest to philosophers, since by developing the power and scope of logic considerably, it seemed to provide for philosophers a new, highly precise instrument for attacking philosophical problems. Russell himself wrote that " . . . logic is what is fundamental in philosophy, and . . . schools should be characterized rather by their logic than by their metaphysics." Russell, both before and after the publication of the *Principia*, attempted to bring to bear the results of his logical studies upon the traditional problems of metaphysics.

One major difference between Moore and Russell and their respective approaches to philosophy can be brought out by citing Russell's reasons for rejecting the doctrine of the Internality of Relations. Although Russell's reasons for rejecting the doctrine so crucial to the Idealists are complex and involved, they nevertheless are characteristic of the early Russell's approach to philosophical problems. One of Russell's main arguments is that the doctrine must be false because of its consequences for mathematics. If all relations are internal, he says, then the Idealists are right in saying that ultimately Reality is One and there is only One Truth. But this entails, Russell argues, that the propositions of mathematics are not even partial truths, which is an unacceptable consequent. The doctrine of the Internality of Relations is false, Russell concludes, and the metaphysical views that are deduced from it are fundamentally mistaken. The Idealist error is at bottom a *logical* error; they failed to see that not all meaningful propositions are of the subject-predicate form; that is, an adequate logic (such as the logical system developed in the *Principia*) must include an independent logic of relations as well as a logic of predication. The metaphysical question of the nature of relations, in other words, was settled by Russell primarily in terms of mathematical and logical considerations.

Russell's interest in mathematics and the need to secure its foundations was equaled by his respect for the procedures of science. He seems to have come to the opinion early that philosophical problems could be successfully solved only when philosophy became more like science in method. By using the symbolic techniques he had done so much to perfect, he hoped to introduce into philosophy some of the precision and the success of the natural sciences. The results of his attempt to make philosophy more scientific in method are to be found in a series of influential books which he wrote during the first decades of this century.

Russell and Moore succeeded in time in bringing to an end the dominance of Idealism in British philosophy. Younger philosophers were influenced by their distinctive approach, and many of them found Idealism quite indefensible against the repeated attacks of Moore and Russell. In time their writings became known in America, and in part because of their affinity with the writings of the American Pragmatists C. S. Peirce (1839–1914) and William James (1842–1910), found a sympathetic audience.

Despite their mutual rejection of Idealism, neither Russell nor Moore seriously doubted the possibility of eventually solving at least some metaphysical problems. They continued to believe that metaphysical truth of a sort is not only possible, but each believed himself to have arrived at some. Their main dissatisfaction concerned the ways used in the past by philosophers to resolve metaphysical questions. Analysis, whether by means of the techniques of symbolic logic or by an appeal to ordinary language, was for them primarily a tool to be used to sharpen and clarify philosophical problems so that they could be more readily solved. Probably neither of them realized that their writings were to prepare the ground for the next, more extreme phase of the revolution.

It was Russell's brilliant student, Ludwig Wittgenstein, who, building upon the work of Russell and to a lesser extent Moore, was the first analyst to argue the more extreme thesis that metaphysical questions are from their very nature unanswerable. The real difficulty, Wittgenstein argued in his cryptic but extremely influential *Tractatus Logico-Philosophicus* (1921), with metaphysical problems is not that philosophers have up to now failed to find adequate ways of solving them, but rather that they are *not questions at all*, since they fail to fulfill the minimal conditions of meaningfulness. All meaningful discourse, he attemped to show, is empirical in nature. Metaphysics is not empirical, so it is not meaningful, and the philosopher's search for metaphysical truth must forever prove abortive. The necessity of the propositions of mathematics and logic follows from the fact that they are tautologous, making no reference to the world. Since the sentences of metaphysicians (Russell and Moore included) are neither propositions of empirical science nor tautologies of logic or mathematics, they are nonsensical.

Philosophy, Wittgenstein said, is primarily the activity of clarifying language; it is not a source of truth about the universe the way science is. The philosopher's only proper task is to show the person who is puzzled by a metaphysical question that it is meaningless and unanswerable. It is clear that Wittgenstein at that time considered philosophy as it has been traditionally practiced since its origin a vain undertaking. The famous last sentence of the *Tractatus*, "Whereof one cannot speak, thereof one must be silent," expresses elegantly the essential doctrine of Wittgenstein's early view.

The impact of the *Tractatus* on the philosophical world was to be enormous. Although few philosophers have claimed to understand completely what

Wittgenstein was attempting to say, the book within a few years had wide circulation and was the subject of considerable discussion. It was clear that, despite his affinities with Russell, Wittgenstein had gone far beyond both Russell and Moore in the position he adopted in the *Tractatus*. Neither Russell nor Moore could endorse what Wittgenstein wrote without inconsistency.

Other philosophers, however, could and did accept the spirit, if not the letter, of the *Tractatus*. Wittgenstein's work found its most sympathetic audience initially, not in America or England, but on the Continent. In Vienna, beginning around 1923, a group of mathematicians and philosophers, having in common a deep disillusionment with the state of continental philosophy at that time and sharing respect for the achievements of science, had banded together for regular meetings and the communication of ideas. The founder and guiding spirit of this group was the philosopher Moritz Schlick (1882–1936). In addition to having some familiarity with the thought of Wittgenstein, Schlick had himself been developing independently ideas similar to some of those expressed by Wittgenstein. In time the group came to be known as the Vienna Circle. In 1929 they formally organized into a society.

It must not be assumed, however, that Logical Positivism was exclusively an outgrowth of Wittgenstein and Schlick. On the contrary, the original Logical Positivists counted among their sources of inspiration a variety of historical figures: David Hume, Auguste Comte, Ernst Mach, Gottlob Frege, and others. Indeed, the relationship between the Vienna Circle and Wittgenstein is not altogether clear even today, although the facts suggest that the *Tractatus* functioned primarily as a catalyst which served to crystallize ideas already present within the Circle. It is clear, however, that the original members of the Vienna Circle endorsed only some of Wittgenstein's ideas, totally rejecting other aspects of his *Tractatus* view.

Logical Positivism has probably gained wider public recognition than any other part of the analytic movement. Unfortunately, much of this recognition has taken the form of gross misconceptions about what the Logical Positivist's position actually was. Some people, especially critics of the movement, have tended to identify all analysis with Logical Positivism. This is, of course, a serious mistake. From its inception, Logical Positivism has been criticized repeatedly by many prominent analytic philosophers.

Like all significant philosophic movements, Logical Positivism was too diverse and complex a phenomenon to lend itself readily to brief, accurate summary. The reader who is interested in a detailed history of the movement is referred to the appropriate works cited in the Bibliography. Two central theses of the group, however, must be mentioned here to show the role Positivism played in the history of analysis.

It was a central tenet of Positivism that all metaphysical sentences without exception are meaningless. The Positivists agreed with Wittgenstein (although for different reasons) that metaphysical questions, the attempted answers to which make up the bulk of the history of philosophy, are pseudo-questions and unanswerable. One of the major figures of Positivism, Rudolf Carnap, defined metaphysical propositions as those "which claim to represent knowledge about something which is over or beyond all experience." What cannot be experienced, even in principle, the Positivists held, cannot be known nor even spoken about in meaningful language. Secondly, most of the members of the Vienna Circle tended to identify philosophy with analysis, especially the analysis of the language of science.

Schlick and Carnap were probably the two most famous members of the Circle. Carnap, from roughly 1928 on, published a series of books and articles on logic and the foundations of science which exerted great influence, especially in America. His *Logical Syntax of Language* (1934) was one of the first and most complete attempts to carry out in detail certain important parts of the Positivist's program. Many of the problems which were to occupy the attention of Positivists for decades were first articulated by Carnap.

There were, however, other members of the Circle who contributed substantially to the progress of Positivism. Some of the more famous names were H. Feigl, F. Waismann, K. Gödel, O. Neurath, H. Hahn, and P. Frank. In addition, the formal organization of the Circle allowed it to establish contact with like-minded philosophers elsewhere, e.g., the so-called "Berlin School," including H. Reichenbach, C. Hempel, K. Grelling, and R. von Mises, and the very productive school of Polish logicians.

In England the most famous Logical Positivist was A. J. Ayer. His youthful *Language, Truth and Logic* (1936) stated his conception of Positivism with uncompromising clarity and zeal. The book soon became a storm center of controversy. Ayer himself repudiated or modified many of the views which he expressed in that book within a short time. Yet, there is no doubt that it was extremely influential in bringing Positivism to the attention of philosophers and educated laymen alike.

Ayer placed great emphasis upon what he called "The Principle of Verification." According to this principle (which appears in other formulations in other Positivistic writers) a sentence cannot be deemed literally meaningful unless it satisfies certain specified conditions. Metaphysical sentences, Ayer hoped, because they failed to meet those conditions, could thus be shown to be meaningless. Philosophy, he argued at that time, is nothing but the analysis of language and the exposure of metaphysical nonsense for what it is. In many ways, Ayer's statement of the Positivistic program was the clearest available, although its clarity rendered it especially vulnerable to the attacks of the critics of Positivism.

The Vienna Circle had a relatively short lifespan. The rise of Fascism in Germany and Austria brought an end to free thought and discussion. Even before the outbreak of World War II most of the important members of the Circle had left Vienna. Many of them emigrated to the United States where they soon came to occupy positions in universities across the country. The end of the Circle as a formal movement was hastened by the death of its moving spirit, Moritz Schlick, who was tragically shot to death by one of his students in 1936. By the beginning of the war, the Vienna Circle, as an organized movement, had all but ceased to exist.

The influence of Positivism, however, did not come to an end with the demise of the Circle. The ideas articulated by the original Positivists became topics of discussion throughout the world. By insisting that all metaphysics is nonsense, Positivism posed a serious threat to established religion, since most religion includes theology, and theology was considered a kind of metaphysics. Defenders of the Faith arose in many places to do battle with the Devil of Positivism. This confrontation of traditional theological thought with anti-metaphysical Positivism led eventually to many lively, fruitful debates, which clarified the kind of attack Positivism was directing against theology. Unfortunately, disputes between the Positivist and the defender of religion often ended other times in fruitless, emotion-laden bickering.

Other philosophers, who were not committed to the defense of religious dogma, also felt the sting of the Positivist attack. By attempting to identify all philosophy with the analysis of language, Positivism left no room for traditional metaphysical investigation in philosophy. Philosophers who felt that the practice of metaphysics was important had first to show the error in the Positivistic program.

Original Positivism, however, was not destroyed either by its many critics or by the end of the Vienna Circle. The fact that few philosophers today would identify themselves with the tenets of the Circle is primarily due to a realization on the part of the Positivists themselves that some of their basic views, as originally stated, were unsound. The Verifiability Criterion of Meaning, for example, on which many early Positivists put such emphasis, was eventually abandoned or modified beyond recognition by its early defenders. Without relinquishing their antimetaphysical attitude, many Positivists began to seek more defensible ways of demonstrating the impossibility of metaphysics. Certain philosophers, for example, Gustav Bergmann, turned their attention to the attempt to construct "Ideal" languages, with the hope that by so doing they could clarify metaphysical questions to the point where they either could be seen to be meaningless or could be answered by making use of the more precise language. "Neo-Positivism" is the name often given to that group of philosophers who share many affinities with Original Positivism, but who in most cases have moved quite a distance from the pioneer position.

In the United States, where Positivism almost from its inception had found many sympathetic listeners, the original doctrines of the Circle have often been combined with the tradition of American Pragmatism. Since Pragmatism and Positivism have always shared many features, it is not surprising that some philosophers have been able to write in both traditions simultaneously. W. V. O. Quine is an excellent example of an original thinker who shows in his writings the influence of both Positivism and Pragmatism upon his thought.

Logical Positivism is one major direction that analytic thought has taken. There is, however, another main stream of analysis which developed more slowly than Positivism, but which has become at least as important. It is usually referred to as "Linguistic Analysis." It can be considered a "movement" only in the broadest sense of that word. Unlike Positivism, Linguistic Analysis has never had any formal organization comparable to the Vienna Circle. The name "Linguistic Analysis" perhaps is best used as a general name used to refer to a number of diverse philosophers all of whom share certain common interests in philosophy. (There is no sharp border line, incidentally, between Neo-Positivism and Linguistic Analysis; there are philosophers who write in both traditions simultaneously.)

The most important figure in the early development of Linguistic Analysis was Ludwig Wittgenstein. Within a few years after completing the *Tractatus*, Wittgenstein began to repudiate many of the basic views he had expressed in that book. Not since Plato has a philosopher been so harsh a critic of his earlier opinions. From roughly 1930 until his death, Wittgenstein expounded a new approach to philosophizing which has had the widest of influences. The distinction between his early and his later views is often made by referring to the "Early Wittgenstein" and the "Later Wittgenstein."

Although Wittgenstein did not publish any of his new ideas until after his death, he did dictate some lectures to his students which were circulated in typescript and eventually published as *The Blue and Brown Books*. It was not until 1953 that his *magnum opus, Philosophical Investigations*, was published. By then, as he himself wrote, many of his new ideas ". . . variously understood, more or less mangled . . ." were topics of discussion in many places.

There is no agreement among scholars concerning the full meaning of Wittgenstein's later writings. Like the *Tractatus*, the *Philosophical Investigations* is written in an original, but often difficult, style which does not lend itself readily to exegesis. A brief summary of his later views, however, is required here in order to give a fair account of the history of analysis. The reader should, however, keep in mind that the brief account that follows is only one of the several possible interpretations of what Wittgenstein was saying.

Wittgenstein had never accepted the basic tenets of Positivism. In the *Tractatus* he had spoken of the need for a logically perfect language, and many Positivists had interpreted him to be referring to the kind of symbolic calculi they were attempting to construct to expedite their analysis of scientific language. Whether or not Wittgenstein had such calculi in mind when he wrote the *Tractatus* is less important than the fact that in his later writings he clearly rejects the construction of artificial symbolic calculi as important for the resolution of philosophical problems. Influenced probably by Moore, he concentrated his attention primarily upon the analysis of the forms of ordinary discourse. His later writings abound with brilliant, subtle descriptions of language as it is ordinarily used.

Moore was interested in analyzing ordinary language in order to clarify metaphysical theses to facilitate their evaluation. Moore never seems to have doubted that at least most metaphysical questions have answers. Wittgenstein, on the contrary, came to believe that metaphysical perplexity arises out of a deep-seated failure to understand the complex functioning of our language. This failure to understand the way our language works gives rise to a kind of "linguistic anxiety" which expresses itself in the temptation to try to ask and answer metaphysical questions. Such questions are not real questions, Wittgenstein believed; they cannot be answered. What must be done is to find the source of the "anxiety" by a careful imaginative description of how our language actually operates. Philosophical problems will not be solved; they will be *dis*solved.

Thus, in his later writings, Wittgenstein still maintained the cardinal conclusion of the *Tractatus*: Metaphysical problems are not real problems and cannot be solved. His whole approach toward showing this, however, changed radically. The task of the philosopher is still to clarify language and remove confusion, but he must do it not merely by demonstrating to the metaphysician that his question is meaningless, but also by describing those features of language which gave rise to the temptation to pose the metaphysical question in the first place.

Brief and incomplete as this sketch of Wittgenstein's later views is, it perhaps serves to show how his later work stimulated a way of approaching philosophical problems quite different from that practiced by the Positivists. Although Wittgenstein never said that the description of ordinary language is the *only* valuable way of resolving philosophical problems, it was clear that he placed great importance on it. Linguistic Analysts all share with Wittgenstein a respect for ordinary language analysis and its fruitfulness for philosophy. Wittgenstein also believed that, in time, philosophical questions would completely disappear if his new procedures were properly applied. There is no residue of "philosophical truth" which would remain after all philosophical problems have been "dissolved."

Although Wittgenstein was the dominant figure in the development of Linguistic Analysis, he was not at that time the only philosopher thinking along such lines. The fact of the matter seems to be that many of the ideas he expounded were in the air at that time, so it is not surprising that other philosophers were developing independently views quite similar in many respects to the ones Wittgenstein was presenting to his students.

The two most important philosophers who helped to spread respect for Linguistic Analysis from its inception were Gilbert Ryle and John Wisdom. Although their respective approaches to philosophical problems were different in many respects, they shared a common interest in the analysis, as each of them understood the word, of ordinary forms of speech.

Ryle's major work, *The Concept of Mind*, attempts to show that the mental-physical dichotomy, which has dominated much metaphysical speculation since Descartes, is the result of a basic confusion about our use of mentalistic terms. This book and the various articles which Ryle wrote exploring other problems in similar ways have been enormously influential in spreading interest in the methods of Linguistic Analysis.

John Wisdom, on the other hand, was a student of Wittgenstein's. But, in a series of articles and books over the past thirty years, he has brought to Linguistic Analysis an original and exciting new kind of philosophical procedure. Unwilling to reject metaphysics as *merely* nonsense, he attempts to understand why the metaphysician feels compelled to talk in his linguistically odd ways. By putting stress upon the imperfect similarities between various kinds of statements in our language, he hopes to discover what is and is not valuable in the various attempts to solve metaphysical questions.

Despite Wittgenstein's great influence upon the present generation of philosophers, it is interesting that few of them have been willing to commit themselves completely to his later views. In part this may be due to a lack of general agreement on what those views are. More important, however, is the reluctance on the part of many analysts to accept the seemingly nihilistic import of Wittgenstein's remarks about the future of philosophy. Wittgenstein seems to say that there is no proper role for the philosopher beyond the dissolution of linguistic confusion. Many philosophers cannot accept this conclusion as the inevitable result of analysis.

One of the most discussed of the younger analysts, P. F. Strawson, has argued that there is no real antithesis between linguistic analysis and a certain kind of metaphysics. He distinguishes two kinds of metaphysics: that which only attempts to describe the conceptual boundaries of our language (*descriptive* metaphysics) and that which attempts to revise them (*revisionary* metaphysics). In his book *Individuals,* which he subtitled "An Essay in Descriptive Metaphysics," Strawson attempts to show, among other things, that certain general conclusions about the world can be gained from an analysis of how we speak. Presumably, this is the very thing that Wittgenstein was saying could not be done.

One other major figure of analysis must be mentioned to complete this general survey. John Austin, like Wittgenstein, published little during his lifetime but exerted great influence on his students. Austin shared with other analysts the conviction that the study of language is of the greatest value in dealing with philosophical questions. Like Wittgenstein and Wisdom, he also believed that a great deal of what philosophers have written is not so much false as it is misleading and confused. However, Austin's procedure for dispelling this confusion is unique. Especially in his later writings, Austin concentrated his attention upon the rich complex of grammatical distinctions to be found in the English language. He displayed an amazing talent for articulating the subtle shifts of meaning which result from the most minute grammatical changes. He was clearly of the opinion that the study of grammar is philosophically important, and he attempted to demonstrate this in his later works.

Austin, however, made few general pronouncements about the import or implications of his grammatical investigations. He does at times speak of the need for "a science of language," implying that such a science will supersede a great deal of what is now done by analytic philosophers. It seems to have been Austin's belief that the time is not yet ripe for speculation in philosophy. We must first become as clear as possible about how our language operates before we attempt to settle philosophical problems or even speculate on whether any of them can be solved. Thus, in spite of his general similarity to Wittgenstein, Austin never endorsed Wittgenstein's speculations about the ultimate fate of philosophy.

Sixty years is a relatively short time as man's history goes. Yet, the changes in philosophical interests and procedures within that period have been enormous. One has only to compare the works of Russell with the later writings of Wittgenstein or Austin to see the extent of the revolution which has occurred in philosophy. It is doubtful that this revolution has come to an end. Only future historians of philosophy will be in a position to judge the ultimate merit of the direction which philosophy has taken in our times. One thing can be said now, however: Philosophers can never again, except at their peril, ignore the importance of language when attempting to resolve philosophical problems. This is a minimal, but lasting, accomplishment of analysis. Whether future philosophical investigation of language will in the end lead to the dissolution of all philosophical puzzles, as Wittgenstein seems to have believed, or whether it will issue in a new, linguistically oriented metaphysics, as Strawson suggests, is in many ways the most important question confronting philosophy today.

part i **THE EARLY ANALYSTS**

1

Bertrand Russell DESCRIPTIONS

Russell's theory of descriptions has been called by F. P. Ramsey a "paradigm of philosophy." It is considered by many an ideal example of how philosophical problems ought to be resolved. The earliest version of the theory was presented in a famous paper, "On Denoting," which appeared in *Mind*, Vol. XIV (1905). The most complete formulation of the theory is to be found in *Principia Mathematica*, I, 66 ff., and I, 14. Although the version reprinted below is not as technical as the others, it nevertheless presents in a lucid manner the essential features of the theory.

Russell's problem was to find a way of interpreting expressions such as "A man walked down the street" or "The round square is round" without having to presuppose that such propositions are talking about strange entities like "a man" or "the round square." Some philosophers, in particular Alexius Meinong, had held that the meaningfulness of such sentences requires that the descriptive components of them refer to something. Since there are no round squares, the words "the round square" must refer to an entity which does not exist.

Russell attempts to avoid the necessity for believing in such odd entities by showing that descriptive phrases such as "a so-and-so" and "the so-and-so" can be meaningful when they occur in sentences even though they do not refer to any nonexistent entities.

The most famous attempt to show that Russell's theory is inadequate is P. F. Strawson's "On Referring" (selection 14); see also Russell's reply to Strawson (selection 15).

Additional discussion of the problem may be found, among other places, in the following articles:

Moore, G. E.: "Russell's 'Theory of Descriptions'" in *The Philosophy of Bertrand Russell*,[1] and in Moore's *Philosophical Papers*.
Geach, P. T.: "Russell's Theory of Description," *Analysis*, 1950.

From *Introduction to Mathematical Philosophy* by Bertrand Russell, chap. XVI. Copyright 1919. George Allen and Unwin, Ltd.; U.S.A.: The Macmillan Company. Used by permission.
[1] Publishing data for works cited in the Introductions are given in the Selected Bibliography.

Lazerowitz, M.: "Knowledge by Description," *Philosophical Review*, 1937.

For a discussion of Meinong's arguments see J. N. Findlay's *Meinong's Theory of Objects and Values*, 2d ed. (Oxford: Clarendon Press, 1963).

We dealt in the preceding chapter with the words *all* and *some;* in this chapter we shall consider the word *the* in the singular, and in the next chapter we shall consider the word *the* in the plural. It may be thought excessive to devote two chapters to one word, but to the philosophical mathematician it is a word of very great importance: like Browning's Grammarian with the enclitic δϵ, I would give the doctrine of this word if I were "dead from the waist down" and not merely in a prison.

We have already had occasion to mention "descriptive functions," *i.e.,* such expressions as "the father of x" or "the sine of x." These are to be defined by first defining "descriptions."

A "description" may be of two sorts, definite and indefinite (or ambiguous). An indefinite description is a phrase of the form "a so-and-so," and a definite description is a phrase of the form "the so-and-so" (in the singular). Let us begin with the former.

"Who did you meet?" "I met a man." "That is a very indefinite description." We are therefore not departing from usage in our terminology. Our question is: What do I really assert when I assert "I met a man"? Let us assume, for the moment, that my assertion is true, and that in fact I met Jones. It is clear that what I assert is *not* "I met Jones." I may say "I met a man, but it was not Jones"; in that case, though I lie, I do not contradict myself, as I should do if when I say I met a man I really mean that I met Jones. It is clear also that the person to whom I am speaking can understand what I say, even if he is a foreigner and has never heard of Jones.

But we may go further: not only Jones, but no actual man, enters into my statement. This becomes obvious when the statement is false, since then there is no more reason why Jones should be supposed to enter into the proposition than why anyone else should. Indeed the statement would remain significant, though it could not possibly be true, even if there were no man at all. "I met a unicorn" or "I met a sea-serpent" is a perfectly significant assertion, if we know what it would be to be a unicorn or a sea-serpent, *i.e.,* what is the definition of these fabulous monsters. Thus it is only what we may call the *concept* that enters into the proposition. In the case of "unicorn," for example, there is only the concept: there is not also, somewhere among the shades, something unreal which may be called "a unicorn." Therefore, since it is significant (though false) to say "I met a unicorn," it is clear that this proposition, rightly analyzed, does not contain a constituent "a unicorn," though it does contain the concept "unicorn."

The question of "unreality," which confronts us at this point, is a very important one. Misled by grammar, the great majority of those logicians who have dealt with this question have dealt with it on mistaken lines. They have regarded grammatical form as a surer guide in analysis than, in fact, it is. And they have not known what differences in grammatical form are important.

"I met Jones" and "I met a man" would count traditionally as propositions of the same form, but in actual fact they are of quite different forms: the first names an actual person, Jones; while the second involves a propositional function, and becomes, when made explicit: "The function 'I met x and x is human' is sometimes true." (It will be remembered that we adopted the convention of using "sometimes" as not implying more than once.) This proposition is obviously not of the form "I met x," which accounts for the existence of the proposition "I met a unicorn" in spite of the fact that there is no such thing as "a unicorn."

For want of the apparatus of propositional functions, many logicians have been driven to the conclusion that there are unreal objects. It is argued, *e.g.*, by Meinong,[2] that we can speak about "the golden mountain," "the round square," and so on; we can make true propositions of which these are the subjects; hence they must have some kind of logical being, since otherwise the propositions in which they occur would be meaningless. In such theories, it seems to me, there is a failure of that feeling for reality which ought to be preserved even in the most abstract studies. Logic, I should maintain, must no more admit a unicorn than zoology can; for logic is concerned with the real world just as truly as zoology, though with its more abstract and general features. To say that unicorns have an existence in heraldry, or in literature, or in imagination, is a most pitiful and paltry evasion. What exists in heraldry is not an animal, made of flesh and blood, moving and breathing of its own initiative. What exists is a picture, or a description in words. Similarly, to maintain that Hamlet, for example, exists in his own world, namely, in the world of Shakespeare's imagination, just as truly as (say) Napoleon existed in the ordinary world, is to say something deliberately confusing, or else confused to a degree which is scarcely credible. There is only one world, the "real" world: Shakespeare's imagination is part of it, and the thoughts that he had in writing Hamlet are real. So are the thoughts that we have in reading the play. But it is of the very essence of fiction that only the thoughts, feelings, etc., in Shakespeare and his readers are real, and that there is not, in addition to them, an objective Hamlet. When you have taken account of all the feelings roused by Napoleon in writers and readers of history, you have not touched the actual man; but in the case of Hamlet you have come to the end of him. If no one thought about Hamlet, there would be nothing left of him; if no one had thought about Napoleon, he would have soon seen to it that some one did. The sense of reality is vital in logic, and whoever juggles with it by pretending that Hamlet has another kind of reality is doing a disservice to thought. A robust sense of reality is very necessary in framing a correct analysis of propositions about unicorns, golden mountains, round squares, and other such pseudo-objects.

In obedience to the feeling of reality, we shall insist that, in the analysis of propositions, nothing "unreal" is to be admitted. But, after all, if there *is* nothing unreal, how, it may be asked, *could* we admit anything unreal? The reply is that, in dealing with propositions, we are dealing in the first instance with symbols, and if we attribute significance to groups of symbols which have no significance, we shall fall into the error of admitting unrealities, in the only

[2] *Untersuchungen zur Gegenstandstheorie und Psychologie,* 1904.

sense in which this is possible, namely, as objects described. In the proposition "I met a unicorn," the whole four words together make a significant proposition, and the word "unicorn" by itself is significant, in just the same sense as the word "man." But the *two* words "a unicorn" do not form a subordinate group having a meaning of its own. Thus if we falsely attribute meaning to these two words, we find ourselves saddled with "a unicorn," and with the problem how there can be such a thing in a world where there are no unicorns. "A unicorn" is an indefinite description which describes nothing. It is not an indefinite description which describes something unreal. Such a proposition as "x is unreal" only has meaning when "x" is a description, definite or indefinite; in that case the proposition will be true if "x" is a description which describes nothing. But whether the description "x" describes something or describes nothing, it is in any case not a constituent of the proposition in which it occurs; like "a unicorn" just now, it is not a subordinate group having a meaning of its own. All this results from the fact that, when "x" is a description, "x is unreal" or "x does not exist" is not nonsense, but is always significant and sometimes true.

We may now proceed to define generally the meaning of propositions which contain ambiguous descriptions. Suppose we wish to make some statement about "a so-and-so," where "so-and-so's" are those objects that have a certain property ϕ, *i.e.*, those objects x for which the propositional function ϕx is true. (*E.g.*, if we take "a man" as our instance of "a so-and-so," ϕx will be "x is human.") Let us now wish to assert the property ψ of "a so-and-so," *i.e.*, we wish to assert that "a so-and-so" has that property which x has when ψx is true. (*E.g.*, in the case of "I met a man," ψx will be "I met x.") Now the proposition that "a so-and-so" has the property ψ is *not* a proposition of the form "ψx." If it were, "a so-and-so" would have to be identical with x for a suitable x; and although (in a sense) this may be true in some cases, it is certainly not true in such a case as "a unicorn." It is just this fact, that the statement that a so-and-so has the property ψ is not of the form ψx, which makes it possible for "a so-and-so" to be, in a certain clearly definable sense, "unreal." The definition is as follows:

The statement that "an object having the property ϕ has the property ψ"

means:

The joint assertion of ϕx and ψx is not always false.

So far as logic goes, this is the same proposition as might be expressed by "some ϕ's are ψ's"; but rhetorically there is a difference, because in the one case there is a suggestion of singularity, and in the other case of plurality. This, however, is not the important point. The important point is that, when rightly analysed, propositions verbally about "a so-and-so" are found to contain no constituent represented by this phrase. And that is why such propositions can be significant even when there is no such thing as a so-and-so.

The definition of *existence*, as applied to ambiguous descriptions, results from what was said at the end of the preceding chapter. We say that "men exist" or "a man exists" if the propositional function "x is human" is sometimes true; and generally "a so-and-so" exists if "x is so-and-so" is sometimes true. We may put this in other language. The proposition "Socrates is a man" is no doubt *equivalent* to "Socrates is human," but it is not the very same proposition. The *is* of "Socrates is human" expresses the relation of subject and predicate; the *is* of "Socrates is a man" expresses identity. It is a disgrace to the human race that it has chosen to employ the same word "is" for these two entirely different ideas—a disgrace which a symbolic logical language of course remedies. The identity in "Socrates is a man" is identity between an object named (accepting "Socrates" as a name, subject to qualifications explained later) and an object ambiguously described. An object ambiguously described will "exist" when at least one such proposition is true, *i.e.*, when there is at least one true proposition of the form "x is a so-and-so," where "x" is a name. It is characteristic of ambiguous (as opposed to definite) descriptions that there may be any number of true propositions of the above form—Socrates is a man, Plato is a man, etc. Thus "a man exists" follows from Socrates, or Plato, or anyone else. With definite descriptions, on the other hand, the corresponding form of proposition, namely, "x is the so-and-so" (where "x" is a name), can only be true for one value of x at most. This brings us to the subject of definite descriptions, which are to be defined in a way analogous to that employed for ambiguous descriptions, but rather more complicated.

We come now to the main subject of the present chapter, namely, the definition of the word *the* (in the singular). One very important point about the definition of "a so-and-so" applies equally to "the so-and-so"; the definition to be sought is a definition of propositions in which this phrase occurs, not a definition of the phrase itself in isolation. In the case of "a so-and-so," this is fairly obvious: no one could suppose that "a man" was a definite object, which could be defined by itself. Socrates is a man, Plato is a man, Aristotle is a man, but we cannot infer that "a man" means the same as "Socrates" means and also the same as "Plato" means and also the same as "Aristotle" means, since these three names have different meanings. Nevertheless, when we have enumerated all the men in the world, there is nothing left of which we can say, "This is a man, and not only so, but it is *the* 'a man,' the quintessential entity that is just an indefinite man without being anybody in particular." It is of course quite clear that whatever there is in the world is definite: if it is a man it is one definite man and not any other. Thus there cannot be such an entity as "a man" to be found in the world, as opposed to specific men. And accordingly it is natural that we do not define "a man" itself, but only the propositions in which it occurs.

In the case of "the so-and-so" this is equally true, though at first sight less obvious. We may demonstrate that this must be the case, by a consideration of the difference between a *name* and a *definite description*. Take the proposition, "Scott is the author of *Waverley*." We have here a name, "Scott," and a description, "the author of *Waverley*," which are asserted to apply to the same person. The distinction between a name and all other symbols may be explained as follows:

A name is a simple symbol whose meaning is something that can only occur as subject, *i.e.*, something of the kind that, in Chapter XIII, we defined as an "individual" or a "particular." And a "simple" symbol is one which has no parts that are symbols. Thus "Scott" is a simple symbol, because, though it has parts (namely, separate letters), these parts are not symbols. On the other hand, "the author of *Waverley*" is not a simple symbol, because the separate words that compose the phrase are parts which are symbols. If, as may be the case, whatever *seems* to be an "individual" is really capable of further analysis, we shall have to content ourselves with what may be called "relative individuals," which will be terms that, throughout the context in question, are never analysed and never occur otherwise than as subjects. And in that case we shall have correspondingly to content ourselves with "relative names." From the standpoint of our present problem, namely, the definition of descriptions, this problem, whether these are absolute names or only relative names, may be ignored, since it concerns different stages in the hierarchy of "types," whereas we have to compare such couples as "Scott" and "the author of *Waverley*," which both apply to the same object, and do not raise the problem of types. We may, therefore, for the moment, treat names as capable of being absolute; nothing that we shall have to say will depend upon this assumption, but the wording may be a little shortened by it.

We have, then, two things to compare: (1) a *name*, which is a simple symbol, directly designating an individual which is its meaning, and having this meaning in its own right, independently of the meanings of all other words; (2) a *description*, which consists of several words, whose meanings are already fixed, and from which results whatever is to be taken as the "meaning" of the description.

A proposition containing a description is not identical with what that proposition becomes when a name is substituted, even if the name names the same object as the description describes. "Scott is the author of *Waverley*" is obviously a different proposition from "Scott is Scott": the first is a fact in literary history, the second a trivial truism. And if we put anyone other than Scott in place of "the author of *Waverley*," our proposition would become false, and would therefore certainly no longer be the same proposition. But, it may be said, our proposition is essentially of the same form as (say) "Scott is Sir Walter," in which two names are said to apply to the same person. The reply is that, if "Scott is Sir Walter" really means "the person named 'Scott' is the person named 'Sir Walter,' " then the names are being used as descriptions: *i.e.*, the individual, instead of being named, is being described as the person having that name. This is a way in which names are frequently used in practice, and there will, as a rule, be nothing in the phraseology to show whether they are being used in this way or *as* names. When a name is used directly, merely to indicate what we are speaking about, it is no part of the *fact* asserted, or of the falsehood if our assertion happens to be false: it is merely part of the symbolism by which we express our thought. What we want to express is something which might (for example) be translated into a foreign language; it is something for which the actual words are a vehicle, but of which they are no part. On the other hand, when we make a proposition about "the person called 'Scott,' " the actual name "Scott" enters into what we are asserting, and not merely into the language used in making the assertion. Our proposition will now be a different one if we substitute "the person called 'Sir Walter.'" But so long as we are using names *as* names, whether we say "Scott" or whether we say "Sir Walter" is as irrelevant to what we are asserting as whether we speak English or French. Thus so long as names are used *as* names, "Scott is Sir Walter" is the same trivial proposition as "Scott is Scott." This completes the proof that "Scott is the author of *Waverley*" is not the same proposition as results from substituting a name for "the author of *Waverley*," no matter what name may be substituted.

When we use a variable, and speak of a propositional function, ϕx say, the process of applying general statements about x to particular cases will consist in substituting a name for the letter "x," assuming that ϕ is a function which has individuals for its arguments. Suppose, for example, that ϕx is "always true"; let it be, say, the "law of identity," $x = x$. Then we may substitute for "x" any name we choose, and we shall obtain a true proposition. Assuming for the moment that "Socrates," "Plato," and "Aristotle" are names (a very rash assumption), we can infer from the law of identity that Socrates is Socrates, Plato is Plato, and Aristotle is Aristotle. But we shall commit a fallacy if we attempt to infer, without further premisses, that the author of *Waverley* is the author of *Waverley*. This results from what we have just proved, that, if we substitute a name for "the author of *Waverley*" in a proposition, the proposition we obtain is a different one. That is to say, applying the result to our present case: If "x" is a name, "$x = x$" is not the same proposition as "the author of *Waverley* is the author of *Waverley*," no matter what name "x" may be. Thus from the fact that all propositions of the form "$x = x$" are true we cannot infer, without more ado, that the author of *Waverley* is the author of *Waverley*. In fact, propositions of the form "the so-and-so is the so-and-so" are not always true: it is necessary that the so-and-so should *exist* (a term which will be explained shortly). It is false that the present King of France is the present King of France, or that the round square is the round square. When we substitute a description for a name, propositional functions which are "always true" may become false, if the description describes nothing. There is no mystery in this as soon as we realise (what was proved in the preceding paragraph) that when we substitute a description the result is not a value of the propositional function in question.

We are now in a position to define propositions in which a definite description occurs. The only thing that distinguishes "the so-and-so" from "a so-and-so" is the implication of uniqueness. We cannot speak of "*the* inhabitant of London," because inhabiting London is an attribute which is not unique. We cannot speak about "the present King of France," because there is none; but we can speak about "the present King of England." Thus propositions about "the so-and-so" always imply the corresponding propositions about "a so-and-so," with the addendum that there is not more than one so-and-so. Such a proposition as "Scott is the author of Waverley" could not be true if *Waverley* had never been written, or if several people had written it; and no more could any other proposition resulting from a propositional function x by the substitution of "the author of *Waverley*" for "x." We may say that "the author of *Waverley*" means "the value of x for which 'x wrote *Waverley*' is true." Thus the proposition "the author of *Waverley* was Scotch," for example, involves:

$(\exists x)(y)(wy \equiv y=x \quad \&$

1. "x wrote *Waverley*" is not always false;
2. "if x and y wrote *Waverley*, x and y are identical" is always true;
3. "if x wrote *Waverley*, x was Scotch" is always true.

These three propositions, translated into ordinary language, state:

1. at least one person wrote *Waverley;*
2. at most one person wrote *Waverley;*
3. Whoever wrote *Waverley* was Scotch.

All these three are implied by "the author of *Waverley* was Scotch." Conversely, the three together (but no two of them) imply that the author of *Waverley* was Scotch. Hence the three together may be taken as defining what is meant by the proposition "the author of *Waverley* was Scotch."

We may somewhat simplify these three propositions. The first and second together are equivalent to: "There is a term c such that 'x wrote *Waverley*' is true when x is c and is false when x is not c." In other words, "There is a term c such that 'x wrote *Waverley*' is always equivalent to 'x is c.'" (Two propositions are "equivalent" when both are true or both are false.) We have here, to begin with, two functions of x, "x wrote *Waverley*" and "x is c," and we form a function of c by considering the equivalence of these two functions of x for all values of x; we then proceed to assert that the resulting function of c is "sometimes true," i.e., that it is true for at least one value of c. (It obviously cannot be true for more than one value of c.) These two conditions together are defined as giving the meaning of "the author of *Waverley* exists."

We may now define "the term satisfying the function ϕx exists." This is the general form of which the above is a particular case. "The author of *Waverley*" is "the term satisfying the function 'x wrote *Waverley*.'" And "the so-and-so" will always involve reference to some propositional function, namely, that which defines the property that makes a thing a so-and-so. Our definition is as follows:

"The term satisfying the function ϕx exists" means:
"There is a term c such that ϕx is always equivalent to 'x is c.'"

In order to define "the author of *Waverley* was Scotch," we have still to take account of the third of our three propositions, namely, "Whoever wrote *Waverley* was Scotch." This will be satisfied by merely adding that the c in question is to be Scotch. Thus "the author of *Waverley* was Scotch" is:

There is a term c such that (1) "x wrote *Waverley*" is always equivalent to "x is c," (2) c is Scotch.

And generally: "the term satisfying ϕx satisfies ψx" is defined as meaning:

There is a term c such that (1) ϕx is always equivalent to "x is c," (2) ψc is true.

This is the definition of propositions in which descriptions occur.

It is possible to have much knowledge concerning a term described, *i.e.*, to know many propositions concerning "the so-and-so," without actually knowing what the so-and-so is, *i.e.*, without knowing any proposition of the form "*x* is the so-and-so," where "*x*" is a name. In a detective story propositions about "the man who did the deed" are accumulated, in the hope that ultimately they will suffice to demonstrate that it was A who did the deed. We may even go so far as to say that, in all such knowledge as can be expressed in words—with the exception of "this" and "that" and a few other words of which the meaning varies on different occasions—no names, in the strict sense, occur, but what seem like names are really descriptions. We may inquire significantly whether Homer existed, which we could not do if "Homer" were a name. The proposition "the so-and-so exists" is significant, whether true or false; but if *a* is the so-and-so (where "*a*" is a name), the words "*a* exists" are meaningless. It is only of descriptions—definite or indefinite—that existence can be significantly asserted; for, if "*a*" is a name, it *must* name something: what does not name anything is not a name, and therefore, if intended to be a name, is a symbol devoid of meaning, whereas a description, like "the present King of France," does not become incapable of occurring significantly merely on the ground that it describes nothing, the reason being that it is a *complex* symbol, of which the meaning is derived from that of its constituent symbols. And so, when we ask whether Homer existed, we are using the word "Homer" as an abbreviated description: we may replace it by (say) "the author of the *Iliad* and the *Odyssey*." The same considerations apply to almost all uses of what look like proper names.

When descriptions occur in propositions, it is necessary to distinguish what may be called "primary" and "secondary" occurrences. The abstract distinction is as follows. A description has a "primary" occurrence when the proposition in which it occurs results from substituting the description for "*x*" in some propositional function ϕx; a description has a "secondary" occurrence when the result of substituting the description for *x* in ϕx gives only *part* of the proposition concerned. An instance will make this clearer. Consider "the present King of France is bald." Here "the present King of France" has a primary occurrence, and the proposition is false. Every proposition in which a description which describes nothing has a primary occurrence is false. But now consider "the present King of France is not bald." This is ambiguous. If we are first to take "*x* is bald," then substitute "the present King of France" for "*x*," and then deny the result, the occurrence of "the present King of France" is secondary and our proposition is true; but if we are to take "*x* is not bald" and substitute "the present King of France" for "*x*," then "the present King of France" has a primary occurrence and the proposition is false. Confusion of primary and secondary occurrences is a ready source of fallacies where descriptions are concerned.

Descriptions occur in mathematics chiefly in the form of *descriptive functions*, *i.e.*, "the term having the relation R to *y*," or "the R of *y*" as we may say, on the analogy of "the father of *y*" and similar phrases. To say "the father of *y* is rich," for example, is to say that the following propositional function of *c*: "*c* is rich, and '*x* begat *y*' is always equivalent to '*x* is *c*,'" is "sometimes true," *i.e.*, is true for at least one value of *c*. It obviously cannot be true for more than one value.

The theory of descriptions, briefly outlined in the present chapter, is of the utmost importance both in logic and in theory of knowledge. But for purposes of mathematics, the more philosophical parts of the theory are not essential, and have therefore been omitted in the above account, which has confined itself to the barest mathematical requisites.

Bertrand Russell   WHAT THERE IS

Logical Atomism, as Russell conceived it, was the metaphysical theory which resulted from introducing the scientific method and the techniques of symbolic logic into philosophy. The most complete statement of the ontology of Russell's version of Logical Atomism is to be found in the last lecture of his "Lectures on Logical Atomism" (1918), which is reprinted in this selection. Many of the views expressed by Russell in the following pages were either rejected or modified by him in his later writings, but he appears never to have wholly abandoned the general way of approaching philosophical problems exemplified there.

Russell's empiricistic commitment can be clearly seen as he attempts to state what kinds of things there are in the world. Our knowledge and belief about the world must be based upon data, and in the last analysis, according to Russell, those data can be gained only through experience. He suggests that assertions about material objects and persons are analyzable into complicated assertions about series of classes of sense contents. In a sense, material objects and persons are "constructs" out of the more basic sense-data, which are the basis of all our knowledge of the world. A considerable part of Russell's later writings in philosophy is devoted to an attempt to resolve the difficulties inherent in his version of empiricism.

The lectures are important also insofar as they show the influence exerted by Wittgenstein upon Russell at that time. It is certain that Wittgenstein (who allowed his *Tractatus Logico-Philosophicus* to be published in 1921) did not accept most of Russell's substantive metaphysical conclusions. Wittgenstein's version of Logical Atomism was radically different in important respects from the version endorsed by Russell.

For additional discussion of Russell's metaphysical views during this period consult C. A. Fritz's *Bertrand Russell's Construction of the External World* (London: Routledge and Kegan Paul, 1952).

I come now to the last lecture of this course, and I propose briefly to point to a few of the morals that are to be gathered from what has gone before, in the way of suggesting the bearing of the doctrines that I have been advocating

From "The Philosophy of Logical Atomism" in *Logic and Knowledge*, R. C. Marsh (ed.), chap. 8. Copyright 1956. George Allen and Unwin, Ltd. Used by permission.

upon various problems of metaphysics. I have dealt hitherto upon what one may call philosophical grammar, and I am afraid I have had to take you through a good many very dry and dusty regions in the course of that investigation, but I think the importance of philosophical grammar is very much greater than it is generally thought to be. I think that practically all traditional metaphysics is filled with mistakes due to bad grammar, and that almost all the traditional problems of metaphysics and traditional results—supposed results—of metaphysics are due to a failure to make the kind of distinctions in what we may call philosophical grammar with which we have been concerned in these previous lectures.

Take, as a very simple example, the philosophy of arithmetic. If you think that 1, 2, 3, and 4, and the rest of the numbers, are in any sense entities, if you think that there are objects, having those names, in the realm of being, you have at once a very considerable apparatus for your metaphysics to deal with, and you have offered to you a certain kind of analysis of arithmetical propositions. When you say, e.g., that 2 and 2 are 4, you suppose in that case that you are making a proposition of which the number 2 and the number 4 are constituents, and that has all sorts of consequences, all sorts of bearings upon your general metaphysical outlook. If there has been any truth in the doctrines that we have been considering, all numbers are what I call logical fictions. Numbers are classes of classes, and classes are logical fictions, so that numbers are, as it were, fictions at two removes, fictions of fictions. Therefore you do not have, as part of the ultimate constituents of your world, these queer entities that you are inclined to call numbers. The same applies in many other directions.

One purpose that has run through all that I have said, has been the justification of analysis, i.e., the justification of logical atomism, of the view that you can get down in theory, if not in practice, to ultimate simples, out of which the world is built, and that those simples have a kind of reality not belonging to anything else. Simples, as I tried to explain, are of an infinite number of sorts. There are particulars and qualities and relations of various orders, a whole hierarchy of different sorts of simples, but all of them, if we were right, have in their various ways some kind of reality that does not belong to anything else. The only other sort of object you come across in the world is what we call *facts,* and facts are the sort of things that are asserted or denied by propositions, and are not properly entities at all in the same sense in which their constituents are. That is shown in the fact that you cannot name them. You can only deny, or assert, or consider them, but you cannot name them because they are not there to be named, although in another sense it is true that you cannot know the world unless you know the facts that make up the truths of the world; but the knowing of facts is a different sort of thing from the knowing of simples.

Another purpose which runs through all that I have been saying is the purpose embodied in the maxim called Occam's Razor. That maxim comes in, in practice, in this way: take some science, say physics. You have there a given body of doctrine, a set of propositions expressed in symbols—I am including words among symbols—and you think that you have reason to believe that on the whole those propositions, rightly interpreted, are fairly true, but you do not know what is the actual meaning of the symbols that you are using. The meaning they have *in use* would have to be explained in some pragmatic way: they have a certain kind of practical or emotional significance to you which is a datum, but the logical significance is not a datum, but a thing to be sought, and you go through, if you are analysing a science like physics, these propositions with a view to finding out what is the smallest empirical apparatus—or the smallest apparatus, not necessarily wholly empirical—out of which you can build up these propositions. What is the smallest number of simple undefined things at the start, and the smallest number of undemonstrated premises, out of which you can define the things that need to be defined and prove the things that need to be proved? That problem, in any case that you like to take, is by no means a simple one, but on the contrary an extremely difficult one. It is one which requires a very great amount of logical technique; and the sort of thing that I have been talking about in these lectures is the preliminaries and first steps in that logical technique. You cannot possibly get at the solution of such a problem as I am talking about if you go at it in a straightforward fashion with just the ordinary acumen that one accumulates in the course of reading or in the study of traditional philosophy. You do need this apparatus of symbolical logic that I have been talking about. (The description of the subject as symbolical logic is an inadequate one. I should like to describe it simply as logic, on the ground that nothing else really is logic, but that would sound so arrogant that I hesitate to do so.)

Let us consider further the example of physics for a moment. You find, if you read the works of physicists, that they reduce matter down to certain elements—atoms, ions, corpuscles, or what not. But in any case the sort of thing that you are aiming at in the physical analysis of matter is to get down to very little bits of matter that still are just like matter in the fact that they persist through time, and that they travel about in space. They have in fact all the ordinary everyday properties of physical matter, not the matter that one has in ordinary life—they do not taste or smell or appear to the naked eye— but they have the properties that you very soon get to when you travel toward physics from ordinary life. Things of that sort, I say, are not the ultimate constituents of matter in any metaphysical sense. Those things are all of them, as I think a very little reflection shows, logical fictions in the sense that I was speaking of. At least, when I say they are, I speak somewhat too dogmatically. It is possible that there may be all these things that the physicist talks about in actual reality, but it is impossible that we should ever have any reason whatsoever for supposing that there are. That is the situation that you arrive at generally in such analyses. You find that a certain thing which has been set up as a metaphysical entity can either be assumed dogmatically to be real, and then you will have no possible argument either for its reality or against its reality; or, instead of doing that, you can construct a logical fiction having the same formal properties, or rather having formally analogous formal properties to those of the supposed metaphysical entity and itself composed of empirically given things, and that logical fiction can be substituted for your supposed metaphysical entity and will fulfill all the scientific purposes that anybody can desire. With atoms and the rest it is so, with all the metaphysical entities whether of science or of metaphysics. By metaphysical entities I mean those things which are supposed to be part of the ultimate constituents of the world, but not to be the kind of thing that is ever empirically given—I do not say merely not being itself empirically given, but not being the *kind* of thing that is empirically given. In the case of matter, you can start from what is empirically given, what one sees and hears and smells and so forth, all the ordinary data of sense, or you can start with some definite ordinary object, say this desk, and you can ask yourselves, "What do I mean by saying that this desk that I am looking at now is the same as the one I was looking at a week ago?" The first simple ordinary answer would be that it *is* the same desk, it is actually identical, there is a perfect identity of substance, or whatever you like to call it. But when that apparently simple answer is suggested, it is important to observe that you cannot have an empirical reason for such a view as that, and if you hold it, you hold it simply because you like it and for no other reason whatever. All that you really know is such facts as that what you see now, when you look at the desk, bears a very close similarity to what you saw a week ago when you looked at it. Rather more than that one fact of similarity I admit you know, or you may know. You might have paid some one to watch the desk continuously throughout the week, and might then have discovered that it was presenting appearances of the same sort all through that period, assuming that the light was kept on all through the night. In that way you could have established continuity. You have not in fact done so. You do not in fact know that that desk has gone on looking the same all the time, but we will assume that. Now the essential point is this: What is the empirical reason that makes you call a number of appearances, appearances of the same desk? What makes you say on successive occasions, I am seeing the same desk? The first thing to notice is this, that it does not matter what is the answer, so long as you have realized that the answer consists in something empirical and not in a recognized metaphysical identity of substance. There is something given in experience which makes you call it the same desk, and having once grasped that fact, you can go on and say, it is that something (whatever it is) that makes you call it the same desk which shall be *defined* as *constituting* it the same desk, and there shall be no assumption of a metaphysical substance which is identical throughout. It is a little easier to the untrained mind to conceive of an identity than it is to conceive of a system of correlated particulars, hung one to another by relations of similarity and continuous change and so on. That idea is apparently more complicated, but that is what is empirically given in the real world, and substance, in the sense of something which is continuously identical in the same desk, is not given to you. Therefore in all cases where you seem to have a continuous entity persisting through changes, what you have to do is to ask yourself what makes you consider the successive appearances as belonging to one thing. When you have found out what makes you take the view that they belong to the same thing, you will then see that that which has made you say so, is all that is *certainly* there in the way of unity. Anything that there may be over and above that, I shall recognize as something I cannot know. What I can know is that there are a certain series of appearances linked together, and the series of those appearances I shall define as being a desk. In that way the desk is reduced to being a logical fiction, because a series is a logical fiction. In that way all the ordinary objects of daily life are extruded from the world of what there is, and in their place as what there is you find a number of passing particulars of the kind that one is immediately conscious of in sense. I want to make clear that I am not *denying* the existence of anything; I am only refusing to affirm it. I refuse to affirm the existence of anything for which there is no evidence, but I equally refuse to deny the existence of anything against which there is no evidence. Therefore I neither affirm nor deny it, but merely say, that is not in the realm of the knowable and is certainly not a part of physics; and physics, if it is to be interpreted, must be interpreted in terms of the sort of thing that can be empirical. If your atom is going to serve purposes in physics, as it undoubtedly does, your atom has got to turn out to be a construction, and your atom will in fact turn out to be a series of classes of particulars. The same process which one applies to physics, one will also apply elsewhere. The application to physics I explained briefly in my book on the *External World*, Chapters III and IV.

I have talked so far about the unreality of the things we think real. I want to speak with equal emphasis about the reality of things we think unreal, such as phantoms and hallucinations. Phantoms and hallucinations, considered in themselves, are, as I explained in the preceding lectures, on exactly the same level as ordinary sense-data. They differ from ordinary sense-data only in the fact that they do not have the usual correlations with other things. In themselves they have the same reality as ordinary sense-data. They have the most complete and absolute and perfect reality that anything can have. They are part of the ultimate constituents of the world, just as the fleeting sense-data are. Speaking of the fleeting sense-data, I think it is very important to remove out of one's instincts any disposition to believe that the real is the permanent. There has been a metaphysical prejudice always that if a thing is really real, it has to last either forever or for a fairly decent length of time. That is to my mind an entire mistake. The things that are really real last a very short time. Again I am not denying that there *may* be things that last forever, or for thousands of years; I only say that those are not within our experience, and that the real things that we know by experience last for a very short time, one tenth or half a second, or whatever it may be. Phantoms and hallucinations are among those, among the ultimate constituents of the world. The things that we call real, like tables and chairs, are systems, series of classes of particulars, and the particulars are the real things, the particulars being sense-data when they happen to be given to you. A table or chair will be a series of classes of particulars, and therefore a logical fiction. Those particulars will be on the same level of reality as a hallucination or a phantom. I ought to explain in what sense a chair is a series of classes. A chair presents at each moment a number of different appearances. All the appearances that it is presenting at a given moment make up a certain class. All those sets of appearances vary from time to time. If I take a chair and smash it, it will present a whole set of different appearances from what it did before, and without going as far as that, it will always be changing as the light changes, and so on. So you get a series in time of different sets of appearances, and that is what I mean by saying that a chair is a series of classes. That explanation is too crude, but I leave out the niceties, as that is not the actual topic I am dealing with. Now each single particular which is part of this whole system is linked up with the others in the system. Supposing, e.g., I take as my particular the appearance which that chair is presenting to me at this moment. That is linked up first of all with the appearance which the same chair is presenting to any one of you at the same moment, and with the appearance which it is going to present to me at later moments. There you get at once two journeys that you can take away from that particular, and that particular will be correlated in certain definite ways with the other particulars which also belong to that chair. That is what you mean by saying—or what you ought to mean by saying—that what I see before me is a real thing as opposed to a phantom. It means that it has a whole set of correlations of different kinds. It means that that particular, which is the appearance of the chair to me at this moment, is not isolated but is connected in a certain well-known familiar fashion with others, in the sort of way that makes it answer one's expectations. And so, when you go and buy a chair, you buy not only the appearance which it presents to you at that moment, but also those other appearances that it is going to present when it gets home. If it were a phantom chair, it would not present any appearances when it got home, and would not be the sort of thing you would want to buy. The sort one calls real is one of a whole correlated system, whereas the sort you call hallucinations are not. The respectable particulars in the world are all of them linked up with other particulars in respectable, conventional ways. Then sometimes you get a wild particular, like a merely visual chair that you cannot sit on, and say it is a phantom, a hallucination, you exhaust all the vocabulary of abuse upon it. That is what one means by calling it unreal, because 'unreal' applied in that way is a term of abuse and never would be applied to a thing that *was* unreal because you would not be so angry with it.

I will pass on to some other illustrations. Take a person. What is it that makes you say, when you meet your friend Jones, "Why, this is Jones"? It is clearly not the persistence of a metaphysical entity inside Jones somewhere, because even if there be such an entity, it certainly is not what you see when you see Jones coming along the street; it certainly is something that you are not acquainted with, not an empirical datum. Therefore plainly there is something in the empirical appearances which he presents to you, something in their relations one to another, which enables you to collect all these together and say, "These are what I call the appearances of one person," and that something that makes you collect them together is not the persistence of a metaphysical subject, because that, whether there be such a persistent subject or not, is certainly not a datum, and that which makes you say "Why, it is Jones" is a datum. Therefore Jones is not constituted as he is known by a sort of pin-point ego that is underlying his appearances, and you have got to find some correlations among the appearances which are of the sort that make you put all those appearances together and say, they are the appearances of one person. Those are different when it is other people and when it is yourself. When it is yourself, you have more to go by. You have not only what you look like, you have also your thoughts and memories and all your organic sensations, so that you have a much richer material and are therefore much less likely to be mistaken as to your own identity than as to some one else's. It happens, of course, that there are mistakes even as to one's own identity, in cases of multiple personality and so forth, but as a rule you will know that it is you because you have more to go by than other people have, and you would know it is you, not by a consciousness of the ego at all but by all sorts of things, by memory, by the way you feel and the way you look and a host of things. But all those are empirical data, and those enable you to say that the person to whom something happened yesterday was yourself. So you can collect a whole set of experiences into one string as all belonging to you, and similarly other people's experiences can be collected together as all belonging to them by relations that actually are observable and without assuming the existence of the persistent ego. It does not matter in the least to what we are concerned with, what exactly is the given empirical relation between two experiences that makes us say, "These are two experiences of the same person." It does not matter precisely what that relation is, because the logical formula for the construction of the person is the same whatever that relation may be, and because the mere fact that you can know that two experiences belong to the same person proves that there is such an empirical relation to be ascertained by analysis. Let us call the relation R. We shall say that when two experiences have to each other the relation R, then they are said to be experiences of the same person. That is a definition of what I mean by "experiences of the same person." We proceed here just in the same way as when we are defining numbers. We first define what is meant by saying that two classes "have the same number," and then define what a number is. The person who has a given experience x will be the class of all those experiences which are "experiences of the same person" as the one who experiences x. You can say that two events are co-personal when there is between them a certain relation R, namely that relation which makes us say that they are experiences of the same person. You can define the person who has a certain experience as being those experiences that are co-personal with that experience, and it will be better perhaps to take them as a series than as a class, because you want to know which is the beginning of a man's life and which is the end. Therefore we shall say that a person is a certain series of experiences. We shall not deny that there may be a metaphysical ego. We shall merely say that it is a question that does not concern us in any way, because it is a matter about which we know nothing and can know nothing, and therefore it obviously cannot be a thing that comes into science in any way. What we know is this string of experiences that makes up a person, and that is put together by means of certain empirically given relations, such, e.g., as memory.

 I will take another illustration, a kind of problem that our method is useful in helping to deal with. You all know the American theory of neutral monism, which derives really from William James and is also suggested in the work of Mach, but in a rather less developed form. The theory of neutral monism maintains that the distinction between the mental and the physical is entirely an affair of arrangement, that the actual material arranged is exactly the same in the case of the mental as it is in the case of the physical, but they differ merely in the fact that when you take a thing as belonging in the same context with certain other things, it will belong to psychology, while when you take it in a certain other context with other things, it will belong to physics, and the difference is as to what you consider to be its context, just the same sort of difference as there is between arranging the people in London alphabetically or geographically. So, according to William James, the actual material of the world can be arranged in two different ways, one of which gives you physics and the other psychology. It is just like rows or columns: in an arrangement of rows and columns, you can take an item as either a member of a certain row or a member of a certain column; the item is the same in the two cases, but its context is different.

If you will allow me a little undue simplicity I can go on to say rather more about neutral monism, but you must understand that I am talking more simply than I ought to do because there is not time to put in all the shadings and qualifications. I was talking a moment ago about the appearances that a chair presents. If we take any one of these chairs, we can all look at it, and it presents a different appearance to each of us. Taken all together, taking all the different appearances that that chair is presenting to all of us at this moment, you get something that belongs to physics. So that, if one takes sense-data and arranges together all those sense-data that appear to different people at a given moment and are such as we should ordinarily say are appearances of the same physical object, then that class of sense-data will give you something that belongs to physics, namely, the chair at this moment. On the other hand, if instead of taking all the appearances that that chair presents to all of us at this moment, I take all the appearances that the different chairs in this room present to me at this moment, I get quite another group of particulars. All the different appearances that different chairs present to me now will give you something belonging to psychology, because that will give you my experiences at the present moment. Broadly speaking, according to what one may take as an expansion of William James, that should be the definition of the difference between physics and psychology.

We commonly assume that there is a phenomenon which we call seeing the chair, but what I call my seeing the chair according to neutral monism is merely the existence of a certain particular, namely the particular which is the sense-datum of that chair at that moment. And I and the chair are both logical fictions, both being in fact a series of classes of particulars, of which one will be that particular which we call my seeing the chair. That actual appearance that the chair is presenting to me now is a member of me and a member of the chair, I and the chair being logical fictions. That will be at any rate a view that you can consider if you are engaged in vindicating neutral monism. There is no simple entity that you can point to and say: this entity is physical and not mental. According to William James and neutral monists that will not be the case with any simple entity that you may take. Any such entity will be a member of physical series and a member of mental series. Now I want to say that if you wish to test such a theory as that of neutral monism, if you wish to discover whether it is true or false, you cannot hope to get any distance with your problem unless you have at your fingers' ends the theory of logic that I have been talking of. You never can tell otherwise what can be done with a given material, whether you can concoct out of a given material the sort of logical fictions that will have the properties you want in psychology and in physics. That sort of thing is by no means easy to decide. You can only decide it if you really have a very considerable technical facility in these matters. Having said that, I ought to proceed to tell you that I have discovered whether neutral monism is true or not, because otherwise you may not believe that logic is any use in the matter. But I do not profess to know whether it is true or not. I feel more and more inclined to think that it may be true. I feel more and more that the difficulties that occur in regard to it are all of the sort that may be solved by ingenuity. But nevertheless there *are* a number of difficulties; there are a number of problems, some of which I have spoken about in the course of these lectures. One is the question of belief and the other sorts of facts involving two verbs. If there are such facts as this, that, I think, may make neutral monism rather difficult, but as I was pointing out, there is the theory that one calls behaviourism, which belongs logically with neutral monism, and that theory would altogether dispense with those facts containing two verbs, and would therefore dispose of that argument against neutral monism. There is, on the other hand, the argument from emphatic particulars, such as "this" and "now" and "here" and such words as that, which are not very easy to reconcile, to my mind, with the view which does not distinguish between a particular and experiencing that particular. But the argument about emphatic particulars is so delicate and so subtle that I cannot feel quite sure whether it is a valid one or not, and I think the longer one pursues philosophy, the more conscious one becomes how extremely often one has been taken in by fallacies, and the less willing one is to be quite sure that an argument is valid if there is anything about it that is at all subtle or elusive, at all difficult to grasp. That makes me a little cautious and doubtful about all these arguments, and therefore although I am quite sure that the question of the truth or falsehood of neutral monism is not to be solved except by these means, yet I do not profess to know whether neutral monism is true or is not. I am not without hopes of finding out in the course of time, but I do not profess to know yet.

As I said earlier in this lecture, one thing that our technique does, is to give us a means of constructing a given body of symbolic propositions with the minimum of apparatus, and every diminution in apparatus diminishes the risk of error. Suppose, e.g., that you have constructed your physics with a certain number of entities and a certain number of premises; suppose you discover that by a little ingenuity you can dispense with half of those entities and half of those premises, you clearly have diminished the risk of error, because if you had before 10 entities and 10 premises, then the 5 you have now would be all right, but it is not true conversely that if the 5 you have now are all right, the 10 must have been. Therefore you diminish the risk of error with every diminution of entities and premises. When I spoke about the desk and said I was not going to assume the existence of a persistent substance underlying its appearances, it is an example of the case in point. You have anyhow the successive appearances, and if you can get on without assuming the metaphysical and constant desk, you have a smaller risk of error than you had before. You would not necessarily have a smaller risk of error if you were tied down to *denying* the metaphysical desk. That is the advantage of Occam's Razor, that it diminishes your risk of error. Considered in that way you may say that the whole of our problem belongs rather to science than to philosophy. I think perhaps that is true, but I believe the only difference between science and philosophy is, that science is what you more or less know and philosophy is what you do not know. Philosophy is that part of science which at present people choose to have opinions about, but which they have no knowledge about. Therefore every advance in knowledge robs philosophy of some problems which formerly it had, and if there is any truth, if there is any value in the kind of procedure of mathematical logic, it will follow that a number of problems which had belonged to philosophy will have ceased to belong to philosophy and will belong to science. And of course the moment they become soluble, they become to a large class of philosophical minds uninteresting, because to many of the people who like philosophy, the charm of it consists in the speculative freedom, in the fact that you can play with hypotheses. You can think out this or that which *may* be true, which is a very valuable exercise until you discover what *is* true; but when you discover what is true the whole fruitful play of fancy in that region is curtailed, and you will abandon that region and pass on. Just as there are families in America who from the time of the Pilgrim Fathers onward had always migrated westward, toward the backwoods, because they did not like civilized life, so the philosopher has an adventurous disposition and likes to dwell in the region where there are still uncertainties. It is true that the transferring of a region from philosophy into science will make it distasteful to a very important and useful type of mind. I think that is true of a good deal of the applications of mathematical logic in the directions that I have been indicating. It makes it dry, precise, methodical, and in that way robs it of a certain quality that it had when you could play with it more freely. I do not feel that it is my place to apologize for that, because if it is true, it is true. If it is not true, of course, I do owe you an apology; but if it is, it is not my fault, and therefore I do not feel I owe any apology for any sort of dryness or dullness in the world. I would say this too, that for those who have any taste for mathematics, for those who like symbolic constructions, that sort of world is a very delightful one, and if you do not find it otherwise attractive, all that is necessary to do is to acquire a taste for mathematics, and then you will have a very agreeable world, and with that conclusion I will bring this course of lectures to an end.

3

Bertrand Russell CHARACTERISTICS
OF MENTAL PHENOMENA

The Analysis of Mind, from which this selection is taken, was published in 1921, a few years after Russell had given his lectures on Logical Atomism. Characteristically, Russell's views concerning the nature of mind and its relation to matter had altered in the interim. He had come to accept as true the doctrine known as "Neutral Monism." Stated generally, this metaphysical doctrine holds that there is no fundamental, intrinsic difference between what we call mental and what we call physical. The distinction we draw between the mental and the physical is not a distinction between two different kinds of "stuffs," but rather it is a way of distinguishing between different kinds of relations into which a more basic, neutral "stuff" can enter. This view is monistic insofar as it maintains that there is only one kind of entity in the universe. Anyone holding this view must explain why we tend to think of the mental and the physical as quite different. Russell differentiates the two in terms of the difference between the laws of psychology and the laws of physics.

In time, Russell abandoned Neutral Monism, although his later views bear many similarities to the position expressed in the following pages.

This selection should be read in conjunction with selections 6, Part III of 11, and 13.

For further reading on the topic see the following:

Fritz, C. A.: *Bertrand Russell's Construction of the External World.*
Russell, B.: "On the Nature of Acquaintance," in *Logic and Knowledge.*
Schilpp, P. A.: *The Philosophy of Bertrand Russell* (articles by Stace, Boodin, and Laird).

At the end of our journey it is time to return to the question from which we set out, namely: What is it that characterizes mind as opposed to matter? Or, to state

Reprinted with permission of the publisher from *The Analysis of Mind* by Bertrand Russell. Lecture XV. First published in 1921 by The Macmillan Company; London: George Allen and Unwin.

the same question in other terms: How is psychology to be distinguished from physics? The answer provisionally suggested at the outset of our inquiry was that psychology and physics are distinguished by the nature of their causal laws, not by their subject matter. At the same time we held that there is a certain subject matter, namely images, to which only psychological causal laws are applicable; this subject matter, therefore, we assigned exclusively to psychology. But we found no way of defining images except through their causation; in their intrinsic character they appeared to have no universal mark by which they could be distinguished from sensations.

In this last lecture I propose to pass in review various suggested methods of distinguishing mind from matter. I shall then briefly sketch the nature of that fundamental science which I believe to be the true metaphysic, in which mind and matter alike are seen to be constructed out of a neutral stuff, whose causal laws have no such duality as that of psychology, but form the basis upon which both physics and psychology are built.

In search for the definition of "mental phenomena," let us begin with "consciousness," which is often thought to be the essence of mind. In the first lecture I gave various arguments against the view that consciousness is fundamental, but I did not attempt to say what consciousness is. We must find a definition of it, if we are to feel secure in deciding that it is not fundamental. It is for the sake of the proof that it is not fundamental that we must now endeavour to decide what it is.

"Consciousness," by those who regard it as fundamental, is taken to be a character diffused throughout our mental life, distinct from sensations and images, memories, beliefs and desires, but present in all of them. Dr. Henry Head, in an article which I quoted in Lecture III, distinguishing sensations from purely physiological occurrences, says: "Sensation, in the strict sense of the term, demands the existence of consciousness." This statement, at first sight, is one to which we feel inclined to assent, but I believe we are mistaken if we do so. Sensation is the sort of thing of which we *may* be conscious, but not a thing of which we *must* be conscious. We have been led, in the course of our inquiry, to admit unconscious beliefs and unconscious desires. There is, so far as I can see, no class of mental or other occurrences of which we are always conscious whenever they happen.

The first thing to notice is that consciousness must be *of* something. In view of this, I should define "consciousness" in terms of that relation of an image or a word to an object which we defined as "meaning." When a sensation is followed by an image which is a "copy" of it, I think it may be said that the existence of the image constitutes consciousness of the sensation, provided it is accompanied by that sort of belief which, when we reflect upon it, makes us feel that the image is a "sign" of something other than itself. This is the sort of belief which, in the case of memory, we expressed in the words "this occurred"; or which, in the case of a judgment of perception, makes us believe in qualities correlated with present sensations, as e.g., tactile and visual qualities are correlated. The addition of some element of belief seems required, since mere imagination does not involve consciousness of anything, and there can be no consciousness which is not of something. If images alone constituted consciousness of their prototypes, such imagination-images as in fact have prototypes would involve consciousness of them; since this is not the case, an element of belief must be added to the images in defining consciousness. The belief must be of that sort that constitutes objective reference, past or present. An image, together with a belief of this sort concerning it, constitutes, according to our definition, consciousness of the prototype of the image.

But when we pass from consciousness of sensations to consciousness of objects of perception, certain further points arise which demand an addition to our definition. A judgment of perception, we may say, consists of a core of sensation, together with associated images, with belief in the present existence of an object to which sensation and images are referred in a way which is difficult to analyse. Perhaps we might say that the belief is not fundamentally in any *present* existence, but is of the nature of an expectation: for example, when we see an object, we expect certain sensations to result if we proceed to touch it. Perception, then, will consist of a present sensation together with expectations of future sensations. (This, of course, is a reflective analysis, not an account of the way perception appears to unchecked introspection.) But all such expectations are liable to be erroneous, since they are based upon correlations which are usual but not invariable. Any such correlation may mislead us in a particular case, for example, if we try to touch a reflection in a looking-glass under the impression that it is "real." Since memory is fallible, a similar difficulty arises as regards consciousness of past objects. It would seem odd to say that we can be "conscious" of a thing which does not or did not exist. The only way to avoid this awkwardness is to add to our definition the proviso that the beliefs involved in consciousness must be *true*.

In the second place, the question arises as to whether we can be conscious of images. If we apply our definition to this case, it seems to demand images of images. In order, for example, to be conscious of an image of a cat, we shall require, according to the letter of the definition, an image which is a copy of our image of the cat, and has this image for its prototype. Now, it hardly seems probable, as a matter of observation, that there are images of images, as opposed to images of sensations. We may meet this difficulty in two ways, either by boldly denying consciousness of images, or by finding a sense in which, by means of a different accompanying belief, an image, instead of meaning its prototype, can mean another image of the same prototype.

The first alternative, which denies consciousness of images, has already been discussed when we were dealing with Introspection in Lecture VI. We then decided that there must be, in some sense, consciousness of images. We are therefore left with the second suggested way of dealing with knowledge of images. According to this second hypothesis, there may be two images of the same prototype, such that one of them means the other, instead of meaning the prototype. It will be remembered that we defined meaning by association: a word or image means an object, we said, when it has the same associations as the object. But this definition must not be interpreted too absolutely: a word or image will not have *all* the same associations as the object which it means. The word "cat" may be associated with the word "mat," but it would not happen except by accident that a cat would be associated with a mat. And in like manner an image may have certain associations which its prototype will not have, e.g., an association with the word "image." When these associations are active, an image means an image, instead of meaning its prototype. If I have had images of a given prototype many times, I can mean one of these, as opposed to the rest, by recollecting the time and place or any other distinctive association of that one occasion. This happens, for example, when a place recalls to us some thought we previously had in that place, so that we remember a thought as opposed to the occurrence to which it referred. Thus we may say that we think of an image A when we have a similar image B associated with recollections of circumstances connected with A, but not with its prototype or with other images of the same prototype. In this way we become aware of images without the need of any new store of mental contents, merely by the help of new associations. This theory, so far as I can see, solves the problems of introspective knowledge, without requiring heroic measures such as those proposed by Knight Dunlap, whose views we discussed in Lecture VI.

According to what we have been saying, sensation itself is not an instance of consciousness, though the immediate memory by which it is apt to be succeeded is so. A sensation which is remembered becomes an object of consciousness as soon as it begins to be remembered, which will normally be almost immediately after its occurrence (if at all); but while it exists it is not an object of consciousness. If, however, it is part of a perception, say of some familiar person, we may say that the person perceived is an object of consciousness. For in this case the sensation is a *sign* of the perceived object in much the same way in which a memory-image is a sign of a remembered object. The essential practical function of "consciousness" and "thought" is that they enable us to act with reference to what is distant in time or space, even though it is not at present stimulating our senses. This reference to absent objects is possible through association and habit. Actual sensations, in themselves, are not cases of consciousness, because they do not bring in this reference to what is absent. But their connection with consciousness is very close, both through immediate memory, and through the correlations which turn sensations into perceptions.

Enough has, I hope, been said to show that consciousness is far too complex and accidental to be taken as the fundamental characteristic of mind. We have seen that belief and images both enter into it. Belief itself, as we saw in an earlier lecture, is complex. Therefore, if any definition of mind is suggested by our analysis of consciousness, images are what would naturally suggest themselves. But since we found that images can only be defined causally, we cannot deal with this suggestion, except in connection with the difference between physical and psychological causal laws.

I come next to those characteristics of mental phenomena which arise out of mnemic causation. The possibility of action with reference to what is not sensibly present is one of the things that might be held to characterize mind. Let us take first a very elementary example. Suppose you are in a familiar room at night, and suddenly the light goes out. You will be able to find your way to the door without much difficulty by means of the picture of the room which you have in your mind. In this case visual images serve, somewhat imperfectly it is true, the purpose which visual sensations would otherwise serve. The stimulus to the production of visual images is the desire to get out of the room, which consists essentially of present sensations and motor impulses caused by them. Again, words heard or read enable you to act with reference to the matters about which they give information; here, again, a present sensible stimulus, in virtue of habits formed in the past, enables you to act in a manner appropriate to an object which is not sensibly present. The whole essence of the practical efficiency of "thought" consists in sensitiveness to *signs:* the sensible presence of A, which is a sign of the present or future existence of B, enables us to act in a manner appropriate to B. Of this, words are the supreme example, since their effects as signs are prodigious, while their intrinsic interest as sensible occurrences on their own account is usually very slight.

The operation of signs may or may not be accompanied by consciousness. If a sensible stimulus A calls up an image of B, and we then act with reference to B, we have what may be called consciousness of B. But habit may enable us to act in a manner appropriate to B as soon as A appears, without ever having an image of B. In that case, although A operates as a sign, it operates without the help of consciousness. Broadly speaking, a very familiar sign tends to operate directly in this manner, and the intervention of consciousness marks an imperfectly established habit.

The power of acquiring experience, which characterizes men and animals, is an example of the general law that, in mnemic causation, the causal unit is not one event at one time, but two or more events at two or more times. A burnt child fears the fire, that is to say, the neighbourhood of fire has a different effect upon a child which has had the sensations of burning than upon one which has not. More correctly, the observed effect, when a child which has been burnt is put near a fire, has for its cause, not merely the neighbourhood of the fire, but this together with the previous burning. The general formula, when an animal has acquired experience through some event A, is that, when B occurs at some future time, the animal to which A has happened acts differently from an animal which A has not happened. Thus A and B together, not either separately, must be regarded as the cause of the animal's behaviour, unless we take account of the effect which A has had in altering the animal's nervous tissue, which is a matter not patent to external observation except under very special circumstances. With this possibility, we are brought back to causal laws, and to the suggestion that many things which seem essentially mental are really neural. Perhaps it is the nerves that acquire experience rather than the mind. If so, the possibility of acquiring experience cannot be used to define mind.

Very similar considerations apply to memory, if taken as the essence of mind. A recollection is aroused by something which is happening now, but is different from the effect which the present occurrence would have produced if the recollected event had not occurred. This may be accounted for by the physical effect of the past event on the brain, making it a different instrument from that which would have resulted from a different experience. The causal peculiarities of memory *may*, therefore, have a physiological explanation. With every special class of mental phenomena this possibility meets us afresh. If psychology is to be a separate science at all, we must seek a wider ground for its separateness than any that we have been considering hitherto.

We have found that "consciousness" is too narrow to characterize mental phenomena, and that mnemic causation is too wide. I come now to a characteristic which, though difficult to define, comes much nearer to what we require, namely subjectivity.

Subjectivity, as a characteristic of mental phenomena, was considered in Lecture VII, in connection with the definition of perception. We there decided that those particulars which constitute the physical world can be collected into sets in two ways, one of which makes a bundle of all those particulars that are appearances of a given thing from different places, while the other makes a bundle of all those particulars which are appearances of different things from a given place. A bundle of this latter sort, at a given time, is called a "perspective"; taken throughout a period of time, it is called a "biography." Subjectivity is the characteristic of perspectives and biographies, the characteristic of giving the view of the world from a certain place. We saw in Lecture VII that this characteristic involves none of the other characteristics that are commonly associated with mental phenomena, such as consciousness, experience and memory. We found in fact that it is exhibited by a photographic plate, and, strictly speaking, by any particular taken in conjunction with those which have the same "passive" place in the sense defined in Lecture VII. The particulars forming one perspective are connected together primarily by simultaneity; those forming one biography, primarily by the existence of direct time-relations between them. To these are to be added relations derivable from the laws of perspective. In all this we are clearly not in the region of psychology, as commonly understood; yet we are also hardly in the region of physics. And the definition of perspectives and biographies, though it does not yet yield anything that would be commonly called "mental," is presupposed in mental phenomena, for example in mnemic causation: the causal unit in mnemic causation, which gives rise to Semon's engram, is the whole of one perspective—not of *any* perspective, but of a perspective in a place where there is nervous tissue, or at any rate living tissue of some sort. Perception also, as we saw, can only be defined in terms of perspectives. Thus the conception of subjectivity, i.e., of the "passive" place of a particular, though not alone sufficient to define mind, is clearly an essential element in the definition.

I have maintained throughout these lectures that the data of psychology do not differ in their intrinsic character from the data of physics. I have maintained that sensations are data for psychology and physics equally, while images, which may be in some sense exclusively psychological data, can only be distinguished from sensations by their correlations, not by what they are in themselves. It is now necessary, however, to examine the notion of a "datum," and to obtain, if possible, a definition of this notion.

The notion of "data" is familiar throughout science, and is usually treated by men of science as though it were perfectly clear. Psychologists, on the other hand, find great difficulty in the conception. "Data" are naturally defined in terms of theory of knowledge: they are those propositions of which the truth is known without demonstration, so that they may be used as premises in proving other propositions. Further, when a proposition which is a datum asserts the existence of something, we say that the something is a datum, as well as the proposition asserting its existence. Thus those objects of whose existence we become certain through perception are said to be data.

There is some difficulty in connecting this epistemological definition of "data" with our psychological analysis of knowledge; but until such a connection has been effected, we have no right to use the conception "data."

It is clear, in the first place, that there can be no datum apart from a belief. A sensation which merely comes and goes is not a datum; it only becomes a datum when it is remembered. Similarly, in perception, we do not have a datum unless we have a *judgment* of perception. In the sense in which objects (as opposed to propositions) are data, it would seem natural to say that those objects of which we are conscious are data. But consciousness, as we have seen, is a complex notion, involving beliefs, as well as mnemic phenomena such as are required for perception and memory. It follows that no datum is theoretically indubitable, since no belief is infallible; it follows also that every datum has a greater or less degree of vagueness, since there is always some vagueness in memory and the meaning of images.

Data are not those things of which our consciousness is earliest in time. At every period of life, after we have become capable of thought, some of our beliefs are obtained by inference, while others are not. A belief may pass from either of these classes into the other, and may therefore become, or cease to be, a belief giving a datum. When, in what follows, I speak of data, I do not mean the things of which we feel sure before scientific study begins, but the things which, when a science is well advanced, appear as affording grounds for other parts of the science, without themselves being believed on any ground except observation. I assume, that is to say, a trained observer, with an analytic attention, knowing the sort of thing to look for, and the sort of thing that will be important. What he observes is, at the stage of science which he has reached, a datum for his science. It is just as sophisticated and elaborate as the theories which he bases upon it, since only trained habits and much practice enable a man to make the kind of observation that will be scientifically illuminating. Nevertheless, when once it has been observed, belief in it is not based on inference and reasoning, but merely upon its having been seen. In this way its logical status differs from that of the theories which are proved by its means.

In any science other than psychology the datum is primarily a perception, in which only the sensational core is ultimately and theoretically a datum, though some such accretions as turn the sensation into a perception are practically unavoidable. But if we postulate an ideal observer, he will be able to isolate the sensation, and treat this alone as datum. There is, therefore, an important sense in which we may say that, if we analyse as much as we ought, our data, outside psychology, consist of sensations, which include within themselves certain spatial and temporal relations.

Applying this remark to physiology, we see that the nerves and brain as physical objects are not truly data; they are to be replaced, in the ideal structure of science, by the sensations through which the physiologist is said to perceive them. The passage from these sensations to nerves and brain as physical objects belongs really to the initial stage in the theory of physics, and ought to be placed in the reasoned part, not in the part supposed to be observed. To say we see the nerves is like saying we hear the nightingale; both are convenient but inaccurate expressions. We hear a sound which we believe to be causally connected with the nightingale, and we see a sight which we believe to be causally connected with a nerve. But in each case it is only the sensation that ought, in strictness, to be called a datum. Now, sensations are certainly among the data of psychology. Therefore all the data of the physical sciences are also psychological data. It remains to inquire whether all the data of psychology are also data of physical science, and especially of physiology.

If we have been right in our analysis of mind, the ultimate data of psychology are only sensations and images and their relations. Beliefs, desires, volitions, and so on, appeared to us to be complex phenomena consisting of sensations and images variously interrelated. Thus (apart from certain relations) the occurrences which seem most distinctively mental, and furthest removed from physics, are, like physical objects, constructed or inferred, not part of the original stock of data in the perfected science. From both ends, therefore, the difference between physical and psychological data is diminished. Is there ultimately no difference, or do images remain as irreducibly and exclusively psychological? In view of the causal definition of the difference between images and sensations, this brings us to a new question, namely: Are the causal laws of psychology different from those of any other science, or are they really physiological?

Certain ambiguities must be removed before this question can be adequately discussed.

First, there is the distinction between rough approximate laws and such as appear to be precise and general. I shall return to the former presently; it is the latter that I wish to discuss now.

Matter, as defined at the end of Lecture V, is a logical fiction, invented because it gives a convenient way of stating causal laws. Except in cases of perfect regularity in appearances (of which we can have no experience), the actual appearances of a piece of matter are not members of that ideal system of regular appearances which is defined as being the matter in question. But the matter is, after all, inferred from its appearances, which are used to *verify* physical laws. Thus, in so far as physics is an empirical and verifiable science, it must assume or prove that the inference from appearances to matter is, in general, legitimate, and it must be able to tell us, more or less, what appearances to expect. It is through this question of verifiability and empirical applicability to experience that we are led to a theory of matter such as I advocate. From the consideration of this question it results that physics, in so far as it is an empirical science, not a logical phantasy, is concerned with particulars of just the same sort as those which psychology considers under the name of sensations. The causal laws of physics, so interpreted, differ from those of psychology only by the fact that they connect a particular with other appearances in the same piece of matter, rather than with other appearances in the same perspective. That is to say, they group together particulars having the same "active" place, while psychology groups together those having the same "passive" place. Some particulars, such as images, have no "active" place, and therefore belong exclusively to psychology.

We can now understand the distinction between physics and psychology.

The nerves and brain are matter: our visual sensations when we look at them may be, and I think are, members of the system constituting irregular appearances of this matter, but are not the whole of the system. Psychology is concerned, *inter alia*, with our sensations when we see a piece of matter, as opposed to the matter which we see. Assuming, as we must, that our sensations have physical causes, their causal laws are nevertheless radically different from the laws of physics, since the consideration of a single sensation requires the breaking up of the group of which it is a member. When a sensation is used to verify physics, it is used merely as a sign of a certain material phenomenon, i.e., of a group of particulars of which it is a member. But when it is studied by psychology, it is taken away from that group and put into quite a different context, where it causes images or voluntary movements. It is primarily this different grouping that is characteristic of psychology as opposed to all the physical sciences, including physiology; a secondary difference is that images, which belong to psychology, are not easily to be included among the aspects which constitute a physical thing or piece of matter.

There remains, however, an important question, namely: Are mental events causally dependent upon physical events in a sense in which the converse dependence does not hold? Before we can discuss the answer to this question, we must first be clear as to what our question means.

When, given A, it is possible to infer B, but given B, it is not possible to infer A, we say that B is dependent upon A in a sense in which A is not dependent upon B. Stated in logical terms, this amounts to saying that, when we know a many-one relation of A to B, B is dependent upon A in respect of this relation. If the relation is a causal law, we say that B is causally dependent upon A. The illustration that chiefly concerns us is the system of appearances of a physical object. We can, broadly speaking, infer distant appearances from near ones, but not vice versa. All men look alike when they are a mile away, hence when we see a man a mile off we cannot tell what he will look like when he is only a yard away. But when we see him a yard away, we can tell what he will look like a mile away. Thus the nearer view gives us more valuable information, and the distant view is causally dependent upon it in a sense in which it is not causally dependent upon the distant view.

It is this greater causal potency of the near appearance that leads physics to state its causal laws in terms of that system of regular appearances to which the nearest appearances increasingly approximate, and that makes it value information derived from the microscope or telescope. It is clear that our sensations, considered as irregular appearances of physical objects, share the causal dependence belonging to comparatively distant appearances; therefore in our sensational life we are in causal dependence upon physical laws.

This, however, is not the most important or interesting part of our question. It is the causation of images that is the vital problem. We have seen that they are subject to mnemic causation, and that mnemic causation may be reducible to ordinary physical causation in nervous tissue. This is the question upon which our attitude must turn towards what may be called materialism. One sense of materialism is the view that all mental phenomena are causally dependent upon physical phenomena in the above-defined sense of causal dependence. Whether this is the case or not, I do not profess to know. The question seems to me the same as the question whether mnemic causation is ultimate, which we considered without deciding in Lecture IV. But I think the bulk of the evidence points to the materialistic answer as the more probable.

In considering the causal laws of psychology, the distinction between rough generalizations and exact laws is important. There are many rough generalizations in psychology, not only of the sort by which we govern our ordinary behaviour to each other, but also of a more nearly scientific kind. Habit and association belong among such laws. I will give an illustration of the kind of law that can be obtained. Suppose a person has frequently experienced A and B in close temporal contiguity, an association will be established, so that A, or an image of A, tends to cause an image of B. The question arises: will the association work in either direction, or only from the one which has occurred earlier to the one which has occurred later? In an article by Mr. Wohlgemuth, called "The Direction of Associations" (*British Journal of Psychology*, vol. v, part iv, March, 1913), it is claimed to be proved by experiment that, in so far as motor memory (i.e., memory of movements) is concerned, association works only from earlier to later, while in visual and auditory memory this is not the case, but the later of two neighbouring experiences may recall the earlier as well as the earlier the later. It is suggested that motor memory is physiological, while visual and auditory memory are more truly psychological. But that is not the point which concerns us in the illustration. The point which concerns us is that a law of association, established by purely psychological observation, is a purely psychological law, and may serve as a sample of what is possible in the way of discovering such laws. It is, however, still no more than a rough generalization, a statistical average. It cannot tell us what will result from a given cause on a given occasion. It is a law of tendency, not a precise and invariable law such as those of physics aim at being.

If we wish to pass from the law of habit, stated as a tendency or average, to something more precise and invariable, we seem driven to the nervous system. We can more or less guess how an occurrence produces a change in the brain, and how its repetition gradually produces something analogous to the channel of a river, along which currents flow more easily than in neighbouring paths. We can perceive that in this way, if we had more knowledge, the tendency to habit through repetition might be replaced by a precise account of the effect of each occurrence in bringing about a modification of the sort from which habit would ultimately result. It is such considerations that make students of psychophysiology materialistic in their methods, whatever they may be in their metaphysics. There are, of course, exceptions, such as Professor J. S. Haldane,[1] who maintains that it is theoretically impossible to obtain physiological explanations of psychical phenomena, or physical explanations of physiological phenomena. But I think the bulk of expert opinion, in practice, is on the other side.

The question whether it is possible to obtain precise causal laws in which the causes are psychological, not material, is one of detailed investigation. I

[1] See his book, *The New Physiology and Other Addresses* (Charles Griffin & Co., 1919).

have done what I could to make clear the nature of the question, but I do not believe that it is possible as yet to answer it with any confidence. It seems to be by no means an insoluble question, and we may hope that science will be able to produce sufficient grounds for regarding one answer as much more probable than the other. But for the moment I do not see how we can come to a decision.

I think, however, on grounds of the theory of matter explained in Lectures V and VII, that an ultimate scientific account of what goes on in the world, if it were ascertainable, would resemble psychology rather than physics in what we found to be the decisive difference between them. I think, that is to say, that such an account would not be content to speak, even formally, as though matter, which is a logical fiction, were the ultimate reality. I think that, if our scientific knowledge were adequate to the task, which it neither is nor is likely to become, it would exhibit the laws of correlation of the particulars constituting a momentary condition of a material unit, and would state the causal laws [*] of the world in terms of these particulars, not in terms of matter. Causal laws so stated would, I believe, be applicable to psychology and physics equally; the science in which they were stated would succeed in achieving what metaphysics has vainly attempted, namely a unified account of what really happens, wholly true even if not the whole truth, and free from all convenient fictions or unwarrantable assumptions of metaphysical entities. A causal law applicable to particulars would count as a law of physics if it could be stated in terms of those fictitious systems of regular appearances which are matter; if this were not the case, it would count as a law of psychology if one of the particulars were a sensation or an image, i.e., were subject to mnemic causation. I believe that the realization of the complexity of a material unit, and its analysis into constituents analogous to sensations, is of the utmost importance to philosophy, and vital for any understanding of the relations between mind and matter, between our perceptions and the world which they perceive. It is in this direction, I am convinced, that we must look for the solution of many ancient perplexities.

It is probable that the whole science of mental occurrences, especially where its initial definitions are concerned, could be simplified by the development of the fundamental unifying science in which the causal laws of particulars are sought, rather than the causal laws of those systems of particulars that constitute the material units of physics. This fundamental science would cause physics to become derivative, in the sort of way in which theories of the constitution of the atom make chemistry derivative from physics; it would also cause psychology to appear less singular and isolated among sciences. If we are right in this, it is a wrong philosophy of matter which has caused many of the difficulties in the philosophy of mind—difficulties which a right philosophy of matter would cause to disappear.

The conclusions at which we have arrived may be summed up as follows:

I. Physics and psychology are not distinguished by their material. Mind and matter alike are logical constructions; the particulars out of which they are constructed, or from which they are inferred, have various relations, some of

[*] In a perfected science, causal laws will take the form of differential equations—or of finite-difference equations, if the theory of quanta should prove correct.

which are studied by physics, others by psychology. Broadly speaking, physics group particulars by their active places, psychology by their passive places.

II. The two most essential characteristics of the causal laws which would naturally be called psychological are *subjectivity* and *mnemic causation;* these are not unconnected, since the causal unit in mnemic causation is the group of particulars having a given passive place at a given time, and it is by this manner of grouping that subjectivity is defined.

III. Habit, memory and thought are all developments of mnemic causation. It is probable, though not certain, that mnemic causation is derivative from ordinary physical causation in nervous (and other) tissue.

IV. Consciousness is a complex and far from universal characteristic of mental phenomena.

V. Mind is a matter of degree, chiefly exemplified in number and complexity of habits.

VI. All our data, both in physics and psychology, are subject to psychological causal laws; but physical causal laws, at least in traditional physics, can only be stated in terms of matter, which is both inferred and constructed, never a datum. In this respect psychology is nearer to what actually exists.

4

G. E. *Moore* A DEFENCE
OF COMMON SENSE

Moore's defense of "the Common Sense view of the world" is without doubt a masterpiece of analytic philosophy. Since 1925, when it first appeared, until today, philosophers have been impressed, baffled, or irritated (frequently all three) at Moore's unique
attempt to establish the truth of certain of our common sense beliefs. Special attention
should be paid to the import of Moore's contention that it is not philosophy's role to
question the truth of common sense beliefs, but rather to seek their proper analysis.
The comparison of Moore's view as it is expressed here with that of Russell in selection 2 throws light on some of the basic differences between the two philosophers.

   An excellent discussion of Moore's argument is to be found in "Moore's 'Defence
of Common Sense'" by A. E. Murphy in *The Philosophy of G. E. Moore.* Moore's
"A Reply to My Critics" in the same volume is also worth consulting. A. R. White's
G. E. Moore: A Critical Exposition (Oxford: Blackwell, 1958) contains an interesting
chapter on Moore's attitude toward common sense and ordinary language. See also
the July, 1958, issue of *Philosophy,* which is devoted almost exclusively to articles on
Moore's philosophy.

In what follows I have merely tried to state, one by one, some of the most important points in which my philosophical position differs from positions which
have been taken up by *some* other philosophers. It may be that the points which
I have had room to mention are not really the most important, and possibly some
of them may be points as to which no philosopher has ever really differed from
me. But, to the best of my belief, each is a point as to which many have really
differed; although (in most cases, at all events) each is also a point as to which
many have agreed with me.

From *Contemporary British Philosophy,* 2d series, edited by J. H. Muirhead.
Copyright 1925. George Allen and Unwin; U.S.A.: The Macmillan Company. Used
by permission.

I. The first point is a point which embraces a great many other points. And it is one which I cannot state as clearly as I wish to state it, except at some length. The method I am going to use for stating it is this. I am going to begin by enunciating, under the heading 1, a whole long list of propositions, which may seem, at first sight, such obvious truisms as not to be worth stating: they are, in fact, a set of propositions, every one of which (in my own opinion) I *know,* with certainty, to be true. I shall, next, under the heading 2, state a single proposition which makes an assertion about a whole set of *classes* of propositions—each class being defined, as the class consisting of all propositions which resemble *one* of the propositions in 1 in a certain respect. 2, therefore, is a proposition which could not be stated, until the list of propositions in 1, or some similar list, had already been given. 2 is itself a proposition which may seem such an obvious truism as not to be worth stating: and it is also a proposition which (in my own opinion) I *know,* with certainty, to be true. But, nevertheless, it is, to the best of my belief, a proposition with regard to which many philosophers have, for different reasons, differed from me; even if they have not directly denied 2 itself, they have held views incompatible with it. My first point, then, may be said to be that 2, together with all its implications, some of which I shall expressly mention, is true.

1. I begin, then, with my list of truisms, every one of which (in my own opinion) I *know,* with certainty, to be true. The propositions to be included in this list are the following:

There exists at present a living human body, which is *my* body. This body was born at a certain time in the past, and has existed continuously ever since, though not without undergoing changes; it was, for instance, much smaller when it was born, and for some time afterwards, than it is now. Ever since it was born, it has been either in contact with or not far from the surface of the earth; and, at every moment since it was born, there have also existed many other things, having shape and size in three dimensions (in the same familiar sense in which it has), from which it has been *at various distances* (in the familiar sense in which it is now at a distance both from that mantelpiece and from that bookcase, and at a greater distance from the bookcase than it is from the mantelpiece); also there have (very often, at all events) existed some other things of this kind with which it was *in contact* (in the familiar sense in which it is now in contact with the pen I am holding in my right hand and with some of the clothes I am wearing). Among the things which have, in this sense, formed part of its environment (i.e., have been either in contact with it, or at *some* distance from it, however *great*) there have, at every moment since its birth, been large numbers of other living human bodies, each of which has, like it, (*a*) at some time been born, (*b*) continued to exist from some time after birth, (*c*) been, at every moment of its life after birth, either in contact with or not far from the surface of the earth; and many of these bodies have already died and ceased to exist. But the earth had existed also for many years before my body was born; and for many of these years, also, large numbers of human bodies had, at every moment, been alive upon it; and many of these bodies had died and ceased to exist before it was born. Finally (to come to a different class of propositions), I am a human being, and I have, at different times since my body was born, had many different experiences, of each of many different kinds: e.g., I have often perceived both my own body and other things which formed part of its environment, including other human bodies; I have not only perceived things of this kind, but have also observed facts about them, such as, for instance, the fact which I am now observing, that that mantelpiece is at present nearer to my body than that bookcase; I have been aware of other facts, which I was not at the time observing, such as, for instance, the fact, of which I am now aware, that my body existed yesterday and was then also for some time nearer to that mantelpiece than to that bookcase; I have had expectations with regard to the future, and many beliefs of other kinds, both true and false; I have thought of imaginary things and persons and incidents, in the reality of which I did not believe; I have had dreams; and I have had feelings of many different kinds. And, just as my body has been the body of a human being, namely myself, who has, during his lifetime, had many experiences of each of these (and other) different kinds; so, in the case of very many of the other human bodies which have lived upon the earth, each has been the body of a different human being, who has, during the lifetime of that body, had many different experiences of each of these (and other) different kinds.

2. I now come to the single truism which, as will be seen, could not be stated except by reference to the whole list of truisms, just given in 1. This truism also (in my own opinion) I *know*, with certainty, to be true; and it is as follows:

In the case of *very many* (I do not say *all*) of the human beings belonging to the class (which includes myself) defined in the following way, i.e., as human beings who have had human bodies, that were born and lived for some time upon the earth, and who have, during the lifetime of those bodies, had many different experiences of each of the kinds mentioned in 1, it is true that each has frequently, during the life of his body, known, with regard to *himself* or *his* body, and with regard to some time earlier than any of the times at which I wrote down the propositions in 1, a proposition *corresponding* to each of the propositions in 1, in the sense that it asserts with regard to *himself* or *his* body and the earlier time in question (namely, in each case, the time at which he knew it), just what the corresponding proposition in 1 asserts with regard to *me* or *my* body and the time at which I wrote that proposition down.

In other words what 2 asserts is only (what seems an obvious enough truism) that each of *us* (meaning by "us," very many human beings of the class defined) has frequently *known*, with regard to *himself* or *his* body and the time at which he knew it, everything which, in writing down my list of propositions in 1, I was claiming to know about *myself* or *my* body and the time at which I wrote that proposition down, i.e., just as *I* knew (when I wrote it down) "There exists at present a living human body which is my body," so each of us has frequently known with regard to himself and some other time the different but corresponding proposition, which *he* could *then* have properly expressed by, "There exists *at present* a human body which is *my* body"; just as *I* know "Many human bodies other than mine have before now lived on the earth," so each of us has frequently known the different but corresponding proposition "Many human bodies other than *mine* have before *now* lived on the earth"; just as *I* know "Many human beings other than myself have before now perceived, and dreamed, and felt," so each of *us* has frequently known the different but corresponding proposition "Many human beings other than *myself* have before *now* perceived, and dreamed, and felt"; and so on, in the case of *each* of the propositions enumerated in 1.

I hope there is no difficulty in understanding, so far, what this proposition 2 asserts. I have tried to make clear by examples what I mean by "propositions *corresponding* to each of the propositions in 1." And what 2 asserts is merely that each of us has frequently known to be true a proposition *corresponding* (in that sense) to each of the propositions in 1—a *different* corresponding proposition, of course, at each of the times at which he knew such a proposition to be true.

But there remain two points, which, in view of the way in which some philosophers have used the English language, ought, I think, to be expressly mentioned, if I am to make quite clear exactly how much I am asserting in asserting 2.

The first point is this. Some philosophers seem to have thought it legitimate to use the word "true" in such a sense that a proposition which is partially false may nevertheless also be true; and some of these, therefore, would perhaps *say* that propositions like those enumerated in 1 are, in their view, true, when all the time they believe that every such proposition is partially false. I wish, therefore, to make it quite plain that I am not using "true" in any such sense. I am using it in such a sense (and I think this is the ordinary usage) that if a proposition is partially false, it follows that it is *not* true, though, of course, it may be *partially* true. I am maintaining, in short, that all the propositions in 1, and also many propositions corresponding to each of these, are *wholly* true; I am asserting this in asserting 2. And hence any philosopher, who does in fact believe, with regard to any or all of these classes of propositions, that every proposition of the class in question is partially false, is, in fact, disagreeing with me and holding a view incompatible with 2, even though he may think himself justified in *saying* that he believes some propositions belonging to all of these classes to be "true."

And the second point is this. Some philosophers seem to have thought it legitimate to use such expressions as, e.g., "The earth has existed for many years past," as if they expressed something which they really believed, when in fact they believe that every proposition, which such an expression would *ordinarily* be understood to express, is, at least partially, false; and all they really believe is that there is some *other* set of propositions, related in a certain way to those which such expressions do actually express, which, unlike these, really are true. That is to say, they use the expression "The earth has existed for many years past" to express, not what it would ordinarily be understood to express, but the proposition that some proposition, related to this in a certain way, is true; when all the time they believe that the proposition, which this expression would ordinarily be understood to express, is, at least partially, false. I wish, therefore, to make it quite plain that I was not using the expressions I used in 1 in any such subtle sense. I meant by each of them precisely what every reader, in reading them, will have understood me to mean. And any philosopher, therefore, who hólds that any of these expressions, if understood in this popular manner, expresses a proposition which embodies some popular error, is disagreeing with me and holding a view incompatible with 2, even though he may hold that there is some *other*, true, proposition which the expression in question might be legitimately used to express.

In what I have just said, I have assumed that there is some meaning which is *the* ordinary or popular meaning of such expressions as "The earth has existed for many years past." And this, I am afraid, is an assumption which some philosophers are capable of disputing. They seem to think that the question "Do you believe that the earth has existed for many years past?" is not a plain question, such as should be met either by a plain "Yes" or "No," or by a plain "I can't make up my mind," but is the sort of question which can be properly met by: "It all depends on what you mean by 'the earth' and 'exists' and 'years': if you mean so and so, and so and so, and so and so, then I do; but if you mean so and so, and so and so, and so and so, or so and so, and so and so, and so and so, or so and so, and so and so, and so and so, then I don't, or at least I think it is extremely doubtful." It seems to me that such a view is as profoundly mistaken as any view can be. Such an expression as "The earth has existed for many years past" is the very type of an unambiguous expression, the meaning of which we all understand. Anyone who takes a contrary view must, I suppose, be confusing the question whether we understand its meaning (which we all certainly do) with the entirely different question whether we *know what it means,* in the sense that we are able to *give a correct analysis* of its meaning. The question what is the correct analysis of *the* proposition meant *on any occasion* (for, of course, as I insisted in defining 2, a different proposition is meant at every different time at which the expression is used) by "The earth has existed for many years past" is, it seems to me, a profoundly difficult question, and one to which, as I shall presently urge, no one knows the answer. But to hold that we do not know what, in certain respects, is the analysis of what we understand by such an expression, is an entirely different thing from holding that we do not understand the expression. It is obvious that we cannot even raise the question how what we do understand by it is to be analysed, unless we do understand it. So soon, therefore, as we know that a person who uses such an expression is using it in its ordinary sense, we understand his meaning. So that in explaining that I was using the expressions used in 1 in their ordinary sense (those of them which have an ordinary sense, which is not the case with quite all of them), I have done all that is required to make my meaning clear.

But now, assuming that the expressions which I have used to express 2 are understood, I think, as I have said, that many philosophers have really held views incompatible with 2. And the philosophers who have done so may, I think, be divided into two main groups. A. What 2 asserts is, with regard to a whole set of *classes* of propositions, that we have, each of us, frequently *known* to be true propositions belonging to *each* of these classes. And one way of holding a view incompatible with this proposition is, of course, to hold, with regard to one or more of the classes in question, that *no* propositions of that class *are* true— that all of them are, at least partially, false; since if, in the case of any one of these classes, *no* propositions of that class *are* true, it is obvious that nobody can have *known* any propositions of that class to be true, and therefore that *we* cannot have known to be true propositions belonging to *each* of these classes. And my first group of philosophers consists of philosophers who have held views incompatible with 2 for this reason. They have held, with regard to one or more of the classes in question, simply that no propositions of that class *are* true. Some of them have held this with regard to *all* the classes in question; some only with regard to *some* of them. But, of course, whichever of these two views they have held, they have been holding a view inconsistent with 2. B. Some philosophers, on the other hand, have not ventured to assert, with regard to *any* of the classes in 2, that no propositions of that class *are* true, but what they have asserted is that, in the case of some of these classes, no human being has ever *known*, with certainty, that any propositions of the class in question are true. That is to say, they differ profoundly from philosophers of group A, in that they hold that propositions of *all* these classes *may* be true; but nevertheless they hold a view incompatible with 2 since they hold, with regard to some of these classes, that none of us has ever *known* a proposition of the class in question to be true.

A. I said that some philosophers, belonging to this group, have held that no propositions belonging to *any* of the classes in 2 are wholly true, while others have only held this with regard to *some* of the classes in 2. And I think the chief division of this kind has been the following. Some of the propositions in 1 (and, therefore, of course, all propositions belonging to the corresponding classes in 2) are propositions which cannot be true, unless some *material things* have existed and have stood *in spatial relations* to one another: that is to say, they are propositions which, *in a certain sense,* imply *the reality of material things,* and *the reality of Space.* E.g., the proposition that my body has existed for many years past, and has, at every moment during that time been either in contact with or not far from the earth, is a proposition which implies both the *reality of material things* (provided you use "material things" in such a sense that to deny the reality of material things implies that no proposition which asserts that human bodies have existed, or that the earth has existed, is wholly true) and also the *reality of Space* (provided, again, that you use "Space" in such a sense that to deny the reality of Space implies that no proposition which asserts that anything has ever been in contact with or at a distance from another, in the familiar senses pointed out in 1, is wholly true). But others among the propositions in 1 (and, therefore, propositions belonging to the corresponding classes in 2), do not (at least obviously) imply either the reality of material things or the reality of Space: e.g., the propositions that I have often had dreams, and have had many different feelings at different times. It is true that propositions of this second class do imply one thing which is also implied by all propositions of the first, namely that (*in a certain sense*) *Time is real,* and imply also one thing not implied by propositions of the first class, namely that (*in a certain sense*) *at least one Self is real.* But I think there are some philosophers, who, while denying that (in the senses in question) either material things or Space are real, have been willing to admit that Selves and Time are real, in the sense required. Other philosophers, on the other hand, have used the expression "Time is not real," to express some view that they held; and some, at least, of these have, I think, meant by this expression something which is incompatible with the truth of *any* of the propositions in 1—they have meant, namely, that *every* proposition of the sort that is expressed by the use of "now" or "at present," e.g., "I am now both seeing and hearing" or "There exists at present a living human body," or by the use of a *past* tense, e.g., "I *have* had many experiences in the past," or "The earth *has* existed for many years," are, at least partially, false.

All the four expressions I have just introduced, namely, "Material things are not real," "Space is not real," "Time is not real," "The Self is not real," are, I think, unlike the expressions I used in 1, really ambiguous. And it may be that, in the case of each of them, some philosopher has used the expression in question to express some view he held which was not incompatible with 2. With such philosophers, if there are any, I am not, of course, at present concerned. But it seems to me that the most natural and proper usage of each of these expressions is a usage in which it *does* express a view incompatible with 2; and, in the case of each of them, some philosophers have, I think, really used the expression in question to express such a view. All such philosophers have, therefore, been holding a view incompatible with 2.

All such views, whether incompatible with *all* of the propositions in 1, or only with *some* of them, seem to me to be quite certainly false; and I think the following points are specially deserving of notice with regard to them:

(*a*) If *any* of the classes of propositions in 2 is such that no proposition of that class is true, then no philosopher has ever existed, and therefore none can ever have held with regard to any such class, that no proposition belonging to it is true. In other words, the proposition that some propositions belonging to each of these classes are true is a proposition which has the peculiarity, that, if any philosopher has ever denied it, it follows from the fact that he has denied it, that he must have been wrong in denying it. For when I speak of "philosophers" I mean, of course (as we all do), exclusively philosophers who have been human beings, with human bodies that have lived upon the earth, and who have at different times had many different experiences. If, therefore, there have been any philosophers, there have been human beings of this class; and if there have been human beings of this class, all the rest of what is asserted in 1 is certainly true too. Any view, therefore, incompatible with the proposition that many propositions corresponding to each of the propositions in 1 are true, can only be true, on the hypothesis that no philosopher has ever held any such view. It follows, therefore, that, in considering whether this proposition is true, I cannot consistently regard the fact that many philosophers, whom I respect, have, to the best of my belief, held views incompatible with it, as having any weight at all against it. Since, if I know that they have held such views, I am, *ipso facto*, knowing that they were mistaken; and, if I have no reason to believe that the proposition in question is true, I have still less reason to believe that they have held views incompatible with it; since I am more certain that they have existed and held *some* views, i.e., that the proposition in question is true, than that they have held any views incompatible with it.

(*b*) It is, of course, the case that all philosophers who have held such views have repeatedly, even in their philosophical works, expressed other views inconsistent with them: i.e., no philosopher has ever been able to hold such views consistently. One way in which they have betrayed this inconsistency is by alluding to the existence of other philosophers. Another way is by alluding to the existence of the human race, and in particular by using "we" in the sense in which I have already constantly used it, in which any philosopher who asserts that "we" do so and so, e.g., that "*we* sometimes believe propositions that are not true," is asserting not only that he himself has done the thing in question, but that *very many other human beings, who have had bodies and lived upon the earth,* have done the same. The fact is, of course, that all philosophers have belonged to the class of human beings which exists only if 2 be true: that is to say, to the class of human beings who have frequently *known* propositions corresponding to each of the propositions in 1. In holding views incompatible with the proposition that propositions of all these classes are true, they have, therefore, been holding views inconsistent with propositions which they themselves *knew* to be true; and it was, therefore, only to be expected that they should sometimes betray their knowledge of such propositions. The strange thing is that philosophers should have been able to hold sincerely, as part of their philosophical creed, propositions inconsistent with what they themselves *knew* to be true; and yet, so far as I can make out, this has really frequently happened. My position, therefore, on this first point, differs from that of philosophers belonging to this group A, not in that I hold anything which they don't hold, but only in that I don't hold, as part of my philosophical creed, things which they do hold as part of theirs—that is to say, propositions inconsistent with some which they and I both hold in common. But this difference seems to me to be an important one.

(*c*) Some of these philosophers have brought forward, in favour of their position, arguments designed to show, in the case of some or all of the propositions in 1, that no propositions of that type can possibly be wholly true, because every such proposition entails both of two incompatible propositions. And I admit, of course, that if any of the propositions in 1 did entail both of two incompatible propositions it could not be true. But it seems to me I have an absolutely conclusive argument to show that none of them does entail both of two incompatible propositions. Namely this: All of the propositions in 1 are true; no true proposition entails both of two incompatible propositions; therefore, none of the propositions in 1 entails both of two incompatible propositions.

(*d*) Although, as I have urged, no philosopher who has held with regard to any of these types of proposition that no propositions of that type are true, has failed to hold also other views inconsistent with his view in this respect, yet I do not think that the view, with regard to any or all of these types, that no proposition belonging to them is true, is *in itself* a self-contradictory view, i.e., entails both of two incompatible propositions. On the contrary, it seems to me quite clear that it *might* have been the case that Time was not real, material things not real, Space not real, selves not real. And in favour of my view that none of these things, which might have been the case, *is* in fact the case, I have, I think, no better argument than simply this—namely, that all the propositions in 1 are, in fact, true.

B. This view, which is usually considered a much more modest view than A, has, I think, the defect that, unlike A, it really is self-contradictory, i.e., entails both of two mutually incompatible propositions.

Most philosophers who have held this view, have held, I think, that though each of us knows propositions corresponding to *some* of the propositions in 1, namely to those which merely assert that *I* myself have had in the past experiences of certain kinds at many different times, yet none of us knows *for certain* any propositions either of the type (*a*) which assert the existence of *material things* or of the type (*b*) which assert the existence of *other* selves, beside myself, and that *they* also have had experiences. They admit that we do in fact *believe* propositions of both these types, and that they *may* be true: some would even say that we know them to be highly probable; but they deny that we ever know them, *for certain,* to be true. Some of them have spoken of such beliefs as "beliefs of Common Sense," expressing thereby their conviction that beliefs of this kind are very commonly entertained by mankind: but they are convinced that these things are, in all cases, only *believed,* not known for certain; and some have expressed this by saying that they are matters of Faith, not of Knowledge.

Now the remarkable thing which those who take this view have not, I think, in general duly appreciated, is that, in each case, the philosopher who takes it is making an assertion about "us"—that is to say, not merely about himself, but about *many other human beings as well.* When he says "No human being has ever *known* of the existence of other human beings," he is saying: "There have been many other human beings beside myself, and none of them (including myself) has ever known of the existence of other human beings." If he says: "These beliefs are beliefs of Common Sense, but they are not matters of *knowledge,*" he is saying: "There have been many other human beings, beside myself, who have shared these beliefs, but neither I nor any of the rest has ever known them to be true." In other words, he asserts with confidence that these beliefs *are* beliefs of Common Sense, and seems often to fail to notice that, *if* they are, they must be true; since the proposition that they are beliefs of Common Sense is one which logically entails propositions both of type (*a*) and of type (*b*); it logically entails the proposition that many human beings, beside the philosopher himself, have had human bodies, which lived upon the earth, and have had various experiences, including beliefs of this kind. This is why this position, as contrasted with positions of group A, seems to me to be self-contradictory. Its difference from A consists in the fact that it is making a proposition about *human knowledge* in general, and therefore is actually asserting the existence of many human beings, whereas philosophers of group A in stating their position are not doing this: they are only contradicting *other* things which they hold. It is true that a philosopher who says "There have existed many human beings beside myself, and none of us has ever known of the existence of any human beings beside himself," is only contradicting himself if what he holds is "There have *certainly* existed many human beings beside myself" or, in other words, "*I* know that there have existed other human beings beside myself." But this, it seems to me, is what such philosophers have in fact been generally doing. They seem to me constantly to betray the fact that they regard the proposition that those beliefs *are* beliefs of Common Sense, or the proposition that they themselves are not the only members of the human race, as not merely true, but *certainly* true; and *certainly* true it cannot be, unless one member, at least, of the human race, namely themselves, has *known* the very things which that member is declaring that no human being has ever known.

Nevertheless, my position, that I *know*, with certainty, to be true all of the propositions in 1, is certainly not a position, the denial of which entails both of two incompatible propositions. If I do *know* all these propositions to be true, then, I think, it is quite certain that other human beings also have known corresponding propositions: that is to say 2 also *is* true, and *I* know it to be true. But do I really *know* all the propositions in 1 to be true? Isn't it possible that I merely believe them? Or know them to be highly probable? In answer to this question, I think I have nothing better to say than that it seems to me that I *do* know them, with certainty. It is, indeed, obvious that, in the case of most of them, I do not know them *directly*: that is to say, I only know them because, in the past, I have known to be true *other* propositions which were evidence for them. If, for instance, I do know that the earth had existed for many years before I was born, I certainly only know this because I have known other things in the past which were evidence for it. And I certainly do not know exactly what the evidence was. Yet all this seems to me to be no good reason for doubting that I do know it. We are all, I think, in this strange position that we do *know* many things, with regard to which we *know* further that we must have had evidence for them, and yet we do not know *how* we know them, i.e., we do not know what the evidence was. If there is any "we," and if we know that there is, this must be so: for that there is a "we" is one of the things in question. And that I do know that there is a "we," that is to say, that many other human beings, with human bodies, have lived upon the earth, it seems to me that I do know, for certain.

If this first point in my philosophical position, namely, my belief in 2, is to be given any name, which has actually been used by philosophers in classifying the positions of other philosophers, it would have, I think, to be expressed by saying that I am one of those philosophers who have held that the "Common Sense view of the world" is, in certain fundamental features, *wholly* true. But it must be remembered that, according to me, *all* philosophers, without exception, have agreed with me in holding this: and that the real difference, which is commonly expressed in this way, is only a difference between those philosophers, who have *also* held views inconsistent with these features in "the Common Sense view of the world," and those who have not.

The features in question (namely, propositions of any of the classes defined in defining 2) are all of them features, which have this peculiar property— namely, that *if we know that they are features in the "Common Sense view of the world," it follows that they are true:* it is self-contradictory to maintain that *we* know them to be features in the Common Sense view, and that yet they are not true; since to say that *we* know this, is to say that they are true. And many of them also have the further peculiar property that, *if they are features in the Common Sense view of the world (whether "we" know this or not), it follows that they are true,* since to say that there is a "Common Sense view of the world," is to say that they are true. The phrases "Common Sense view of the world" or "Common Sense beliefs" (as used by philosophers) are, of course, extraordinarily vague; and, for all I know, there may be many propositions which may be properly called features in "the Common Sense view of the world" or "Common Sense beliefs," which are not true, and which deserve to be mentioned with the contempt with which some philosophers speak of "Common Sense beliefs." But to speak with contempt of those "Common Sense beliefs" which I have mentioned is quite certainly the height of absurdity. And there are, of course, enormous numbers of other features in "the Common Sense view of the world" which, if these are true, are quite certainly true too: e.g., that there have lived upon the surface of the earth not only human beings, but also many different species of plants and animals, etc., etc.

II. What seems to me the next in importance of the points in which my philosophical position differs from positions held by *some* other philosophers, is one which I will express in the following way. I hold, namely, that there is no good reason to suppose either (A) that *every* physical fact is *logically* dependent upon some mental fact or (B) that *every* physical fact is *causally* dependent upon some mental fact. In saying this, I am not, of course, saying that there *are* any physical facts which are wholly independent (i.e., both logically and causally) of mental facts: I do, in fact, believe that there are; but that is not what I am asserting. I am only asserting that there is *no good reason* to suppose the contrary; by which I mean, of course, that none of the human beings, who have had human bodies that lived upon the earth, have, during the lifetime of their bodies, had any good reason to suppose the contrary. Many philosophers have, I think, not only believed either that *every* physical fact is *logically* dependent upon some mental fact ("physical fact" and "mental fact" being understood in the sense in which I am using these terms) or that *every* physical fact is *causally* dependent upon some mental fact, or both, but also that they themselves had good reason for these beliefs. In this respect, therefore, I differ from them.

In the case of the term "physical fact," I can only explain how I am using it by giving examples. I mean by "physical facts," facts *like* the following: "That mantelpiece is at present nearer to this body than that bookcase is," "The earth has existed for many years past," "The moon has at every moment for many years past been nearer to the earth than to the sun," "That mantelpiece is of a light colour." But, when I say "facts *like* these," I mean, of course, facts like them *in a certain respect;* and what this respect is I cannot define. The term "physical fact" is, however, in common use; and I think that I am using it in its ordinary sense. Moreover, there is no need for a definition to make my point clear; since among the examples I have given there are some with regard to which I hold that there is no reason to suppose *them* (i.e., these particular physical facts) either logically or causally dependent upon any mental fact.

"Mental fact," on the other hand, is a much more unusual expression, and I am using it in a specially limited sense, which, though I think it is a natural one, does need to be explained. There may be many other senses in which the term can be properly used, but I am only concerned with this one; and hence it is essential that I should explain what it is.

There may, possibly, I hold, be "mental facts" of three different kinds,

It is only with regard to the first kind that I am sure that there are facts of that kind; but if there were any facts of either of the other two kinds, they would be "mental facts" in my limited sense, and therefore I must explain what is meant by the hypothesis that there are facts of those two kinds.

(a) My first kind is this. I am conscious now; and also I am seeing something now. These two facts are both of them mental facts of my first kind; and my first kind consists exclusively of facts which resemble one or other of the two *in a certain respect*.

(α) The fact that I am conscious now is obviously, in a certain sense, a fact, with regard to a particular individual and a particular time, to the effect that that individual is conscious at that time. And every fact which resembles this one in that respect is to be included in my first kind of mental fact. Thus the fact that I was also conscious at many different times yesterday is not itself a fact of this kind: but it entails that there *are* (or, as we should commonly say, because the times in question are past times, "were") many other facts of this kind, namely, each of the facts, which, at each of the times in question, I could have properly expressed by "I am conscious *now*." *Any* fact which is, in this sense, a fact with regard to an individual and a time (whether the individual be myself or another, and whether the time be past or present), to the effect that that individual *is* conscious at that time, is to be included in my first kind of mental fact: and I call such facts, facts of class (α).

(β) The second example I gave, namely, the fact that I am seeing something now, is obviously related to the fact that I am conscious now in a peculiar manner. It not only *entails* the fact that I am conscious now (for from the fact that I am seeing something it *follows* that I am conscious: I *could* not have been seeing anything, unless I had been conscious, though I might quite well have been conscious without seeing anything) but it also is a fact, with regard to a *specific way* (or mode) of being conscious, to the effect that I am conscious in that way: in the same sense in which the proposition (with regard to any particular thing) "This is red" both entails the proposition (with regard to the same thing) "This is coloured," and is also a proposition, with regard to a *specific way* of being coloured, to the effect that that thing is coloured in that way. And any fact which is related in this peculiar manner to any fact of class (α), is also to be included in my first kind of mental fact, and is to be called a fact of class (β). Thus the fact that I am hearing now is, like the fact that I am seeing now, a fact of class (β); and so is any fact, with regard to myself and a past time, which could at that time have been properly expressed by "I am dreaming now," "I am imagining now," "I am at present aware of the fact that . . . ," etc., etc. In short, any fact which is a fact with regard to a particular individual (myself or another), a particular time (past or present), and *any particular kind of experience,* to the effect that that individual is having at that time an experience of that particular kind, is a fact of class (β): and only such facts are facts of class (β).

My first kind of mental facts consists exclusively of facts of classes (α) and (β), and consists of *all* facts of either of these kinds.

(b) That there are many facts of classes (α) and (β) seems to me perfectly certain. But many philosophers seem to me to have held a certain view with regard to the *analysis* of facts of class (α), which is such that, if it were true, there would be facts of another kind, which I should wish also to call "mental facts." I don't feel at all sure that this analysis is true; but it seems to me that it *may* be true; and since we can understand what is meant by the supposition that it is true, we can also understand what is meant by the supposition that there are "mental facts" of this second kind.

Many philosophers have, I think, held the following view as to the analysis of what each of us knows, when he knows (at any time) "I am conscious now." They have held, namely, that there is a certain intrinsic property (with which we are all of us familiar and which might be called that of "being an experience") which is such that, at any time at which any man knows "I am conscious now," he is knowing, with regard to that property and himself and the time in question, "There is occurring now an event which has this property (i.e., 'is an experience') and which is an experience of *mine*," and such that this fact is what he expresses by "I am conscious now." And if this view is true, there must be many facts of each of three kinds, each of which I should wish to call "mental facts"; viz., (1) facts with regard to some event, which has this supposed intrinsic property, and to some time, to the effect that that event is occurring at that time, (2) facts with regard to this supposed intrinsic property and some time, to the effect that *some* event which has that property is occurring at that time, and (3) facts with regard to some property, which is a *specific way* of having the supposed intrinsic property (in the sense above explained in which "being red" is a specific way of "being coloured") and some time, to the effect that some event which has that specific property is occurring at that time. Of course, there not only are not, but *cannot* be, facts of any of these kinds, unless there is an intrinsic property related to what each of us (on any occasion) expresses by "I am conscious now," in the manner defined above; and I feel very doubtful whether there is any such property; in other words, although I know for certain both that I have had many experiences, and that I have had experiences of many different kinds, I feel very doubtful whether to say the first is the same thing as to say that there have been many events, each of which was an experience and an experience of mine, and whether to say the second is the same thing as to say that there have been many events, each of which was an experience of mine, and each of which also had a different property, which was a specific way of being an experience. The proposition that I have had experiences does not necessarily entail the proposition that there have been any events which were experiences; and I cannot satisfy myself that I am acquainted with any events of the supposed kind. But yet it seems to me possible that the proposed analysis of "I am conscious now" is correct: that I am really acquainted with events of the supposed kind, though I cannot see that I am. And *if* I am, then I should wish to call the three kinds of facts defined above "mental facts." Of course, if there are "experiences" in the sense defined, it would be possible (as many have held) that there *can* be no experiences which are not *some individual's* experiences; and in that case any fact of any of these three kinds would be logically dependent on, though not necessarily identical with, some fact of class (α) or class (β). But it seems to me also a possibility that, if there are "experiences," there might be experiences which did not belong to any individual; and, in that case, there would be "mental facts" which were neither identical with nor logically dependent on any fact of class (α) or class (β).

(c) Finally some philosophers have, so far as I can make out, held that there are or may be facts which are facts with regard to some individual, to the effect that he is conscious, or is conscious in some specific way, but which differ from facts of classes (α) and (β), in the important respect that they are not facts *with regard to any time·* they have conceived the possibility that there may be one or more individuals, who are *timelessly* conscious, and timelessly conscious in specific modes. And others, again, have, I think, conceived the hypothesis that the intrinsic property defined in (b) may be one which does not belong only to *events*, but may also belong to one or more wholes, which do *not* occur at any time: in other words, that there may be one or more *timeless* experiences, which might or might not be the experiences of some individual. It seems to me very doubtful whether any of these hypotheses are even possibly true; but I cannot see for certain that they are not possible: and, if they are possible, then I should wish to give the name "mental fact" to any fact (if there were any) of any of the five following kinds, viz., (1) to any fact which is the fact, with regard to any individual, that he is *timelessly* conscious, (2) to any fact which is the fact, with regard to any individual, that he is *timelessly* conscious in any specific way, (3) to any fact which is the fact with regard to a *timeless* experience that it exists, (4) to any fact which is the fact with regard to the supposed intrinsic property "being an experience," that something timelessly exists which has that property, and (5) to any fact which is the fact, with regard to any property, which is a specific mode of this supposed intrinsic property, that something timelessly exists which has that property.

I have, then, defined three different kinds of facts, each of which is such that, if there *were* any facts of that kind (as there certainly *are*, in the case of the first kind), the facts in question *would be* "mental facts" in my sense; and to complete the definition of the limited sense in which I am using "mental facts," I have only to add that I wish also to apply the name to one *fourth* class of facts: namely, to any fact, which is the fact, with regard to any of these three kinds of facts, or any kinds included in them, *that there are facts of the kind in question*; i.e., not only will each individual fact of class (α) be, in my sense, a "mental fact," but also the general fact "that there are facts of class (α)," will itself be a "mental fact"; and similarly in all other cases: e.g., not only will the fact that I am now perceiving (which is a fact of class β) be a "mental fact," but also the general fact that *there are* facts, with regard to individuals and times, to the effect that the individual in question is perceiving at the time in question, will be a "mental fact."

A. Understanding "physical fact" and "mental fact" in the senses just explained, I hold, then, that there is no good reason to suppose that *every* physical fact is *logically* dependent upon some mental fact. And I use the phrase, with regard to two facts, F_1 and F_2, "F_1 is *logically dependent* on F_2," wherever and only where F_1 *entails* F_2, either in the sense in which the proposition "I am seeing now" *entails* the proposition "I am conscious now," or the proposition (with regard to any particular thing) "This is red" entails the proposition (with regard to the same thing) "This is coloured," or else in the more strictly logical sense in which (for instance) the conjunctive proposition "All men are mortal, and Mr. Baldwin is a man" entails the proposition "Mr. Baldwin is mortal." To say, then, of two facts, F_1 and F_2, that F_1 is *not* logically dependent upon F_2, is only to say that F_1 *might* have been a fact, even if there had been no such fact as F_2; or that the conjunctive proposition "F_1 is a fact, but there is no such fact as F_2," is a proposition which is not self-contradictory, i.e., does not entail both of two mutually incompatible propositions.

I hold, then, that, in the case of *some* physical facts, there is no good reason to suppose that there is some mental fact, such that the physical fact in question could not have been a fact unless the mental fact in question had also been one. And my position is perfectly definite, since I hold that this is the case with all the four physical facts, which I have given as examples of physical facts. For example, there is no good reason to suppose that there is any mental fact whatever, such that the fact that that mantelpiece is at present nearer to my body than that bookcase could not have been a fact, unless the mental fact in question had also been a fact; and, similarly, in all the other three cases.

In holding this I am certainly differing from some philosophers. I am, for instance, differing from Berkeley, who held that that mantelpiece, that bookcase, and my body are, all of them, either "ideas" or "constituted by ideas," and that no "idea" can possibly exist without being perceived. He held, that is, that this physical fact is logically dependent upon a mental fact of my fourth class: namely, a fact which is the fact that there is at least one fact, which is a fact with regard to an individual and the present time, to the effect that that individual is now perceiving something. He does not say that this physical fact is logically dependent upon any fact which is a fact of any of my first three classes, e.g., on any fact which is the fact, with regard to a particular individual and the present time, that *that* individual is now perceiving something: what he does say is that the physical fact couldn't have been a fact, unless it had been a fact that there was *some* mental fact of this sort. And it seems to me that many philosophers, who would perhaps disagree either with Berkeley's assumption that my body is an "idea" or "constituted by ideas," or with his assumption that "ideas" cannot exist without being perceived, or with both, nevertheless would agree with him in thinking that this physical fact is logically dependent upon *some* "mental fact": e.g., they might say that it could not have been a fact, unless there had been, at some time or other, or, were timelessly, *some* "experience." Many, indeed, so far as I can make out, have held that *every* fact is logically dependent on every other fact. And, of course, they have held in the case of their opinions, as Berkeley did in the case of his, that they had good reasons for them.

B. I also hold that there is no good reason to suppose that *every* physical fact is *causally* dependent upon some mental fact. By saying that F_1 is *causally* dependent on F_2, I mean only that F_1 *wouldn't* have been a fact unless F_2 had been; *not* (which is what "logically dependent" asserts) that F_1 *couldn't conceivably* have been a fact, unless F_2 had been. And I can illustrate my meaning by reference to the example which I have just given. The fact that that mantel-piece is at present nearer to my body than that bookcase, is (as I have just explained) so far as I can see, not *logically* dependent upon any mental fact; it *might* have been a fact, even if there had been no mental facts. But it certainly is *causally* dependent on many mental facts: my body *would* not have been here unless I had been conscious in various ways in the past; and the mantelpiece and the bookcase certainly *would* not have existed, unless other men had been conscious too.

But with regard to two of the facts, which I gave as instances of physical facts, namely the fact that the earth has existed for many years past, and the fact that the moon has for many years past been nearer to the earth than to the sun, I hold that there is no good reason to suppose that these are *causally* dependent upon any mental fact. So far as I can see, there is no reason to suppose that there is any mental fact of which it could be truly said: unless this fact had been a fact, the earth would not have existed for many years past. And in holding this, again, I think I differ from some philosophers. I differ, for instance, from those who have held that all material things were created by God, and that they had good reasons for supposing this.

III. I have just explained that I differ from those philosophers who have held that there is good reason to suppose that all material things were created by God. And it is, I think, an important point in my position, which should be mentioned, that I differ also from all philosophers who have held that there is good reason to suppose that there is a God at all, whether or not they have held it likely that he created all material things.

And similarly, whereas some philosophers have held that there is good reason to suppose that we, human beings, shall continue to exist and to be conscious after the death of our bodies, I hold that there is no good reason to suppose this.

IV. I now come to a point of a very different order.

As I have explained under II, I am not at all sceptical as to the *truth* of such propositions as "The earth has existed for many years past," "Many human bodies have each lived for many years upon it," i.e., propositions which assert the existence of material things: on the contrary, I hold that we all know, with certainty, many such propositions to be true. But I am very sceptical as to what, in certain respects, the correct *analysis* of such propositions is. And this is a matter as to which I think I differ from many philosophers. Many seem to hold that there is no doubt at all as to their *analysis*, nor, therefore, as to the analysis of the proposition "Material things have existed," in certain respects in which I hold that the analysis of the propositions in question is extremely doubtful; and some of them, as we have seen, while holding that there is no doubt as to their *analysis*, seem to have doubted whether any such propositions are *true*. I, on the other hand, while holding that there is no doubt whatever that many such propositions are wholly true, hold also that no philosopher, hitherto, has succeeded in suggesting an analysis of them, as regards certain important points, which comes anywhere near to being certainly true.

what does "simpler" mean here?

It seems to me quite evident that the question how propositions of the type I have just given are to be analysed depends on the question how propositions of another and simpler type are to be analysed. I know, at present, that I am perceiving a human hand, a pen, a sheet of paper, etc.; and it seems to me that I cannot know how the proposition "Material things exist" is to be analysed, until I know how, in certain respects, these simpler propositions are to be analysed. But even these are not simple enough. It seems to me quite evident that my knowledge that I am now perceiving a human hand is a deduction from a pair of propositions simpler still—propositions which I can only express in the form "I am perceiving *this*" and "*This* is a human hand." It is the analysis of propositions of the latter kind which seems to me to present such great difficulties, while nevertheless the whole question as to the *nature* of material things obviously depends upon their analysis. It seems to me a surprising thing that so few philosophers, while saying a great deal as to what material things *are* and as to what it is to perceive them, have attempted to give a clear account as to what precisely they suppose themselves to *know* (or to *judge*, in case they have held that we don't *know* any such propositions to be true, or even that no such propositions *are* true) when they know or judge such things as "This is a hand," "That is the sun," "This is a dog," etc., etc., etc.

Two things only seem to me to be quite certain about the analysis of such propositions (and even with regard to these I am afraid some philosophers would differ from me), namely, that whenever I know, or judge, such a proposition to be true, (1) there is always some *sense-datum* about which the proposition in question is a proposition—some sense-datum which is *a* subject (and, in a certain sense, the principal or ultimate subject) of the proposition in question, and (2) that, nevertheless, *what* I am knowing or judging to be true about this sense-datum is not (in general) that it is *itself* a hand, or a dog, or the sun, etc., etc., as the case may be.

Some philosophers have I think doubted whether there are any such things as other philosophers have meant by "sense-data" or "sensa." And I think it is quite possible that some philosophers (including myself, in the past) have used these terms in senses such that it is really doubtful whether there are any such things. But there is no doubt at all that there are sense-data, in the sense in which I am now using that term. I am at present seeing a great number of them, and feeling others. And in order to point out to the reader what sort of things I mean by sense-data, I need only ask him to look at his own right hand. If he does this he will be able to pick out something (and, unless he is seeing double, *only* one thing) with regard to which he will see that it is, at first sight, a natural view to take that that thing is identical, not, indeed, with his whole right hand, but with that part of its surface which he is actually seeing, but will also (on a little reflection) be able to see that it is doubtful whether it can be identical with the part of the surface of his hand in question. Things *of the sort* (in a certain respect) of which this thing is, which he sees in looking at his hand, and with regard to which he can understand how some philosophers should have supposed it to *be* the part of the surface of his hand which he is seeing, while others have supposed that it can't be, are what I mean by "sense-data." I therefore define the term in such a way that it is an open ques-

... are what I mean by "rubber glove"

O. K. Bouwsma

(reported by David McNaughton)

tion whether the sense-datum which I now see in looking at my hand and which is a sense-datum of my hand is or is not identical with that part of its surface which I am now actually seeing.

That what I know, with regard to this sense-datum, when I know "This is a human hand," is not that it is *itself* a human hand, seems to me certain because I know that my hand has many parts (e.g., its other side, and the bones inside it), which are quite certainly *not* parts of this sense-datum.

I think it certain, therefore, that the analysis of the proposition "This is a human hand" is, roughly at least, of the form "There is a thing, and only one thing, of which it is true both that it is a human hand and that *this surface* is a part of its surface." In other words, to put my view in terms of the phrase "theory of representative perception," I hold it to be quite certain that I do not *directly* perceive *my hand;* and that when I am said (as I may be correctly said) to "perceive" it, that I "perceive" it means that I perceive (in a different and more fundamental sense) something which is (in a suitable sense) *representative* of it, namely, a certain part of its surface.

This is all that I hold to be *certain* about the analysis of the proposition "This is a human hand." We have seen that it includes in its analysis a proposition of the form "This is part of the surface of a human hand" (where "This," of course, has a different meaning from that which it has in the original proposition which has now been analysed). But this proposition also is undoubtedly a proposition about the sense-datum, which I am seeing, which is a sense-datum *of* my hand. And hence the further question arises: *What,* when I know *"This is part of the surface of* a human hand," am I knowing about the sense-datum in question? Am I, in this case, really knowing about the sense-datum in question that it *itself* is part of the surface of a human hand? Or, just as we found in the case of "This is a human hand," that what I was knowing about the sense-datum was certainly not that it *itself* was a human hand, so, is it perhaps the case, with this new proposition, that even here I am not knowing, with regard to the sense-datum, that it is *itself* part of the surface of a hand? And, if so, what is it that I am knowing about the sense-datum itself?

This is the question to which, as it seems to me, no philosopher has hitherto suggested an answer which comes anywhere near to being *certainly* true.

There seem to me to be three, and only three, alternative types of answer possible; and to any answer yet suggested, of any of these types, there seem to me to be very grave objections.

1. Of the first type, there is but one answer: namely, that in this case what I am knowing really is that the sense-datum *itself* is part of the surface of a human hand. In other words that, though I don't perceive *my hand* directly, I do *directly* perceive part of its surface; that the sense-datum itself *is* this part of its surface and not merely something which (in a sense yet to be determined) "represents" this part of its surface; and that hence the sense in which I "perceive" this part of the surface of my hand, is not in its turn a sense which needs to be defined by reference to yet a third more ultimate sense of "perceive," which is the only one in which perception is direct, namely, that in which I perceive the sense-datum.

If this view is true (as I think it may just possibly be), it seems to me certain that we must abandon a view which has been held to be certainly true by most philosophers, namely, the view that our sense-data always really have the qualities which they sensibly appear to us to have. For I know that if another man were looking through a microscope at the same surface which I am seeing with the naked eye, the sense-datum which he saw would sensibly appear to him to have qualities very different from and incompatible with those which my sense-datum sensibly appears to me to have: and yet, if my sense-datum is identical with the surface we are both of us seeing, his must be identical with it also. My sense-datum can, therefore, be identical with this surface only on condition that it is identical with his sense-datum; and, since his sense-datum sensibly appears to him to have qualities incompatible with those which mine sensibly appears to me to have, his sense-datum can be identical with mine only on condition that the sense-datum in question either has not got the qualities which it sensibly appears to me to have, or has not got those which it sensibly appears to him to have.

I do not, however, think that this is a fatal objection to this first type of view. A far more serious objection seems to me to be that, when we see a thing double (have what is called "a double image" of it), we certainly have *two* sense-data each of which is *of* the surface seen, and which cannot therefore both be identical with it; and that yet it seems as if, if any sense-datum is ever identical with the surface *of* which it is a sense-datum, each of these so-called "images" must be so. It looks, therefore, as if every sense-datum is, after all, only "representative" of the surface, *of* which it is a sense-datum.

2. But, if so, what relation has it to the surface in question?

This second type of view is one which holds that when I know "This is part of the surface of a human hand," what I am knowing with regard to the sense-datum which is *of* that surface, is, *not* that it is *itself* part of the surface of a human hand, but something of the following kind. There is, it says, *some* relation, R, such that what I am knowing with regard to the sense-datum is either "There is one thing and only one thing, of which it is true both that it is a part of the surface of a human hand, and that it has R to this sense-datum," or else "There are a set of things, of which it is true both that that set, taken collectively, *are* part of the surface of a human hand, and also that each member of the set has R to this sense-datum, and that nothing which is not a member of the set has R to it."

Obviously, in the case of this second type, many different views are possible, differing according to the view they take as to what the relation R is. But there is only one of them, which seems to me to have any plausibility; namely, that which holds that R is an ultimate and unanalysable relation, which might be expressed by saying that "xRy" means the same as "y is an appearance or manifestation of x." I.e., the analysis which this answer would give of "This is part of the surface of a human hand" would be "There is one and only one thing of which it is true both that it is part of the surface of a human hand, and that this sense-datum is an appearance or manifestation of it."

To this view also there seem to me to be very grave objections, chiefly drawn from a consideration of the questions how we can possibly *know* with regard to any of our sense-data that there is one thing and one thing only which has to them such a supposed ultimate relation; and how, if we do, we can possibly *know* anything further about such things, e.g., of what size or shape they are.

3. The third type of answer, which seems to me to be the only possible alternative if 1 and 2 are rejected, is the type of answer which J. S. Mill seems to have been implying to be the true one when he said that material things are "permanent possibilities of sensation." He seems to have thought that when I know such a fact as "This is part of the surface of a human hand," what I am knowing with regard to the sense-datum which is the principal subject of that fact, is not that it is itself part of the surface of a human hand, nor yet, with regard to any relation, that *the* thing which has to it that relation is part of the surface of a human hand, but a whole set of hypothetical facts each of which is a fact of the form "If *these* conditions had been fulfilled, I should have been perceiving a sense-datum intrinsically related to *this* sense-datum in *this* way," "If *these* (other) conditions had been fulfilled, I should have been perceiving a sense-datum intrinsically related to *this* sense-datum in *this* (other) way," etc., etc.

With regard to this third type of view as to the analysis of propositions of the kind we are considering, it seems to me, again, just *possible* that it is a true one; but to hold (as Mill himself and others seem to have held) that it is *certainly*, or nearly certainly, true, seems to me as great a mistake, as to hold with regard either to 1 or to 2, that they are *certainly*, or nearly certainly, true. There seem to me to be very grave objections to it; in particular the three, (*a*) that though, in general, when I know such a fact as "This is a hand," I certainly do know some hypothetical facts of the form "If *these* conditions had been fulfilled, I should have been perceiving a sense-datum of *this* kind, which would have been a sense-datum of the same surface of which *this* is a sense-datum," it seems doubtful whether any conditions with regard to which I know this are not themselves conditions of the form "If this and that *material thing* had been in those positions and conditions . . . ," (*b*) that it seems again very doubtful whether there is any intrinsic relation, such that my knowledge that (under *these* conditions) I should have been perceiving a sense-datum of *this* kind, which would have been a sense-datum of the same surface of which *this* is a sense-datum, is equivalent to a knowledge, with regard to that relation, that I should, under those conditions, have been perceiving a sense-datum related by it to *this* sense-datum, and (*c*) that, if it were true, the sense in which a material surface is "round" or "square," would necessarily be utterly different from that in which our sense-data sensibly appear to us to be "round" or "square."

V. Just as I hold that the proposition "There are and have been material things" is quite certainly true, but that the question how this proposition is to be analysed is one to which no answer that has been hitherto given is anywhere near certainly true; so I hold that the proposition "There are and have been many Selves" is quite certainly true, but that here again all the analyses of this proposition that have been suggested by philosophers are highly doubtful.

That I am now perceiving many different sense-data, and that I have at many times in the past perceived many different sense-data, I know for certain

—that is to say, I know that there are mental facts of class (β), connected in a way which it is proper to express by saying that they are all of them facts about *me;* but how this kind of connection is to be analysed, I do not know for certain, nor do I think that any other philosopher knows with any approach to certainty. Just as in the case of the proposition "This is part of the surface of a human hand," there are several extremely different views as to its analysis, each of which seems to me *possible,* but none nearly certain, so also in the case of the proposition "This, that and that sense-datum are all at present being perceived by *me,*" and still more so in the case of the proposition "*I* am now perceiving this sense-datum, and *I* have in the past perceived sense-data of these other kinds." Of the *truth* of these propositions there seems to me to be no doubt, but as to what is the correct analysis of them there seems to me to be the gravest doubt—the true analysis may, for instance, *possibly* be quite as paradoxical as is the third view given above under IV as to the analysis of "This is part of the surface of a human hand"; but whether it *is* as paradoxical as this seems to me to be quite as doubtful as in that case. Many philosophers, on the other hand, seem to me to have assumed that there is little or no doubt as to the correct analysis of such propositions; and many of these, just reversing my position, have also held that the propositions themselves are not true.

5

G. E. Moore PROOF
OF AN EXTERNAL WORLD

Moore published "Proof of an External World" in 1939. Like his earlier "Defence of Common Sense," this essay has aroused a considerable amount of discussion and controversy. A hasty reading may make it seem as if Moore believes he can settle the ancient problem concerning the existence of an external world merely by raising his hands. A close reading of the essay, however, discloses that Moore's proof is much more complicated and quite worthy of serious consideration.

As in his earlier essay, Moore relies heavily upon his basic belief that he, as well as other people, does *know* many things of a nonanalytic nature (e.g., "This is a hand"). If Moore does not know such things, then the proof fails. An equally important problem arising out of the essay, according to some philosophers, is to state exactly *what*, if anything, Moore has proved to exist by his argument. Has any philosopher ever denied the existence of the external world Moore claims to have proved to exist?

A discussion of Moore's proof is to be found in "Moore's 'Proof of an External World' " by Alice Ambrose in *The Philosophy of G. E. Moore*, P. A. Schilpp (ed.). Also see Moore's reply to Ambrose in "A Reply to My Critics" in the same volume.

In the preface to the second edition of Kant's *Critique of Pure Reason* some words occur, which, in Professor Kemp Smith's translation, are rendered as follows:

> It still remains a scandal to philosophy . . . that the existence of things outside of us . . . must be accepted merely on *faith*, and that, if anyone thinks good to doubt their existence, we are unable to counter his doubts by any satisfactory proof.[1]

From *Proceedings of the British Academy*, Vol. XXV, 1939, pp. 273–300. Published for the British Academy by Humphrey Milford, Oxford University Press, London.

[1] B xxxix, note: Kemp Smith, p. 34. The German words are "so bleibt es immer ein Skandal der Philosophie . . . , das Dasein der Dinge ausser uns . . . bloss auf *Glauben* annehmen zu müssen, und wenn es jemand einfällt es zu bezweifeln, ihm keinen genugtuenden Beweis entgegenstellen zu können."

It seems clear from these words that Kant thought it a matter of some importance to give a proof of "the existence of things outside of us" or perhaps rather (for it seems to me possible that the force of the German words is better rendered in this way) of "the existence of *the* things outside of us"; for had he not thought it important that a proof should be given, he would scarcely have called it a "scandal" that no proof had been given. And it seems clear also that he thought that the giving of such a proof was a task which fell properly within the province of philosophy; for, if it did not, the fact that no proof had been given could not possibly be a scandal to *philosophy*.

Now, even if Kant was mistaken in both of these two opinions, there seems to me to be no doubt whatever that it is a matter of some importance and also a matter which falls properly within the province of philosophy to discuss the question what sort of proof, if any, can be given of "the existence of things outside of us." And to discuss this question was my object when I began to write the present lecture. But I may say at once that, as you will find, I have only, at most, succeeded in saying a very small part of what ought to be said about it.

The words "it . . . remains a scandal to philosophy . . . that we are unable . . ." would, taken strictly, imply that, at the moment at which he wrote them, Kant himself was unable to produce a satisfactory proof of the point in question. But I think it is unquestionable that Kant himself did not think that he personally was at the time unable to produce such a proof. On the contrary, in the immediately preceding sentence, he has declared that he has, in the second edition of his *Critique*, to which he is now writing the Preface, given a "rigorous proof" of this very thing; and has added that he believes this proof of his to be "the only possible proof." It is true that in this preceding sentence he does not describe the proof which he has given as a proof of "the existence of things outside of us" or of "the existence of the things outside of us," but describes it instead as a proof of "the objective reality of outer intuition." But the context leaves no doubt that he is using these two phrases, "the objective reality of outer intuition" and "the existence of things (*or* 'the things') outside of us," in such a way that whatever is a proof of the first is also necessarily a proof of the second. We must, therefore, suppose that when he speaks as if *we* are unable to give a satisfactory proof, he does not mean to say that he himself, as well as others, is *at the moment* unable; but rather that, until he discovered the proof which he has given, both he himself and everybody else *were* unable. Of course, if he is right in thinking that he has given a satisfactory proof, the state of things which he describes came to an end as soon as his proof was published. As soon as that happened, anyone who read it was able to give a satisfactory proof by simply repeating that which Kant had given, and the "scandal" to philosophy had been removed once for all.

If, therefore, it were certain that the proof of the point in question given by Kant in the second edition is a satisfactory proof, it would be certain that at least one satisfactory proof can be given; and all that would remain of the question which I said I proposed to discuss would be, firstly, the question as to what *sort* of a proof this of Kant's is, and secondly the question whether (contrary to Kant's own opinion) there may not perhaps be other proofs, of the same or of a different sort, which are also satisfactory. But I think it is by no means certain that Kant's proof is satisfactory. I think it is by no means certain that he did succeed in removing once for all the state of affairs which he considered to be a scandal to philosophy. And I think, therefore, that the question whether it is possible to give *any* satisfactory proof of the point in question still deserves discussion.

But what is the point in question? I think it must be owned that the expression "things outside of us" is rather an odd expression, and an expression the meaning of which is certainly not perfectly clear. It would have sounded less odd if, instead of "things outside of us" I had said "external things," and perhaps also the meaning of this expression would have seemed to be clearer; and I think we make the meaning of "external things" clearer still if we explain that this phrase has been regularly used by philosophers as short for "things external to *our minds*." The fact is that there has been a long philosophical tradition, in accordance with which the three expressions "external things," "things external to *us*," and "things external to *our minds*" have been used as equivalent to one another, and have, each of them, been used as if they needed no explanation. The origin of this usage I do not know. It occurs already in Descartes; and since he uses the expressions as if they needed no explanation, they had presumably been used with the same meaning before. Of the three, it seems to me that the expression "external to *our minds*" is the clearest, since it at least makes clear that what is meant is not "external to *our bodies*"; whereas both the other expressions might be taken to mean this: and indeed there has been a good deal of confusion, even among philosophers, as to the relation of the two conceptions "external things" and "things external to *our bodies*." But even the expression "things external to our minds" seems to me to be far from perfectly clear; and if I am to make really clear what I mean by "proof of the existence of things outside of us," I cannot do it by merely saying that by "outside of us" I mean "external to our minds."

There is a passage in which Kant himself says that the expression "outside of us" "carries with it an unavoidable ambiguity." He says that "sometimes it means something which exists *as a thing in itself* distinct from us, and sometimes something which merely belongs to external *appearance*"; he calls things which are "outside of us" in the first of these two senses "objects which might be called external in the transcendental sense," and things which are so in the second "*empirically external* objects"; and he says finally that, in order to remove all uncertainty as to the latter conception, he will distinguish empirically external objects from objects which might be called "external" in the transcendental sense, "by calling them outright things which are *to be met with in space*."

I think that this last phrase of Kant's, "things which are to be met with in space," does indicate fairly clearly what sort of things it is with regard to which I wish to inquire what sort of proof, if any, can be given that there are any things of that sort. My body, the bodies of other men, the bodies of animals, plants of all sorts, stones, mountains, the sun, the moon, stars, and planets, houses and other buildings, manufactured articles of all sorts—chairs, tables, pieces of paper, etc., are all of them "things which are to be met with in space." In short, all things of the sort that philosophers have been used to call "physical objects," "material things," or "bodies" obviously come under this head. But the phrase "things that are to be met with in space" can be naturally understood as applying also in cases where the names "physical object," "material thing," or "body" can hardly be applied. For instance, shadows are sometimes to be met with in space, although they could hardly be properly called "physical objects," "material things," or "bodies"; and although in one usage of the term "thing" it would not be proper to call a shadow a "thing," yet the phrase "things which are to be met with in space" can be naturally understood as synonymous with "whatever can be met with in space," and this is an expression which can quite properly be understood to include shadows. I wish the phrase "things which are to be met with in space" to be understood in this wide sense; so that if a proof can be found that there ever have been as many as two different shadows it will follow at once that there have been at least two "things which were to be met with in space," and this proof will be as good a proof of the point in question as would be a proof that there have been at least two "physical objects" of no matter what sort.

The phrase "things which are to be met with in space" can, therefore, be naturally understood as having a very wide meaning—a meaning even wider than that of "physical object" or "body," wide as is the meaning of these latter expressions. But wide as is its meaning, it is not, in one respect, so wide as that of another phrase which Kant uses as if it were equivalent to this one; and a comparison between the two will, I think, serve to make still clearer what sort of things it is with regard to which I wish to ask what proof, if any, can be given that there are such things.

The other phrase which Kant uses as if it were equivalent to "things which are to be met with in space" is used by him in the sentence immediately preceding that previously quoted in which he declares that the expression "things outside of us" "carries with it an unavoidable ambiguity." In this preceding sentence he says that an "empirical object" "is called *external*, if it is presented (*vorgestellt*) *in space*." He treats, therefore, the phrase "presented in space" as if it were equivalent to "to be met with in space." But it is easy to find examples of "things," of which it can hardly be denied that they are "presented in space," but of which it could, quite naturally, be emphatically denied that they are "to be met with in space." Consider, for instance, the following description of one set of circumstances under which what some psychologists have called a "negative after-image" and others a "negative after-sensation" can be obtained. "If, after looking steadfastly at a white patch on a black ground, the eye be turned to a white ground, a grey patch is seen for some little time." (Foster's *Text-book of Physiology*, iv, iii, 3, page 1266; quoted in Stout's *Manual of Psychology*, 3rd edition, page 280.) Upon reading these words recently, I took the trouble to cut out of a piece of white paper a four-pointed star, to place it on a black ground, to "look steadfastly" at it, and then to turn my eyes to a white sheet of paper: and I did find that I saw a grey patch for some little time—I not only saw a grey patch, but I saw it *on* the white ground, and also this grey patch was of roughly the same shape as the white four-pointed star at which I had "looked steadfastly" just before—it also was a four-pointed star. I repeated the simple experiment successfully several times. Now each of those grey four-pointed stars, one of which I saw in each experiment, was what is called an "after-image" or "after-sensation"; and can anybody deny that each of these after-images can be quite properly said to have been "presented in space"? I saw each of them on a real white background, and, if so, each of them was "presented" on a real white background. But though they were "presented in space" everybody, I think, would feel that it was gravely misleading to say that they were "to be met with in space." The white star at which I "looked steadfastly," the black ground on which I saw it, and the white ground on which I saw the after-images, were, of course, "to be met with in space": they were, in fact, "physical objects" or surfaces of physical objects. But one important difference between them, on the one hand, and the grey after-images, on the other, can be quite naturally expressed by saying that the latter were *not* "to be met with in space." And one reason why this is so is, I think, plain. To say that so and so was at a given time "to be met with in space" naturally suggests that there are conditions such that *anyone* who fulfilled them might, conceivably, have "perceived" the "thing" in question—might have seen it, if it was a visible object, have felt it, if it was a tangible one, have heard it, if it was a sound, have smelt it, if it was a smell. When I say that the white four-pointed paper star, at which I looked steadfastly, was a "physical object" and was "to be met with in space," I am implying that *anyone*, who had been in the room at the time, and who had normal eyesight and a normal sense of touch, might have seen and felt it. But, in the case of those grey after-images which I saw, it is not conceivable that anyone besides myself should have seen any one of them. It is, of course, quite conceivable that other people, if they had been in the room with me at the time, and had carried out the same experiment which I carried out, would have seen grey after-images *very like* one of those which I saw: there is no absurdity in supposing even that they might have seen after-images *exactly* like one of those which I saw. But there is an absurdity in supposing that any one of the after-images which I saw could also have been seen by anyone else: in supposing that two different people can ever see the *very same* after-image. One reason, then, why we should say that none of those grey after-images which I saw was "to be met with in space," although each of them was certainly "presented in space" to me, is simply that none of them could conceivably have been seen by anyone else. It is natural so to understand the phrase "to be met with in space," that to say of anything which a man perceived that it was to be met with in space is to say that it might have been perceived by *others* as well as by the man in question.

Negative after-images of the kind described are, therefore, one example of "things" which, though they must be allowed to be "presented in space," are nevertheless *not* "to be met with in space," and are *not* "external to our minds" in the sense with which we shall be concerned. And two other important examples may be given.

The first is this. It is well known that people sometimes see things double, an occurrence which has also been described by psychologists by saying that they have a "double image," or two "images," of some object at which they are looking. In such cases it would certainly be quite natural to say that each of the two "images" is "presented in space": they are seen, one in one place, and the other in another, in just the same sense in which each of those grey after-images which I saw was seen at a particular place on the white background at which I was looking. But it would be utterly unnatural to say that, when I have a double image, each of the two images is "to be met with in space." On the contrary it is quite certain that *both* of them are not "to be met with in space." If both were, it would follow that somebody else might see the *very same* two images which I see; and, though there is no absurdity in supposing that another person might see a pair of images exactly similar to a pair which I see, there is an absurdity in supposing that anyone else might see the *same identical pair*. In every case, then, in which anyone sees anything double, we have an example of at least one "thing" which, though "presented in space" is certainly not "to be met with in space."

And the second important example is this. Bodily pains can, in general, be quite properly said to be "presented in space." When I have a toothache, I feel it *in* a particular region of my jaw or *in* a particular tooth; when I make a cut on my finger smart by putting iodine on it, I feel the pain in a particular place in my finger; and a man whose leg has been amputated may feel a pain *in* a place where his foot might have been if he had not lost it. It is certainly perfectly natural to understand the phrase "presented in space" in such a way that if, in the sense illustrated, a pain is felt *in* a particular place, that pain is "presented in space." And yet of pains it would be quite unnatural to say that they are "to be met with in space," for the same reason as in the case of after-images or double images. It is quite conceivable that another person should feel a pain exactly like one which I feel, but there is an absurdity in supposing that he could feel *numerically the same* pain which I feel. And pains are in fact a typical example of the sort of "things" of which philosophers say that they are *not* "external" to our minds, but "within" them. Of any pain which *I* feel they would say that it is necessarily *not* external to my mind but *in* it.

And finally it is, I think, worth while to mention one other class of "things," which are certainly not "external" objects and certainly not "to be met with in space," in the sense with which I am concerned, but which yet some philosophers would be inclined to say are "presented in space," though they are not "presented in space" in quite the same sense in which pains, double images, and negative after-images of the sort I described are so. If you look at an electric light and then close your eyes, it sometimes happens that you see, for some little time, against the dark background which you usually see when your eyes are shut, a bright patch similar in shape to the light at which you have just been looking. Such a bright patch, if you see one, is another example of what some psychologists have called "after-images" and others "after-sensations"; but, unlike the negative after-images of which I spoke before, it is seen when your eyes are shut. Of such an after-image, seen with closed eyes, some philosophers might be inclined to say that this image too was "presented in space," although it is certainly not "to be met with in space." They would be inclined to say that it is "presented in space," because it certainly is presented as at some little distance from the person who is seeing it: and how can a thing be presented as at some little distance from me without being "presented in space"? Yet there is an important difference between such after-images, seen with closed eyes, and after-images of the sort I previously described—a difference which might lead other philosophers to deny that these after-images, seen with closed eyes, are "presented in space" at all. It is a difference which can be expressed by saying that when your eyes are shut, you are not seeing any part of *physical* space at all—of the space which is referred to when we talk of "things which are to be met with in *space*." An after-image seen with closed eyes certainly is presented in *a* space, but it may be questioned whether it is proper to say that it is presented in *space*.

It is clear, then, I think, that by no means everything which can naturally be said to be "presented in space" can also be naturally said to be a "thing which is to be met with in space." Some of the "things," which are presented in space, are very emphatically *not* to be met with in space: or, to use another phrase, which may be used to convey the same notion, they are emphatically *not* "physical realities" at all. The conception "presented in space" is therefore, in one respect, much wider than the conception "to be met with in space": many "things" fall under the first conception which do not fall under the second—many after-images, one at least of the pair of "images" seen whenever anyone sees double, and most bodily pains, are "presented in space," though none of them are to be met with in space. From the fact that a "thing" is presented in space, it by no means follows that it is to be met with in space. But just as the first conception is, in one respect, wider than the second, so, in another, the second is wider than the first. For there are many "things" to be met with in space, of which it is not true that they are presented in space. From the fact that a "thing" is to be met with in space, it by no means follows that it is presented in space. I have taken "to be met with in space" to imply, as I think it naturally may, that a "thing" *might be* perceived; but from the fact that a thing *might be* perceived, it does not follow that it *is* perceived; and if it is not actually perceived, then it will not be presented in space. It is characteristic of the sorts of "things," including shadows, which I have described as "to be met with in space," that there is no absurdity in supposing with regard to any one of them which *is*, at a given time, perceived, both (1) that it might have existed at that very time, without being perceived; (2) that it might have existed at another time, without being perceived at that other time; and (3) that during the whole period of its existence, it need not have been perceived at any time at all. There is, therefore, no absurdity in supposing that many things, which were at one time to be met with in space, never were "presented" at any time at all, and that many things which *are* to be met with in space now, are not now "presented" and also never were and never will be. To use a Kantian phrase, the conception of "things which are to be met with in space" embraces not only objects of actual experience, but also objects of *possible* experience; and from the fact that a thing is or was an object of *possible* experience, it by no means follows that it either was or is or will be "presented" at all.

I hope that what I have now said may have served to make clear enough what sorts of "things" I was originally referring to as "things outside us" or "things external to our minds." I said that I thought that Kant's phrase "things that are to be met with in space" indicated fairly clearly the sorts of "things" in question; and I have tried to make the range clearer still, by pointing out that this phrase only serves the purpose, if (*a*) you understand it in a sense, in which many "things," e.g., after-images, double images, bodily pains, which might be said to be "presented in space," are nevertheless *not* to be reckoned as "things that are to be met with in space," and (*b*) you realize clearly that there is no contradiction in supposing that there have been and are "to be met with in space" things which never have been, are not now, and never will be perceived, nor in supposing that among those of them which have at some time been perceived many existed at times at which they were not being perceived. I think it will now be clear to everyone that, since I do not reckon as "external things" after-images, double images, and bodily pains, I also should not reckon as "external things," any of the "images" which we often "see with the mind's eye" when we are awake, nor any of those which we see when we are asleep and dreaming; and also that I was so using the expression "external" that from the fact that a man was at a given time having a visual hallucination, it will follow that he was seeing at that time something which was *not* "external" to his mind, and from the fact that he was at a given time having an auditory hallucination, it will follow that he was at the time hearing a sound which was *not* "external" to his mind. But I certainly have not made my use of these phrases, "external to our minds" and "to be met with in space," so clear that in the case of every kind of "thing" which might be suggested, you would be able to tell at once whether I should or should not reckon it as "external to our minds" and "to be met with in space." For instance, I have said nothing which makes it quite clear whether a reflection which I see in a looking-glass is or is not to be regarded as "a thing that is to be met with in space" and "external to our minds," nor have I said anything which makes it quite clear whether the sky is or is not to be so regarded. In the case of the sky, everyone, I think, would feel that it was quite inappropriate to talk of it as "a thing that is to be met with in space"; and most people, I think, would feel a strong reluctance to affirm, without qualification, that reflections which people see in looking-glasses are "to be met with in space." And yet neither the sky nor reflections seen in mirrors are in the same position as bodily pains or after-images in the respect which I have emphasized as a reason for saying of these latter that they are *not* to be met with in space—namely, that there is an absurdity in supposing that *the very same* pain which I feel could be felt by someone else or that *the very same* after-image which I see could be seen by someone else. In the case of reflections in mirrors we should quite naturally, in certain circumstances, use language which implies that another person may see the same reflection which we see. We might quite naturally say to a friend: "Do you see that reddish reflection in the water there? I can't make out what it's a reflection of," just as we might say, pointing to a distant hill-side: "Do you see that white speck on the hill over there? I can't make out what it is." And in the case of the sky, it is quite obviously *not* absurd to say that other people see it as well as I.

It must, therefore, be admitted that I have not made my use of the phrase "things to be met with in space," nor therefore that of "external to our minds," which the former was used to explain, so clear that in the case of every kind of "thing" which may be mentioned, there will be no doubt whatever as to whether things of that kind are or are not "to be met with in space" or "external to our minds." But this lack of a clear-cut definition of the expression "things that are to be met with in space," does not, so far as I can see, matter for my present purpose. For my present purpose it is, I think, sufficient if I make clear, in the case of many kinds of things, that I am so using the phrase "things that are to be met with in space," that, in the case of each of these kinds, from the proposition that there are things of that kind it *follows* that there are things to be met with in space. And I have, in fact, given a list (though by no means an exhaustive one) of kinds of things which are related to my use of the expression "things that are to be met with in space" in this way. I mentioned among others the bodies of men and of animals, plants, stars, houses, chairs, and shadows; and I want now to emphasize that I am so using "things to be met with in space" that, in the case of each of these kinds of "things," from the proposition that there are "things" of that kind it *follows* that there are things to be met with in space: e.g., from the proposition that there are plants or that plants exist it *follows* that there are things to be met with in space, from the proposition that shadows exist, it *follows* that there are things to be met with in space, and so on, in the case of all the kinds of "things" which I mentioned in my first list. That this should be clear is sufficient for my purpose, because, if it is clear, then it will also be clear that, as I implied before, if you have proved that two plants exist, or that a plant and a dog exist, or that a dog and a shadow exist, etc., etc., you will *ipso facto* have proved that there are things to be met with in space: you will not require *also* to give a separate proof that from the proposition that there are plants it *does* follow that there are things to be met with in space.

Now with regard to the expression "things that are to be met with in space" I think it will readily be believed that I may be using it in a sense such that no proof is required that from "plants exist" there follows "there are things to be met with in space"; but with regard to the phrase "things external to our minds" I think the case is different. People may be inclined to say: "I can see quite clearly that from the proposition 'At least two dogs exist at the present moment' there *follows* the proposition 'At least two things are to be met with in space at the present moment,' so that if you can prove that there are two dogs in existence at the present moment you will *ipso facto* have proved that two things at least are to be met with in space at the present moment. I can see that you do not also require a separate proof that from 'Two dogs exist' 'Two things are to be met with in space' does *follow;* it is quite obvious that there couldn't be a dog which wasn't to be met with in space. But it is not by any means so clear to me that if you can prove that there are two dogs or two shadows, you will *ipso facto* have proved that there are two things *external to our minds*. Isn't it possible that a dog, though it certainly must be 'to be met with in space,' might *not* be an external object—an object external to our minds? Isn't a separate proof required that anything that is to be met with in space must be external to our minds? Of course, if you are using 'external' as a mere synonym for 'to be met with in space,' no proof will be required that dogs are external objects: in that case, if you can prove that two dogs exist, you will *ipso facto* have proved that there are some external things. But I find it difficult to believe that you, or anybody else, do really use 'external' as a mere synonym for 'to be met with in space'; and if you don't, isn't some proof required that whatever is to be met with in space must be external to our minds?"

Now Kant, as we saw, asserts that the phrases "outside of us" or "external" are in fact used in two very different senses; and with regard to one of these two senses, that which he calls the "transcendental" sense, and which he tries to explain by saying that it is a sense in which "external" means "existing *as a thing in itself* distinct from us," it is notorious that he himself held that things which are to be met with in space are *not* "external" in that sense. There is, therefore, according to him, *a* sense of "external," a sense in which the word has been commonly used by philosophers—such that, if "external" be used in that sense, then from the proposition "Two dogs exist" it will *not* follow that there are some external things. What this supposed sense is I do not think that Kant himself ever succeeded in explaining clearly; nor do I know of any reason for supposing that philosophers ever have used "external" in a sense, such that in *that* sense things that are to be met with in space are *not* external. But how about the other sense, in which, according to Kant, the word "external" has been commonly used—that which he calls "empirically external"? How is this conception related to the conception "to be met with in space"? It may be noticed that, in the passages which I quoted, Kant himself does not tell us at all clearly what he takes to be the proper answer to this question. He only makes the rather odd statement that, in order to remove all uncertainty as to the conception "empirically external," he will distinguish objects to which it applies from those which might be called "external" in the transcendental sense, by "calling them outright things which are *to be met with in space*." These odd words certainly suggest, as one possible interpretation of them, that in Kant's opinion the conception "empirically external" is *identical* with the conception "to be met with in space" —that he does think that "external," when used in this second sense, is a mere synonym for "to be met with in space." But, if this is his meaning, I do find it very difficult to believe that he is right. Have philosophers, in fact, ever used "external" as a mere synonym for "to be met with in space"? Does he himself do so?

I do not think they have, nor that he does himself; and, in order to explain how they have used it, and how the two conceptions "external to our minds" and "to be met with in space" are related to one another, I think it is important expressly to call attention to a fact which hitherto I have only referred to incidentally: namely, the fact that those who talk of certain things as "external to" our minds, do, in general, as we should naturally expect, talk of other "things," with which they wish to contrast the first, as "in" our minds. It has, of course, been often pointed out that when "in" is thus used, followed by "my mind," "your mind," "his mind," etc., "in" is being used metaphorically. And there are some metaphorical uses of "in," followed by such expressions, which occur in common speech, and which we all understand quite well. For instance, we all understand such expressions as "I had you in mind when I made that arrangement" or "I had you in mind when I said that there are some people who can't bear to touch a spider." In these cases "I was thinking of you" can be used to mean the same as "I had you in mind." But it is quite certain that this particular metaphorical use of "in" is not the one in which philosophers are using it when they contrast what is "in" my mind with what is "external" to it. On the contrary, in their use of "external," you will be external to my mind even at a moment when I have you in mind. If we want to discover what this peculiar metaphorical use of "*in* my mind" is, which is such that nothing, which is, in the sense we are now concerned with, "external" to my mind, can ever be "in" it, we need, I think, to consider instances of the sort of "things" which they would say are "in" my mind in this special sense. I have already mentioned three such instances, which are, I think, sufficient for my present purpose: any bodily pain which I feel, any after-image which I see with my eyes shut, and any image which I "see" when I am asleep and dreaming, are typical examples of the sort of "thing" of which philosophers have spoken as *"in* my mind." And there is no doubt, I think, that when they have spoken of such things as my body, a sheet of paper, a star—in short "physical objects" generally—as "external," they have meant to emphasize some important difference which they feel to exist between such things as these and such "things" as a pain, an after-image seen with closed eyes, and a dream-image. But *what* difference? What difference do they feel to exist between a bodily pain which I feel or an after-image which I see with closed eyes, on the one hand, and my body itself, on the other—what difference which leads them to say that whereas the bodily pain and the after-image are "in" my mind, my body itself is *not* "in" my mind—not even when I am feeling it and seeing it or thinking of it? I have already said that one difference which there is between the two, is that my body is to be met with in space, whereas the bodily pain and the after-image are not. But I think it would be quite wrong to say that this is *the* difference which has led philosophers to speak of the two latter as "in" my mind, and of my body as *not* "in" my mind.

The question what the difference is which has led them to speak in this way, is not, I think, at all an easy question to answer; but I am going to try to give, in brief outline, what I *think* is a right answer.

It should, I think, be noted, first of all, that the use of the word "mind," which is being adopted when it is said that any bodily pains which I feel are "in my mind," is one which is not quite in accordance with any usage common in ordinary speech, although we are very familiar with it in philosophy. Nobody, I think, would say that bodily pains which I feel are "in my mind", unless he was also prepared to say that it is *with* my mind that I feel bodily pains; and to say this latter is, I think, not quite in accordance with common non-philosophic usage. It is natural enough to say that it is with my mind that I remember, and think, and imagine, and feel *mental* pains—e.g., disappointment, but not, I think, quite so natural to say that it is with my mind that I feel *bodily* pains, e.g., a severe headache; and perhaps even less natural to say that it is with my mind that I see and hear and smell and taste. There is, however, a well-established philosophical usage according to which seeing, hearing, smelling, tasting, and having a bodily pain are just as much *mental* occurrences or processes as are remembering, or thinking, or imagining. This usage was, I think, adopted by philosophers, because they saw a real resemblance between such statements as "I saw a cat," "I heard a clap of thunder," "I smelt a strong smell of onions," "My finger smarted horribly," on the one hand, and such statements as "I remembered having seen him," "I was thinking out a plan of action," "I pictured the scene to myself," "I felt bitterly disappointed," on the other—a resemblance which puts all these statements in one class together, as contrasted with other statements in which "I" or "my" is used, such as, e.g., "I was less than four feet high," "I was lying on my back," "My hair was very long." What is the resemblance in question? It is a resemblance which might be expressed by say-ing that all the first eight statements are the sort of statements which furnish data for psychology, while the three latter are not. It is also a resemblance which may be expressed, in a way now common among philosophers, by saying that in the case of all the first eight statements, if we make the statement more specific by adding a date, we get a statement such that, if it is true, then if *follows* that I was "having an experience" at the date in question, whereas this does not hold for the three last statements. For instance, if it is true that I saw a cat between 12 noon and 5 minutes past, today, it *follows* that I was "having some experience" between 12 noon and 5 minutes past, today; whereas from the proposition that I was less than four feet high in December 1877, it does not *follow* that I had any experiences in December 1877. But this philosophic use of "having an experi-ence" is one which itself needs explanation, since it is not identical with any use of the expression that is established in common speech. An explanation, however, which is, I think, adequate for the purpose, can be given by saying that a phi-losopher, who was following this usage, would say that I was at a given time "having an experience" if and only if either (1) I was conscious at the time or (2) I was dreaming at the time or (3) something else was true of me at the time, which resembled what is true of me when I am conscious and when I am dream-ing, in a certain very obvious respect in which what is true of me when I am dreaming resembles what is true of me when I am conscious, and in which what would be true of me, if at any time, for instance, I had a vision, would resemble both. This explanation is, of course, in some degree vague; but I think it is clear enough for our purpose. It amounts to saying that, in this philosophic usage of "having an experience," it would be said of me that I was, at a given time, having *no* experience, if I was at the time neither conscious nor dreaming nor having a vision nor *anything else of the sort;* and, of course, this is vague in so far as it has not been specified what else would be *of the sort:* this is left to be gathered from the instances given. But I think this is sufficient: often at night when I am asleep, I am neither conscious nor dreaming nor having a vision nor *anything else of the sort*—that is to say, I am having no experiences. If this explanation of this philosophic usage of "having an experience" is clear enough, then I think that what has been meant by saying that any pain which I feel or any after-image which I see with my eyes closed is "*in* my mind," can be ex-plained by saying that what is meant is neither more nor less than that there would be a contradiction in supposing *that very same pain* or *that very same after-image* to have existed at a time at which I was having no experience; or, in other words, that from the proposition, with regard to any time, that *that* pain or *that* after-image existed at that time, it *follows* that I was having some experience at the time in question. And if so, then we can say that the felt difference between bodily pains which I feel and after-images which I see, on the one hand, and my body on the other, which has led philosophers to say that any such pain or after-image is "*in* my mind," whereas my body *never* is but is always "outside of" or "external to" my mind, is just this, that whereas there is a contradiction in supposing a pain which I feel or an after-image which I see to exist at a time when I am having no experience, there is no contradiction in supposing my body to exist at a time when I am having no experience; and we can even say, I think, that just this and nothing more is what they have meant by these puzzling and misleading phrases "in my mind" and "external to my mind."

But now, if to say of anything, e.g., my body, that it is external to *my* mind, means merely that from a proposition to the effect that it existed at a specified time, there in no case follows the further proposition that *I* was having an experience at the time in question, then to say of anything that it is external to *our* minds, will mean similarly that from a proposition to the effect that it existed at a specified time, it in no case follows that any of *us* were having experiences at the time in question. And if by *our* minds be meant, as is, I think, usually meant, the minds of human beings living on the earth, then it will follow that any pains which animals may feel, any after-images they may see, any experiences they may have, though not external to *their* minds, yet are external to *ours*. And this at once makes plain how different is the conception "external to our minds" from the conception "to be met with in space"; for, of course, pains which animals feel or after-images which they see are no more to be met with in space than are pains which *we* feel or after-images which *we* see. From the proposition that there are external objects—objects that are not in any of *our* minds, it does *not* follow that there are things to be met with in space; and hence "external to our minds" is not a mere synonym for "to be met with in space": that is to say, "external to our minds" and "to be met with in space" are two different conceptions. And the true relation between these conceptions seems to me to be this. We have already seen that there are ever so many kinds of "things," such that, in the case of each of these kinds, from the proposition that there is at least one thing of that kind there *follows* the proposition that there is at least one thing to be met with in space: e.g., this follows from "There is at least one star," from "There is at least one human body," from "There is at least one shadow," etc. And I think we can say that of every kind of thing of which this is true, it is also true that from the proposition that there is at least one "thing" of that kind there *follows* the proposition that there is at least one thing external to our minds: e.g., from "There is at least one star" there follows not only "There is at least one thing to be met with in space" but also "There is at least one external thing," and similarly in all other cases. My reason for saying this is as follows. Consider any kind of thing, such that anything of that kind, if there is anything of it, must be "to be met with in space": e.g., consider the kind "soap-bubble." If I say of anything which I am perceiving, "That is a soap-bubble," I am, it seems to me, certainly implying that there would be no contradiction in asserting that it existed before I perceived it and that it will continue to exist, even if I cease to perceive it. This seems to me to be part of what is meant by saying that it is a real soap-bubble, as distinguished, for instance, from an hallucination of a soap-bubble. Of course, it by no means follows, that if it really is a soap-bubble, it did in fact exist before I perceived it or will continue to exist after I cease to perceive it: soap-bubbles are an example of a kind of "physical object" and "thing to be met with in space," in the case of which it is notorious that particular specimens of the kind often do exist only so long as they are perceived by a particular person. But a thing which I perceive would not be a soap-bubble unless its existence at any given time were *logically independent* of my perception of it at that time; unless that is to say, from the proposition, with regard to a particular time, that it existed at that time, it *never* follows that I perceived it at that time. But, if it is true that it would not be a soap-bubble, unless it *could* have existed at any given time without being perceived by me at that time, it is certainly also true that it would not be a soap-bubble, unless it *could* have existed at any given time, without its being true that I was having any experience of any kind at the time in question: it would not be a soap-bubble, unless, whatever time you take, from the proposition that it existed at that time it does *not* follow that I was having any experience at that time. That is to say, from the proposition with regard to anything which I am perceiving that it is a soap-bubble, there *follows* the proposition that it is external to *my* mind. But if, when I say that anything which I perceive is a soap-bubble, I am implying that it is external to *my* mind, I am, I think, certainly also implying that it is also external to all other minds: I am implying that it is not a thing of a sort such that things of that sort *can* only exist at a time when somebody is having an experience. I think, therefore, that from any proposition of the form "There's a soap-bubble!" there does really *follow* the proposition "There's an external object!" "There's an object external to *all* our minds!" And, if this is true of the kind "soap-bubble," it is certainly also true of any other kind (including the kind "unicorn") which is such that, if there are any things of that kind, it follows that there are *some* things to be met with in space.

I think, therefore, that in the case of all kinds of "things," which are such that if there is a pair of things, both of which are of one of these kinds, or a pair of things one of which is of one of them and one of them of another, then it will follow at once that there are some things to be met with in space, it is true also that if I can prove that there are a pair of things, one of which is of one of these kinds and another of another, or a pair both of which are of one of them, then I shall have proved *ipso facto* that there are at least two "things outside of us." That is to say, if I can prove that there exist now both a sheet of paper and a human hand, I shall have proved that there are now "things outside of us"; if I can prove that there exist now both a shoe and sock, I shall have proved that there are now "things outside of us"; etc.; and similarly I shall have proved it, if I can prove that there exist now two sheets of paper, or two human hands, or two shoes, or two socks, etc. Obviously, then, there are thousands of different things such that, if, at any time, I can prove any one of them, I shall have proved the existence of things outside of us. Cannot I prove any of these things?

It seems to me that, so far from its being true, as Kant declares to be his opinion, that there is only one possible proof of the existence of things outside of us, namely the one which he has given, I can now give a large number of different proofs, each of which is a perfectly rigorous proof; and that at many other times I have been in a position to give many others. I can prove now, for instance, that two human hands exist. How? By holding up my two hands and saying, as I make a certain gesture with the right, "Here is one hand," and adding, as I make a certain gesture with the left, "and here is another." And if, by doing this, I have proved *ipso facto* the existence of external things, you will all see that I can also do it now in numbers of other ways: there is no need to multiply examples.

But did I prove just now that two human hands were then in existence? I do want to insist that I did; that the proof which I gave was a perfectly rigorous one; and that it is perhaps impossible to give a better or more rigorous proof of anything whatever. Of course, it would not have been a proof unless three conditions were satisfied; namely, (1) unless the premiss which I adduced as proof of the conclusion was different from the conclusion I adduced it to prove; (2) unless the premiss which I adduced was something which I *knew* to be the case, and not merely something which I believed but which was by no means certain, or something which, though in fact true, I did not know to be so; and (3) unless the conclusion did really follow from the premiss. But all these three conditions were in fact satisfied by my proof. (1) The premiss which I adduced in proof was quite certainly different from the conclusion, for the conclusion was merely "Two human hands exist at this moment," but the premiss was something far more specific than this—something which I expressed by showing you my hands, making certain gestures, and saying the words "Here is one hand, and here is another." It is quite obvious that the two were different, because it is quite obvious that the conclusion might have been true, even if the premiss had been false. In asserting the premiss I was asserting much more than I was asserting in asserting the conclusion. (2) I certainly did at the moment *know* that which I expressed by the combination of certain gestures with saying the words "There is one hand and here is another." I *knew* that there was one hand in the place indicated by combining a certain gesture with my first utterance of "here" and that there was another in the different place indicated by combining a certain gesture with my second utterance of "here." How absurd it would be to suggest that I did not know it, but only believed it, and that perhaps it was not the case! You might as well suggest that I do not know that I am now standing up and talking—that perhaps after all I'm not, and that it's not quite certain that I am! And finally (3) it is quite certain that the conclusion did follow from the premiss. This is as certain as it is that if there is one hand here and another here *now*, then it follows that there are two hands in existence *now*.

My proof, then, of the existence of things outside of us did satisfy three of the conditions necessary for a rigorous proof. Are there any other conditions necessary for a rigorous proof, such that perhaps it did not satisfy one of them? Perhaps there may be; I do not know; but I do want to emphasize that, so far as I can see, we all of us do constantly take proofs of this sort as absolutely conclusive proofs of certain conclusions—as finally settling certain questions, as to which we were previously in doubt. Suppose, for instance, it were a question whether there were as many as three misprints on a certain page in a certain book. A says there are, B is inclined to doubt it. How could A prove that he is right? Surely he *could* prove it by taking the book, turning to the page, and pointing to three separate places on it, saying "There's one misprint here, another here, and another here": surely that is a method by which it *might* be proved! Of course, A would not have proved, by doing this, that there were at least three misprints on the page in question, unless it was certain that there was a misprint in each of the places to which he pointed. But to say that he *might* prove it in this way, is to say that it *might* be certain that there was. And if such a thing as that could ever be certain, then assuredly it was certain just now that there was one hand in one of the two places I indicated and another in the other.

I did, then, just now, give a proof that there were *then* external objects;

and obviously, if I did, I could *then* have given many other proofs of the same sort that there were external objects *then,* and could now give many proofs of the same sort that there are external objects *now.*

But, if what I am asked to do is to prove that external objects have existed *in the past,* then I can give many different proofs of this also, but proofs which are in important respects of a different sort from those just given. And I want to emphasize that, when Kant says it is a scandal not to be able to give a proof of the existence of external objects, a proof of their existence in the past would certainly *help* to remove the scandal of which he is speaking. He says that, if it occurs to anyone to question their existence, we ought to be able to confront him with a satisfactory proof. But by a person who questions their existence, he certainly means not merely a person who questions whether any exist at the moment of speaking, but a person who questions whether any have *ever* existed; and a proof that some have existed in the past would certainly therefore be relevant to *part* of what such a person is questioning. How then can I prove that there have been external objects in the past? Here is one proof. I can say: "I held up two hands above this desk not very long ago; therefore two hands existed not very long ago; therefore at least two external objects have existed at some time in the past, Q.E.D." This is a perfectly good proof, provided I *know* what is asserted in the premiss. But I *do* know that I held up two hands above this desk not very long ago. As a matter of fact, in this case you all know it too. There's no doubt whatever that I did. Therefore I have given a perfectly conclusive proof that external objects have existed in the past; and you will all see at once that, if this is a conclusive proof, I could have given many others of the same sort, and could now give many others. But it is also quite obvious that this sort of proof differs in important respects from the sort of proof I gave just now that there were two hands existing *then.*

I have, then, given two conclusive proofs of the existence of external objects. The first was a proof that two human hands existed at the time when I gave the proof; the second was a proof that two human hands had existed at a time previous to that at which I gave the proof. These proofs were of a different sort in important respects. And I pointed out that I could have given, then, many other conclusive proofs of both sorts. It is also obvious that I could give many others of both sorts now. So that, if these are the sort of proof that is wanted, nothing is easier than to prove the existence of external objects.

But now I am perfectly well aware that, in spite of all that I have said, many philosophers will still feel that I have not given any satisfactory proof of the point in question. And I want briefly, in conclusion, to say something as to why this dissatisfaction with my proofs should be felt.

One reason why, is, I think, this. Some people understand "proof of an external world" as including a proof of things which I haven't attempted to prove and haven't proved. It is not quite easy to say *what* it is that they want proved— *what* it is that is such that unless they got a proof of it, they would not say that they had a proof of the existence of external things; but I can make an approach to explaining what they want by saying that if I had proved the propositions which I used as *premisses* in my two proofs, then they would perhaps admit that I had proved the existence of external things, but, in the absence of such a proof (which, of course, I have neither given nor attempted to give), they will say that I have not given what they mean by a proof of the existence of external things. In other words, they want a proof of what I assert *now* when I hold up my hands and say "Here's one hand and here's another"; and, in the other case, they want a proof of what I assert *now* when I say "I did hold up two hands above this desk just now." Of course, what they really want is not merely a proof of these two propositions, but something like a general statement as to how *any* propositions of this sort may be proved. This, of course, I haven't given; and I do not believe it can be given: if this is what is meant by proof of the existence of external things, I do not believe that any proof of the existence of external things is possible. Of course, in some cases what might be called a proof of propositions which seem like these can be got. If one of you suspected that one of my hands was artificial he might be said to get a proof of my proposition "Here's one hand, and here's another," by coming up and examining the suspected hand close up, perhaps touching and pressing it, and so establishing that it really was a human hand. But I do not believe that any proof is possible in nearly all cases. How am I to prove now that "Here's one hand, and here's another"? I do not believe I can do it. In order to do it, I should need to prove for one thing, as Descartes pointed out, that I am not now dreaming. But how can I prove that I am not? I have, no doubt, conclusive reasons for asserting that I am not now dreaming; I have conclusive evidence that I am awake: but that is a very different thing from being able to prove it. I could not tell you what all my evidence is; and I should require to do this at least, in order to give you a proof.

But another reason why some people would feel dissatisfied with my proofs is, I think, not merely that they want a proof of something which I haven't proved, but that they think that, if I cannot give such extra proofs, then the proofs that I have given are not conclusive proofs at all. And this, I think, is a definite mistake. They would say: "If you cannot prove your premiss that here is one hand and here is another, then you do not know it. But you yourself have admitted that, if you did not know it, then your proof was not conclusive. Therefore your proof was not, as you say it was, a conclusive proof." This view that, if I cannot prove such things as these, I do not know them, is, I think, the view that Kant was expressing in the sentence which I quoted at the beginning of this lecture, when he implies that so long as we have no proof of the existence of external things, their existence must be accepted merely on *faith*. He means to say, I think, that if I cannot prove that there is a hand here, I must accept it merely as a matter of faith—I cannot know it. Such a view, though it has been very common among philosophers, can, I think, be shown to be wrong—though shown only by the use of premisses which are not known to be true, unless we do know of the existence of external things. I can know things, which I cannot prove; and among things which I certainly did know, even if (as I think) I could not prove them, were the premisses of my two proofs. I should say, therefore, that those, if any, who are dissatisfied with these proofs merely on the ground that I did not know their premisses, have no good reason for their dissatisfaction.

6

C. D. Broad THE TRADITIONAL PROBLEM
OF BODY AND MIND

The Mind and Its Place in Nature, from which this selection is taken, is generally recognized as one of the most important books of analytic philosophy. Although Broad never attracted the following that philosophers such as Russell, Wittgenstein, or Austin have, his influence upon the philosophical world has been considerable. In *The Mind and Its Place in Nature* he takes up several related problems of mind and attempts to clarify both the problem and the possible solutions to it. Typical of Broad's approach to philosophical problems is the final chapter of the book where he painstakingly lists seventeen possible theories about the relation of mind and matter and carefully evaluates them. Like Russell, Broad felt that it is part of philosophy's task to theorize in a way not too unlike that of science.

The third chapter of *The Mind and Its Place in Nature* is devoted to a detailed discussion of the traditional mind-body problem. This problem arises for anyone who holds that mind and body are fundamentally different in nature. How can there be interaction between the mental and the physical when they seem to have such different properties? In the selection which follows, Broad states several possible views concerning the relation of mind and matter and evaluates the strong and weak points of each.

Broad's approach to the mind-body problem should be contrasted with Russell's views as expressed in selection 3, and especially with Ryle's quite different approach in selection 13.

Recommended additional reading on the subject includes:

Ducasse, C. J.: *Nature, Mind and Death*
Wisdom, J.: *Problems of Mind and Matter*

See also the Selected Bibliography for Part IV in Edwards, P., and Pap, A.: *A Modern Introduction to Philosophy.*

In the last Chapter we considered organisms simply as complicated material systems which behave in certain characteristic ways. We did not consider the fact that some organisms are animated by minds, and that all the minds of whose existence we are certain animate organisms. And we did not deal with those features in the behaviour of certain organisms which are commonly supposed to be due to the mind which animates the organism. It is such facts as these, and certain problems to which they have given rise, which I mean to discuss in the present Chapter. There is a question which has been argued about for some centuries now under the name of "Interaction"; this is the question whether minds really do act on the organisms which they animate, and whether organisms really do act on the minds which animate them. (I must point out at once that I imply no particular theory of mind or body by the word "to animate." I use it as a perfectly neutral name to express the fact that a certain mind is connected in some peculiarly intimate way with a certain body, and, under normal conditions with no other body. This is a fact even on a purely behaviouristic theory of mind; on such a view to say that the mind M animates the body B would mean that the body B, in so far as it behaves in certain ways, *is* the mind M. A body which did not act in these ways would be said not to be animated by a mind. And a different Body B', which acted in the same general way as B, would be said to be animated by a different mind M'.)

The problem of Interaction is generally discussed at the level of enlightened common-sense; where it is assumed that we know pretty well what we mean by "mind," by "matter," and by "causation." Obviously no solution which is reached at that level can claim to be ultimate. If what we call "matter" should turn out to be a collection of spirits of low intelligence, as Leibniz thought, the argument that mind and body are so unlike that their interaction is impossible would become irrelevant. Again, if causation be nothing but regular sequence and concomitance, as some philosophers have held, it is ridiculous to regard psychoneural parallelism and interaction as mutually exclusive alternatives. For interaction will mean no more than parallelism, and parallelism will mean no less than interaction. Nevertheless I am going to discuss the arguments here at the common-sense level, because they are so incredibly bad and yet have imposed upon so many learned men.

We start then by assuming a developed mind and a developed organism as two distinct things, and by admitting that the two are now intimately connected in some way or other which I express by saying that "this mind *animates* this organism." We assume that bodies are very much as enlightened common-sense believes them to be; and that, even if we cannot define "causation," we have some means of recognising when it is present and when it is absent. The question then is: "Does a mind ever act on the body which it animates, and does a body ever act on the mind which animates it?" The answer which common-sense would give to both questions is: "Yes, certainly." On the face of it my body acts on my mind whenever a pin is stuck into the former and a painful sensation thereupon arises in the latter. And, on the face of it, my mind acts on my body whenever a desire to move my arm arises in the former and is followed by this movement in the latter. Let us call this common-sense view "Two-sided Interaction." Although it seems so obvious it has been denied by probably a majority of philosophers and a majority of physiologists. So the question is: "Why should so many distinguished men, who have studied the subject, have denied the apparently obvious fact of Two-sided Interaction?"

The arguments against Two-sided Interaction fall into two sets:—Philosophical and Scientific. We will take the philosophical arguments first; for we shall find that the professedly scientific arguments come back in the end to the principles or prejudices which are made explicit in the philosophical arguments.

PHILOSOPHICAL ARGUMENTS AGAINST TWO-SIDED INTERACTION. No one can deny that there is a close correlation between certain bodily events and certain mental events, and conversely. Therefore anyone who denies that there is action of mind on body and of body on mind must presumably hold (*a*) that concomitant variation is not an adequate criterion of causal connexion, and (*b*) that the other feature which is essential for causal connexion is absent in the case of body and mind. Now the common philosophical argument is that minds and mental states are so extremely unlike bodies and bodily states that it is inconceivable that the two should be causally connected. It is certainly true that, if minds and mental events are just what they seem to be to introspection and nothing more, and if bodies and bodily events are just what enlightened common-sense thinks them to be and nothing more, the two *are* extremely unlike, And this fact is supposed to show that, however closely correlated certain pairs of events in mind and body respectively may be, they cannot be causally connected.

Evidently the assumption at the back of this argument is that concomitant variation, together with a high enough degree of likeness, is an adequate test for causation; but that no amount of concomitant variation can establish causation in the absence of a high enough degree of likeness. Now I am inclined to admit part of this assumption. I think it is practically certain that causation does not simply *mean* concomitant variation. (And, if it did, *cadit quæstio*.) Hence the existence of the latter is not *ipso facto* a proof of the presence of the former. Again, I think it is almost certain that concomitant variation between A and B is not in fact a sufficient sign of the presence of a *direct* causal relation between the two. (I think it may perhaps be a sufficient sign of *either* a direct causal relation between A and B *or* of several causal relations which indirectly unite A and B through the medium of other terms C, D, etc.) So far I agree with the assumptions of the argument. But I cannot see the least reason to think that the other characteristic, which must be added to concomitant variation before we can be sure that A and B are causally connected, is a high degree of likeness between the two. One would like to know just how unlike two events may be before it becomes impossible to admit the existence of a causal relation between them. No one hesitates to hold that draughts and colds in the head are causally connected, although the two are extremely unlike each other. If the unlikeness of draughts and colds in the head does not prevent one from admitting a causal connexion between the two, why should the unlikeness of volitions and voluntary movements prevent one from holding that they are causally connected? To sum up. I am willing to admit that an adequate criterion of causal connexion needs some other relation between a pair of events beside concomitant variation; but I do not believe for a moment that this other relation is that of qualitative likeness.

This brings us to a rather more refined form of the argument against Interaction. It is said that, whenever we admit the existence of a causal relation between two events, these two events (to put it crudely) must also form parts of a single substantial whole. E.g., all physical events are spatially related and form one great extended whole. And the mental events which would commonly be admitted to be causally connected are always events in a single mind. A mind is a substantial whole of a peculiar kind too. Now it is said that between bodily events and mental events there are no relations such as those which unite physical events in different parts of the same Space or mental events in the history of the same mind. In the absence of such relations, binding mind and body into a single substantial whole, we cannot admit that bodily and mental events can be causally connected with each other, no matter how closely correlated their variations may be.

This is a much better argument than the argument about qualitative likeness and unlikeness. If we accept the premise that causal relations can subsist only between terms which form parts of a single substantial whole must we deny that mental and bodily events can be causally connected? I do not think that we need. (i) It is of course perfectly true that an organism and the mind which animates it do not form a physical whole, and that they do not form a mental whole; and these, no doubt, are the two kinds of substantial whole with which we are most familiar. But it does not follow that a mind and its organism do not form a substantial whole of *some* kind. There, plainly, is the extraordinary intimate union between the two which I have called "animation" of the one by the other. Even if the mind be just what it seems to introspection, and the body be just what it seems to perception aided by the more precise methods of science, this seems to me to be enough to make a mind and its body a substantial whole. Even so extreme a dualist about Mind and Matter as Descartes occasionally suggests that a mind and its body together form a quasi-substance; and, although we may quarrel with the language of the very numerous philosophers who have said that the mind is "the form" of its body, we must admit that such language would never have seemed plausible unless a mind and its body together had formed something very much like a single substantial whole.

(ii) We must, moreover, admit the possibility that minds and mental events have properties and relations which do not reveal themselves to introspection, and that bodies and bodily events may have properties and relations which do not reveal themselves to perception or to physical and chemical experiment. In virtue of these properties and relations the two together may well form a single substantial whole of the kind which is alleged to be needed for causal interaction. Thus, if we accept the premise of the argument, we have no right to assert that mind and body *cannot* interact; but only the much more modest proposition that introspection and perception do not suffice to assure us that mind and body are so interrelated that they *can* interact.

(iii) We must further remember that the Two-sided Interactionist is under no obligation to hold that the *complete* conditions of any mental event are bodily or that the complete conditions of any bodily event are mental. He needs only to assert that some mental events include certain bodily events among their necessary conditions, and that some bodily events include certain mental events among their necessary conditions. If I am paralysed my volition may not move my arm; and, if I am hypnotised or intensely interested or frightened, a wound may not produce a painful sensation. Now, if the complete cause and the complete effect in all interaction include both a bodily and a mental factor, the two wholes will be related by the fact that the mental constituents belong to a single mind, that the bodily constituents belong to a single body, and that this mind animates this body. This amount of connexion should surely be enough to allow of causal interaction.

This will be the most appropriate place to deal with the contention that, in voluntary action, and there only, we are immediately acquainted with an instance of causal connexion. If this be true the controversy is of course settled at once in favour of the Interactionist. It is generally supposed that this view was refuted once and for all by Mr. Hume in his *Enquiry concerning Human Understanding* (Sect. VII, Part I). I should not care to assert that the doctrine in question is true; but I do think that it is plausible, and I am quite sure that Mr. Hume's arguments do not refute it. Mr. Hume uses three closely connected arguments. (1) The connexion between a successful volition and the resulting bodily movement is as mysterious and as little self-evident as the connexion between any other event and its effect. (2) We have to learn from experience which of our volitions will be effective and which will not. *E.g.*, we do not know, until we have tried, that we can voluntarily move our arms and cannot voluntarily move our livers. And again, if a man were suddenly paralysed, he would still expect to be able to move his arm voluntarily, and would be suprised when he found that it kept still in spite of his volition. (3) We have discovered that the immediate consequence of a volition is a change in our nerves and muscles, which most people know nothing about; and is not the movement of a limb, which most people believe to be its immediate and necessary consequence.

The second and third arguments are valid only against the contention that we know immediately that a volition to make a certain movement is the *sufficient* condition for the happening of that movement. They are quite irrelevant to the contention that we know immediately that the volition is a *necessary* condition for the happening of just that movement at just that time. No doubt many other conditions are also necessary, *e.g.*, that our nerves and muscles shall be in the right state; and these other necessary conditions can be discovered only by special investigation. Since our volitions to move our limbs are in fact followed in the vast majority of cases by the willed movement, and since the other necessary conditions are not very obvious, it is natural enough that we should think that we know immediately that our volition is the *sufficient* condition of the movement of our limbs. If we think so, we are certainly wrong; and Mr. Hume's arguments prove that we are. But they prove nothing else. It does not follow that we are wrong in thinking that we know, without having to wait for the result, that the volition is a *necessary* condition of the movement.

It remains to consider the first argument. Is the connexion between cause and effect as mysterious and as little self-evident in the case of the voluntary production of bodily movement as in all other cases? If so, we must hold that the first time a baby wills to move its hand it is just as much surprised to find its hand moving as it would be to find its leg moving or its nurse bursting into flames. I do not profess to know anything about the infant mind; but it seems to me that this is a wildly paradoxical consequence, for which there is no evidence or likelihood. But there is no need to leave the matter there. It is perfectly plain that, in the case of volition and voluntary movement, there is a connexion between the cause and the effect which is not present in other cases of causation, and which does make it plausible to hold that in this one case the nature of the effect can be foreseen by merely reflecting on the nature of the cause. The peculiarity of a volition as a cause-factor is that it involves as an essential part of it the idea of the effect. To say that a person has a volition to move his arm involves saying that he has an idea of his arm (and not of his leg or his liver) and an idea of the position in which he wants his arm to be. It is simply silly in view of this fact to say that there is no closer connexion between the desire to move my arm and the movement of my arm than there is between this desire and the movement of my leg or my liver. We cannot detect any analogous connexion between cause and effect in causal transactions which we view wholly from outside, such as the movement of a billiard-ball by a cue. It is therefore by no means unreasonable to suggest that, in the one case of our own voluntary movements, we can see without waiting for the result that such and such a volition is a necessary condition of such and such a bodily movement.

It seems to me then that Mr. Hume's arguments on this point are absolutely irrelevant, and that it may very well be true that in volition we positively know that our desire for such and such a bodily movement is a necessary (though not a sufficient) condition of the happening of just that movement at just that time. On the whole then I conclude that the philosophical arguments certainly do not disprove Two-sided Interaction, and that they do not even raise any strong presumption against it. And, while I am not prepared definitely to commit myself to the view that, in voluntary movement, we positively *know* that the mind acts on the body, I do think that this opinion is quite plausible when properly stated and that the arguments which have been brought against it are worthless. I pass therefore to the scientific arguments.

SCIENTIFIC ARGUMENTS AGAINST TWO–SIDED INTERACTION.   There are, so far as I know, two of these. One is supposed to be based on the physical principle of the Conservation of Energy, and on certain experiments which have been made on human bodies. The other is based on the close analogy which is said to exist between the structures of the physiological mechanism of reflex action and that of voluntary action. I will take them in turn.

1. The Argument from Energy.   It will first be needful to state clearly what is asserted by the principle of the Conservation of Energy. It is found that, if we take certain material systems, *e.g.*, a gun, a cartridge, and a bullet, there is a certain magnitude which keeps approximately constant throughout all their changes. This is called "Energy." When the gun has not been fired it and the bullet have no motion, but the explosive in the cartridge has great chemical energy. When it has been fired the bullet is moving very fast and has great energy of movement. The gun, though not moving fast in its recoil, has also great energy of movement because it is very massive. The gases produced by the explosion have some energy of movement and some heat-energy, but much less chemical energy than the unexploded charge had. These various kinds of energy can be measured in common units according to certain conventions. To an innocent mind there seems to be a good deal of "cooking" at this stage, *i.e.*, the conventions seem to be chosen and various kinds and amounts of concealed energy seem to be postulated in order to make the principle come out right at the end. I do not propose to go into this in detail, for two reasons. In the first place, I think that the conventions adopted and the postulates made, though somewhat suggestive of the fraudulent company-promoter, can be justified by their coherence with certain experimental facts, and that they are not simply made *ad hoc*. Secondly, I shall show that the Conservation of Energy is absolutely irrelevant to the question at issue, so that it would be waste of time to treat it too seriously in the present connexion. Now it is found that the total energy of all kinds in this system, when measured according to these conventions, is approximately the same in amount though very differently distributed after the explosion and before it. If we had confined our attention to a part of this system and *its* energy this would not have been true. The bullet, *e.g.*, had no energy at all before the explosion and a great deal afterwards. A system like the bullet, the gun, and the charge, is called a "Conservative System"; the bullet alone, or the gun and the charge, would be called "Non-conservative Systems." A conservative system might therefore be defined as one whose total energy is redistributed, but not altered in amount, by changes that happen within it. Of course a given system might be conservative for some kinds of change and not for others.

So far we have merely defined a "Conservative System," and admitted that there are systems which, for some kinds of change at any rate, answer approximately to our definition. We can now state the Principle of the Conservation of Energy in terms of the conceptions just defined. The principle asserts that every material system is either itself conservative, or, if not, is part of a larger material system which is conservative. We may take it that there is good inductive evidence for this proposition.

The next thing to consider is the experiments on the human body. These tend to prove that a living body, with the air that it breathes and the food that it eats, forms a conservative system to a high degree of approximation. We can measure the chemical energy of the food given to a man, and that which enters his body in the form of Oxygen breathed in. We can also, with suitable apparatus, collect, measure, and analyse the air breathed out, and thus find its chemical energy. Similarly, we can find the energy given out in bodily movement, in heat, and in excretion. It is alleged that, on the average, whatever the man may do, the energy of his bodily movements is exactly accounted for by the energy given to him in the form of food and of Oxygen. If you take the energy put in food and Oxygen, and subtract the energy given out in waste-products, the balance is almost exactly equal to the energy put out in bodily movements.

Such slight differences as are found are as often on one side as on the other, and are therefore probably due to unavoidable experimental errors. I do not propose to criticise the interpretation of these experiments in detail, because, as I shall show soon, they are completely irrelevant to the problem of whether mind and body interact. But there is just one point that I will make before passing on. It is perfectly clear that such experiments can tell us only what happens on the average over a long time. To know whether the balance was accurately kept at every moment we should have to kill the patient at each moment and analyse his body so as to find out the energy present then in the form of stored-up products. Obviously we cannot keep on killing the patient in order to analyse him, and then reviving him in order to go on with the experiment. Thus it would seem that the results of the experiment are perfectly compatible with the presence of quite large excesses or defects in the total bodily energy at certain moments, provided that these average out over longer periods. However, I do not want to press this criticism; I am quite ready to accept for our present purpose the traditional interpretation which has been put on the experiments.

We now understand the physical principle and the experimental facts. The two together are generally supposed to prove that mind and body cannot interact. What precisely is the argument, and is it valid? I imagine that the argument, when fully stated, would run somewhat as follows: "I will to move my arm, and it moves. If the volition has anything to do with causing the movement we might expect energy to flow from my mind to my body. Thus the energy of my body ought to receive a measurable increase, not accounted for by the food that I eat and the Oxygen that I breathe. But no such physically unaccountable increases of bodily energy are found. Again, I tread on a tin-tack, and a painful sensation arises in my mind. If treading on the tack has anything to do with causing the sensation we might expect energy to flow from my body to my mind. Such energy would cease to be measurable. Thus there ought to be a noticeable decrease in my bodily energy, not balanced by increases anywhere in the physical system. But such unbalanced decreases of bodily energy are not found." So it is concluded that the volition has nothing to do with causing my arm to move, and that treading on the tack has nothing to do with causing the painful sensation.

Is this argument valid? In the first place it is important to notice that the conclusion does not follow from the Conservation of Energy and the experimental facts alone. The real premise is a tacitly assumed proposition about causation; viz., that, if a change in A has anything to do with causing a change in B, energy must leave A and flow into B. This is neither asserted nor entailed by the Conservation of Energy. What it says is that, if energy leaves A, it must appear in something else, say B; so that A and B together form a conservative system. Since the Conservation of Energy is not itself the premise for the argument against Interaction, and since it does not entail that premise, the evidence for the Conservation of Energy is not evidence against Interaction. Is there any independent evidence for the premise? We may admit that it is true of many, though not of all, transactions within the physical realm. But there are cases where it is not true even of purely physical transactions; and, even if it were always true in the physical realm, it would not follow that it must also be true of transphysical causation. Take the case of a weight swinging at the end of a string hung from a fixed point. The total energy of the weight is the same at all positions in its course. It is thus a conservative system. But at every moment the direction and velocity of the weight's motion are different, and the proportion between its kinetic and its potential energy is constantly changing. These changes are caused by the pull of the string, which acts in a different direction at each different moment. The string makes no difference to the total energy of the weight; but it makes all the difference in the world to the particular way in which the weight moves and the particular way in which the energy is distributed between the potential and the kinetic forms. This is evident when we remember that the weight would begin to move in an utterly different course if at any moment the string were cut.

Here, then, we have a clear case even in the physical realm where a system is conservative but is continually acted on by something which affects its movement and the distribution of its total energy. Why should not the mind act on the body in this way? If you say that you can see how a string can affect the movement of a weight, but cannot see how a volition could affect the movement of a material particle, you have deserted the scientific argument and have gone back to one of the philosophical arguments. Your real difficulty is either that volitions are so very unlike movements, or that the volition is in your mind whilst the movement belongs to the physical realm. And we have seen how little weight can be attached to these objections.

The fact is that, even in purely physical systems, the Conservation of Energy does not explain what changes will happen or when they will happen. It merely imposes a very general limiting condition on the changes that are possible. The fact that the system composed of bullet, charge, and gun, in our earlier example, is conservative does not tell us that the gun ever will be fired, or when it will be fired if at all, or what will cause it to go off, or what forms of energy will appear if and when it does go off. The change in this case is determined by pulling the trigger. Likewise the mere fact that the human body and its neighbourhood form a conservative system does not explain any particular bodily movement; it does not explain why I ever move at all, or why I sometimes write, sometimes walk, and sometimes swim. To explain the happening of these particular movements at certain times it seems to be essential to take into account the volitions which happen from time to time in my mind; just as it is essential to take the string into account to explain the particular behaviour of the weight, and to take the trigger into account to explain the going off of the gun at a certain moment. The difference between the gun-system and the body-system is that a little energy does flow into the former when the trigger is pulled, whilst it is alleged that none does so when a volition starts a bodily movement. But there is not even this amount of difference between the body-system and the swinging weight.

Thus the argument from energy has no tendency to disprove Two-sided Interaction. It has gained a spurious authority from the august name of the Conservation of Energy. But this impressive principle proves to have nothing to do with the case. And the real premise of the argument is not self-evident, and is not universally true even in purely intra-physical transactions. In the end this scientific argument has to lean on the old philosophic arguments; and we have seen that these are but bruised reeds. Nevertheless, the facts brought forward by the argument from energy do throw some light on the *nature* of the interaction between mind and body, assuming this to happen. They do suggest that all the energy of our bodily actions comes out of and goes back into the physical world, and that minds neither add energy to nor abstract it from the latter. What they do, if they do anything, is to determine that at a given moment so much energy shall change from the chemical form to the form of bodily movement; and they determine this, so far as we can see, without altering the total amount of energy in the physical world.

2. **The Argument from the Structure of the Nervous System.**   There are purely reflex actions, like sneezing and blinking, in which there is no reason to suppose that the mind plays any essential part. Now we know the nervous structure which is used in such acts as these. A stimulus is given to the outer end of an afferent nerve; some change or other runs up this nerve, crosses a synapsis between this and an afferent nerve, travels down the latter to a muscle, causes the muscle to contract, and so produces a bodily movement. There seems no reason to believe that the mind plays any essential part in this process. The process may be irreducibly vital, and not merely physico-chemical; but there seems no need to assume anything more than this. Now it is said that the whole nervous system is simply an immense complication of interconnected nervous arcs. The result is that a change which travels inwards has an immense number of alternative paths by which it may travel outwards. Thus the reaction to a given stimulus is no longer one definite movement, as in the simple reflex. Almost any movement may follow any stimulus according to the path which the afferent disturbance happens to take. This path will depend on the relative resistance of the various synapses at the time. Now a variable response to the same stimulus is characteristic of deliberate as opposed to reflex action.

These are the facts. The argument based on them runs as follows. It is admitted that the mind has nothing to do with the causation of purely reflex actions. But the nervous structure and the nervous processes involved in deliberate action do not differ in kind from those involved in reflex action; they differ only in degree of complexity. The variability which characterises deliberate action is fully explained by the variety of alternative paths and the variable resistances of the synapses. So it is unreasonable to suppose that the mind has any more to do with causing deliberate actions than it has to do with causing reflex actions.

I think that this argument is invalid. In the first place I am pretty sure that the persons who use it have before their imagination a kind of picture of how mind and body must interact if they interact at all. They find that the facts do not answer to this picture, and so they conclude that there is no interaction. The picture is of the following kind. They think of the mind as sitting somewhere in a hole in the brain, surrounded by telephones. And they think of the afferent disturbance as coming to an end at one of these telephones and there affecting the mind. The mind is then supposed to respond by sending an afferent impulse down another of these telephones. As no such hole, with afferent nerves stopping at its walls and afferent nerves starting from them, can be found, they conclude that the mind can play no part in the transaction. But another alternative is that this picture of how the mind must act if it acts at all is wrong. To put it shortly, the mistake is to confuse a gap in an explanation with a spatio-temporal gap, and to argue from the absence of the latter to the absence of the former.

The Interactionist's contention is simply that there is a gap in any purely physiological explanation of deliberate action; *i.e.*, that all such explanations fail to account completely for the facts because they leave out one necessary condition. It does not follow in the least that there must be a spatio-temporal breach of continuity in the physiological conditions, and that the missing condition must fill this gap in the way in which the movement of a wire fills the spatio-temporal interval between the pulling of a bell-handle and the ringing of a distant bell. To assume this is to make the mind a kind of physical object, and to make its action a kind of mechanical action. Really, the mind and its actions are not literally in Space at all, and the time which is occupied by the mental event is no doubt *also* occupied by some part of the physiological process. Thus I am inclined to think that much of the force which this argument actually exercises on many people is simply due to the presupposition about the *modus operandi* of interaction, and that it is greatly weakened when this presupposition is shown to be a mere prejudice due to our limited power of envisaging unfamiliar alternative possibilities.

We can, however, make more detailed objections to the argument than this. There is a clear introspective difference between the mental accompaniment of voluntary action and that of reflex action. What goes on in our minds when we decide with difficulty to get out of a hot bath on a cold morning is obviously extremely different from what goes on in our minds when we sniff pepper and sneeze. And the difference is qualitative; it is not a mere difference of complexity. This difference has to be explained somehow; and the theory under discussion gives no plausible explanation of it. The ordinary view that, in the latter case, the mind is not acting on the body at all; whilst, in the former, it is acting on the body in a specific way, does at least make the introspective difference between the two intelligible.

Again, whilst it is true that deliberate action differs from reflex action in its greater variability of response to the same stimulus, this is certainly not the whole or the most important part of the difference between them. The really important difference is that, in deliberate action, the response is varied *appropriately* to meet the special circumstances which are supposed to exist at the time or are expected to arise later; whilst reflex action is not varied in this way, but is blind and almost mechanical. The complexity of the nervous system explains the *possibility* of variation; it does not in the least explain why the alternative which actually takes place should as a rule be appropriate and not merely haphazard. And so again it seems as if some factor were in operation in deliberate action which is not present in reflex action; and it is reasonable to suppose that this factor is the volition in the mind.

It seems to me that this second scientific argument has no tendency to disprove interaction; but that the facts which it brings forward do tend to suggest the particular form which interaction probably takes if it happens at all. They suggest that what the mind does to the body in voluntary action, if it does anything, is to lower the resistance of certain synapses and to raise that of others. The result is that the nervous current follows such a course as to produce the particular movement which the mind judges to be appropriate at the time. In such a view the difference between reflex, habitual, and deliberate actions for the present purpose becomes fairly plain. In pure reflexes the mind cannot voluntarily affect the resistance of the synapses concerned, and so the action takes place in spite of it. In habitual action it deliberately refrains from interfering with the resistance of the synapses, and so the action goes on like a complicated reflex. But it *can* affect these resistances if it wishes, though often only with difficulty; and it is ready to do so if it judges this to be expedient. Finally, it may lose the power altogether. This would be what happens when a person becomes a slave to some habit, such as drug-taking.

I conclude that, at the level of enlightened common-sense at which the ordinary discussion of Interaction moves, no good reason has been produced for doubting that the mind acts on the body in volition, and that the body acts on the mind in sensation. The philosophic arguments are quite inconclusive; and the scientific arguments, when properly understood, are quite compatible with Two-sided Interaction. At most they suggest certain conclusions as to the form which interaction probably takes if it happens at all.

DIFFICULTIES IN THE DENIAL OF INTER-ACTION . I propose now to consider some of the difficulties which would attend the denial of Interaction, still keeping the discussion at the same common-sense level. If a man denies the action of body on mind he is at once in trouble over the causation of new sensations. Suppose that I suddenly tread on an unsuspected tin-tack. A new sensation suddenly comes into my mind. This is an event, and it presumably has some cause. Now, however carefully I introspect and retrospect, I can find no other mental event which is adequate to account for the fact that just that sensation has arisen at just that moment. If I reject the common-sense view that treading on the tack is an essential part of the cause of the sensation, I must suppose either that it is uncaused, or that it is caused by other events in my mind which I cannot discover by introspection or retrospection, or that it is caused telepathically by other finite minds or by God. Now enquiry of my neighbours would show that it is not caused telepathically by any event in their minds which they can introspect or remember. Thus anyone who denies the action of body on mind, and admits that sensations have causes, must postulate either (a) immense numbers of unobservable states in his own mind; or (b) as many unobservable states in his neighbours' minds, together with telepathic action; or (c) some non-human spirit together with telepathic action. I must confess that the difficulties which have been alleged against the action of body on mind seem to be mild compared with those of the alternative hypotheses which are involved in the denial of such action.

The difficulties which are involved in the denial of the action of mind on body are at first sight equally great; but I do not think that they turn out to be so serious as those which are involved in denying the action of body on mind. The *prima facie* difficulty is this. The world contains many obviously artificial objects, such as books, bridges, clothes, etc. We know that, if we go far enough back in the history of their production, we always do in fact come on the actions of some human body. And the minds connected with these bodies did design the objects in question, did will to produce them, and did believe that they were initiating and guiding the physical process by means of these designs and volitions. If it be true that the mind does not act on the body, it follows that the designs and volitions in the agents' minds did not in fact play any part in the production of books, bridges, clothes, etc. This appears highly paradoxical. And it is an easy step from it to say that anyone who denies the action of mind on body must admit that <u>books, bridges, and other such objects *could* have been produced even though there had been no minds</u>, no thought of these objects and no desire for them. This consequence seems manifestly absurd to common-sense, and it might be argued that it reflects its absurdity back on the theory which entails it.

The man who denies that mind can act on body might deal with this difficulty in two ways: (1) He might deny that the conclusion *is* intrinsically absurd. He might say that human bodies are extraordinarily complex physical objects, which probably obey irreducible laws of their own, and that we really do not know enough about them to set limits to what their unaided powers could accomplish. This is the line which Spinoza took. The conclusion, it would be argued, *seems* absurd only because the state of affairs which it contemplates is so very unfamiliar. We find it difficult to imagine a body like ours without a mind like ours; but, if we could get over this defect in our powers of imagination, we might have no difficulty in admitting that such a body could do all the things which our bodies do. I think it must be admitted that the difficulty is not so great as that which is involved in denying the action of body on mind. There we had to postulate *ad hoc* utterly unfamiliar entities and modes of action; here it is not certain that we should have to do this.

(2) The other line of argument would be to say that the alleged consequence does not necessarily follow from denying the action of mind on body. I assume that both parties admit that causation is something more than mere *de facto* regularity of sequence and concomitance. If they do not, of course the whole controversy between them becomes futile; for there will certainly be causation between mind and body and between body and mind, in the only sense in which there is causation anywhere. This being presupposed, the following kind of answer is logically possible. When I say that B could not have happened unless A had happened, there are two alternative possibilities. (*a*) A may itself be an indispensable link in any chain of causes which ends up with B. (*b*) A may not itself be a link in any chain of causation which ends up with B. But there may be an indispensable link *a* in any such chain of causation, and A may be a necessary accompaniment or sequel of *a*. These two possibilities may be illustrated by diagrams. (*a*) is represented by the figure below:

$$A_0 \xrightarrow{\quad} A \xrightarrow{\quad} A_1 \xrightarrow{\quad} A_2 \xrightarrow{\quad} B$$

The two forms of (*b*) are represented by the two figures below:

$$A_0 \qquad A \qquad A_1 \qquad A_2 \qquad B$$

$$\cdot \longrightarrow \; \cdot \longrightarrow \; \cdot \longrightarrow \; \cdot \longrightarrow \cdot$$

$$a$$

and

$$A_0 \qquad\qquad \cdot A \atop A_1 \qquad A_2 \qquad B$$

$$\cdot \longrightarrow \; \cdot \longrightarrow \; \cdot \longrightarrow \; \cdot \longrightarrow \cdot$$

$$a$$

Evidently, if B cannot happen unless a precedes, and if a cannot happen without A accompanying or immediately following it, B will not be able to happen unless A precedes it. And yet A will have had no part in causing B. It will be noticed that, on this view, a has a complex effect AA_1, of which a certain part, viz., A_1 is sufficient by itself to produce A_2 and ultimately B. Let us apply this abstract possibility to our present problem. Suppose that B is some artificial object, like a book or a bridge. If we admit that this could not have come into existence unless a certain design and volition had existed in a certain mind, we could interpret the facts in two ways. (*a*) We could hold that the design and volition are themselves an indispensable link in the chain of causation which ends in the production of a bridge or a book. This is the common view, and it requires us to admit the action of mind on body. (*b*) We might hold that the design and the volition are not themselves a link in the chain of causation which ends in the production of the artificial object; but that they are a necessary accompaniment or sequent of something which *is* an indispensable link in this chain of causation. On this view the chain consists wholly of physical events; but one of these physical events (viz., some event in the brain) has a complex consequent. One part of this consequent is purely physical, and leads by purely physical causation to the ultimate production of a bridge or a book. The other is purely mental, and consists of a certain design and volition in the mind which animates the human body concerned. If this has any consequences they are purely mental. Each part of this complex consequent follows with equal necessity; this particular brain-state could no more have existed without such and such a mental state accompanying or following it than it could have existed without such and such a bodily movement following it. If we are willing to take some such view as this, we can admit that certain objects could not have existed unless there had been designs of them and desires for them; and yet we could consistently deny that these desires and designs have any effect on the movements of our bodies.

It seems to me then that the doctrine which I will call "One-sided Action of Body on Mind" is logically possible; *i.e.*, a theory which accepts the action of body on mind but denies the action of mind on body. But I do not see the least reason to accept it, since I see no reason to deny that mind acts on body in volition. One-sided Action has, I think, generally been held in the special form called "Epiphenomenalism." I take this doctrine to consist of the following four propositions: (1) Certain bodily events cause certain mental events. (2) No mental event plays any part in the causation of any bodily event. (3) No mental event plays any part in the causation of any other mental event. Consequently (4) all mental events are caused by bodily events and by them only. Thus Epiphenomenalism is just One-sided Action of Body on Mind, together with a special theory about the nature and structure of mind. This special theory does not call for discussion here, where I am dealing only with the relations between minds and bodies, and am not concerned with a detailed analysis of mind. In a later chapter we shall have to consider the special features of Epiphenomenalism.

ARGUMENTS IN FAVOUR OF INTERACTION. The only arguments *for* One-sided Action of Body on Mind or for Parallelism are the arguments *against* Two-sided Interaction; and these, as we have seen, are worthless. Are there any arguments in favour of Two-sided Interaction? I have incidentally given two which seem to me to have considerable weight. In favour of the action of mind on body is the fact that we seem to be immediately aware of a causal relation when we voluntarily try to produce a bodily movement, and that the arguments to show that this cannot be true are invalid. In favour of the action of body on mind are the insuperable difficulties which I have pointed out in accounting for the happening of new sensations on any other hypothesis. There are, however, two other arguments which have often been thought to prove the action of mind on body. These are (1) an evolutionary argument, first used, I believe, by William James; and (2) the famous "telegram argument." They both seem to me to be quite obviously invalid.

(1) The evolutionary argument runs as follows: It is a fact, which is admitted by persons who deny Two-sided Interaction, that minds increase in complexity and power with the growth in complexity of the brain and nervous system. Now, if the mind makes no difference to the actions of the body, this development of the mental side is quite unintelligible from the point of view of natural selection. Let us imagine two animals whose brains and nervous systems were of the same degree of complexity; and suppose, if possible, that one had a mind and the other had none. If the mind makes no difference to the behaviour of the body the chance of survival and of leaving descendants will clearly be the same for the two animals. Therefore natural selection will have no tendency to favour the evolution of mind which has actually taken place. I do not think that there is anything in this argument. Natural selection is a purely negative process; it simply tends to eliminate individuals and species which have variations unfavourable to survival. Now, by hypothesis, the possession of a mind is not *unfavourable* to survival; it simply makes no difference. Now it may be that the existence of a mind of such and such a kind is an inevitable consequence of the existence of a brain and nervous system of such and such a degree of complexity. Indeed we have seen that some such view is essential if the opponent of Two-sided Interaction is to answer the common-sense objection that artificial objects could not have existed unless there had been a mind which designed and desired them. On this hypothesis there is no need to invoke natural selection twice over, once to explain the evolution of the brain and nervous system, and once to explain the evolution of the mind.

If natural selection will account for the evolution of the brain and nervous system, the evolution of the mind will follow inevitably, even though it adds nothing to the survival-value of the organism. The plain fact is that natural selection does not account for the origin or for the growth in complexity of anything whatever; and therefore it is no objection to any particular theory of the relations of mind and body that, if it were true, natural selection would not explain the origin and development of mind.

(2) The "telegram argument" is as follows: Suppose there were two telegrams, one saying "Our son has been killed," and the other saying: "Your son has been killed." And suppose that one or other of them was delivered to a parent whose son was away from home. As physical stimuli they are obviously extremely alike, since they differ only in the fact that the letter "Y" is present in one and absent in the other. Yet we know that the reaction of the person who received the telegram might be very different according to which one he received. This is supposed to show that the reactions of the body cannot be wholly accounted for by bodily causes, and that the mind must intervene causally in some cases. Now I have very little doubt that the mind does play a part in determining the action of the recipient of the telegram; but I do not see why this argument should prove it to a person who doubted or denied it. If two very similar stimuli are followed by two very different results, we are no doubt justified in concluding that these stimuli are not the complete causes of the reactions which follow them. But of course it would be admitted by every one that the receipt of the telegram is not the complete cause of the recipient's reaction. We all know that his brain and nervous system play an essential part in any reaction that he may make to the stimulus. The question then is whether the minute structure of his brain and nervous system, including in this the supposed traces left by past stimuli and past reactions, is not enough to account for the great difference in his behaviour on receiving two very similar stimuli. Two keys may be very much alike, but one may fit a certain lock and the other may not. And, if the lock be connected with the trigger of a loaded gun, the results of "stimulating" the system with one or other of the two keys will be extremely different. We know that the brain and nervous system are very complex, and we commonly suppose that they contain more or less permanent traces and linkages due to past stimuli and reactions. If this be granted, it is obvious that two very similar stimuli may produce very different results, simply because one fits in with the internal structure of the brain and nervous system whilst the other does not. And I do not see how we can be sure that anything more is needed to account for the mere difference of reaction adduced by the "telegram argument."

THE POSITIVE THEORY OF PARALLELISM. The doctrine of Psycho-physical Parallelism, or, as I prefer to call it, "Psycho-neural Parallelism," has two sides to it. One is negative; it is the denial that mind acts on body and the denial that body acts on mind. With this side of it I have now dealt to the best of my ability, and have argued that there is no reason to believe it and tolerably good reason to disbelieve it. But Psycho-neural Parallelism has also a positive side, which might be accepted by one who rejected its negative side. The positive assertion of Parallelism is that there is a one-one correlation between events in a mind and events in the brain and nervous system of the body which it animates. Is there any reason to believe this on empirical grounds?

I think we must say that it *may* be true, but that it is a perfectly enormous assumption unless there be some general metaphysical ground for it; and that the empirical evidence for it is, and will always remain, quite inadequate. The assertion is that to every particular change in the mind there corresponds a certain change in the brain which this mind animates, and that to every change in the brain there corresponds a certain change in the mind which animates this brain. What kind of empirical evidence *could* there be for such an assertion? At best the evidence would be of the following kind: "I have observed a number of brains and the minds which animate them; and I have never found a change in either which was not correlated with a specific change in the other. And all other people who have made similar observations have found the same thing." *If* we had evidence of this sort the positive side of Parallelism would be a straightforward inductive generalisation of it; *i.e.*, an argument from "A has never been observed to happen without B" to "A never does happen without B." But actually we have *no* evidence whatever of this kind. No one person in the world ever has observed, or probably ever will observe, a brain and *its* mind. The only mind that he can observe is his own and the only brains that he can observe are those of others. Nor is this the worst. We can very rarely observe other men's brains at all, and never when they are alive and in a state of normal consciousness. Thus the actual empirical data for the positive side of Parallelism consist of observations on brains which are no longer animated by minds at all or whose animating minds are in abeyance. And these minds could not be directly observed by us even if they were present and functioning normally.

It will therefore be worth while to consider carefully what amount of parallelism we really are justified on empirical grounds in assuming. (1) We have fairly good reasons for thinking that the existence and general integrity of a brain and nervous system is a necessary condition for the manifestation of a mind to itself and to other minds. We do not positively know that it is a sufficient condition; and the question whether it be so or not will have to be discussed later in this book. Our evidence is all of the following kind: (i) In the absence of a brain and nervous system we see none of those external actions which we know in our own case to be accompanied by consciousness. (ii) The brain and nervous system are known to increase in complexity up to a certain age, and we have observed in ourselves and can infer from the behaviour of others a corresponding growth in mental complexity. (iii) Soon after men have ceased to show signs of consciousness by their external behaviour their brains and nervous systems break up. It must be admitted that it might be maintained with almost equal plausibility that these last facts show that the integrity of the brain and nervous system is dependent on the presence of the mind. We might just as well argue that the brain begins to break up because the mind has ceased to animate it, as that the mind has ceased to manifest itself because the brain has begun to break up. In fact, seeing the order in which we actually get our knowledge of the two facts, the former is *prima facie* the more plausible interpretation. (iv) In many cases where men's behaviour has been so odd as to suggest that their minds are abnormal, it is known that their brains have been injured or it has been found after their death that their brains were in an abnormal state. On the other hand, it must be admitted that the brains in some lunatics on dissection show no systematic differences from those of normal people. It would obviously be absurd to talk of "Parallelism" in reference to this very general relation between the integrity and complexity of the brain and nervous system, on the one hand, and the manifestation of a human mind, on the other.

(2) There is, however, empirical evidence which goes rather further than this. It is found that wounds in certain parts of the brain make specific differences to the mind. E.g., a wound in one part may be followed by a loss of memory for spoken words, and so on. Unfortunately, similar results can often be produced by causes like hypnotism or like those which psycho-analysts discuss. And here there is no positive empirical evidence that these specific areas of the brain are affected. Again, there seems to be some evidence that, after a time and within certain limits, another part of the brain can take over the functions of a part that has been injured. Thus the most that we can say is that the general integrity of certain parts of the brain seems to be at least a temporarily necessary condition for the manifestation of certain specific kinds of mental activity. It remains doubtful how far any given area is indispensable for a given kind of mental activity, and whether there may not be some kinds of activity which, though dependent like all others on the general integrity of the brain, are not specially correlated with any particular area. We might sum up these facts by saying that there is good evidence for a considerable amount of "Departmental Parallelism" between mind and brain.

(3) The orthodox Parallelist, however, goes much further than this, and much beyond the most rigid departmental parallelism. He would hold, not merely that there is a strict correlation between each distinguishable *department* of mental life and some specific *area* of the brain, but also that there is a strict parallelism of *events*. E.g., he holds, not merely that I could not remember at all unless a certain area of my brain were intact, but also that if I now remember eating my breakfast there is a certain event in this area uniquely correlated with this particular mental event. And by "unique correlation" he means that if some other mental state had happened now instead of this particular memory there would necessarily have been a different brain-event, and conversely. So far as I know there is not, and could not possibly be, any empirical evidence for this "Parallelism of Events," as I will call it. For (i), while a man is conscious and can observe events in his own mind, his brain is not open to inspection by himself or by anyone else. And, when his brain is open to inspection, he is not likely to be in a position to introspect or to tell others what is going on in his mind, even if something is happening there at the time. (ii) In any case the events in the brain which are supposed to correspond to particular events in the mind would be admitted to be too minute to be observable even under the most favourable circumstances. They are as purely hypothetical as the motions of electrons, without the advantage that the assumption of them

enables us to predict better than we could otherwise do what states of mind a man will probably have under given circumstances.

It seems to me then that there is no empirical evidence at all for a Parallelism of Events between mind and brain. If this doctrine is to be held, the grounds for it must be general. *E.g.*, psycho-*neural* parallelism might be plausible if, on other grounds, we saw reason to accept psycho-*physical* parallelism; *i.e.*, the doctrine that *every* physical event is correlated with a specific mental event, and conversely. And the wider doctrine might be defended as helping to explain the apparent origin of life and mind from apparently non-living and non-conscious matter. This is a question which we shall have to discuss later; all that I am concerned to argue at present is that, at the level of enlightened common-sense and apart from some general metaphysical theory of the nature of matter and mind, there is no adequate evidence for a psycho-neural parallelism of events. And, as parallelism has commonly been defended on the ground that it is established by empirical scientific investigation of the brain and nervous system, this fact is worth pointing out.

If there is no reason *for* psycho-neural parallelism of events, is there any positive reason *against* it? Some philosophers have held that there is. They have held that, while it is possible and even probable that *some* mental events are correlated with specific neural events, it is impossible that this should be true of *all* mental events. Those who take this view generally hold that there probably is psycho-neural parallelism of events for sensations, but that there certainly cannot be such parallelism for comparison, introspection, attentive inspection, and so on. This view is taken by Mr. Johnson in his *Logic* (Part III); and it will be worth while to consider his arguments. They are contained in Chapter VII, §6 of that work. Mr. Johnson's argument, if I rightly understand it, comes to this: We must distinguish, *e.g.*, between the *fact* that I am having two sensations, one of which is light red and the other dark red, and my *recognition* that both are red and that one is darker than the other. We must likewise distinguish, *e.g.*, between the *fact* that the dark one started before the light one, and my recognition of this fact; and between the *fact* that the dark one is to the left of the light one in my visual field and my recognition of this fact. Finally, we must notice that we have to distinguish different degrees of clearness and determinateness with which a perfectly determinate fact may be recognised. We may merely judge that one sensum is separate from another, or we may judge that one is to the left of the other, or we may judge that the first is as much to the left of the second as the second is to the right of a third, and so on. Now Mr. Johnson contends that the sensations themselves have neural correlates, and that the determinate qualities and relations which the sensations actually have are determined by the qualities and relations of these neural correlates. But he holds that there is then nothing left on the neural side for the *recognition* of these qualities and relations to be correlated with. Still less is there anything left on the neural side to be correlated with the infinitely numerous different degrees of determinateness with which the qualities and relations of the sensations may be apprehended. Hence he concludes that mental events above the level of sensations *cannot* be correlated one to one with specific neural eveι.ts. He does not explicitly draw the distinction which I have done between Departmental Parallelism and Parallelism of Events; but I think it is plain that his argument is meant only to deny the latter. He would probably admit that, if certain specific areas of our brains were injured, we should lose altogether the power of making judgments of comparison and of recognising spatio-temporal relations; but he would hold that, given the general integrity of those areas, there is not some one specific event within them corresponding to each particular judgment of comparison or of spatio-temporal relation.

Before criticising this argument we must notice that Mr. Johnson does not explicitly distinguish sensations and sensa. By a "sensation" I think he means what I should call a "sensed sensum." And he thinks that, from the nature of the case, there can be no unsensed sensa. Thus a sensation for him is a sensum, regarded as existentially mind-dependent; and, in virtue of its supposed existential mind-dependence, it counts as a mental event belonging to the mind on which its existence depends. If we like to distinguish between mental *states* and mental *acts* we can say that a sensation, for Mr. Johnson, is apparently a mental *state* having certain sensible qualities, such as colour, position in the visual field, and so on. To recognize that one is having a sensation, that it is of such and such a kind, and that it stands in such and such spatio-temporal relations to other sensations, would be to perform a cognitive mental *act*. And his contention is that, whilst there is a parallelism of events for mental states, there cannot for this very reason be also a parallelism of events for mental acts. This at least is how I understand him.

Now I must confess that Mr. Johnson's argument seems to me to be so extremely weak that (knowing Mr. Johnson) I hesitate to believe that I can have properly understood it. Let us suppose that the actual relative position of two sensa s_1 and s_2 in a visual sense-field is determined by the relative position of two excited areas in the brain, b_1 and b_2. Let us suppose that the actual relative date of the two sensa in the sense-history of the experiment is determined by the relative date of the excitement of these areas. And let us suppose that the determinate sensible qualities of the two sensa (*e.g.*, the particular shade of the particular colour possessed by each) is determined by the particular kind of movement which is going on in the microscopic particles within these two areas. Mr. Johnson's contention seems to be that, when we have mentioned the positions of the excited areas, the dates at which they begin to be excited, and the particular kind of movement which is going on within them, we have said all that can be said about the neural events. There is nothing left on the neural side to be correlated with our acts of recognition, of qualitative comparison, and of spatio-temporal judgment; and therefore these events can have no special neural correlate. To this there are two answers which seem so obvious that I am almost ashamed to make them.

1. At the very utmost the argument would show only that there is nothing left *within the two areas* b_1 and b_2 to be correlated with any judgments which we happen to make about the sensations s_1 and s_2. But these two areas do not exhaust the whole of the brain and nervous system. Why our acts of judgment about these two sensations should not have neural correlates in some other part of the brain I cannot imagine. The situation on the mental side is that we may,

but need not, make these judgments if we do have the sensations; and that we cannot make them unless we have the sensations. This is exactly what we might expect if the neural correlates of the acts of judgment were in a different part of the brain from the neural correlates of the sensations themselves; and if a certain kind of disturbance in the latter were a necessary but insufficient condition of a certain kind of disturbance in the former.

neural

2. But we could answer the argument without needing even to assume that the neutral correlates of judgments about sensations are in a different area of the brain from the neural correlates of the sensations themselves. We have to remember that the same area may contain at the same time microscopic events of different scales of magnitude. Let us take a purely physical analogy. The same piece of metal may be at once hot and glowing. We have extremely good reasons to believe that *both* these apparent characteristics are correlated with microscopic motions which are going on throughout the whole volume occupied by the bit of metal. The heat is supposed to be correlated with the random movements of molecules and the light with the jumps of electrons from one stable orbit to another. The large-scale events can go on without the small-scale events (a body may be hot without glowing); but the more violent the large-scale events the more frequent will be the small-scale events (a body begins to glow if it be heated enough). Now I cannot imagine why the same thing might not be true of the neural correlates of sensations and the neural correlates of our judgments about our sensations. Suppose that the neural correlates of sensations were large-scale events in a certain area of the brain; and suppose that the neural correlates of our judgments about these sensations were small-scale events in the same area. Then I should expect to find that sensations could happen without our making judgments about them; that we could not make the judgments unless we had the sensations; and that it would be more difficult not to make the judgments as the sensations became more intense, other things being equal. And this is exactly what I do find. It seems to me then, either that I have altogether misunderstood Mr. Johnson's argument, or that there is nothing whatever in it.

There remains one other point to be discussed before leaving the subject. It is true, as Mr. Johnson points out, that we make judgments of various degrees of determinateness about the same perfectly determinate fact. Does this raise any particular difficulty against the view that every act of judgment has a specific neural correlate? I do not think that it does, if we avoid certain confusions into which it is very easy to fall. I suppose that the difficulty that is felt is this: "Every neural event is perfectly determinate; how can an indeterminate judgment have a determinate neural correlate; and how can there be different determinate neural correlates for all the different degrees of determinateness in judgments?" To this I should answer (i) that of course the differences on the neural side which would correspond to different degrees of determinateness in the judgment are not themselves differences of determinateness. But why should they be? The differences on the neural side which correspond to differences of shade in sensations of colour are not themselves differences of shade. If, *e.g.*, the area which is correlated with judgments about our sensations be different from the area which is correlated with the sensations themselves, we might suppose that differences in the determinateness of the judgment were correlated with differences in the extent or the intensity of the disturbance within this area. If, on the other hand, we supposed that our sensations were correlated with large-scale events, and our judgments about these sensations with small-scale events in the same region of the brain, we might suppose that differences in the determinateness of the judgment are correlated with differences in the frequency of these small-scale events. There is thus no difficulty, so far as I can see, in providing neural correlates to every different degree of determinateness in our judgments. (ii) It is perhaps necessary to point out that what is called an "indeterminate judgment" is not an indeterminate event; every event, whether mental or physical, is no doubt perfectly determinate of its kind. *E.g.*, whether I merely judge that *some one* has been in the room or make the more determinate judgment that *John Smith* has been in the room, either judgment as a psychical event has perfectly determinate forms of all the physical determinables under which it falls. The indefiniteness is in what is asserted, not in the act of asserting as such. Hence the problem is not, as it might seem to a careless observer, to find a determinate neural correlate to an indeterminate psychical event; the problem is merely to find a determinate neural correlate to a determinate psychical event which consists in the asserting of a relatively indeterminate characteristic.

I conclude then that no adequate reason has been produced by Mr. Johnson to prove that there *cannot* be specific neural correlates to mental *acts* as well as to mental *states*. I have also tried to show that there neither is nor is likely to be any empirical evidence *for* the doctrine that all mental events have specific neural events as their correlates. Hence the positive doctrine of Psycho-neural Parallelism of Events seems to me to be a perfectly open question. This is not perhaps a wildly exciting result. But it is not altogether to be despised, since it leaves us with a perfectly free hand when we try to construct a speculative theory of the relations of matter and mind which shall do justice to all the known facts. For the known facts neither require nor preclude complete Psycho-neural Parallelism of Events.

SUMMARY AND CONCLUSIONS. I wish to make quite clear what I do and what I do not claim to have done in this chapter. I have definitely assumed that the body and the mind are two distinct entities, which are now in a very intimate union, which I express by saying that the former is "animated by" the latter. I have raised no question about the exact nature or origin of this relation of "animation"; and I have not considered the apparent growth of mind in the individual or the apparent development of consciousness from the non-conscious in the course of the earth's history. Again, I have taken the body to be very much as common-sense, enlightened by physical science, but not by philosophical criticism, takes it to be; I have supposed that we know pretty well what a mind is; and I have assumed that causation *is* not simply regular sequence and concomitant variation, though these are more or less trustworthy *signs* of the presence of a causal relation. These are the assumptions on which the question of Interaction has commonly been discussed by philosophers and by scientists; and it would be idle for me to conceal my opinion that it has been discussed extraordinarily badly. The problem seems to have exercised a most unfortunate effect on those who have treated it; for I have rarely met with a collection of worse arguments on all sides. I can only hope that I have not provided yet another instance in support of this generalisation.

My conclusion is that, subject to the assumptions just mentioned, no argument has been been produced which should make any reasonable person doubt that mind acts on body in volition and that body acts on mind in sensation. I have tried to show the extreme difficulties which are involved in attempting to deny that body acts on mind. And I have tried to show that the apparently equal difficulties which seem to be involved in attempting to deny that mind acts on body could be evaded with a little ingenuity. Thus One-sided Action of Body on Mind is a possible theory. But there seems to me to be no positive reason for accepting it, and at least one reason for doubting it, viz, the conviction which many men have (and which Mr. Hume's arguments fail altogether to refute) that we *know* directly that our volitions are necessary conditions for the occurrence of our voluntary movements.

If these conclusions be sound, Parallelism, considered as an *alternative* which excludes Interaction, has no leg left to stand upon. But Parallelism has a positive side to it which is perfectly compatible with Interaction, and is therefore worth discussing for its own sake. I distinguished between the metaphysical doctrine of Psycho-*physical* Parallelism and the more restricted doctrine of Psycho-*neural* Parallelism. And I divided the latter into Departmental Parallelism and Parallelism of Events. It seemed to me that there was good empirical evidence for a considerable amount of Departmental Parallelism, but that there was not and is not likely to be adequate empirical evidence for Parallelism of Events. On the other hand, I came to the conclusion that Mr. Johnson's arguments to prove that complete parallelism between mental and neural events is *impossible* were quite unsound.

This, I think, is as far as the discussion can be carried at this level. One thing seems to me to emerge clearly even at this point. If interaction has to be denied at a later stage it can only be because the relation between mind and body turns out to be so intimate that "interaction" is an unsuitable expression for the connection between a particular mental event and its correlated bodily event. This would be so if, *e.g.*, Materialism were true, so that the mind was just some part of the body. It might be so on a Double-aspect Theory, or on a theory of Neutral Monism. But we cannot decide between such general theories until we know more about the true nature of Mind and of Matter, and have taken into consideration questions about origin and development of minds which we have hitherto explicitly left out of account. Thus the final discussion of the question can come only near the end of the book.

part ii LOGICAL POSITIVISM

7

part i

A. J. Ayer THE ELIMINATION
OF METAPHYSICS

Language, Truth and Logic, which first appeared in 1936, quickly took on the status of a classic. Although, as Ayer admits, it was a "young man's book," overly confident and iconoclastic in tone, it nevertheless set forth in a most readable style Ayer's conception of the basic tenets of Logical Positivism. In 1946 a revised edition appeared to which Ayer appended an introduction stating how he had modified his original views in the light of the criticisms which had been directed against them.

Central to Ayer's version of Positivism is the Principle of Verification. Ayer intended it as a criterion of meaning, through which significant discourse could be distinguished from senseless combinations of words. Metaphysics, he was confident, could on the basis of the criterion be shown to fall in the latter class.

In the first chapter of the book, which is reprinted in this selection, Ayer states the Principle of Verification and attempts to clarify how it is to be understood and how it can be used to demonstrate the literal meaninglessness of metaphysical sentences. Many of the substantive points which he makes in this chapter are discussed in greater detail in later chapters.

Further reading on the topic includes:

Ayer, A. J.: "Demonstration of the Impossibility of Metaphysics," *Mind,* 1934.
Lazerowitz, M.: "The Principle of Verification," *Mind,* 1937.
Stace, W. T.: "Positivism," *Mind,* 1944.
Wisdom, J.: "Metaphysics and Verification" in *Philosophy and Psycho-analysis.*

See also the bibliographical footnotes in Chapter 16 of Passmore's *A Hundred Years of Philosophy.*

The traditional disputes of philosophers are, for the most part, as unwarranted as they are unfruitful. The surest way to end them is to establish beyond question what should be the purpose and method of a philosophical enquiry. And this is by no means so difficult a task as the history of philosophy would lead one to suppose. For if there are any questions which science leaves it to philosophy to answer, a straightforward process of elimination must lead to their discovery.

We may begin by criticising the metaphysical thesis that philosophy affords us knowledge of a reality transcending the world of science and common sense. Later on, when we come to define metaphysics and account for its existence, we shall find that it is possible to be a metaphysician without believing in a transcendent reality; for we shall see that many metaphysical utterances are due to the commission of logical errors, rather than to a conscious desire on the part of their authors to go beyond the limits of experience. But it is convenient for us to take the case of those who believe that it is possible to have knowledge of a transcendent reality as a starting-point for our discussion. The arguments which we use to refute them will subsequently be found to apply to the whole of metaphysics.

One way of attacking a metaphysician who claimed to have knowledge of a reality which transcended the phenomenal world would be to enquire from what premises his propositions were deduced. Must he not begin, as other men do, with the evidence of his senses? And if so, what valid process of reasoning can possibly lead him to the conception of a transcendent reality? Surely from empirical premises nothing whatsoever concerning the properties, or even the existence, of anything super-empirical can legitimately be inferred. But this objection would be met by a denial on the part of the metaphysician that his assertions were ultimately based on the evidence of his senses. He would say that he was endowed with a faculty of intellectual intuition which enabled him to know facts that could not be known through sense-experience. And even if it could be shown that he was relying on empirical premises, and that his venture into a non-empirical world was therefore logically unjustified, it would not follow that the assertions which he made concerning this non-empirical world could not be true. For the fact that a conclusion does not follow from its putative premise is not sufficient to show that it is false. Consequently one cannot overthrow a system of transcendent metaphysics merely by criticising the way in which it comes into being. What is required is rather a criticism of the nature of the actual statements which comprise it. And this is the line of argument which we shall, in fact, pursue. For we shall maintain that no statement which refers to a "reality" transcending the limits of all possible sense-experience can possibly have any literal significance; from which it must follow that the labours of those who have striven to describe such a reality have all been devoted to the production of nonsense.

It may be suggested that this is a proposition which has already been proved by Kant. But although Kant also condemned transcendent metaphysics, he did so on different grounds. For he said that the human understanding was so constituted that it lost itself in contradictions when it ventured out beyond the limits of possible experience and attempted to deal with things in themselves. And thus he made the impossibility of a transcendent metaphysic not, as we do, a matter of logic, but a matter of fact. He asserted, not that our minds could not conceivably have had the power of penetrating beyond the phenomenal world, but merely that they were in fact devoid of it. And this leads the critic to ask how, if it is possible to know only what lies within the bounds of sense-experience, the author can be justified in asserting that real things do exist beyond, and how he can tell what are the boundaries beyond which the human understanding may not venture, unless he succeeds in passing them himself. As Wittgenstein says, "in order to draw a limit to thinking, we should have to think both sides of this limit," [1] a truth to which Bradley gives a special twist in maintaining that the man who is ready to prove that metaphysics is impossible is a brother metaphysician with a rival theory of his own. [2]

Whatever force these objections may have against the Kantian doctrine, they have none whatsoever against the thesis that I am about to set forth. It cannot here be said that the author is himself overstepping the barrier he maintains to be impassable. For the fruitlessness of attempting to transcend the limits of possible sense-experience will be deduced, not from a pyschological hypothesis concerning the actual constitution of the human mind, but from the rule which determines the literal significance of language. Our charge against the metaphysician is not that he attempts to employ the understanding in a field where it cannot profitably venture, but that he produces sentences which fail to conform to the conditions under which alone a sentence can be literally significant. Nor are we ourselves obliged to talk nonsense in order to show that all sentences of a certain type are necessarily devoid of literal significance. We need only formulate the criterion which enables us to test whether a sentence expresses a genuine proposition about a matter of fact, and then point out that the sentences under consideration fail to satisfy it. And this we shall now proceed to do. We shall first of all formulate the criterion in somewhat vague terms, and then give the explanations which are necessary to render it precise.

The criterion which we use to test the genuineness of apparent statements of fact is the criterion of verifiability. We say that a sentence is factually significant to any given person, if and only if, he knows how to verify the proposition which it purports to express—that is, if he knows what observations would lead him, under certain conditions, to accept the proposition as being true, or reject it as being false. If, on the other hand, the putative proposition is of such a character that the assumption of its truth, or falsehood, is consistent with any assumption whatsoever concerning the nature of his future experience, then, as far as he is concerned, it is, if not a tautology, a mere pseudo-proposition. The sentence expressing it may be emotionally significant to him; but it is not literally significant. And with regard to questions the procedure is the same. We enquire in every case what observations would lead us to answer the question, one way or the other; and, if none can be discovered, we must conclude that the sentence under consideration does not, as far as we are concerned, express a genuine question, however strongly its grammatical appearance may suggest that it does.

As the adoption of this procedure is an essential factor in the argument of this book, it needs to be examined in detail.

[1] *Tractatus Logico-Philosophicus,* Preface.
[2] Bradley, *Appearance and Reality,* 2d ed., p. 1.

In the first place, it is necessary to draw a distinction between practical verifiability, and verifiability in principle. Plainly we all understand, in many cases believe, propositions which we have not in fact taken steps to verify. Many of these are propositions which we could verify if we took enough trouble. But there remain a number of significant propositions, concerning matters of fact, which we could not verify even if we chose; simply because we lack the practical means of placing ourselves in the situation where the relevant observations could be made. A simple and familiar example of such a proposition is the proposition that there are mountains on the farther side of the moon.[3] No rocket has yet been invented which would enable me to go and look at the farther side of the moon, so I am unable to decide the matter by actual observation. But I do know what observations would decide it for me, if, as is theoretically conceivable, I were once in a position to make them. And therefore I say that the proposition is verifiable in principle, if not in practice, and is accordingly significant. On the other hand, such a metaphysical pseudo-proposition as "the Absolute enters into, but is itself incapable of, evolution and progress," [4] is not even in principle verifiable. For one cannot conceive of an observation which would enable one to determine whether the Absolute did, or did not, enter into evolution and progress. Of course it is possible that the author of such a remark is using English words in a way in which they are not commonly used by English-speaking people, and that he does, in fact, intend to assert something which could be empirically verified. But until he makes us understand how the proposition that he wishes to express would be verified, he fails to communicate anything to us. And if he admits, as I think the author of the remark in question would have admitted, that his words were not intended to express either a tautology or a proposition which was capable, at least in principle, of being verified, then it follows that he has made an utterance which has no literal significance even for himself.

A further distinction which we must make is the distinction between the "strong" and the "weak" sense of the term "verifiable." A proposition is said to be verifiable, in the strong sense of the term, if, and only if, its truth could be conclusively established in experience. But it is verifiable, in the weak sense, if it is possible for experience to render it probable. In which sense are we using the term when we say that a putative proposition is genuine only if it is verifiable?

It seems to me that if we adopt conclusive verifiability as our criterion of significance, as some positivists have proposed,[5] our argument will prove too much. Consider, for example, the case of general propositions of law—such propositions, namely, as "arsenic is poisonous"; "all men are mortal"; "a body tends to expand when it is heated." It is of the very nature of these propositions that their truth cannot be established with certainty by any finite series of observations. But if it is recognised that such general propositions of law are designed to cover an infinite number of cases, then it must be admitted that they cannot, even in principle, be verified conclusively. And then, if we adopt con-

---

[3] This example has been used by Professor Schlick to illustrate the same point.

[4] A remark taken at random from *Appearance and Reality*, by F. H. Bradley.

[5] E.g., M. Schlick, "Positivismus und Realismus," *Erkenntnis*, vol. I, 1930. F. Waismann, "Logische Analyse des Warscheinlichkeitsbegriffs," *Erkenntnis*, vol. 1, 1930.

clusive verifiability as our criterion of significance, we are logically obliged to treat these general propositions of law in the same fashion as we treat the statements of the metaphysician.

In face of this difficulty, some positivists [6] have adopted the heroic course of saying that these general propositions are indeed pieces of nonsense, albeit an essentially important type of nonsense. But here the introduction of the term "important" is simply an attempt to hedge. It serves only to mark the authors' recognition that their view is somewhat too paradoxical, without in any way removing the paradox. Besides, the difficulty is not confined to the case of general propositions of law, though it is there revealed most plainly. It is hardly less obvious in the case of propositions about the remote past. For it must surely be admitted that, however strong the evidence in favour of historical statements may be, their truth can never become more than highly probable. And to maintain that they also constituted an important, or unimportant, type of nonsense would be unplausible, to say the very least. Indeed, it will be our contention that no proposition, other than a tautology, can possibly be anything more than a probable hypothesis. And if this is correct, the principle that a sentence can be factually significant only if it expresses what is conclusively verifiable is self-stultifying as a criterion of significance. For it leads to the conclusion that it is impossible to make a significant statement of fact at all.

Nor can we accept the suggestion that a sentence should be allowed to be factually significant if, and only if, it expresses something which is definitely confutable by experience.[7] Those who adopt this course assume that, although no finite series of observations is ever sufficient to establish the truth of a hypothesis beyond all possibility of doubt, there are crucial cases in which a single observation, or series of observations, can definitely confute it. But, as we shall show later on, this assumption is false. A hypothesis cannot be conclusively confuted any more than it can be conclusively verified. For when we take the occurrence of certain observations as proof that a given hypothesis is false, we presuppose the existence of certain conditions. And though, in any given case, it may be extremely improbable that this assumption is false, it is not logically impossible. We shall see that there need be no self-contradiction in holding that some of the relevant circumstances are other than we have taken them to be, and consequently that the hypothesis has not really broken down. And if it is not the case that any hypothesis can be definitely confuted, we cannot hold that the genuineness of a proposition depends on the possibility of its definite confutation.

Accordingly, we fall back on the weaker sense of verification. We say that the question that must be asked about any putative statement of fact is not, Would any observations make its truth or falsehood logically certain? but simply, Would any observations be relevant to the determination of its truth or falsehood? And it is only if a negative answer is given to this second question that we conclude that the statement under consideration is nonsensical.

To make our position clearer, we may formulate it in another way. Let us call a proposition which records an actual or possible observation an experiential

---

[6] E.g., M. Schlick, "Die Kausalität in der gegenwärtigen Physik," *Naturwissenschaft*, vol. 19, 1931.

[7] This has been proposed by Karl Popper in his *Logik der Forschung*.

proposition. Then we may say that it is the mark of a genuine factual proposition, not that it should be equivalent to an experiential proposition, or any finite number of experiential propositions, but simply that some experiential propositions can be deduced from it in conjunction with certain other premises without being deducible from those other premises alone.[8]

This criterion seems liberal enough. In contrast to the principle of conclusive verifiability, it clearly does not deny significance to general propositions or to propositions about the past. Let us see what kinds of assertion it rules out.

A good example of the kind of utterance that is condemned by our criterion as being not even false but nonsensical would be the assertion that the world of sense-experience was altogether unreal. It must, of course, be admitted that our senses do sometimes deceive us. We may, as the result of having certain sensations, expect certain other sensations to be obtainable which are, in fact, not obtainable. But, in all such cases, it is further sense-experience that informs us of the mistakes that arise out of sense-experience. We say that the senses sometimes deceive us, just because the expectations to which our sense-experiences give rise do not always accord with what we subsequently experience. That is, we rely on our senses to substantiate or confute the judgements which are based on our sensations. And therefore the fact that our perceptual judgements are sometimes found to be erroneous has not the slightest tendency to show that the world of sense-experience is unreal. And, indeed, it is plain that no conceivable observation, or series of observations, could have any tendency to show that the world revealed to us by sense-experience was unreal. Consequently, anyone who condemns the sensible world as a world of mere appearance, as opposed to reality, is saying something which, according to our criterion of significance, is literally nonsensical.

An example of a controversy which the application of our criterion obliges us to condemn as fictitious is provided by those who dispute concerning the number of substances that there are in the world. For it is admitted both by monists, who maintain that reality is one substance, and by pluralists, who maintain that reality is many, that it is impossible to imagine any empirical situation which would be relevant to the solution of their dispute. But if we are told that no possible observation could give any probability either to the assertion that reality was one substance or to the assertion that it was many, then we must conclude that neither assertion is significant. We shall see later on that there are genuine logical and empirical questions involved in the dispute between monists and pluralists. But the metaphysical question concerning "substance" is ruled out by our criterion as spurious.

A similar treatment must be accorded to the controversy between realists and idealists, in its metaphysical aspect. A simple illustration, which I have made use of in a similar argument elsewhere,[9] will help to demonstrate this. Let us suppose that a picture is discovered and the suggestion made that it was painted by Goya. There is a definite procedure for dealing with such a question. The experts examine the picture to see in what way it resembles the accredited works

[8] This is an over-simplified statement, which is not literally correct. I give what I believe to be the correct formulation in the Introduction.

[9] Vide "Demonstration of the Impossibility of Metaphysics," *Mind*, 1934, p. 339.

of Goya, and to see if it bears any marks which are characteristic of a forgery; they look up contemporary records for evidence of the existence of such a picture, and so on. In the end, they may still disagree, but each one knows what empirical evidence would go to confirm or discredit his opinion. Suppose, now, that these men have studied philosophy, and some of them proceed to maintain that this picture is a set of ideas in the perceiver's mind, or in God's mind, others that it is objectively real. What possible experience could any of them have which would be relevant to the solution of this dispute one way or the other? In the ordinary sense of the term "real," in which it is opposed to "illusory," the reality of the picture is not in doubt. The disputants have satisfied themselves that the picture is real, in this sense, by obtaining a correlated series of sensations of sight and sensations of touch. Is there any similar process by which they could discover whether the picture was real, in the sense in which the term "real" is opposed to "ideal"? Clearly there is none. But, if that is so, the problem is fictitious according to our criterion. This does not mean that the realist-idealist controversy may be dismissed without further ado. For it can legitimately be regarded as a dispute concerning the analysis of existential propositions, and so as involving a logical problem which can be definitively solved. What we have just shown is that the question at issue between idealists and realists becomes fictitious when, as is often the case, it is given a metaphysical interpretation.

There is no need for us to give further examples of the operation of our criterion of significance. For our object is merely to show that philosophy, as a genuine branch of knowledge, must be distinguished from metaphysics. We are not now concerned with the historical question how much of what has traditionally passed for philosophy is actually metaphysical. We shall, however, point out later on that the majority of the "great philosophers" of the past were not essentially metaphysicians, and thus reassure those who would otherwise be prevented from adopting our criterion by considerations of piety.

As to the validity of the verification principle, in the form in which we have stated it, a demonstration will be given in the course of this book. For it will be shown that all propositions which have factual content are empirical hypotheses; and that the function of an empirical hypothesis is to provide a rule for the anticipation of experience. And this means that every empirical hypothesis must be relevant to some actual, or possible, experience, so that a statement which is not relevant to any experience is not an empirical hypothesis, and accordingly has no factual content. But this is precisely what the principle of verifiability asserts.

It should be mentioned here that the fact that the utterances of the metaphysician are nonsensical does not follow simply from the fact that they are devoid of factual content. It follows from that fact, together with the fact that they are not *a priori* propositions. And in assuming that they are not *a priori* propositions, we are once again anticipating the conclusions of a later chapter in this book. For it will be shown there that *a priori* propositions, which have always been attractive to philosophers on account of their certainty, owe this certainty to the fact that they are tautologies. We may accordingly define a metaphysical sentence as a sentence which purports to express a genuine proposition, but does, in fact, express neither a tautology nor an empirical hypothesis. And as tautologies and empirical hypotheses form the entire class of significant propositions, we are justified in concluding that all metaphysical assertions are nonsensical. Our next task is to show how they come to be made.

The use of the term "substance," to which we have already referred, provides us with a good example of the way in which metaphysics mostly comes to be written. It happens to be the case that we cannot, in our language, refer to the sensible properties of a thing without introducing a word or phrase which appears to stand for the thing itself as opposed to anything which may be said about it. And, as a result of this, those who are infected by the primitive superstition that to every name a single real entity must correspond assume that it is necessary to distinguish logically between the thing itself and any, or all, of its sensible properties. And so they employ the term "substance" to refer to the thing itself. But from the fact that we happen to employ a single word to refer to a thing, and make that word the grammatical subject of the sentences in which we refer to the sensible appearances of the thing, it does not by any means follow that the thing itself is a "simple entity," or that it cannot be defined in terms of the totality of its appearances. It is true that in talking of "its" appearances we appear to distinguish the thing from the appearances, but that is simply an accident of linguistic usage. Logical analysis shows that what makes these "appearances" the "appearances of" the same thing is not their relationship to an entity other than themselves, but their relationship to one another. The metaphysician fails to see this because he is misled by a superficial grammatical feature of his language.

A simpler and clearer instance of the way in which a consideration of grammar leads to metaphysics is the case of the metaphysical concept of Being. The origin of our temptation to raise questions about Being, which no conceivable experience would enable us to answer, lies in the fact that, in our language, sentences which express existential propositions and sentences which express attributive propositions may be of the same grammatical form. For instance, the sentences "Martyrs exist" and "Martyrs suffer" both consist of a noun followed by an intransitive verb, and the fact that they have grammatically the same appearance leads one to assume that they are of the same logical type. It is seen that in the proposition "Martyrs suffer," the members of a certain species are credited with a certain attribute, and it is sometimes assumed that the same thing is true of such a proposition as "Martyrs exist." If this were actually the case, it would, indeed, be as legitimate to speculate about the Being of martyrs as it is to speculate about their suffering. But, as Kant pointed out,[10] existence is not an attribute. For, when we ascribe an attribute to a thing, we covertly assert that it exists: so that if existence were itself an attribute, it would follow that all positive existential propositions were tautologies, and all negative existential propositions self-contradictory; and this is not the case.[11] So that those who raise questions about Being which are based on the assumption that existence is an attribute are guilty of following grammar beyond the boundaries of sense.

[10] Vide *The Critique of Pure Reason,* "Transcendental Dialectic," Book II, chap. iii, section 4.

[11] This argument is well stated by John Wisdom, *Interpretation and Analysis,* pp. 62, 63.

A similar mistake has been made in connection with such propositions as "Unicorns are fictitious." Here again the fact that there is a superficial grammatical resemblance between the English sentences "Dogs are faithful" and "Unicorns are fictitious," and between the corresponding sentences in other languages, creates the assumption that they are of the same logical type. Dogs must exist in order to have the property of being faithful, and so it is held that unless unicorns in some way existed they could not have the property of being fictitious. But, as it is plainly self-contradictory to say that fictitious objects exist, the device is adopted of saying that they are real in some non-empirical sense—that they have a mode of real being which is different from the mode of being of existent things. But since there is no way of testing whether an object is real in this sense, as there is for testing whether it is real in the ordinary sense, the assertion that fictitious objects have a special non-empirical mode of real being is devoid of all literal significance. It comes to be made as a result of the assumption that being fictitious is an attribute. And this is a fallacy of the same order as the fallacy of supposing that existence is an attribute, and it can be exposed in the same way.

In general, the postulation of real non-existent entities results from the superstition, just now referred to, that, to every word or phrase that can be the grammatical subject of a sentence, there must somewhere be a real entity corresponding. For as there is no place in the empirical world for many of these "entities," a special non-empirical world is invoked to house them. To this error must be attributed, not only the utterances of a Heidegger, who bases his metaphysics on the assumption that "Nothing" is a name which is used to denote something peculiarly mysterious,[12] but also the prevalence of such problems as those concerning the reality of propositions and universals whose senselessness, though less obvious, is no less complete.

These few examples afford a sufficient indication of the way in which most metaphysical assertions come to be formulated. They show how easy it is to write sentences which are literally nonsensical without seeing that they are nonsensical. And thus we see that the view that a number of the traditional "problems of philosophy" are metaphysical, and consequently fictitious, does not involve any incredible assumptions about the psychology of philosophers.

Among those who recognize that if philosophy is to be accounted a genuine branch of knowledge it must be defined in such a way as to distinguish it from metaphysics, it is fashionable to speak of the metaphysician as a kind of misplaced poet. As his statements have no literal meaning, they are not subject to any criteria of truth or falsehood: but they may still serve to express, or arouse, emotion, and thus be subject to ethical or æsthetic standards. And it is suggested that they may have considerable value, as means of moral inspiration, or even as works of art. In this way, an attempt is made to compensate the metaphysician for his extrusion from philosophy.[13]

[12] Vide *Was ist Metaphysik*, by Heidegger: criticised by Rudolf Carnap in his "Überwindung der Metaphysik durch logische Analyse der Sprache," *Erkenntnis*, vol. II, 1932.

[13] For a discussion of this point, see also C. A. Mace, "Representation and Expression," *Analysis*, vol. I, no. 3; and "Metaphysics and Emotive Language," *Analysis*, vol. II, nos. 1 and 2.

I am afraid that this compensation is hardly in accordance with his deserts. The view that the metaphysician is to be reckoned among the poets appears to rest on the assumption that both talk nonsense. But this assumption is false. In the vast majority of cases the sentences which are produced by poets do have literal meaning. The difference between the man who uses language scientifically and the man who uses it emotively is not that the one produces sentences which are incapable of arousing emotion, and the other sentences which have no sense, but that the one is primarily concerned with the expression of true propositions, the other with the creation of a work of art. Thus, if a work of science contains true and important propositions, its value as a work of science will hardly be diminished by the fact that they are inelegantly expressed. And similarly, a work of art is not necessarily the worse for the fact that all the propositions comprising it are literally false. But to say that many literary works are largely composed of falsehoods, is not to say that they are composed of pseudo-propositions. It is, in fact, very rare for a literary artist to produce sentences which have no literal meaning. And where this does occur, the sentences are carefully chosen for their rhythm and balance. If the author writes nonsense, it is because he considers it most suitable for bringing about the effects for which his writing is designed.

The metaphysician, on the other hand, does not intend to write nonsense. He lapses into it through being deceived by grammar, or through committing errors of reasoning, such as that which leads to the view that the sensible world is unreal. But it is not the mark of a poet simply to make mistakes of this sort. There are some, indeed, who would see in the fact that the metaphysician's utterances are senseless a reason against the view that they have æsthetic value. And, without going so far as this, we may safely say that it does not constitute a reason for it.

It is true, however, that although the greater part of metaphysics is merely the embodiment of humdrum errors, there remain a number of metaphysical passages which are the work of genuine mystical feeling; and they may more plausibly be held to have moral or æsthetic value. But, as far as we are concerned, the distinction between the kind of metaphysics that is produced by a philosopher who has been duped by grammar, and the kind that is produced by a mystic who is trying to express the inexpressible, is of no great importance: what is important to us is to realise that even the utterances of the metaphysician who is attempting to expound a vision are literally senseless; so that henceforth we may pursue our philosophical researches with as little regard for them as for the more inglorious kind of metaphysics which comes from a failure to understand the workings of our language.

A. J. Ayer   THE PRINCIPLE

OF VERIFICATION

Ayer had attempted in the first edition of *Language, Truth and Logic* to state the Principle of Verification with sufficient precision and clarity so that it could be used to show the literal meaninglessness of metaphysics. It soon became clear, however, that the criterion was not acceptable as it had been stated. In the Introduction to the second edition, part of which is reprinted below, Ayer attempted to answer some of the criticisms which had been directed against his original formulation. He restates the criterion in an amended form, attempting to avoid the failings of the original statement.

Hempel's essay (selection 10) contains a discussion of later developments in the attempt to formulate an adequate meaning criterion. See also Carnap's discussion in selection 8 and Wittgenstein's provocative remarks in the concluding pages of Part I of selection 11.

The principle of verification is supposed to furnish a criterion by which it can be determined whether or not a sentence is literally meaningful. A simple way to formulate it would be to say that a sentence had literal meaning if and only if the proposition it expressed was either analytic or empirically verifiable. To this, however, it might be objected that unless a sentence was literally meaningful it would not express a proposition;[1] for it is commonly assumed that every proposition is either true or false, and to say that a sentence expressed what was either true or false would entail saying that it was literally meaningful. Accordingly, if the principle of verification were formulated in this way, it might be argued not only that it was incomplete as a criterion of meaning, since it would not cover the case of sentences which did not express any propositions at all, but

[1] Vide M. Lazerowitz, "The Principle of Verifiability," *Mind,* 1937, pp. 372–378.

also that it was otiose, on the ground that the question which it was designed to answer must already have been answered before the principle could be applied. It will be seen that when I introduce the principle in this book I try to avoid this difficulty by speaking of "putative propositions" and of the proposition which a sentence "purports to express"; but this device is not satisfactory. For, in the first place, the use of words like "putative" and "purports" seems to bring in psychological considerations into which I do not wish to enter, and secondly, in the case where the "putative proposition" is neither analytic nor empirically verifiable, there would, according to this way of speaking, appear to be nothing that the sentence in question could properly be said to express. But if a sentence expresses nothing there seems to be a contradiction in saying that what it expresses is empirically unverifiable; for even if the sentence is adjudged on this ground to be meaningless, the reference to "what it expresses" appears still to imply that something is expressed.

This is, however, no more than a terminological difficulty, and there are various ways in which it might be met. One of them would be to make the criterion of verifiability apply directly to sentences, and so eliminate the reference to propositions altogether. This would, indeed, run counter to ordinary usage, since one would not normally say of a sentence, as opposed to a proposition, that it was capable of being verified, or, for that matter, that it was either true or false; but it might be argued that such a departure from ordinary usage was justified, if it could be shown to have some practical advantage. The fact is, however, that the practical advantage seems to lie on the other side. For while it is true that the use of the word "proposition" does not enable us to say anything that we could not, in principle, say without it, it does fulfil an important function; for it makes it possible to express what is valid not merely for a particular sentence s but for any sentence to which s is logically equivalent. Thus, if I assert, for example, that the proposition p is entailed by the proposition q I am indeed claiming implicitly that the English sentence s which expresses p can be validly derived from the English sentence r which expresses q, but this is not the whole of my claim. For, if I am right, it will also follow that any sentence, whether of the English or any other language, that is equivalent to s can be validly derived, in the language in question, from any sentence that is equivalent to r; and it is this that my use of the word "proposition" indicates. Admittedly, we could decide to use the word "sentence" in the way in which we now use the word "proposition," but this would not be conducive to clarity, particularly as the word "sentence" is already ambiguous. Thus, in a case of repetition, it can be said either that there are two different sentences or that the same sentence has been formulated twice. It is in the latter sense that I have so far been using the word, but the other usage is equally legitimate. In either usage, a sentence which was expressed in English would be accounted a different sentence from its French equivalent, but this would not hold good for the new usage of the word "sentence" that we should be introducing if we substituted "sentence" for "proposition." For in that case we should have to say that the English expression and its French equivalent were different formulations of the same sentence. We might indeed be justified in increasing the ambiguity of the word "sentence" in this way if we thereby avoided any of the difficulties that have been thought to be attached to the use of the word "proposition"; but I do not think that this is to be achieved by the mere substitution of one verbal token for another. Accordingly, I conclude that this technical use of the word "sentence," though legitimate in itself, would be likely to promote confusion, without securing us any compensatory advantage.

A second way of meeting our original difficulty would be to extend the use of the word "proposition," so that anything that could properly be called a sentence would be said to express a proposition, whether or not the sentence was literally meaningful. This course would have the advantage of simplicity, but it is open to two objections. The first is that it would involve a departure from current philosophical usage; and the second is that it would oblige us to give up the rule that every proposition is to be accounted either true or false. For while, if we adopted this new usage, we should still be able to say that anything that was either true or false was a proposition, the converse would no longer hold good; for a proposition would be neither true nor false if it was expressed by a sentence which was literally meaningless. I do not myself think that these objections are very serious, but they are perhaps sufficiently so to make it advisable to solve our terminological problem in some other way.

The solution that I prefer is to introduce a new technical term; and for this purpose I shall make use of the familiar word "statement," though I shall perhaps be using it in a slightly unfamiliar sense. Thus I propose that any form of words that is grammatically significant shall be held to constitute a sentence, and that every indicative sentence, whether it is literally meaningful or not, shall be regarded as expressing a statement. Furthermore, any two sentences which are mutually translatable will be said to express the same statement. The word "proposition," on the other hand, will be reserved for what is expressed by sentences which are literally meaningful. Thus, the class of propositions becomes, in this usage, a sub-class of the class of statements, and one way of describing the use of the principle of verification would be to say that it provided a means of determining when an indicative sentence expressed a proposition, or, in other words, of distinguishing the statements that belonged to the class of propositions from those that did not.

It should be remarked that this decision to say that sentences express statements involves nothing more than the adoption of a verbal convention; and the proof of this is that the question, "What do sentences express?" to which it provides an answer is not a factual question. To ask of any particular sentence what it is that it expresses may, indeed, be to put a factual question; and one way of answering it would be to produce another sentence which was a translation of the first. But if the general question, "What do sentences express?" is to be interpreted factually, all that can be said in answer is that, since it is not the case that all sentences are equivalent, there is not any one thing that they all express. At the same time, it is useful to have a means of referring indefinitely to "what sentences express" in cases where the sentences themselves are not particularly specified; and this purpose is served by the introduction of the word "statement" as a technical term. Accordingly, in saying that sentences express statements, we are indicating how this technical term is to be understood, but we are not thereby conveying any factual information in the sense in which we should be conveying factual information if the question we were answering was empirical. This may, indeed, seem a point too obvious to be worth making; but the question, "What do sentences express?" is closely analogous to the question, "What do sentences mean?" and, as I have tried to show elsewhere,[2] the question, "What do sentences mean?" has been a source of confusion to philosophers because they have mistakenly thought it to be factual. To say that indicative sentences mean propositions is indeed legitimate, just as it is legitimate to say that they express statements. But what we are doing, in giving answers of this kind, is to lay down conventional definitions; and it is important that these conventional definitions should not be confused with statements of empirical fact.

Returning now to the principle of verification, we may, for the sake of brevity, apply it directly to statements rather than to the sentences which express them, and we can then reformulate it by saying that a statement is held to be literally meaningful if and only if it is either analytic or empirically verifiable. But what is to be understood in the context by the term "verifiable"? I do indeed attempt to answer this question in the first chapter of this book; but I have to acknowledge that my answer is not very satisfactory.

To begin with, it will be seen that I distinguish between a "strong" and a "weak" sense of the term "verifiable," and that I explain this distinction by saying that "a proposition is said to be verifiable in the strong sense of the term, if and only if its truth could be conclusively established in experience," but that "it is verifiable, in the weak sense, if it is possible for experience to render it probable." And I then give reasons for deciding that it is only the weak sense of the term that is required by my principle of verification. What I seem, however, to have overlooked is that, as I represent them, these are not two genuine alternatives.[3] For I subsequently go on to argue that all empirical propositions are hypotheses which are continually subject to the test of further experience; and from this it would follow not merely that the truth of any such proposition never was conclusively established but that it never could be; for however strong the evidence in its favour, there would never be a point at which it was impossible for further experience to go against it. But this would mean that my "strong" sense of the term "verifiable" had no possible application, and in that case there was no need for me to qualify the other sense of "verifiable" as weak; for on my own showing it was the only sense in which any proposition could conceivably be verified.

If I do not now draw this conclusion, it is because I have come to think that there is a class of empirical propositions of which it is permissible to say that they can be verified conclusively. It is characteristic of these propositions, which I have elsewhere [4] called "basic propositions," that they refer solely to the content of a single experience, and what may be said to verify them conclusively is the occurrence of the experience to which they uniquely refer. Furthermore, I

[2] In *The Foundations of Empirical Knowledge*, pp. 92–104.
[3] Vide M. Lazerowitz, "Strong and Weak Verification," *Mind*, 1939, pp. 202–213.
[4] "Verification and Experience," *Proceedings of the Aristotelian Society*, vol. XXXVII; cf. also *The Foundations of Empirical Knowledge*, pp. 80–84.

should now agree with those who say that propositions of this kind are "incorrigible," assuming that what is meant by their being incorrigible is that it is impossible to be mistaken about them except in a verbal sense. In a verbal sense, indeed, it is always possible to misdescribe one's experience; but if one intends to do more than record what is experienced without relating it to anything else, it is not possible to be factually mistaken; and the reason for this is that one is making no claim that any further fact could confute. It is, in short, a case of "nothing venture, nothing lose." It is, however, equally a case of "nothing venture, nothing win," since the mere recording of one's present experience does not serve to convey any information either to any other person or indeed to oneself; for in knowing a basic proposition to be true one obtains no further knowledge than what is already afforded by the occurrence of the relevant experience. Admittedly, the form of words that is used to express a basic proposition may be understood to express something that is informative both to another person and to oneself, but when it is so understood it no longer expresses a basic proposition. It was for this reason, indeed, that I maintained, in the fifth chapter of this book, that there could not be such things as basic propositions, in the sense in which I am now using the term; for the burden of my argument was that no synthetic proposition could be purely ostensive. My reasoning on this point was not in itself incorrect, but I think that I mistook its purport. For I seem not to have perceived that what I was really doing was to suggest a motive for refusing to apply the term "proposition" to statements that "directly recorded an immediate experience"; and this is a terminological point which is not of any great importance.

Whether or not one chooses to include basic statements in the class of empirical propositions, and so to admit that some empirical propositions can be conclusively verified, it will remain true that the vast majority of the propositions that people actually express are neither themselves basic statements, nor deducible from any finite set of basic statements. Consequently, if the principle of verification is to be seriously considered as a criterion of meaning, it must be interpreted in such a way as to admit statements that are not so strongly verifiable as basic statements are supposed to be. But how then is the word "verifiable" to be understood?

It will be seen that, in this book, I begin by suggesting that a statement is "weakly" verifiable, and therefore meaningful, according to my criterion, if "some possible sense-experience would be relevant to the determination of its truth or falsehood." But, as I recognize, this itself requires interpretation; for the word "relevant" is uncomfortably vague. Accordingly, I put forward a second version of my principle, which I shall restate here in slightly different terms, using the phrase "observation-statement," in place of "experiential proposition," to designate a statement "which records an actual or possible observation." In this version, then, the principle is that a statement is verifiable, and consequently meaningful, if some observation-statement can be deduced from it in conjunction with certain other premises, without being deducible from those other premises alone.

I say of this criterion that it "seems liberal enough," but in fact it is far too liberal, since it allows meaning to any statement whatsoever. For, given any statement "*S*" and an observation-statement "*O*," "*O*" follows from "*S*" and "if *S* then *O*" without following from "if *S* then *O*" alone. Thus, the statements "the Absolute is lazy" and "if the Absolute is lazy, this is white" jointly entail the observation-statement "this is white," and since "this is white" does not follow from either of these premises, taken by itself, both of them satisfy my criterion of meaning. Furthermore, this would hold good for any other piece of nonsense that one cared to put, as an example, in place of "the Absolute is lazy," provided only that it had the grammatical form of an indicative sentence. But a criterion of meaning that allows such latitude as this is evidently unacceptable.[5]

It may be remarked that the same objection applies to the proposal that we should take the possibility of falsification as our criterion. For, given any statement "*S*" and any observation-statement "*O*," "*O*" will be incompatible with the conjunction of "*S*" and "if *S* then not *O*." We could indeed avoid the difficulty, in either case, by leaving out the stipulation about the other premises. But as this would involve the exclusion of all hypotheticals from the class of empirical propositions, we should escape from making our criteria too liberal only at the cost of making them too stringent.

Another difficulty which I overlooked in my original attempt to formulate the principle of verification is that most empirical propositions are in some degree vague. Thus, as I have remarked elsewhere,[6] what is required to verify a statement about a material thing is never the occurrence of precisely this or precisely that sense-content, but only the occurrence of one or other of the sense-contents that fall within a fairly indefinite range. We do indeed test any such statement by making observations which consist in the occurrence of particular sense-contents; but, for any test that we actually carry out, there is always an indefinite number of other tests, differing to some extent in respect either of their conditions or their results, that would have served the same purpose. And this means that there is never any set of observation-statements of which it can truly be said that precisely they are entailed by any given statement about a material thing.

Nevertheless, it is only by the occurrence of some sense-content, and consequently by the truth of some observation-statement, that any statement about a material thing is actually verified; and from this it follows that every significant statement about a material thing can be represented as entailing a disjunction of observation-statements, although the terms of this disjunction, being infinite, can not be enumerated in detail. Consequently, I do not think that we need be troubled by the difficulty about vagueness, so long as it is understood that when we speak of the "entailment" of observation-statements, what we are considering to be deducible from the premises in question is not any particular observation-statement, but only one or other of a set of such statements, where the defining characteristic of the set is that all its members refer to sense-contents that fall within a certain specifiable range.

There remains the more serious objection that my criterion, as it stands,

[5] Vide I. Berlin, "Verifiability in Principle," *Proceedings of the Aristotelian Society,* vol. XXXIX.

[6] *The Foundations of Empirical Knowledge,* pp. 240–241.

allows meaning to any indicative statement whatsoever. To meet this, I shall emend it as follows. I propose to say that a statement is directly verifiable if it is either itself an observation-statement, or is such that in conjunction with one or more observation-statements it entails at least one observation-statement which is not deducible from these other premises alone; and I propose to say that a statement is indirectly verifiable if it satisfies the following conditions: first, that in conjunction with certain other premises it entails one or more directly verifiable statements which are not deducible from these other premises alone; and secondly, that these other premises do not include any statement that is not either analytic, or directly verifiable, or capable of being independently established as indirectly verifiable. And I can now reformulate the principle of verification as requiring of a literally meaningful statement, which is not analytic, that it should be either directly or indirectly verifiable, in the foregoing sense.

It may be remarked that in giving my account of the conditions in which a statement is to be considered indirectly verifiable, I have explicitly put in the proviso that the "other premises" may include analytic statements; and my reason for doing this is that I intend in this way to allow for the case of scientific theories which are expressed in terms that do not themselves designate anything observable. For while the statements that contain these terms may not appear to describe anything that anyone could ever observe, a "dictionary" may be provided by means of which they can be transformed into statements that are verifiable; and the statements which constitute the dictionary can be regarded as analytic. Were this not so, there would be nothing to choose between such scientific theories and those that I should dismiss as metaphysical; but I take it to be characteristic of the metaphysician, in my somewhat pejorative sense of the term, not only that his statements do not describe anything that is capable, even in principle, of being observed, but also that no dictionary is provided by means of which they can be transformed into statements that are directly or indirectly verifiable.

Metaphysical statements, in my sense of the term, are excluded also by the older empiricist principle that no statement is literally meaningful unless it describes what could be experienced, where the criterion of what could be experienced is that it should be something of the same kind as actually has been experienced.[7] But, apart from its lack of precision, this empiricist principle has, to my mind, the defect of imposing too harsh a condition upon the form of scientific theories; for it would seem to imply that it was illegitimate to introduce any term that did not itself designate something observable. The principle of verification, on the other hand, is, as I have tried to show, more

[7] Cf. Bertrand Russell, *The Problems of Philosophy*, p. 91: "Every proposition which we can understand must be composed wholly of constituents with which we are acquainted." And, if I understand him correctly, this is what Professor W. T. Stace has in mind when he speaks of a "Principle of Observable Kinds." Vide his "Positivism," *Mind*, 1944. Stace argues that the principle of verification "rests upon" the principle of observable kinds, but this is a mistake. It is true that every statement that is allowed to be meaningful by the principle of observable kinds is also allowed to be meaningful by the principle of verification: but the converse does not hold.

liberal in this respect, and in view of the use that is actually made of scientific theories which the other would rule out, I think that the more liberal criterion is to be preferred.

It has sometimes been assumed by my critics that I take the principle of verification to imply that no statement can be evidence for another unless it is part of its meaning; but this is not the case. Thus, to make use of a simple illustration, the statement that I have blood on my coat may, in certain circumstances, confirm the hypothesis that I have committed a murder, but it is not part of the meaning of the statement that I have committed a murder that I should have blood upon my coat, nor, as I understand it, does the principle of verification imply that it is. For one statement may be evidence for another, and still neither itself express a necessary condition of the truth of this other statement, nor belong to any set of statements which determines a range within which such a necessary condition falls; and it is only in these cases that the principle of verification yields the conclusion that one statement is part of the meaning of the other. Thus, from the fact that it is only by the making of some observation that any statement about a material thing can be directly verified it follows, according to the principle of verification, that every such statement contains some observation-statement or other as part of its meaning, and it follows also that, although its generality may prevent any finite set of observation-statements from exhausting its meaning, it does not contain anything as part of its meaning that cannot be represented as an observation-statement; but there may still be many observation-statements that are relevant to its truth or falsehood without being part of its meaning at all. Again, a person who affirms the existence of a deity may try to support his contention by appealing to the facts of religious experience; but it does not follow from this that the factual meaning of his statement is wholly contained in the propositions by which these religious experiences are described. For there may be other empirical facts that he would also consider to be relevant; and it is possible that the descriptions of these other empirical facts can more properly be regarded as containing the factual meaning of his statement than the descriptions of the religious experiences. At the same time, if one accepts the principle of verification, one must hold that his statement does not have any other factual meaning than what is contained in at least some of the relevant empirical propositions; and that if it is so interpreted that no possible experience could go to verify it, it does not have any factual meaning at all.

In putting forward the principle of verification as a criterion of meaning, I do not overlook the fact that the word "meaning" is commonly used in a variety of senses, and I do not wish to deny that in some of these senses a statement may properly be said to be meaningful even though it is neither analytic nor empirically verifiable. I should, however, claim that there was at least one proper use of the word "meaning" in which it would be incorrect to say that a statement was meaningful unless it satisfied the principle of verification; and I have, perhaps tendentiously, used the expression "literal meaning" to distinguish this use from the others, while applying the expression "factual meaning" to the case of statements which satisfy my criterion without being analytic. Furthermore, I suggest that it is only if it is literally meaningful, in this sense, that a statement can properly be said to be either true or false. Thus, while I wish the principle of verification itself to be regarded, not as an empirical hypothesis, but as a definition, it is not supposed to be entirely arbitrary. It is indeed open to anyone to adopt a different criterion of meaning and so to produce an alternative definition which may very well correspond to one of the ways in which the word "meaning" is commonly used. And if a statement satisfied such a criterion, there is, no doubt, some proper use of the word "understanding" in which it would be capable of being understood. Nevertheless, I think that, unless it satisfied the principle of verification, it would not be capable of being understood in the sense in which either scientific hypotheses or common-sense statements are habitually understood. I confess, however, that it now seems to me unlikely that any metaphysician would yield to a claim of this kind; and although I should still defend the use of the criterion of verifiability as a methodological principle, I realize that for the effective elimination of metaphysics it needs to be supported by detailed analyses of particular metaphysical arguments.

8

Rudolf Carnap TESTABILITY

AND MEANING

"Testability and Meaning" is perhaps the most famous of Carnap's shorter works. It first appeared in *Philosophy of Science* in 1936 and 1937. Among the many topics dealt with by Carnap in the essay, the following are of special interest: his discussion of meaning criteria and the requirements of an empiricistic language, the use of reduction sentences for analyzing assertions about dispositional properties, and physicalism as a basis for reconstructing the language of science. Although parts of this essay can be fully understood only by a person trained in symbolic notation, the attentive reader without such a background should be able to gain much from a careful reading of it.

Carnap's discussion of meaning criteria can be profitably compared with Ayer's discussion in Parts I and II of selection 7 and Hempel's summary in selection 10. Carnap's sections on Physicalism should be compared with selections 3, 6, and 13.

I. INTRODUCTION[1]

1. Our Problem: Confirmation, Testing, and Meaning

Two chief problems of the theory of knowledge are the question of meaning and the question of verification. The first question asks under what conditions a sentence has meaning, in the sense of cognitive, factual meaning. The second one asks how we get to know something, how we can find out whether a given sentence is true or false. The second question presupposes the first one. Obviously we must understand a sentence, i.e., we must know its meaning, before we can try to find out whether it is true or not. But, from the point of view of empiricism, there is a still closer connection between the two problems. In a certain sense, there is only one answer to the two questions.

From volumes III and IV of *Philosophy of Science*. Copyright 1936, 1937. The Williams and Wilkins Company. Used by permission.

[1] In 1950 Professor Carnap made some corrections and additions to the original version of this article. These have been incorporated in the text as reprinted here.

If we knew what it would be for a given sentence to be found true then we would know what its meaning is. And if for two sentences the conditions under which we would have to take them as true are the same, then they have the same meaning. Thus the meaning of a sentence is in a certain sense identical with the way we determine its truth or falsehood; and a sentence has meaning only if such a determination is possible.

If by verification is meant a definitive and final establishment of truth, then no (synthetic) sentence is ever verifiable, as we shall see. We can only confirm a sentence more and more. Therefore we shall speak of the problem of *confirmation* rather than of the problem of verification. We distinguish the *testing* of a sentence from its confirmation, thereby understanding a procedure —e.g., the carrying out of certain experiments—which leads to a confirmation in some degree either of the sentence itself or of its negation. We shall call a sentence *testable* if we know such a method of testing for it; and we call it *confirmable* if we know under what conditions the sentence would be confirmed. As we shall see, a sentence may be confirmable without being testable; e.g., if we know that our observation of such and such a course of events would confirm the sentence, and such and such a different course would confirm its negation without knowing how to set up either this or that observation.

In what follows, the problems of confirmation, testing, and meaning will be dealt with. After some preliminary discussions in this Introduction, a logical analysis of the chief concepts connected with confirmation and testing will be carried out in Chapter I, leading to the concept of reducibility. Chapter II contains an empirical analysis of confirmation and testing, leading to a definition of the terms "confirmable" and "testable" mentioned before. The difficulties in discussions of epistemological and methodological problems are, it seems, often due to a mixing up of logical and empirical questions; therefore it seems desirable to separate the two analyses as clearly as possible. Chapter III uses the concepts defined in the preceding chapters for the construction of an empiricist language, or rather a series of languages. Further, an attempt will be made to formulate the principle of empiricism in a more exact way, by stating a requirement of confirmability or testability as a criterion of meaning. Different requirements are discussed, corresponding to different restrictions of the language; the choice between them is a matter of practical decision.

2. The Older Requirement of Verifiability

The connection between meaning and confirmation has sometimes been formulated by the thesis that a sentence is meaningful if and only if it is verifiable, and that its meaning is the method of its verification. The historical merit of this thesis was that it called attention to the close connection between the meaning of a sentence and the way it is confirmed. This formulation thereby helped, on the one hand, to analyze the factual content of scientific sentences, and, on the other hand, to show that the sentences of trans-empirical metaphysics have no cognitive meaning. But from our present point of view, this formulation, although acceptable as a first approximation, is not quite correct. By its oversimplification, it led to a too narrow restriction of scientific language, excluding not only metaphysical sentences but also certain scientific sentences having factual meaning. Our present task could therefore be formulated as that of a modification of the requirement of verifiability. It is a question of a modification, not of an entire rejection of that requirement. For among empiricists there seems to be full agreement that at least some more or less close relation exists between the meaning of a sentence and the way in which we may come to a verification or at least a confirmation of it.

The requirement of verifiability was first stated by Wittgenstein,[2] and its meaning and consequences were exhibited in the earlier publications of our Vienna Circle;[3] it is still held by the more conservative wing of this Circle.[4] The thesis needs both explanation and modification. What is meant by "verifiability" must be said more clearly. And then the thesis must be modified and transformed in a certain direction.

Objections from various sides have been raised against the requirement mentioned not only by anti-empiricist metaphysicians but also by some empiricists, e.g., by Reichenbach,[5] Popper,[6] Lewis,[7] Nagel,[8] and Stace.[9] I believe that these criticisms are right in several respects; but on the other hand, their formulations must also be modified. The theory of confirmation and testing which will be explained in the following chapters is certainly far from being an entirely satisfactory solution. However, by more exact formulation of the problem, it seems to me, we are led to a greater convergence with the views of the authors mentioned and with related views of other empiricist authors and groups. The points of agreement and of still existing differences will be evident from the following explanations.

A first attempt at a more detailed explanation of the thesis of verifiability has been made by Schlick[10] in his reply to Lewis' criticisms. Since "verifiability" means "possibility of verification" we have to answer two questions:

---

[2] Wittgenstein [1].

[3] I use this geographical designation because of lack of a suitable name for the movement itself represented by this Circle. It has sometimes been called Logical Positivism, but I am afraid this name suggests too close a dependence upon the older Positivists, especially Comte and Mach. We have indeed been influenced to a considerable degree by the historical positivism, especially in the earlier stage of our development. But today we would like a more general name for our movement, comprehending the groups in other countries which have developed related views (see: Congress [1], [2]). The term "Scientific Empiricism" (proposed by Morris [1], p. 285) is perhaps suitable. In some historical remarks in the following, concerned chiefly with our original group I shall however use the term "Vienna Circle."

[4] Schlick [1], p. 150, and [4]; Waismann [1], p. 229.

[5] Reichenbach [1] and earlier publications; [3].

[6] Popper [1].

[7] Lewis [2] has given the most detailed analysis and criticism of the requirement of verifiability.

[8] Nagel [1].

[9] Stace [1].

[10] Schlick [4].

(1) what is meant in this connection by "possibility"? and (2) what is meant by "verification"? Schlick—in his explanation of "verifiability"—answers the first question, but not the second one. In his answer to the question: what is meant by "verifiability of a sentence S," he substitutes the fact described by S for the process of verifying S. Thus he thinks, e.g., that the sentence S_1: "Rivers flow up-hill," is verifiable, because it is logically possible that rivers flow up-hill. I agree with him that this fact is logically possible and that the sentence S_1 mentioned above is verifiable—or, rather, confirmable, as we prefer to say for reasons to be explained soon. But I think his reasoning which leads to this result is not quite correct. S_1 is confirmable, not because of the logical possibility of the fact described in S_1, but because of the physical possibility of the process of confirmation; it is possible to test and to confirm S_1 (or its negation) by observations of rivers with the help of survey instruments.

Except for some slight differences, e.g., the mentioned one, I am on the whole in agreement with the views of Schlick explained in his paper.[10] I agree with his clarification of some misunderstandings concerning positivism and so-called methodological solipsism. When I used the last term in previous publications I wished to indicate by it nothing more than the simple fact [11] that everybody in testing any sentence empirically cannot do otherwise than refer finally to his own observations; he cannot use the results of other people's observations unless he has become acquainted with them by his own observations, e.g., by hearing or reading the other man's report. No scientist, as far as I know, denies this rather trivial fact. Since, however, the term "methodological solipsism"—in spite of all explanations and warnings—is so often misunderstood, I shall prefer not to use it any longer. As to the fact intended, there is, I think, no disagreement among empiricists; the apparent differences are due only to the unfortunate term. A similar remark is perhaps true concerning the term "autopsychic basis" ("eigenpsychische Basis").

Another point may be mentioned in which I do not share Schlick's view. He includes in the range of meaningful sentences only synthetic and analytic sentences but not contradictory ones (for an explanation of these terms see §5). In my view—and perhaps also in his—this question is not a theoretical question of truth but a practical question of decision concerning the form of the language-system, and especially the formative rules. Therefore I do not say that Schlick is wrong, but only, that I am not inclined to accept his proposal concerning the limitation of the range of sentences acknowledged as meaningful. This proposal would lead to the following consequences which seem to me to be very inconvenient. In certain cases (namely, if S_1 is analytic, S_2 is contradictory, S_3 and S_4 are synthetic and incompatible with each other) the following occur: (1) the negation of a meaningful sentence S_1 is taken as meaningless; (2) the negation of a meaningless series of symbols S_2 is taken as a meaningful sentence; (3) the conjunction of two meaningful and synthetic sentences S_3 and S_4 is taken as meaning-

[11] Comp.: Erkenntnis [2], p. 461.

less. By the use of technical terms of logical syntax the objection can be expressed more precisely: if we decide to include in the range of (meaningful) sentences of our language only analytic and synthetic sentences (or even only synthetic sentences),[12] then the formative rules of our language become indefinite.[13] That means that in this case we have no fixed finite method of distinguishing between the meaningful and the meaningless, i.e., between sentences and expressions which are not sentences. And this would obviously be a serious disadvantage.

3. Confirmation instead of Verification

If verification is understood as a complete and definitive establishment of truth then a universal sentence, e.g., a so-called law of physics or biology, can never be verified, a fact which has often been remarked. Even if each single instance of the law were supposed to be verifiable, the number of instances to which the law refers—e.g., the space-time-points—is infinite and therefore can never be exhausted by our observations which are always finite in number. We cannot verify the law, but we can test it by testing its single instances, i.e., the particular sentences which we derive from the law and from other sentences established previously. If in the continued series of such testing experiments no negative instance is found but the number of positive instances increases then our confidence in the law will grow step ·by step. Thus, instead of verification, we may speak here of gradually increasing *confirmation* of the law.

Now a little reflection will lead us to the result that there is no fundamental difference between a universal sentence and a particular sentence with regard to verifiability but only a difference in degree. Take for instance the following sentence: "There is a white sheet of paper on this table." In order to ascertain whether this thing is paper, we may make a set of simple observations and then, if there still remains some doubt, we may make some physical and chemical experiments. Here as well as in the case of the law, we try to examine sentences which we infer from the sentence in question. These inferred sentences are predictions about future observations. The number of such predictions which we can derive from the sentence given is infinite; and therefore the sentence can never be completely verified. To be sure, in many cases we reach a practically sufficient certainty after a small number of positive instances, and then we stop experimenting. But there is always the theoretical possibility of continuing the series of test-observations. Therefore here also *no complete verification is possible* but only a process of gradually increasing *confirmation*. We may, if we wish, call a sentence disconfirmed [14] in a certain degree if its negation is confirmed in that degree.

The impossibility of absolute verification has been pointed out and ex-

---

[12] Comp.: Carnap [6], p. 32, 34.

[13] Comp.: Carnap [4], §45.—About the indefinite character of the concepts "analytic" and "contradictory" comp.: Carnap [7], p. 163; or [4b] §§34a and 34d.

[14] "Erschüttert," Neurath [6].

plained in detail by Popper.[15] In this point our present views are, it seems to me, in full accordance with Lewis [16] and Nagel.[17]

Suppose a sentence S is given, some test-observations for it have been made, and S is confirmed by them in a certain degree. Then it is a matter of practical decision whether we will consider that degree as high enough for our acceptance of S, or as low enough for our rejection of S, or as intermediate between these so that we neither accept nor reject S until further evidence will be available. Although our decision is based upon the observations made so far, nevertheless it is not uniquely determined by them. There is no general rule to determine our decision. Thus the acceptance and the rejection of a (synthetic) sentence always contains a *conventional component*. That does not mean that the decision—or, in other words, the question of truth and verification—is conventional. For, in addition to the conventional component there is always the non-conventional component—we may call it, the objective one—consisting in the observations which have been made. And it must certainly be admitted that in very many cases this objective component is present to such an overwhelming extent that the conventional component practically vanishes. For such a simple sentence as, e.g., "There is a white thing on this table," the degree of confirmation, after a few observations have been made, will be so high that we practically cannot help accepting the sentence. But even in this case there remains still the theoretical possibility of denying the sentence. Thus even here it is a matter of decision or convention.

The view that no absolute verification but only gradual confirmation is possible, is sometimes formulated in this way: every sentence is a probability-sentence; e.g., by Reichenbach [18] and Lewis.[19] But it seems advisable to separate the two assertions. Most empiricists today will perhaps agree with the first thesis, but the second is still a matter of dispute. It presupposes the thesis that the degree of confirmation of a hypothesis can be interpreted as the degree of probability in the strict sense which this concept has in the calculus of probability, i.e., as the limit of relative frequency. Reichenbach [20] holds this thesis. But so far he has not worked out such an interpretation in detail, and today it is still questionable whether it can be carried out at all. Popper [21] has explained the difficulties of such a frequency interpretation of the degree of confirmation; the chief difficulty lies in how we are to determine for a given hypothesis the series of "related" hypotheses to which the concept of frequency is to apply. It seems to me that at present it is not yet clear

[15] Popper [1].
[16] Lewis [2], p. 137, note 12: "No verification of the kind of knowledge commonly stated in propositions is ever absolutely complete and final."
[17] Nagel [1], pp. 144f.
[18] Reichenbach [1].
[19] Lewis [2], p. 133.
[20] Reichenbach [2], pp. 271ff.; [3], pp. 154ff.
[21] Popper [1], chap. VIII; for the conventional nature of the problem compare my remark in Erkenntnis vol. 5, p. 292.

whether the concept of degree of confirmation can be defined satisfactorily as a quantitative concept, i.e., a magnitude having numerical values. Perhaps it is preferable to define it as a merely topological concept, i.e. by defining only the relations: "S_1 has the same (or, a higher) degree of confirmation than S_2," but in such a way that most of the pairs of sentences will be incomparable. We will use the concept in this way—without however defining it—only in our informal considerations which serve merely as a preparation for exact definitions of other terms. We shall later on define the concepts of complete and incomplete reducibility of confirmation as syntactical concepts, and those of complete and incomplete confirmability as descriptive concepts.

4. The Material and the Formal Idioms

It seems to me that there is agreement on the main points between the present views of the Vienna Circle, which are the basis of our following considerations, and those of Pragmatism, as interpreted, e.g., by Lewis.[22] This agreement is especially marked with respect to the view that every (synthetic) sentence is a hypothesis, i.e., can never be verified completely and definitively. One may therefore expect that the views of these two empiricist movements will continue to converge to each other in their further development; Morris[23] believes that this convergence is a fact and, moreover, tries to promote it.

However, in spite of this agreement on many important points, there is a difference between our method of formulation and that which is customary in other philosophical movements, especially in America and England. This difference is not as unimportant as are the differences in formulation in many other cases. For the difference in formulation depends on the difference between the material and the formal idioms.[24] The use of the material idiom is very common in philosophy; but it is a dangerous idiom, because it sometimes leads to pseudo-questions. It is therefore advisable to translate questions and assertions given in the material idiom into the formal idiom. In the material idiom occur expressions like "facts," "objects," "the knowing subject," "relation between the knowing subject and the known subject," "the given," "sense-data," "experiences," etc. The formal idiom uses syntactical terms instead, i.e., terms concerning the formal structure of linguistic expressions. Let us take an example. It is a pseudo-thesis of idealism and older positivism, that a

---

[22] Lewis [2], especially p. 133.

[23] Morris [1], [2].

[24] Here I can give no more than some rough indications concerning the material and the formal idioms. For detailed explanations compare Carnap [4], chap. V. A shorter and more easily understandable exposition is contained in [5], pp. 85–88.—What I call the formal and the material idioms or modes of speech, is not the same as what Morris ([1], p. 8) calls the formal and the empirical modes of speech. To Morris's empirical mode belong what I call the real object-sentences; and these belong neither to the formal nor to the material mode in my sense (comp. Carnap [4], §74, and [5], p. 61). The distinction between the formal and the material idioms does not concern the usual sentences of science but chiefly those of philosophy, especially those of epistemology or methodology.

physical object (e.g., the moon) is a construction out of sense-data. Realism on the other hand asserts, that a physical object is not constructed but only cognized by the knowing subject. We—the Vienna Circle—neither affirm nor deny any of these theses, but regard them as pseudo-theses, i.e., as void of cognitive meaning. They arise from the use of the material mode, which speaks about "the object"; it thereby leads to such pseudo-questions as the "nature of this object," and especially as to whether it is a mere construction or not. The formulation in the formal idiom is as follows: "A physical object-name (e.g., the *word* 'moon') is reducible to sense-data predicates (or perception predicates)." Lewis [25] seems to believe that logical positivism—the Vienna Circle—accepts the idealistic pseudo-thesis mentioned. But that is not the case. The misunderstanding can perhaps be explained as caused by an unintentional translation of our thesis from the formal into the more accustomed material idiom, whereby it is transformed into the idealistic pseudo-thesis.

The same is true concerning our thesis: "My testing of any sentence, even one which contains another man's name and a psychological predicate (e.g., 'Mr. X is now cheerful'), refers back ultimately to my own observation-sentences." If we translate it into: "Your mind is nothing more than a construction which I put upon certain data of my own experience," we have the pseudo-thesis of solipsism, formulated in the material idiom. But this is not our thesis.

The formulation in the material idiom makes many epistemological sentences and questions ambiguous and unclear. Sometimes they are meant as psychological questions. In this case clearness could be obtained by a formulation in the psychological language. In other cases questions are not meant as empirical, factual questions, but as logical ones. In this case they ought to be formulated in the language of logical syntax. In fact, however, epistemology in the form it usually takes—including many of the publications of the Vienna Circle—is an unclear mixture of psychological and logical components. We must separate it into its two kinds of components if we wish to come to clear, unambiguous concepts and questions. I must confess that I am unable to answer or even to understand many epistemological questions of the traditional kind because they are formulated in the material idiom. The following are some examples taken from customary discussions: "Are you more than one of my ideas?" "Is the past more than the present recollection?" "Is the future more than the present experience of anticipation?" "Is the self more than one of those ideas I call mine?" "If a robot is exhibiting all the behavior appropriate to tooth-ache, is there a pain connected with that behavior or not?" etc.

I do not say that I have not the least understanding of these sentences. I see some possibilities of translating them into unambiguous sentences of the formal idiom. But unfortunately there are several such translations, and hence I can only make conjectures as to the intended meaning of the questions. Let me take another example. I find the following thesis [26] formulated in the material mode: "Any reality must, in order to satisfy our empirical concept

[25] Lewis [2], pp. 127–128.
[26] Lewis [2], p. 138.

of it, transcend the concept itself. A construction imposed upon given data cannot be identical with a real object; the thing itself must be more specific, and in comparison with it the construction remains abstract." As a conjecture, selected from a great number of possibilities, I venture the following translation into the formal idiom: "For any object-name and any given finite class C of sentences (or: of sentences of such and such a kind), there are always sentences containing that name such that neither their confirmation nor that of their negation is completely reducible to that of C (in syntactical terminology: there are sentences each of which is neither a consequence of C nor incompatible with C)." Our present views, by the way—as distinguished from our previous ones—are in agreement with this thesis, provided my interpretation hits the intended meaning. The translation shows that the thesis concerns the structure of language and therefore depends upon a convention, namely the choice of the language-structure. This fact is concealed by the formulation in the material mode. There the thesis seems to be independent of the choice of language, it seems to concern a certain character which "reality" either does or does not possess. Thus the use of material idiom leads to a certain absolutism, namely to the neglect of the fact that the thesis is relative to the chosen language-system. The use of the formal idiom reveals that fact. And indeed our present agreement with the thesis mentioned is connected with our admission of incompletely confirmable sentences, which will be explained later on.

The dangers of the material idiom were not explicitly noticed by our Vienna Circle in its earlier period. Nevertheless we used this idiom much less frequently than is customary in traditional philosophy; and when we used it, we did so in most cases in such a way that it was not difficult to find a translation into the formal idiom. However, this rather careful use was not deliberately planned, but was adopted intuitively, as it were. It seems to me that most of the formulations in the material idiom which are considered by others as being theses of ours have never been used by us. In recent years we have become increasingly aware of the disadvantages of the material idiom. Nevertheless we do not try to avoid its use completely. For sometimes its use is preferable practically, as long as this idiom is still more customary among philosophers. But perhaps there will come a time when this will no longer be the case. Perhaps some day philosophers will prefer to use the formal idiom—at least in those parts of their works which are intended to present decisive arguments rather than general preliminary explanations.

II. LOGICAL ANALYSIS OF CONFIRMATION AND TESTING

5. Some Terms and Symbols of Logic

In carrying out methodological investigations especially concerning verification, confirmation, testing, etc., it is very important to distinguish clearly between logical and empirical, e.g., psychological questions. The frequent lack of such a distinction in so-called epistemological discussions has caused a great deal of ambiguity and misunderstanding. In order to make quite clear the meaning and nature of our definitions and explanations, we will separate the two kinds of definitions. In this Chapter II we are concerned with logical analysis. We shall define concepts belonging to logic, or more precisely, to logical syntax, although the choice of the concepts to be defined and of the way in which they are defined is suggested in some respects by a consideration of empirical questions—as is often the case in laying down logical definitions. The logical concepts defined here will be applied later on, in Chapter III, in defining concepts of an empirical analysis of confirmation. These descriptive, i.e., non-logical, concepts belong to the field of biology and psychology, namely, to the theory of the use of language as a special kind of human activity.[27]

In the following logical analysis we shall make use of some few *terms of logical syntax*, which may here be explained briefly.[28] The terms refer to a language-system, say L, which is supposed to be given by a system of rules of the following two kinds. The formative rules state how to construct sentences of L out of the symbols of L. The transformative rules state how to deduce a sentence from a class of sentences, the so-called premisses, and which sentences are to be taken as true unconditionally, i.e., without reference to premisses. The transformative rules are divided into those which have a logico-mathematical nature; they are called logical rules or L-rules (this "L-" has nothing to do with the name "L" of the language); and those of an empirical nature, e.g., physical or biological laws stated as postulates; they are called physical rules or P-rules.

We shall take here "S," "S_1," "S_2," etc., as designations of sentences (not as abbreviations for sentences). We use "~S" as designation of the negation of S. (Thus, in this connection, "~" is not a symbol of negation but a syntactical symbol, an abbreviation for the words "the negation of.") If a sentence S can be deduced from the sentences of a class C according to the rules of L, S is called a *consequence* of C; and moreover an L-consequence, if the L-rules are sufficient for the deduction, otherwise a P-consequence. S_1 and S_2 are called *equipollent* (with each other) if each is a consequence of the other. If S can be shown to be true on the basis of the rules of L, S is called *valid* in L; and moreover L-valid or *analytic*, if true on the basis of the L-rules alone, otherwise P-valid. If, by application of the rules of L, S can be shown to be false, S is called *contravalid;* and L-contravalid or *contradictory*, if by L-rules alone, otherwise P-contravalid. If S is neither valid nor contravalid S is called *indeterminate*. If S is neither analytic nor contradictory, in other words, if its truth or falsehood cannot be determined by logic alone, but needs reference either to P-rules or to the facts outside of language, S is called

---

[27] [1950 Note: According to present terminology, we divide the theory of language (semiotic) into three parts: pragmatics, semantics, and logical syntax. The descriptive concepts mentioned belong to pragmatics; logical analysis belongs either to semantics (if referring to meaning and interpretation) or to syntax (if formalized).]

[28] For more exact explanations of these terms see Carnap [4]; some of them are explained also in [5].

synthetic. Thus the totality of the sentences of L is classified in the following way:

L-concepts:

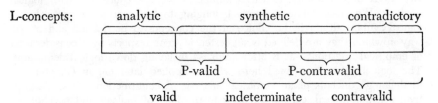

A sentence S_1 is called incompatible with S_2 (or with a class C of sentences) if the negation $\sim S_1$ is a consequence of S_2 (or of C, respectively). The sentences of a class are called mutually independent if none of them is a consequence of, or incompatible with, any other of them.

The most important kind of predicates occurring in a language of science is that of the predicates attributed to space-time-points (or to small space-time-regions). For the sake of simplicity we shall restrict the following considerations—so far as they deal with predicates—to those of this kind. The attribution of a certain value of a physical function, e.g., of temperature, to a certain space-time-point can obviously also be expressed by a predicate of this kind. The following considerations, applied here to such predicates only, can easily be extended to descriptive terms of any other kind.

In order to be able to formulate examples in a simple and exact way we will use the following symbols. We take "a," "b," etc., as names of space-time-points (or of small space-time-regions), i.e., as abbreviations for quadruples of space-time-coördinates; we call them *individual constants.* "x," "y," etc., will be used as corresponding variables; we will call them *individual variables.* We shall use "P," "P_1," "P_2," etc., and "Q," "Q_1," etc., as *predicates;* if no other indication is given, they are supposed to be predicates of the kind described. The sentence "$Q_1(b)$" is to mean: "The space-time-point b has the property Q_1." Such a sentence consisting of a predicate followed by one or several individual constants as arguments will be called a *full sentence* of that predicate.

Connective symbols: "$\sim$" for "not" (negation), "$\vee$" for "or" (disjunction), "$\cdot$" for "and" (conjunction), "$\supset$" for "if—then" (implication), "$\equiv$" for "if—then—, and if not—then not—" (equivalence). "$\sim Q(a)$" is the negation of a full sentence of "Q"; it is sometimes also called a full sentence of the predicate "$\sim Q$."

Operators: "$(x)P(x)$" is to mean: "every point has the property P" (*universal* sentence; the first "(x)" is called the universal *operator,* and the sentential function "$P(x)$" its *operand*). "$(\exists x)P(x)$" is to mean: "There is at least one point having the property P" (*existential* sentence; "$(\exists x)$" is called the existential operator and "$P(x)$" its operand). (In what follows, we shall not make use of any other operators than universal and existential operators with individual variables, as described here.) In our later examples we shall use the following abbreviated notation for universal sentences of a certain form occurring very frequently. If **the sentence** "$(x)[\text{———}]$" is such that "———" consists of several partial sentences which are connected by "$\sim$," "$\vee$," etc., and each of which consists of a predicate with "x" as argument, we allow omission of the operator and the arguments. Thus, e.g., instead of "$(x)(P_1(x) \supset P_2(x))$" we shall write shortly "$P_1 \supset P_2$"; and instead of "(x) $[Q_1(x) \supset (Q_3(x) \equiv Q_2(x))]$" simply "$Q_1 \supset (Q_3 \equiv Q_2)$." The form "$P_1 \supset P_2$" is that of the simplest physical laws; it means: "If any space-time-point has the property P_1, it has also the property P_2."

6. Reducibility of Confirmation

The number of sentences for which, at a certain moment, we have found a confirmation of some degree or other is always finite. If now a class C of sentences contains a finite sub-class C' such that the sentence S is a consequence of C', then, if the sentences of C' are found to be confirmed to a certain degree, S will be confirmed to at least the same degree. In this case we have, so to speak, a complete confirmation of S by C'. (It is to be noticed that "complete" is not meant here in an absolute sense, but in a relative sense with respect to certain premisses.) On the other hand, suppose that S is not a consequence of any finite sub-class of C, but each sentence of an infinite sub-class C'' of C is a consequence of S—e.g., if S is a universal sentence and C'' the class of its instances. In this case, no complete confirmation of S by sentences of C is possible; nevertheless, S will be confirmed by the confirmation of sentences of C'' at least to some degree, though not necessarily to the same degree. Suppose moreover that the sentences of C'' are mutually independent. Since their number is infinite, they cannot be exhausted. Therefore the degree of confirmation of S will increase by the confirmation of more and more sentences of C'' but without ever coming to a complete confirmation. On the basis of these considerations we will lay down the definitions 1 to 6. In Definitions 1 and 2 C is a class of sentences. The terms defined in Definitions 1 a, b and c are only auxiliary terms for Definition 2.

Definition 1. a. We will say that the confirmation of S is completely reducible to that of C, if S is a consequence of a finite subclass of C.

b. We will say that the confirmation of *a non-contravalid sentence* S is directly incompletely reducible to that of C, if the confirmation of S is not completely reducible to that of C but if there is an infinite sub-class C' of C such that the sentences of C' are mutually independent and are consequences of S *by substitution alone.*

c. We will say that the confirmation of S is directly reducible to that of C, if it is either completely reducible or directly incompletely reducible to that of C.

Definition 2. a. We will say that the *confirmation* of S is *reducible* to that of C, if there is a finite series of classes $C_1, C_2, \ldots C_n$ such that the relation of directly reducible confirmation subsists (1) between S and C_1, (2) between every sentence of C_1 and C_{i+1} ($i = 1$ to $n-1$), and (3) between every sentence of C_n and C.

b. We will say that the *confirmation* of S is *incompletely reducible* to that of C, if it is reducible but not completely reducible to that of C.

Definition 3. We will say that the confirmation of S is reducible (or completely reducible, or incompletely reducible) to that of a class C of predicates (or to that of its members) if it is reducible (or completely reducible, or incompletely reducible, respectively) to a not contravalid sub-class of the class which contains the full sentences of the predicates of C and the negations of these sentences. The sub-class is required not to be contravalid because any sentence whatever is a consequence of a contravalid class, as, e.g., {"P(a)," "~P(a)"}, and hence its confirmation is reducible to that of this class.

The following definitions concerning predicates are analogous to the previous ones concerning sentences.

Definition 4. We will say that the confirmation of a *predicate* "Q" is reducible (or completely reducible, or incompletely reducible) to that of a class C of predicates, say "P_1," "P_2," etc., if the confirmation of every full sentence of "Q" with a certain argument, e.g., "Q(a)," is reducible (or completely reducible, or incompletely reducible, respectively) to that of a non-contradictory sub-class of the class C' consisting of the full sentences of the predicates of C with the same argument and the negations of those sentences ("$P_1(a)$," "~$P_1(a)$," "$P_2(a)$," "~$P_2(a)$," etc.).

Definition 5. A *predicate* "Q" is called *reducible* (or completely reducible, or incompletely reducible) to a class C of predicates or to its members, if the confirmation both of "Q" and of "~Q" is reducible (or completely reducible, or incompletely reducible, respectively) to C.

When we speak of sentential functions, sentences are understood to be included because a sentence may be taken as a special case of a sentential function with the number zero of free variables. Therefore the following definitions are also applied to sentences.

Definition 6. A sentential function is said to have *atomic form* if it consists of one predicate followed by one or several arguments (individual constants or variables). Examples: "P(x)," "Q(a, x)," "P(a)."

Definition 7. A sentential function is said to have *molecular form* if it is constructed out of one or several sentential functions with the help of none, one or several connective symbols (but without operators).

Definition 8. a. A sentential function is said to have *generalized form* if it contains at least one (unrestricted) operator.

b. A sentential function is said to have *essentially generalized form* if it has generalized form and cannot be transformed into a molecular form containing the same descriptive predicates.

We have to distinguish between a sentence of atomic form and an atomic sentence (see Definition 15a, §9; here the predicate occurring must fulfill certain conditions); and likewise between a sentence of molecular form and a molecular sentence (see Definition 15b, §9). Since the sentences of atomic form are included in those of molecular form, the important distinction is that between molecular and (essentially) generalized form.

In what follows we will apply the concepts of reducibility of confirmation, defined before, first to molecular sentences and then to generalized sentences.

Theorem 1. If the confirmation both of S_1 and of S_2 is completely reducible to that of a class C of predicates, then the confirmation both of their disjunction and of their conjunction, provided the latter is not contravalid, is also completely reducible to that of C.

Proof. The disjunction is a consequence of S_1; the conjunction is a consequence of S_1 and S_2.

Theorem 2. If S is a non-contravalid sentence of *molecular form* and the descriptive predicates occurring in S belong to C, the confirmation of S is completely reducible to that of C.

Proof. Let C′ be the class of the full sentences of the predicates of C and their negations. According to a well-known theorem of logic, S can be transformed into the so-called disjunctive normal form,[29] i.e., into a disjunction of non-contravalid conjunctions of sentences of C′. Now, the confirmation of a sentence of C′ is completely reducible to that of C. Therefore, according to Theorem 1, the confirmation of each of the conjunctions is also completely reducible to that of C, and, again according to Theorem 1, the same is true for the disjunction of these conjunctions, and hence for S.

The application of the concepts defined before to sentences of generalized form may be explained by the following examples.

S_1: $'(x)P(x)'$

S_2: $'(x) \sim P(x)'$ (in words: every point has the property not P; in other words: no point has the property P).

C_1 may be taken as the class of the full sentences of "P," i.e., the class of the particular sentences "P(a), "P(b)," etc.; C_2 as the class of the negations of these sentences: "$\sim$P(a)," etc.; and C as the sum of C_1 and C_2. Then, according to a well-known result (see §3), the confirmation of S_1 is directly reducible to that of C_1 and hence to that of C, but only incompletely, because S_1 is not a consequence of any finite sub-class of C, however large this may be. On the other hand, $\sim S_1$ is a consequence of each sentence of C_2, e.g., of "$\sim$P(a)." Therefore the confirmation of $\sim S_1$ is completely reducible to that of C_2 and hence to that of C.

S_2 bears the same relation to C_2 as S_1 does to C_1. Therefore the confirmation of S_2 is incompletely reducible to that of C_2, and the confirmation of $\sim S_2$

	Two formulations	The confirmation of S is reducible					
		to that of C_1 ("P(a)" etc.)		to that of C_2 ("$\sim$P(a)" etc.)		to that of C (= C_1 + C_2)	
		compl.	incompl.	compl.	incompl.	compl.	incompl.
S_1	$(x)P(x)$; $\sim(\exists x)\sim P(x)$	—	+	—	—	—	+
$\sim S_1$	$\sim(x)P(x)$; $(\exists x)(\sim P(x))$	—	—	+	—	+	—
S_2	$(x)\sim P(x)$; $\sim(\exists x)P(x)$	—	—	—	+	—	+
$\sim S_2$	$\sim(x)\sim P(x)$; $(\exists x)P(x)$	+	—	—	—	+	—

[29] Compare *Hilbert* [1], p. 13.

is completely reducible to that of C_1. This can easily be seen when we transform $\sim S_2$ into the existential sentence "$(\exists x)P(x)$" which is a consequence of each sentence of C_1, e.g., of "$P(a)$." The results of these considerations may be exhibited by the table on page 143, which gives two formulations for each of the four sentences, one containing a universal operator and the other an existential operator. Some of the results, which we need later on, are formulated in the following Theorems 3 and 4.

Theorem 3. Let S be the *universal sentence* "$(x)P(x)$." The confirmation of S is incompletely reducible to that of the full sentences of "P" and hence to that of "P." The confirmation of $\sim S$ is completely reducible to that of the negation of any full sentence of "P" and hence to that of "P."

Theorem 4. Let S be the existential sentence "$(\exists x)P(x)$." The confirmation of S is completely reducible to that of any full sentence of "P" and hence to that of "P." The confirmation of $\sim S$ is incompletely reducible to that of the negations of the full sentences of "P" and hence to that of "P."

The Theorems 3 and 4 correspond to the following usual, but not quite correct formulations: (1) "A universal sentence is not verifiable but falsifiable," (2) "An existential sentence is verifiable but not falsifiable." Still closer corresponding theorems will be stated later on (Theorems 19 and 20, §24).

7. Definitions

By an (explicit) definition of a descriptive predicate "Q" with one argument we understand a sentence of the form

(D:) $Q(x) \equiv \ldots x \ldots$

where at the place of "$\ldots x \ldots$" a sentential function—called the definiens—stands which contains "x" as the only free variable. For several arguments the form is analogous. We will say that a definition D is based upon the class C of predicates if every descriptive symbol occurring in the definiens of D belongs to C. If the predicates of a class C are available in our language we may introduce other predicates by a chain of definitions of such a kind that each definition is based upon C and the predicates defined by previous definitions of the chain.

Definition 9. A definition is said to have atomic (or molecular, or generalized, or essentially generalized) form, if its definiens has atomic (or molecular, or generalized, or essentially generalized, respectively) form.

Theorem 5. If "P" is defined by a definition D based upon C, "P" is reducible to C. If D has molecular form, "P" is completely reducible to C. If D has essentially generalized form, "P" is incompletely reducible to C.

Proof. "P" may be defined by "$P(x) \equiv \ldots x \ldots$" Then, for any b, "$P(b)$" is equipollent to "$\ldots b \ldots$" and hence in the case of molecular form, according to Theorem 2, completely reducible to C, and in the other case, according to Theorems 3 and 4, reducible to C.

Let us consider the question whether the so-called *disposition-concepts* can be defined, i.e., predicates which enunciate the disposition of a point or body for reacting in such and such a way to such and such conditions, e.g., "visible," "smellable," "fragile," "tearable," "soluble," "indissoluble," etc. We shall see that such disposition-terms cannot be defined by means of the terms by which these conditions and reactions are described, but they can be introduced by sentences of another form. Suppose we wish to introduce the predicate "Q_3" meaning "soluble in water." Suppose further, that "Q_1" and "Q_2" are already defined in such a way that "$Q_1(x, t)$" means "the body x is placed into water at the time t," and "$Q_2(x, t)$" means "the body x dissolves at the time t." Then one might perhaps think that we could define "soluble in water" in the following way: "x is soluble in water" is to mean "whenever x is put into water, x dissolves," in symbols:

(D:) $$Q_3(x) \equiv (t)[Q_1(x, t) \supset Q_2(x, t)]$$

But this definition would not give the intended meaning of "Q_3." For, suppose that c is a certain match which I completely burnt yesterday. As the match was made of wood, I can rightly assert that it was not soluble in water; hence the sentence "$Q_3(c)$" (S_1) which asserts that the match c is soluble in water, is false. But if we assume the definition D, S_1 becomes equipollent with "(t) $[Q_1(c, t) \supset Q_2(c, t)]$" ($S_2$). Now the match c has never been placed into water and on the hypothesis made never can be so placed. Thus any sentence of the form "$Q_1(c, t)$" is false for any value of "t." Hence S_2 is true, and, because of D, S_1 also is true, in contradiction to the intended meaning of S_1. "Q_3" cannot be defined by D, nor by any other definition. But we can introduce it by the following sentence:

(R:) $$(x)(t)[Q_1(x, t) \supset (Q_3(x) \equiv Q_2(x, t))]$$

in words: "if any thing x is put into water at any time t, then, if x is soluble in water, x dissolves at the time t, and if x is not soluble in water, it does not." This sentence belongs to that kind of sentences which we shall call reduction sentences.

8. Reduction Sentences

Suppose we wish to introduce a new predicate "Q_3" into our language and state for this purpose a pair of sentences of the following form:

(R_1) $\qquad\qquad\qquad Q_1 \supset (Q_2 \supset Q_3)$
(R_2) $\qquad\qquad\qquad Q_4 \supset (Q_5 \supset \sim Q_3)$

Here, "Q_1" and "Q_4" may describe experimental conditions which we have to fulfill in order to find out whether or not a certain space-time-point b has the property Q_3, i.e., whether "$Q_3(b)$" or "$\sim Q_3(b)$" is true. "Q_2" and "Q_5" may describe possible results of the experiments. Then R_1 means: if we realize the experimental condition Q_1 then, if we find the result Q_2, the point has the property Q_3. By the help of R_1, from "$Q_1(b)$" and "$Q_2(b)$," "$Q_3(b)$" follows.

R_2 means: if we satisfy the condition Q_4 and then find Q_5 the point has not the property Q_3. By the help of R_2, from "$Q_4(b)$" and "$Q_5(b)$," "$\sim Q_3(b)$" follows. We see that the sentences R_1 and R_2 tell us how we may determine whether or not the predicate "Q_3" is to be attributed to a certain point, provided we are able to determine whether or not the four predicates "Q_1," "Q_2," "Q_4," and "Q_5" are to be attributed to it. By the statement of R_1 and R_2 "Q_3" is reduced in a certain sense to those four predicates; therefore we shall call R_1 and R_2 reduction sentences for "Q_3" and "$\sim Q_3$" respectively. Such a pair of sentences will be called a reduction pair for "Q_3." By R_1 the property Q_3 is attributed to the points of the class $Q_1 \cdot Q_2$, by R_2 the property $\sim Q_3$ to the points of the class $Q_4 \cdot Q_5$. If by the rules of the language—either logical rules or physical laws—we can show that no point belongs to either of these classes (in other words, if the universal sentence "$\sim [(Q_1 \cdot Q_2) \vee (Q_4 \cdot Q_5)]$" is valid) then the pair of sentences does not determine Q_3 nor $\sim Q_3$ for any point and therefore does not give a reduction for the predicate Q_3. Therefore, in the definition of "reduction pair" to be stated, we must exclude this case.

In special cases "Q_4" coincides with "Q_1," and "Q_5" with "$\sim Q_2$." In that case the reduction pair is "$Q_1 \supset (Q_2 \supset Q_3)$" and "$Q_1 \supset (\sim Q_2 \supset \sim Q_3)$"; the latter can be transformed into "$Q_1 \supset (Q_3 \supset Q_2)$." Here the pair can be replaced by the one sentence "$Q_1 \supset (Q_3 \equiv Q_2)$" which means: if we accomplish the condition Q_1, then the point has the property Q_3 if and only if we find the result Q_2. This sentence may serve for determining the result "$Q_3(b)$" as well as for "$\sim Q_3(b)$"; we shall call it a bilateral reduction sentence. It determines Q_3 for the points of the class $Q_1 \cdot Q_2$, and $\sim Q_3$ for those of the class $Q_1 \cdot \sim Q_2$; it does not give a determination for the points of the class $\sim Q_1$. Therefore, if "$(x)(\sim Q_1(x))$" is valid, the sentence does not give any determination at all. To give an example, let "$Q'_1(b)$" mean "the point b is both heated and not heated," and "$Q''_1(b)$": "the point b is illuminated by light-rays which have a speed of 400,000 km/sec." Here for any point c "$Q'_1(c)$" and "$Q''_1(c)$" are contravalid—the first contradictory and the second P-contravalid; therefore, "$(x) (\sim Q'_1(x))$" and "$(x)(\sim Q''_1(x))$" are valid—the first analytic and the second P-valid; in other words, the conditions Q'_1 and Q''_1 are impossible, the first logically and the second physically. In this case, a sentence of the form "$Q'_1 \supset (Q_3 \equiv Q_2)$" or "$Q''_1 \supset (Q_3 \equiv Q_2)$" would not tell us anything about how to use the predicate "Q_3" and therefore could not be taken as a reduction sentence. These considerations lead to the following definitions.

Definition 10. a. A universal sentence of the form

(R) $$Q_1 \supset (Q_2 \supset Q_3)$$

is called a *reduction sentence* for "Q_3" provided "$\sim (Q_1 \cdot Q_2)$" is not valid.

b. A pair of sentences of the forms

(R_1) $$Q_1 \supset (Q_2 \supset Q_3)$$
(R_2) $$Q_4 \supset (Q_5 \supset \sim Q_3)$$

is called a *reduction pair* for "Q_3" provided "$\sim [(Q_1 \cdot Q_2) \vee (Q_4 \cdot Q_5)]$" is not valid.

c. A sentence of the form

(R$_b$)
$$Q_1 \supset (Q_3 \equiv Q_2)$$

is called a *bilateral reduction sentence* for "Q$_3$" provided "$(x)(\sim Q_1(x))$" is not valid.

Every statement about reduction pairs in what follows applies also to bilateral reduction sentences, because such sentences are comprehensive formulations of a special case of a reduction pair.

If a reduction pair for "Q$_3$" of the form given above is valid—i.e., either laid down in order to introduce "Q$_3$" on the basis of "Q$_1$," "Q$_2$," "Q$_4$," and "Q$_5$," or consequences of physical laws stated beforehand—then for any point c "Q$_3$(c)" is a consequence of "Q$_1$(c)" and "Q$_2$(c)," and "$\sim$Q$_3$(c)" is a consequence of "Q$_4$(c)" and "Q$_5$(c)." Hence "Q$_3$" is completely reducible to those four predicates.

Theorem 6. If a reduction pair for "Q" is valid, then "Q" is completely reducible to the four (or two, respectively) other predicates occurring.

We may distinguish between logical reduction and physical reduction, dependent upon the reduction sentence being analytic or P-valid, in the latter case for instance a valid physical law. Sometimes not only the sentence "Q$_1$ $\supset$ (Q$_3$ $\equiv$ Q$_2$)" is valid, but also the sentence "Q$_3$ $\equiv$ Q$_2$." (This is, e.g., the case if "(x)Q$_1$(x)" is valid.) Then for any b, "Q$_3$(b)" can be transformed into the equipollent sentence "Q$_2$(b)," and thus "Q$_3$" can be eliminated in any sentence whatever. If "Q$_3$ $\equiv$ Q$_2$" is not P-valid but analytic it may be considered as an explicit definition for "Q$_3$." Thus an *explicit definition* is a special kind of a logical bilateral reduction sentence. A logical bilateral reduction sentence which does not have this simple form, but the general form "Q$_1$ $\supset$ (Q$_3$ $\equiv$ Q$_2$)," may be considered as a kind of conditional definition.

If we wish to construct a language for science we have to take some descriptive (i.e., non-logical) terms as primitive terms. Further terms may then be introduced not only by explicit definitions but also by other reduction sentences. The possibility of *introduction by laws*, i.e., by physical reduction, is, as we shall see, very important for science, but so far not sufficiently noticed in the logical analysis of science. On the other hand the terms introduced in this way have the disadvantage that in general it is not possible to eliminate them, i.e., to translate a sentence containing such a term into a sentence containing previous terms only.

Let us suppose that the term "Q$_3$" does not occur so far in our language, but "Q$_1$," "Q$_2$," "Q$_4$," and "Q$_5$" do occur. Suppose further that either the following reduction pair R$_1$, R$_2$ for "Q$_3$":

(R$_1$) $Q_1 \supset (Q_2 \supset Q_3)$
(R$_2$) $Q_4 \supset (Q_5 \supset \sim Q_3)$

or the following bilateral reduction sentence for "Q$_3$":

(R$_b$) $Q_1 \supset (Q_3 \equiv Q_2)$

is stated as valid in order to introduce "Q$_3$," i.e., to give meaning to this new term of our language. Since, on the assumption made, "Q_3" has no antecedent meaning, we do not assert anything about facts by the statement of R_b. This statement is not an assertion but a convention. In other words, the factual content of R_b is empty; in this respect, R_b is similar to a definition. On the other hand, the pair R_1, R_2 has a positive content. By stating it as valid, beside stating a convention concerning the use of the term "Q_3," we assert something about facts that can be formulated in the following way without the use of "Q_3." If a point c had the property $Q_1 \cdot Q_2 \cdot Q_4 \cdot Q_5$, then both "$Q_3(c)$" and "$\sim Q_3(c)$" would follow. Since this is not possible for any point, the following universal sentence S which does not contain "Q_3," and which in general is synthetic, is a consequence of R_1 and R_2:

(S:) $$\sim (Q_1 \cdot Q_2 \cdot Q_4 \cdot Q_5).$$

In the case of the bilateral reduction sentence R_b, "Q_4" coincides with "Q_1" and "Q_5" with "$\sim Q_2$." Therefore in this case S degenerates to "$\sim (Q_1 \cdot Q_2 \cdot Q_1 \cdot \sim Q_2)$" and hence becomes analytic. Thus a bilateral reduction sentence, in contrast to a reduction pair, has no factual content.

9. Introductive Chains

For the sake of simplicity we have considered so far only the introduction of a predicate by one reduction pair or by one bilateral reduction sentence. But in most cases a predicate will be introduced by either several reduction pairs or several bilateral reduction sentences. If a property or physical magnitude can be determined by different methods then we may state one reduction pair or one bilateral reduction sentence for each method. The intensity of an electric current can be measured, for instance, by measuring the heat produced in the conductor, or the deviation of a magnetic needle, or the quantity of silver separated out of a solution, or the quantity of hydrogen separated out of water, etc. We may state a set of bilateral reduction sentences, one corresponding to each of these methods. The factual content of this set is not null because it comprehends such sentences as, e.g., "If the deviation of a magnetic needle is such and such then the quantity of silver separated in one minute is such and such, and vice versa," which do not contain the term "intensity of electric current," and which obviously are synthetic.

If we establish one reduction pair (or one bilateral reduction sentence) as valid in order to introduce a predicate "Q_3," the meaning of "Q_3" is not established completely, but only for the cases in which the test condition is fulfilled. In other cases, e.g., for the match in our previous example, neither the predicate nor its negation can be attributed. We may diminish this region of indeterminateness of the predicate by adding one or several more laws which contain the predicate and connect it with other terms available in our language. These further laws may have the form of reduction sentences (as in the example of the electric current) or a different form. In the case of the predicate "soluble in water" we may perhaps add the law stating that two bodies of the same substance are either both soluble or both not soluble. This law would help in the instance of the match; it would, in accordance with common usage, lead to the result "the match c is not soluble," because other pieces of wood are found to be insoluble on the basis of the first reduction sentence. Nevertheless, a region of indeterminateness remains, though a smaller one. If a body b consists of such a substance that for no body of this substance has the test-condition—in the above example: "being placed into water"—ever been fulfilled, then neither the predicate nor its negation can be attributed to b. This region may then be diminished still further, step by step, by stating new laws. These laws do not have the conventional character that definitions have; rather are they discovered empirically within the region of meaning which the predicate in question received by the laws stated before. But these laws are extended by convention into a region in which the predicate had no meaning previously; in other words, we decided to use the predicate in such a way that these laws which are tested and confirmed in cases in which the predicate has a meaning, remain valid in other cases.

We have seen that a new predicate need not be introduced by a definition, but may equally well be introduced by a set of reduction pairs. (A bilateral reduction sentence may here be taken as a special form of a reduction pair.) Consequently, instead of the usual chain of definitions, we obtain a chain of sets of sentences, each consisting either of one definition or of one or several reduction pairs. By each set a new predicate is introduced.

Definition 11. A (finite) chain of (finite) sets of sentences is called an *introductive chain* based upon the class C of predicates if the following conditions are fulfilled. Each set of the chain consists either of one definition or of one or more reduction pairs for one predicate, say "Q"; every reduction pair is valid; every predicate occurring in the set, other than "Q," either belongs to C or is such that one of the previous sets of the chain is either a definition for it or a set of reduction pairs for it.

Definition 12. If the last set of a given introductive chain based upon C either consists in a definition for "Q" or in a set of reduction pairs for "Q," "Q" is said to be *introduced* by this chain on the basis of C.

For our purposes we will suppose that a reduction sentence always has the simple form "$Q_1 \supset (Q_2 \supset Q_3)$" and not the analogous but more complicated form "$(x) [\_ \_ \_ x \_ \_ \_ \supset (\ldots x \ldots \supset Q_3(x))]$" where "$\_ \_ \_ x \_ \_ \_$" and "$\ldots x \ldots$" indicate sentential functions of a non-atomic form. This supposition does not restrict the generality of the following considerations because a reduction sentence of the compound form indicated may always be replaced by two definitions and a reduction sentence of the simple form, namely, by:

$$Q_1 \equiv \_ \_ \_ x \_ \_ \_$$
$$Q_2 \equiv \ldots x \ldots$$
$$Q_1 \supset (Q_2 \supset Q_3).$$

The above supposition once made, the nature of an introductive chain is chiefly dependent upon the form of the definitions occurring. Therefore we define as follows.

Definition 13. An introductive chain is said to have atomic form (or molecular form) if every definition occurring in it has atomic form (or molecular form, respectively); it is said to have generalized form (or essentially generalized form) if at least one definition of generalized form (or essentially generalized form, respectively) occurs in it.

Theorem 7. If "P" is introduced by an introductive chain based upon C, "P" is reducible to C. If the chain has molecular form, "P" is completely reducible to C; if the chain has essentially generalized form, "P" is incompletely reducible to C. This follows from Theorems 5 (§7) and 6 (§8).

We call *primitive symbols* those symbols of a language L which are introduced directly, i.e., without the help of other symbols. Thus there are the following kinds of symbols of L:

1. *primitive symbols of L,*
2. *indirectly introduced symbols* i.e., those introduced by introductive chains based upon primitive symbols; here we distinguish:
   a. *defined symbols,* introduced by chains of definitions,
   b. *reduced symbols,* i.e., those introduced by introductive chains containing at least one reduction sentence; here we may further distinguish:
      α. *L-reduced symbols,* whose chains contain only L-reduction pairs,
      β. *P-reduced symbols,* whose chains contain at least one P-reduction pair.

Definition 14. a. An *introductive chain* based upon primitive predicates of a language L and having atomic (or molecular, or generalized, or essentially generalized, respectively) form is called an atomic (or molecular, or generalized, or essentially generalized, respectively) introductive chain of L.

b. A *predicate* of L is called an *atomic* (or *molecular*) predicate if it is either a primitive predicate of L or introduced by an atomic (or molecular, respectively) introductive chain of L; it is called a *generalized* (or essentially generalized) predicate if it is introduced by a generalized (or essentially generalized, respectively) introductive chain of L.

Definition 15. a. A sentence S is called an *atomic sentence* if S is a full sentence of an atomic predicate. b. S is called a *molecular sentence* if S has molecular form and contains only molecular predicates. c. S is called a *generalized sentence* if S contains an (unrestricted) operator or a generalized predicate. d. S is called an essentially generalized sentence if S is a generalized sentence and is not equipollent with a molecular sentence.

It should be noticed that the term "atomic sentence," as here defined, is not at all understood to refer to ultimate facts.[30] Our theory does not assume anything like ultimate facts. It is a matter of convention which predicates are taken as primitive predicates of a certain language L; and hence likewise, which

---

[30] In contradistinction to the term "atomic sentence" or "elementary sentence" as used by Russell or Wittgenstein.

predicates are taken as atomic predicates and which sentences as atomic sentences.

10. Reduction and Definition

In §8 the fact was mentioned that in some cases, for instance in the case of a disposition-term, the reduction cannot be replaced by a definition. We now are in a position to see the situation more clearly. Suppose that we introduce a predicate "Q" into the language of science first by a reduction pair and that, later on, step by step, we add more such pairs for "Q" as our knowledge about "Q" increases with further experimental investigations. In the course of this procedure the range of indeterminateness for "Q," i.e., the class of cases for which we have not yet given a meaning to "Q," becomes smaller and smaller. Now at each stage of this development we could lay down a definition for "Q" corresponding to the set of reduction pairs for "Q" established up to that stage. But, in stating the definition, we should have to make an arbitrary decision concerning the cases which are not determined by the set of reduction pairs. A definition determines the meaning of the new term once for all. We could either decide to attribute "Q" in the cases not determined by the set, or to attribute "$\sim$Q" in these cases. Thus for instance, if a bilateral reduction sentence R of the form "$Q_1 \supset (Q_3 \equiv Q_2)$" is stated for "$Q_3$," then the predicate "$Q_3$" is to be attributed to the points of the class $Q_1 \cdot Q_2$, and "$\sim Q_3$" to those of the class $Q_1 \cdot \sim Q_2$, while for the points of the class $\sim Q_1$ the predicate "Q_3" has no meaning. Now we might state one of the following two definitions:

$$(D_1) \qquad\qquad Q_3 \equiv (Q_1 \cdot Q_2)$$
$$(D_2) \qquad\qquad Q_3 \equiv (\sim Q_1 \vee Q_2)$$

If c is a point of the undetermined class, on the basis of D_1 "$Q_3(c)$" is false, and on the basis of D_2 it is true. Although it is possible to lay down either D_1 or D_2, neither procedure is in accordance with the intention of the scientist concerning the use of the predicate "Q_3." The scientist wishes neither to determine all the cases of the third class positively, nor all of them negatively; he wishes to leave these questions open until the results of further investigations suggest the statement of a new reduction pair; thereby some of the cases so far undetermined become determined positively and some negatively. If we now were to state a definition, we should have to revoke it at such a new stage of the development of science, and to state a new definition, incompatible with the first one. If, on the other hand, we were now to state a reduction pair, we should merely have to add one or more reduction pairs at the new stage; and these pairs will be compatible with the first one. In this latter case we do not correct the determinations laid down in the previous stage but simply supplement them.

Thus, if we wish to introduce a new term into the language of science, we have to distinguish two cases. If the situation is such that we wish to fix the meaning of the new term once for all, then a definition is the appropriate form. On the other hand, if we wish to determine the meaning of the term at the present time for some cases only, leaving its further determination for other cases to decisions which we intend to make step by step, on the basis of empirical knowledge which we expect to obtain in the future, then the method of reduction is the appropriate one rather than that of a definition. A set of reduction pairs is a partial determination of meaning only and can therefore not be replaced by a definition. Only if we reach, by adding more and more reduction pairs, a stage in which all cases are determined, may we go over to the form of a definition.

We will examine in greater detail the situation in the case of several reduction pairs for "Q_3":

(R_1) $Q_1 \supset (Q_2 \supset Q_3)$
(R_2) $Q_4 \supset (Q_5 \supset \sim Q_3)$
(R'_1) $Q'_1 \supset (Q'_2 \supset Q_3)$
(R'_2) $Q'_4 \supset (Q'_5 \supset \sim Q_3)$
etc.

Then "Q_3" is determined by R_1 for the points of the class $Q_1 \cdot Q_2$, by R'_1 for the class $Q'_1 \cdot Q'_2$, etc., and therefore, by the totality of reduction sentences for "Q_3," for the class $(Q_1 \cdot Q_2) \vee (Q'_1 \cdot Q'_2) \vee \ldots$. This class may shortly be designated by "$Q_{1,2}$." Analogously "$\sim Q_3$" is determined by the reduction sentences for "$\sim Q_3$" for the points of the class $(Q_4 \cdot Q_5) \vee (Q'_4 \cdot Q'_5) \vee \ldots$, which we designate by "$Q_{4,5}$." Hence "Q_3" is determined either positively or negatively for the class $Q_{1,2} \vee Q_{4,5}$. Therefore the universal sentence "$Q_{1,2} \vee Q_{4,5}$" means, that for every point either "Q_3" or "$\sim Q_3$" is determined. If this sentence is true, the set of reduction sentences is complete and may be replaced by the definition "$Q_3 \equiv Q_{1,2}$." For the points of the class $\sim (Q_{1,2} \vee Q_{4,5})$, "$Q_3$" is not determined, and hence, in the stage in question, "Q_3" is without meaning for these points. If on the basis of either logical rules or physical laws it can be shown that all points belong to this class, in other words, if the universal sentence "$\sim (Q_{1,2} \vee Q_{4,5})$" is valid—either analytic or P-valid—then neither "Q_3" nor "$\sim Q_3$" is determined for any point and hence the given set of reduction pairs does not even partly determine the meaning of "Q_3" and therefore is not a suitable means of introducing this predicate.

The given set of reduction pairs asserts that a point belonging to the class $Q_{4,5}$ has the property $\sim Q_3$ and hence not the property Q_3, and therefore cannot belong to $Q_{1,2}$ because every point of this class has the property Q_3. What the set asserts can therefore be formulated by the universal sentence saying that no point belongs to both $Q_{1,2}$ and $Q_{4,5}$, i.e., the sentence "$\sim (Q_{1,2} \cdot Q_{4,5})$." This sentence represents, so to speak, the factual content of the set. In the case of one reduction pair this representative sentence is "$\sim (Q_1 \cdot Q_2 \cdot Q_4 \cdot Q_5)$"; in the case of one bilateral reduction sentence this becomes "$\sim (Q_1 \cdot Q_2 \cdot Q_1 \cdot \sim Q_2)$" or (x) $(\sim Q_{1(x)} \vee Q_{2(x)} \vee \sim Q_{2(x)})$, which is analytic.

The following diagram shows the tripartition of the class of all points by a reduction pair (or a bilateral reduction sentence, or a set of reduction pairs, respectively). For the first class "Q_3" is determined, for the second class "$\sim Q_3$." The third class lies between them and is not yet determined; but some of its points may be determined as belonging to Q_3 and some others as belonging to $\sim Q_3$ by reduction pairs to be stated in the future.

reduction pair:	$Q_1 \cdot Q_2$	$\sim[(Q_1 \cdot Q_2) \vee (Q_4 \cdot Q_5)]$	$Q_4 \cdot Q_5$
bilat. reduction sentence:	$Q_1 \cdot Q_2$	$\sim Q_1$	$Q_1 \cdot \sim Q_2$
set of reduction pairs:	$Q_{1,2}$	$\sim(Q_{1,2} \vee Q_{4,5})$	$Q_{4,5}$

$$\underbrace{}_{Q_3} \quad \underbrace{}_{\text{not determined}} \quad \underbrace{}_{\sim Q_3}$$

If we establish a set of *reduction pairs* as new valid sentences for the introduction of a new predicate "Q_3," are these valid sentences *analytic or P-valid?* Moreover, which other sentences containing "Q_3" are analytic? The distinction between analytic and P-valid sentences refers primarily to those sentences only in which all descriptive terms are primitive terms. In this case the criterion is as follows: [31] a valid sentence S is analytic if and only if every sentence S′ is also valid which is obtained from S when any descriptive term wherever it occurs in S is replaced by any other term whatever of the same type; otherwise it is P-valid. A sentence S containing defined terms is analytic if the sentence S′ resulting from S by the elimination of the defined terms is analytic; otherwise it is P-valid. A definition, e.g., "$Q(x) \equiv \ldots x \ldots$" is, according to this criterion, itself analytic; for, after it has been stated as a valid sentence, by the elimination of "Q" we get from it "$\ldots x \ldots \equiv \ldots x \ldots$," which is analytic.

In the case of a new descriptive term introduced by a set of reduction pairs, the situation is not as simple as in the case of a definition because elimination is here not possible. Let us consider the question how the criterion is to be stated in this case. The introduction of a new term into a language is, strictly speaking, the construction of a new language on the basis of the original one. Suppose that we go over from the language L_1, which does not contain "Q," to the language L_2 by introducing "Q" by a set R of reduction pairs, whose representative sentence (in the sense explained before) may be taken to be S. Then S as not containing "Q" is a sentence of L_1 also; its logical character within L_1 does not depend upon "Q" and may therefore be supposed to be determined already. By stating the sentences of R as valid in L_2, S becomes also valid in L_2 because it is a consequence of R in L_2. If now S is analytic in L_1, it is also analytic in L_2; in this case R does not assert anything about facts, and we must therefore take its sentences as analytic. According to this, every bilateral reduction sentence is analytic, because its representative sentence is analytic, as we have seen before. If S is either P-valid or indeterminate in L_1,

[31] Carnap [4], §51.

it is valid and moreover P-valid in L_2 in consequence of our stating R as valid in L_2. In this case every sentence of R is valid; it is P-valid unless it fulfills the general criterion of analyticity stated before (referring to all possible replacements of the descriptive terms). If S is either P-contravalid or contradictory in L_1, it has the same property in L_2 and is simultaneously valid in L_2. It may be analytic in L_2, if it fulfills the general criterion. In this case every sentence of R is both valid and contravalid, and hence L_2 is inconsistent.[32] If S is contradictory in L_1 and at least one sentence of R is analytic according to the general criterion, then L_2 is not only inconsistent but also L-inconsistent. The results of these considerations may be exhibited by the following table; column

The representative sentence S		A reduction sentence of R (in L_2)	L_2
in L_1	in L_2		
1. analytic	analytic	analytic	consistent (if L_1 is consistent)
2. P-valid	P-valid	valid *	
3. indeterminate	P-valid	valid *	
4. P-contravalid	valid and P-contravalid	valid * and P-contravalid	inconsistent
5. contradictory	valid and contradictory	valid * and contradictory	inconsistent †

  * Analytic if fulfilling the general criterion (p. 153); otherwise P-valid.

  † and moreover L-inconsistent if at least one sentence of R is analytic on the basis of the general criterion (p. 153).

Now the *complete criterion for "analytic"* can be stated as follows:

Nature of S	Criterion for S being *analytic*
1. S does not contain any descriptive symbol.	S is valid.
2. All descriptive symbols of S are primitive.	Every sentence S′ which results from S when we replace any descriptive symbol at all places where it occurs in S by any symbol whatever of the same type—and hence S itself also—is valid.
3. S contains a defined descriptive symbol "Q."	The sentence S′ resulting from S · by the elimination of "Q" is valid.
4. S contains a descriptive symbol "Q" introduced by a set R of reduction pairs; let L′ be the sublanguage of L not containing "Q," and S′ the representative sentence of R (comp. p. 152).	S′ is analytic in L′, and S is an L-consequence of R (e.g., one of the sentences of R); in other words, the implication sentence containing the conjunction of the sentences of R as first part and S as second part is analytic (i.e., every sentence resulting from this implication sentence where we replace "Q" at all places by any symbol of the same type occurring in L′ is valid in L′).

  [32] Compare Carnap [4], §59.

(1) gives a complete classification of the sentences of a language (see the diagram in §5).

III. EMPIRICAL ANALYSIS OF CONFIRMATION AND TESTING

11. Observable and Realizable Predicates

In the preceding chapter we analyzed logically the relations which subsist among sentences or among predicates if one of them may be confirmed with the help of others. We defined some concepts of a syntactical kind, based upon the concept "consequence" as the chief concept of logical syntax. In what follows we shall deal with *empirical methodology*. Here also we are concerned with the questions of confirming and testing sentences and predicates. These considerations belong to a theory of language just as the logical ones do. But while the logical analysis belongs to an analytic theory of the formal, syntactical structure of language, here we will carry out an empirical analysis of the application of language. Our considerations belong, strictly speaking, to a biological or psychological theory of language as a kind of human behavior, and especially as a kind of reaction to observations. We shall see, however, that for our purposes we need not go into details of biological or psychological investigations. In order to make clear what is understood by empirically testing and confirming a sentence and thereby to find out what is to be required for a sentence or a predicate in a language having empirical meaning, we can restrict ourselves to using very few concepts of the field mentioned. We shall take two descriptive, i.e., non-logical, terms of this field as *basic terms* for our following considerations, namely, "*observable*" and "*realizable*." All other terms, and above all the terms "confirmable" and "testable," which are the chief terms of our theory, will be defined on the basis of the two basic terms mentioned; in the definitions we shall make use of the logical terms defined in the foregoing chapter. The two basic terms are of course, as basic ones, not defined within our theory. Definitions for them would have to be given within psychology, and more precisely, within the behavioristic theory of language. We do not attempt such definitions, but we shall give at least some rough explanations for the terms, which will make their meaning clear enough for our purposes.

Explanation 1. A predicate "P" of a language L is called *observable* for an organism (e.g., a person) N, if, for suitable arguments, e.g., "b," N is able under suitable circumstances to come to a decision with the help of few observations about a full sentence, say "P(b)," i.e., to a confirmation of either "P(b)" or "$\sim$P(b)" of such a high degree that he will either accept or reject "P(b)."

This explanation is necessarily vague. There is no sharp line between observable and non-observable predicates because a person will be more or less able to decide a certain sentence quickly, i.e., he will be inclined after a certain period of observation to accept the sentence. For the sake of simplicity we will here draw a sharp distinction between observable and non-observable predicates. By thus drawing an arbitrary line between observable and non-observable predicates in a field of continuous degrees of observability we partly determine in advance the possible answers to questions such as whether or not a certain predicate is observable by a given person. Nevertheless the general philosophical, i.e., methodological question about the nature of meaning and testability will, as we shall see, not be distorted by our oversimplification. Even particular questions as to whether or not a given sentence is confirmable, and whether or not it is testable by a certain person, are affected, as we shall see, at most to a very small degree by the choice of the boundary line for observable predicates.

According to the explanation given, for example, the predicate "red" is observable for a person N possessing a normal colour sense. For a suitable argument, namely, a space-time point c sufficiently near to N, say a spot on the table before N, N is able under suitable circumstances—namely, if there is sufficient light at c—to come to a decision about the full sentence "the spot c is red" after few observations—namely, by looking at the table. On the other hand, the predicate "red" is not observable by a colour-blind person. And the predicate "an electric field of such and such an amount" is not observable to anybody, because, although we know how to test a full sentence of this predicate, we cannot do it directly, i.e., by a few observations; we have to apply certain instruments and hence to make a great many preliminary observations in order to find out whether the things before us are instruments of the kind required.

Explanation 2. A predicate "P" of a language L is called *"realizable"* by N, if for a suitable argument, e.g., "b," N is able under suitable circumstances to make the full sentence "P(b)" true, i.e., to produce the property P at the point b.

When we use the terms *"observable," "realizable," "confirmable,"* etc., without explicit reference to anybody, it is to be understood that they are meant with respect to the people who use the language L to which the predicate in question belongs.

Examples. Let "$P_1(b)$" mean: "the space-time-point b has the temperature 100°C." "P_1" is realizable by us because we know how to produce that temperature at the point b, if b is accessible to us. "$P_2(b)$" may mean: "there is iron at the point b." "P_2" is realizable because we are able to carry a piece of iron to the point b if b is accessible. If "$P_3(b)$" means: "at the point b is a substance whose index of light refraction is 10," "P_3" is not realizable by anybody at the present time, because nobody knows at present how to produce such a substance.

12. Confirmability

In the preceding chapter we have dealt with the concept of reducibility of a predicate "P" to a class C of other predicates, i.e., the logical relation which subsists between "P" and C if the confirmation of "P" can be carried out by that of predicates of C. Now, if confirmation is to be feasible at all, this process of referring back to other predicates must terminate at some point. The reduction must finally come to predicates for which we can come to a confirmation directly, i.e., without reference to other predicates. According to Explanation 1, the observable predicates can be used as such a basis. This consideration leads us to the following definition of the concept "confirmable." This concept is a descriptive one, in contradistinction to the logical concept "reducible to C"— which could be named also "confirmable with respect to C."

Definition 16.[*] A *sentence* S is called *confirmable* (or completely confirmable, or incompletely confirmable) if the confirmation of S is reducible (or completely reducible, or incompletely reducible, respectively) to that of a class of observable predicates.

Definition 17. A sentence S is called *bilaterally confirmable* (or bilaterally completely confirmable) if both S and ∼S are confirmable (or completely confirmable, respectively).

Definition 18. A *predicate* "P" is called *confirmable* (or completely confirmable, or incompletely confirmable) if "P" is reducible (or completely reducible, or incompletely reducible, respectively) to a class of observable predicates.

Hence, if "P" **is** confirmable (or completely confirmable) the full sentences of "P" are bilaterally confirmable (or bilaterally completely confirmable, respectively).

When we call a sentence S confirmable, we do not mean that it is possible to arrive at a confirmation of S under the circumstances as they actually exist. We rather intend this possibility under some *possible circumstances,* whether they be real or not. Thus, e.g., because my pencil is black and I am able to make out by visual observation that it is black and not red, I cannot come to a positive confirmation of the sentence "My pencil is red." Nevertheless we call this sentence confirmable and moreover completely confirmable for the reason that we are able to indicate the—actually non-existent, but possible—observations which would confirm that sentence. Whether the real circumstances are such that the testing of a certain sentence S leads to a positive result, i.e., to a confirmation of S, or such that it leads to a negative result, i.e., to a confirmation of ∼S, is irrelevant for the questions of confirmability, testability and meaning of the sentence though decisive for the question of truth, i.e., sufficient confirmation.

Theorem 8. If "P" is introduced on the basis of observable predicates, "P" is confirmable. If the introductive chain has molecular form, "P" is completely confirmable. This follows from Theorem 7 (§9).

Theorem 9. If S is a sentence of molecular form and all predicates occurring in S are confirmable (or completely confirmable), S is bilaterally confirmable (or bilaterally completely confirmable, respectively). From Theorem 2 (§6).

Theorem 10. If the sentence S is constructed out of confirmable predicates with the help of connective symbols and universal or existential operators, S is bilaterally confirmable. From Theorems 2, 3, and 4 (§6).

13. Method of Testing

If "P" is confirmable then it is not impossible that for a suitable point *b* we may find a confirmation of "P(b)" or of "∼P(b)." But it is not necessary that

---

[*] [1950 Note: Today I should prefer to replace Def. 16 by the following definition, based on Def. 18: A *sentence* S is *confirmable* (or completely confirmable, or incompletely confirmable) if every descriptive predicate occurring in S is confirmable (or completely confirmable, or incompletely confirmable).]

we know a method for finding such a confirmation. If such a procedure can be given—we may call it a *method of testing*—then "P" is not only confirmable but—as we shall say later on—testable. The following considerations will deal with the question how to formulate a method of testing and thereby will lead to a definition of "testable."

The description of a method of testing for "Q_3" has to contain two other predicates of the following kinds:

1. A predicate, say "Q_1," describing a *test-condition* for "Q_3," i.e., an experimental situation which we have to create in order to test "Q_3" at a given point.

2. A predicate, say "Q_2," describing a *truth-condition* for "Q_3" with respect to "Q_1," i.e., a possible experimental result of the test-condition Q_1 at a given point b of such a kind that, if this result occurs, "Q_3" is to be attributed to b. Now the connection between "Q_1," "Q_2," and "Q_3" is obviously as follows: if the test-condition is realized at the given point b then, if the truth-condition is found to be fulfilled at b, b has the property to be tested; and this holds for any point. Thus the method of testing for "Q_3" is to be formulated by the universal sentence "$Q_1 \supset (Q_2 \supset Q_3)$," in other words, by a reduction sentence for "Q_3." But this sentence, beside being a reduction sentence, must fulfill the following two additional requirements:

1. "Q_1" must be realizable because, if we did not know how to produce the test-condition, we could not say that we had a method of testing.

2. We must know beforehand how to test the truth condition Q_2; otherwise we could not test "Q_3" although it might be confirmable. In order to satisfy the second requirement, "Q_2" must be either observable or explicitly defined on the basis of observable predicates or a method of testing for it must have been stated. If we start from observable predicates—which, as we know, can be tested without a description of a method of testing being necessary—and then introduce other predicates by explicit definitions or by such reduction sentences as fulfill the requirements stated above and hence are descriptions of a method of testing, then we know how to test each of these predicates. Thus we are led to the following definitions.

Definition 19. An introductive chain based upon observable predicates of such a kind that in each of its reduction sentences, say "$Q_1 \supset (Q_2 \supset Q_3)$" or "$Q_4 \supset (Q_5 \supset \sim Q_3)$," the first predicate—"$Q_1$" or "$Q_4$," respectively—is realizable, is called a *test chain*. A reduction sentence (or a reduction pair, or a bilateral reduction sentence) belonging to a test chain is called a *test sentence* (or a *test pair*, or a *bilateral test sentence*, respectively).

A test pair for "Q," and likewise a bilateral test sentence for "Q," describes a method of testing for both "Q" and "$\sim$Q." A bilateral test sentence, e.g., "$Q_1 \supset (Q_3 \equiv Q_2)$" may be interpreted in words in the following way. "If at a space-time-point x the test-condition Q_1 (consisting perhaps in a certain experimental situation, including suitable measuring instruments) is realized then we will attribute the predicate "Q_3" to the point x if and only if we find at x the state Q_2 (which may be a certain result of the experiment, e.g., a certain position of the pointer on the scale)." To give an example, let "$Q_3(b)$" mean: "The fluid at the space-time-point b has a temperature of 100°"; "$Q_1(b)$"; "A mercury thermometer is put at b; we wait, while stirring the liquid, until the mercury comes to a standstill"; "$Q_2(b)$": "The head of the mercury column of the thermometer at b stands at the mark 100 of the scale." If here "Q_3" is introduced by "$Q_1 \supset (Q_3 \equiv Q_2)$" obviously its testability is assured.

14. Testability

Definition 20.   If a predicate is either observable or introduced by a test chain it is called *testable*. A testable predicate is called *completely testable* if it is either observable or introduced by a test chain having molecular form; otherwise *incompletely testable*.

Let us consider the question under what conditions a set of laws, e.g., of physics, which contain a predicate "Q" can be transformed into a set of reduction-sentences or of test-sentences for "Q." Suppose a set of laws is given which contain "Q" and have the following form. Each of the laws is a universal sentence containing only individual variables (no predicate variables); "Q" is followed wherever it occurs in the sentence by the same set of variables, which are bound by universal operators applying to the whole sentence. Thus each of the laws has the form ("x)[$...Q(x)...Q(x)...$]." The majority of the laws of classical physics can be brought into this form. Now the given set of laws can be transformed in the following way. First we write down the conjunction of the laws of the given set and transform it into one universal sentence "$(x)[...Q(x)... Q(x)...]$." Then we transform the function included in square brackets into the so-called conjunctive normal form,[34] i.e., a conjunction of say n disjunctions of such a kind that "Q" occurs only in partial sentences which are members of such disjunctions and have either the form "$Q(x)$" or "$\sim Q(x)$." Finally we dissolve the whole universal sentence into n universal sentences in accordance with the rule that "$(x)[P_1(x) \cdot P_2(x) \cdot ... \cdot P_n(x)]$" can be transformed into "$(x)P_1(x)$. $(x) \cdot P_2(x) \cdot ... (x)P_n(x)$." Thus we have a set of n universal sentences; each of them is a disjunction having among its members either "$Q(x)$" or "$\sim Q(x)$" or both. If we employ "$\sim P(x)$" as abbreviation for the disjunction of the remaining members not containing "Q" these sentences have one of the following forms:

1. $Q \vee \sim P$
2. $\sim Q \vee \sim P$
3. $Q \vee \sim Q \vee \sim P$

A sentence of the form (3) is analytic and can therefore be omitted without changing the content of the set. (1) can be given the form "$P \supset Q$" and, by analysing "P" in some way or other into a conjunction "$P_1 \cdot P_2$," the form "$(P_1 \cdot P_2)$ $\supset Q$" and hence "$P_1 \supset (P_2 \supset Q)$" which is a reduction sentence of the first form. In the same way (2) can be transformed into "$P \supset \sim Q$" and hence into "$(P_1 \cdot P_2) \supset \sim Q$" and into "$P_1 \supset (P_2 \supset \sim Q)$" which is a reduction sentence of the second form. An analysis of "P" into "$P_1 \cdot P_2$" is obviously always possible;

[34] Compare Hilbert [1], p. 13; Carnap [4b], §34b, RR 2.

if not otherwise then in the trivial way of taking an analytic predicate as "P_1" and "P" itself as "P_2." If "P" is testable then we may look for such an analysis that "P_1" is realizable. If we can find such a one then—since "P_2" is also testable in this case—the reduction sentence "$P_1 \supset (P_2 \supset Q)$" or "$P_1 \supset (P_2 \supset {\sim}Q)$" is a test-sentence.

Thus we have seen that a set of laws of the form here supposed can always be transformed into a set of reduction sentences for "Q," and, if a special condition is fulfilled, into a set of test-sentences. This condition is fulfilled in very many and perhaps most of the cases actually occurring in physics because nearly all predicates used in physics are testable and perhaps most of them are realizable.

Theorem 11.   If a predicate is testable it is confirmable; if it is completely testable it is completely confirmable. By Theorem 8, §12.

On the other hand, "P" may be *confirmable without being testable.* This is the case, if "P" is introduced by an introductive chain based upon observable predicates but containing a reduction sentence "$Q_1 \supset (Q_2 \supset Q_3)$" of such a kind that "$Q_1$," although it is of course confirmable and may even be testable, is not realizable. If this should be the case, there is a possibility that by a happy chance the property Q_3 will be found at a certain point, although we have no method which would lead us with certainty to such a result. Suppose that "Q_1" and "Q_2" are completely confirmable, i.e., completely reducible to observable predicates—they may even be observable themselves—and that "Q_3" is introduced by "$Q_1 \supset (Q_3 \equiv Q_2)$." Let c be a point in our spatio-temporal neighborhood such that we are able to observe its properties. Then by happy chance "$Q_1(c)$" may be true. If so, we are able to find this out by observation and then, by either finding "$Q_2(c)$" or "${\sim}Q_2(c)$," to arrive at the conclusion either of "$Q_3(c)$" or of "${\sim}Q_3(c)$." But if that stroke of luck does not happen, i.e., if "$Q_1(c)$" is false—no matter whether we find that out by our observations or not —we are not in a position to determine the truth or falsehood of "$Q_3(c)$," and it is impossible for us to come to a confirmation of either "$Q_3(c)$" or "${\sim}Q_3(c)$" in any degree whatsoever. To give an example, let "$Q_1(c)$" mean that at the space-time point c there is a person with a certain disease. We suppose that we know symptoms both for the occurrence of this disease as well as for its non-occurrence; hence "Q_1" is confirmable. It may even be the case that we know a method by which we are able to find out with certainty whether or not a given person at a given time has this disease; if we know such a method "Q_1" is not only confirmable but testable and moreover completely testable. We will suppose, however, that "Q_1" is not realizable, i.e., we do not know at present any method of producing this disease; whether or not "${\sim}Q_1$" is realizable, in other words, whether or not we are able to cure the disease, does not matter for our considerations. Let us suppose further that clinical observations of the cases of this disease show that there are two classes of such cases, one characterized by the appearance of a certain symptom, i.e., a testable or even observable predicate, say "Q_2," the other by the lack of this symptom, i.e., by "${\sim}Q_2$." If this distinction turns out to be relevant for the further development of the disease and for its consequences, physicians may wish to classify all persons into two classes: those who are disposed to show the symptom Q_2 in case they acquire the disease Q_1, and those who do not, i.e., those who show ${\sim}Q_2$ if they get Q_1. The first class may be designated by "Q_3," and hence the second by "$\sim Q_3$." Then "Q_3" can be introduced by the bilateral reduction sentence "$Q_1 \supset (Q_3 \equiv Q_2)$." The classification by "Q_3" and "$\sim Q_3$" will be useful if observations of a long series of cases of this disease show that a person who once belongs to the class Q_3 (or $\sim Q_3$) always belongs to this class. Moreover, other connections between Q_3 and other biological properties may be discovered; these connections will then be formulated by laws containing "Q_3"; under suitable circumstances these laws can be given the form of supplementary reduction pairs for "Q_3." Thus "Q_3" may turn out to be a useful and important concept for the formulation of the results of empirical investigation. But "Q_3" is not testable, not even incompletely, because we do not know how to decide a given sentence "$Q_3(a)$," i.e., how to make experiments in order to find out whether a given person belongs to the class Q_3 or not; all we can do is to wait until this person happens to get the disease Q_1 and then to find out whether he shows the symptom Q_2 or not. It may happen, however, in the further development of our investigations, that we find that every person for whom we find "Q_1" and "Q_2" and to whom we therefore attribute "Q_3" shows a certain constant testable property Q_4, e.g., a certain chemical property of the blood, and that every person for whom we find "Q_1" and "$\sim Q_2$" and whom we therefore classify into $\sim Q_3$, does not show Q_4. On the basis of such results we would state the law "$Q_3 \equiv Q_4$." By this law, "Q_3" becomes synonymous—not L-synonymous, but P-synonymous—with the testable predicate "Q_4" and hence becomes itself testable. But until we are in a position to state a law of this or a similar kind, "Q_3" is not testable.

This example shows that a non-testable predicate can nevertheless be confirmable, and even completely confirmable, and its introduction and use can be helpful for the purposes of empirical scientific investigation.

Definition 21. If a *sentence* S is confirmable (or completely confirmable) and all predicates occurring in S are testable (or completely testable), S is called *testable* (or completely testable, respectively). If S is testable but not completely testable it is called incompletely testable. If S is bilaterally confirmable (or bilaterally completely confirmable) and all predicates occurring in it are testable (or completely testable), S is called *bilaterally testable* (or bilaterally completely testable, respectively).

Theorem 12. If S is a full sentence of a testable (or completely testable) predicate, S is bilaterally testable (or bilaterally completely testable, respectively).

Theorem 13. If S is a sentence of molecular form and all predicates occurring in S are testable (or completely testable) S is bilaterally testable (or bilaterally completely testable, respectively). By Theorems 11 and 9 (§ 12).

Theorem 14. If the sentence S is constructed out of testable predicates with the help of connective symbols and universal or existential operators, S is bilaterally testable. From Theorems 11 and 10 (§ 12).

15. A Remark about Positivism and Physicalism

One of the fundamental theses of *positivism* may perhaps be formulated in this way: every term of the whole language L of science is reducible to what we may call sense-data terms or perception terms. By a perception term we understand a predicate "P" such that "P(b)" means: "the person at the space-time-place b has a perception of the kind P." (Let us neglect here the fact that the older positivism would have referred in a perception sentence not to a space-time-place, but to an element of "consciousness"; let us here take the physicalistic formulation given above.) I think that this thesis is true if we understand the term "reducible" in the sense in which we have defined it here. But previously reducibility was not distinguished from definability. Positivists therefore believed that every descriptive term of science could be defined by perception terms, and hence, that every sentence of the language of science could be translated into a sentence about perceptions. This opinion is also expressed in the former publications of the Vienna Circle, including mine of 1928 (Carnap [1]), but I now think, that it is not entirely adequate. Reducibility can be asserted, but not unrestricted possibility of elimination and re-translation; the reason being that the method of introduction by reduction pairs is indispensable.

Because we are here concerned with an important correction of a widespread opinion let us examine in greater detail the reduction and retranslation of sentences as positivists previously regarded them. Let us take as an example a simple sentence about a physical thing:

(1) "On May 6, 1935, at 4 P.M., there is a round black table in my room."

According to the usual positivist opinion, this sentence can be translated into the conjunction of the following conditional sentences (2) about (possible) perceptions. (For the sake of simplicity we eliminate in this example only the term "table" and continue to use in these sentences some terms which are not perception terms e.g.," "my room," "eye," etc., which by further reduction would have to be eliminated also.)

(2a) "If on May . . . somebody is in my room and looks in such and such direction, he has a visual perception of such and such a kind."

(2a'), (2a''), etc. Similar sentences about the other possible aspects of the table.

(2b) "If . . . somebody is in my room and stretches out his hands in such and such a direction, he has touch perceptions of such and such a kind."

(2b'), (2b''), etc. Similar sentences about the other possible touchings of the table.

(2c), etc. Similar sentences about possible perceptions of other senses.

It is obvious that no single one of these sentences (2) nor even a conjunction of some of them would suffice as a translation of (1); we have to take the whole series containing all possible perceptions of that table. Now the first difficulty of this customary positivistic reduction consists in the fact that it is not certain that the series of sentences (2) is finite. If it is not, then there exists no conjunction of them; and in this case the original sentence (1) cannot be translated into one perception sentence. But a more serious objection is the following one. Even the whole class of sentences (2)—no matter whether it be finite or infinite—is not equipollent with (1), because it may be the case that (1) is false, though every single sentence of the class (2) is true. In order to construct such a case, suppose that at the time stated there is neither a round black table in my room, nor any observer at all. (1) is then obviously false. (2a) is a universal implication sentence:

"(x)   [(x is ... in my room and looks ...) $\supset$ (x perceives ...)]"

which we may abbreviate in this way:

(3) $(x)[P(x) \supset Q(x)]$

which can be transformed into
(4) $(x)[\sim P(x) \lor Q(x)]$

((2a) can be formulated in words in this way: "For anybody it is either not the case that he is in my room on May . . . and looks . . . or he has a visual perception of such and such a kind.") Now, according to our assumption, for every person x it is false that x is at that time in my room and looks . . . ; in symbols:

(5) $(x) \; (\sim P(x))$

Therefore (4) is true, and hence (2a) also, and analogously every one of the other sentences of the class (2), while (1) is false. In this way the positivistic reduction in its customary form is shown to be invalid. The example dealt with is a sentence about a directly perceptible thing. If we took as examples sentences about atoms, electrons, electric field and the like, it would be even clearer that the positivistic translation into perception terms is not possible.

Let us look at the consequences which these considerations have for the construction of a scientific language on a positivistic basis, i.e., with perception terms as the only primitive terms. The most important consequence concerns the method of introduction of further terms. In introducing terms of perceptible things (e.g., "table") and *a fortiori* the abstract terms of scientific physics, we must not restrict the introductive method to definitions but must also use reduction. If we do this the positivistic thesis concerning reducibility above mentioned can be shown to be true.

Let us give the name *"thing-language"* to that language which we use in every-day life in speaking about the perceptible things surrounding us. A sentence of the thing-language describes things by stating their observable properties or observable relations subsisting between them. What we have called observable predicates are predicates of the thing-language. (They have to be clearly distinguished from what we have called perception terms; if a person sees a round red spot on the table the perception term "having a visual perception of something round and red" is attributed to the person while the observable predicate "round and red" is attributed to the space-time point on the table.) Those predicates of the thing-language which are not observable, e.g., disposition terms, are reducible to observable predicates and hence confirmable. We have seen this in the example of the predicate "soluble" (§7).

Let us give the name *"physical language"* to that language which is used in physics. It contains the thing-language and, in addition, those terms of a scientific terminology which we need for a scientific description of the processes in inorganic nature. While the terms of the thing-language for the most part serve only for a qualitative description of things, the other terms of the physical language are designed increasingly for a quantitative description. For every term of the physical language physicists know how to use it on the basis of their observations. Thus every such term is reducible to observable predicates and hence confirmable. Moreover, nearly every such term is testable, because for every term—perhaps with the exception of few terms considered as preliminary ones—physicists possess a method of testing; for the quantitative terms this is a method of measurement.

The so-called thesis of *Physicalism* [85] asserts that every term of the language of science—including beside the physical language those sub-languages which are used in biology, in psychology, and in social science—is reducible to terms of the physical language. Here a remark analogous to that about positivism has to be made. We may assert reducibility of the terms, but not—as was done in our former publications—definability of the terms and hence translatability of the sentences.

In former explanations of physicalism we used to refer to the physical language as a basis of the whole language of science. It now seems to me that what we really had in mind as such a basis was rather the thing-language, or, even more narrowly, the observable predicates of the thing-language. In looking for a new and more correct formulation of the thesis of physicalism we have to consider the fact mentioned that the method of definition is not sufficient for the introduction of new terms. Then the question remains: can every term of the language of science be introduced on the basis of observable terms of the thing-language by using only definitions and test-sentences, or are reduction sentences necessary which are not test sentences? In other words, which of the following formulations of the thesis of physicalism is true?

1. *Thesis of Physicalistic Testability:* "Every descriptive predicate of the language of science is testable on the basis of observable thing-predicates."

2. *Thesis of Physicalistic Confirmability:* "Every descriptive predicate of the language of science is confirmable on the basis of observable thing-predicates."

If we had been asked the question at the time when we first stated physicalism, I am afraid we should perhaps have chosen the first formulation. Today I hesitate to do this, and I should prefer the weaker formulation (2). The reason is that I think scientists are justified to use and actually do use terms which are confirmable without being testable, as the example in §14 shows.

We have sometimes formulated the thesis of physicalism in this way: "The language of the whole of science is a physicalistic language." We used to say: a language L is called a physicalistic language if it is constructed out of the physical language by introducing new terms. (The introduction was supposed to

[85] Comp. Neurath [1], [2], [3]; Carnap [2], [8].

be made by definition; we know today that we must employ reduction as well.) In this definition we could replace the reference to the physical language by a reference to the thing-language or even to the observable predicates of the thing-language. And here again we have to decide whether to admit for the reduction only test-chains or other reduction chains as well; in other words, whether to define "physicalistic language" as "a language whose descriptive terms are testable on the basis of observable thing-predicates" or ". . . are confirmable. . . ."

16. Sufficient Bases

A class C of descriptive predicates of a language L such that every descriptive predicate of L is reducible to C is called a *sufficient reduction basis* of L; if in the reduction only definitions are used, C is called a *sufficient definition basis*. If C is a sufficient reduction basis of L and the predicates of C—and hence all predicates of L—are confirmable, C is called a *sufficient confirmation basis* of L; and if moreover the predicates of C are completely testable, for instance observable, and every predicate of L is reducible to C by a test chain—and hence is testable—C is called a *sufficient test basis* of L.

As we have seen, positivism asserts that the class of perception-terms is a sufficient basis for the language of science; physicalism asserts the same for the class of physical terms, or, in our stronger formulation, for the class of observable thing-predicates. Whether positivism and physicalism are right or not, at any rate it is clear that there can be several and even mutually exclusive bases. The classes of terms which positivism and physicalism assert to be sufficient bases, are rather comprehensive. Nevertheless even these bases are not sufficient definition bases but only sufficient reduction bases. Hence it is obvious that, if we wish to look for narrower sufficient bases, they must be reduction bases. We shall find that there are sufficient reduction bases of the language of science which have a far narrower extension than the positivistic and the physicalistic bases.

Let L be the physical language. We will look for sufficient reduction bases of L. If physicalism is right, every such basis of L is also a basis of the total scientific language; but here we will not discuss the question of physicalism. We have seen that the class of the observable predicates is a sufficient reduction basis of L. In what follows we will consider only bases consisting of observable predicates; hence they are *confirmation bases of the physical language* L. Whether they are also test bases depends upon whether all confirmable predicates of L are also testable; this question may be left aside for the moment. The visual sense is the most important sense; and we can easily see that it is sufficient for the confirmation of any physical property. A deaf man for instance is able to determine pitch, intensity and timbre of a physical sound with the help of suitable instruments; a man without the sense of smell can determine the olfactory properties of a gas by chemical analysis; etc. That all physical functions (temperature, electric field, etc.) can be determined by the visual sense alone is obvious. Thus we see that the predicates of the visual sense, i.e., the colour-predicates as functions of space-time-places, are a sufficient confirmation basis of the physical language L.

But the basis can be restricted still more. Consider a man who cannot perceive colours, but only differences of brightness. Then he is able to determine all physical properties of things or events which we can determine from photographs; and that means, all properties. Thus he determines, e.g., the colour of a light with the help of a spectroscope or a spectrograph. Hence the class of predicates which state the degree of brightness at a space-time-place—or the class consisting of the one functor [36] whose value is the degree of brightness—is a sufficient basis of L.

Now imagine a man whose visual sense is still more restricted. He may be able to distinguish neither the different colours nor the different degree of brightness, but only the two qualities bright and dark (= not bright) with their distribution in the visual field. What he perceives corresponds to a bad phototype which shows no greys but only black and white. Even this man is able to accomplish all kinds of determinations necessary in physics. He will determine the degree of brightness of a light by an instrument whose scale and pointer form a black-white-picture. Hence the one predicate "bright" is a sufficient basis of L.

But even a man who is completely blind and deaf, but is able to determine by touching the spatial arrangements of bodies, can determine all physical properties. He has to use instruments with palpable scale-marks and a palpable pointer (such as, e.g., watches for the blind). With such a spectroscope he can determine the colour of a light; etc. Let "Solid" be a predicate such that "Solid (b)" means: "There is solid matter at the space-time-point b." Then this single predicate "Solid" is a sufficient basis of L.

Thus we have found several very narrow bases which are sufficient confirmation bases for the physical language and simultaneously sufficient test bases for the testable predicates of the physical language. And, if physicalism is right, they are also sufficient for the total language of science. Some of these bases consist of one predicate only. And obviously there are many more sufficient bases of such a small extent. This result will be relevant for our further considerations. It may be noticed that this result cannot at all be anticipated *a priori*; neither the fact of the existence of so small sufficient bases nor the fact that just the predicates mentioned are sufficient, is a logical necessity. Reducibility depends upon the validity of certain universal sentences, and hence upon the system of physical laws; thus the facts mentioned are special features of the structure of that system, or—expressed in the material idiom—special features of the causal structure of the real world. Only after constructing a system of physics can we determine what bases are sufficient with respect to that system.

IV. THE CONSTRUCTION OF A LANGUAGE-SYSTEM

17. The Problem of a Criterion of Meaning

It is not the aim of the present essay to defend the principle of empiricism against apriorism or anti-empiricist metaphysics. Taking empiricism [37] for

---

[36] Compare Carnap [4], §3.

[37] The words "empiricism" and "empiricist" are here understood in their widest sense, and not in the narrower sense of traditional positivism or sensationalism or any other doctrine restricting empirical knowledge to a certain kind of experience.

granted, we wish to discuss, the question what is meaningful. The word "meaning" will here be taken in its empiricist sense; an expression of language has meaning in this sense if we know how to use it in speaking about empirical facts, either actual or possible ones. Now our problem is what expressions are meaningful in this sense. We may restrict this question to sentences because expressions other than sentences are meaningful if and only if they can occur in a meaningful sentence.

Empiricists generally agree, at least in general terms, in the view that the question whether a given sentence is meaningful is closely connected with the questions of the possibility of verification, confirmation or testing of that sentence. Sometimes the two questions have been regarded as identical. I believe that this identification can be accepted only as a rough first approximation. Our real problem now is to determine the precise relation between the two questions, or generally, to state the criterion of meaning in terms of verification, confirmation or testing.

I need not emphasize that here we are concerned only with the problem of meaning as it occurs in methodology, epistemology or applied logic,[38] and not with the psychological question of meaning. We shall not consider here the questions whether any images and, if so, what images are connected with a given sentence. That these questions belong to psychology and do not touch the methodological question of meaning, has often been emphasized.[39]

It seems to me that the question about the criterion of meaning has to be construed and formulated in a way different from that in which it is usually done. In the first place we have to notice that this problem concerns the structure of language. (In my opinion this is true for all philosophical questions, but that is beyond our present discussion.) Hence a clear formulation of the question involves reference to a certain language; the usual formulations do not contain such a reference and hence are incomplete and cannot be answered. Such a reference once made, we must above all distinguish between two main kinds of questions about meaningfulness; to the first kind belong the questions referring to a historically given language-system, to the second kind those referring to a language-system which is yet to be constructed. These two kinds of questions have an entirely different character. A question of the first kind is a theoretical one; it asks, what is the actual state of affairs; and the answer is either true or false. The second question is a practical one; it asks, how shall we proceed; and the answer is not an assertion but a proposal or decision. We shall consider the two kinds one after the other.

A *question of the first kind* refers to a given language-system L and concerns an expression E of L (i.e., a finite series of symbols of L). The question is, whether E is meaningful or not. This question can be divided into two parts: (a) "Is E a sentence of L?" and (b) "If so, does E fulfill the empiricist criterion of meaning?" Question (a) is a formal question of logical syntax; question (b) belongs to the field of methodology. It would be advisable to avoid the terms

---

[38] Our problem of meaning belongs to the field which *Tarski* [1] calls *Semantic;* this is the theory of the relations between the expressions of a language and things, properties, facts, etc., described in the language.

[39] Comp., e.g., Schlick [4], p. 355.

"meaningful" and "meaningless" in this and in similar discussions—because these expressions involve so many rather vague philosophical associations—and to replace them by an expression of the form "a . . . sentence of L"; expressions of this form will then refer to a specified language and will contain at the place ". . ." an adjective which indicates the methodological character of the sentence, e.g., whether or not the sentence (and its negation) is verifiable or completely or incompletely confirmable or completely or incompletely testable and the like, according to what is intended by "meaningful."

18. The Construction of a Language-System L

A *question of the second kind* concerns a language-system L which is being proposed for construction. In this case the rules of L are not given, and the problem is how to choose them. We may construct L in whatever way we wish. There is no question of right or wrong, but only a practical question of convenience or inconvenience of a system form, i.e., of its suitability for certain purposes. In this case a theoretical discussion is possible only concerning the consequences which such and such a choice of rules would have; and obviously this discussion belongs to the first kind. The special question whether or not a given choice of rules will produce an empiricist language, will then be contained in this set of questions.

In order to make the problem more specific and thereby more simple, let us suppose that we wish to construct L as a physical language, though not as a language for all science. The problems connected with specifically biological or psychological terms, though interesting in themselves, would complicate our present discussion unnecessarily. But the main points of the philosophical discussions of meaning and testability already occur in this specialized case.

In order to formulate the rules of an intended language L, it is necessary to use a language L' which is already available. L' must be given at least practically and need not be stated explicitly as a language-system, i.e., by formulated rules. We may take as L' the English language. In constructing L, L' serves for two different purposes. First, L' is the syntax-language [40] in which the rules of the object-language L are to be formulated. Secondly, L' may be used as a basis for comparison for L, i.e., as a first object-language with which we compare the second object-language L, as to richness of expressions, structure and the like. Thus we may consider the question, to which sentences of the English language (L') do we wish to construct corresponding sentences in L, and to which not. For example, in constructing the language of Principia Mathematica, Whitehead and Russell wished to have available translations for the English sentences of the form "There is something which has the property φ"; they therefore constructed their language-system so as to contain the sentence-form "$(\exists x) \cdot \varphi x$." A difficulty occurs because the English language is not a language-system in the strict sense (i.e., a system of fixed rules) so that the concept of translation cannot be used here in its exact syntactical sense. Nevertheless this concept is sufficiently clear for our present practical purpose. The comparison of L with L' belongs to the rather vague, preliminary considerations which lead to decisions about the

[40] Comp. Carnap [4], §1; [5], p. 39.

system L. Subsequently the result of these decisions can be exactly formulated as rules of the system L.

It is obvious that we are not compelled to construct L so as to contain sentences corresponding to all sentences of L'. If, e.g., we wish to construct a language of economics, then its sentences correspond only to a small part of the sentences of the English language L'. But even if L were to be a language adequate for all science there would be many—and I among them—who would not wish to have in L a sentence corresponding to every sentence which usually is considered as a correct English sentence and is used by learned people. We should not wish, e.g., to have corresponding sentences to many or perhaps most of the sentences occurring in the books of metaphysicians. Or, to give a non-metaphysical example, the members of our Circle did not wish in former times to include into our scientific language a sentence corresponding to the English sentence

S_1: "This stone is now thinking about Vienna."

But at present I should prefer to construct the scientific language in such a way that it contains a sentence S_2 corresponding to S_1. (Of course I should then take S_2 as false, and hence $\sim S_2$ as true.) I do not say that our former view was wrong. Our mistake was simply that we did not recognize the question as one of decision concerning the form of the language; we therefore expressed our view in the form of an assertion—as is customary among philosophers—rather than in the form of a proposal. We used to say: "S_1 is not false but meaningless"; but the careless use of the word "meaningless" has its dangers and is the second point in which we would like at present to modify the previous formulation.

We return to the question how we are to proceed in constructing a physical language L, using as L' the English physical language.

The following list shows the items which have to be decided in constructing a language L.

    I. *Formative rules* (= definition of "sentence in L").
        A. Atomic sentences.
            1. The form of atomic sentences.
            2. The atomic predicates.
                a. Primitive predicates.
                b. Indirectly introduced atomic predicates.
        B. Formative operations of the first kind: Connections; Molecular sentences.
        C. Formative operations of the second kind: Operators.
            1. Generalized sentences. (This is the *critical point*.)
            2. Generalized predicates.
    II. *Transformative rules* (= definition of "consequence in L").
        A. L-rules. (The rules of logical deduction.)
        B. P-rules. (The physical laws stated as valid.)

In the following sections we shall consider in succession items of the kind I, i.e., the formative rules. We will choose these rules for the language L from the point of view of empiricism; and we shall try, in constructing this empiricist language L, to become clear about what is required for a sentence to have meaning.

19. Atomic Sentences: Primitive Predicates

The suitable method for stating formative rules does not consist in describing every single form of sentence which we wish to admit in L. That is impossible because the number of these forms is infinite. The best method consists in fixing

1. The forms of some sentences of a simple structure; we may call them (elementary or) *atomic sentences* (IA);

2. Certain *operations* for the formation of compound sentences (IB,C).

IA1. Atomic Sentences. As already mentioned, we will consider only predicates of that type which is most important for physical language, namely, those predicates whose arguments are individual constants, i.e., designations of space-time-points. (It may be remarked that it would be possible and even convenient to admit also full sentences of physical functors as atomic sentences of L, e.g., "te(a) = r," corresponding to the sentence of L′: "The temperature at the space-time-point *a* is r." For the sake of simplicity we will restrict the following considerations to predicate-sentences. The results can easily be applied to functor-sentences also.) An atomic sentence is a full sentence of an atomic predicate (Definition 15a, §9). An atomic predicate is either primitive or introduced by an atomic chain (Definition 14b, §9). Therefore we have to answer the following questions in order to determine the form of the atomic sentences of L:

IA2.   (a) Which predicates shall we admit as primitive predicates of L?
       (b) Which forms of atomic introductive chains shall we admit?

IA2a: Primitive Predicates.   Our decision concerning question (a) is obviously very important for the construction of L. It might be thought that the richness of language L depends chiefly upon how rich is the selection we make of primitive predicates. If this were the case the philosophical discussion of what sentences were to be included in L—which is usually formulated as: what sentences are meaningful?—would reduce to this question of the selection of primitive predicates. But in fact this is not the case. As we shall see, the main controversy among philosophers concerns the formation of sentences by operators (IC1). About the selection of primitive predicates agreement can easily be attained, even among representatives of the most divergent views regarding what is meaningful and what is meaningless. This is easily understood if we remember our previous considerations about sufficient bases. If a suitable predicate is selected as the primitive predicate of L, all other physical predicates can be introduced by reduction chains.

To illustrate how the selection of primitive predicates could be carried out, let us suppose that the person N_1 who is constructing the language L trusts his sense of sight more than his other senses. That may lead him to take the colour-predicates (attributed to things or space-time-points, not to acts of perception) as primitive predicates of L. Since all other physical predicates are reducible to them, N_1 will not take any other primitive predicates. It is just at this point in selecting primitive predicates, that N_1 has to face the question of observability. If N_1 possesses a normal colour sense each of the selected predicates, e.g., "red," is observable by him in the sense explained before (§11). Further, if N_1 wishes to share the language L with other people—as is the case in practice—N_1 must inquire whether the predicates selected by him are also observable by them; he must investigate whether they are able to use these predicates in sufficient agreement with him—whether it be subsequent to training by him or not. We may suppose that N_1 will come to a positive result on the basis of his experience with English-speaking people. Exact agreement, it is true, is not obtainable; but that is not demanded. Suppose however that N_1 meets a completely colour-blind man N_2. N_1 will find that he cannot get N_2 to use the colour predicates in sufficient agreement with him, in other words, that these predicates are not observable by N_2. If nevertheless N_1 wishes to have N_2 in his language-community, N_1 must change his selection of primitive predicates. Perhaps he will take the brightness-predicates which are also observable by him. But there might be a completely blind man N_3, for whom not one of the primitive predicates selected by N_1 is observable. Is N_3 now unable to take part in the total physical language of N_1? No, he is not. N_1 and N_3 might both take, e.g., the predicate "solid" as primitive predicate for their common language L. This predicate is observable both for N_3 and N_1, and it is a sufficient confirmation basis for the physical language L, as we have seen above. Or, if N_1 prefers to keep visual predicates as primitive predicates for L, he may suggest to N_3 that he take "solid" as primitive predicate of N_3's language L_3 and then introduce the other predicates by reduction in such a way that they agree with the predicates of N_1's language L. Then L and L_3 will be completely congruent even as to the stock of predicates, though the selections of primitive predicates are different. How far N_1 will go in accepting people with restricted sensual faculties into his language-community is a matter of practical decision. For our further considerations we shall suppose that only observable predicates are selected as primitive predicates of L. Obviously this restriction is not a necessary one. But, as empiricists, we want every predicate of our scientific language to be confirmable, and we must therefore select observable predicates as primitive ones. For the following considerations we suppose that the primitive predicates of L are observable without fixing a particular selection.

Decision 1.   Every primitive descriptive predicate of L is observable.

20. The Choice of a Psychological or a Physical Basis

In selecting the primitive predicates for the physical language L, we must pay attention to the question whether they are observable, i.e., whether they can be directly tested by perceptions. Nevertheless we need not demand the existence of sentences in L—either atomic or other kinds—corresponding to perception-sentences of L' (e.g., "I am now seeing a round, red patch"). L may be a physical language constructed according to the demands of empiricism, and may nevertheless contain no perception-sentences at all.

If we choose a basis for the whole scientific language and if we decide as empiricists, to choose observable predicates, two (or three) different possibilities still remain open for specifying more completely the basis, apart from the question of taking a narrower or wider selection. For, if we take the concept "observable" in the wide sense explained before (§11) we find two quite different kinds of observable predicates, namely physical and psychological ones.

1. Observable *physical predicates of the thing-language,* attributed to perceived things of any kind or to space-time-points. All examples of primitive predicates of L mentioned before belong to this kind. Examples of full sentences of such predicates: "This thing is brown," "This spot is quadrangular," "This space-time-point is warm," "At this space-time-point is a solid substance."

2. Observable *psychological predicates.* Examples: "having a feeling of anger," "having an imagination of a red triangle," "being in the state of thinking about Vienna," "remembering the city hall of Vienna." The perception predicates also belong to this kind, e.g., "having a perception (sensation) of red," ". . . of sour"; these perception predicates have to be distinguished from the corresponding thing-predicates belonging to the first kind. These predicates are observable in our sense in so far as a person N who is in such a state can, under normal conditions, be aware of this state and can therefore directly confirm a sentence attributing such a predicate to himself. Such an attribution is based upon that kind of observation which psychologists call introspection or self-observation, and which philosophers sometimes have called perception by the inner sense. These designations are connected with and derived from certain doctrines to which I do not subscribe and which will not be assumed in the following; but the fact referred to by these designations seems to me to be beyond discussion. Concerning these observable psychological predicates we have to distinguish two interpretations or modes of use, according to which they are used either in a phenomenological or in a physicalistic language.

2a. Observable psychological predicates *in a phenomenological language.* Such a predicate is attributed to a so-called state of consciousness with a temporal reference (but without spatial determination, in contradistinction to 2b). Examples of full sentences of such predicates (the formulation varies according to the philosophy of the author): "My consciousness is now in a state of anger" (or: "I am now . . . ," or simply: "Now anger"); and analogously with "such and such an imagination," ". . . remembrance," ". . . thinking," ". . . perception," etc. These predicates are here interpreted as belonging to a phenomenological language, i.e., a language about conscious phenomena as non-spatial events. However, such a language is a purely subjective one, suitable for soliloquy only, while the intersubjective thing-language is suitable for use among different subjects. For the construction of a subjective language predicates of this kind may be taken as primitive predicates. Several such subjective languages constructed by several subjects may then be combined for the construction of an intersubjective language. But the predicates of this kind cannot be taken directly as observable primitive predicates of an intersubjective language.

2b. Observable psychological predicates *in a physicalistic language.* Such a predicate is attributed to a person as a thing with spatio-temporal determination. (I believe that this is the use of psychological predicates in our language of everyday life, and that they are used or interpreted in the phenomenological way only by philosophers.) Examples of full sentences: "Charles was angry yesterday at noon," "I (i.e., this person, known as John Brown) have now a perception of red," etc. Here the psychological predicates belong to an intersubjective language. And they are intersubjectively confirmable. N_2 may succeed in confirming such a sentence as "N_1 is now thinking of Vienna" (S), as is constantly done in everyday life as well as in psychological investigations in the laboratory. However, the sentence S is confirmable by N_2 only incompletely, ✶ although it is completely confirmable by N_1. [It seems to me that there is general agreement about the fact that N_1 can confirm more directly than N_2 a sentence concerning N_1's feelings, thoughts, etc. There is disagreement only concerning the question whether this difference is a fundamental one or only a difference in degree. The majority of philosophers, including some members of our Circle in former times, hold that the difference is fundamental inasmuch as there is a certain field of events, called the consciousness of a person, which is absolutely inaccessible to any other person. But we now believe, on the basis of physicalism, that the difference, although very great and very important for practical life, is only a matter of degree and that there are predicates for which the directness of confirmation by other persons has intermediate degrees (e.g., "sour" and "quadrangular" or "cold" when attributed to a piece of sugar in my mouth). But this difference in opinion need not be discussed for our present purposes.] We may formulate the fact mentioned by saying that the psychological predicates in a physicalistic language are intersubjectively confirmable but only *subjectively observable*. [As to testing, the difference is still greater. The sentence S is certainly not completely testable by N_2; and it seems doubtful whether it is at all testable by N_2, although it is cer- 7. tainly confirmable by N_2.] This feature of the predicates of kind 2b is a serious disadvantage and constitutes a reason against their choice as primitive predicates of an intersubjective language. Nevertheless we would have to take them as primitive predicates in a language of the whole of science if they were not reducible to predicates of the kind 1, because in such a language we require them in any case. But, if physicalism is correct they are in fact reducible and hence dispensable as primitive predicates of the whole language of science. And certainly for the physical language L under construction we need not take them as primitive.

According to these considerations, it seems to be preferable to choose the primitive predicates from the predicates of kind 1, i.e., of the observable thing-predicates. These are the only intersubjectively observable predicates. In this case, therefore, the same choice can be accepted by the different members of the language community. We formulate our decision concerning L, as a supplement to Decision 1:

Decision 2. <u>Every primitive predicate of L is a thing predicate.</u>

The choice of primitive predicates is meant here as the choice of a basis for possible confirmation. Thus, in order to find out whether the choice of primitive predicates of the kind 1 or 2a or 2b corresponds to the view of a certain philosopher, we have to examine what he takes as the basis for empirical knowledge, for confirmation or testing. Mach, by taking the sensa-tion elements ("Empfindungselemente") as basis, can be interpreted as a representative of the standpoint 2a; and similarly other positivists, sensa-tionalists and idealists. The views held in the first period of the Vienna Circle were very much influenced by positivists and above all by Mach, and hence also show an inclination to the view 2a. I myself took elementary experiences ("Elementarerlebnisse") as basis (in [1]). Later on, when our Circle made the step to physicalism, we abandoned the phenomenological language recognizing its subjective limitation.[41] Neurath[42] requires for the basic sentences ("Protokollsätze"), i.e., those to which all confirmation and testing finally goes back, the occurrence of certain psychological terms of the kind 2b—or: of biological terms, as we may say with Neurath in order to stress the physicalistic interpretation—namely, designations of actions of perception (as physicalistic terms). He does not admit in these basic sentences such a simple expression as, e.g., "a black round table" which is observable in our sense but requires instead "a black round table per-ceived (or: seen) by Otto." This view can perhaps be interpreted as the choice of predicates of the kind 2b as primitive ones. We have seen above the disadvantages of such a choice of the basis. Popper[43] rejects for his basic sentences reference to mental events, whether it be in the introspec-tive, phenomenological form, or in physicalistic form. He characterizes his basic sentences with respect to their form as singular existential sentences and with respect to their content as describing observable events; he de-mands that a basic sentence must be intersubjectively testable by observa-tion. Thus his view is in accordance with our choice of predicates of the kind 1 as primitive ones. He was, it seems to me, the first to hold this view. (The only inconvenient point in his choice of basic sentences seems to me to be the fact that the negations of his basic sentences are not basic sen-tences in his sense.)

I wish to emphasize the fact that I am in agreement with Neurath not only in the general outline of empiricism and physicalism but also in regard to the question what is to be required for empirical confirmation. Thus I do not deny—as neither Popper nor any other empiricist does, I believe—that a certain connection between the basic sentences and our perceptions is required. But, it seems to me, it is sufficient that the biological designations of perceptive activity occur in the formulation of the me-thodological requirement concerning the basic sentences—as, e.g., in our formulation "The primitive descriptive predicates have to be observable," where the term "observable" is a biological term referring to perceptions—and that they need not occur in the basic sentences themselves. Also a lan-guage restricted to physics as, e.g., our language L without containing any biological or perception terms may be an empiricist language provided its primitive descriptive predicates are observable; it may even fulfill the re-

[41] Comp. Carnap [2], §6.
[42] Neurath [5], and [6], p. 361.
[43] Popper [1], pp. 57ff.

quirement of empiricism in its strictest form inasmuch as all predicates are completely testable. And this language is in its nature quite different from such a language as, e.g., that of theoretical physics. The latter language—although as a part of the whole language of science, it is an empiricist language because containing only confirmable terms—does not contain observable predicates of the thing-language and hence does not include a confirmation basis. On the other hand, a physical language like L contains within itself its basis for confirmation and testing.

21. Introduced Atomic Predicates
Beside the question just discussed concerning the choice of a psychological or a physical basis no problems of a fundamental, philosophical nature arise in selecting   primitive predicates. In practice, an agreement about the selection can easily be obtained, because every predicate whose observability could be doubted—as, e.g., electric field or the like—can easily be dispensed with. As mentioned before, the whole situation described here is not logically necessary, but a contingent character of the system of predicates in their relation to reducibility and consequently to the laws of science. This character of the system of science explains the historical fact that nearly all controversies among contemporary philosophers—at least among those who reject trans-empirical speculative metaphysics—about the limitation of language do not concern the selection of primitive predicates but the selection of formative operations to be admitted. These operations will be considered later on.

As we have seen, the question of observability has to be decided only for the predicates to be chosen as primitive predicates. Our description of the process of their selection has shown that it is an empirical question, not a logical one. All other questions of confirmability of a given predicate concern indirect confirmation, which depends upon the logical, i.e., syntactical relations between the predicate in question and observable predicates. Thus these further questions of confirmability concern the structure of the language, namely, the form of definitions and reduction sentences. However, the question of testability of a given predicate involves, in addition, another empirical question, namely, whether certain confirmable predicates are realizable.

IA2b.   Indirectly Introduced Atomic Predicates.   In addition to the primitive predicates of the physical language L other predicates have to be introduced by introductive chains. We have to decide—first for atomic predicates, and later on also for predicates of other kinds—whether to admit in introductive chains definitions only, or also reduction sentences of the general form. In our previous considerations we have seen that the introduction by reduction is practically indispensable. Therefore we decide to admit it. There are two possibilities: we may or may not restrict the introductive chains in L to test chains. We will leave this point undecided and formulate the two possible forms of our decision:
Decision 3.   Introductive chains containing reduction pairs are admitted in L, either (a) *only* in the form of *test chains*, or (b) without restriction to test chains.

Theorem 15. If the primitive predicates of a language are observable—as, e.g., in our language L according to Decision 1—all atomic predicates are completely confirmable; moreover, they are completely testable if only test chains are admitted—as, e.g., in L in the case of Decision 3a. This follows from Theorem 8 (§12).

22. Molecular Sentences

After considering the question of the atomic sentences of L (IA in the list of p. 169, we have to consider the second part of the formative rules, namely, the rules determining what operations for the formation of compound sentences are to be admitted. We have to distinguish two main kinds of such operations:

1. the formation of molecular sentences with the aid of connections (IB);
2. the formation of generalized sentences with the aid of operators (IC).

IB: Connections. There are two kinds of sentential connections. The so-called extensional connections or truth-functions are characterized by the fact that the truth-value of any compound sentence constructed with their help depends only upon the truth-values of the component sentences. The connections of the usual sentential calculus mentioned before are extensional (see §5): negation, disjunction, conjunction, implication, equivalence. The non-extensional connections are called intensional [44]; to them belong, e.g., Lewis' strict implication [45] and the so-called modal functions.[46] In the case of an intensional connection the truth-value of a compound sentence depends upon the truth-values as well as the forms of the component sentences. (Here it is presupposed that sufficient L-rules are stated for the connective symbol in question; if that is not the case the symbol is, strictly speaking, not a logical, but a descriptive one [47] and hence would have to be introduced on the basis of the primitive descriptive predicates.)

That the extensional connections are admissible and even necessary (at least a sufficient selection of one or two of them by which the others can be defined if desired) is not in doubt. But whether or not they are sufficient, i.e., whether or not intensional connections are also desirable or perhaps necessary for the expressiveness of the language, is still discussed by logicians. I believe that we can dispense with them without making the language poorer.[48] However, the question is not important for our present problem concerning meaningfulness, because those who prefer not to introduce the connections of this kind, do not deny that they are meaningful.

---

[44] For the lack of better terms I keep Russell's terms "extensional" and "intensional"; it is to be noticed that here they have only the above given meaning, not the meaning they have in traditional philosophy.

[45] C. I. Lewis and C. H. Langford [1].

[46] Comp. Carnap [4], §69.

[47] Comp. Carnap [4], §50 and 62.

[48] Comp. Carnap [4], §70.

For the sake of simplicity we will not use intensional connections in language L.

Decision 4. The sentential connections in L are extensional. This decision seems to be justified by the fact that so far no concept needed for a language of science is known which could not be expressed in a language having extensional connections only; e.g., the concept of probability can also be expressed extensionally. Of course this decision is here made only for the language L as an object of our present considerations and does not at all intend to dispose of the whole problem. The restriction to extensional predicates was presupposed in our former definitions of "molecular form," "molecular predicate," "molecular sentence"; hence these definitions can now be applied to L.

Theorem 16. If the primitive predicates of a language are observable— as they are, e.g., in L according to Decision 1—the following is true. a. All molecular predicates are completely confirmable and all molecular sentences are bilaterally completely confirmable. b. If only test chains are admitted, as, e.g., in L in the case of Decision 3a—all molecular predicates are completely testable and all molecular sentences are bilaterally completely testable. This follows from Theorems 8 and 9 (§12).

A universal or existential sentence which is restricted to a finite field (as, e.g., the sentences constructed with restricted operators in the languages I and II dealt with in Carnap [4]) can be transformed into a conjunction or a disjunction respectively and therefore has the same character as a molecular sentence. It is also completely confirmable, if the predicates occurring are completely confirmable. If such sentences occurred in L it would be convenient to include them among the molecular sentences. But we will suppose that L does not contain sentences of this kind.

23. Molecular Languages

The fact that the molecular sentences are completely confirmable and, in the case of Decision 3a, also completely testable is an important advantage of these sentences over the essentially generalized sentences. Let us call a language limited to molecular sentences exclusively a *molecular language.* Such a language fulfills the requirements of confirmability and testability in its most radical form. Hence we understand the fact that certain epistemologists, especially positivists, propose or demand a molecular language as the language of science. We shall regard as examples the views of Russell, Wittgenstein, Schlick and Ramsey.

In a molecular language unrestricted universality cannot be expressed. Therefore, if such a language is chosen, we have to face the problem of how to deal with the physical laws. There seem to be in the main two possible ways. A law may be expressed in the form of a molecular sentence, namely, a restricted universal sentence or a conjunction, concerning those instances of the law which have been observed so far. On the other hand a law may be taken, not as a sentence, but as a rule of inference according to which one molecular sentence (e.g., a prediction about a future event) can be inferred from other ones (e.g., sentences about observed events). Each of these ways has actually been followed, as we shall see.

Russell asserts the following thesis in discussing the "question of the verifiability of physics" [49]: "Empirical knowledge is confined to what we actually observe." [50] This view is perhaps influenced by Mach's positivism.[51] If we wish to interpret this thesis we have to make it clearer by translating it from the material idiom into a formal (or a semi-formal) one (comp. §4): "The assertions of empirical science are confined to those sentences which are deducible from stated observation-sentences" (i.e., from sentences about actual observations). As this thesis is true for a molecular language of a certain kind, but not for a language containing physical laws in the form of unrestricted universal sentences, we may interpret Russell's view as presupposing a molecular language.

Wittgenstein, perhaps influenced by Mach and Russell, requires that every sentence must be completely verifiable.[52] Thus we might expect him to acknowledge as legitimate only a molecular language. And indeed he asserts that "propositions are truth-functions of elementary propositions," [53] "all propositions are results of truth-operations on the elementary propositions";[54] here truth-functions are conceived as not including general operators.[55] In consequence of this, Wittgenstein does not acknowledge physical laws as sentences in the proper sense, but takes them as rules for forming (or rather, stating) sentences, thus choosing the second of the two ways mentioned above. This view of Wittgenstein is reported by Schlick who is himself in agreement with it.[56]

Ramsey propounds a quite similar view, perhaps influenced by Wittgenstein. A universal sentence like "All men are mortal"—he calls it a variable hypothetical—is not a conjunction, because "it cannot be written out as one"; [57] "if then it is not a conjunction, it is not a proposition at all";[58] "variable hypo-

[49] Russell [2] p. 110.
[50] l. c., p. 112.
[51] Comp. l. c., p. 123.
[52] Comp. Waismann [1], p. 229.
[53] Wittgenstein [1], prop. 5, p. 103.
[54] l. c., prop. 5.3, p. 119.
[55] l. c., prop. 5.521, p. 135.
[56] Schlick [1], p. 150: "A definitive verification" of a natural law "is, strictly speaking, impossible"; it follows from this that a law, "logically considered, does not have the character of an assertion, for a genuine assertion must admit of being definitively verified." It follows from the fact "that one can never actually speak of an absolute verification of a natural law" that "a natural law essentially does not possess the logical character of an 'assertion,' but rather presents an 'instruction for the formation of assertions' (I am indebted to Ludwig Wittgenstein for these ideas and terms)" (l. c., p. 151). "Instructions of this kind occur grammatically in the guise of ordinary sentences." By this explanation, "the problem of induction becomes pointless," i.e., "the question of the logical justification of universal sentences about reality." "We recognize with Hume that there is no logical justification for them; there can be none because they are not genuine sentences. Natural laws are not 'general implications' (to use the language of the logician); because they cannot be verified for *all* cases; rather, they are prescriptions, rules of procedure for the investigator to discover true sentences" (l. c., p. 156).
[57] Ramsey [1], p. 237.
[58] l. c., p. 238.

theticals are not judgments but rules for judging 'If I meet a ϕ, I shall regard it as a ψ' ";[59] a variable hypothetical "is not strictly a proposition at all, but a formula from which we derive propositions." [60]

Previously, influenced also by Mach and Russell, I too accepted a molecular language.[61] According to the positivistic principle of testability in its most radical form, I restricted the atomic sentences to sentences about actual experiences. The laws of physics as well as all predictions were interpreted as records of present and (remembered) past experiences, namely those experiences from which the law or the prediction is usually said to be inferred by induction. Thus I followed the first of the two ways mentioned above; the physical laws also were interpreted as molecular sentences. At present I no longer hold this view. But I do not think—as Lewis and Schlick do—that it was false. I think it is true concerning a molecular language (of a special kind). But I was wrong in thinking that the language I dealt with was *the* language, i.e., the only legitimate language,—as Wittgenstein, Schlick and Lewis likewise seem to think concerning the language-forms accepted by them. Consequently I made the mistake of formulating my epistemological view in the form of an assertion—as most philosophers do—instead of in the form of a suggestion concerning the form of language. At present I think that the whole question is a matter of choice, of convention; and further, that a molecular language can be chosen as the language of science, but that a non-molecular, generalized one is much more suitable and, in addition, closer to the actual practice of science. This will soon be explained.

It may be mentioned that in the discussion about the logical foundations of mathematics, some finitists or intuitionists, e.g., Weyl, Brouwer and Kaufmann, sometimes express opinions which are related to those just quoted and which may be understood as arguing in favor of a molecular language. Thus for instance Kaufmann [62] rejects unrestricted universal sentences (except the *a priori* ones), because they are not verifiable. In Weyl's [63] opinion a pure existential judgment (as he calls it) is not a proper judgment, but a "judgment-abstract," similar to a description of a hidden treasure without indication of its place; and a universal judgment is not a proper judgment, but a rule for judgments ("Urteilsanweisung"). We will not analyse here the views of these authors in detail, because they are chiefly concerned with mathematics rather than empirical science.

24. The Critical Problem: Universal and Existential Sentences

So far we have considered the first kind of operations by which compound sentences may be constructed out of atomic sentences, namely, the construction of molecular sentences by the help of connections. Now we have to deal with the second kind of operations, namely, the construction of generalized sentences with the aid of universal and existential operators.

[59] l. c., p. 241.
[60] l. c., p. 251.
[61] Carnap [1].
[62] Kaufmann [1], p. 10.
[63] Weyl [1], p. 19.

We shall suppose, that no sentences occur in language L with finitely restricted operators or with free variables. As mentioned before, the former ones
have the same character as molecular sentences; the latter ones have the same
character as sentences with universal operators. For the sake of simplicity we
will consider in the following only operators of the lowest type, i.e., those with
individual variables, not with predicate- or functor-variables. The operators of
the lowest type are the most important ones in physics and generally in science;
and all fundamental problems of meaning, confirmation and testing discussed
in present philosophy already arise in connection with these operators. Accordingly the term "operator (in L)" is to be understood in the following as "operator
(not finitely restricted) with an individual variable."

The purpose of the following considerations is to enable us to decide
whether or not we will admit the application of operators in L and, if so, to what
extent. In the following, "M_1," "M_2," etc., are taken as molecular predicates. Any
molecular sentence can be transformed into (i.e., is equipollent to) a full sentence of a molecular predicate defined in a suitable way.

If we at all admit operators in L we may allow beside generalized sentences
of the simplest form, such as "$(x)M(x)$" and "$(\exists x)M(x)$," also those with a
more complicated form, as, e.g., "$(\exists x)(y)M_1(x,y)$" or "$(x)(\exists y)(z)M_2(x,y,z)$."
The last example corresponds to the English sentence (of L'): "For every point
x there exists a point y such that for every point z $M_2(x,y,z)$."

In Theorem 3, §6, we stated a certain relation between "$(x)P_1(x)$" (S_1)
and the full sentences of "P_1." Now the same relation subsists between
"$(x)(y)P_2(x,y)$" (S_2) and the full sentences of "P_2" because "$P_2(a,b)$" is a
consequence of "$(y)P_2(a,y)$"; this last is a consequence of S_2, so that "$P_2(a,b)$"
is itself a consequence of S_2, although S_2 is not a consequence of any finite
class of full sentences of "P_2." Furthermore, the relation which we stated in
Theorem 4 (§6) between "$(\exists x)P_1(x)$" (S_3) and the full sentences of "P_1"
also subsists between "$(\exists x)(\exists y)P_2(x,y)$" ($S_4$) and the full sentences of
"P_2"; for S_4 is a consequence of "$(\exists y)P_2(a,y)$," which is a consequence of
"$P_2(a,b)$," so that S_4 is a consequence of "$P_2(a,b)$," although $\sim S_4$ is not a
consequence of any finite class of negations of full sentences of "P_2." Thus we
see that for the question of confirmation a series of several operators of the
same kind—that is to say all of them universal or all of them existential—has
the same character as one operator of that kind.

First we will deal with only such generalized sentences of L as contain
molecular predicates only. A sentence of this kind is constructed out of molecular
predicates with the help of connections and operators. As is well-known such a
sentence can be transformed into the so-called normal form [64] consisting of an
operand which does not contain operators and is preceded by a series of operators without negation symbols. With the help of a molecular predicate defined
in a suitable way we may transform the operand into "$M(x, \ldots)$." We next divide the series of operators of such a sentence S into sub-series each containing
one or several operators of the same kind, that is to say, all of them universal or
all of them existential; we call these sub-series the operator sets of S. Finally,
we classify the sentences of the form described in the following way. The class

---

[64] Comp. Hilbert [1], p. 63; Carnap [4b], §34b, RR 9.

of those sentences which have n operator-sets is called U_n, if the first operator is a universal one, and E_n, if the first operator is an existential one. The class U_0 is the same as E_0; it is the class of the molecular sentences. Instead of "a sentence of the form U_n" we shall write shortly "a U_n"; and analogously "an E_n." A U_1 has one or more universal operators only, an E_1 one or more existential operators. To U_2 belong the sentences of the form "$(x) (\exists y) M(x,y)$," but likewise "$(x_1) (x_2) (\exists y_1) (\exists y_2) (\exists y_3) M(x_1, x_2, y_1, y_2, y_3)$," etc., and generally every sentence consisting of a set of universal operators succeeded by a set of existential operators and by a molecular operand. To U_3 belongs every sentence constructed in the following way: first a set of universal operators, then a set of existential operators, then a set of universal operators, and finally a molecular operand.

Theorem 17. If S is a U_{n+1}, the confirmation of S is incompletely reducible to that of certain E_n, and the confirmation of $\sim$S is completely reducible to that of each among certain U_n.

Proof. For n = o, this follows easily from Theorem 3 (§6). For n > o, let S be "$(x_1)(\exists x_2)(x_3) \ldots x_{n+1}) M(x_1, \ldots x_{n+1})$." We define "P" by "$P(x_1) \equiv (\exists x_2)(x_3) \ldots x_{n+1}) M(x_1, \ldots x_{n+1})$." Then S can be transformed into "$(x_1) P(x_1)$." Therefore, according to Theorem 3 (§6), the confirmation of S is incompletely reducible to that of the full sentences of "P"; and the confirmation of $\sim$S is completely reducible to anyone of their negations. Now a full sentence of "P," say "$P(a)$," can be transformed into "$(\exists x_2)(x_3) \ldots x_{n+1}) M(a, x_2, \ldots x_{n+1})$" and is therefore an E_n. "$\sim P(a)$" can be transformed into "$(x_2)(\exists x_3) \ldots x_{n+1}) [\sim M(a, x_2, \ldots x_{n+1})]$" and is therefore a U_n.

Theorem 18. If S is an E_{n+1}, the confirmation of S is completely reducible to that of each among certain U_n, and the confirmation of $\sim$S is incompletely reducible to that of certain E_n.

Proof. For n =o, this follows easily from Theorem 4 (§6). For n > o, let S be "$(\exists x_1)(x_2)(\exists x_3) \ldots x_{n+1}) M(x_1, \ldots x_{n+1})$." We define "P" by "$P(x_1) \equiv (x_2)(\exists x_3) \ldots x_{n+1}) M(x_1, \ldots x_{n+1})$." Then S can be transformed into "$(\exists x_1) P(x_1)$." Therefore, according to Theorem 4 (§6), the confirmation of S is completely reducible to that of any full sentence of "P"; and the confirmation of $\sim$S is incompletely reducible to that of the negations of the full sentences of "P." A full sentence "$P(a)$" can be transformed into "$(x_2)(\exists x_3) \ldots x_{n+1}) M(a, x_2, \ldots x_{n+1})$" and is therefore a U_n. "$\sim P(a)$" can be transformed into "$(\exists x_2)(x_3) \ldots x_{n+1}) [\sim M(a, x_2, \ldots x_{n+1})]$" and is therefore an E_n.

Theorem 19. If the primitive predicates of a language are observable—as they are, e.g., in L—and if S is a U_1, i.e., of the form "$(x) M(x)$," the following is true. a. S is incompletely confirmable and $\sim$S completely confirmable. b. If only test chains are admitted—as, e.g., in L in the case of Decision 3a—S is incompletely testable and $\sim$S completely testable. This follows from Theorem 3 (§6) and Theorem 16 (§22).

Theorem 20. If the primitive predicates of a language are observable—as they are, e.g., in L—and if S is an E_1, i.e., of the form "$(\exists x) M(x)$," the following is true. a. S is completely confirmable and $\sim$S incompletely confirmable. b. If only test chains are admitted—as, e.g., in L in the case of Decision 3a—S is completely testable and $\sim$S incompletely testable. This follows from Theorem 4 (§6) and Theorem 16 (§22).

The Theorems 19 and 20 correspond to the customary but not quite correct formulation: "a universal sentence is not verifiable but falsifiable; an existential sentence is verifiable but not falsifiable."

Theorem 21. If the primitive predicates of a language are observable—as they are, e.g., in L—and if S is a U_n or an E_n with $n > 1$, thus containing at least one universal operator and simultaneously at least one existential operator, the following is true. a. Both S and $\sim$S are incompletely confirmable, and hence S is bilaterally confirmable. b. If only test chains are admitted both S and $\sim$S are incompletely testable, and hence S is bilaterally testable. This follows from Theorems 17 and 18.

Thus we have seen that all generalized sentences of L of the forms described before are confirmable, and, in the case of Decision 3a, testable. The E_1 and the negations of U_1 are completely confirmable (or completely testable, respectively); all the other generalized sentences—provided they are essentially generalized—are only incompletely confirmable (or incompletely testable, respectively). No essentially generalized sentence is bilaterally completely confirmable or bilaterally completely testable.

25. The Scale of Languages

This being the case, how shall we decide about admitting of generalized sentences in the language L? This is the most critical question. In regard to it there are fundamental differences among philosophers, which are very sharply discussed. There is an infinite number of possible answers, i.e., of possible choices concerning the limitation of language. Among the possible language-forms we may choose the chief ones and order them in a series with regard to the highest degree of complexity admitted in them. But how may we determine this degree? It is natural to assume, if $m > n$, that a U_m is more complicated than a U_n, and an E_m as more so than an E_n. But how are we to decide the order of U_n with respect to E_n? We may do so by establishing the convention to take U_n as simpler than E_n. This convention is practically justified by the fact that some philosophers admit U_1 but not E_1, or U_2 but not E_2; the attempt to give theoretical reasons for this convention has been made by Popper, as we shall see. Thus we obtain a progression of languages L_0, L_1, etc., starting with the molecular language L_0 and going on to languages of greater and greater extentions. Every language in the table on page 183 contains the sentences of the previous languages and, in addition, the sentences of the class given in the second column. After this endless series we may put the language $L\infty$ which is to contain all the sentences of the languages of the series $L_0, L_1 \ldots L_n, \ldots$ (with finite n) but no others.

Note on L_0, molecular language. We have considered above some examples of philosophers who propose or require L_0, that is, who demand the limitation to molecular sentences. From our last considerations it is clear that to accept the requirement of complete confirmability or that of complete testability means to exclude generalized sentences and hence to state L_0. The step of dropping that requirement and choosing one of the wider languages instead of L_0 is a decisive one. One of the chief reasons in favour of this decision is the fact, that both methods of interpreting physical laws in the case of L_0 which we

Language	Sentences of maximal complexity admitted in L_n	
	Class	Example
L_0	U_0, E_0 (both molecular)	$M_1(a)$
L_1	U_1	$(x)M_1(x)$
L_2	E_1	$(\exists x)M_1(x)$
L_3	U_2	$(x)(\exists y)M_2(x,y)$
L_4	E_2	$(\exists x)(y)M_2(x,y)$
L_5	U_3	$(x)(\exists y)(z)M_3(x,y,z)$
L_6	E_3	$(\exists x)(y)(\exists z)M_3(x,y,z)$
.	.	.
.	.	.
.	.	.
$L\infty$	no maximal complexity; sentences of any such class with any number of operator sets are admitted.	

mentioned above (§23) are not very convenient for practical use and, above all, are not in close conformity with the actual method adopted by physicists. For in the first place, in actual practice laws are not dealt with as reports; and secondly, they are connected with one another or with singular sentences in a form of a disjunction or conjunction or implication or equivalence, etc.; in other words: they are manipulated like sentences, not like rules. (These reasons are not proofs for an assertion, but motives for a decision.)

I believe that Morris [65] is right in saying that by the step described, i.e., the adoption of a generalized language which is able to express physical laws in a satisfactory way, we ("logical positivists") come to a closer agreement with pragmatism. Morris [66] considers the two movements as complementary in their views, and as convergent in the directions of their present development.

Note on L_1. We may take Popper's [67] *principle of falsifiability* as an example of the choice of this language. Popper is however very cautious in the formulation of his limiting principle ("Abgrenzungskriterium"); he does not call the sentences E_1 meaningless, but only non-empirical and metaphysical. (Perhaps he wishes to exclude existential sentences and other metaphysical sentences ? P. 174 not from the language altogether, but only from the language of empirical science.) At first sight, universal and existential sentences seem to be coördinate with each other. In pure logic there is indeed a complete symmetry between them (principle of duality), but in epistemology, i.e., in applied logic considered from the point of view of confirmation and testing, there is difference [68] which has often been noticed. Also some intuitionists object more to existential than to universal sentences, and sometimes only to the former ones. Therefore they may

[65] Morris [1], p. 6.
[66] l. c., p. 1.
[67] Popper [1], pp. 12, 33.
[68] Popper ([1], chaps. II and IV) especially has emphasized the fact that for scientific testing falsifiability is more important than verifiability, and therefore (in our terminology:) sentences whose negations are completely confirmable are preferable to those whose negations are only incompletely confirmable though they are themselves completely confirmable, and hence U_1 preferable to E_1.

perhaps be taken as supporters of L_1. I [69] have stated a language which contains U_1 (with free variables, not with operators) but not E_1 and therefore may also be taken as an example of L_1; but this language has not been proposed as the language of science.

Note on L_3. While Popper in theory states the principle of falsifiability and in consequence takes the language-form L_1, in practice he seems to me to take the more liberal form L_3. He shows that probability-sentences are sentences of the form U_2 which he calls existential hypotheses ("Es-gibt-Hypothesen" [70]). He admits that probability-sentences are essential for physics, and therefore he includes them into the language of physics, which thus seem to have the form L_3. The way in which he tries to show that the admission of existential hypotheses is compatible with his requirement of falsifiability, is less important for our present consideration. He admits that they are neither falsifiable nor verifiable [71]—in our terminology: neither their negations nor they themselves are completely confirmable—but he tries to show that according to certain methodological rules they are manipulated like falsifiable sentences and actually are sometimes falsified.[72]

Note on $L\infty$. I am at present inclined to accept this most liberal form of language, including sentences with any number of operator-sets. If one sees, e.g., from Popper's explanations, how convenient and even essential the sentences U_2 are for physics, and if in consequence one decides to admit this form, then it seems rather arbitrary to limit the number of operator-sets to two or any fixed higher number and not to admit more complicated forms. It is true that the greater the number of operator-sets in a sentence S is, the greater is the distance of S from the empirical basis, i.e., from the atomic sentences, and hence the more indirect and incomplete is the possibility of confirming or testing S and $\sim$S. But there is no number of operator-sets for which the connection with the empirical basis would completely vanish. If operators once are admitted and thereby the requirement of complete confirmability or complete testability is dropped, there seems to me to be no natural limit at any finite number of operator-sets.

After any one of the languages $L_0, L_1 \ldots L\infty$ is chosen we may decide between Decision 3a and 3b (§21). In the case of Decision 3a all introductive chains are test chains and hence all predicates and all sentences of the language are *testable*. A language L_n restricted in this way may be designated by "L^t_n." Thus we have a second series of languages: $L^t_0, L^t_1, L^t_2, \ldots L^t\infty$.

1 C 2: Generalized Predicates. If we have a language in which operators are admitted then we may also admit them in definitions, i.e., state generalized definitions and general introductive chains containing such definitions.

We have considered so far only such generalized sentences as have a molecular operand. We did this for the sake of simplicity, because the definition of the

---

[69] Carnap [4], Language I.
[70] Popper [1], p 135.
[71] l. c., p. 134.
[72] l. c., pp. 140, 144.

single languages of the series L_0, L_1, etc., can be stated more easily in this case. But if we come to language $L\infty$ in which the use of operators is not limited then for this language we may also admit the occurrence of any number of generalized predicates in the operand.

26. Incompletely Confirmable Hypotheses in Physics

Now let us consider under what circumstances a physicist might find it necessary or desirable to state an hypothesis in a generalized form. Let us begin with one operator. The full sentences of a molecular predicate "M_1" (i.e., "M_1(a)," etc.) are bilaterally completely confirmable. Suppose some of them are confirmed by observations, but not the negation of any of them so far. This fact may suggest to the physicist the sentence "$(x)M_1(x)$" of U_1 as a physical law to be adopted, i.e., a hypothesis whose negation is completely confirmable and which leads to completely confirmable predictions as consequences of it (e.g., "$M_1(b)$," etc.) If more and more such predictions are confirmed by subsequent observations, but not the negation of any of them, we may say that the hypothesis, though never confirmed completely, is confirmed in a higher and higher degree.

Considerations of this kind are very common; they are often used in order to explain that the admission of not completely confirmable ("unverifiable") universal hypotheses does not infringe the principle of empiricism. Such considerations are, I think, agreed to by all philosophers except those who demand complete confirmability ("verifiability") and thereby the limitation to a molecular language.

Now it seems to me that a completely analogous consideration applies to sentences with any number of operator sets, i.e., to sentences of U_n or E_n for any n. The diagram on page 186 may serve as an example. A *broken* arrow running from a sentence S to a class C of sentences indicates that the confirmation of S is *incompletely* reducible to that of C. S is in this case a universal sentence and C the class of its instances; each sentence of C is therefore a consequence of S, but S is not a consequence of any finite sub-class of C. A *solid* arrow running from S_1 to S_2 indicates that the confirmation of S_1 is *completely* reducible to that of S_2. In this case, S_1 is an existential sentence and a consequence of S_2. The relation of reducibility of confirmation as indicated in the diagram is in accordance with Theorems 17 and 18 (§24), but, for these cases, can easily be seen by glancing at the sentences. At the left side are indicated the classes to which the sentences belong.

Let us start at the bottom of the diagram. The sentences of C_1 are molecular, and hence bilaterally completely testable. Let us suppose that a physicist confirms by his observations a good many of the sentences of C_1 without finding a confirmation for the negation of any sentence of C_1. According to the customary procedure described above, these experiences will suggest to him the adoption of S_1 as a well-confirmed hypothesis, which, by further confirmation of more and more sentences of C_1, may acquire an even higher degree of confirmation. Let us suppose that likewise the sentences of C_2 are confirmed by observations, further those of C_3, etc. Then the physicist will state S_2, S_3, etc., as well-confirmed hypotheses. If now sentences of the form E_2 are admitted in L, then the first sentence of C is a sentence of L, is also a consequence of S_1 and is therefore confirmed at least to the same degree as S_1. In order to make feasible the formulation of this well-confirmed hypothesis the physicist will be inclined to admit

U_4:
$$(x)P'(x)$$
$$(S':) \ (v)(\exists w)(x)(\exists y)(z)M'(v, w, x, y, z)$$

$$\downarrow$$

$$C'$$

E_4:
$$P'(d_1) \qquad\qquad P'(d_2) \quad P'(d_3)\ldots$$
$$(\exists w)(x)(\exists y)(z)M'(d_1, w, x, y, z)$$

$$\downarrow$$

U_3:
$$(x)(\exists y)(z)M'(d_1, e_1, x, y, z)$$
$$(x)P(x)$$
$$(S:) \ (x)(\exists y)(z)M(x, y, z)$$

$$\downarrow$$

$$C$$

E_2:
$$P(a_1) \qquad\qquad P(a_2) \qquad\qquad P(a_3)$$
$$(\exists y)(z)M(a_1, y, z) \quad (\exists y)(z)M(a_2, y, z) \quad (\exists y)(z)M(a_3, y, z)\ldots$$

$$\downarrow\qquad\qquad\downarrow\qquad\qquad\downarrow$$

U_1:
$$(S_1:)(z)M(a_1, b_1, z) \quad (S_2:)(z)M(a_2, b_2, z) \quad (S_3:)(z)M(a_3, b_3, z)\ldots$$

$$\downarrow\qquad\qquad\downarrow\qquad\qquad\downarrow$$

$$C_1 \qquad\qquad\qquad C_2 \qquad\qquad\qquad C_3$$

$U_0 (E_0)$:
(molecular)
$$M(a_1, b_1, c_1) \qquad M(a_2, b_2, c_2) \qquad M(a_3, b_3, c_3)$$
$$M(a_1, b_1, c_1') \qquad M(a_2, b_2, c_2') \qquad M(a_3, b_3, c_3') \qquad \ldots$$
$$M(a_1, b_1, c_1'') \qquad M(a_2, b_2, c_2'') \qquad M(a_3, b_3, c_3'')$$

the sentences of E_2 in L. If he does so he can go one step further. He will adopt the second sentence of C as a consequence of the stated hypothesis S_2, the third one as a consequence of S_3, etc. If now the sentences of a sufficient number of classes of the series C_1, C_2, etc., are confirmed by observations, the corresponding number of sentences of the series S_1, S_2, etc., and likewise of sentences of C will be stated as well-confirmed hypotheses. If we define "P" by "$P(x) \equiv (\exists y)(z) M(x,y,z)$," we may abbreviate the sentences of C by "$P(a_1)$," "$P(a_2)$," etc. The fact that these sentences are well-confirmed hypotheses will suggest to the physicist the sentence "$(x)P(x)$," that is S, as a hypothesis to be adopted provided he admits at all sentences of the form U_3 in L. The statement of S as confirmed by C is quite analogous to that of S_1 as confirmed by C_1. If somebody asserted that S— belonging to U_3—is meaningless while the sentences of C—belonging to E_2— are meaningful, he would thereby assert that it is meaningless to assume hypothetically that a certain condition which we have already assumed to subsist at several points a_1, a_2, a_3, etc., subsists at every point. Thus no reason is to be seen for prohibiting sentences of U_3, if sentences of E_2 are admitted.

This same procedure can be continued to higher and higher levels. Suppose that in the definition of "M" two individual constants occur, say "d_1" and "e_1"; then we may write S in the form "$(x) (\exists y) (z)M'(d_1,e_1,x,y,z)$." According to our previous supposition this is a hypothesis which is incompletely confirmed to a certain degree by our observations, namely, by the sentences of C_1, C_2, etc. Then the first sentence of C', being a consequence of S, is confirmed to at least the same degree. If we define "P'" by "$P' (v) \equiv (\exists w)(x)(\exists y)(z)M'(v,w,x,y,z)$" we may abbreviate the first sentence of C' by "$P'(d_1)$." Now let us suppose that analogous sentences for d_2, d_3, etc., are likewise found to be confirmed by our observations. Then by these sentences of C' (belonging to E_4) S' (belonging to U_5) is incompletely confirmed.

On the basis of these considerations it seems natural and convenient to make the following decisions.

Decision 5. Let S be a universal sentence (e.g., "$(x)Q(x)$")—which is being considered either for admission to or exclusion from L—and C be the class of the corresponding full sentences ("$Q(a_1)$," "$Q(a_2)$," etc.). Then obviously the sentences of C are consequences of S, and the confirmation of S is incompletely reducible to that of C. If the sentences of C are admitted in L we will admit the sentences of the form S, i.e., a class U_n for a certain n $(n > o)$.

Decision 6. Let S be an existential sentence (e.g., "$(\exists x)Q(x)$")— which is being considered either for admission to or exclusion from L—and C be the class of the corresponding full sentences ("$Q(a_1)$," "$Q (a_2)$," etc.) Then obviously S is a consequence of every sentence of C, and hence the confirmation of S is completely reducible to that of C. If the sentences of C are admitted in L we will admit the sentences of the form S, i.e., a class E_n for a certain n $(n > o)$.

The acceptance of Decisions 5 and 6 leads in the first place, as shown by the example explained before, to the admission of U_1, E_2, U_3, E_4, U_5, etc., in L; and it also leads to the admission of E_1, U_2, E_3, U_4, etc. Hence the result is the choice of a language $L\infty$ or, if Decision 3a is made, language $L\overset{t}{\infty}$.

As an objection to our proposal of language $L\infty$ the remark will perhaps be made that the statement of hypotheses of a high complexity, say U_{10} or E_{10}, will never be necessary or desirable in science, and that therefore we need not choose $L\infty$. Our reply is, that the proposal of $L\infty$ by no means requires the statement of hypotheses of such a kind; it simply proposes not to prohibit their statement *a priori* by the formative rules of the language. It seems convenient to give the scientist an open field for possible formulations of hypotheses. Which of these ad-mitted possibilities will actually be applied, must be learned from the further evolution of science,—it cannot be foreseen from general methodological considerations.

27. The Principle of Empiricism

It seems to me that it is preferable to formulate the principle of empiricism not in the form of an assertion—"all knowledge is empirical" or "all synthetic sentences that we can know are based on (or connected with) experiences" or the like—but rather in the form of a proposal or requirement. As empiricists, we require the language of science to be restricted in a certain way; we require that descriptive predicates and hence synthetic sentences are not to be admitted unless they have some connection with possible observations, a connection which has to be characterized in a suitable way. By such a formulation, it seems to me, greater clarity will be gained both for carrying on discussion between empiricists and anti-empiricists as well as for the reflections of empiricists.

We have seen that there are many different possibilities in framing an empiricist language. According to our previous considerations there are in the main four different requirements each of which may be taken as a possible formu-lation of empiricism; we will omit here the many intermediate positions which have been seen to consist in drawing a rather arbitrary boundary line.

RCT. Requirement of Complete Testability: "Every synthetic sentence must be completely testable." I.e., if any synthetic sentence S is given, we must know a method of testing for every descriptive predicate occurring in S so that we may determine for suitable points whether or not the predicate can be attributed to them; moreover, S must have such a form that at least certain sen-tences of this form can possibly be confirmed in the same degree as particular sentences about observable properties of things. This is the strongest of the four requirements. If we adopt it, we shall get a *testable molecular language* like L_0^t, i.e., a language restricted to molecular sentences and to test chains as the only introductive chains, in other words, to those reduction sentences whose first predicate is realizable.

RCC. Requirement of Complete Confirmability: "Every synthetic sentence must be completely confirmable." I.e., if any synthetic sentence S is given, there must be for every descriptive predicate occurring in S the possibility of our finding out for suitable points whether or not they have the property designated by the predicate in question; moreover, S must have a form such as is required in RCT, and hence be molecular. Thus the only difference between RCC and RCT concerns predicates. By RCC predicates are admitted which are introduced by the help of reduction sentences which are not test sentences. By the admission of the predicates of this kind the language is enlarged to a *confirmable molecular language* like L_0. The advantages of the admission of such predicates have been explained in §14. It seems however that there are not very many predicates of this kind in the language of science and hence that the practical difference between RCT and RCC is not very great. But the difference in the methodo-logical character of L_0^t and L_0 may seem important to those who wish to state RCT.

RT. Requirement of Testability: "Every synthetic sentence must be test-able." RT is more liberal than RCT, but in another direction than RCC. RCC and RT are incomparable inasmuch as each of them contains predicates not admitted in the other one. RT admits incompletely testable sentences—these are chiefly universal sentences to be confirmed incompletely by their instances—and thus leads to a *testable generalized language,* like L_∞^t. Here the new sentences in comparison with L_0^t are very many; among them are the laws of science in the form of unrestricted universal sentences. Therefore the difference of RCT and RT, i.e., of L_0^t and L_∞^t, is of great practical importance. The advantages of this comprehensive enlargement have been explained in §§25 and 26.

RC. Requirement of Confirmability: "Every synthetic sentence must be confirmable." Here both restrictions are dispensed with. Predicates which are confirmable but not testable are admitted; and generalized sentences are ad-mitted. This simultaneous enlargement in both directions leads to a *confirmable generalized language* like L_∞. L_∞ contains not only L_0^t but also L_0 and L_∞^t as proper sub-languages. RC is the most liberal of the four requirements. But it suf-fices to exclude all sentences of a non-empirical nature, e.g., those of transcenden-tal metaphysics, inasmuch as they are not confirmable, not even incompletely. Therefore it seems to me that RC suffices as a formulation of the principle of em-piricism; in other words, if a scientist chooses any language fulfilling this require-ment no objection can be raised against this choice from the point of view of empiricism. On the other hand, that does not mean that a scientist is not allowed to choose a more restricted language and to state one of the more restricting requirements for himself—though not for all scientists. There are no theoretical objections against these requirements, that is to say, objections condemning them as false or incorrect or meaningless or the like; but it seems to me that there are practical objections against them as being inconvenient for the purpose of science.

The following table shows the four requirements and their chief consequences.

Requirement	Restriction to *molecular* sentences	Restriction to *test* chains	Language
RCT: complete testability	+	+	L_0^t
RCC: complete confirmability	+	−	L_0
RT: testability	−	+	L_∞^t
RC: confirmability	−	−	L_∞

28. Confirmability of Predictions

Let us consider the nature of a *prediction,* a sentence about a future event, from the point of view of empiricism, i.e., with respect to confirmation and test-ing. Modifying our previous symbolism, we will take "c" as the name of a certain physical system, "x" as a corresponding variable, "t" as the time-variable, "t_0" as a value of "t" designating a moment at which we have made observations about c, and "d" as a constant designating a certain time interval, e.g., one day or one million years. Now let us consider the following sentences:

(S) $$(t)[P_1(c, t) \supset P_2(c, t + d)]$$

in words: "For every instant t, if the system c has the state P_1 at the time t, then it has the state P_2 at the time t + d";

(S_1) $$P_1(c, t_0)$$

"The system c has the state P_1 at the time t_0 (of our observation)";

(S_2) $$P_2(c, t_0 + d)$$

"The system c will have the state P_2 at the time $t_0 + d$." Now let us make the following suppositions. There is a set C of laws about physical systems of that kind to which c belongs such that S can be derived from C; the predicates occurring in the laws of C, and among them "P_1" and "P_2," are completely testable; the laws of C have been tested very frequently and each tested instance had a positive result; S_1 is confirmed to a high degree by observations. From these suppositions it follows that S_1 and S_2, having molecular form and containing only predicates which are completely testable, are themselves completely testable; that the laws of C are incompletely testable, but (incompletely) confirmed to a rather high degree; that S, being a consequence of C, is also confirmed to a rather high degree; that S_2, being a consequence of S and S_1, is also confirmed to a rather high degree. If we wait until the time $t_0 + d$ it may happen that we shall confirm S_2 by direct observations to a very high degree. But, as we have seen, a prediction like S_2 may have even at the present time a rather high degree of confirmation dependent upon the degree of confirmation of the laws used for the derivation of the prediction. The nature of a prediction like S_2 is, with respect to confirmation and testing, the same as that of a sentence S_3 about a past event not observed by ourselves, and the same as that of a sentence S_4 about a present event not directly observed by us, e.g., a process now going on in the interior of a machine, or a political event in China. S_3 and S_4 are like S_2, derived from sentences based on our direct observations with the help of laws which are incompletely confirmed to some degree or other by previous observations.[78]

To give an example, let c be the planetary system, C the set of the differential equations of celestial mechanics from which S may be derived by integration, S_1 describing the present constellation of c—the positions and the velocities of the bodies—and d the interval of one million years. Let "$P_3(t)$" mean: "There

---

[78] Reichenbach ([3], p. 153) asks what position the Vienna Circle has taken concerning the methodological nature of predictions and other sentences about events not observed, after it gave up its earlier view influenced by Wittgenstein (comp. §23). The view explained above is that which my friends—especially Neurath and Frank—and I have held since about 1931 (compare Frank [1], Neurath [3], Carnap [2a], pp. 443, 464f.; [2b], pp. 55f., 99f.).

are no living beings in the world at the time t," and consider the following sentence.

$$(S_5) \qquad\qquad P_3(t_0 + d) \supset P_2(c, t_0 + d)$$

meaning that if in a million years there will be no living beings in the world then at that time the constellation of the planetary system will be P_2 (i.e., that which is to be calculated from the present constellation with the help of the laws confirmed by past observations). S_5 may be taken as a convenient formulation of the following sentence discussed by Lewis [74] and Schlick:[75] "If all minds (or: living beings) should disappear from the universe, the stars would still go on in their courses." Both Lewis and Schlick assert that this sentence is not verifiable. This is true if "verifiable" is interpreted as "completely confirmable." But the sentence is confirmable and even testable, though incompletely. We have no well-confirmed predictions about the existence or non-existence of organisms at the time $t_0 + d$; but the laws C of celestial mechanics are quite independent of this question. Therefore, irrespective of its first part, S_5 is confirmed to the same degree as its second part, i.e., as S_2, and hence, as C. Thus we see that an indirect and incomplete testing and confirmation of S_2—and thereby of S_5—is neither logically nor physically nor even practically impossible, but has been actually carried out by astronomers. Therefore I agree with the following conclusion of Schlick concerning the sentence mentioned above (though not with his reasoning): "We are as sure of it as of the best founded physical laws that science has discovered." The sentence in question is meaningful from the point of view of empiricism, i.e., it has to be admitted in an empiricist language, provided generalized sentences are admitted at all and complete confirmability is not required. The same is true for any sentence about past, present or future events, which refers to events other than those we have actually observed, provided it is sufficiently connected with such events by confirmable laws.

The object of this essay is not to offer definitive solutions of problems treated. It aims rather to stimulate further investigation by supplying more exact definitions and formulations, and thereby to make it possible for others to state their different views more clearly for the purposes of fruitful discussion. Only in this way may we hope to develop convergent views and so approach the objective of *scientific empiricism* as a movement comprehending all related groups—the development of an increasingly scientific philosophy.

BIBLIOGRAPHY

For the sake of shortness, the following *publications* will be quoted by the here-given figures in square brackets.

Ayer, A. J.[*] [1] Language, Truth and Logic. London, 1936.

[74] Lewis [2], p. 143.
[75] Schlick [4], p. 367.

Bridgman, P. W. [1] The Logic of Modern Physics. New York, 1927.

Carnap, R. [1] Der logische Aufbau der Welt. Berlin (now F. Meiner, Leipzig), 1928.

[2a] Die physikalische Sprache als Universalsprache der Wissenschaft. Erkenntnis, 2, 1932.

[2b] (Translation:) The Unity of Science. Kegan Paul, London, 1934.

[3] Ueber Protokollsätze. Erkenntnis, 3, 1932.

[4a] Logische Syntax der Sprache. Springer, Wien, 1934.

[4b] (Translation) Logical Syntax of Language. Kegan Paul, London, 1937.

[5] Philosophy and Logical Syntax. Kegan Paul, London, 1935.

[6] Formalwissenschaft und Realwissenschaft. Erkenntnis, 5, 1935. (Congress [1]).

[7] Ein Gültigkeitskriterium für die Sätze der klassischen Mathematik. Monatsh. Math. Phys., 42, 1935.

[8] Les Concepts Psychologiques et les Concepts Physiques sont-ils Foncièrement Différents? Revue de Synthèse, 10, 1935.

[9] Wahrheit und Bewährung. In: Congress [3].

[10] Von der Erkenntnistheorie zur Wissenschaftslokig. In: Congress [3].

[11] Ueber die Einheitssprache der Wissenschaft. Logische Bemerkungen zur Enzyklopädie. In: Congress [3].

[12] Existe-t-il des prémisses de la science qui soient incontrôlables?

Congress [1] Einheit der Wissenschaft. Bericht über die Prager Vorkonferenz der Internationalen Kongresse für Einheit der Wissenschaft, Sept., 1934. Erkenntnis, 5, Heft 1–3, 1935.

*[2] Erster Internationaler Kongresse für Einheit der Wissenschaft (Congrès Internat. de Philos. Scientifique), Paris, 1935. [Report of Sessions.] Erkenntnis, 5, Heft 6, 1936.

*[3] Actes du Ier Congrès Internat. de Philos. Scientifique, Paris, 1935. 8 fasc. Hermann & Cie, Paris, 1936.

Ducasse, C. J. *[1] Verification, Verifiability and Meaningfulness. Journ. of Philos., 33, 1936.

Feigl, H. *[1] Sense and Nonsense in Scientific Realism. In: Congress [3].

Frank, Ph. [1] Das Kausalgesetz und seine Grenzen. Springer, Wien, 1932.

Hempel, C. G. [1] Beiträge zur logischen Analyse des Wahrsheinlichkeitsbegriff. Diss. Berlin, 1934.

[2] Ueber den Gehalt von Wahrscheinlichkeitsaussagen. Erkenntnis, 5, 1935.

[3] On the Logical Positivist's Theory of Truth. Analysis 2, 1935.

[4] Some Remarks on Empiricism. Analysis 3, 1936.

Hilbert, D., und Ackermann, W. [1] Grundzüge der theoretischen Logik. Springer, Berlin, 1928.

Kaufmann, F. [1] Das Unendliche in der Mathematik und seine Ausschaltung. Deuticke, Wein, 1930.

Lewis, C. I., [1] with Langford, C. H. Symbolic Logic. The Century Co., New York, 1932.

[2] Experience and Meaning. Philos. Review, 43, 1934.

Morris, Ch. W. [1] Philosophy of Science and Science of Philosophy. Philos. of Sc., 2, 1935.

[2]   The Concept of Meaning in Pragmatism and Logical Positivism. Proc. 8th Internat. Congr. Philos. (1934). Prague, 1936.

[3]   Semiotic and Scientific Empiricism. In: Congress [3].

Nagel, E. [1] Verifiability, Truth, and Verification. Journ. of Philos., 31, 1934.

*[2]   Impressions and Appraisals of Analytic Philosophy in Europe. Journ. of Philos., 33, 1936.

Ness, A.   *[1] Erkenntnis und wissenschaftliches Verhalten. Norske Vid.-Akad. II Hist.-Fil. Kl., No. 1. Oslo, 1936.

Neurath, O. [1] Physicalism. Monist, 41, 1931.

[2]   Physikalismus. Scientia, 50, 1931.

[3]   Soziologie im Physikalismus. Erkenntnis, 2, 1931.

[4]   Protokollsätze. Erkenntnis, 3, 1932.

[5]   Radikaler Physikalismus und "wirkliche Welt." Erkenntnis, 4, 1934.

[6]   Pseudorationalismus der Falsification. Erkenntnis, 5, 1935.

*[7]   Le Développement du Cercle du Vienne et l'Avenir de l'Empirisme Logique. Hermann, Paris, 1935.

*[8]   Einzelwissenschaften, Einheitswissenschaft, Pseudorationalismus. In: Congress [3].

Popper, K. [1] Logik der Forschung. Springer, Wien, 1935.

*[2]   Empirische Methode. In: Congress [3].

Ramsey, F. P. [1] General Propositions and Causality, 1929. Published posthumously in: The Foundations of Mathematics, and other Logical Essays, pp. 237–255. Harcourt, Brace, New York, 1931.

Reichenbach, H. [1] Wahrscheinlichkeitslehre. Sijthoff, Leyden, 1935.

*[2]   Ueber Induktion und Wahrscheinlichkeit. Erkenntnis, 5, 1935.

*[3]   Logistic Empiricism in Germany and the Present State of its Problems. Journ. of Philos., 33, 1936.

*[4]   L'Empirisme Logistique et la Désaggrégation de l'Apriori. In: Congress [3].

Russell, B. [1] see Whitehead.

[2]   Our Knowledge of the External World. Norton, New York, 1914.

Russell, L. J. [1] Communication and Verification. Proc. Arist. Soc., Suppl. vol. 13, 1934.

Schlick, M. [1] Die Kausalität in der gegenwärtigen Physik. Naturwiss., 19, 1931.

[2]   Ueber das Fundament der Erkenntnis. Erkenntnis, 4, 1934.

[3]   Facts and Propositions. Analysis, 2, 1935.

[4]   Meaning and Verification. Philos. Review, 45, 1936.

Stace, W. T. *[1] Metaphysics and Meaning. Mind, 44, 1935.

Stebbing, S. L. [1] Communication and Verification. Proc. Arist. Soc., Suppl. vol. 13, 1934.

Tarski, A. *[1] Der Wahrheitsbegriff in den formalisierten Sprachen. Stud. Philos., 1, 1936.

Waismann, F. [1] Logische Analyse des Wahrscheinlichkeitsbegriffs. Erkenntnis, 1, 1930.

Weyl, H. [1] Die heutige Erkenntnislage in der Mathematik. Symposion, 1, 1925; also published separately.

Whitehead, A. N., and Russell, B. [1] Principia Mathematica. (1910–12) 2d ed. Cambridge, 1925–1927.

Wittgenstein, L. [1] Tractatus Logico-Philosophicus. Harcourt, Brace, New York, 1922.

* Appeared after the writing of this essay.

ADDITIONS TO BIBLIOGRAPHY

[Addition 1950. We list here some later publication in which the same or closely related problems are discussed. Further bibliographical references are given in the books by Feigl & Sellers and by Pap mentioned below, and in *Revue Int. de Philos.*, January, 1950].

Ayer, A. J. [1], 2d ed., 1946.

————: *The Foundations of Empirical Knowledge*, New York, 1940.

Bergmann, G.: "Outline of an Empiricist Philosophy of Physics," *Amer. J. of Physics*, 11, 1943.

————: "Sense Data, Linguistic Convention, and Existence," *Phil. of Science*, 14, 1947.

Bridgman, P. W.: "Operational Analysis," *Phil. of Science*, 5, 1938.

Carnap, R.: "Truth and Confirmation" (1936, 1945) Reprinted in Feigl and Sellers, *Readings*.

————: *Logical Foundations of the Unity of Science* (vol. I, no. 1, of the *International Encyclopedia of Unified Science*), Chicago, 1938. (Also reprinted in Feigl and Sellers, *Readings*.)

————: *Foundations of Logic and Mathematics* (vol. I, no. 3 of the *Encyclopedia of Unified Science*), Chicago, 1939.

————: *Introduction to Semantics*, Cambridge, Mass., 1942.

————: *Logical Foundations of Probability*, Chicago, 1950.

Carnap, R.: "Empiricism, Semantics, and Ontology," *Revue Int. de Philos.*, 4, 1950.

Chisholm, R. M.: "The Contrary-to-Fact Conditional," *Mind*, 55, 1946. Reprinted in Feigl and Sellers, *Readings*.

————: "The Problem of Empiricism," *Journal of Phil.*, 45, 1948.

Church, A.: "Review of Ayer, *Language, Truth, and Logic*," 2d ed., *J. of Symbolic Logic*, 14, 1949.

Ducasse, C. J.: "Verification, Verifiability, and Meaningfulness," *J. of Phil.*, 33, 1936.

Feigl, H., and Sellars, W. S. (editors): *Readings in Philosophical Analysis*, New York, 1949.

Feigl, H.: "Operationism and Scientific Method," *Psychol. Review*, 52, 1945 (Reprinted in *Readings*).

————: "Logical Empiricism" (Reprinted in *Readings*).

————: "Existential Hypotheses; Realistic vs. Phenomenalistic Interpretations," *Phil. of Science*, 17, 1950.

————: "Logical Reconstruction: Realism and Pure Semiotic," *Phil. of Science*, 17, 1950.

————: "The Mind-Body Problem in the Development of Logical Empiricism," *Revue Int. de Phil.*, 4, 1950.

Goodman, N.: "The Problem of Counterfactual Conditionals," *J. of Phil.*, 44, 1947.

Hempel, C. G.: "Studies in the Logic of Confirmation," *Mind*, 54, 1945.

————: "Problems and Changes in the Empiricist Criterion of Meaning," *Revue Int. de Philos.*, 4, 1950.

————: *Principles of Concept Formation in the Empirical Sciences* (forthcoming volume of the *International Encyclopedia of Unified Science*).

Hempel, C. G., and Oppenheim, P.: "Studies in the Logic of Explanation," *Phil. of Science*, 15, 1948.

Kaplan, A.: "Definition and Specification of Meaning," *J. of Phil.*, 43, 1946.

Kaufmann, Felix: *Methodology of the Social Sciences*, Oxford University Press, 1944.

Lewis, C. I.: *An Analysis of Knowledge and Valuation*, La Salle, Ill., 1946.

————: "Prof. Chisholm and Empiricism," *J. of Phil.*, 45, 1948.

Margenau, H.: *The Nature of Physical Reality*, New York, 1950.

Mahlberg, H.: "Positivisme et Science," *Studia Philosophica*, 3, 1948.

Mises, R., von: *Kleines Lehrbuch des Positivismus*, The Hague (also Univ. of Chicago Press), 1939.

Morris, Charles: *Foundations of the Theory of Signs* (vol. I, no. 2, of the *International Encyclopedia of Unified Science*), Chicago, 1938.

————: *Signs, Language, and Behavior*, New York, 1946.

O'Connor, D. J.: "Some Consequences of Professor A. J. Ayer's Verification Principle," *Analysis*, 10, 1950.

Pap, A.: *Elements of Analytic Philosophy*, New York, 1949.

Reichenbach, H.: *Experience and Prediction*, Chicago, 1938.

————: *Symbolic Logic*, New York, 1947.

Russell, B.: *An Inquiry into Meaning and Truth*, New York, 1940.

————: *Human Knowledge; its Scope and Limits*, New York, 1948.

Schlick, M.: *Gesammelte Aufsätze*, Wien, 1938.

Sellars, W. S.: "Realism and the New Way of Words," *Philos. and Phenom. Research*, 8, 1948. (Also reprinted in Feigl and Sellars, *Readings*).

————: "Concepts as Involving Laws and Inconceivable without Them," *Phil. of Science*, 15, 1948.

Stace, W. T.: "Positivism," *Mind*, 53, 1944.

Waismann, F.: "Verifiability," *Proc. Arist. Soc.*, Suppl. 19, 1945.

9

W. V. O. Quine TWO DOGMAS
OF EMPIRICISM

This essay first appeared in *The Philosophical Review* in 1950. It became a subject of controversy immediately. At the time he wrote it, Quine was already well known as a logician and analytic philosopher with positivist sympathies. But, in this essay, he challenges two doctrines which many people feel are central to Logical Positivism: the analytic-synthetic distinction and the belief that there are propositions which future experience can never cause us to reject as false.

The analytic-synthetic distinction has a long history in modern philosophy. The contemporary distinction is foreshadowed in the writings of Leibniz, Hume, and Kant. Logical Positivism made the distinction between logically true and factually true assertions a cornerstone of their account of language. Quine raises a question of whether the distinction can ever be made.

The belief that there are certain propositions which no experience can ever lead us to reject is the second "dogma" of empiricism according to Quine. He argues that although there may be propositions whose truth we would abandon only as a last resort, there are nevertheless no propositions which could not in principle be upset by future experience.

Recommended further reading on the topics discussed by Quine includes the following:

Goodman, N.: "On Likeness of Meaning" in *Semantics and the Philosophy of Language*, L. Linsky (ed.).
Waismann, F.: "Analytic-Synthetic," in six parts, *Analysis*, 1949–1953.
White, M.: "The Analytic and Synthetic: An Untenable Dualism" in *John Dewey: Philosopher of Science and Freedom*, S. Hook (ed.).

See also the bibliographical footnotes on synonymity in Chapter XVII of Passmore's *A Hundred Years of Philosophy*.

Modern empiricism has been conditioned in large part by two dogmas. One is a belief in some fundamental cleavage between truths which are *analytic,* or grounded in meanings independently of matters of fact, and truths which are *synthetic,* or grounded in fact. The other dogma is *reductionism:* the belief that each meaningful statement is equivalent to some logical construct upon terms which refer to immediate experience. Both dogmas, I shall argue, are ill-founded. One effect of abandoning them is, as we shall see, a blurring of the supposed boundary between speculative metaphysics and natural science. Another effect is a shift toward pragmatism.

1. BACKGROUND FOR ANALYTICITY

Kant's cleavage between analytic and synthetic truths was foreshadowed in Hume's distinction between relations of ideas and matters of fact, and in Leibniz's distinction between truths of reason and truths of fact. Leibniz spoke of the truths of reason as true in all possible worlds. Picturesqueness aside, this is to say that the truths of reason are those which could not possibly be false. In the same vein we hear analytic statements defined as statements whose denials are self-contradictory. But this definition has small explanatory value; for the notion of self-contradictoriness, in the quite broad sense needed for this definition of analyticity, stands in exactly the same need of clarification as does the notion of analyticity itself. The two notions are the two sides of a single dubious coin.

Kant conceived of an analytic statement as one that attributes to its subject no more than is already conceptually contained in the subject. This formulation has two shortcomings: it limits itself to statements of subject-predicate form, and it appeals to a notion of containment which is left at a metaphorical level. But Kant's intent, evident more from the use he makes of the notion of analyticity than from his definition of it, can be restated thus: a statement is analytic when it is true by virtue of meanings and independently of fact. Pursuing this line, let us examine the concept of *meaning* which is presupposed.

Meaning, let us remember, is not to be identified with naming. Frege's example of "Evening Star" and "Morning Star," and Russell's of "Scott" and "the author of *Waverley,*" illustrate that terms can name the same thing but differ in meaning. The distinction between meaning and naming is no less important at the level of abstract terms. The terms "9" and "the number of the planets" name one and the same abstract entity but presumably must be regarded as unlike in meaning; for astronomical observation was needed, and not mere reflection on meanings, to determine the sameness of the entity in question.

The above examples consist of singular terms, concrete and abstract. With general terms, or predicates, the situation is somewhat different but parallel. Whereas a singular term purports to name an entity, abstract or concrete, a general term does not; but a general term is *true* of an entity, or of each of many, or of none. The class of all entities of which a general term is true is called the *extension* of the term. Now paralleling the contrast between the meaning of a singular term and the entity named, we must distinguish equally between the meaning of a general term and its extension. The general terms "creature with a heart" and "creature with kidneys," for example, are perhaps alike in extension but unlike in meaning.

Confusion of meaning with extension, in the case of general terms, is less common than confusion of meaning with naming in the case of singular terms. It is indeed a commonplace in philosophy to oppose intension (or meaning) to extension, or, in a variant vocabulary, connotation to denotation.

The Aristotelian notion of essence was the forerunner, no doubt, of the modern notion of intension or meaning. For Aristotle it was essential in men to be rational, accidental to be two-legged. But there is an important difference between this attitude and the doctrine of meaning. From the latter point of view it may indeed be conceded (if only for the sake of argument) that rationality is involved in the meaning of the word "man" while two-leggedness is not; but two-leggedness may at the same time be viewed as involved in the meaning of "biped" while rationality is not. Thus from the point of view of the doctrine of meaning it makes no sense to say of the actual individual, who is at once a man and a biped, that his rationality is essential and his two-leggedness accidental or vice versa. Things had essences, for Aristotle, but only linguistic forms have meanings. Meaning is what essence becomes when it is divorced from the object of reference and wedded to the word.

For the theory of meaning a conspicuous question is the nature of its objects: what sort of things are meanings? A felt need for meant entities may derive from an earlier failure to appreciate that meaning and reference are distinct. Once the theory of meaning is sharply separated from the theory of reference, it is a short step to recognizing as the primary business of the theory of meaning simply the synonymy of linguistic forms and the analyticity of statements; meanings themselves, as obscure intermediary entities, may well be abandoned.

The problem of analyticity then confronts us anew. Statements which are analytic by general philosophical acclaim are not, indeed, far to seek. They fall into two classes. Those of the first class, which may be called *logically true,* are typified by:

(1)   No unmarried man is married.

The relevant feature of this example is that it not merely is true as it stands, but remains true under any and all reinterpretations of "man" and "married." If we suppose a prior inventory of *logical* particles, comprising "no," "un-," "not," "if," "then," "and," etc., then in general a logical truth is a statement which is true and remains true under all reinterpretations of its components other than the logical particles.

But there is also a second class of analytic statements, typified by:

(2)   No bachelor is married.

The characteristic of such a statement is that it can be turned into a logical truth by putting synonyms for synonyms; thus (2) can be turned into (1) by putting "unmarried man" for its synonym "bachelor." We still lack a proper character-ization of this second class of analytic statements, and therewith of analyticity generally, inasmuch as we have had in the above description to lean on a notion of "synonymy" which is no less in need of clarification than analyticity itself.

In recent years Carnap has tended to explain analyticity by appeal to what he calls state-descriptions. A state-description is any exhaustive assignment of truth values to the atomic, or noncompound, statements of the language. All other statements of the language are, Carnap assumes, built up of their com-ponent clauses by means of the familiar logical devices, in such a way that the truth value of any complex statement is fixed for each state-description by specifiable logical laws. A statement is then explained as analytic when it comes out true under every state description. This account is an adaptation of Leibniz's "true in all possible worlds." But note that this version of analyticity serves its purpose only if the atomic statements of the language are, unlike "John is a bachelor" and "John is married," mutually independent. Otherwise there would be a state-description which assigned truth to "John is a bachelor" and to "John is married," and consequently "No bachelors are married" would turn out syn-thetic rather than analytic under the proposed criterion. Thus the criterion of analyticity in terms of state-descriptions serves only for languages devoid of extralogical synonym-pairs, such as "bachelor" and "unmarried man"—synonym-pairs of the type which give rise to the "second class" of analytic statements. The criterion in terms of state-descriptions is a reconstruction at best of logical truth, not of analyticity.

I do not mean to suggest that Carnap is under any illusions on this point. His simplified model language with its state-descriptions is aimed primarily not at the general problem of analyticity but at another purpose, the clarification of probability and induction. Our problem, however, is analyticity; and here the major difficulty lies not in the first class of analytic statements, the logical truths, but rather in the second class, which depends on the notion of synonymy.

2. DEFINITION

There are those who find it soothing to say that the analytic statements of the second class reduce to those of the first class, the logical truths, by *definition;* "bachelor," for example, is *defined* as "unmarried man." But how do we find that "bachelor" is defined as "unmarried man"? Who defined it thus, and when? Are we to appeal to the nearest dictionary, and accept the lexicographer's formu-lation as law? Clearly this would be to put the cart before the horse. The lexicographer is an empirical scientist, whose business is the recording of ante-cedent facts; and if he glosses "bachelor" as "unmarried man" it is because of his belief that there is a relation of synonymy between those forms, implicit in general or preferred usage prior to his own work. The notion of synonymy pre-supposed here has still to be clarified, presumably in terms relating to linguistic behavior. Certainly the "definition" which is the lexicographer's report of an observed synonymy cannot be taken as the ground of the synonymy.

Definition is not, indeed, an activity exclusively of philologists. Philosophers and scientists frequently have occasion to "define" a recondite term by para-phrasing it into terms of a more familiar vocabulary. But ordinarily such a definition, like the philologist's, is pure lexicography, affirming a relation of synonymy antecedent to the exposition in hand.

Just what it means to affirm synonymy, just what the interconnections may be which are necessary and sufficient in order that two linguistic forms be properly describable as synonymous, is far from clear; but, whatever these interconnections may be, ordinarily they are grounded in usage. Definitions reporting selected instances of synonymy come then as reports upon usage.

There is also, however, a variant type of definitional activity which does not limit itself to the reporting of preëxisting synonymies. I have in mind what Carnap calls *explication*—an activity to which philosophers are given, and scientists also in their more philosophical moments. In explication the purpose is not merely to paraphrase the definiendum into an outright synonym, but actually to improve upon the definiendum by refining or supplementing its meaning. But even explication, though not merely reporting a preëxisting synonymy between definiendum and definiens, does rest nevertheless on *other* preëxisting synonymies. The matter may be viewed as follows. Any word worth explicating has some contexts which, as wholes, are clear and precise enough to be useful; and the purpose of explication is to preserve the usage of these favored contexts while sharpening the usage of other contexts. In order that a given definition be suitable for purposes of explication, therefore, what is required is not that the definiendum in its antecedent usage be synonymous with the definiens, but just that each of these favored contexts of the definiendum, taken as a whole in its antecedent usage, be synonymous with the corresponding context of the definiens.

Two alternative definientia may be equally appropriate for the purposes of a given task of explication and yet not be synonymous with each other; for they may serve interchangeably within the favored contexts but diverge elsewhere. By cleaving to one of these definientia rather than the other, a definition of explicative kind generates, by fiat, a relation of synonymy between definiendum and definiens which did not hold before. But such a definition still owes its explicative function, as seen, to preëxisting synonymies.

There does, however, remain still an extreme sort of definition which does not hark back to prior synonymies at all: namely, the explicitly conventional introduction of novel notations for purposes of sheer abbreviation. Here the definiendum becomes synonymous with the definiens simply because it has been created expressly for the purpose of being synonymous with the definiens. Here we have a really transparent case of synonymy created by definition; would that all species of synonymy were as intelligible. For the rest, definition rests on synonymy rather than explaining it.

The word "definition" has come to have a dangerously reassuring sound, owing no doubt to its frequent occurrence in logical and mathematical writings. We shall do well to digress now into a brief appraisal of the role of definition in formal work.

In logical and mathematical systems either of two mutually antagonistic types of economy may be striven for, and each has its peculiar practical utility. On the one hand we may seek economy of practical expression—ease and brevity in the statement of multifarious relations. This sort of economy calls usually for distinctive concise notations for a wealth of concepts. Second, however, and oppositely, we may seek economy in grammar and vocabulary; we may try to find a minimum of basic concepts such that, once a distinctive notation has been appropriated to each of them, it becomes possible to express any desired further concept by mere combination and iteration of our basic notations. This second sort of economy is impractical in one way, since a poverty in basic idioms tends to a necessary lengthening of discourse. But it is practical in another way: it greatly simplifies theoretical discourse *about* the language, through minimizing the terms and the forms of construction wherein the language consists.

Both sorts of economy, though prima facie incompatible, are valuable in their separate ways. The custom has consequently arisen of combining both sorts of economy by forging in effect two languages, the one a part of the other. The inclusive language, though redundant in grammar and vocabulary, is economical in message lengths, while the part, called primitive notation, is economical in grammar and vocabulary. Whole and part are correlated by rules of translation whereby each idiom not in primitive notation is equated to some complex built up of primitive notation. These rules of translation are the so-called *definitions* which appear in formalized systems. They are best viewed not as adjuncts to one language but as correlations between two languages, the one a part of the other.

But these correlations are not arbitrary. They are supposed to show how the primitive notations can accomplish all purposes, save brevity and convenience, of the redundant language. Hence the definiendum and its definiens may be expected, in each case, to be related in one or another of the three ways lately noted. The definiens may be a faithful paraphrase of the definiendum into the narrower notation, preserving a direct synonymy[1] as of antecedent usage; or the definiens may, in the spirit of explication, improve upon the antecedent usage of the definiendum; or finally, the definiendum may be a newly created notation, newly endowed with meaning here and now.

In formal and informal work alike, thus, we find that definition—except in the extreme case of the explicitly conventional introduction of new notations —hinges on prior relations of synonymy. Recognizing then that the notion of definition does not hold the key to synonymy and analyticity, let us look further into synonymy and say no more of definition.

3. INTERCHANGEABILITY

A natural suggestion, deserving close examination, is that the synonymy of two linguistic forms consists simply in their interchangeability in all contexts without change of truth value—interchangeability, in Leibniz's phrase, *salva veritate*. Note that synonyms so conceived need not even be free from vagueness, as long as the vaguenesses match.

But it is not quite true that the synonyms "bachelor" and "unmarried man" are everywhere interchangeable *salva veritate*. Truths which become false under

---

[1] According to an important variant sense of "definition," the relation preserved may be the weaker relation of mere agreement in reference. But definition in this sense is better ignored in the present connection, being irrelevant to the question of synonymy.

substitution of "unmarried man" for "bachelor" are easily constructed with the help of "bachelor of arts" or "bachelor's buttons"; also with the help of quotation, thus:

"Bachelor" has less than ten letters.

Such counterinstances can, however, perhaps be set aside by treating the phrases "bachelor of arts" and "bachelor's buttons" and the quotation "bachelor" each as a single indivisible word and then stipulating that the interchangeability *salva veritate* which is to be the touchstone of synonymy is not supposed to apply to fragmentary occurrences inside of a word. This account of synonymy, supposing it acceptable on other counts, has indeed the drawback of appealing to a prior conception of "word" which can be counted on to present difficulties of formulation in its turn. Nevertheless some progress might be claimed in having reduced the problem of synonymy to a problem of wordhood. Let us pursue this line a bit, taking "word" for granted.

The question remains whether interchangeability *salva veritate* (apart from occurrences within words) is a strong enough condition for synonymy, or whether, on the contrary, some heteronymous expressions might be thus interchangeable. Now let us be clear that we are not concerned here with synonymy in the sense of complete identity in psychological associations or poetic quality; indeed no two expressions are synonymous in such a sense. We are concerned only with what may be called *cognitive* synonymy. Just what this is cannot be said without successfully finishing the present study; but we know something about it from the need which arose for it in connection with analyticity in §1. The sort of synonymy needed there was merely such that any analytic statement could be turned into a logical truth by putting synonyms for synonyms. Turning the tables and assuming analyticity, indeed, we could explain cognitive synonymy of terms as follows (keeping to the familiar example): to say that "bachelor" and "unmarried man" are cognitively synonymous is to say no more nor less than that the statement:

(3)   All and only bachelors are unmarried men

is analytic.[2]

What we need is an account of cognitive synonymy not presupposing analyticity—if we are to explain analyticity conversely with help of cognitive synonymy as undertaken in §1. And indeed such an independent account of cognitive synonymy is at present up for consideration, namely, interchangeability *salva veritate* everywhere except within words. The question before us, to resume the thread at last, is whether such interchangeability is a sufficient

---

[2] This is cognitive synonymy in a primary, broad sense. Carnap and Lewis have suggested how, once this notion is at hand, a narrower sense of cognitive synonymy which is preferable for some purposes can in turn be derived. But this special ramification of concept-building lies aside from the present purposes and must not be confused with the broad sort of cognitive synonymy here concerned.

condition for cognitive synonymy. We can quickly assure ourselves that it is, by examples of the following sort. The statement:

(4)   Necessarily all and only bachelors are bachelors

is evidently true, even supposing "necessarily" so narrowly construed as to be truly applicable only to analytic statements. Then, if "bachelor" and "unmarried man" are interchangeable *salva veritate,* the result:

(5)   Necessarily all and only bachelors are unmarried men

of putting "unmarried man" for an occurrence of "bachelor" in (4) must, like (4), be true. But to say that (5) is true is to say that (3) is analytic, and hence that "bachelor" and "unmarried man" are cognitively synonymous.

Let us see what there is about the above argument that gives it its air of hocus-pocus. The condition of interchangeability *salva veritate* varies in its force with variations in the richness of the language at hand. The above argument supposes we are working with a language rich enough to contain the adverb "necessarily," this adverb being so construed as to yield truth when and only when applied to an analytic statement. But can we condone a language which contains such an adverb? Does the adverb really make sense? To suppose that it does is to suppose that we have already made satisfactory sense of "analytic." Then what are we so hard at work on right now?

Our argument is not flatly circular, but something like it. It has the form, figuratively speaking, of a closed curve in space.

Interchangeability *salva veritate* is meaningless until relativized to a language whose extent is specified in relevant respects. Suppose now we consider a language containing just the following materials. There is an indefinitely large stock of one-place predicates (for example, "*F*" where "*Fx*" means that *x* is a man) and many-place predicates (for example, "*G*" where "*Gxy*" means that *x* loves *y*), mostly having to do with extralogical subject matter. The rest of the language is logical. The atomic sentences consist each of a predicate followed by one or more variables "*x*," "*y*," etc.; and the complex sentences are built up of the atomic ones by truth functions ("not," "and," "or," etc.) and quantification. In effect such a language enjoys the benefits also of descriptions and indeed singular terms generally, these being contextually definable in known ways. Even abstract singular terms naming classes, classes of classes, etc., are contextually definable in case the assumed stock of predicates includes the two-place predicate of class membership. Such a language can be adequate to classical mathematics and indeed to scientific discourse generally, except in so far as the latter involves debatable devices such as contrary-to-fact conditionals or modal adverbs like "necessarily." Now a language of this type is extensional, in this sense: any two predicates which agree extensionally (that is, are true of the same objects) are interchangeable *salva veritate.*

In an extensional language, therefore, interchangeability *salva veritate* is no assurance of cognitive synonymy of the desired type. That "bachelor" and "unmarried man" are interchangeable *salva veritate* in an extensional language assures us of no more than that (3) is true. There is no assurance here that the extensional agreement of "bachelor" and "unmarried man" rests on meaning rather than merely on accidental matters of fact, as does the extensional agreement of "creature with a heart" and "creature with kidneys."

For most purposes extensional agreement is the nearest approximation to synonymy we need care about. But the fact remains that extensional agreement falls far short of cognitive synonymy of the type required for explaining analyticity in the manner of §1. The type of cognitive synonymy required there is such as to equate the synonymy of "bachelor" and "unmarried man" with the analyticity of (3), not merely with the truth of (3).

So we must recognize that interchangeability *salva veritate,* if construed in relation to an extensional language, is not a sufficient condition of cognitive synonymy in the sense needed for deriving analyticity in the manner of §1. If a language contains an intensional adverb "necessarily" in the sense lately noted, or other particles to the same effect, then interchangeability *salva veritate* in such a language does afford a sufficient condition of cognitive synonymy; but such a language is intelligible only in so far as the notion of analyticity is already understood in advance.

The effort to explain cognitive synonymy first, for the sake of deriving analyticity from it afterward as in §1, is perhaps the wrong approach. Instead we might try explaining analyticity somehow without appeal to cognitive synonymy. Afterward we could doubtless derive cognitive synonymy from analyticity satisfactorily enough if desired. We have seen that cognitive synonymy of "bachelor" and "unmarried man" can be explained as analyticity of (3). The same explanation works for any pair of one-place predicates, of course, and it can be extended in obvious fashion to many-place predicates. Other syntactical categories can also be accommodated in fairly parallel fashion. Singular terms may be said to be cognitively synonymous when the statement of identity formed by putting "=" between them is analytic. Statements may be said simply to be cognitively synonymous when their biconditional (the result of joining them by "if and only if") is analytic.[3] If we care to lump all categories into a single formulation, at the expense of assuming again the notion of "word" which was appealed to early in this section, we can describe any two linguistic forms as cognitively synonymous when the two forms are interchangeable (apart from occurrences within "words") *salva* (no longer *veritate* but) *analyticitate.* Certain technical questions arise, indeed, over cases of ambiguity or homonymy; let us not pause for them, however, for we are already digressing. Let us rather turn our backs on the problem of synonymy and address ourselves anew to that of analyticity.

4. SEMANTIC RULES

Analyticity at first seemed most naturally definable by appeal to a realm of meanings. On refinement, the appeal to meanings gave way to an appeal to synonymy or definition. But definition turned out to be a will-o'-the-wisp, and

---

[3] The "if and only if" itself is intended in the truth functional sense.

synonymy turned out to be best understood only by dint of a prior appeal to analyticity itself. So we are back at the problem of analyticity.

I do not know whether the statement "Everything green is extended" is analytic. Now does my indecision over this example really betray an incomplete understanding, an incomplete grasp of the "meanings," of "green" and "extended"? I think not. The trouble is not with "green" or "extended," but with "analytic."

It is often hinted that the difficulty in separating analytic statements from synthetic ones in ordinary language is due to the vagueness of ordinary language and that the distinction is clear when we have a precise artificial language with explicit "semantical rules." This, however, as I shall now attempt to show, is a confusion.

The notion of analyticity about which we are worrying is a purported relation between statements and languages: a statement S is said to be *analytic for* a language L, and the problem is to make sense of this relation generally, that is, for variable "S" and "L." The gravity of this problem is not perceptibly less for artificial languages than for natural ones. The problem of making sense of the idiom "S is analytic for L," with variable "S" and "L," retains its stubbornness even if we limit the range of the variable "L" to artificial languages. Let me now try to make this point evident.

For artificial languages and semantical rules we look naturally to the writings of Carnap. His semantical rules take various forms, and to make my point I shall have to distinguish certain of the forms. Let us suppose, to begin with, an artificial language L_0 whose semantical rules have the form explicitly of a specification, by recursion or otherwise, of all the analytic statements of L_0. The rules tell us that such and such statements, and only those, are the analytic statements of L_0. Now here the difficulty is simply that the rules contain the word "analytic," which we do not understand! We understand what expressions the rules attribute analyticity to, but we do not understand what the rules attribute to those expressions. In short, before we can understand a rule which begins "A statement S is analytic for language L_0 if and only if . . . ," we must understand the general relative term "analytic for"; we must understand "S is analytic for L" where "S" and "L" are variables.

Alternatively we may, indeed, view the so-called rule as a conventional definition of a new simple symbol "analytic-for-L_0," which might better be written untendentiously as "K" so as not to seem to throw light on the interesting word "analytic." Obviously any number of classes K, M, N, etc. of statements of L_0 can be specified for various purposes or for no purpose; what does it mean to say that K, as against M, N, etc., is the class of the "analytic" statements of L_0?

By saying what statements are analytic for L_0 we explain "analytic-for-L_0" but not "analytic," not "analytic for." We do not begin to explain the idiom "S is analytic for L" with variable "S" and "L," even if we are content to limit the range of "L" to the realm of artificial languages.

Actually we do know enough about the intended significance of "analytic" to know that analytic statements are supposed to be true. Let us then turn to a second form of semantical rule, which says not that such and such statements are analytic but simply that such and such statements are included among the truths. Such a rule is not subject to the criticism of containing the un-understood word "analytic"; and we may grant for the sake of argument that there is no difficulty over the broader term "true." A semantical rule of this second type, a rule of truth, is not supposed to specify all the truths of the language; it merely stipulates, recursively or otherwise, a certain multitude of statements which, along with others unspecified, are to count as true. Such a rule may be conceded to be quite clear. Derivatively, afterward, analyticity can be demarcated thus: a statement is analytic if it is (not merely true but) true according to the semantical rule.

Still there is really no progress. Instead of appealing to an unexplained word "analytic," we are now appealing to an unexplained phrase "semantical rule." Not every true statement which says that the statements of some class are true can count as a semantical rule—otherwise all truths would be "analytic" in the sense of being true according to semantical rules. Semantical rules are distinguishable, apparently, only by the fact of appearing on a page under the heading "Semantical Rules"; and this heading is itself then meaningless.

We can say indeed that a statement is *analytic-for-L_0* if and only if it is true according to such and such specifically appended "semantical rules," but then we find ourselves back at essentially the same case which was originally discussed: "S is analytic-for-L_0 if and only if. . . ." Once we seek to explain "S is analytic for L" generally for variable "L" (even allowing limitation of "L" to artificial languages), the explanation "true according to the semantical rules of L" is unavailing; for the relative term "semantical rule of" is as much in need of clarification, at least, as "analytic for."

It may be instructive to compare the notion of semantical rule with that of postulate. Relative to a given set of postulates, it is easy to say what a postulate is: it is a member of the set. Relative to a given set of semantical rules, it is equally easy to say what a semantical rule is. But given simply a notation, mathematical or otherwise, and indeed as thoroughly understood a notation as you please in point of the translations or truth conditions of its statements, who can say which of its true statements rank as postulates? Obviously the question is meaningless—as meaningless as asking which points in Ohio are starting points. Any finite (or effectively specifiable infinite) selection of statements (preferably true ones, perhaps) is as much *a* set of postulates as any other. The word "postulate" is significant only relative to an act of inquiry; we apply the word to a set of statements just in so far as we happen, for the year or the moment, to be thinking of those statements in relation to the statements which can be reached from them by some set of transformations to which we have seen fit to direct our attention. Now the notion of semantical rule is as sensible and meaningful as that of postulate, if conceived in a similarly relative spirit—relative, this time, to one or another particular enterprise of schooling unconversant persons in sufficient conditions for truth of statements of some natural or artificial language L. But from this point of view no one signalization of a subclass of the truths of L is intrinsically more a semantical rule than another; and, if "analytic" means "true by semantical rules," no one truth of L is analytic to the exclusion of another.[4]

---

[4] The foregoing paragraph was not part of the present essay as originally published. It was prompted by R. M. Martin.

It might conceivably be protested that an artificial language *L* (unlike a natural one) is a language in the ordinary sense *plus* a set of explicit semantical rules—the whole constituting, let us say, an ordered pair; and that the semantical rules of *L* then are specifiable simply as the second component of the pair *L*. But, by the same token and more simply, we might construe an artificial language *L* outright as an ordered pair whose second component is the class of its analytic statements; and then the analytic statements of *L* become specifiable simply as the statements in the second component of *L*. Or better still, we might just stop tugging at our bootstraps altogether.

Not all the explanations of analyticity known to Carnap and his readers have been covered explicitly in the above considerations, but the extension to other forms is not hard to see. Just one additional factor should be mentioned which sometimes enters: sometimes the semantical rules are in effect rules of translation into ordinary language, in which case the analytic statements of the artificial language are in effect recognized as such from the analyticity of their specified translations in ordinary language. Here certainly there can be no thought of an illumination of the problem of analyticity from the side of the artificial language.

From the point of view of the problem of analyticity the notion of an artificial language with semantical rules is a *feu follet par excellence*. Semantical rules determining the analytic statements of an artificial language are of interest only in so far as we already understand the notion of analyticity; they are of no help in gaining this understanding.

Appeal to hypothetical languages of an artificially simple kind could conceivably be useful in clarifying analyticity, if the mental or behavioral or cultural factors relevant to analyticity—whatever they may be—were somehow sketched into the simplified model. But a model which takes analyticity merely as an irreducible character is unlikely to throw light on the problem of explicating analyticity.

It is obvious that truth in general depends on both language and extralinguistic fact. The statement "Brutus killed Caesar" would be false if the world had been different in certain ways, but it would also be false if the word "killed" happened rather to have the sense of "begat." Thus one is tempted to suppose in general that the truth of a statement is somehow analyzable into a linguistic component and a factual component. Given this supposition, it next seems reasonable that in some statements the factual component should be null; and these are the analytic statements. But, for all its a priori reasonableness, a boundary between analytic and synthetic statements simply has not been drawn. That there is such a distinction to be drawn at all is an unempirical dogma of empiricists, a metaphysical article of faith.

5. THE VERIFICATION THEORY AND REDUCTIONISM

In the course of these somber reflections we have taken a dim view first of the notion of meaning, then of the notion of cognitive synonymy, and finally of the notion of analyticity. But what, it may be asked, of the verification theory of meaning? This phrase has established itself so firmly as a catchword of empiricism that we should be very unscientific indeed not to look beneath it for a possible key to the problem of meaning and the associated problems.

The verification theory of meaning, which has been conspicuous in the literature from Peirce onward, is that the meaning of a statement is the method of empirically confirming or infirming it. An analytic statement is that limiting case which is confirmed no matter what.

As urged in §1, we can as well pass over the question of meanings as entities and move straight to sameness of meaning, or synonymy. Then what the verification theory says is that statements are synonymous if and only if they are alike in point of method of empirical confirmation or infirmation.

This is an account of cognitive synonymy not of linguistic forms generally, but of statements.[5] However, from the concept of synonymy of statements we could derive the concept of synonymy for other linguistic forms, by considerations somewhat similar to those at the end of §3. Assuming the notion of "word," indeed, we could explain any two forms as synonymous when the putting of the one form for an occurrence of the other in any statement (apart from occurrences within "words") yields a synonymous statement. Finally, given the concept of synonymy thus for linguistic forms generally, we could define analyticity in terms of synonymy and logical truth as in §1. For that matter, we could define analyticity more simply in terms of just synonymy of statements together with logical truth; it is not necessary to appeal to synonymy of linguistic forms other than statements. For a statement may be described as analytic simply when it is synonymous with a logically true statement.

So, if the verification theory can be accepted as an adequate account of statement synonymy, the notion of analyticity is saved after all. However, let us reflect. Statement synonymy is said to be likeness of method of empirical confirmation or infirmation. Just what are these methods which are to be compared for likeness? What, in other words, is the nature of the relation between a statement and the experiences which contribute to or detract from its confirmation?

The most naïve view of the relation is that it is one of direct report. This is *radical reductionism*. Every meaningful statement is held to be translatable into a statement (true or false) about immediate experience. Radical reductionism, in one form or another, well antedates the verification theory of meaning explicitly so called. Thus Locke and Hume held that every idea must either originate directly in sense experience or else be compounded of ideas thus originating; and taking a hint from Tooke we might rephrase this doctrine in semantical jargon by saying that a term, to be significant at all, must be either a name of a sense datum or a compound of such names or an abbreviation of such a compound. So stated, the doctrine remains ambiguous as between sense

---

[5] The doctrine can indeed be formulated with terms rather than statements as the units. Thus Lewis describes the meaning of a term as "*a criterion in mind,* by reference to which one is able to apply or refuse to apply the expression in question in the case of presented, or imagined, things or situations." For an instructive account of the vicissitudes of the verification theory of meaning, centered however on the question of meaning*fulness* rather than synonymy and analyticity, see Hempel.

data as sensory events and sense data as sensory qualities; and it remains vague as to the admissible ways of compounding. Moreover, the doctrine is unnecessarily and intolerably restrictive in the term-by-term critique which it imposes. More reasonably, and without yet exceeding the limits of what I have called radical reductionism, we may take full statements as our significant units—thus demanding that our statements as wholes be translatable into sense-datum language, but not that they be translatable term by term.

This emendation would unquestionably have been welcome to Locke and Hume and Tooke, but historically it had to await an important reorientation in semantics—the reorientation whereby the primary vehicle of meaning came to be seen no longer in the term but in the statement. This reorientation, explicit in Frege, underlies Russell's concept of incomplete symbols defined in use; also it is implicit in the verification theory of meaning, since the objects of verification are statements.

Radical reductionism, conceived now with statements as units, set itself the task of specifying a sense-datum language and showing how to translate the rest of significant discourse, statement by statement, into it. Carnap embarked on this project in the *Aufbau.*

The language which Carnap adopted as his starting point was not a sense-datum language in the narrowest conceivable sense, for it included also the notations of logic, up through higher set theory. In effect it included the whole language of pure mathematics. The ontology implicit in it (that is, the range of values of its variables) embraced not only sensory events but classes, classes of classes, and so on. Empiricists there are who would boggle at such prodigality. Carnap's starting point is very parsimonious, however, in its extralogical or sensory part. In a series of constructions in which he exploits the resources of modern logic with much ingenuity, Carnap succeeds in defining a wide array of important additional sensory concepts which, but for his constructions, one would not have dreamed were definable on so slender a basis. He was the first empiricist who, not content with asserting the reducibility of science to terms of immediate experience, took serious steps toward carrying out the reduction.

If Carnap's starting point is satisfactory, still his constructions were, as he himself stressed, only a fragment of the full program. The construction of even the simplest statements about the physical world was left in a sketchy state. Carnap's suggestions on this subject were, despite their sketchiness, very suggestive. He explained spatio-temporal point-instants as quadruples of real numbers and envisaged assignment of sense qualities to point-instants according to certain canons. Roughly summarized, the plan was that qualities should be assigned to point-instants in such a way as to achieve the laziest world compatible with our experience. The principle of least action was to be our guide in constructing a world from experience.

Carnap did not seem to recognize, however, that his treatment of physical objects fell short of reduction not merely through sketchiness, but in principle. Statements of the form "Quality q is at point-instant x,y,z,t" were, according to his canons, to be apportioned truth values in such a way as to maximize and minimize certain over-all features, and with growth of experience the truth values were to be progressively revised in the same spirit. I think this is a good schematization (deliberately oversimplified, to be sure) of what science really does; but it provides no indication, not even the sketchiest, of how a statement of the form "Quality q is at x,y,z,t" could ever be translated into Carnap's initial language of sense data and logic. The connective "is at" remains an added undefined connective; the canons counsel us in its use but not in its elimination.

Carnap seems to have appreciated this point afterward; for in his later writings he abandoned all notion of the translatability of statements about the physical world into statements about immediate experience. Reductionism in its radical form has long since ceased to figure in Carnap's philosophy.

But the dogma of reductionism has, in a subtler and more tenuous form, continued to influence the thought of empiricists. The notion lingers that to each statement, or each synthetic statement, there is associated a unique range of possible sensory events such that the occurrence of any of them would add to the likelihood of truth of the statement, and that there is associated also another unique range of possible sensory events whose occurrence would detract from that likelihood. This notion is of course implicit in the verification theory of meaning.

The dogma of reductionism survives in the supposition that each statement, taken in isolation from its fellows, can admit of confirmation or infirmation at all. My countersuggestion, issuing essentially from Carnap's doctrine of the physical world in the *Aufbau*, is that our statements about the external world face the tribunal of sense experience not individually but only as a corporate body.

The dogma of reductionism, even in its attenuated form, is intimately connected with the other dogma—that there is a cleavage between the analytic and the synthetic. We have found ourselves led, indeed, from the latter problem to the former through the verification theory of meaning. More directly, the one dogma clearly supports the other in this way: as long as it is taken to be significant in general to speak of the confirmation and infirmation of a statement, it seems significant to speak also of a limiting kind of statement which is vacuously confirmed, *ipso facto*, come what may; and such a statement is analytic.

The two dogmas are, indeed, at root identical. We lately reflected that in general the truth of statements does obviously depend both upon language and upon extralinguistic fact; and we noted that this obvious circumstance carries in its train, not logically but all too naturally, a feeling that the truth of a statement is somehow analyzable into a linguistic component and a factual component. The factual component must, if we are empiricists, boil down to a range of confirmatory experiences. In the extreme case where the linguistic component is all that matters, a true statement is analytic. But I hope we are now impressed with how stubbornly the distinction between analytic and synthetic has resisted any straightforward drawing. I am impressed also, apart from prefabricated examples of black and white balls in an urn, with how baffling the problem has always been of arriving at any explicit theory of the empirical confirmation of a synthetic statement. My present suggestion is that it is nonsense, and the root of much nonsense, to speak of a linguistic component and a factual component in the truth of any individual statement. Taken collectively, science has its double dependence upon language and experience; but this duality is not significantly traceable into the statements of science taken one by one.

The idea of defining a symbol in use was, as remarked, an advance over the impossible term-by-term empiricism of Locke and Hume. The statement, rather than the term, came with Frege to be recognized as the unit accountable to an empiricist critique. But what I am now urging is that even in taking the statement as unit we have drawn our grid too finely. The unit of empirical significance is the whole of science.

6. EMPIRICISM WITHOUT THE DOGMAS

The totality of our so-called knowledge or beliefs, from the most casual matters of geography and history to the profoundest laws of atomic physics or even of pure mathematics and logic, is a man-made fabric which impinges on experience only along the edges. Or, to change the figure, total science is like a field of force whose boundary conditions are experience. A conflict with experience at the periphery occasions readjustments in the interior of the field. Truth values have to be redistributed over some of our statements. Reëvaluation of some statements entails reëvaluation of others, because of their logical interconnections —the logical laws being in turn simply certain further statements of the system, certain further elements of the field. Having reëvaluated one statement we must reëvaluate some others, which may be the statements logically connected with the first or may be the statements of logical connections themselves. But the total field is so underdetermined by its boundary conditions, experience, that there is much latitude of choice as to what statements to reëvaluate in the light of any single contrary experience. No particular experiences are linked with any particular statements in the interior of the field, except indirectly through considerations of equilibrium affecting the field as a whole.

If this view is right, it is misleading to speak of the empirical content of an individual statement—especially if it is a statement at all remote from the experiential periphery of the field. Furthermore it becomes folly to seek a boundary between synthetic statements, which hold contingently on experience, and analytic statements, which hold come what may. Any statement can be held true come what may, if we make drastic enough adjustments elsewhere in the system. Even a statement very close to the periphery can be held true in the face of recalcitrant experience by pleading hallucination or by amending certain statements of the kind called logical laws. Conversely, by the same token, no statement is immune to revision. Revision even of the logical law of the excluded middle has been proposed as a means of simplifying quantum mechanics; and what difference is there in principle between such a shift and the shift whereby Kepler superseded Ptolemy, or Einstein Newton, or Darwin Aristotle?

For vividness I have been speaking in terms of varying distances from a sensory periphery. Let me try now to clarify this notion without metaphor. Certain statements, though *about* physical objects and not sense experience, seem peculiarly germane to sense experience—and in a selective way: some statements to some experiences, others to others. Such statements, especially germane to particular experiences, I picture as near the periphery. But in this relation of "germaneness" I envisage nothing more than a loose association reflecting the relative likelihood, in practice, of our choosing one statement rather than another for revision in the event of recalcitrant experience. For example, we can imagine recalcitrant experiences to which we would surely be inclined to accommodate our system by reëvaluating just the statement that there are brick houses on Elm Street, together with related statements on the same topic. We can imagine other recalcitrant experiences to which we would be inclined to accommodate our system by reëvaluating just the statement that there are no centaurs, along with kindred statements. A recalcitrant experience can, I have urged, be accommodated by any of various alternative reëvaluations in various alternative quarters of the total system; but, in the cases which we are now imagining, our natural tendency to disturb the total system as little as possible would lead us to focus our revisions upon these specific statements concerning brick houses or centaurs. These statements are felt, therefore, to have a sharper empirical reference than highly theoretical statements of physics or logic or ontology. The latter statements may be thought of as relatively centrally located within the total network, meaning merely that little preferential connection with any particular sense data obtrudes itself.

As an empiricist I continue to think of the conceptual scheme of science as a tool, ultimately, for predicting future experience in the light of past experience. Physical objects are conceptually imported into the situation as convenient intermediaries—not by definition in terms of experience, but simply as irreducible posits comparable, epistemologically, to the gods of Homer. For my part I do, qua lay physicist, believe in physical objects and not in Homer's gods; and I consider it a scientific error to believe otherwise. But in point of epistemological footing the physical objects and the gods differ only in degree and not in kind. Both sorts of entities enter our conception only as cultural posits. The myth of physical objects is epistemologically superior to most in that it has proved more efficacious than other myths as a device for working a manageable structure into the flux of experience.

Positing does not stop with macroscopic physical objects. Objects at the atomic level are posited to make the laws of macroscopic objects, and ultimately the laws of experience, simpler and more manageable; and we need not expect or demand full definition of atomic and subatomic entities in terms of macroscopic ones, any more than definition of macroscopic things in terms of sense data. Science is a continuation of common sense, and it continues the common-sense expedient of swelling ontology to simplify theory.

Physical objects, small and large, are not the only posits. Forces are another example; and indeed we are told nowadays that the boundary between energy and matter is obsolete. Moreover, the abstract entities which are the substance of mathematics—ultimately classes and classes of classes and so on up—are another posit in the same spirit. Epistemologically these are myths on the same footing with physical objects and gods, neither better nor worse except for differences in the degree to which they expedite our dealings with sense experiences.

The over-all algebra of rational and irrational numbers is underdetermined by the algebra of rational numbers, but is smoother and more convenient; and it includes the algebra of rational numbers as a jagged or gerrymandered part. Total science, mathematical and natural and human, is similarly but more extremely underdetermined by experience. The edge of the system must be kept squared with experience; the rest, with all its elaborate myths or fictions, has as its objective the simplicity of laws.

Ontological questions, under this view, are on a par with questions of natural science.[6] Consider the question whether to countenance classes as entities. This, as I have argued elsewhere, is the question whether to quantify with respect to variables which take classes as values. Now Carnap has maintained that this is a question not of matters of fact but of choosing a convenient language form, a convenient conceptual scheme or framework for science. With this I agree, but only on the proviso that the same be conceded regarding scientific hypotheses generally. Carnap has recognized that he is able to preserve a double standard for ontological questions and scientific hypotheses only by assuming an absolute distinction between the analytic and the synthetic; and I need not say again that this is a distinction which I reject.

The issue over their being classes seems more a question of convenient conceptual scheme; the issue over there being centaurs, or brick houses on Elm Street, seems more a question of fact. But I have been urging that this difference is only one of degree, and that it turns upon our vaguely pragmatic inclination to adjust one strand of the fabric of science rather than another in accommodating some particular recalcitrant experience. Conservatism figures in such choices, and so does the quest for simplicity.

Carnap, Lewis, and others take a pragmatic stand on the question of choosing between language forms, scientific frameworks; but their pragmatism leaves off at the imagined boundary between the analytic and the synthetic. In repudiating such a boundary I espouse a more thorough pragmatism. Each man is given a scientific heritage plus a continuing barrage of sensory stimulation; and the considerations which guide him in warping his scientific heritage to fit his continuing sensory promptings are, where rational, pragmatic.

[6] "L'ontologie fait corps avec la science elle-même et ne peut en être separée." Meyerson.

10

Carl Hempel PROBLEMS AND CHANGES
IN THE EMPIRICIST
CRITERION OF MEANING

In this essay Hempel summarizes the problems involved in the various attempts
to formulate an adequate meaning criterion. Like many other Positivists, he tends to
the conclusion that the most fruitful approach is to construct an acceptable empiricistic
language; meaningfulness would then be determined by whether or not a given
sentence is translatable into such a language. This selection should be read in conjunction with selections 7 and 8.

Hempel later came to believe that some of the theses defended in this article
needed modification. A brief statement of his later opinion and additional bibliography
are to be found in "Remarks by the Author (1958)," in A. J. Ayer, *Logical Positivism*,
pp. 127–129.

Additional reading about the empiricist meaning criterion can be found in the
books cited by Hempel at the conclusion of this essay. See also the bibliographical footnotes in Chapter 16 of Passmore's *A Hundred Years of Philosophy* and the Selected
Bibliography to Part VIII of Edward and Pap's *A Modern Introduction to Philosophy*.

1. INTRODUCTION

The fundamental tenet of modern empiricism is the view that all non-analytic
knowledge is based on experience. Let us call this thesis the principle of empiricism.[1] Contemporary logical empiricism has added[2] to it the maxim that a

From *Revue Internationale de Philosophie*, vol. IV, no. 11, January 15, 1950.
Used by permission.
[1] This term is used by Benjamin (2) in an examination of the foundations of
empiricism. For a recent discussion of the basic ideas of empiricism see Russell (27),
part Six.
[2] In his stimulating article, "Positivism," W. T. Stace argues, in effect, that the

sentence makes a cognitively meaningful assertion, and thus can be said to be either true or false, only if it is either (1) analytic or self-contradictory or (2) capable, at least in principle, of experiential test. According to this so-called *empiricist criterion of cognitive meaning, or of cognitive significance,* many of the formulations of traditional metaphysics and large parts of epistemology are devoid of cognitive significance—however rich some of them may be in non-cognitive import by virtue of their emotive appeal or the moral inspiration they offer. Similarly certain doctrines which have been, at one time or another, formulated within empirical science or its border disciplines are so contrived as to be incapable of test by any conceivable evidence; they are therefore qualified as pseudo-hypotheses, which assert nothing, and which therefore have no explanatory or predictive force whatever. This verdict applies, for example, to the neo-vitalist speculations about entelechies or vital forces, and to the "telefinalist hypothesis" propounded by Lecomte du Noüy.

The preceding formulations of the principle of empiricism and of the empiricist meaning criterion provide no more, however, than a general and rather vague characterization of a basic point of view, and they need therefore to be elucidated and amplified. And while in the earlier phases of its development, logical empiricism was to a large extent preoccupied with a critique of philosophic and scientific formulations by means of those fundamental principles, there has been in recent years an increasing concern with the positive tasks of analyzing in detail the logic and methodology of empirical science and of clarifying and restating the basic ideas of empiricism in the light of the insights thus obtained. In the present article, I propose to discuss some of the problems this search has raised and some of the results it seems to have established.

2. CHANGES IN THE TESTABILITY CRITERION OF EMPIRICAL MEANING

As our formulation shows, the empiricist meaning criterion lays down the requirement of experiential testability for those among the cognitively meaningful sentences which are neither analytic nor contradictory; let us call them sentences with empirical meaning, or empirical significance. The concept of testability, which is to render precise the vague notion of being based—or rather baseable —on experience, has undergone several modifications which reflect an increasingly refined analysis of the structure of empirical knowledge. In the present section, let us examine the major stages of this development.

For convenience of exposition, we first introduce three auxiliary concepts, namely those of observable characteristic, of observation predicate, and of observation sentence. A property or a relation of physical objects will be called

---

testability criterion of meaning is not logically entailed by the principle of empiricism. (See (29), especially section 11.) This is correct: According to the latter, a sentence expresses knowledge only if it is either analytic or corroborated by empirical evidence; the former goes further and identifies the domain of cognitively significant discourse with that of potential knowledge; i.e., it grants cognitive import only to sentences for which—unless they are either analytic or contradictory—a test by empirical evidence is conceivable.

an *observable characteristic* if, under suitable circumstances, its presence or absence in a given instance can be ascertained through direct observation. Thus, the terms "green," "soft," "liquid," "longer than," designate observable characteristics, while "bivalent," "radioactive," "better electric conductor," and "introvert" do not. Terms which designate observable characteristics will be called *observation predicates*. Finally, by an *observation sentence* we shall understand any sentence which—correctly or incorrectly—asserts of one or more specifically named objects that they have, or that they lack, some specified observable characteristic. The following sentences, for example, meet this condition: "The Eiffel Tower is taller than the buildings in its vicinity," "The pointer of this instrument does not cover the point marked '3' on the scale," and even, "The largest dinosaur on exhibit in New York's Museum of Natural History had a blue tongue"; for this last sentence assigns to a specified object a characteristic— having a blue tongue—which is of such a kind that under suitable circumstances (e.g., in the case of my Chow dog) its presence or absence can be ascertained by direct observation. Our concept of observation sentence is intended to provide a precise interpretation of the vague idea of a sentence asserting something that is "in principle" ascertainable by direct observation, even though it may happen to be actually incapable of being observed by myself, perhaps also by my contemporaries, and possibly even by any human being who ever lived or will live. Any evidence that might be adduced in the test of an empirical hypothesis may now be thought of as being expressed in observation sentences of this kind.[3]

We now turn to the changes in the conception of testability, and thus of empirical meaning. In the early days of the Vienna Circle, a sentence was said to have empirical meaning if it was capable, at least in principle, of complete verification by observational evidence; i.e., if observational evidence could be described which, if actually obtained, would conclusively establish the truth of the sentence.[4] With the help of the concept of observation sentence, we can

---

[3] Observation sentences of this kind belong to what Carnap has called the thing-language (cf., e.g., (7), pp. 52–53). That they are adequate to formulate the data which serve as the basis for empirical tests is clear in particular for the intersubjective testing procedures used in science as well as in large areas of empirical inquiry on the common-sense level. In epistemological discussions, it is frequently assumed that the ultimate evidence for beliefs about empirical matters consists in perceptions and sensations whose description calls for a phenomenalistic type of language. The specific problems connected with the phenomenalistic approach cannot be discussed here; but it should be mentioned that at any rate all the critical considerations presented in this article in regard to the testability criterion are applicable, *mutatis mutandis*, to the case of a phenomenalistic basis as well.

[4] Originally, the permissible evidence was meant to be restricted to what is observable by the speaker and perhaps his fellow-beings during their life times. Thus construed, the criterion rules out, as cognitively meaningless, all statements about the distant future or the remote past, as has been pointed out, among others, by Ayer in (1), chap. I; by Pap in (21), chap. 13, esp. pp. 333 ff.; and by Russell in (27), pp. 445–447. This difficulty is avoided, however, if we permit the evidence to consist of any finite set of "logically possible observation data," each of them formulated in

restate this requirement as follows: A sentence S has empirical meaning if and only if it is possible to indicate a finite set of observation sentences, O_1, O_2, ..., O_n, such that if these are true, then S is necessarily true, too. As stated, however, this condition is satisfied also if S is an analytic sentence or if the given observation sentences are logically incompatible with each other. By the following formulation, we rule these cases out and at the same time express the intended criterion more precisely:

2.1. Requirement of Complete Verifiability in Principle: A sentence has empirical meaning if and only if it is not analytic and follows logically from some finite and logically consistent class of observation sentences.[5]

---

an observation sentence. Thus, e.g., the sentence S_1, "The tongue of the largest dinosaur in New York's Museum of Natural History was blue or black," is completely verifiable in our sense; for it is a logical consequence of the sentence S_2, "The tongue of the largest dinosaur in New York's Museum of Natural History was blue"; and this is an observation sentence, as has been shown above.

And if the concept of *verifiability in principle* and the more general concept of *confirmability in principle,* which will be considered later, are construed as referring to *logically possible evidence* as expressed by observation sentences, then it follows similarly that the class of statements which are verified, or at least confirmable, in principle includes such assertions as that the planet Neptune and the Antarctic Continent existed before they were discovered, and that atomic warfare, if not checked, may lead to the extermination of this planet. The objections which Russell (cf. (27), pp. 445 and 447) raises against the verifiability criterion by reference to those examples do not apply therefore if the criterion is understood in the manner here suggested. Incidentally, statements of the kind mentioned by Russell, which are not actually verifiable by any human being, were explicitly recognized as cognitively significant already by Schlick (in (28), part V), who argued that the impossibility of verifying them was "merely empirical." The characterization of verifiability with the help of the concept of observation sentence as suggested here might serve as a more explicit and rigorous statement of that conception.

[5] As has frequently been emphasized in empiricist literature, the term "verifiability" is to indicate, of course, the conceivability, or better, the logical possibility of evidence of an observational kind which, if actually encountered, would constitute conclusive evidence for the given sentence; it is not intended to mean the technical possibility of performing the tests needed to obtain such evidence, and even less does it mean the possibility of actually finding directly observable phenomena which constitute conclusive evidence for that sentence—which would be tantamount to the actual existence of such evidence and would thus imply the truth of the given sentence. Analogous remarks apply to the terms "falsifiability" and "confirmability." This point has been disregarded in some recent critical discussions of the verifiability criterion. Thus, e.g., Russell (cf. (27), p. 448) construes verifiability as the actual existence of a set of conclusively verifying occurrences. This conception, which has never been advocated by any logical empiricist, must naturally turn out to be inadequate since according to it the empirical meaningfulness of a sentence could not be established without gathering empirical evidence, and moreover enough of it to permit a conclusive proof of the sentences in question! It is not surprising, therefore, that his extraordinary interpretation of verifiability leads Russell to the conclusion: "In fact, that a proposition is verifiable is itself not verifiable" (*l. c.*). Actually, under the empiricist interpretation

This criterion, however, has several serious defects. The first of those here to be mentioned has been pointed out by various writers:

(*a*) The verifiability requirement rules out all sentences of universal form and thus all statements purporting to express general laws; for these cannot be conclusively verified by any finite set of observational data. And since sentences of this type constitute an integral part of scientific theories, the verifiability requirement must be regarded as overly restrictive in this respect. Similarly, the criterion disqualifies all sentences such as "For any substance there exists some solvent," which contain both universal and existential quantifiers (i.e., occurrences of the terms "all" and "some" or their equivalents); for no sentences of this kind can be logically deduced from any finite set of observation sentences.

Two further defects of the verifiability requirement do not seem to have been widely noticed:

(*b*) Suppose that S is a sentence which satisfies the proposed criterion, whereas N is a sentence such as "The absolute is perfect," to which the criterion attributes no empirical meaning. Then the alternation SvN (i.e., the expression obtained by connecting the two sentences by the word "or"), likewise satisfies the criterion; for if S is a consequence of some finite class of observation sentences, then trivially SvN is a consequence of the same class. But clearly, the empiricist criterion of meaning is not intended to countenance sentences of this sort. In this respect, therefore, the requirement of complete verifiability is too inclusive.

(*c*) Let "P" be an observation predicate. Then the purely existential sentence "$(Ex)P(x)$" ("There exists at least one thing that has the property P") is completely verifiable, for it follows from any observation sentence asserting of some particular object that it has the property P. But its denial, being equivalent to the universal sentence "$(x) \sim P(x)$" ("Nothing has the property P") is clearly not completely verifiable, as follows from comment (*a*) above. Hence, under the criterion 2.1, the denials of certain empirically—and thus cognitively —significant sentences are empirically meaningless; and as they are neither analytic nor contradictory they are cognitively meaningless. But however we may

---

of complete verifiability, any statement asserting the verifiability of some sentence S whose text is quoted, is either analytic or contradictory; for the decision whether there exists a class of observation sentences which entail S, i.e., whether such observation sentences can be formulated, no matter whether they are true or false— that decision is a matter of pure logic and requires no factual information whatever.

A similar misunderstanding is in evidence in the following passage in which W. H. Werkmeister claims to characterize a view held by logical positivists: "A proposition is said to be 'true' when it is 'verifiable in principle'; i.e., when we know the conditions which, when realized, will make 'verification' possible (cf. Ayer)." (cf. (31), p. 145). The quoted thesis, which, again, was never held by any logical positivist, including Ayer, is in fact logically absurd. For we can readily describe conditions which, if realized, would verify the sentence "The outside of the Chrysler Building is painted a bright yellow"; but similarly, we can describe verifying conditions for its denial; hence, according to the quoted principle, both the sentence and its denial would have to be considered true. Incidentally, the passage under discussion does not accord with Werkmeister's perfectly correct observation, *l. c.*, p. 40, that verifiability is intended to characterize the meaning of a sentence—which shows that verifiability is meant to be a criterion of cognitive significance rather than of truth.

delimit the domain of significant discourse, we shall have to insist that if a sentence falls within that domain, then so must its denial. To put the matter more explicitly: The sentences to be qualified as cognitively meaningful are precisely those which can be significantly said to be either true or false. But then, adherence to 2.1 would engender a serious dilemma, as is shown by the consequence just mentioned: We would either have to give up the fundamental logical principle that if a sentence is true or false, then its denial is false or true, respectively (and thus cognitively significant); or else, we must deny, in a manner reminiscent of the intuitionistic conception of logic and mathematics, that "$(x) \sim P(x)$" is logically equivalent to the negation of "$(Ex) P(x)$." Clearly, the criterion 2.1, which has disqualified itself on several other counts, does not warrant such drastic measures for its preservation; hence, it has to be abandoned.[6]

Strictly analogous considerations apply to an alternative criterion, which makes complete falsifiability in principle the defining characteristic of empirical significance. Let us formulate this criterion as follows: A sentence has empirical meaning if and only if it is capable, in principle, of complete refutation by a finite number of observational data; or, more precisely:

2.2. Requirement of Complete Falsifiability in Principle: A sentence has empirical meaning if and only if its denial is not analytic and follows logically from some finite logically consistent class of observation sentences.[7]

This criterion qualifies a sentence as empirically meaningful if its denial satisfies the requirement of complete verifiability; as is to be expected, it is therefore inadequate on similar grounds as the latter:

(*a*) It rules out purely existential hypotheses, such as "There exists at least one unicorn," and all sentences whose formulation calls for mixed—i.e., universal and existential—quantification; for none of these can possibly be conclusively falsified by a finite number of observation sentences.

(*b*) If a sentence S is completely falsifiable whereas N is a sentence which

---

[6] The arguments here adduced against the verifiability criterion also prove the inadequacy of a view closely related to it, namely that two sentences have the same cognitive significance if any set of observation sentences which would verify one of them would also verify the other, and conversely. Thus, e.g., under this criterion, any two general laws would have to be assigned the same cognitive significance, for no general law is verified by any set of observation sentences. The view just referred to must be clearly distinguished from a position which Russell examines in his critical discussion of the positivistic meaning criterion. It is "the theory that two propositions whose verified consequences are identical have the same significance" ((27), p. 448). This view is untenable indeed, for what consequences of a statement have actually been verified at a given time is obviously a matter of historical accident which cannot possibly serve to establish identity of cognitive significance. But I am not aware that any logical positivist ever subscribed to that "theory."

[7] The idea of using theoretical falsifiability by observational evidence as the "criterion of demarcation" separating empirical science from mathematics and logic on the one hand and from metaphysics on the other is due to K. Popper, (cf. (22), sections 1-7 and 19-24; also see (23), vol. II, pp. 282-285). Whether Popper would subscribe to the proposed restatement of the falsifiability criterion, I do not know.

is not, then their conjunction, S.N (i.e., the expression obtained by connecting the two sentences by the word "and") is completely falsifiable; for if the denial of S is entailed by some class of observation sentences, then the denial of S.N is, *a fortiori*, entailed by the same class. Thus, the criterion allows empirical significance to many sentences which an adequate empiricist criterion should rule out, such as, say "All swans are white and the absolute is perfect."

(*c*) If "P" is an observation predicate, then the assertion that all things have the property P is qualified as significant, but its denial, being equivalent to a purely existential hypothesis, is disqualified (cf. (*a*)). Hence, criterion 2.2 gives rise to the same dilemma as 2.1.

In sum, then, interpretations of the testability criterion in terms of complete verifiability or of complete falsifiability are inadequate because they are overly restrictive in one direction and overly inclusive in another, and because both of them require incisive changes in the fundamental principles of logic.

Several attempts have been made to avoid these difficulties by construing the testability criterion as demanding merely a partial and possibly indirect confirmability of empirical hypotheses by observational evidence.

2.3. A formulation suggested by Ayer [8] is characteristic of these attempts to set up a clear and sufficiently comprehensive criterion of confirmability. It states, in effect, that a sentence S has empirical import if from S in conjunction with suitable subsidiary hypotheses it is possible to derive observation sentences which are not derivable from the subsidiary hypotheses alone.

This condition is suggested by a closer consideration of the logical structure of scientific testing; but it is much too liberal as it stands. Indeed, as Ayer himself has pointed out in the second edition of his book, *Language, Truth, and Logic*,[9] his criterion allows empirical import to any sentence whatever. Thus, e.g., if S is the sentence "The absolute is perfect," it suffices to choose as a subsidiary hypothesis the sentence "If the absolute is perfect then this apple is red" in order to make possible the deduction of the observation sentence "This apple is red," which clearly does not follow from the subsidiary hypothesis alone.[10]

2.4. To meet this objection, Ayer has recently proposed a modified version of his testability criterion. The modification restricts, in effect, the subsidiary

[8] (1), Chap. I.—The case against the requirements of verifiability and of falsifiability in favor of a requirement of partial confirmability and disconfirmability is very clearly presented also by Pap in (21), Chap. 13.

[9] (1), 2d ed., pp. 11–12.

[10] According to Stace (cf. (29), p. 218), the criterion of partial and indirect testability, which he calls the positivist principle, presupposes (and thus logically entails) another principle, which he terms the *Principle of Observable Kinds:* "A sentence, in order to be significant, must assert or deny facts which are of a kind or class such that it is logically possible directly to observe some facts which are instances of that class or kind. And if a sentence purports to assert or deny facts which are of a class or kind such that it would be logically impossible directly to observe any instance of that class or kind, then the sentence is non-significant." I think the argument Stace offers to prove that this principle is entailed by the requirement of

hypotheses mentioned in 2.3 to sentences which are either analytic or can independently be shown to be testable in the sense of the modified criterion.[11]

But it can readily be shown that this new criterion, like the requirement of complete falsifiability, allows empirical significance to any conjunction S.N, where S satisfies Ayer's criterion while N is a sentence such as "The absolute is perfect," which is to be disqualified by that criterion. Indeed: whatever consequences can be deduced from S with the help of permissible subsidiary hypotheses can also be deduced from S.N by means of the same subsidiary hypotheses, and as Ayer's new criterion is formulated essentially in terms of the deducibility of a certain type of consequence from the given sentence, it countenances S.N together with S. Another difficulty has been pointed out by Professor A. Church, who has shown [12] that if there are any three observation sentences none of which alone entails any of the others, then it follows for any sentence S whatsoever that either it or its denial has empirical import according to Ayer's revised criterion.

3. TRANSLATABILITY INTO AN EMPIRICIST LANGUAGE AS A NEW CRITERION OF COGNITIVE MEANING

I think it is useless to continue the search for an adequate criterion of testability in terms of deductive relationships to observation sentences. The past development of this search—of which we have considered the major stages—seems to warrant the expectation that as long as we try to set up a criterion of testability for individual sentences in a natural language, in terms of logical relationship to observation sentences, the result will be either too restrictive or too inclusive, or both. In particular it appears likely that such criteria would allow empirical import, in the manner of 2.1b or of 2.2b, either to any alternation or to any conjunction of two sentences of which at least one is qualified as empirically

---

testability is inconclusive (mainly because of the incorrect tacit assumption that "on the transformation view of deduction," the premises of a valid deductive argument must be necessary conditions for the conclusion (*l. c.*, p. 225)). Without pressing this point any further, I should like to add here a remark on the principle of observable kinds itself. Professor Stace does not say how we are to determine what "facts" a given sentence asserts or denies, or indeed whether it asserts or denies any "facts" at all. Hence, the exact import of the principle remains unclear. No matter, however, how one might choose the criteria for the factual reference of sentences, this much seems certain: If a sentence expresses any fact at all, say *f*, then it satisfies the requirement laid down in the first sentence of the principle; for we can always form a class containing *f* together with the fact expressed by some observation sentence of our choice, which makes *f* a member of a class of facts at least one of which is capable, in principle, of direct observation. The first part of the principle of observable kinds is therefore all-inclusive, somewhat like Ayer's original formulation of the empiricist meaning criterion.

[11] This restriction is expressed in recursive form and involves no vicious circle. For the full statement of Ayer's criterion, see (1), 2d ed., p. 13.

[12] Church (11).

meaningful; and this peculiarity has undesirable consequences because the liberal grammatical rules of English as of any other natural language countenance as sentences certain expressions ("The absolute is perfect" was our illustration) which even by the most liberal empiricist standards make no assertion whatever; and these would then have to be permitted as components of empirically significant statements.

The predicament would not arise, of course, in an artificial language whose vocabulary and grammar were so chosen as to preclude altogether the possibility of forming sentences of any kind which the empiricist meaning criterion is intended to rule out. Let us call any such language an *empiricist language*. This reflection suggests an entirely different approach to our problem: Give a general characterization of the kind of language that would qualify as empiricist, and then lay down the following:

3.1. Translatability Criterion of Cognitive Meaning: A sentence has cognitive meaning if and only if it is translatable into an empiricist language.

This conception of cognitive import, while perhaps not explicitly stated, seems to underlie much of the more recent work done by empiricist writers; as far as I can see it has its origin in Carnap's essay, *Testability and Meaning* (especially part 4).

As any language, so also any empiricist language can be characterized by indicating its vocabulary and the rules determining its logic; the latter include the syntactical rules according to which sentences may be formed by means of the given vocabulary. In effect, therefore, the translatability criterion proposes to characterize the cognitively meaningful sentences by the vocabulary out of which they may be constructed, and by the syntactical principles governing their construction. What sentences are singled out as cognitively significant will depend, accordingly, on the choice of the vocabulary and of the construction rules. Let us consider a specific possibility:

3.2. We might qualify a language L as empiricist if it satisfies the following conditions:

a. *The vocabulary of L contains:*

1. The customary locutions of logic which are used in the formulation of sentences; including in particular the expressions "no," "and," "or," "if . . . then . . . ," "all," "some," "the class of all things such that . . . ," " . . . is an element of class . . .";

2. Certain *observation predicates*. These will be said to constitute the basic empirical vocabulary of L;

3. Any expression definable by means of those referred to under 1 and 2.

b. *The rules of sentence formation for L* are those laid down in some contemporary logical system such as *Principia Mathematica*.

Since all defined terms can be eliminated in favor of primitives, these rules stipulate in effect that a language L is empiricist if all its sentences are expressible, with the help of the usual logical locutions, in terms of observable characteristics of physical objects. Let us call any language of this sort a thing-language in the narrower sense. Alternatively, the basic empirical vocabulary of an empiricist language might be construed as consisting of phenomenalistic terms, each of them referring to some aspect of the phenomena of perception or sensation. The construction of adequate phenomenalistic languages, however, presents considerable difficulties [13] and in recent empiricism, attention has been focussed primarily on the potentialities of languages whose basic empirical vocabulary consists of observation predicates; for the latter lend themselves more directly to the description of that type of intersubjective evidence which is invoked in the test of scientific hypotheses.

If we construe empiricist languages in the sense of 3.2, then the translatability criterion 3.1 avoids all of the shortcomings pointed out in our discussion of earlier forms of the testability criterion:

(*a*) Our characterization of empiricist languages makes explicit provision for universal and existential quantification, i.e., for the use of the terms "all" and "some"; hence, no type of quantified statement is generally excluded from the realm of cognitively significant discourse;

(*b*) Sentences such as "The absolute is perfect" cannot be formulated in an empiricist language (cf. (*d*) below); hence there is no danger that a conjunction or alternation containing a sentence of that kind as a component might be qualified as cognitively significant;

(*c*) In a language L with syntactical rules conforming to *Principia Mathematica*, the denial of a sentence is always again a sentence of L. Hence, the translatability criterion does not lead to the consequence, which is entailed by both 2.1 and 2.2, that the denials of certain significant sentences are non-significant;

(*d*) Despite its comprehensiveness, the new criterion does not attribute cognitive meaning to *all* sentences; thus, e.g., the sentences "The absolute is perfect" and "Nothingness nothings" cannot be translated into an empiricist language because their key terms are not definable by means of purely logical expressions and observation terms.

4. THE PROBLEM OF DISPOSITION TERMS AND OF THEORETICAL CONSTRUCTS

Yet, the new criterion is still too restrictive—as are, incidentally, also its predecessors—in an important respect which now calls for consideration. If empiricist languages are defined in accordance with 3.2, then, as was noted above, the translatability criterion 3.1 allows cognitive import to a sentence only if its constitutive empirical terms are explicitly definable by means of observation predicates. But as we shall argue presently, many terms even of the physical sciences are not so definable; hence the criterion would oblige us to reject, as devoid of cognitive import, all scientific hypotheses containing such terms—an altogether intolerable consequence.

The concept of temperature is a case in point. At first glance, it seems as though the phrase "Object x has a temperature of c degree centigrade," or briefly "$T(x) = c$" could be defined by the following sentence, (D): $T(x) = c$ if and only if the following condition is satisfied: If a thermometer is in contact with x, then it registers c degrees on its scale.

[13] Important contributions to the problem have been made by Carnap (5) and by Goodman (15).

Disregarding niceties, it may be granted that the definiens given here is formulated entirely in reference to observables. However, it has one highly questionable aspect: In *Principia Mathematica* and similar systems, the phrase "if *p* then *q*" is construed as being synonymous with "not *p* or *q*"; and under this so-called material interpretation of the conditional, a statement of the form "if *p* then *q*" is obviously true if (though not only if) the sentence standing in the place of "*p*" is false. If, therefore, the meaning of "if . . . then . . ." in the definiens of (D) is understood in the material sense, then that definiens is true if (though not only if) *x* is an object not in contact with a thermometer—no matter what numerical value we may give to *c*. And since the definiendum would be true under the same circumstances, the definition (D) would qualify as true the assignment of any temperature value whatsoever to any object not in contact with a thermometer! Analogous considerations apply to such terms as "electrically charged," "magnetic," "intelligent," "electric resistance," etc., in short to all disposition terms, i.e., terms which express the disposition of one or more objects to react in a determinate way under specified circumstances: A definition of such terms by means of observation predicates cannot be effected in the manner of (D), however natural and obvious a mode of definition this may at first seem to be.[14]

There are two main directions in which a resolution of the difficulty might be sought. On the one hand, it could be argued that the definition of disposition terms in the manner of (D) is perfectly adequate provided that the phrase "if . . . then . . ." in the definiens is construed in the sense it is obviously intended to have, namely as implying, in the case of (D), that even if *x* is not actually in contact with a thermometer, still if it *were* in such contact, then the thermometer *would* register *c* degrees. In sentences such as this, the phrase "if . . . then . . ." is said to be used counterfactually; and it is in this "strong" sense, which implies a counterfactual conditional, that the definiens of (D) would have to be construed. This suggestion would provide an answer to the problem of defining disposition terms if it were not for the fact that no entirely satisfactory account of the exact meaning of counterfactual conditionals seems to be available at present. Thus, the first way out of the difficulty has the status of a program rather than that of a solution. The lack of an adequate theory of counterfactual conditionals is all the more deplorable as such a theory is needed also for the analysis of the concept of general law in empirical science and of certain related ideas. A clarification of this cluster of problems constitutes at present one of the urgent desiderata in the logic and methodology of science.[15]

[14] This difficulty in the definition of disposition terms was first pointed out and analyzed by Carnap (in (6); see esp. section 7).

[15] The concept of strict implication as introduced by C. I. Lewis would be of no avail for the interpretation of the strong "if . . . then . . ." as here understood, for it refers to a purely logical relationship of entailment, whereas the concept under consideration will, in general, represent a nomological relationship, i.e., one based on empirical laws. For recent discussions of the problems of counterfactuals and laws, see Langford (18); Lewis (20), pp 210–230; Chisholm (10); Goodman (14); Reichenbach (26), chap. VIII; Hempel and Oppenheim (16), part III; Popper (24).

An alternative way of dealing with the definitional problems raised by disposition terms was suggested, and developed in detail, by Carnap. It consists in permitting the introduction of new terms, within an empiricist language, by means of so-called reduction sentences, which have the character of partial or conditional definitions.[16] Thus, e.g., the concept of temperature in our last illustration might be introduced by means of the following reduction sentence, (R): If a thermometer is in contact with an object x, then T $(x) = c$ if and only if the thermometer registers c degrees.

This rule, in which the conditional may be construed in the material sense, specifies the meaning of "temperature," i.e., of statements of the form "T$(x) = c$," only partially, namely in regard to those objects which are in contact with a thermometer; for all other objects, it simply leaves the meaning of "T$(x) = c$" undetermined. The specification of the meaning of "temperature" may then be gradually extended to cases not covered in (R) by laying down further reduction sentences, which reflect the measurement of temperature by devices other than thermometers.

Reduction sentences thus provide a means for the precise formulation of what is commonly referred to as operational definitions.[17] At the same time, they show that the latter are not definitions in the strict sense of the word, but rather partial specifications of meaning.

The preceding considerations suggest that in our characterization 3.2 of empiricist languages we broaden the provision *a* 3 by permitting in the vocabulary of L all those terms whose meaning can be specified in terms of the basic empirical vocabulary by means of definitions or reduction sentences. Languages satisfying this more inclusive criterion will be referred to as thing-languages in the wider sense.

If the concept of empiricist language is broadened in this manner, then the translatability criterion 3.1. covers—as it should—also all those statements whose constituent empirical terms include "empirical constructs," i.e., terms which do not designate observables, but which can be introduced by reduction sentences on the basis of observation predicates.

Even in this generalized version, however, our criterion of cognitive meaning may not do justice to advanced scientific theories, which are formulated in terms of "theoretical constructs," such as the terms "absolute temperature," "gravitational potential," "electric field," "ψ function," etc. There are reasons to think that neither definitions nor reduction sentences are adequate to introduce these terms on the basis of observation predicates. Thus, e.g., if a system of reduction sentences for the concept of electric field were available, then—to oversimplify the point a little—it would be possible to describe, in terms of observable characteristics, some necessary and some sufficient conditions for the

---

[16] Cf. Carnap (6); a brief elementary exposition of the central idea may be found in Carnap (7), part III. The partial definition (R) formulated above for the expression "T$(x) = c$" illustrates only the simplest type of reduction sentence, the so-called bilateral reduction sentence.

[17] On the concept of operational definition, which was developed by Bridgman, see, for example, Bridgman (3, 4) and Feigl (12).

presence, in a given region, of an electric field of any mathematical description, however complex. Actually, however, such criteria can at best be given only for some sufficiently simple kinds of fields.

Now theories of the advanced type here referred to may be considered as hypothetico-deductive systems in which all statements are logical consequences of a set of fundamental assumptions. Fundamental as well as derived statements in such a system are formulated either in terms of certain theoretical constructs which are not defined within the system and thus play the rôle of primitives, or in terms of expressions defined by means of the latter. Thus, in their logical structure such systems equal the axiomatized uninterpreted systems studied in mathematics and logic. They acquire applicability to empirical subject matter, and thus the status of theories of empirical science, by virtue of an empirical interpretation. The latter is effected by a translation of some of the sentences of the theory—often derived rather than fundamental ones—into an empiricist language, which may contain both observation predicates and empirical constructs. And since the sentences which are thus given empirical meaning are logical consequences of the fundamental hypotheses of the theory, that translation effects, indirectly, a partial interpretation of the latter and of the constructs in terms of which they are formulated.[18]

In order to make translatability into an empiricist language an adequate criterion of cognitive import, we broaden therefore the concept of empiricist language so as to include thing-languages in the narrower and in the wider sense as well as all interpreted theoretical systems of the kind just referred to.[19] With this understanding, 3.1 may finally serve as a general criterion of cognitive meaning.

5. ON "THE MEANING" OF AN EMPIRICAL STATEMENT

In effect, the criterion thus arrived at qualifies a sentence as cognitively meaningful if its non-logical constituents refer, directly or in certain specified indirect

[18] The distinction between a formal deductive system and the empirical theory resulting from it by an interpretation has been elaborated in detail by Reichenbach in his penetrating studies of the relations between pure and physical geometry; cf., e.g., Reichenbach (25). The method by means of which a formal system is given empirical content is characterized by Reichenbach as "coordinating definition" of the primitives in the theory by means of specific empirical concepts. As is suggested by our discussion of reduction and the interpretation of theorical constructs, however, the process in question may have to be construed as a partial interpretation of the non-logical terms of the system rather than as a complete definition of the latter in terms of the concepts of a thing-language.

[19] These systems have not been characterized here as fully and as precisely as would be desirable. Indeed, the exact character of the empirical interpretation of theoretical constructs and of the theories in which they function is in need of further investigation. Some problems which arise in this connection—such as whether, or in what sense, theoretical constructs may be said to denote—are obviously also of considerable epistemological interest. Some suggestions as to the interpretation of theoretical constructs may be found in Carnap (8), section 24, and in Kaplan (17); for an excellent discussion of the epistemological aspects of the problem, see Feigl (13).

ways, to observables. But it does not make any pronouncement on what "the meaning" of a cognitively significant sentence is, and in particular it neither says nor implies that that meaning can be exhaustively characterized by what the totality of possible tests would reveal in terms of observable phenomena. Indeed, *the content of a statement with empirical import cannot, in general, be exhaustively expressed by means of any class of observation sentences.*

For consider first, among the statements permitted by our criterion, any purely existential hypothesis or any statement involving mixed quantification. As was pointed out earlier, under 2.2*a*, statements of these kinds entail no observation sentences whatever; hence their content cannot be expressed by means of a class of observation sentences.

And secondly, even most statements of purely universal form (such as "All flamingoes are pink") entail observation sentences (such as "That thing is pink") only when combined with suitable other observation sentences (such as "That thing is a flamingo").

This last remark can be generalized: The use of empirical hypotheses for the prediction of observable phenomena requires, in practically all cases, the use of subsidiary empirical hypotheses.[20] Thus, e.g., the hypothesis that the agent of tuberculosis is rod-shaped does not by itself entail the consequence that upon looking at a tubercular sputum specimen through a microscope, rod-like shapes will be observed: a large number of subsidiary hypotheses, including the theory of the microscope, have to be used as additional premises in deducing that prediction.

Hence, what is sweepingly referred to as "the (cognitive) meaning" of a given scientific hypothesis cannot be adequately characterized in terms of potential observational evidence alone, nor can it be specified for the hypothesis taken in isolation. In order to understand "the meaning" of a hypothesis within an empiricist language, we have to know not merely what observation sentences it entails alone or in conjunction with subsidiary hypotheses, but also what other, non-observational, empirical sentences are entailed by it, what sentences in the given language would confirm or disconfirm it, and for what other hypotheses the given one would be confirmatory or disconfirmatory. In other words, the cognitive meaning of a statement in an empiricist language is reflected in the totality of its logical relationships to all other statements in that language and not to the observation sentences alone. In this sense, the statements of empirical science have a surplus meaning over and above what can be expressed in terms of relevant observation sentences.[21]

6. THE LOGICAL STATUS OF THE EMPIRICIST CRITERION OF MEANING

What kind of a sentence, it has often been asked, is the empiricist meaning criterion itself? Plainly it is not an empirical hypothesis; but it is not analytic or

---

[20] This point is clearly taken into consideration in Ayer's criteria of cognitive significance, which were discussed in section 2.

[21] For a fuller discussion of the issues here involved cf. Feigl (13) and the comments on Feigl's position which will be published together with that article.

self-contradictory either; hence, when judged by its own standard, is it not devoid of cognitive meaning? In that case, what claim of soundness or validity could possibly be made for it?

One might think of construing the criterion as a definition which indicates what empiricists propose to understand by a cognitively significant sentence; thus understood, it would not have the character of an assertion and would be neither true nor false. But this conception would attribute to the criterion a measure of arbitrariness which cannot be reconciled with the heated controversies it has engendered and even less with the fact, repeatedly illustrated in the present article, that the changes in its specific content have always been determined by the objective of making the criterion a more adequate index of cognitive import. And this very objective illuminates the character of the empiricist criterion of meaning: It is intended to provide a clarification and *explication* of the idea of a sentence which makes an intelligible assertion.[22] This idea is admittedly vague, and it is the task of philosophic explication to replace it by a more precise concept. In view of this difference of precision we cannot demand, of course, that the "new" concept, the explicatum, be strictly synonymous with the old one, the explicandum.[23] How, then, are we to judge the adequacy of a proposed explication, as expressed in some specific criterion of cognitive meaning?

First of all, there exists a large class of sentences which are rather generally recognized as making intelligible assertions, and another large class of which this is more or less generally denied. We shall have to demand of an adequate explication that it take into account these spheres of common usage; hence an explication which, let us say, denies cognitive import to descriptions of past events or to generalizations expressed in terms of observables has to be rejected as inadequate. As we have seen, this first requirement of adequacy has played an important rôle in the development of the empiricist meaning criterion.

But an adequate explication of the concept of cognitively significant statement must satisfy yet another, even more important, requirement: Together with the explication of certain other concepts, such as those of confirmation and of probability, it has to provide the framework for a general theoretical account of the structure and the foundations of scientific knowledge. Explication, as here understood, is not a mere description of the accepted usages of the terms under consideration: it has to go beyond the limitations, ambiguities, and inconsistencies of common usage and has to show how we had better construe the meanings of those terms if we wish to arrive at a consistent and comprehensive theory of knowledge. This type of consideration, which has been largely

[22] In the preface to the second edition of his book, Ayer takes a very similar position: he holds that the testability criterion is a definition which, however, is not entirely arbitrary, because a sentence which did not satisfy the criterion "would not be capable of being understood in the sense in which either scientific hypotheses or common-sense statements are habitually understood" ((1), p. 16).

[23] Cf. Carnap's characterization of explication in his article (9), which examines in outline the explication of the concept of probability. The Frege-Russell definition of integers as classes of equivalent classes, and the semantical definition of truth—cf. Tarski (30)—are outstanding examples of explication. For a lucid discussion of various aspects of logical analysis see Pap (21), chap. 17.

influenced by a study of the structure of scientific theories, has prompted the more recent extensions of the empiricist meaning criterion. These extensions are designed to include in the realm of cognitive significance various types of sentences which might occur in advanced scientific theories, or which have to be admitted simply for the sake of systematic simplicity and uniformity,[24] but on whose cognitive significance or non-significance a study of what the term "intelligible assertion" means in everyday discourse could hardly shed any light at all.

As a consequence, the empiricist criterion of meaning, like the result of any other explication, represents a linguistic proposal which itself is neither true nor false, but for which adequacy is claimed in two respects: First in the sense that the explication provides a reasonably close *analysis* of the commonly accepted meaning of the explicandum—and this claim implies an empirical assertion; and secondly in the sense that the explication achieves a *"rational reconstruction"* of the explicandum, i.e., that it provides, together perhaps with other explications, a general conceptual framework which permits a consistent and precise restatement and theoretical systematization of the contexts in which the explicandum is used—and this claim implies at least an assertion of a logical character.

Though a proposal in form, the empiricist criterion of meaning is therefore far from being an arbitrary definition; it is subject to revision if a violation of the requirements of adequacy, or even a way of satisfying those requirements more fully, should be discovered. Indeed, it is to be hoped that before long some of the open problems encountered in the analysis of cognitive significance will be clarified and that then our last version of the empiricist meaning criterion will be replaced by another, more adequate one.

BIBLIOGRAPHIC REFERENCES

1. Ayer, A. J., *Language, Truth and Logic*, Oxford Univ. Press, 1936; 2d ed., Gollancz, London, 1946.
2. Benjamin, A. C., *Is empiricism self-refuting?* (*Journal of Philos.*, vol. 38, 1941).
3. Bridgman, P. W., *The Logic of Modern Physics*, The Macmillan Co., New York, 1927.
4. ———, *Operational analysis* (*Philos. of Science*, vol. 5, 1938).
5. Carnap, R., *Der logische Aufbau der Welt*, Berlin, 1928.
6. ———, *Testability and meaning* (*Philos. of Science*, vol. 3, 1936, and vol. 4, 1937).
7. ———, *Logical foundations of the unity of science*, In: *Internat. Encyclopedia of Unified Science*, I, 1; Univ. of Chicago Press, 1938.
8. ———, *Foundations of logic and mathematics. Internat. Encyclopedia of Unified Science*, I, 3; Univ. of Chicago Press, 1939.

[24] Thus, e.g., our criterion qualifies as significant certain statements containing, say, thousands of existential or universal quantifiers—even though such sentences may never occur in every-day nor perhaps even in scientific discourse. For indeed, from a systematic point of view it would be arbitrary and unjustifiable to limit the class of significant statements to those containing no more than some fixed number of quantifiers. For further discussion of this point, cf. Carnap (6), sections 17, 24, 25.

9. Carnap, R., *The two concepts of probability* (*Philos. and Phenom. Research*, vol. 5, 1945).

10. Chisholm, R. M., *The contrary-to-fact conditional* (*Mind*, vol. 55, 1946).

11. Church, A., Review of (1), 2d ed. (*The Journal of Symb. Logic*, vol. 14, 1949, pp. 52–53).

12. Feigl, H., *Operationism and scientific method* (*Psychol. Review*, vol. 52, 1945). (Also reprinted in Feigl and Sellars, *Readings in Philosophical Analysis*, New York, 1949.)

13. ———, *Existential hypotheses; realistic vs. phenomenalistic interpretations* (*Philos. of Science*, vol. 17, 1950).

14. Goodman, N., *The problem of counterfactual conditionals* (*Journal of Philos.*, vol. 44, 1947).

15. ———, *The Structure of Appearance*, To be published soon, probably by Harvard University Press.

16. Hempel, C. G., and Oppenheim, P., *Studies in the logic of explanation* (*Philos. of Science*, vol. 15, 1948).

17. Kaplan, A., *Definition and specification of meaning* (*Journal of Philos.*, vol. 43, 1946).

18. Langford, C. H., Review in *The Journal of Symb. Logic*, vol. 6 (1941), pp. 67–68.

19. Lecomte du Noüy, *Human Destiny*, New York, London, Toronto 1947.

20. Lewis, C. I., *An Analysis of Knowledge and Valuation*, Open Court Publ., La Salle, Ill., 1946.

21. Pap, A., *Elements of Analytic Philosophy*, The Macmillian Co., New York, 1949.

22. Popper, K., *Logik der Forschung*, Springer, Wien, 1935.

23. ———, *The Open Society and its Enemies*, 2 vols., Routledge, London, 1945.

24. ———, *A note on natural laws and so-called "contrary-to-fact conditionals"* (*Mind*, vol. 58, 1949).

25. Reichenbach, H., *Philosophie der Raum-Zeit-Lehre*, Berlin, 1928.

26. ———, *Elements of Symbolic Logic*, The Macmillan Co., New York, 1947.

27. Russell, B., *Human Knowledge*, Simon and Schuster, New York, 1948.

28. Schlick, M., *Meaning and Verification* (*Philos. Review*, vol. 45, 1936). (Also reprinted in Feigl and Sellars, *Readings in Philosophical Analysis*, New York, 1949).

29. Stace, W. T., *Positivism* (*Mind*, vol. 53, 1944).

30. Tarski, A., *The semantic conception of truth and the foundations of semantics* (*Philos. and Phenom. Research*, vol. 4, 1944). (Also reprinted in Feigl and Sellars, *Readings in Philosophical Analysis*, New York, 1949.)

31. Werkmeister, W. H., *The Basis and Structure of Knowledge*, Harper, New York and London, 1948.

32. Whitehead, A. N., and Russell, B., *Principia Mathematica*, 3 vols., 2d ed., Cambridge, 1925–1927.

part iii LINGUISTIC ANALYSIS

11

G. E. *Moore* WITTGENSTEIN'S LECTURES IN 1930–1933

The lectures reported on by Moore in the following pages were given by Wittgenstein at Cambridge during the period between 1930 and 1933. Wittgenstein had recently returned to Cambridge from Austria, where he had been teaching school. It is fortunate that we have Moore's careful record of those lectures, since, except for a brief article in the Aristotelian Society Proceedings (1929), Wittgenstein did not himself publish any of his later views until the *Philosophical Investigations* (1953). The lectures are especially important because they show us the state of Wittgenstein's thought at a time when he was just beginning to formulate the view identified with the Later Wittgenstein.

The interested reader will want to follow his reading of this selection with a reading of the *Bluebook*, a set of notes dictated by Wittgenstein to his students. Also recommended is the *Brown Book,* which can be profitably read as preparation for reading in Wittgenstein's masterpiece, the *Philosophical Investigations.*

Expository commentaries on Wittgenstein are just beginning to appear. The following are worth consulting:

On the *Tractatus*
Anscombe, G.E.M.: *An Introduction to Wittgenstein's Tractatus* (London: Hutchinson, 1959).
Black, M.: *A Companion to Wittgenstein's Tractatus* (Ithaca, N.Y.: Cornell University Press, 1964).
Maslow, A.: *A Study in Wittgenstein's Tractatus* (Berkeley, Calif.: University of California Press, 1961).
Stenius, E.: *Wittgenstein's Tractatus* (Oxford: Blackwell and Mott, 1960).

On the Later Wittgenstein
Cavell, S.: "The Availability of Wittgenstein's Later Philosophy," *The Philosophical Review,* January, 1962.
Pitcher, G.: *The Philosophy of Wittgenstein* (Englewood Cliffs, N.J., Prentice-Hall, 1964).
Pole, D.: *The Later Philosophy of Wittgenstein* (London: Athlone Press, 1958).

From *Mind,* vol. LXIII, nos. 249, 251, and 253. Used by permission of the editor.

PART I

In January 1929, Wittgenstein returned to Cambridge after an absence of more than fifteen years. He came with the intention of residing in Cambridge and pursuing there his researches into philosophical problems. Why he chose Cambridge for this latter purpose I do not know: perhaps it was for the sake of having the opportunity of frequent discussion with F. P. Ramsey. At all events he did in fact reside in Cambridge during all three Full Terms of 1929, and was working hard all the time at his researches.[1] He must, however, at some time during that year, have made up his mind that, besides researching, he would like to do a certain amount of lecturing, since on October 16th, in accordance with his wishes, the Faculty Board of Moral Science resolved that he should be invited to give a course of lectures to be included in their Lecture List for the Lent Term of 1930.

During this year, 1929, when he was researching and had not begun to lecture, he took the Ph.D. degree at Cambridge. Having been entered as an "Advanced Student" during his previous period of residence in 1912 and 1913, he now found that he was entitled to submit a dissertation for the Ph.D. He submitted the *Tractatus* and Russell and I were appointed to examine him. We gave him an oral examination on June 6th, an occasion which I found both pleasant and amusing. We had, of course, no doubt whatever that his work deserved the degree: we so reported, and when our report had been approved by the necessary authorities, he received the degree in due course.

In the same month of June in which we examined him, the Council of Trinity College made him a grant to enable him to continue his researches. (They followed this up in December 1930, by electing him to a Research Fellowship, tenable for five years, which they afterwards prolonged for a time.)

In the following July of 1929 he attended the Joint Session of the Mind Association and Arisotelian Society at Nottingham, presenting a short paper entitled "Some Remarks on Logical Form." This paper was the only piece of philosophical writing by him, other than the *Tractatus,* published during his life-time. Of this paper he spoke in a letter to *Mind* (July 1933) as "weak"; and since 1945 he has spoken of it to me in a still more disparaging manner, saying something to the effect that, when he wrote it, he was getting new ideas about which he was still confused, and that he did not think it deserved any attention.

But what is most important about this year, 1929, is that in it he had frequent discussions with F. P. Ramsey—discussions which were, alas! brought to an end by Ramsey's premature death in January 1930.[2] Ramsey had written for *Mind* (October 1923, page 465) a long Critical Notice of the *Tractatus;* and

---

[1] The statement in the Obituary notice in *The Times* for May 2, 1951, that he arrived in Cambridge in 1929 "for a short visit" is very far from the truth. Fortunately I kept a brief diary during the period in question and can therefore vouch for the truth of what I have stated above about his residence in 1929, though there is in fact other evidence.

[2] In the Preface to his posthumously published *Philosophical Investigations,* where Wittgenstein acknowledges his obligations to Ramsey (p. x), Wittgenstein him-

subsequently, during the period when Wittengstein was employed as a village schoolmaster in Austria, Ramsey had gone out to see him, in order to question him as to the meaning of certain statements in the *Tractatus*. He stayed in the village for a fortnight or more, having daily discussions with Wittgenstein. Of these discussions in Austria I only know that Ramsey told me that, in reply to his questions as to the meaning of certain statements, Wittgenstein answered more than once that he had forgotten what he had meant by the statement in question. But after the first half of the discussions at Cambridge in 1929, Ramsey wrote at my request the following letter in support of the proposal that Trinity should make Wittgenstein a grant in order to enable him to continue his researches.

> In my opinion Mr. Wittgenstein is a philosophic genius of a different order from anyone else I know. This is partly owing to his great gift for seeing what is essential in a problem and partly to his overwhelming intellectual vigour, to the intensity of thought with which he pursues a question to the bottom and never rests content with a mere possible hypothesis. From his work more than that of any other man I hope for a solution of the difficulties that perplex me both in philosophy generally and in the foundations of Mathematics in particular.
>
> It seems to me, therefore, peculiarly fortunate that he should have returned to research. During the last two terms I have been in close touch with his work and he seems to me to have made remarkable progress. He began with certain questions in the analysis of propositions which have now led him to problems about infinity which lie at the root of current controversies on the foundations of Mathematics. At first I was afraid that lack of mathematical knowledge and facility would prove a serious handicap to his working in this field. But the progress he has made has already convinced me that this is not so, and that here too he will probably do work of the first importance.
>
> He is now working very hard and, so far as I can judge, he is getting on well. For him to be interrupted by lack of money would, I think, be a great misfortune for philosophy.

The only other thing I know about these discussions with Ramsey at Cambridge in 1929 is that Wittgenstein once told me that Ramsey had said to him "I don't like your method of arguing."

---

self says that he had "innumerable" discussions with Ramsey "during the last two years of his life," which should mean both in 1928 and in 1929. But I think this must be a mistake. I imagine that Wittgenstein, trusting to memory alone, had magnified into a series of discussions continuing for two years, a series which in fact only continued for a single year. It will be noticed that in the letter from Ramsey himself which I am about to quote, and which is dated June 14, 1929, Ramsey states that he had been in close touch with Wittgenstein's work "during the last two terms," i.e. during the Lent and May Terms of 1929, implying that he had not been in close touch with it in 1928. And though I do not know where Wittgenstein was in 1928, he certainly was not resident in Cambridge where Ramsey was resident, so that it is hardly possible that they can have had in that year such frequent discussions as they certainly had in 1929.

Wittgenstein began to lecture in January 1930, and from the first he adopted a plan to which he adhered, I believe, throughout his lectures at Cambridge.[a] His plan was only to lecture once a week in every week of Full Term, but on a later day in each week to hold a discussion class at which what he had said in that week's lecture could be discussed. At first both lecture and discussion class were held in an ordinary lecture-room in the University Arts School; but very early in the first term Mr. R. E. Priestley (now Sir Raymond Priestley), who was then Secretary General of the Faculties and who occupied a set of Fellows' rooms in the new building of Clare, invited Wittgenstein to hold his discussion classes in these rooms. Later on, I think, both lectures and discussion classes were held in Priestley's rooms, and this continued until, in October 1931, Wittgenstein, being then a Fellow of Trinity, was able to obtain a set of rooms of his own in Trinity which he really liked. These rooms were those which Wittgenstein had occupied in the academic year 1912–13, and which I had occupied the year before, and occupied again from October 1913, when Wittgenstein left Cambridge and went to Norway. Of the only two sets which are on the top floor of the gate-way from Whewell's Courts into Sidney Street, they were the set which looks westward over the larger Whewell's Court, and, being so high up, they had a large view of sky and also of Cambridge roofs, including the pinnacles of King's Chapel. Since the rooms were not a Fellow's set, their sitting-room was not large, and for the purpose of his lectures and classes Wittgenstein used to fill it with some twenty plain cane-bottomed chairs, which at other times were stacked on the large landing outside. Nearly from the beginning the discussion classes were liable to last at least two hours, and from the time when the lectures ceased to be given in the Arts School they also commonly lasted at least as long. Wittgenstein always had a blackboard at both lectures and classes and made plenty of use of it.

I attended both lectures and discussion classes in all three terms of 1930 and in the first two terms of 1931. In the Michaelmas Term of 1931 and the Lent Term of 1932 I ceased, for some reason which I cannot now remember, to attend the lectures though I still went to the discussion classes; but in May 1932, I resumed the practice of attending the lectures as well, and throughout the academic year 1932–1933 I attended both. At the lectures, though not at the discussion classes, I took what I think were very full notes, scribbled in notebooks of which I have six volumes nearly full. I remember Wittgenstein once saying to me that he was glad I was taking notes, since, if anything were to happen to him, they would contain some record of the results of his thinking.

My lecture-notes may be naturally divided into three groups, to which I will refer as (I), (II), and (III). (I) contains the notes of his lectures in the Lent and May Terms of 1930; (II) those of his lectures in the academic year 1930–

---

[a] Professor von Wright has subsequently informed me that I was mistaken in believing this: that in 1939, Wittgenstein lectured twice a week and held no discussion class; and that in the Easter Term of 1947, he both gave two lectures a week and also held a discussion class. I have also remembered that at one time (I do not know for how long) he gave, besides his ordinary lectures, a special set of lectures for mathematicians.

1931; and (III) those of lectures which he gave in the May Term of 1932, after I had resumed attending, as well as those of all the lectures he gave in the academic year 1932–1933. The distinction between the three groups is of some importance, since, as will be seen, he sometimes in later lectures corrected what he had said in earlier ones.

The chief topics with which he dealt fall, I think, under the following heads. First of all, in all three periods he dealt (A) with some very general questions about language, (B) with some special questions in the philosophy of Logic, and (C) with some special questions in the philosophy of Mathematics. Next, in (III) and in (III) alone, he dealt at great length, (D) with the difference between the proposition which is expressed by the words "I have got toothache," and those which are expressed by the words "You have got toothache" or "He has got toothache," in which connection he said something about Behaviourism, Solipsism, Idealism, and Realism, and (E) with what he called "the grammar of the word 'God' and of ethical and aesthetic statements." And he also dealt, more shortly, in (I) with (F) our use of the term "primary colour"; in (III) with (G) some questions about Time; and in both (II) and (III) with (H) the kind of investigation in which he was himself engaged, and its difference from and relation to what has traditionally been called "philosophy."

I will try to give some account of the chief things he said under all these heads; but I cannot possibly mention nearly everything, and it is possible that some of the things I omit were really more important than those I mention. Also, though I tried to get down in my notes the actual words he used, it is possible that I may sometimes have substituted words of my own which misrepresent his meaning: I certainly did not understand a good many of the things he said. Moreover, I cannot possibly do justice to the extreme richness of illustration and comparison which he used: he was really succeeding in giving what he called a "synoptic" view of things which we all know. Nor can I do justice to the intensity of conviction with which he said everything which he did say, nor to the extreme interest which he excited in his hearers. He, of course, never read his lectures: he had not, in fact, written them out, although he always spent a great deal of time in thinking out what he proposed to say.

(A) He did discuss at very great length, especially in (II), certain very general questions about language; but he said, more than once, that he did not discuss these questions because he thought that language was the subject-matter of philosophy. He did not think that it was. He discussed it only because he thought that particular philosophical errors or "troubles in our thought" were due to false analogies suggested by our actual use of expressions; and he emphasized that it was only necessary for him to discuss those points about language which, as he thought, led to these particular errors or "troubles."

The general things that he had to say about language fall naturally, I think, under two heads, namely (*a*) what he had to say about the meaning of single words, and (*b*) what he had to say about "propositions."

(*a*) About the meaning of single words, the positive points on which he seemed most anxious to insist were, I think, two, namely (*a*) something which he expressed by saying that the meaning of any single word in a language is "defined," "constituted," "determined," or "fixed" (he used all four expressions in different places) by the "grammatical rules" with which it is used in that language, and (β) something which he expressed by saying that every significant word or symbol must essentially belong to a "system," and (metaphorically) by saying that the meaning of a word is its "place" in a "grammatical system."

But he said in (III) that the sense of "meaning" of which he held these things to be true, and which was the only sense in which he intended to use the word, was only one of those in which we commonly use it: that there was another which he described as that in which it is used "as a name for a process accompanying our use of a word and our hearing of a word." By the latter he apparently meant that sense of "meaning" in which "to know the meaning" of a word means the same as to "understand" the word; and I think he was not quite clear as to the relation between this sense of "meaning" and that in which he intended to use it, since he seemed in two different places to suggest two different and incompatible views of this relation, saying in (II) that "the rules applying to negation actually describe my experience in using 'not,' i.e. describe my understanding of the word," and in one place in (III), on the other hand, saying, "perhaps there is a causal connection between the rules and the feeling we have when we hear 'not'." On the former occasion he added that "a logical investigation doesn't teach us anything about the meaning of negation: we can't get any clearer about its meaning. What's difficult is to make the rules explicit."

Still later in (III) he made the rather queer statement that "the idea of meaning is in a way obsolete, except in such phrases as 'this means the same as that' or 'this has no meaning'," having previously said in (III) that "the mere fact that we have the expression 'the meaning' of a word is bound to lead us wrong: we are led to think that the rules are responsible to something not a rule, whereas they are only responsible to rules."

As to (a) although he had said, at least once, that the meaning of a word was "constituted" by the grammatical rules which applied to it, he explained later that he did not mean that the meaning of a word *was* a list of rules; and he said that though a word "carried its meaning with it," it did not carry with it the grammatical rules which applied to it. He said that the student who had asked him whether he meant that the meaning of a word *was* a list of rules would not have been tempted to ask that question but for the false idea (which he held to be a common one) that in the case of a substantive like "the meaning" you have to look for something at which you can point and say "This is the meaning." He seemed to think that Frege and Russell had been misled by the same idea, when they thought they were bound to give an answer to the question "What *is* the number 2?" As for what he meant by saying that the meaning of a word is "determined by" (this was the phrase which he seemed to prefer) the "grammatical rules" in accordance with which it is used, I do not think he explained further what he meant by this phrase.

(β) As to what he meant by saying that, in order that a word or other sign should have meaning, it must belong to a "system," I have not been able to arrive at any clear idea. One point on which he insisted several times in (II) was that if a word which I use is to have meaning, I must "commit myself" by its use. And he explained what he meant by this by saying "If I commit myself, that means that if I use, e.g., 'green' in this case, I have to use it in others," adding "If you commit yourself, there are consequences." Similarly he said a little later, "If a word is to have significance, we must commit ourselves," adding "There is no use in correlating noises to facts, unless we commit ourselves to using the noise in a particular way again—unless the correlation has consequences," and going on to say that it must be possible to be "led by a language." And when he expressly raised, a little later, the question "What is there in this talk of a 'system' to which a symbol must belong?" he answered that we are concerned with the phenomenon of "being guided by." It looked, therefore, as if one use which he was making of the word "system" was such that in order to say that a word or other sign "belonged to a system," it was not only necessary but *sufficient* that it should be used in the same way on several different occasions. And certainly it would be natural to say that a man who habitually used a word in the same way was using it "systematically."

But he certainly also frequently used "system" in such a sense that *different* words or other expressions could be said to belong to the *same* "system"; and where, later on, he gave, as an illustration of what he meant by "Every symbol must essentially belong to a system," the proposition "A crotchet can only give information on what note to play in a system of crotchets," he seemed to imply that for a sign to have significance it is *not* sufficient that we should "commit ourselves" by its use, but that it is also necessary that the sign in question should belong to the same "system" with other signs. Perhaps, however, he only meant, not that for a sign to have *some* meaning, but that for *some* signs to have *the significance which they actually have in a given language,* it is necessary that they should belong to the same "system" with other signs. This word "system" was one which he used very very frequently, and I do not know what conditions he would have held must be satisfied by two different signs in order that they may properly be said to belong to the same "system." He said in one place in (II) that the "system of projection" by which "2 + 3" can be projected into "5" is "in no way inferior" to the "system" by which "11 + 111" can be projected into "11111," and I think one can see, in this case, that "2 + 3 = 5" can be properly said to belong to the same "system" as, e.g., "2 + 2 ≠ 4," and also can properly be said to belong to a different "system" from that to which "11 + 111 = 11111" and "11 + 11 = 1111" both belong, though I have no clear idea as to the sense in which these things can properly be said. Nor do I know whether Wittgenstein would have held, e.g., that in the case of *every* English word, it could not have the significance which it actually has in English unless it belonged to the same "system" as other English words, or whether he would have held that this is only true of *some* English words, e.g. of the words "five" and "four," and of the words "red" and "green."

But besides these two positive things, (*a*) and (*β*), which he seemed anxious to say about the meaning of words, he also insisted on three negative things, i.e. that three views which have sometimes been held are mistakes. The first of these mistakes was (*γ*) the view that the meaning of a word was some image which it calls up by association—a view to which he seemed to refer as the "causal" theory of meaning. He admitted that sometimes you cannot understand a word unless it calls up an image, but insisted that, even where this is the case, the image is just as much a "symbol" as the word is. The second mistake was (δ) the view that, where we can give an "ostensive" definition of a word, the object pointed at is the meaning of the word. Against this view, he said, for one thing, that, in such a case "the gesture of pointing together with the object pointed at can be used *instead* of the word," i.e. is itself something which has meaning and has the same meaning as the word has. In this connection he also pointed out that you may point at a red book, either to show the meaning of "book" or to show the meaning of "red," and that hence in "This is a book" and "This is the colour 'red'," "this" has quite a different meaning; and he emphasized that, in order to understand the ostensive definition "This is 'red'," the hearer must already understand what is meant by "colour." And the third mistake was (ε) that a word is related to its meaning in the same way in which a proper name is related to the "bearer" of that name. He gave as a reason for holding that this is false that the bearer of a name can be ill or dead, whereas we cannot possibly say that the meaning of the name is ill or dead. He said more than once that the bearer of a name can be "substituted" for the name, whereas the meaning of a word can never be substituted for that word. He sometimes spoke of this third mistake as the view that words are "representative" of their meanings, and he held that in no case is a word "representative" of its meaning, although a proper name is "representative" of its bearer (if it has one). He added in one place: "The meaning of a word is no longer for us an object corresponding to it."

On the statement "Words, except in propositions, have no meaning" he said that this "is true or false, as you understand it"; and immediately went on to add that, in what he called "language games," single words "have meanings by themselves," and that they may have meaning by themselves even in our ordinary language "if we have provided one." In this connection he said, in (II), that he had made a mistake (I think he meant in the *Tractatus*) in supposing that a proposition must be complex. He said the truth was that we can replace a proposition by a simple sign, but that the simple sign must be "part of a system."

(*b*) About "propositions," he said a great deal in many places as to answers which might be given to the question "What is a proposition?"—a question which he said we do not understand clearly. But towards the end of (III) he had definitely reached the conclusion "It is more or less arbitrary what we call a 'proposition'," adding that "therefore Logic plays a part different from what I and Russell and Frege supposed it to play"; and a little later he said that he could not give a general definition of "proposition" any more than of "game": that he could only give examples, and that any line he could draw would be "arbitrary, in the sense that nobody would have decided whether to call so-and-so a 'proposition' or not." But he added that we are quite right to use the word "game," so long as we don't pretend to have drawn a definite outline.

In (II), however, he had said that the word "proposition," "as generally understood," includes both "what I call propositions," also "hypotheses," and also mathematical propositions; that the distinction between these three "kinds" is a "logical distinction," and that therefore there must be some grammatical rules, in the case of each kind, which apply to that kind and not to the other two; but that the "truth-function" rules apply to all three, and that that is why they are all called "propositions."

He went on to illustrate the difference between the first two kinds by saying that "There seems to me to be a man here" is of the first kind, whereas "There is a man here" is a "hypothesis"; and said that one rule which applies to the first and not to the second is that I can't say "There seems to me to seem to me to be a man here" whereas I can say "There seems to me to be a man here." But, soon after, he said that the word "proposition" is used in *two* different ways, a wider and a narrower, meaning by the wider that in which it included all three of the kinds just distinguished, and by the narrower, apparently, that in which it included the first two kinds, but not the third. For propositions in this narrower sense he seemed later very often to use the expression "experiential propositions," and accordingly I will use this expression to include propositions of both the first two kinds. The things which he had to say about experiential propositions, thus understood, were extremely different from those which he had to say about the third kind; and I will therefore treat these two subjects separately.

(*a*) Of experiential propositions he said in (I) that they could be "compared with reality" and either "agreed or disagreed with it." He pointed out very early something which he expressed by saying "Much of language needs outside help," giving as an example your use of a specimen of a colour in order to explain what colour you want a wall painted; but he immediately went on to say (using "language" in a different sense) that in such a case the specimen of a colour is "a part of your language." He also pointed out (as in the *Tractatus*) that you can assert a proposition or give an order without using any words or symbols (in the ordinary sense of "symbol"). One of the most striking things about his use of the term "proposition" was that he apparently so used it that in giving an order you are necessarily expressing a "proposition," although, of course, an order can be neither true nor false, and can be "compared with reality" only in the different sense that you can look to see whether it is carried out or not.

About propositions, understood in this sense, he made a distinction in (II) between what he called "the sign" and what he called "the symbol," saying that whatever was necessary to give a "sign" significance was a part of "the symbol," so that where, for instance, the "sign" is a sentence, the "symbol" is something which contains both the sign and also everything which is necessary to give that sentence sense. He said that a "symbol," thus understood, *is* a "proposition" and "cannot be nonsensical, though it can be either true or false." He illustrated this by saying that if a man says "I am tired" his mouth is part of the symbol; and said that any explanation of a sign "completes the symbol."

Here, therefore, he seemed to be making a distinction between a proposition and a sentence, such that no sentence can be identical with any proposition, and that no proposition can be without sense. But I do not think that in his actual use of the term "proposition" he adhered to this distinction. He seemed to me sometimes so to use "proposition" that every significant sentence *was* a proposition, although, of course, a significant sentence does not contain everything which is necessary to give it significance. He said, for instance, that signs with different meanings must *be* different "symbols." And very often he seemed to me to follow the example of Russell in the Introduction to *Principia Mathematica* in so using the word "proposition" that "propositions," and not merely sentences, could be without sense; as, for instance, when he said at the beginning of (II) that his object was to give us some "firm ground" such as "If a proposition has a meaning, its negation must have a meaning." And, towards the end of (III), in connection with the view at which he had then arrived that the words "proposition," "language," and "sentence" are all "vague," he expressly said that the answer to the question whether, when you say "A unicorn looks like this" and point at a picture of a unicorn, the picture is or is not a part of the proposition you are making, was "You can say which you please." He was, therefore, now rejecting his earlier view that a proposition must contain everything which is necessary to make a sentence significant, and seemed to be implying that the use of "proposition" to mean the same as "sentence" was a perfectly correct one.

In connection with the *Tractatus* statement that propositions, in the "narrower" sense with which we are now concerned, are "pictures," he said he had not at that time noticed that the word "picture" was vague; but he still, even towards the end of (III), said that he thought it "useful to say 'A proposition is a picture *or something like one*'" although in (II) he had said he was willing to admit that to call a proposition a "picture" was misleading; that propositions are not pictures "in any ordinary sense"; and that to say that they are, "merely stresses a certain aspect of the grammar of the word 'proposition'—merely stresses that our uses of the words 'proposition' and 'picture' follow similar rules."

In connection with this question of the similarity between experiential "propositions" and pictures, he frequently used the words "project" and "projection." Having pointed out that it is paradoxical to say that the words "Leave the room" is a "picture" of what a boy does if he obeys the order, and having asserted that it is, in fact, *not* a "picture" of the boy's action "in any ordinary sense," he nevertheless went on to say that it is "as much" a picture of the boy's action as "2 + 3" is of "5," and that "2 + 3" really is a picture of "5" "*with reference to a particular system of projection*," and that this system is "in no way inferior" to the system in which "11 + 111" is projected into "11111," only that "the method of projection is rather queer." He had said previously that the musical signs "♯" and "♭" are obviously not pictures of anything you do on the keyboard of a piano; that they differ in this respect from what,

e.g., " 𝄞 " would be, if you had the rule that the second crotchet is to stand for the white key on the piano that is next to the right of that for which the first crotchet stands, and similarly for the third and second crotchet; but nevertheless, he said, "♯" and "♭" "work in exactly the same way" as these crotchets would work, and added that "almost all our words work as they do." He explained this by saying that a "picture" must have been given by an explanation of how "♯" and "♭" are used, and that an explanation is always of the same kind as a definition, viz. "replacing one symbol by another." He went on to say that when a man reads on a piano from a score, he is "led" or "guided" by the position of the crotchets, and that this means that he is "following a general rule," and that this rule, though not "contained" in the score, nor in the result, nor in both together, must be "contained" in his intention. But he said, that though the rule is "contained" in the intention, the intention obviously does not "contain" any *expression* of the rule, any more than, when I read aloud, I am conscious of the rules I follow in translating the printed signs into sounds. He said that what the piano player does is "to see the rule in the score," and that, even if he is playing automatically, he is still "guided by" the score, provided that he *would* use the general rule to judge whether he had made a mistake or not. He even said in one place that to say that a man is "guided" by the score "means" that he *would justify* what he played by reference to the score. He concluded by saying that, if he plays correctly, there is *a* "similarity" between what he does on the piano and the score, "though we usually confine 'similarity' to projection according to certain rules only"; and that in the same sense there is *a* "similarity" between automatic traffic signals and the movements of traffic which are guided by them. Later on he said that for any sign whatever there *could* be a method of projection such that it made sense, but that when he said of any particular expression "That means nothing" or "is nonsense," what he meant was "*With the common method of projection* that means nothing," giving as an instance that when he called the sentence "It is due to human weakness that we can't write down all the cardinal numbers" "meaningless," he meant that it is meaningless if the person who says it is using "due to human weakness" as in "It's due to human weakness that we can't write down a billion cardinal numbers." Similarly, he said that surely Helmholtz must have been talking nonsense when he said that in happy moments he could imagine four-dimensional space, because *in the system he was using* those words make no sense, although "I threw the chalk into four-dimensional space" would make sense, if we were not using the words on the analogy of throwing from one room into another, but merely meant "It first disappeared and then appeared again." He insisted more than once that we are apt to think that we are using a new system of projection which would give sense to our words, when in fact we are not using a new system at all: "any expression" he said "*may* make sense, but you may think you are using it with sense, when in fact you are not."

One chief view about propositions to which he was opposed was a view which he expressed as the view that a proposition is a sort of "shadow" intermediate between the expression which we use in order to assert it and the fact (if any) which "verifies" it. He attributed this view to W. E. Johnson, and he said of it that it was an attempt to make a distinction between a proposition and a sentence. (We have seen that he himself had in (II) made a different attempt to do this.) He said that it regarded the supposed "shadow" as something "similar" to the fact which verifies it, and in that way different from the expression which expresses it, which is not "similar" to the fact in question; and he said that, even if there were such a "shadow" it would not "bring us any nearer to the fact," since "it would be susceptible of different interpretations just as the expression is." He said, "You can't give any picture which can't be misinterpreted" and "No interpolation between a sign and its fulfilment does away with a sign." He added that the only description of an expectation "which is relevant for us" is "the expression of it," and that "the expression of an expectation contains a description of the fact that would fulfil it," pointing out that if I expect to *see a red patch* my expectation is fulfilled if and only if I do *see a red patch,* and saying that the words "see a red patch" have the same meaning in both expressions.

Near the beginning of (I) he made the famous statement, "The sense of a proposition is the way in which it is verified"; but in (III) he said this only meant "You can determine the meaning of a proposition by asking how it is verified" and went on to say, "This is necessarily a mere rule of thumb, because 'verification' means different things, and because in some cases the question 'How is that verified?' makes no sense." He gave as an example of a case in which that question "makes no sense" the proposition "I've got toothache," of which he had already said that it makes no sense to ask for a verification of it —to ask "How do you know that you have?" I think that he here meant what he said of "I've got toothache" to apply to all those propositions which he had originally distinguished from "hypotheses" as "what I call propositions"; although in (II) he had distinguished the latter from "hypotheses" by saying that they had "a definite verification or falsification." It would seem, therefore, that in (III) he had arrived at the conclusion that what he had said in (II) was wrong, and that in the case of "what he called propositions," so far from their having "a definite verification," it was senseless to say that they had a verification at all. His "rule of thumb," therefore, could only apply, if at all, to what he called "hypotheses"; and he went on to say that, in many cases, it does not apply even to these, saying that statements in the newspapers could verify the "hypothesis" that Cambridge had won the boat-race, and that yet these statements "only go a very little way towards explaining the meaning of 'boat-race' "; and that similarly "The pavement is wet" may verify the proposition "It has been raining," and that yet "it gives very little of the grammar of 'It has been raining'." He went on to say "Verification determines the meaning of a proposition only where it gives the grammar of the proposition in question"; and in answer to the question "How far is giving a verification of a proposition a grammatical statement about it?" he said that, whereas "When it rains the pavement gets wet" is not a grammatical statement at all, if we say "The fact that the pavement is wet is a *symptom* that it has been raining" this statement is "a matter of grammar."

PART II

(β) The third kind of "proposition" mentioned in Part I of which at the very beginning of (I) Wittgenstein gave mathematical propositions as an example, saying that they are a "very different sort of instrument" from, e.g. "There is a piece of chalk here," and of which he sometimes said that they are not propositions at all, were those which have been traditionally called "necessary," as opposed to "contingent." They are propositions of which the negation would be said to be, not merely false, but "impossible," "unimaginable," "unthinkable" (expressions which he himself often used in speaking of them). They include not only the propositions of pure Mathematics, but also those of Deductive

Logic, certain propositions which would usually be said to be propositions about colours, and an immense number of others.

Of these propositions he undoubtedly held that, unlike "experiential" propositions, they cannot be "compared with reality," and do not "either agree or disagree" with it. But I think the most important thing he said about them, and certainly one of the most important things he said anywhere in these lectures, was an attempt to explain exactly how they differed from experiental propositions. And this attempt, so far as I can see, consisted in maintaining with regard to them two things, viz. (β') that the sentences, which would commonly be said to express them, do in fact, when used in this way, "say nothing" or "are without sense," and (β'') that this supposed fact that such sentences, when so used, are without sense, is due to the fact that they are related in a certain way to "rules of grammar." But *what*, precisely, was the relation to grammatical rules, which he held to be the reason why they had no sense? This question still puzzles me extremely.

For a time I thought (though I felt that this was doubtful) that he held so-called necessary propositions to be *identical* with certain grammatical rules—a view which would have yielded the conclusion that sentences, which would commonly be said to express necessary propositions, are in fact always merely expressing rules of grammar. And I think he did in fact hold that the very same expressions, which would commonly be said to express necessary propositions, can also be properly used in such a way that, when so used, they merely express rules of grammar. But I think he must have been aware (though I think he never expressly pointed this out) that, if so, then, *when* such expressions are being used merely to express rules of grammar they are being used in a very different way from that in which, on his view, they are being used when they would commonly be said to be expressing necessary propositions. For he certainly held, if I am not mistaken, of *all* expressions which would commonly be said to be expressing necessary propositions, what in the *Tractatus* he had asserted to be true of the particular case of "tautologies," viz. both (1) that, when so used, they are "without sense" and "say nothing," and (2) that, nevertheless, they are, in a certain sense "true," though he made plain, in these lectures, that he thought that the sense in which they are "true" was very different from that in which experiential propositions may be "true." (As I have said, he seemed to me often to use the words "proposition" and "sentence" as if they meant the same, perhaps partly because the German word "*Satz*" may be properly used for either; and therefore often talked as if sentences could *be* "true".) But of the same expressions, when used, as he thought they might be, merely to express rules, though he might perhaps have said that they "say nothing," since he insisted strongly of one particular class of them, namely, those which express rules of deduction, that they are neither true nor false, he cannot, I think, have held that they are "without sense"; indeed he said, at least once, of an expression which would commonly be said to express a necessary proposition, "if it is to have any meaning, it must be a mere rule of a game"—thus implying that, if it is used to express a rule, it has a meaning. But in what sense was he using "rules," when he insisted that his own "rules of inference" were neither true nor false? I think this is an important question, because he seems to me to have used the expression "rules of grammar" in two different senses, the difference between which he never expressly pointed out, and one of which is such that a grammatical rule, in that sense, will be true or false. He often spoke as if rules of grammar *allowed* you to use certain expressions and *forbade* you to use others, and he gave me the impression that, when so speaking, he was giving the name of "rules" to actual statements that you are allowed or forbidden to use certain expressions—that, for instance, he would have called the statement, "You can't say 'Two men *was* working in that field' " a rule of English grammar. This use of "can't" is, indeed, one which is quite natural and familiar in the case of rules of games, to which he constantly compared rules of grammar; e.g., a chess-player might quite naturally say to an opponent, who was a beginner and was not yet familiar with the rules of chess, "You can't do that" or "You can't make that move," if the beginner moved a pawn, from its position at the beginning of the game, three squares forward instead of only two. But, if we so use "rule" that the expression "You can't do that," when thus used, is expressing a rule, then surely a rule *can* be true or false; for it is possible to be mistaken as to whether you can or can't make a certain move at chess, and "You can't do that" will be true, if it is an *established* rule in chess not to make the kind of move in question, and will be false if there is no such established rule. But if we ask: What is the rule which *is* established in such a case? we come upon a very different sense of "rule"; for the answer to this question will consist in describing or specifying a way in which somebody *might* act, whether anybody ever does so act or not; and with this sense of "rule" it seems to me obvious that a rule cannot be true or false, and equally obvious that any expression which specifies it will have sense. In the case of rules of grammar, the possible action which such a rule specifies, will, of course, be a way of using words or forms of sentence in speaking or writing; and I think that the fact that "rule" may be used in this sense, in which a "rule" can obviously be neither true nor false, may have been partly responsible for Wittgenstein's assertion that his "rules of inference" were neither true nor false. It is perhaps worth noting that the statement that such a rule is an *established* rule in a given language (as is implied for English by, e.g., the statement, "You can't say 'Two men *was* working in that field' "), which really is true or false, is, of course, an experiential proposition about the way in which words or forms of sentence are actually used in the language in question; and that, therefore, if we suppose that the very same expression which is sometimes used to express a necessary proposition can also be used to express such an experiential proposition, then the ways in which it is used in these two cases must be very different; just as the ways in which the same expression is used, if used sometimes to express a necessary proposition and sometimes merely to specify a possible way of speaking or writing, must also be very different.

I think, therefore, that Wittgenstein cannot possibly have held that expressions which are being used in the way in which they would commonly be said to be expressing necessary propositions, are being used in the same way in which they are being used when used to express rules of grammar. But, if so, to *what* relation to rules of grammar did he hold it was due that expressions which are being used in the former way, have no sense? I am still extremely puzzled as to the answer to this question, for the following reason.

He seemed often to suggest that any sentence which is "constructed in accordance with" (this is his own phrase) the rules of grammar of the language to which the sentence belongs, always has sense; e.g., that any English sentence which is constructed in accordance with the rules of English grammar, has sense. But, if so, since he held that, e.g., the sentences "2 + 2 = 4" or "The proposition with regard to any two propositions that they are not both false follows logically from the proposition that they are both true," both of which would certainly be commonly said to express necessary propositions, are, when so used, without sense, he must have held that these two sentences, when so used, are not constructed in accordance with the rules of English grammar. Can he possibly have held that they are not? I think it is possible he did; but I do not know. In Helmholtz's statement that he could imagine the fourth dimension, he seemed to be saying that if Helmholtz was "projecting" the sentence "I can imagine a piece of chalk being thrown into the fourth dimension" "with the common method of projection," then he was talking nonsense, but that if he had been "projecting" that sentence in an unusual way, so that it meant the same as "I can imagine a piece of chalk first disappearing and then appearing again," then he would have been talking sense.

But is not "projecting with the common method of projection" merely a metaphorical way of saying "using in accordance with the established rules of grammar"? If so, then Wittgenstein was here saying that a sentence used in accordance with the established rules of grammar may nevertheless *not* make sense, and even implying that, in particular cases, the fact that it does not make sense is (partly) due to the fact that it *is* being used in accordance with the usual rules. I think, however, that possibly he intended to distinguish between "projecting with the common method" and "using in accordance with the usual rules," since he insisted strongly in at least one passage that any rule can be "interpreted" in different ways, and also (if I have not misunderstood him) that it is impossible to add to any rule an unambiguous rule as to how it is to be interpreted. Possibly, therefore, he meant by "projecting with the common method," *not* "using in accordance with the usual rules," but "*interpreting* in the usual manner"—a distinction which would apparently allow him to hold that, when Helmholtz uttered his nonsensical sentence, he was *not* using that sentence in accordance with the usual rules, though he *was* interpreting in the usual manner the rules, whatever they may have been, in accordance with which he was using it. But I am very puzzled as to how this distinction could be used. Suppose, for instance, a person were to use "I can imagine a piece of chalk being thrown into the fourth dimension" in such a way that it meant the same as "I can imagine a piece of chalk first disappearing and then appearing again," how on earth could anyone (including the person in question) possibly decide whether in such a case the speaker or writer was doing what Wittgenstein called elsewhere "changing his grammar," i.e. using the first expression *not* in accordance with the usual rules, but in accordance with rules such that it meant the same as the second means, or whether he was merely "interpreting" in an unusual way the rules, whatever they may have been, in accordance with which he was using the first expression? I suspect, therefore, that when Wittgenstein said that Helmholtz must have been using the "common method of projection," when he uttered his nonsensical sentence, he was not distinguishing this from using the sentence in accordance with the ordinary rules, and was therefore implying that a sentence constructed in accordance with the ordinary rules might nevertheless be without sense. But, if so, his view may have been that, e.g., "$2 + 2 = 4$," when used in the way in which it would commonly be said to express a necessary proposition, *is* used in accordance with the ordinary rules of grammar, and is nevertheless "without sense," and is so partly *because* it *is* used in accordance with the ordinary rules; for he certainly would not have denied that that expression *might* be used in such a way that it had sense. But I do not know whether this was his view or not.

But finally there is still another reason why I am puzzled as to what his view was about sentences, which would commonly be said to express necessary propositions. His view was, if I am right, one which he expressed by the use of the expressions, (β') "without sense," as equivalent to which he often used the expressions "nonsense," "meaningless," and even "useless" and (β'') "rules of grammar"; and these two expressions were used by him constantly throughout these lectures. And my last puzzle is due to the fact that I think there is reason to suspect that he was not using either expression in any ordinary sense, and that I have not been able to form any clear idea as to how he was using them.

(β') With regard to the expression "without sense" I think there is no doubt that he was using it in the same way in which he used it in the *Tractatus*, 4.461, when he said that a "tautology" is without sense (sinnlos). In that passage he gave as an example of the supposed fact that a "tautology" is without sense the statement "I know nothing about the weather, if I know that either it is raining or it is not"; and in these lectures he used a very similar example to show the same thing. Also in that passage of the *Tractatus* he said that a "tautology" "says nothing," and seemed to mean by this the same as what he meant by saying that it was "without sense"; and this expression he also used in these lectures, and apparently in the same sense. And I think it is clearly true that we could say correctly of a man who only knew that either it was raining or it was not, that he knew nothing *about the present state of the weather*. But could we also say correctly of such a man that he knew *nothing at all?* I do not think we could; and yet, so far as I can see, it is only if we could say this correctly that we should be justified in saying that the sentence "Either it is raining or it is not" "says nothing" or is "without sense." I think, therefore, that Wittgenstein can only have been right in saying that "tautologies" and other sentences, which would commonly be said to express necessary propositions, are "without sense" and "say nothing," if he was using these two expressions in some peculiar way, different from any in which they are ordinarily used. So far as I can see, if we use "make sense" in any way in which it is ordinarily used, "Either it's raining or it's not" *does* make sense, since we should certainly say that the meaning of this sentence is different from that of "Either it's snowing or it's not," thus implying that since they have different meanings, both of them have *some* meaning; and similarly, if "say nothing" is used in any sense in which it is ordinarily used, Wittgenstein's proposition in *Tractatus* 5.43 that "All the 'Sätze' of Logic say the same, namely, nothing" seems to me to be certainly untrue. And that he was using these expressions in some peculiar way seems to me to be also suggested by the fact that in *Tractatus* 4.461, he seems to be saying that "contradictions" are "without sense" in the same sense in which "tautologies" are, in spite of the fact that in the very same passage he asserts that the latter are "unconditionally true," while the former are "true under no condition." But, if he was using these expressions (and also "meaningless" and "nonsense," which, as I have said, he often used as equivalent to them) in some peculiar sense, what was that sense? Later in (III) he expressly raised the questions "What is meant by the decision that a sentence makes or does not make sense?" and "What is the criterion of making sense?" having said that, in order to answer these questions, he must "plunge into something terrible," and that he must do this in order to "put straight" what he had just been saying, which, he said, he had not "put correctly." In trying to answer these questions or this question (for I think he was using the two expressions to mean the same) he said many things, including the statement that he had himself been "misled" by the expression "sense"; and he went on to say that his present view was that " 'sense' was correlative to 'proposition' " (meaning, apparently, here by "proposition" what he had formerly called "proposition in the narrower sense," i.e. "experiential proposition," thus excluding, e.g., mathematical "propositions") and that hence, if "proposition" was not "sharply bounded," "sense" was not "sharply bounded" either. He went on to say about "proposition" the things which I have already quoted (pages 240–241); and then implied that where we say "This makes no sense" we always mean "This makes nonsense *in this particular game*"; and in answer to the question "Why do we call it 'nonsense'? what does it mean to call it so?" said that when we call a sentence "nonsense," it is "because of some similarity to sentences which have sense," and that "nonsense always arises from forming symbols analogous to certain uses, where they have no use." He concluded finally that " 'makes sense' is vague, and will have different senses in different cases," but that the expression "makes sense" is useful just as "game" is useful, although, like "game," it "alters its meaning as we go from proposition to proposition"; adding that, just as "sense" is vague, so must be "grammar," "grammatical rule," and "syntax."

But all this, it seems to me, gives no explanation of how he was using the expression "without sense" in the particular case of "tautologies" and other sentences which would commonly be said to express necessary propositions: it only tells us that he might be using it in a different sense in that case from that in which he used it in other cases. The only explanation which, so far as I know, he did give as to how he was using it in the particular case of "tautologies," was where he asked in (III), "What does the statement that a tautology 'says nothing' mean?" and gave as an answer, that to say that "$q \supset q$" "says nothing" means that $p \cdot (q \supset q) = p$; giving as an example that the logical product "It's raining and I've either got grey hair or I've not" $=$ "It's raining." If he did mean this, and if, as he seemed to be, he was using "says nothing" to mean the same as "is without sense," one important point would follow, namely, that he was not using "without sense" in the same way in the case of "tautologies" as in the case of "contradictions," since he would certainly not have said that $p \cdot (q.\sim q) = p$. But it gives us no further explanation of how he *was* using "without sense" in the case of "tautologies." For if he was using that expression in any ordinary way, then I think he was wrong in saying that "It's raining, and I've either got grey hair or I've not" = "It's raining," since, in any ordinary usage, we should say that the "sense" of "either I've got grey hair or I've not" was different from that of, e.g., "either I'm six feet high or I'm not," and should not say, as apparently he would, that both sentences say nothing, and therefore say the same.

In connection with his use of the phrase "without sense," one other thing which he said or implied more than once should, I think, be mentioned, because it may give a partial explanation of why he thought that both "contradictions" and "tautologies" are without sense. He said in (I) that "the linguistic expression" of "This line can be bisected" is " 'This line *is* bisected' has sense," while at the same time insisting that "the linguistic expression" of "This line is infinitely divisible" is not " 'This line is infinitely divided' has sense" (he held that "This line *is* infinitely divided" is senseless) but is "an infinite possibility in language." He held, therefore, that in many cases the "linguistic expression" of "It is possible that p should be true" or "should have been true" is "The sentence 'p' has sense." And I think there is no doubt that he here meant by "possible" what is commonly called, and was called by him on a later occasion, "logically possible." But to say that a sentence "p" is the "linguistic expression" of a *proposition* "q," would naturally mean that the sentence "p" and the *sentence* "q" have the same meaning, although for some reason or other "p" can be called a "linguistic expression," though the sentence "q" cannot. And that he did hold that, if an expression "p" is "the linguistic expression" of a *proposition* "q," then the expression "p" and the *expression* "q" have the same meaning was also suggested by a passage late in (III), where, having explained that by "possible" he here meant "logically possible," he asked the question "Doesn't 'I can't feel his toothache' mean that 'I feel his toothache' has no sense?" obviously implying that the right answer to this question is "Yes, it does." And he also, in several other places, seemed to imply that "p can't be the case," where this means "It is logically impossible that p should be the case" means the same as "The sentence 'p' has no sense." I think that his view in the *Tractatus* that "contradictions" are "without sense" (sinnlos) may have been a deduction from this proposition. But why should he have held that "tautologies" also are "without sense"? I think that this view of his may have been, in part, a deduction from the conjunction of the proposition that "It is logically impossible that p" means the same as "The sentence 'p' has no sense" with his principle, which I have already had occasion to mention and which he said "gave us some firm ground," that "If a proposition has meaning, its negation also has meaning," where, as I pointed out, he seemed to be using "proposition" to mean the same as "sentence." For it is logically impossible that the negation of a tautology should be true, and hence, if it is true that "It is logically impossible that p" means the same as "The sentence 'p' has no sense," then it will follow from the conjunction of this proposition with his principle, that a "tautology" (or should we say "any sentence which expresses a tautology"?) also has none. But why he thought (if he did) that "It is logically impossible that p" means the same as "The sentence '*p*' has no sense," I cannot explain. And it seems to me that if, as he certainly held, the former of these two propositions entails the latter, then the sentence "It is logically impossible that *p*" must also have no sense; for can this sentence have any sense if the sentence "*p*" has none? But, if "It is logically impossible that *p*" has no sense, then, so far as I can see, it is quite impossible that it can mean the same as "The sentence '*p*' has no sense," for this latter expression certainly has sense, if "having sense" is being used in any ordinary way.

(*β″*) With regard to the expressions "rules of grammar" or "grammatical rules" he pointed out near the beginning of (I), where he first introduced the former expression, that when he said "grammar should not allow me to say 'greenish red'," he was "making things belong to grammar, which are not commonly supposed to belong to it"; and he immediately went on to say that the arrangement of colours in the colour octahedron "is really a part of grammar, not of psychology"; that "There is such a colour as a greenish blue" is "grammar"; and that Euclidean Geometry is also "a part of grammar." In the interval between (II) and (III) I wrote a short paper for him in which I said that I did not understand how he was using the expression "rule of grammar" and gave reasons for thinking that he was not using it in its ordinary sense; but he, though he expressed approval of my paper, insisted at that time that he was using the expression in its ordinary sense. Later, however, in (III), he said that "any explanation of the use of language" was "grammar," but that if I explained the meaning of "flows" by pointing at a river "we shouldn't naturally call this a rule of grammar." This seems to suggest that by that time he was doubtful whether he was using "rule of grammar" in quite its ordinary sense; and the same seems to be suggested by his saying, earlier in (III), that we should be using his "jargon" if we said that whether a sentence made sense or not depended on "whether or not it was constructed according to the rules of grammar."

I still think that he was not using the expression "rules of grammar" in any ordinary sense, and I am still unable to form any clear idea as to how he was using it. But, apart from his main contention (whatever that may have been) as to the connection between "rules of grammar" (in his sense) and necessary propositions, there were two things upon which he seemed mainly anxious to insist about "rules of grammar," namely (*γ′*), that they are all "arbitrary" and (*γ″*) that they "treat only of the symbolism"; and something ought certainly to be said about his treatment of these two points.

As for (*γ′*) he often asserted without qualification that all "rules of grammar" are arbitrary. But in (II) he expressly mentioned two senses of "arbitrary" in which he held that some grammatical rules are *not* arbitrary, and in one place in (III) he said that the sense in which all were arbitrary was a "peculiar" one. The two senses, of which he said in (II) that some grammatical rules were *not* arbitrary in those senses, were (1) a sense in which he said that rules about the use of single words were always "in part" *not* arbitrary—a proposition which he thought followed from his proposition, which I have mentioned before (page 238), that all single words are significant only if "we commit ourselves" by using them, and (2) a sense in which to say that a rule is an established rule in the language we are using is to say that it is not arbitrary: he gave, as an example, that if we followed a rule according to which "hate" was an intransitive verb, this rule would be arbitrary, whereas "if we use it in the sense in which we do use it," then the rule we are following is not arbitrary. But what, then, was the sense in which he held that all grammatical rules *are* arbitrary? This was a question to which he returned again and again in (II), trying to explain what the sense was, and to give reasons for thinking that in that sense they really are arbitrary. He first tried to express his view by saying that it is impossible to "justify" any grammatical rule—a way of expressing it to which he also recurred later; but he also expressed it by saying that we can't "give reasons" for grammatical rules, soon making clear that what he meant by this was that we can't give reasons for *following* any particular rule rather than a different one. And in trying to explain why we can't give reasons for following any particular rule, he laid very great stress on an argument, which he put differently in different places, and which I must confess I do not clearly understand. Two of the premisses of this argument are, I think, clear enough. One was (1) that any reason "would have to be a description of reality": this he asserted in precisely those words. And the second was (2) that "any description of reality must be capable of truth and falsehood" (these again were his own words), and it turned out, I think, that part of what he meant by this was that any false description must be significant. But to complete the argument he had to say something like (what again he actually said in one place) "and, if it were false, it would have to be said in a language not using this grammar"; and this is what I do not clearly understand. He gave as an illustration of his meaning that it cannot be because of a "quality in reality" that "I use sweet" in such a way that "sweeter" has meaning, but "identical" in such a way that "more identical" has none; giving as a reason "If it were because of a 'quality' in reality, it must be possible to say that reality hasn't got this quality, which grammar forbids." And he had said previously "I can't say what reality would have to be like, in order that what makes nonsense should make sense, because in order to do so I should have to use this new grammar." But, though I cannot put clearly the whole of his argument, I think one important point results from what I have quoted—a point which he himself never expressly pointed out. It results, namely, that he was using the phrases "description of reality" and "quality in reality" in a restricted sense—a sense, such that no statement to the effect that a certain expression is actually used in a certain way is a "description of reality" or describes "a quality in reality." He was evidently so using these terms that statements about the actual use of an expression, although such statements are obviously experiential propositions, are not to be called "descriptions of reality." He was confining the term "descriptions of reality" to expressions in which no term is used as a name for itself. For if he were not, it is obviously perfectly easy to say what reality would have to be like in order that "more identical," which is nonsense, should make sense: we can say that if "more identical" were used to mean what we now mean by "sweeter," then it would make sense; and the proposition that "more identical" is used in that way, even if it is a false one (and I do not know for certain that the very words "more identical" are not used in that way in, e.g., some African language) it is certainly not one which English grammar "forbids" us to make—it is certainly untrue that the sentence which expresses it has no significance in English.

It seems, therefore, that though in (II) he had said that what he meant by saying that all "grammatical rules" are "arbitrary" was that we cannot "give reasons" for following any particular rule rather than a different one, what he meant was only that we cannot give reasons for so doing which are both (*a*) "descriptions of reality" and (*b*) "descriptions of reality" *of a particular sort,* viz. descriptions of reality which do not *mention,* or say anything *about,* any particular word or other expression, though of course they must *use* words or other expressions. And that this was his meaning is made, I think, plainer from a passage late in (III) in which he compared rules of deduction with "the fixing of a unit of length" (or, as he said later, a "standard" of length). He there said "The reasons (if any) for fixing a unit of length do not make it 'not arbitrary,' in the sense in which a statement that so-and-so is the length of this object is not arbitrary," adding "Rules of deduction are analogous to the fixing of a unit of length," and (taking "3 + 3 = 6" as an instance of a rule of deduction) " '3 + 3 = 6' is a rule as to the way we are going to talk . . . it is a preparation for a description, just as fixing a unit of length is a preparation for measuring." He seemed, therefore, here to be admitting that reasons *of a sort* can sometimes be given for following a particular "grammatical rule," only not reasons of the special sort which a well-conducted operation of measurement may give (once the meaning of "foot" has been fixed), for, e.g., the statement that a particular rod is less than four feet long. He did in fact mention in this connection that some "grammatical rules" follow from others; in which case, of course, that they do so follow may be given as a reason for speaking in accordance with them. In this case, however, he would no doubt have said that the reason given is not a "description of reality." But it is obvious that reasons which are, in any ordinary sense, "descriptions of reality" can also be given for following a particular rule; e.g., a particular person may give, as a reason for calling a particular length a "foot," the "description of reality" which consists in saying that that is how the word "foot," when used for a unit of length, is generally used in English. And, in this case, of course, it may also be said that the reason why the word "foot" was originally used, in English, as a name for the particular length which we do in fact so call, was that the length in question is not far from the length of those parts of a grown man's body which, in English, are called his "feet." In these cases, however, I think he might have urged with truth both (*a*) that the reason given, though a "description of reality," is a description which "mentions" or says something *about* the word "foot" and does not merely *use* that word, and also (*b*) that it is not a reason for following the rule of calling that particular length a "foot" in the same sense of the word "reason" as that in which a well-conducted measurement may give a "reason" for the statement that a particular rod is less than four feet long. It is surely obvious that a "reason" for *acting* in a particular way, e.g. in this case, for using the word "foot" for a particular length, cannot be a reason for so doing in the same sense of the word "reason" as that in which a reason for thinking that so-and-so is the case may be a reason for so thinking. I think, therefore, if all these explanations are given, it becomes pretty clear in what sense Wittgenstein was using the word "arbitrary" when he said that all gram-matical rules were arbitrary.

But there remains one thing which he said in this connection which has puzzled me extremely. He actually introduced his comparison between rules of deduction and the fixing of a unit of length by saying: "The statement that rules of deduction are neither true nor false is apt to give an uncomfortable feeling." It appeared, therefore, as if he thought that this statement that they are neither true nor false followed from the statement that they are arbitrary, and that the comparison of them with the fixing of a unit of length would tend to remove this uncomfortable feeling, i.e. to make you see that they really are neither true nor false.

Now, in connection with his comparison between rules of deduction and the fixing of a unit of length, he gave (among other examples) as an example of a rule of deduction "$3 + 3 = 6$," and said a good deal about this example. And it certainly does give me a very uncomfortable feeling to be told that "$3 + 3 = 6$" is neither true nor false. But I think this uncomfortable feeling only arises because one thinks, if one is told this, that the *expression* "$3 + 3 = 6$" is being used in the way in which it most commonly is used, i.e. in the way in which it would commonly be said to be expressing a necessary proposition. And I think this uncomfortable feeling would completely vanish if it were clearly explained that the person who says this, is *not* using the expression "$3 + 3 = 6$" in this way, but in the very different way which I tried to distinguish above (page 246), i.e., the way in which it is merely used to specify a possible way of speaking and writing, which might or might not be actually adopted, although in this case the rule of speaking and writing in the way specified is, as a matter of fact, a well-established rule. I said that Wittgenstein never, so far as I knew, in these lectures expressly distinguished these two different ways of using the same expression (e.g., the expression "$3 + 3 = 6$"), but that I thought he did hold that, e.g., the expression "$3 + 3 = 6$" could be properly used in the second way as well as in the first, and that his thinking this might be partly respon-sible for his declaration that rules of deduction are neither true nor false (page 246). For it seemed to me quite obvious that, if the expression "$3 + 3 = 6$" is used in this second way, then it cannot possibly be either true or false. But I cannot help thinking that in this passage in (III) in which he compared rules of deduction with the fixing of a unit of length, he actually meant to say that even when used in the first way, i.e., in the way in which it would commonly be said to express a necessary proposition, it still expresses neither a true nor a false proposition.

In what he actually said about "$3 + 3 = 6$" in this passage, I think it is necessary to distinguish three different propositions which he made, of which the first two seem to me certainly true, but the third not to follow from the first two, and to be extremely doubtful. (1) He began by asking the question, "Is 'I've put 6 apples on the mantelpiece' the same as 'I've put 3 there, and also another 3 there'?" and then, after pointing out that counting up to 3 in the case of each of two different groups, and arriving at the number "6" by count-ing *all* the apples, are "three different experiences," he said "You can imagine putting two groups of 3 there, and then finding only 5." And the two propositions which seem to me certainly true are (*a*) that you can imagine this which he said you can imagine, and (*b*) (which he also said) that "3 + 3 = 6" does not "prophesy" that, when you have had the two experiences of counting up to 3 in the case of each of two groups of apples which you certainly have put on the mantelpiece, you will also have the third experience of finding that there are 6 there, when you come to count *all* the apples that are there; or, in other words, he was saying that the proposition "3 + 3 = 6" is quite consistent with finding, by your third experience of counting, that there are only 5 there. This second proposition seems to me also true, because it seems to me clear that it is a mere matter of experience, that when you have put two groups of 3 apples on a mantelpiece, you will, under the circumstances Wittgenstein was considering (e.g., that no apple has been taken away) find that there are 6 there; or, in other words, it is a mere matter of experience that apples don't simply vanish with no apparent cause; and it surely should be obvious that "3 + 3 = 6" certainly entails no more than that, *if* at any time there were in any place two different groups, each numbering 3 apples, then *at that time* there were 6 apples in the place in question: it entails nothing about any future time. But (2) Wittgenstein went on to add that if, on having put two groups of 3 on the mantelpiece, and finding that there were only 5 there, you were to say (as you certainly might under the circumstances he was considering) "one must have vanished," this latter statement "*only means* 'If you keep to the arithmetical rule "3 + 3 = 6" ' you *have to say* 'One must have vanished'." And it is this assertion of his that, under the supposed circumstances, "One must have vanished" *only means* that, if you keep to a certain rule, you must *say so,* which seems to me questionable and not to follow from the two true propositions I have given under (1). (He had already said something similar in (I) in connection with his very paradoxical proposition that Euclidean Geometry is "a part of grammar"; for he there said that what Euclid's proposition "The three angles of a triangle are equal to two right angles" asserts is "If by measurement you get any result for the sum of the three angles other than 180°, you *are going to say* that you've made a mistake.")

But I have been a good deal puzzled as to what he meant and implied by this assertion that, under these circumstances the words "One must have vanished" *only mean* "If you keep to the arithmetical rule '3 + 3 = 6,' you have to say so." And, of course, my view that it is very doubtful whether what he meant and implied is true depends on my view as to what he did mean and imply.

Of course, the circumstances under which he said that "One must have vanished" *only means* this, are extremely unusual: possibly they never have happened and never will happen: but, as I have said, I fully agree with him that they *might* happen—that I can *imagine* their happening; and the question whether, if they did, then the words "One must have vanished" would *only mean* what he says, seems to me to raise an extremely important question, which does not only concern what would happen under these extremely unlikely circumstances, but concerns what is the case under circumstances which constantly do occur.

I will first try to state as accurately as I can what I take to be the cir-

cumstances he was supposing, and I will put them in the form of what he was
supposing would be true of me, if I had been in those circumstances. He was
supposing, I take it, (1) that I should know, because I had counted correctly,
that I did put on the mantelpiece two groups of apples, each of which contained 3 apples and no more, (2) that I should know, by counting *at a subsequent time,* that there were *at that time* only 5 apples on the mantelpiece,
(3) that I should also know, because I was watching all the time, that nothing
had happened which would account in any normal way for the fact that, though
I put 3 + 3 there, there are only 5 there now, e.g. I should know, in this way,
that nobody had taken one away, that none had fallen off the mantelpiece, and
that none had visibly flown away, and finally, (4) (and this, if I am not mistaken, was very essential to his point) that I should *not* know, by any operation
of counting performed either by myself or by any other person who had told
me his result, that I did put 6 apples on the mantelpiece, so that, if I asserted
that I did put 6, this could only be a deduction from the proposition that I did
put 3 + 3 there, which (1) asserts that I *have* found to be true by counting.

   Under the circumstances stated in (1) and (3) I certainly should be very
much surprised to find that what is stated in (2) was true, and I might quite
naturally assert that one must have vanished, though I think I might equally
naturally express my surprise by the use of words which contain no "must,"
e.g. by saying "Why! one has vanished!" And it is under these circumstances,
if I am not mistaken, that Wittgenstein was asserting that if I did use the words
"One must have vanished" to make an assertion, these words would *"only mean"*
"If I keep to the arithmetical rule '3 + 3 = 6' I have to say that one must have
vanished."

   And, first of all, I have felt some doubts on two separate points as to what
he meant by the words "you have to say so." The first is this. I at first thought
that he might be using the words "say so," rather incorrectly, to mean "say
the words 'One must have vanished'" (or, of course, any equivalent words,
e.g., in another language). But I now think there is no reason to suppose that
he was not using the word "say" quite correctly (i.e., as we usually do), to
mean the same as "assert," and there is some positive reason to suppose that
he was doing so. One positive reason is that, among the circumstances which
he was supposing was that which I have called (1), viz., that I should *know*
that I did put 3 + 3 apples on the mantelpiece; and I think he was certainly
supposing that if I knew this, I should not merely say the words "I put 3 + 3
there," but should *assert* that I did—a proposition which does not seem to me
certainly true, though, if I knew it, I should certainly be *willing* to assert it,
unless I wanted to tell a lie. The second point is this: What did he mean by
"have to" in "I should *have to* say so"? These words might naturally mean that
I should be failing to keep to the rule "3 + 3 = 6" if I merely failed to assert
that one must have vanished—if, for instance, I merely made no assertion. But
I feel sure he did not mean to assert that I should be failing to keep to the rule
(which I will in future call, for short, "violating" the rule) if I merely omitted
to say that one must have vanished. I think he certainly meant that I should be
violating the rule only if I made some assertion the making of which was in-

consistent with asserting that one must have vanished, e.g., if I asserted that none had vanished.

If I am right on these two points, his view as to what the words "One must have vanished" would "only mean" under the supposed circumstances, could be expressed more clearly as the view that these words would only mean "If I assert that I put $3 + 3$ on the mantelpiece, I shall be keeping to the rule '$3 + 3 = 6$' if I also assert that one must have vanished, and shall be violating that rule, if I make any assertion the making of which is inconsistent with asserting that one must have vanished." And I will, in future, assume that this was his view.

But now the question arises: Why should he have held that, under the supposed circumstances, the words "One must have vanished" would "only mean" a proposition which mentioned the arithmetical proposition "$3 + 3 = 6$"? How does "6" come in? I think the answer to this question is that he was assuming that among the propositions from which, under the supposed circumstances, the proposition that one had vanished would be a deduction (the "must have," of course, indicates, as "must" often does, that it would be a deduction from *some* propositions) would be not only the propositions given as known by me in (1), (2), and (3) of my description of the circumstances, but also the proposition "I put 6 apples on the mantelpiece," which, according to (4) in my description is *not* known by me as a result of any operation of counting, but only, if at all, as a deduction from "I put $3 + 3$." And I think his reason for asserting that, under the supposed circumstances "One must have vanished" would "only mean" what he said it would only mean, was that he was supposing that this sentence "I put 6 on the mantelpiece" would *not*, under the circumstances described in (1) and (4), mean what it would mean if I had discovered, by counting *all* the apples I was putting on the mantelpiece, that I was putting 6, but, since I had not done this, would "only mean" "I shall be keeping to the rule '$3 + 3 = 6$', if I assert that I put 6, and shall be violating that rule if I make any assertion inconsistent with asserting that I put 6"—a proposition which to avoid clumsy repetitions, I will in future call "B." I think, therefore, he was implying that under the circumstances (1) and (4), the words "I put 6 apples on the mantelpiece" would "only mean" B. And I think the important question raised by his assertion as to what "One must have vanished" would "only mean" under circumstances (1), (2), (3), and (4), is this question as to whether, under circumstances (1) and (4), which might quite often occur, "I put 6" would "only mean" B—"only mean" being used, of course, in the same sense (whatever that may have been) in which he used it with regard to "One must have vanished."

But then the question arises: In what sense was he using the expression "only mean"? If anyone tells us that, under the circumstances (1) and (4), the sentence "I put 6 on the mantelpiece," if used to make an assertion, would "only mean" B, I think the most natural interpretation of these words would be that anyone who, under circumstances (1) and (4), used this sentence to make an assertion would be using it to assert B. But I think it is quite incredible that anyone would ever actually use the expression "I put 6" to assert B; and equally incredible that anyone would ever use the expression "One must have vanished" to assert what Wittgenstein said would be their "only meaning" under circumstances (1), (2), (3), and (4). In both cases the assertion which is said to be the 'only meaning' of a given expression is an assertion *about* the ordinary meaning of the expression in question, to the effect that you will be speaking in accordance with a certain rule if you use the expression in question to assert what it would be usually used to mean, and will be violating that rule if you make any assertion inconsistent with that ordinary meaning. And I think it is quite incredible that anybody would ever use a given expression to make such an assertion *about* the ordinary meaning of the expression in question; and, in both our cases, quite clear that anybody who did use the expression in question to make an assertion, would be using it to *make* the assertion which it would ordinarily mean, and not to make the assertion *about* its ordinary meaning which Wittgenstein said or implied would be its "only meaning" under the circumstances described. And I do not think that he ever meant to make either of these incredible statements: he was not intending to say that the sentence "One must have vanished" ever would be used, or could be properly used, to make the assertion which he says would be its "only meaning" under the supposed circumstances. But, if so, how was he using the expression "only mean"? I think he was using it, not in its most natural sense, but loosely, in a more or less natural sense, to say that the assertion which he said would be its "only meaning" under the circumstances described, would be *the* true proposition which resembled most closely a proposition which he held to be false, but which he knew was commonly held to be true. In the case of "I put 6," if he implied, as I think he did, that, under circumstances (1) and (4), "I put 6" would "only mean" B, the proposition which he held to be false was the proposition that if I put $3 + 3$, it is *necessarily* also true that I put 6, and the proposition which he held to be *the* true proposition which most closely resembled this false proposition, and which might therefore have misled those who think to be true this proposition which he held to be false, was that, if "I put $3 + 3$" was true, then B would be true. I think, in fact, he was holding that the proposition that in putting $3 + 3$ on the mantelpiece, I was *necessarily* putting 6 there, was false; that I can imagine that in putting $3 + 3$ there, I was, e.g., only putting 5, and that, if there ever were $3 + 3$ on the mantelpiece, nevertheless, if anybody had counted correctly how many there were altogether *at that very time,* he would possibly have found that there were only 5.

But whether or not he held, as I think he did, that in putting $3 + 3$ apples on the mantelpiece, I was not necessarily putting 6, I think it is quite certain that he held another proposition, about the relation of which to this one I am not clear. He held, namely, that the expression "$3 + 3 = 6$" is *never* used in Arithmetic, not therefore even when it would commonly be held to express a necessary proposition, to express a proposition from which it follows that if I put $3 + 3$, I necessarily put 6. And this view seems to me to follow from his two views (1) that (as is suggested by his phrase "the arithmetical *rule* '$3 + 3 = 6$'") the expression "$3 + 3 = 6$," as used in Arithmetic, *always* only expresses a "rule of grammar," and (2) that rules of grammar "treat only of the symbolism." I shall shortly have to point out that there seems to me to be a serious difficulty in understanding exactly what he meant by saying that, e.g., "3 + 3 = 6" "treats only of the symbolism"; but I think there is no doubt he meant at least this: that you will be speaking in accordance with that rule if, when you *assert* that you put 3 + 3, you also *assert* that you put 6, and violating it if, having *asserted* the former, you make any assertion the making of which is incompatible with asserting the latter, but that it by no means follows that, if you keep to the rule, what you assert will be *true*, nor yet that, if you violate it, what you assert will be *false*: in either case, he held, what you assert *may* be true, but also *may* be false. And I think his reason for this view of his can be made plainer by noticing that since (as he implies by his phrase "the arithmetical rule '3 + 3 = 6'") "3 + 3 = 6" is a well-established rule (if a rule of grammar at all), it will follow that, if you keep to that rule, you will be using language "correctly" (or, with his use of "grammar," speaking "grammatically"), and that, if you violate it you will be speaking "incorrectly" (or, with his use of "grammar," guilty of bad grammar); and that from the fact that you are using language correctly, in the sense of "in accordance with an established rule," it by no means follows that what you assert, by this correct use of language, is "correct" in the very different sense in which "That is correct" = "That is true," nor from the fact that you are using language incorrectly that what you assert by this incorrect use of language is "incorrect" in the very different sense in which "That is incorrect" = "That is false." It is obvious that you may be using language just as correctly when you use it to assert something false as when you use it to assert something true, and that when you are using it incorrectly, you may just as easily be asserting something true by this incorrect use as something false. It by no means follows, for instance, from the fact that you are using the word "foot" "correctly," i.e. for the length for which it is usually used in English, that when you make such an assertion as "This rod is less than four feet long," your assertion is true; and, if you were to use it "incorrectly" for the length which is properly called in English an "inch" or for that which is properly called a "yard," it would by no means follow that any assertion you made by this incorrect use of the word "foot" was false. I think Wittgenstein thought that similarly you will be using the phrase "I put 6" correctly, if, when you assert that you put 3 + 3, you also assert that you put 6, and incorrectly if, when you assert that you put 3 + 3, you deny that you put 6, or even assert that it is possible that you did not put 6; and that this is *the* true proposition which has led people to assume, what he thought false, that the expression "3 + 3 = 6" is used in Arithmetic to express a proposition from which it follows that if I put 3 + 3, I necessarily put 6.

And I think this view of his also gives the chief explanation of what he meant by the puzzling assertion that 3 + 3 = 6 (and *all* rules of deduction, similarly) is neither true nor false. I think what he chiefly meant by saying this was not, as I suggested above (page 246) that 3 + 3 = 6 was a "rule" in the sense in which rules can obviously be neither true nor false, but that he was using "true" in a restricted sense, in which he would have said that 3 + 3 = 6 was only "true" if it followed from it (as he denied to be the case) that if I put 3 + 3 on the mantelpiece, I necessarily put 6; in a sense, therefore, in which, even if, as I suggested (page 246), he sometimes used "rule" in a sense in which the proposition "You can't *say* that you put 3 + 3, and *deny* that you put 6"—a

proposition which he held to be true in any ordinary sense, he would nevertheless have said that this proposition was not "true," because it was a proposition
about how words are actually used. I think he was using "true" and "false" in a
restricted sense, just as he was using "description of reality" in a restricted sense
(above, page 253), i.e., in a sense in which no propositions about how words are
used can be said to be "true" or "false."

And the reason why I think it very doubtful whether he was right in holding
(if he did hold) that it is not true that in putting $3 + 3$ on the mantelpiece, I
necessarily also put 6, is that I do not think I can imagine that in putting $3 + 3$,
I was not putting 6. I have already said (page 255) that I agree with him that I
can imagine that, having put $3 + 3$ there, I should find at *a subsequent time* that
there were only 5 there, even under the circumstances described in (3) of my
description of the circumstances he was supposing: I can imagine, I think, that
one has really vanished. But it seems to be quite a different question whether I
can imagine that, in putting $3 + 3$, I was not putting 6, or that, if at any time
there were $3 + 3$ on the mantelpiece, there were *at that time* not 6 there. I admit,
however, that the propositions that I was putting 6, or that there were 6 on the
mantelpiece, do seem to me to entail that, *if* anybody had counted correctly,
he would have found that there were 6; I am, therefore, implying that I cannot
imagine these hypothetical propositions not to be true: but I do not think I can
imagine this. And I also can see no reason to think that the expression "$3 + 3 =
6$" is never used in Arithmetic to express a proposition from which it follows that
if I put $3 + 3$, I put 6. I am not convinced that this expression, in Arithmetic,
always only expresses a "grammatical rule," i.e., a rule as to what language it
will be correct to use, even if it sometimes does. Wittgenstein has not succeeded
in removing the "uncomfortable feeling" which it gives me to be told that "$3 +
3 = 6$" and "$(p \supset q \cdot p)$ entails q" are neither true nor false.

(γ'') As for the proposition that rules of grammar "treat only of the symbolism,"
he never, at least while I was present, expressly pointed out that such an expression as "$2 = 1 + 1$" can be used to express at least three very different propositions. It can be used (1) in such a way that anybody could understand what
proposition or rule it was being used to express, provided only he understood how
the sign "$=$" was being used, and did not understand either the expression "2"
or the expression "$1 + 1$" except as names for themselves (what has been called
"autonymously"). But it can be used (2) in such a way that nobody could understand what proposition or rule it was being used to express, unless he understood
non-autonymously both the sign "$=$" and also the expression "$1 + 1$," but need
not understand the expression "2" other than autonymously. Or (3) it can be
used in such a way that nobody could understand what proposition or rule it was
being used to express, unless he understood non-autonymously *both* the expression "2" and the expression "$1 + 1$," as well as the expression "$=$." But, though he
did not expressly point out that, e.g., "$2 = 1 + 1$" could be used in each of these
three very different ways, he said things which seem to me to imply the view
that in Arithmetic it was *only* used in the first way. He said, for instance, in (II)
"To explain the meaning of a sign means only to substitute one sign for another,"
and again, later on, "An explanation of a proposition is always of the same kind as
a definition, i.e., replacing one symbol by another." In making these statements,

he seems to me to have been confusing the true proposition that you can only explain the meaning of one sign by *using* other signs, with the proposition, which seems to me obviously false, that, when you explain the meaning of one sign by *using* another, all you are asserting is that the two signs have the same meaning or can be substituted for one another: he seems in fact to have been asserting that propositions, which are in fact of form (2), are only of form (1). And this mistake seems to be responsible for the astounding statement which he actually made in (III) that Russell had been mistaken in thinking that "= Def." had a different meaning from "=." It seems to me obvious that a statement can only be properly called a "definition" or "explanation" of the meaning of a sign, if, in order to understand what statement you are making by the words you use, it is necessary that the hearer or reader should understand the *definiens*, and not merely take it as a name for itself. When, for instance, *Principia Mathematica* defines the meaning of the symbol "⊃" by saying that "$p \supset q$" is to mean "$\sim p \lor q$," it is surely obvious that nobody can understand what statement is being made as to how "⊃" will be used, unless he understands the expression "$\sim p \lor q$," and does not take it merely as a name for itself; and that therefore the statement which is being made is not merely a statement of form (1), to the effect that the two different expressions "$p \supset q$" and "$\sim p \lor q$" have the same meaning or can be substituted for one another, but a statement of form (2), i.e., that the *definiens* "$\sim p \lor q$" is *not* being used autonomously, though the *definiendum* "⊃" *is* being used autonomously.

But the most serious difficulty in understanding what he meant by saying that, e.g., "$3 + 3 = 6$" "treats only of the symbolism" seems to me to arise from a question with which he only dealt briefly at the end of (I), and with which he there dealt only in a way which I certainly do not at all completely understand; namely, the question: Of *what* symbols did he suppose that "$3 + 3 = 6$" was treating? He did indeed actually assert in (III) that the proposition "red is a primary colour" was a proposition about the word "red"; and, if he had seriously held this, he might have held similarly that the proposition or rule "$3 + 3 = 6$" was merely a proposition or rule about the particular expressions "$3 + 3$" and "6." But he cannot have held seriously either of these two views, because the *same* proposition which is expressed by the words "red is a primary colour" can be expressed in French or German by words which say nothing about the English word "red"; and similarly the *same* proposition or rule which is expressed by "$3 + 3 = 6$" was undoubtedly expressed in Attic Greek and in Latin by words which say nothing about the Arabic numerals "3" and "6." And this was a fact which he seemed to be admitting in the passage at the end of (I) to which I refer. In this passage, which he introduced by saying that he would answer objections to the view (which he held) that the arithmetical calculus "is a game," he began by saying, very emphatically, that it is *not* a game "with ink and paper"; by which he perhaps meant (but I do not know) that it is not a game with the Arabic numerals. He went on to say that Frege had concluded from the fact that Mathematics is not a game "with ink and paper" that it dealt not with the symbols but with "what is symbolized"—a view with which he apparently disagreed. And he went on to express his own alternative view by saying "What is essential to the rules is the logical multiplicity which all the different possible symbols have in common"; and here, by speaking of "all the different possible symbols," I take it he was admitting, what is obvious, that the *same* rules which are expressed by the use of the Arabic numerals may be expressed by ever so many different symbols. But if the rules "treat only of the symbolism" how can two rules which treat of *different* symbols, e.g., of "3" and "III," possibly be the *same* rule? I suppose he must have thought that we use the word "same" in such a sense that two rules, which are obviously *not* the same, in that they treat of different symbols, are yet said to be the same, provided only that the rules for their use have the same "logical multiplicity" (whatever that may mean). But he never, I think, at least while I was present, returned to this point, or tried to explain and defend his view.

He did, however, in this passage, compare the rules of Arithmetic to the rules of chess, and used of chess the phrase, "What is chacteristic of chess is the logical multiplicity of its rules" just as he used of Mathematics the phrase "What is essential to its rules is the logical multiplicity which all the different possible symbols have in common." I doubt, however, whether he was right in what he meant by saying "*What* is characteristic of chess is the logical multiplicity of its rules," which, of course, implies that this is sufficient to characterize chess. He was undoubtedly right in saying that the material and the shape of which the different pieces are commonly made is irrelevant to chess: chess could certainly be played with pieces of any material and any shape, e.g., with pieces of paper which were all of the same shape. But if by "the rules of chess" he meant, as I think he probably did, the rules which govern the moves which may be made by pieces of different sorts, e.g., by pawns and bishops, and was suggesting that the "logical multiplicity" of the rules which govern the possible moves of a pawn and a bishop is sufficient to distinguish a pawn from a bishop, I think he was wrong. The rule that a pawn can only make certain moves certainly, I think, does not mean that any piece the rules for the moves of which have a certain "logical multiplicity" (whatever that may mean) may only make the moves in question, even if he was right in holding that the rules for the moves of pawns have a different "logical multiplicity" from those for the moves of bishops; and similarly in the case of all the other different kinds of pieces. Though a pawn is certainly not necessarily distinguished from a bishop or a knight by its shape, as it usually is, it seems to me that it is necessarily distinguished by the positions which it may occupy at the beginning of the game, so that a rule which states that pawns can only make such and such moves, states that pieces which occupy certain positions at the beginning of the game can only make such and such moves; and similarly with all the other different kinds of piece: they are all necessarily distinguished from one another by the positions which they occupy at the beginning of the game, where "necessarily" means that it would not be chess that you were playing, if the pieces to which different kinds of move are allowed, did not occupy certain positions relatively to one another at the beginning of the game. Of course, if you did play chess with pieces of paper which were all of the same shape, it would be necessary that the pieces should have some mark to show what positions they had occupied at the beginning of the game, as might be done, for instance, by writing "pawn" on those pieces which had occupied certain positions, and, e.g., "bishop" on those which had occupied others; and it would also be necessary to distinguish by some mark (what is usually done by a difference of colour) those pieces which belonged to one of the two players from those which belonged to the other, as could, e.g., be easily done by writing an "O" on all the pieces which belonged to one player, and a "+" on all which belonged to the other. I think, therefore, he was probably wrong in holding, as he apparently did, that the rules of chess are completely analogous, in respect of their relation to "logical multiplicity," to what he held to be true of the rules of Arithmetic.

There remains one other matter which should be mentioned in treating of his views about necessary propositions. He made a good deal of use, especially in (II) in discussing rules of deduction, of the expression "internal relation," even asserting in one place "What justifies inference is an internal relation." He began the discussion in which he made this assertion by saying that "following" is called a "relation" as if it were like "fatherhood"; but said that where, for example, it is said that a proposition of the form "$p \lor q$" "follows" from the corresponding proposition of the form "$p \cdot q$," the so-called "relation" is "entirely determined by the two propositions in question," and that, this being so, the so-called "relation" is "entirely different from other relations." But it soon became plain that, when he said this about "following," it was only one of the proper uses of the word "follow" in English, as between two propositions, of which he was speaking, namely, that use which is sometimes called "follows logically": he did, in fact, constantly use the word "inference" as if it meant the same as "deductive inference." How he made plain that what he was talking of as "following" was only "following logically," was that he immediately went on to say that the kind of "following" of which he was speaking, and which he exemplified by the sense in which any propositions of the form "$p \lor q$" "follows" from the corresponding proposition of the form "$p \cdot q$," was "quite different" from what is meant when, e.g., we say that a wire of a certain material and diameter *can't* support a piece of iron of a certain weight—a proposition which he actually expressed in the next lecture (quite correctly according to English usage) as the proposition that "it *follows* from the weight of the piece of iron and the material and diameter of the wire, that the wire will break if you try to support that piece of iron by it." He went on to express the difference between these two uses of "follow," by saying that, in the case of the wire and the piece of iron, both (*a*) "it remains *thinkable* that the wire will not break," and (*b*) that "from the weight of the piece of iron and the material and diameter of the wire *alone*, I can't know that the wire will break," whereas in the case of a proposition of the form "$p \lor q$" and the corresponding proposition of the form "$p \cdot q$" "following" is an "internal relation," which, he said, means "roughly speaking" "that it is *unthinkable* that the relation should not hold between the terms." And he immediately went on to say that the *general* proposition "$p \lor q$ follows from $p \cdot q$" "is not wanted"; that "if you can't see," by looking at two propositions of these forms that the one follows from the other, "the general proposition won't help you"; that, if I say of a proposition of the form "$p \lor q$" that it follows from the corresponding proposition of the form "$p \cdot q$" "everything here is useless, except the two propositions themselves";

and that if another proposition were needed to justify our statement that the first follows from the second, "we should need an infinite series." He finally concluded "A rule of inference" (meaning "deductive inference") "never justifies an inference."

In the next lecture, which he began, as he often did, by repeating (sometimes in a slightly different form and, if necessary, with added explanations and corrections) the main points which he had intended to make at the end of the preceding one, he said that to say of one proposition "q" that it "follows" from another "p" "*seems* to say that there is a relation between them which justifies passing from one to the other," but that "what makes one suspicious about this is that we perceive the relation by merely looking at the propositions concerned—that it is 'internal' and not like the proposition that 'This wire will break' follows from the weight of the iron and the material and diameter of the wire"; and here he immediately went on to add that the expression "internal relation" is misleading, and that he used it "only because others had used it"; and he proceeded to give a slightly different formulation of the way in which the expression had been used, viz. "A relation which holds if the terms are what they are, and which cannot therefore be imagined not to hold." He also, shortly afterwards, gave some further explanation of what he had meant by saying that if a rule were needed to justify the statement that one proposition follows (logically) from another, we should need an infinite series. He said that if a rule r, were needed to justify an inference from p to q, q would follow from the conjunction of p and r, so that we should need a fresh rule to justify the inference from this conjunction to q, and so on *ad infinitum*. Hence, he said, "an inference can only be justified by what we see," and added that "this holds throughout Mathematics." He then gave his truth-table notation for "$p \lor q$" and "$p \cdot q$," and said that the "criterion" for the statement that the former follows from the latter was that "to every T in the latter there corresponds a T in the former." He said that, in saying this, he had stated "a rule of inference," but that this rule was only a "rule of grammar" and "treated only of the symbolism." A little later he said that the relation of "following" can be "represented" by "tautologies" (in his special sense), but that the tautology "$(p \cdot q) \supset (p \lor q)$" does not *say* that $p \lor q$ follows from $p \cdot q$, because it says nothing, but that the fact that it is a tautology *shows* that $p \lor q$ follows from $p \cdot q$. And a little later still he said that the relation of following "can be seen by looking at the *signs*," and seemed to identify this with saying that it is "internal"; and the fact that he here said that it can be seen by looking at the *signs*, whereas he had previously said that it can be seen by looking at the *propositions*, seems to me to show that, as I said (page 242) seemed to be often the case, he was identifying "sentences" with "propositions." Finally he introduced a new phrase, in explanation of his view that the expression "internal relation" is misleading, saying that internal and external relations are "categorically" different; and he used the expression "belong to different categories" later on in (III), where he said that "follows" and "implies" (a word which he here used, as Russell had done, as if it meant the same as the *Principia* symbol "$\supset$") "belong to different categories"; adding the important remark that whether one proposition "follows" from another "cannot depend at all upon their truth or falsehood," and saying that it only depends on "an internal *or grammatical* relation."

PART III

(B) In the case of Logic, there were two most important matters with regard to which he said that the views he had held when he wrote the *Tractatus* were definitely wrong.

(1) The first of these concerned what Russell called "atomic" propositions and he himself in the *Tractatus* had called "Elementarsätze." He said in (II) that it was with regard to "elementary" propositions and their connection with truth-functions or "molecular" propositions that he had had to change his opinions most; and that this subject was connected with the use of the words "thing" and "name." In (III) he began by pointing out that neither Russell nor he himself had produced any examples of "atomic" propositions; and said that there was something wrong indicated by this fact, though it was difficult to say exactly what. He said that both he and Russell had the idea that non-atomic propositions could be "analysed" into atomic ones, but that we did not yet know what the analysis was: that, e.g., such a proposition as "It is raining" might, if we knew its analysis, turn out to be molecular, consisting, e.g., of a conjunction of "atomic" propositions. He said that in the *Tractatus* he had objected to Russell's assumption that there certainly were atomic propositions which asserted two-termed relations—that he had refused to prophesy as to what would be the result of an analysis, if one were made, and that it might turn out that no atomic proposition asserted less than, e.g., a four-termed relation, so that we could not even talk of a two-termed relation. His present view was that it was senseless to talk of a "final" analysis, and he said that he would now treat as atomic all propositions in the expression of which neither "and," "or," nor "not" occurred, nor any expression of generality, provided we had not expressly given an exact definition, such as we might give of "It's rotten weather," if we said we were going to use the expression "rotten" to mean "both cold and damp."

In saying this he seemed to me to be overlooking both the fact that a man often says that he is going to use an expression in a certain definite way and then does not in fact so use it, and also the fact that many common words, e.g., father, mother, sister, brother, etc., are often so used that such a sentence as "This is my father" undoubtedly expresses a molecular proposition, although a person who so uses it has never expressly stated that he will so use it. These two facts, however, of course, do not prove that he was wrong in thinking that it is senseless to talk of a "final" or "ultimate" analysis.

(2) The second important logical mistake which he thought he had made at the time when he wrote the *Tractatus* was introduced by him in (III) in connection with the subject of "following" (by which he meant, as usual, *deductive* following or "entailment"—a word which I think he actually used in this discussion) from a "general" proposition to a particular instance and from a particular instance to a "general" proposition. Using the notation of *Principia*

Mathematica, he asked us to consider the two propositions "$(x) \cdot fx$ entails fa" and "fa entails $(\exists x) \cdot fx$." He said that there was a temptation, to which he had yielded in the *Tractatus,* to say that $(x) \cdot fx$ is identical with the logical product "$fa \cdot fb \cdot fc \ldots$," and $(\exists x) \cdot fx$ identical with the logical sum "$fa \lor fb \lor fc \ldots$"; but that this was in both cases a mistake. In order to make clear exactly where the mistake lay, he first said that in the case of such a universal proposition as "Everybody in this room has a hat" (which I will call "A"), he had known and actually said in the *Tractatus,* that, even if Smith, Jones, and Robinson are the only people in the room, the logical product "Smith has a hat, Jones has a hat, and Robinson has a hat" cannot possibly be identical with A, because in order to get a proposition which entails A, you obviously have to add "and Smith, Jones, and Robinson are the only people in the room." But he went on to say that if we are talking of "individuals" in Russell's sense (and he actually here mentioned atoms as well as colours, as if they were "individuals" in this sense), the case is different, because, in that case, there is no proposition analogous to "Smith, Jones, and Robinson are the only people in the room." The class of things in question, if we are talking of "individuals," is, he said, in this case, determined not by a proposition but by our "dictionary": it is "defined by grammar." For example, he said that the class "primary colour" is "defined by grammar," not by a proposition; that there is no such proposition as "red is a primary colour," and that such a proposition as "In this square there is one of the primary colours" really is identical with the logical sum "In this square there is either red or green or blue or yellow"; whereas in the case of Smith, Jones, and Robinson, there is such a proposition as "Smith is in this room" and hence also such a proposition as "Smith, Jones, and Robinson are the only people in this room." He went on to say that one great mistake which he made in the *Tractatus* was that of supposing that in the case of *all* classes "defined by grammar," general propositions were identical either with logical products or with logical sums (meaning by this logical products or sums of the propositions which are values of fx) as, according to him, they really are in the case of the class "primary colours." He said that, when he wrote the *Tractatus,* he had supposed that *all* such general propositions were "truth-functions"; but he said now that in supposing this he was committing a fallacy, which is common in the case of Mathematics, e.g., the fallacy of supposing that $1 + 1 + 1 \ldots$ is a sum, whereas it is only a *limit,* and that dx/dy is a quotient, whereas it also is only a *limit.* He said he had been misled by the fact that $(x) \cdot fx$ can be replaced by $fa \cdot fb \cdot fc \ldots$, having failed to see that the latter expression is not always a logical product: that it is only a logical product if the dots are what he called "the dots of laziness," as where we represent the alphabet by "A, B, C $\ldots$," and therefore the whole expression can be replaced by an enumeration; but that it is not a logical product where, e.g., we represent the cardinal numbers by 1, 2, 3, $\ldots$, where the dots are not the "dots of laziness" and the whole expression cannot be replaced by an enumeration. He said that, when he wrote the *Tractatus,* he would have defended the mistaken view which he then took by asking the question: How can $(x) \cdot fx$ possibly entail $fa,$ if $(x) \cdot fx$ is not a logical product? And he said that the answer to this question is that where $(x) \cdot fx$ is not a logical product, the proposition "$(x) \cdot fx$

entails *fa*" is "taken as a primary proposition," whereas where it is a logical product this proposition is deduced from other primary propositions.

The point which he here made in saying that where we talk of the cardinal numbers we are not talking of a logical product was a point which he had made earlier, in (I), though he did not there point out that in the *Tractatus* he had made the mistake of supposing that an infinite series was a logical product— that it *could* be enumerated, though we were unable to enumerate it. In this passage in (I) he began by saying that by the proposition "there are an infinite number of shades of grey between black and white" we "mean something entirely different" from what we mean by, e.g., "I see three colours in this room," because, whereas the latter proposition can be verified by counting, the former cannot. He said that "There are an infinite number" does not give an answer to the question "How many are there?" whereas "There are three" does give an answer to this question. He went on to discuss infinite divisibility in the case of space, and said that the "linguistic expression" of "This line can be bisected" was "The words 'This line has been bisected' have sense," but that the "linguistic expression" of "This line can be infinitely divided" is certainly not "The words 'This line has been infinitely divided' have sense." He said that if we express "has been bisected," "has been trisected," "has been quadrisected," etc., by f $(1 + 1)$, $f(1 + 1 + 1)$, $f(1 + 1 + 1 + 1)$, etc., we see that an internal relation holds between successive members of this series and that the series has no end; and he concluded by saying that the "linguistic expression" of an infinite possibility is an infinite possibility in language. He also pointed out that $\Sigma 1 + \frac{1}{2} + \frac{1}{4} \ldots$ approaches a limit, whereas a logical product does not approach any limit. And he said finally that the cases to which the *Principia* notations $(x) \cdot \phi x$ and $(\exists x)$ ϕx apply, i.e., cases in which the former can be regarded as a logical product and the latter as a logical sum of propositions of the form ϕa, ϕb, ϕc, etc., are comparatively rare; that oftener we have propositions, such as "I met a man," which do not "presuppose any totality"; that the cases to which the *Principia* notations apply are only those in which we could give proper names to the entities in question; and that giving proper names is only possible in very special cases.

Besides these two cardinal cases, in which he said that the views which he had held at the time when he wrote the *Tractatus* were certainly wrong, I think that the chief logical points which he made were as follows.

(3) One point which he made was that Russell was quite wrong in supposing that, if expressions of the form "$p \supset q$" are used with the meaning which is given to "$\supset$" in *Principia Mathematica,* then it follows that from a false proposition we *can infer* every other proposition, and that from a true one we *can infer* any other true one. He said that Russell's holding this false opinion was partly due to his supposing that "$p \supset q$" can be translated by "If p, then q." He said that we never use "If p, then q" to mean merely what is meant by "$p \supset q$"; and that Russell had admitted this, but still maintained that in the case of what he called "formal implications," i.e., propositions of the form $(x) \cdot \phi x \supset \psi x$, such a proposition can be properly translated by "If . . . , then . . ." Wittgenstein said that this also was a mistake, giving as a reason that if, e.g., we substitute "is a man" for ϕ and "is mortal" for ψ, then the mere fact that there were no men would

verify $(x) \cdot \phi x \supset \psi x$, but that we never so use "If . . . , then . . ." that the mere fact that there were no men would verify "If anything is a man, then that thing is mortal."

(4) He also, on more than one occasion, said something about Sheffer's "stroke notation," and, on one occasion, about Tarski's "3-valued" Logic.[4]

About the former he said that it resembled what are called mathematical "discoveries" in respect of the fact that Sheffer had no rule for discovering an answer to the question "Is there only one logical constant?" whereas there is a rule for discovering, e.g., the answer to a multiplication sum. He said that, where there is no rule, it is misleading to use the word "discovery," though this is constantly done. He said that Russell or Frege might quite well have used the expression "p/q" as short for "$\sim p \cdot \sim q$," and yet still maintained that they had two primitive ideas, "and" and "not," and not one only. Plainly, therefore, he thought that Sheffer, though he admitted that Sheffer had actually defined "p/q" as meaning "$\sim p \cdot \sim q$," had done something else. But what else? He said that Sheffer's "discovery" consisted in finding a "new aspect" of certain expressions. But I am sorry to say that I did not and do not understand what he meant by this.

On Tarski's 3-valued Logic he said that it was all right "as a calculus"—that Tarski had really "discovered" a new calculus. But he said that "true" and "false" could not have in it the meaning which they actually have; and he particularly emphasized that Tarski had made the mistake of supposing that his third value, which he called "doubtful," was identical with what we ordinarily mean by "doubtful."

(C) Of problems which are specifically problems in the philosophy of Mathematics, I think that those which he most discussed are the three following. But in this case I should like to remind the reader of what I said in the first part of this article (page 237) that I cannot possibly mention nearly everything which he said, and that it is possible that some things which I omit were really more important than what I mention; and also to give the warning that in this case it is particularly likely that I may have misunderstood or may misrepresent him, since my own knowledge of Mathematics is very small. But I think that what I say will at least give some idea of the *kind* of questions which he was eager to discuss.

(1) In (I) he said that there were two very different kinds of proposition used in Mathematics, "neither of them at all like what are usually called propositions." These were (1) propositions proved by a chain of equations, in which you proceed from axioms to other equations, by means of axioms, and (2) propositions proved by "mathematical induction." And he added in (III) that proofs of the second kind, which he there called "recursive proofs," are not proofs in the same *sense* as are proofs of the first kind. He added that people constantly commit the fallacy of supposing that "true," "problem," "looking for," "proof" always mean the same, whereas in fact these words "mean entirely different things" in different case.

As an example of a proposition of the second kind he took the Associative Law for the addition of numbers, namely, "$a + (b + c) = (a + b) + c$"; and

---

[4] See Moore's *Philosophical Papers*, p. 324, for a correction of this point.

he discussed the proof of this proposition at considerable length on two separate occasions, first in (I) and then later in (III). On both occasions he discussed a proof of it given by Skolem, though in (I) he did not expressly say that the proof discussed was Skolem's. He said in (I) that the proof seemed to assume at one point the very proposition which it professed to prove, and he pointed out in (III) that in one of the steps of his proof Skolem did actually assume the Associative Law. He said that since Skolem professed to be giving a proof, one would have expected him to prove it from other formulae, but that in fact the proof begins in an entirely different way, namely with a definition—the definition "$a + (b + 1) = (a + b) + 1$"; and he maintained both in (I) and in (III) that it was quite unnecessary for Skolem to assume the Associative Law in one step of his proof, saying in (I) that the proof "really rests entirely on the definition," and in (III) that you don't in fact use the Associative Law in the proof at all. He wrote the proof "in his own way" in order to show this, saying that if you write the definition in the form "$\phi 1 = \psi 1$," then all that is proved is the two formulae $(a)\phi(c + 1) = \phi c + 1$ and $(b)\psi(c + 1) = \psi c + 1$, and that to prove these two formulae is the same thing as what is called "proving the Associative Law *for all numbers.*" He went on to say that the fact that this proof proves all we want "shows that we are not dealing with an extension at all"; that instead of talking of a *finite part* of the series "1, 2, 3 . . . ,'" on the one hand, and of the *whole* series on the other hand, we should talk of a bit of the series and of *the Law which generates it;* that proving the Associative Law "for all numbers" can't mean the same sort of thing as proving it, e.g., for three numbers, since, in order to do this latter, you would have to give a separate proof for each of the three; and that what we have in the proof is a general *form* of proof for *any* number. Finally he said that the generality which is misleadingly expressed by saying that we have proved the Associative Law for "*all* cardinals," really comes in the definition, which might have been written in the form of a series, viz "$1 + (1 + 1) = (1 + 1) + 1$" "$1 + (2 + 1) = (1 + 2) + 1$" "$2 + (1 + 1) = (2 + 1) + 1$" *and so on*; and that this series is not a logical product of which the examples given are a part, but a *rule,* and that "the examples are only there to explain the rule."

(2) Another problem in the philosophy of Mathematics, which he discussed on no less than three separate occasions, was what we are to say of the apparent question "Are there anywhere in the development of π three consecutive 7's?" (Sometimes he took the question "Are there *five* consecutive 7's?" instead of "Are there three?") He first dealt with this apparent question in (I), in connection with Brouwer's view that the Law of Excluded Middle does not apply to some mathematical propositions; i.e. that some mathematical propositions are neither true nor false; that there is an alternative to being either true or false, viz. being "undecidable." And on this occasion he said that the words "There are three consecutive 7's in the development of π" are nonsense, and that hence not only the Law of Excluded Middle does not apply in this case, but that no laws of Logic apply in it; though he admitted that if someone developed π for ten years and actually found three consecutive 7's in the development, this would prove that there were three consecutive 7's *in a ten years' development,* and seemed to be admitting, therefore, that it is possible that there might be. The

next time he discussed the question, early in (III), he said that if anyone actually found three consecutive 7's this would prove that there are, but that if no one found them that wouldn't prove that there are not; that, therefore, it is something for the truth of which we have provided a test, but for the falsehood of which we have provided none; and that therefore it must be a quite different sort of thing from cases in which a test for both truth and falsehood is provided. He went on to discuss the apparent question in a slightly new way. He said we seem to be able to define π' as the number which, if there are three consecutive 7's in the development of π, differs from π in that, in the place in which three consecutive 7's occur in π, there occur in it three consecutive 1's instead, but which, if there are not, does not differ from π at all; and that we seem to be able to say that π', so defined, either is identical with π or is not. But he said here that, since we have no way of finding out whether π' is identical with π or not, the question whether it is or not "has no meaning"; and, so far as I can see, this entails the same view which he had expressed in (I), viz. that the words "There are *not* three consecutive 7's anywhere in the development of π" have no meaning, since, if these words had a meaning, it would seem to follow that "$\pi' = \pi$" also has one, and that therefore the question "Is π' identical with π?" also has one. In the second passage in (III) in which he discussed this apparent question he expressly said that though the words (1) "There are five consecutive 7's in the first thousand digits of π" have sense, yet the words (2) "There are five consecutive 7's *somewhere* in the development" have none, that "we can't say that (2) makes sense because (2) follows from (1)." But in the very next lecture he seemed to have changed his view on this point, since he there said "We ought not to say 'There are five 7's in the development' has no sense," having previously said "It has whatever sense its grammar allows," and having emphasized that "it has a very curious grammar" since "it is compatible with there not being five consecutive 7's in any development you can give." If it has sense, although a "very curious" one, it does presumably express a proposition to which the Law of Excluded Middle and the other rules of Formal Logic do apply; but Wittgenstein said nothing upon this point. What he did say was that "All big mathematical problems are of the nature of 'Are there five consecutive 7's in the development of π?'" and that "they are therefore quite different from multiplication sums, and not comparable in respect of difficulty."

He said many other things about this question, but I cannot give them all, and some of them I certainly did not and do not understand. But one puzzling thing which he seemed to say in (III) was that, if we express the proposition that there is, in the development of π, a number of digits which is immediately followed by five consecutive 7's, by "$(\exists n) \cdot fn$," then there are two conceivable ways of proving $(\exists n) \cdot fn$, namely, (1) by *finding* such a number, and (2) by proving that $\sim(\exists n) \cdot fn$ is self-contradictory; but that the $(\exists n) \cdot fn$ proved in the latter way could not be the same as that proved in the former. In this connection he said that there is no "opposite" to the first method of proof. He said also that "$\exists n$" means something different where it is possible to "look for" a number which proves it, from what it means where this is not possible; and, generally, that "The proof of an existence theorem gives the meaning of 'existence' in that theorem," whereas the meaning of "There's a man in the next room" does not depend on the method of proof.

(3) This last problem is connected, and was connected by him, with a general point which he discussed more than once in connection with the question "How can we look for a method of trisecting an angle by rule and compasses, if there is no such thing?" He said that a man who had spent his life in trying to trisect an angle by rule and compasses would be inclined to say "If you understand both what is meant by 'trisection' and what is meant by 'bisection by rule and compasses,' you must understand what is meant by 'trisection by rule and compasses' " but that this was a mistake; that we can't imagine trisecting an angle by rule and compasses, whereas we can imagine dividing an angle into eight equal parts by rule and compasses; that "looking for" a trisection by rule and compasses is not like "looking for" a unicorn, since "There are unicorns" has sense, although in fact there are no unicorns, whereas "There are animals which show on their foreheads a construction by rule and compasses of the trisection of an angle" is just nonsense like "There are animals with three horns, but also with only one horn": it does not give a description of any possible animal. And Wittgenstein's answer to the original question was that by proving that it is impossible to trisect an angle by rule and compasses "we change a man's idea of trisection of an angle" but that we should say that what has been proved impossible is the very thing which he had been trying to do, because "we are willingly led in this case to identify two different things." He compared this case to the case of calling what he was doing "philosophy," saying that it was not the same kind of thing as Plato or Berkeley had done, but that we may feel that what he was doing "takes the place" of what Plato and Berkeley did, though it is really a different thing. He illustrated the same point in the case of the "construction" of a regular pentagon, by saying that if it were proved to a man who had been trying to find such a construction that there isn't any such thing, he would say "That's what I was trying to do" because "his idea has shifted on a rail on which he is ready to shift it." And he insisted here again that (*a*) to have an idea of a regular pentagon and (*b*) to know what is meant by constructing by rule and compasses, e.g., a square, do not in combination enable you to know what is meant by constructing, by rule and compasses, a regular pentagon. He said that to explain what is meant by "construction" we can give two series of "construction," viz. (*a*) equilateral triangle, regular hexagon, etc., and (*b*) square, regular octagon, etc., but that neither of these would give meaning to the construction of a regular pentagon, since they don't give any rule which applies to the number 5. He said that in a sense the result wanted is clear, but the means of getting at it is not; but in another sense, the result wanted is itself not clear, since "constructed pentagon" is not the same as "measured pentagon" and that whether the same figure will be both "depends on our physics": why we call a construction a construction of a regular pentagon is "because of the physical properties of our compasses, etc."

In (I) he had said that in the case of Logic and Mathematics (and "Sense-data") you can't know the same thing in two independent ways; and that it was in the case of "hypotheses" and *nowhere else,* that there are different evidences for the same thing. But in (III) he said that even in the case of hypotheses, e.g., the proposition that there is a cylindrical object on the mantelpiece, he himself preferred to say that if the evidence was different, the proposition was also different, but that "you can say which you please." He did not say whether, in the case of Logic and Mathematics also, he now held that "you can say which you please."

(D) He spent, as I have said in the first part of this article (page 237), a great deal of time on this discussion, and I am very much puzzled as to the meaning of much that he said, and also as to the connection between different things which he said. It seems to me that his discussion was rather incoherent, and my account of it must be incoherent also, because I cannot see the connection between different points which he seemed anxious to make. He said very early in the discussion that the whole subject is "extraordinarily difficult" because "the whole field is full of misleading notations"; and that its difficulty was shown by the fact that the question at issue is the question between Realists, Idealists, and Solipsists. And he also said, more than once, that many of the difficulties are due to the fact that there is a great temptation to confuse what are merely experiential propositions, which might, therefore, not have been true, with propositions which are necessarily true or are, as he once said, "tautological or grammatical statements." He gave, as an instance of a proposition of the latter sort, "I can't feel your toothache," saying that "If you feel it, it isn't mine" is a "matter of grammar," and also that "I can't feel your toothache" means the same as " 'I feel your toothache' has no sense"; and he contrasted this with "I hear my voice coming from somewhere near my eyes," which he said we think to be necessary, but which in fact is not necessary "though it always happens." In this connection he gave the warning "Don't be prejudiced by anything which *is* a fact, but which *might* be otherwise." And he seemed to be quite definite on a point which seems to me certainly true, viz., that I might see without physical eyes, and even without having a body at all; that the connection between seeing and physical eyes is merely a fact learnt by experience, not a necessity at all; though he also said that "the visual field" has certain internal properties, such that you can describe the motion of certain things in it as motions towards or away from "your eye"; but that here "your eye" does not mean your physical eye, nor yet anything whatever which is *in* the visual field. He called "your eye," in this sense, "the eye of the visual field," and said that the distinction between motion towards it and away from it was "on the same level" as "the distinction between 'curved' and 'straight'."

However, he began the discussion by raising a question, which he said was connected with Behaviourism, namely, the question "When we say 'He has toothache' is it correct to say that his toothache is only his behaviour, whereas when I talk about my toothache I am not talking about my behaviour?"; but very soon he introduced a question expressed in different words, which is perhaps not merely a different formulation of the same question, viz., "Is another person's toothache 'toothache' in the same sense as mine?" In trying to find an answer to this question or these questions, he said first that it was clear and admitted that what verifies or is a criterion for "I have toothache" is quite different from what verifies or is a criterion for "He has toothache," and soon added that, since this is so, the *meanings* of "I have toothache" and "he has toothache" must be different. In this connection he said later, first, that the meaning of "verification" is different, when we speak of verifying "I have" from what it is when we speak of verifying "He has," and then, later still, that there is no such thing as a verification for "I have," since the question "How do you know that you have toothache?" is nonsensical. He criticized two answers which might be given to this last question by people who think it is not nonsensical, by saying (1) that the answer "Because I feel it" won't do, because "I feel it" means the same as "I have it," and (2) that the answer "I know it by inspection" also won't do, because it implies that I can "look to see" whether I have it or not, whereas "looking to see whether I have it or not" has no meaning. The fact that it is nonsense to talk of verifying the fact that I have it, puts, he said, "I have it" on "a different level" in grammar from "he has it." And he also expressed his view that the two expressions are on a different grammatical level by saying that they are not both values of a single propositional function "x has toothache"; and in favour of this view he gave two definite reasons for saying that they are not, namely, (1) that "I don't know whether I have toothache" is always absurd or nonsense, whereas "I don't know whether he has toothache" is not nonsense, and (2) that "It seems to me that I have toothache" is nonsense, whereas "It seems to me that he has" is not.

He said, that when he said this, people supposed him to be saying that other people never really have what he has, but that, if he did say so, he would be talking nonsense; and he seemed quite definitely to reject the behaviourist view that "he has toothache" means only that "he" is behaving in a particular manner; for he said that "toothache" doesn't in fact only mean a particular kind of behaviour, and implied that when we pity a man for having toothache, we are not pitying him for putting his hand to his cheek; and, later on, he said that we *conclude* that another person has toothache from his behaviour, and that it is legitimate to conclude this on the analogy of the resemblance of his behaviour to the way in which we behave when we have toothache. It seemed, therefore, that just as to his first question he meant to give definitely the answer "No," so to his second question he meant to give definitely the answer "Yes"; the word "toothache" is used in the same sense when we say that he has it (or "you have it") as when we say that I have it, though he never expressly said so; and though he seemed to throw some doubt on whether he meant this by saying "I admit that other people do have toothache—this having *the meaning which we have given it.*"

It seemed, therefore, that he did not think that the difference between "I have toothache" and "He has toothache" was due to the fact that the word "toothache" was used in a different sense in the two sentences. What then was it due to? Much that he said seemed to suggest that his view was that the difference was due to the fact that in "He has toothache" we were necessarily talking of a physical body, whereas in "I have toothache" we were not. As to the first of these two propositions he did not seem quite definite; for though at first he said that "my voice" means "the voice which comes from my mouth," he seemed afterwards to suggest that in "He has toothache" (or "You have") we were not necessarily referring to a *body,* but might be referring only to a *voice,* identified as "his" or "yours" without reference to a body. But as to the second proposition, the one about "I have toothache," the point on which he seemed most anxious to insist was that what we call "having toothache" is what he called a "primary experience" (he once used the phrase "direct experience" as equivalent to this one); and he said that "what characterizes 'primary experience' " is that in its case " 'I' does not denote a possessor." In order to make clear what he meant by this he compared "I have toothache" with "I see a red patch"; and said of what he called "visual sensations" generally, and in particular of what he called "the visual field," that "the idea of a person doesn't enter into the description of it, just as a (physical) eye doesn't enter into the description of what is seen"; and he said that similarly "the idea of a person" doesn't enter into the description of "having toothache." How was he here using the word "person"? He certainly meant to deny that the idea of a physical body enters necessarily into the description; and in one passage he seemed to imply that he used "person" to mean the same as "physical body," since he said "A description of a sensation does not contain a description of a sense-organ, nor, *therefore,* of a person." He was, therefore, still maintaining apparently that one distinction between "I have toothache" and "He has toothache" was due to the fact that the latter necessarily refers to a physical body (or, perhaps, to a voice instead) whereas the former does not. But I think this was not the only distinction which he had in mind, and that he was not always using "person" to mean the same as physical body (or, perhaps, a voice instead). For he said that "Just as no (physical) eye is involved in seeing, so no Ego is involved in thinking or in having toothache"; and he quoted, with apparent approval, Lichtenberg's saying "Instead of 'I think' we ought to say 'It thinks' " ("it" being used, as he said, as "Es" is used in "Es blitzet"); and by saying this he meant, I think, something similar to what he said of "the eye of the visual field" when he said that it is not anything which is *in* the visual field. Like so many other philosophers, in talking of "visual sensations" he seemed not to distinguish between "what I see" and "my seeing of it"; and he did not expressly discuss what appears to be a possibility, namely, that though no person enters into what I see, yet some "person" other than a physical body or a voice, may "enter into" my seeing of it.

In this connection, that in "I have toothache" "I" does not "denote a possessor," he pointed out that, when I talk of "*my* body," the fact that the body in question is "mine" or "belongs to me," cannot be verified by reference to that body itself, thus seeming to imply that when I say "This body belongs to me," "me" is used in the second of the senses which he distinguished for "I," viz., that in which, according to him, it does not "denote a possessor." But he did not seem to be quite sure of this, since he said in one place "*If* there is an ownership such that I possess a body, this isn't verified by reference to a body," i.e., that "This is *my* body" can't possibly mean "This body belongs to this body." He said that, where "I" is replaceable by "this body" "I" and "he" are "on the same (grammatical) level." He was quite definite that the word 'I' or "any other word which denotes a subject" is used in "two utterly different ways," one in which it is "on a level with other people," and one in which it is not. This difference, he said, was a difference in "the grammar of our ordinary language." As an instance of one of these two uses, he gave "I've got a match-box" and "I've got a bad tooth," which he said were "on a level" with "Skinner has a match-box" and "Skinner has a bad tooth." He said that in these two cases "I have . . ." and "Skinner has . . ." really were values of the same propositional function, and that "I" and "Skinner" were both "possessors." But in the case of "I have toothache" or "I see a red patch" he held that the use of "I" is utterly different.

In speaking of these two senses of "I" he said, as what he called "a final thing," "In one sense 'I' and 'conscious' are equivalent, but not in another," and he compared this difference to the difference between what can be said of the pictures on a film in a magic lantern and of the picture on the screen; saying that the pictures in the lantern are all "on the same level" but that the picture which is at any given time on the screen is not "on the same level" with any of them, and that if we were to use "conscious" to say of one of the pictures in the lantern that it was at that time being thrown on the screen, it would be meaningless to say of the picture on the screen that it was "conscious." The pictures on the film, he said, "have neighbours," whereas that on the screen has none. And he also compared the "grammatical" difference between the two different uses of "I" with the difference between the meaning of "has blurred edges" as applied to the visual field, and the meaning of the same expression as applied to any drawing you might make of the visual field: your drawing might be imagined to have sharp edges instead of blurred ones, but this is unimaginable in the case of the visual field. The visual field, he said, has no outline or boundary, and he equated this with "It has no sense to say that it has one."

In connection with his statement that "I," in one of its uses, is equivalent to "conscious," he said something about Freud's use of the terms "conscious" and "unconscious." He said that Freud had really discovered phenomena and connections not previously known, but that he talked as if he had found out that there were in the human mind "unconscious" hatreds, volitions, etc., and that this was very misleading, because we think of the difference between a "conscious" and an "unconscious" hatred as like that between a "seen" and an "unseen" chair. He said that, in fact, the grammar of "felt" and "unfelt" hatred is quite different from that of "seen" and "unseen" chair, just as the grammar of "artificial" flower is quite different from that of "blue" flower. He suggested that "unconscious toothache," if "unconscious" were used as Freud used it, might be necessarily bound up with a physical body, whereas "conscious toothache" is not so bound up."

As regards Solipsism and Idealism he said that he himself had been often tempted to say "All that is real is the experience of the present moment" or "All that is certain is the experience of the present moment"; and that anyone who is at all tempted to hold Idealism or Solipsism knows the temptation to say "The only reality is the present experience" or "The only reality is *my* present experience." Of these two latter statements he said that both were equally absurd, but that, though both were fallacious, "the idea expressed by them is of enormous importance." Both about Solipsism and about Idealism he had insisted earlier that neither of them pretends that what it says is learnt by experience—that the arguments for both are of the form "you can't" or "you must," and that both these expressions "cut (the statement in question) out of our language." Elsewhere he said that both Solipsists and Idealists would say they "couldn't imagine it otherwise," and that, in reply to this, he would say, "If so, your statement has no sense" since "nothing can characterize reality, except as opposed to something else which is not the case." Elsewhere he had said that the Solipsist's statement "Only my experience is real" is absurd "as a statement of fact," but that the Solipsist sees that a person who says "No: my experience is real too" has not really refuted him, just as Dr. Johnson did not refute Berkeley by kicking a stone. Much later he said that Solipsism is right if it merely says that "I have toothache" and "He has toothache" are "on quite a different level," but that "if the Solipsist says that he has something which another hasn't, he is absurd and is making the very mistake of putting the two statements on the same level." In this connection he said that he thought that both the Realist and the Idealist were "talking nonsense" in the particular sense in which "nonsense is produced by trying to express by the use of language what ought to be embodied in the grammar"; and he illustrated this sense by saying that "I can't feel his toothache" means " 'I feel his toothache' has no sense" and therefore does not "express a fact" as "I can't play chess" may do.

(E) He concluded (III) by a long discussion which he introduced by saying "I have always wanted to say something about the grammar of ethical expressions, or, e.g., of the word 'God'." But in fact he said very little about the grammar of such words as "God," and very little also about that of ethical expressions. What he did deal with at length was not Ethics but Aesthetics, saying, however, "Practically everything which I say about 'beautiful' applies in a slightly different way to 'good'." His discussion of Aesthetics, however, was mingled in a curious way with criticism of assumptions which he said were constantly made by Frazer in the *Golden Bough,* and also with criticism of Freud.

About "God" his main point seemed to be that this word is used in many *grammatically* different senses. He said, for instance, that many controversies about God could be settled by saying "I'm not using the word in such a sense that you can say . . . ," and that different religions "treat things as making sense which others treat as nonsense, and don't merely deny some proposition which another religion affirms"; and he illustrated this by saying that if people use "god" to mean something like a human being, then "God has four arms" and "God has two arms" will both have sense, but that others so use "God" that "God has arms" is nonsense—would say "God *can't* have arms." Similarly, he said of the expression "the soul," that sometimes people so use that expression that "the soul is a gaseous human being" has sense, but sometimes so that it has not. To explain what he meant by "grammatically" different senses, he said we wanted terms which are not "comparable," as, e.g., "solid" and "gaseous" are comparable, but which differ as, e.g., "chair" differs from "permission to sit on a chair," or "railway" from "railway accident."

He introduced his whole discussion of Aesthetics by dealing with one problem about the meaning of words, with which he said he had not yet dealt.

He illustrated this problem by the example of the word "game," with regard to which he said both (1) that, even if there is something common to all games, it doesn't follow that this is what we mean by calling a particular game a "game," and (2) that the reason why we call so many different activities "games" need not be that there is anything common to them all, but only that there is "a gradual transition" from one use to another, although there may be nothing in common between the two ends of the series. And he seemed to hold definitely that there is nothing in common in our different uses of the word "beautiful," saying that we use it "in a hundred different games"—that, e.g., the beauty of a face is something different from the beauty of a chair or a flower or the binding of a book. And of the word "good" he said similarly that each different way in which one person, A, can convince another, B, that so-and-so is "good" fixes the meaning in which "good" is used in that discussion—"fixes the grammar of that discussion"; but that there will be "gradual transitions," from one of these meanings to another, "which take the place of something in common." In the case of "beauty" he said that a difference of meaning is shown by the fact that "you can say more" in discussing whether the arrangement of flowers in a bed is "beautiful" than in discussing whether the smell of lilac is so.

He went on to say that specific colours in a certain spatial arrangement are not merely "symptoms" that what has them *also* possesses a quality which we call "being beautiful," as they would be, if we meant by "beautiful," e.g., "causing stomach-ache," in which case we could learn by experience whether such an arrangement did always cause stomach-ache or not. In order to discover how we use the word "beautiful" we need, he said, to consider (1) what an actual aesthetic controversy or inquiry is like, and (2) whether such inquiries are in fact psychological inquiries "though they look so very different." And on (1) he said that the actual word "beautiful" is hardly ever used in aesthetic controversies: that we are more apt to use "right," as, e.g., in "That doesn't look quite right yet," or when we say of a proposed accompaniment to a song "That won't do: it isn't right." And on (2) he said that if we say, e.g., of a bass "It is too heavy; it moves too much," we are not saying "If it moved less, it would be more agreeable to me": that, on the contrary, that it should be quieter is an "end in itself," not a means to some other end; and that when we discuss whether a bass "will do," we are no more discussing a psychological question than we are discussing psychological questions in Physics; that what we are trying to do is to bring the bass "nearer to an ideal," though we haven't an ideal before us which we are trying to copy; that in order to show what we want, we might point to another tune, which we might say is "perfectly right." He said that in aesthetic investigations "the one thing we are not interested in is causal connections, whereas this is the only thing we are interested in in Psychology." To ask "Why is this beautiful?" is not to ask for a causal explanation: that, e.g., to give a causal explanation in answer to the question "Why is the smell of a rose pleasant?" would not remove our "aesthetic puzzlement."

Against the particular view that "beautiful" means "agreeable" he pointed out that we may refuse to go to a performance of a particular work on such a ground as "I can't stand its greatness," in which case it is disagreeable rather than agreeable; that we may think that a piece of music which we in fact prefer is "just nothing" in comparison to another to which we prefer it; and that the fact that we go to see "King Lear" by no means proves that that experience is agreeable: he said that, even if it is agreeable, that fact "is about the least important thing you can say about it." He said that such a statement as "That bass moves too much" is not a statement about human beings at all, but is more like a piece of Mathematics; and that, if I say of a face which I draw "It smiles too much," this says that it could be brought closer to some "ideal," not that it is not yet agreeable enough, and that to bring it closer to the "ideal" in question would be more like "solving a mathematical problem." Similarly, he said, when a painter tries to improve his picture, he is not making a psychological experiment on himself, and that to say of a door "It is top-heavy" is to say what is wrong with it, *not* what impression it gives you. The question of Aesthetics, he said, was not "Do you like this?" but "*Why* do you like it?"

What Aesthetics tries to do, he said, is to give *reasons*, e·g., for having this word rather than that in a particular place in a poem, or for having this musical phrase rather than that in a particular place in a piece of music. Brahms's *reason* for rejecting Joachim's suggestion that his Fourth Symphony should be opened by two chords was not that that wouldn't produce the feeling he wanted to produce, but something more like "That isn't what I meant." *Reasons,* he said, in Aesthetics, are "of the nature of further descriptions": e.g., you can make a person see what Brahms was driving at by showing him lots of different pieces by Brahms, or by comparing him with a contemporary author; and all that Aesthetics does is "to draw your attention to a thing," to "place things side by side." He said that if, by giving "reasons" of this sort, you make another person "see what you see" but it still "doesn't appeal to him," that is "an end" of the discussion; and that what he, Wittgenstein, had "at the back of his mind" was "the idea that aesthetic discussions were like discussions in a court of law," where you try to "clear up the circumstances" of the action which is being tried, hoping that in the end what you say will "appeal to the judge." And he said that the same sort of "reasons" were given, not only in Ethics, but also in Philosophy.

As regards Frazer's *Golden Bough,* the chief points on which he seemed to wish to insist were, I think, the three following: (1) That it was a mistake to suppose that there was *only one* "reason," in the sense of "motive," which led people to perform a particular action—to suppose that there was "one motive, which was *the* motive." He gave as an instance of this sort of mistake Frazer's statement, in speaking of Magic, that when primitive people stab an effigy of a particular person, they believe that they have hurt the person in question. He said that primitive people do not *always* entertain this "false scientific belief," though in some cases they may: that they may have quite different reasons for stabbing the effigy. But he said that the tendency to suppose that there is "one motive which is *the* motive" was "enormously strong," giving as an instance that there are theories of play each of which gives *only one* answer to the question "Why do children play?" (2) That it was a mistake to suppose that *the* motive is always "to get something useful." He gave as an instance of this mistake Frazer's supposition that "people at a certain stage thought it useful to kill a person, in order to get a good crop." (3) That it was a mistake to suppose that why, e.g., the account of the Beltane Festival "impresses us so much" is because it has "developed from a festival in which a real man was burnt." He accused Frazer of thinking that this was the reason. He said that our puzzlement as to why it impresses us is not diminished by giving the *causes* from which the festival arose, but is diminished by finding other similar festivals: to find these may make it seem "natural," whereas to give the causes from which it arose cannot do this. In this respect he said that the question "Why does this impress us?" is like the aesthetic questions "Why is this beautiful?" or "Why will this bass not do?"

He said that Darwin, in his "expression of the Emotions," made a mistake similar to Frazer's, e.g., in thinking that "because our ancestors, when angry, wanted to bite" is a sufficient explanation of why we show our teeth when angry. He said you might say that what is satisfactory in Darwin is not such "hypotheses," but his "putting the facts in a system"—helping us to make a "synopsis" of them.

As for Freud, he gave the greater part of two lectures to Freud's investigation of the nature of a "joke" (Witz), which he said was an "aesthetic investigation." He said that Freud's book on this subject was a very good book for looking for philosophical mistakes, and that the same was true of his writings in general, because there are so many cases in which one can ask how far what he says is a "hypothesis" and how far merely a good way of representing a fact —a question as to which he said Freud himself is constantly unclear. He said, for instance, that Freud encouraged a confusion between getting to know the *cause* of your laughter and getting to know the *reason* why you laugh, because what he says sounds as if it were science, when in fact it is only a "wonderful representation." This last point he also expressed by saying "It is all excellent similes, e.g., the comparison of a dream to a rebus." (He had said earlier that all Aesthetics is of the nature of "giving a good simile.") He said that this confusion between *cause* and *reason* had led to the disciples of Freud making "an abominable mess": that Freud did not in fact give any method of analysing dreams which was analogous to the rules which will tell you what are the causes of stomach-ache; that he had genius and therefore might sometimes by psycho-analysis find the *reason* of a certain dream, but that what is most striking about him is "the enormous field of psychical facts which he arranges."

As for what Freud says about jokes, he said first that Freud makes the two mistakes (1) of supposing that there is something common to all jokes, and (2) of supposing that this supposed common character is the meaning of "joke." He said it is not true, as Freud supposed, that *all* jokes enable you to do covertly what it would not be seemly to do openly, but that "joke," like "proposition," "has a rainbow of meanings." But I think the point on which he was most anxious to insist was perhaps that psycho-analysis does not enable you to discover the *cause* but only the *reason* of, e.g., laughter. In support of this statement he asserted that a psycho-analysis is successful only if the patient agrees to the explanation offered by the analyst. He said there is nothing analogous to this in Physics; and that what a patient agrees to can't be a *hypothesis* as to the *cause* of his laughter, but only that so-and-so was the *reason* why he laughed. He explained that the patient who agrees did not think of this reason at the moment when he laughed, and that to say that he thought of it "subconsciously" "tells you nothing as to what was happening at the moment when he laughed."

(F) In (I), rather to my surprise, he spent a good deal of time in discussing what would usually be called a question about colours, namely, the question how the four "saturated" colours, pure yellow, pure red, pure blue and pure green, which he called "primary," are distinguished from those "saturated" colours which are not "primary." He drew a circle on the blackboard to represent the arrangement of the saturated colours, with a vertical diameter joining "yellow" at the top to "blue" at the bottom, and a horizontal diameter joining "green" on the left to "red" on the right. And he seemed to be maintaining with regard to these four colours that they are distinguished from the other saturated colours in the two following ways, viz., (1) that the sense in which any purple is "between" pure red and pure blue, and in which any orange is "between" pure yellow and pure red is very different from the sense of "between" in which pure red is "between" any orange and any purple; a difference which he also expressed by saying that whereas an orange can be properly called a "mixture" of yellow and red, red cannot possibly be called a "mixture" of orange and purple; and (2) that whereas pure red can be properly said to be "midway" between pure yellow and pure blue, there is no colour which is "midway" between pure red and pure blue, or "midway" between pure yellow and pure red, etc. He said that, for these reasons, the arrangement of the saturated colours in a square, with the four "primaries" at the four corners, is a better picture of their relations than the arrangement of them in a circle.

I say only that he *seemed* to be making these assertions, because he emphasized from the beginning that "primary" is not an adjective to "colour" in the sense in which "black" may be an adjective to "gown," but that the distinction between "primary" and "not primary" is a "logical" distinction—an expression which he explained later on by saying that, just as sounds are not distinguished from colours by the fact that something is true of the one which is not true of the other, so red, blue, green, and yellow are not distinguished from the other saturated colours by the fact that anything is true of them which is not true of the others. He emphasized to begin with that the sentences "blue is not primary" and "violet is primary" are both of them "nonsense," and I think there is no doubt he held that, since this is so, their contradictories "blue is primary" and "violet is not primary" are also nonsense, though there is a sense in which the two last are true, and the two former false. In other words, I think he certainly held that "blue is primary" is a "necessary proposition"—that we can't imagine its not being true—and that therefore, as he said (page 276), it "has no sense." It would seem to follow that if, as he seemed to be, he was really talking about the *colours*, red, blue, green, and yellow, all that he said about them was "nonsense." According to what he said elsewhere, he could only have been talking sense if he was talking, not about the colours, but about certain words used to express them; and accordingly he did actually go on to say that "red is primary" was only a proposition about the use of the English word "red," which, as I said (page 261), he cannot seriously have held. The question I am here raising is the question which I discussed at length in the second part of this article, and I have nothing to add except to give one quotation which I ought to have given there. He actually said, in one place in (II), "What corresponds to a necessity in the world must be what in language seems an arbitrary rule." I do not think he had succeeded in getting quite clear as to what relation he wished to assert to hold between what he called "rules of grammar," on the one hand, and "necessary propositions," on the other.

(G) With questions about Time he dealt, at considerable length, in two places in (III).

The earlier discussion was in connection with his view that the "troubles in our thought" which he was concerned to remove, arise from our thinking that sentences which we do not use with any practical object, sound as if they "ought to have sense," when in fact they have none. And in this connection his main point seemed to be that, since we talk of Time "flowing" as well as of a river "flowing," we are tempted to think that Time "flows" in a certain "direction," as a river does, and that therefore it has sense to suppose that Time might flow in the opposite direction, just as it certainly has sense to suppose that a river might. He said, in one place, that some philosophers have actually made the muddle of thinking that Time has a "direction" which might conceivably be reversed. Later on he made a distinction, as to the meaning of which I am not clear, between what he called "memory-time" and what he called "information-time," saying that in the former there is only earlier and later, not past and future, and that it has sense to say that I remember that which in "information-time" is future. This distinction seemed to be connected with one he had made earlier, when he said, that if we imagine a river with logs floating down it at equal spatial distances from one another, the interval between the time at which, e.g., the 120th log passed us and that at which, e.g., the 130th passed, might *seem* to be equal to that between the time at which the 130th passed us and that at which the 140th passed us, although, *measured by a clock*, these intervals were not equal. He went on to ask: "Supposing all events had come to an end, what is the criterion for saying that Time would have come to an end too, or that it still went on?" and to ask: "If there were no events earlier than a hundred years ago, would there have been no time before that?" He said that what we need to do is to notice how we use the expression "Time"; and that people ask "Has Time been created?" although the question "Has 'before' been created?" has absolutely no meaning.

But he said a good many things in this discussion which I have failed to understand, and I may easily have omitted points which he would have considered of the first importance.

In his second discussion he was trying to show what was wrong with the following statement which Russell made in his *Outline of Philosophy:*

> Remembering, which occurs now, cannot possibly prove that what is remembered occurred at some other time, because the world might have sprung into being five minutes ago, full of acts of remembering which were entirely misleading.

But I cannot help thinking that, in what he said about this statement, he made two quite definite mistakes as to what Russell was implying by it. In order to explain why I think so I must, however, first explain what I take it that Russell was implying.

It will be noted that Russell speaks as if "acts of remembering" could be "entirely misleading"; and he seems not to have noticed that we so use the term "remember" that if an act, which resembles an act of remembering, turns out to be entirely misleading, we say that it was not an act of remembering. For instance "I remember that I had breakfast this morning" is so used that, if it turns out that I did not have breakfast this morning, it *follows logically* that I do *not* remember that I did: from "I remember that I had it" it *follows logically* that I did have it, so that "acts of remembering, which are entirely misleading" is a contradiction in terms; if an act is entirely misleading, it is not an act of remembering. It is plain, therefore, that Russell was using the expression "acts of remembering" in a different sense from any in which it can be correctly used; and his view could be more correctly expressed as the view that it is *logically possible* that we never remember anything. I say "logically possible," because when he says "the world *might* have sprung into being five minutes ago," I think he certainly means by "might," merely that it is *logically possible* that it did.

Now Wittgenstein pointed out, quite justly, that when Russell says "The world might have sprung into being five minutes ago" his choice of "five minutes ago" as the time when the world might have "sprung into being" is "arbitrary": Russell's view requires that it is equally true that it might have "sprung into being" two minutes ago or one minute ago, or, says Wittgenstein, that it might have begun to exist *now:* he actually said that Russell *ought* to have said "The world might have been created *now.*" And I think it is true that Russell does imply this. But Wittgenstein said that in the statement quoted, Russell was "committing the precise fallacy of Idealism." And surely this is a complete mistake! From what I have quoted (page 276), it appears clear that what Wittgenstein regarded as the "fallacy of Idealism" was some such statement as "It is logically *im*possible that anything should be real except the present experience." And Russell's statement certainly does not imply this. It looks to me as if, for the moment, Wittgenstein was confusing the two entirely different propositions, (1) "It is logically possible that nothing exists except the present experience" which Russell may be said to imply, and (2) "It is logically *im*possible that anything should exist except the present experience," which he certainly does not imply.

But it seems to me that he also made another complete mistake as to what Russell's view implied; and this was a criticism into which he went at some length. He began by asking us to consider the question "What is the verification for the proposition 'The world began to exist five minutes ago'?" saying that, if you admit no criterion for its truth, that sentence is "useless," or, as he afterwards said, "meaningless." And his criticism of Russell here consisted in saying that "Russell is refusing to admit as evidence for 'the world began more than five minutes ago' what we all admit as such evidence, and is therefore making that statement meaningless." He compared Russell's statement to the statement "There is a rabbit between A and B, whenever nobody is looking" which he said "seems to have sense, but is in fact meaningless, because it cannot be refuted by experience." But surely Russell would admit, and can perfectly consistently admit, that some of those events, which he calls incorrectly "acts of remembering" do constitute very strong evidence that the world existed more than five minutes ago. He is not concerned to deny that they constitute *strong* evidence, but only that they constitute *absolutely conclusive* evidence—that they "prove" that it did. In other words, he is only asserting that it is *logically possible* that the world did not. Wittgenstein seems to me to have overlooked the distinction between denying that we have *any* evidence which Russell does not do, and denying that we have *absolutely conclusive* evidence, which I think Russell certainly meant to do.

But later on Wittgenstein seemed to me to be suggesting another quite different argument, which, if he did mean what he seemed to mean, and if what he seemed to mean is true, would really be a valid refutation of Russell's statement. He introduced again the phrase "memory-time," saying that a certain order of events might be so called, and then going on to say that all these events "approach a point such that it will have no sense to say 'B occurred after the present in memory-time'"; that "now" "should be a point in an order"; and that when we say "The clock is striking now," "now" means "the present of our memory-time," and cannot mean, e.g., "at 6.7" because it has sense to say "It is 6.7 *now*." I think all this suggests that his view was that "now," in the sense in which we commonly use it, and in which Russell was undoubtedly using it, has a meaning such that part of what we are saying when we say that an event is happening "now," is that it was preceded by other events which we remember; and, if this is true, it would certainly follow that Russell was wrong in implying that it is logically possible that nothing should have happened before *now*.

(H) I was a good deal surprised by some of the things he said about the difference between "philosophy" in the sense in which what he was doing might be called "philosophy" (he called this "modern philosophy"), and what has traditionally been called "philosophy." He said that what he was doing was a "new subject," and not merely a stage in a "continuous development"; that there was now, in philosophy, a "kink" in the "development of human thought," comparable to that which occurred when Galileo and his contemporaries invented dynamics; that a "new method" had been discovered, as had happened when "chemistry was developed out of alchemy"; and that it was now possible for the first time that there should be "skilful" philosophers, though of course there had in the past been "great" philosophers.

He went on to say that, though philosophy had now been "reduced to a matter of skill," yet this skill, like other skills, is very difficult to acquire. One difficulty was that it required a "sort of thinking" to which we are not accustomed and to which we have not been trained—a sort of thinking very different from what is required in the sciences. And he said that the required skill could not be acquired merely by hearing lectures: discussion was essential. As regards his own work, he said it did not matter whether his results were true or not: what mattered was that "a method had been found."

In answer to the question why this "new subject" should be called "philosophy" he said in (III) that though what he was doing was certainly different from what, e.g., Plato or Berkeley had done, yet people might feel that it "takes the place of" what they had done—might be inclined to say "This is what I really wanted" and to identify it with what they had done, though it is really different, just as (as I said above, page 271) a person who had been trying to trisect an angle by rule and compasses might, when shown the proof that this is impossible, be inclined to say that this impossible thing was the very thing he had been trying to do, though what he had been trying to do was really different. But in (II) he had also said that the "new subject" did really resemble what had been traditionally called "philosophy" in the three respects that (1) it was very general, (2) it was fundamental both to ordinary life and to the sciences, and (3) it was independent of any special results of science; that therefore the application to it of the word "philosophy" was not purely arbitrary.

He did not expressly try to tell us exactly what the "new method" which had been found was. But he gave some hints as to its nature. He said, in (II), that the "new subject" consisted in "something like putting in order our notions as to what can be said about the world," and compared this to the tidying up of a room where you have to move the same object several times before you can get the room really tidy. He said also that we were "in a muddle about things," which we had to try to clear up; that we had to follow a certain instinct which leads us to ask certain questions, though we don't even understand what these questions mean; that our asking them results from "a vague mental uneasiness," like that which leads children to ask "Why?"; and that this uneasiness can only be cured "either by showing that a particular question is not permitted, or by answering it." He also said that he was not trying to teach us any new facts: that he would only tell us "trivial" things—"things which we all know already"; but that the difficult thing was to get a "synopsis" of these trivialities, and that our "intellectual discomfort" can only be removed by a synopsis of *many* trivialities—that "if we leave out any, we still have the feeling that something is wrong." In this connection he said it was misleading to say that what we wanted was an "analysis," since in science to "analyse" water means to discover some new fact about it, e.g., that it is composed of oxygen and hydrogen, whereas in philosophy "we know at the start all the facts we need to know." I imagine that it was in this respect of needing a "synopsis" of trivialities that he thought that philosophy was similar to Ethics and Aesthetics (page 278).

I ought, perhaps, finally to repeat what I said in the first part of this article (page 237), namely, that he held that though the "new subject" must say a great deal about language, it was only necessary for it to deal with those points about language which have led, or are likely to lead, to definite philosophical puzzles or errors. I think he certainly thought that some philosophers nowadays have been misled into dealing with linguistic points which have no such bearing, and the discussion of which therefore, in his view, forms no part of the proper business of a philosopher.

John Wisdom PHILOSOPHY

AND PSYCHO-ANALYSIS

Although John Wisdom's writings in philosophy show clearly the influence of Wittgenstein, they nevertheless also display a marked originality. Despite the complexity and difficulty of his style, a careful reading of Wisdom is seldom unprofitable. His is a unique kind of genius in philosophy.

The essay which follows is an excellent example of Wisdom's repeated attempts to explore the ultimate bases of philosophical perplexity. A great deal of the time, Wisdom is primarily interested in finding out why metaphysicians feel compelled to utter such strange sentences (e.g., "Time is unreal," "There are no material things," etc.). According to Wisdom, such sentences are both false (and perhaps meaningless) and yet illuminating. Even more than Wittgenstein, Wisdom has stressed the "therapeutic" conception of philosophy, a view that comes out clearly in the following pages where he emphasizes the analogy between philosophical and neurotic distress, contrasting them with other kinds of problems.

The reader who is interested in gaining a fuller acquaintance with Wisdom's thought is referred to his famous article "Gods" in *Philosophy and Psycho-analysis*. *Other Minds* is Wisdom's most sustained discussion of a single topic and is in many ways his finest work.

I. PHILOSOPHICAL CONFLICT

Wittgenstein once said that he "holds no opinions in philosophy" and, again that he tries to remove "a feeling of puzzlement, to cure a sort of mental cramp." This emphasizes much more what evil philosophy removes than what good it brings. Nevertheless, all who have felt the old philosophical puzzles know the cramp Wittgenstein refers to. Indeed if one thinks of a philosopher one thinks of a man who talks like this, for example:

We fancy we sometimes know what other creatures are thinking and how they are feeling. But all we really know is how they nod and smile at this, bark and frown at that. No reasoning from such information will justify a conclusion about how they think and feel; it won't even tell us that they think and feel at all, much less will it tell us what goes on in the souls behind their faces. True we can infer from the faces of clocks what goes on within. But that is different. For some of us have sometimes noted a clock's face and quickly looked within. None of us has ever noted a friend's face and then quickly looked within. Maybe we have looked within his body and found a decayed tooth or other sand in the transmission. But not in the happiest days have we ever viewed the landscapes he alone can view. And yet though it seems we *can't* know how others think and feel surely we often *do* know.

The trouble spreads. The philosopher soon finds himself saying:

Not only do I not know how or whether anything else thinks or feels but also I cannot really know what is happening in any place hidden from me, in the inside of a clock, for example, or beyond the horizon. I can open some clocks quickly but none quickly enough. On Tuesday at 2 p.m., I know only what is happening near me, within the walls of my room, in my own little ark. For what is happening far away on the waste of waters or in the roaring Strand, I am obliged to rely on doves and telephones. However fast I hurry to the place I'm always late. The dove brings a leaf perhaps, but by the time I reach the distant Spring the leaves are turning or it's full Summer. For, if not, it wasn't Spring but still Winter when I started. Finding fallen leaves in November I may say I was right when in April, in Germany, I thought it was Spring in England. But the fallen leaves are not the Spring of which I dreamed in April. That is now for ever in the past. Even that I don't really know, obliged as I am to rely for all knowledge of the past upon dead leaves, bones, stones, documents and the faded photos in the family album and my memory. Nor do I know the future. For even if I knew what had happened this wouldn't guarantee what will happen.

And now if I know nothing of the past and nothing of the future then all I seem to see and hear may have no more substance than a dream. For just as a phoenix is not a phoenix unless it renews itself in its own ashes so bread that comes down from Heaven isn't bread but manna, and a dagger than vanishes is not a dagger but an image.

Further, even if I knew the future and could with perfect propriety predict to all eternity the pattern of my sensations, would this give substance to the shadows in a mirror that mirrors nothing?

And yet, surely, I do know these things it seems I can't know? I do know that where there's smoke there's fire, that the stone I kick is real, that the friend who speaks with me is not a talking doll.

So spreads and swings the philosophic hesitation. Driven by a caricature of curiosity which is kept for ever hungry by an inexorable desire to be logically perfect and factually infallible the philosopher diminishes his claims to knowledge; agnosticism about the minds of others becomes agnosticism about all things but his own thought as he thinks it—in other words Solipsism. And Solipsism soon becomes Scepticism, the "claim" that we know nothing. For when the philosopher become Solipsist fancies himself about to reap the reward of his logical purity in perfect knowledge, limited indeed but invulnerable, just then the statement he had hoped to make dwindles to the senseless whimper of an elderly infant in the mansions of the dead.[1] I don't mean, of course, that all philosophers in the end become Sceptics and find peace in death. On the contrary, no philosopher becomes really a Sceptic; because if a man really feels what the Sceptic says he feels then he is said to have "a sense of unreality" and is removed to a home. In fact the sceptical philosopher never succeeds in killing his primitive credulities which, as Hume says, reassert themselves the moment he takes up the affairs of life and ceases to murmur the incantations which generate his philosophic doubt. More than that, most philosophers refuse to be Sceptics even in their philosophic moments; these travellers on the road to Nothing mostly look back and would return whence they have come, but cannot. In this sad case, some talk of trans-sensual spheres glimpsed by a trans-sensual awareness, an apprehension of Reality mediated by, but not limited to, the sights and sounds, the headaches and the heartaches to which we seem confined; others, the Realists, pretend that nothing's happened, that everything's all right, that fine-spun argument can never shake the common sense they had and hold; others, the Phenomenalists, say that everything's all right because the ideal of knowledge of reality beyond appearance is only unattainable because it's unintelligible; others hurry agitatedly from one cult to another; others stand poised "betwixt a world destroyed and world restored," paralysed in the cramp of conflict.

We have come upon these people before—in other difficulties; indeed they are ourselves. And none of them is at ease. This comes out plainly in those who say they are not. But even those who have erected a temple for tranquility have often a hidden fear of its falling about their ears. The Transcendentalist must constantly defend himself against the Sceptic and even against the Realist, who are the more menacing because they are not only outside him but also within. The realist must keep forgetting the philosophic qualms which though crammed down into Tartarus are not dead—the confidence he professes is never what it was before he ate of the forbidden tree· The phenomenalist protests too much that there was no baby in the bath water he threw away. None of them is easy—or if he is, he shouldn't be. This last qualification reminds us of the incompleteness in the description of the proper philosopher as one who tries to cure uneasiness. He may set himself to disturb complacency. So may a psycho-analyst. We may recognize this without forgetting how much philosophy and analytic work by patient and analyst is conflict and the cure of it.

[1] With apologies to Paul Nash. For fuller treatment see *Other Minds*, VII, John Wisdom.

II. PHILOSOPHICAL AND OBSESSIONAL DOUBT

I have used words with a clinical flavour in the sketch of philosophers which I have just given because I want to bring out likenesses, connections, between states of philosophical stress and other states of stress arising from internal sources as opposed to states of stress arising from external sources. A general or a business man who has to decide what to do in a complicated situation may go over the many relevant considerations carefully and may do so many times. A judge considers carefully, even anxiously, the arguments of contending counsel. But the general, the business man and the judge may consider their problems very patiently and still be very different from the neurotic. The neurotic may discuss his problems—he may indeed—but he never means business; the discussion is not a means to action, to something other than itself; on the contrary, after a while we get the impression that in spite of his evident unhappiness and desire to come from hesitation to decision he also desires the discussion never to end and dreads its ending. Have you not quite often had this impression with philosophers?—philosophers other than ourselves, for we, of course, are never neurotic. I once discussed with a man in a mental hospital whether he should continue to starve himself and study the Scriptures or take more nourishment and lend a hand at home. He put the matter well and with an admirable impartiality, but some months later I learned that he had died in the hospital, still, I believe, unable to settle the issue. And we have all read of the man who cannot be sure that he has turned off the tap or the light. He must go again to make sure, and then perhaps he must go again because though he knows the light's turned off he yet can't *feel* sure. He is obsessed by a chronic doubt. Has he done what he ought about the light or the tap? Perhaps his doubt is less limited, perhaps he is constantly questioning himself as to whether he has done what he ought. Such a man will often want rules of life to save him from continual conflict. Or again, his doubt may be less a matter of whether he has done this or that, or what he ought, and more a doubt as to what is happening where he can't see. He has slammed his front door, he hasn't much time to catch his train, but still he turns back because he wants to feel perfectly sure that things are all right behind the door—to which fortunately he has a key. At least he has a key until, like a philosopher, he wishes to see behind the door without opening it. Instantly it becomes "a veil past which I cannot see" and in the darkness of the cave one cannot tell whether She smiles or frowns. If we are watching shadows on a wall and want to know whether the shadows are telling the truth about what is going on behind our backs we can turn our heads and look; we aren't like an infant who, helpless in his cradle, cannot turn his head and cries when his mother goes out of sight; nor like philosophers who perpetually feel they don't know what's going on behind their backs, and who, still like the child, dread to know, cling to their ignorance. God or the gods know what really is so, what goes on among "objective realities," but we know only what goes on among our own toys, copies of real things. The gods know but they never tell us anything, as James Forsyte continually complained when age now instead of youth confined him to his bed. The gods know but they tell us nothing—a conspiracy of silence among the arch-deceivers.

Yesterday a man just beginning philosophy told me that he had said to a friend: "Some philosophers don't believe in material things and I am now not sure that I do." His friend said, taking hold of the table, "You don't believe there's a table here? You're mad."

I said:

> Your friend's right. There is something very odd about the situation when a philosopher says "I don't believe there's a table here" or "I doubt whether there's a table here." It's not that his question is odd, I mean it's not simply his uttering these words "I'm not sure whether there's a table here" which strikes us as odd. If when you are seeking water in the desert someone gazes at what looks like water in the distance and says "I doubt whether there's really water there," you don't think him absurd. But the philosopher says "I am not sure" while he's drinking the water; he says it when no one would, or when no one but a madman would, or when no one but a madman or a philosopher would. And then also he is queer in that he doesn't act, doesn't feel, doesn't anticipate the future in the way his words suggest. In this he is at once more and less queer than a madman. The madman says, perhaps, "I shouldn't open that door" and his eyes widen in almost furious terror. You say "Why not?" and continue to walk towards the door. He clutches your arm and says, softly, "There's a tiger in there." You say "Nonsense, I've only just been in the room. You don't suppose a furniture firm has just driven up outside, erected a ladder, and slipped a tiger in through the window, do you?" "Ah!" the madman says, "He hides" or "You can't see him."

This is the psychotic and he is different from the neurotic who says that he must make sure that he hasn't left the lights on but that, of course, it's all nonsense and that he really knows he has turned them off, or that he must make quite sure that his hands are quite clean although it is true he has only just washed them. The neurotic, we might say, doesn't believe what he says. Still he does go back at the risk of losing his train to make sure that the lights are off. The philosopher doesn't. His acts and feelings are even less in accordance with his words than are the acts and feelings of the neurotic. He, even more than the neurotic and much more than the psychotic, doesn't believe what he says, doesn't doubt when he says he's not sure. (Compare wishes when he says he doesn't, i.e. unconsciously wishes.) But if we say that the philosopher doesn't believe what he says, that he's only pretending to doubt, then we must remember that he's very different from someone who, wishing to deceive us, pretends. The philosopher isn't one who merely makes it seem to others that he is in doubt; he also seems to himself to doubt. In other words, although many of his acts and feelings are unsuitable to his words, some are suitable and, in particular, as he speaks he has much of the feeling characteristic of doubt.

When he says "Perhaps it's all in my mind," he feels something of the relief or disappointment of one who fearing this, hoping that, says "Maybe it's all a dream."

But now what is it that makes philosophers go on in the way they do?

III. THE PHILOSOPHER IS DIFFERENT

There is a big difference between the philosopher and both the psychotic and the obsessional neurotic. It lies in the flow of justificatory talk, of rationalization, which the philosopher produces when asked why he takes the extraordinary line he does. It is true that both the psychotic and neurotic listen to reason and defend themselves. The philosopher defends himself more elaborately. But this is not the point. The point is, aren't his rationalizations reasons?

When we call justifying talk "rationalization" we hint that we are not impressed by it and do not expect others to be. But we are impressed by the philosopher's talk, it has a universal effect, reluctantly we are impressed by it. The trouble is that it doesn't impress us quite enough to make us satisfied with his conclusions while yet it impresses us; the reasons seem not quite good enough and not quite bad enough and—connected fact—it seems the same with the reasons for opposing conclusions. At the same time the position is not what it is in science or crime where some evidence lends probability to one hypothesis and other evidence lends probability to another and we may contentedly wait for more evidence to tip the scales. For the philosopher's proofs profess to be *proofs* or nothing. And yet, too, we cannot, as in mathematics or logic, bring the conflict to an end by finding the slip in one of the calculations which purport to demonstrate the conflicting conclusions. There's something queer about philosophical reasons and the reasoning goes on too long.

IV. FIRST AS TO THE QUEERNESS OF PHILOSOPHICAL REASONS AND CONFLICT

Contrast a logical conflict. Lately it was reported in the Press that a railway official upon being asked the cause of a recent run of accidents replied, "Well, the men are tired, the rolling stock a little the worse for wear, but it's not so much that as the working out of the law of averages." This explanation is based on the logical doctrine that the longer a die has been thrown without a six the more probable is a six on the next throw, and we may imagine someone who argues for this as follows: when a die is about to be thrown 100 times the probability of at least one six being thrown is very great, namely .999999988 approximately. It may happen, however, that no six has appeared in the first 25 throws. In such a case unless a six appears in the next 75 throws there will have been 100 throws without a six and this, as we have seen, is improbable to the degree .000000012. Therefore it is improbable to the degree .000000012 that no six will appear in the next 75 throws. Again, if it should happen that no six appears in the first 99 throws then unless a six appears in the next throw there will have been 100 throws without a six and this is improbable to the degree .000000012. Therefore it is then improbable to the degree .000000012 that there will not be a six on the next throw, while before the throws started this was not improbable but probable to the degree 5/6.

This reasoning may temporarily impress us but we soon reply: The probability of a six after a long run of anything but sixes is still one in six if we assume that the die is not loaded, while if we do not assume this the probability of a six, so far from having increased as you suggest, has decreased, for the long run of throws without a six suggests that there is something about the die which prevents its falling six uppermost. Your reasoning in favour of the increasing probability of a six is tempting but it's fallacious. When you say "It may happen that no six has appeared in the first 25 throws—in such a case, unless a six appears in the next 75 throws there will have been 100 throws without a six and this, as we have seen, is improbable to the degree .000000012"—do you mean that we have seen that given only that a die is about to be thrown 100 times then it is improbable to a degree .000000012 that there will be no sixes? or do you mean that we have seen that given that a die has been thrown 25 times without a six and that it will be thrown another 75 times, then it is improbable to a degree .000000012 that at the end there will have been no six thrown? The former is true, the latter is false. For given that a die has been thrown 25 times without a six and that it will be thrown another 75 times, the improbability that at the end of the 100 throws no six will have been thrown is the improbability of throwing a six in the next 75 throws, that is $1 - (\frac{5}{6})^{75}$.[2] And when 99 throws have been made and another is about to be made, the improbability of this series of 100 throws not including a six, is the improbability of not throwing a six in the next throw, that is 5/6.

Here the difficulty is cleared up; one proof is definitely mistaken and the mistake is found; the other proof is sound and the matter is settled. So much for the Monte Carlo fallacy.

It may seem a pity that philosophy cannot be conducted on these lines. But it cannot. A philosophical conflict is like a logical or arithmetical conflict. But it's different too. The peculiarity of philosophical conflicts has only lately been grasped. Philosophical theories such as "Matter (or Mind) does not exist" are neither theories nor theorems; they are what they sound like—paradoxes; and philosophical questions are not questions (scientific) nor problems (logic) —but are more like riddles such as

> Can one man do what another does? Surely he can. And yet surely it can't be that he can. For suppose A scratches his head. Then if B scratches his head he doesn't do what A does since it's not B's head but A's that A scratches. But if B scratches A's head then again he doesn't do what A does since A scratches his own head and B scratches someone else's.

But here drinks are served all round. For now nobody cares whether we say

[2] Neglecting the fact that the 25 throws without a six suggest slightly that the die is loaded. This, negligible in a small number of throws, is not negligible in a large number of throws. It is this, I think, and not the explanation offered in Keynes's *Probability*, p. 316, which is the main source of the Petersbourg Paradox.

"No man can do what another man does," or say "If a man, A, scratches his head and a man, B, also scratches his, B's, head then each does what the other does," or say "If a man, A, scratches his head and a man, B, also scratches A's head then each does what the other does." And now that nobody cares, the original paradox "No man can do what another does" cannot be mistaken for a theory about human powers like "No man can play billiards like Lindrum." And, what is more, now that everybody understands, now that everybody has explained his reasons, the doctrine "No man can do what another does" can no longer be mistaken for a theorem like "No man can draw isosceles triangles with the angles at the base unequal." In fact the paradox now appears as a paradox though in doing so it ceases to be one. For it now appears that one who says "No man can do what another does" cuts a caper and encourages us to do likewise, not pointlessly but in order to reveal a concealed curiosity, namely that one man does what another does only when he does something different. One who says "No man can do what another does" introduces a new logic to show up a hidden feature of the old, uses language oddly in order to show up an oddity in our usual use. And one who says "No man can know the mind of another as he does his own" or "No one can really know the mind of another" does the same sort of thing. His statement doesn't come out of experience in the way "No one can know what a Red man feels" comes out of experience; and it doesn't come out of ordinary language in the way "No one can know what a good poker player is thinking" or "No one can marry his widow's sister" does. It is not a statement of fact nor of logic. It comes out of language and out of experience—but in its own way—like "Tyger, tyger! burning bright." It comes from extraordinary experience of the ordinary calling for extraordinary use of ordinary language. And to burst this way the bonds of habitual modes of projection is no more extraordinary than a caricature, or a picture that is not a photograph.

The consequence is that paradoxes are not established by experiment and statistics and cannot be proved by conclusive-deductive reasoning. They can be supported by inconclusive-deductive reasoning. The reasoning cannot be conclusive for, if it were, then the opposite of the paradox could not also be supported, and if its opposite could not be supported it would not be a paradox. And the reasoning will not be effective unless it leads to or comes from a new apprehension of the familiar—without that it will be dead words, for after all tigers don't burn even in forests at night.

A paradox is a flag which declares a discovery—not a new continent nor a cure for pneumonia but a discovery in the familiar—but often it is also the Blue Peter of a new voyage. For often we don't properly understand a paradox until, beginning by regarding it literally, we have noted objections to it and held to it because of the reasons for it, and again noted objections and again held to it, and have come by this route to a state where we are no longer driven to assert it or to deny it. There's no short cut to this; for if *before* treating a paradox and its denial as incompatible and arguing for a win we say "No doubt there's much in both" this leaves us entirely vague as to what is in either. No—the journey to the new freedom is mostly long and arduous, the work of bringing to light and setting in order with respect to one another what drives us to accept, and what forces us to deny, a paradox, what makes it so fascinating, so attractive and so repugnant, may fairly take a long time. But it can take too long.

V. PHILOSOPHICAL DISPUTE CAN GO ON TOO LONG

It may fairly take a woman a long time to decide which of two men is the right one for her to marry and it may take a man a long time to decide which of two professions is the right one for him to take up. But again in each case it may take too long. At first as we review with our friend the many considerations that bear on the issue we accompany him with interest, later with patience, but at last with irritation. For in time we feel that the difficulty is no longer a matter of coming to know his own mind, but of making up his mind. He still represents himself as ignorant of what would suit him and in this way conceals his incapacity to choose. "Win or a place, win or a place" shout those who quote the possible investments, but still he hesitates. And why can't he decide? Not merely because the considerations are so balanced. There's often nothing to choose on looks, form, breeding, and price between one horse and another, but this doesn't prevent people deciding before the flags go down which one to back. No, his chronic indecision, whether it takes the form of enthusiastic oscillation or melancholy inactivity, is due to the fact that besides the reasons revealed in the course of talking the matter over there are others which remain hidden. Family disputes are often very interminable and often have an unpleasant sweetness because they are conducted wholly in terms of what is "right" or "reasonable" while each disputant knows that forces quite other than those mentioned are at work and often knows the other knows. It is not that the things mentioned, the things brought up in the discussion, are not at work but that other things unmentioned and unmentionable are also at work and being unmentioned do not work themselves out, so the disputes get their character—unpleasantly sweet and interminable.

The man I mentioned earlier who died in hospital discussing with himself an issue between altruism and the development of the true self, analysed himself in vain. Had he overweighted this? Had he neglected that? We struggle to pass from conflict into harmony, to find, as Aristotle said, the proper point between opposites. But unlike Aristotle we cannot face the prospect of choices without end and feel we must have rules to live by. To represent a difficult choice as ignorance of our duty in the situation we are in enables us to escape from facing the hidden sources of our hesitation. How much more can we escape into the wider inquiries of what acts, in general, are right and what, in general, makes good things good. Here we may wander for ever and when darkness begins to fall still build an altar to an unknown god.

When earlier I introduced the Monte Carlo fallacy I did so because I thought of it as one which arises purely from linguistic sources, as one which can be removed by turning the light on to linguistic confusion. And it is true that this trouble is more completely curable by linguistic treatment than are more philosophical troubles where the relevant facts of language form such a labyrinth that pressed in one quarter one may always take cover in another.

But now it strikes me how very persistent and how very prevalent is even the simple Monte Carlo fallacy. One constantly hears people say "Ah! that was too good to last" or "When we were having all the fine weather I thought we should have to pay for it" or again, after a run of misadventures, "Something will turn up. The luck must turn." Of course, to expect specially bad weather after specially good is not irrational if records show that regularly soon after specially good weather specially bad weather comes. But so far as I know there are no such records and so far as the people who use this argument know there are no such records. What they rely upon is "the laws of chance working themselves out"; what they rely upon is their feeling that though they don't know what card Fate will next deal them they do know what pack she holds so that if till now there have been no aces there'll be a lot of them soon to make up. True, there are people who when all has gone well for a long time feel more confident than ever; *they* feel that this just shows that Fate is with them. But there are others who begin to feel that they've had more than they deserve and that Fate will soon remind them that they are mortals, Polycrates and Amasis. And this last feeling finds expression, "justification," rationalization, in talk about the laws of chance—confused talk because without the confusion it wouldn't express the way they feel. It's the same when things go badly; some fall into despair, others feel that they have been punished enough and that even the most implacable Fate will now be prepared to "give them a break." So it appears how even this very purely logical paradox is not purely logical. It is true that the reasoning which leads to it, though fallacious, is plausible, it impresses us, and it does so partly because we have not a very firm and adequate understanding of the use of our linguistic tools in many discussions about probabilities; *but it does so also because the resulting paradox suits many people and suits something in most of us.* Gambling has a peculiar and half-secret fascination for many people; so also for many has the most theoretical talk about probability and chance. I submit that though the logical or linguistic explanation of the Monte Carlo fallacy is very adequate we would have a still more adequate explanation were we able to bring out not only the features of language that make for the committing of that fallacy but also other causes hidden beneath the flow of talk. And *if this is true of the Monte Carlo fallacy it is much more true of the philosophical paradoxes.*

Chance and Necessity, Freedom and Deity, Mind and Matter, Space and Time—these words have in them the detachment of the intellect but also echoes from the heart, and the fascination of them is not confined to professional philosophers. I remember how years ago one night in the "Elephant" a gentleman who, it was plain, had already been there some time took me aside in order to explain to me something of the connection between Mind and Matter. The big words of metaphysics have an appeal which is wide and deep and old and we cannot fully understand and resolve the riddles they present without understanding that appeal. In this sketch of philosophers I have been hinting at this. I have been hinting at connections with what psycho-analysts try to bring into the light. True, philosophy has never been merely a psychogenic disorder nor is the new philosophical technique merely a therapy. There's a difference. Philosophers reason for and against their doctrines and in doing so show us not new things but old things anew. Nevertheless, having recognized how different is philosophy from therapy it is worth noticing the connections: (*a*) how philosophical discussion is the bringing out of latent opposing forces like arriving at a decision and not like learning what is behind a closed door or whether $235 \times 6 = 1420$; (*b*) how, often, when the reasoning is done we find that besides the latent linguistic sources there are others non-linguistic and much more hidden which subtly co-operate with the features of language to produce philosophies; (*c*) how, in consequence, a purely linguistic treatment of philosophical conflicts is often inadequate; (*d*) how the non-linguistic sources are the same as those that trouble us elsewhere in our lives so that the riddles written on the veil of appearance are indeed riddles of the Sphinx.

13

part i

Gilbert Ryle DESCARTES' MYTH

The Concept of Mind was first published in 1949. Although the thesis of the book bears many similarities to Wittgenstein's views in the *Bluebook* and the *Philosophical Investigations*, it is a unique and original contribution to the philosophy of mind. Its influence within the philosophical community has been great.

Ryle's major work is a sustained attempt to plot the "logical geography" of the words we use in our language to describe mental activity. "Descartes' myth," which he attempts to expose in the first chapter of the book, has been, according to Ryle, the source of confusion in philosophy for centuries. This confusion can be in part eliminated, Ryle believes, by paying careful attention to the ways in which we actually use mentalistic terms in our language. Our daily use of them does not imply any kind of dualism between two different "substances," mind and body. The logic of mentalistic terms is quite different from the logic of physicalistic terms; it is a kind of "category mistake" to try to assimilate the two as most philosophers have, in one way or another, done.

This selection should be contrasted with Russell's account of mind in selection 3, Broad's discussion in 6, and Wittgenstein's discussion in Part III of selection 11.

For commentary on Ryle's thesis see Passmore's bibliographical footnotes in Chapter XVIII of *A Hundred Years of Philosophy*.

1. THE OFFICIAL DOCTRINE

There is a doctrine about the nature and place of minds which is so prevalent among theorists and even among laymen that it deserves to be described as the official theory. Most philosophers, psychologists, and religious teachers subscribe, with minor reservations, to its main articles and, although they admit certain theoretical difficulties in it, they tend to assume that these can be overcome without serious modifications being made to the architecture of the theory. It will be argued here that the central principles of the doctrine are unsound and

From *The Concept of Mind*, Chap. 1, by Gilbert Ryle (1949) by permission of The Hutchinson Publishing Group.

conflict with the whole body of what we know about minds when we are not speculating about them.

The official doctrine, which hails chiefly from Descartes, is something like this. With the doubtful exceptions of idiots and infants in arms every human being has both a body and a mind. Some would prefer to say that every human being is both a body and a mind. His body and his mind are ordinarily harnessed together, but after the death of the body his mind may continue to exist and function.

Human bodies are in space and are subject to the mechanical laws which govern all other bodies in space. Bodily processes and states can be inspected by external observers. So a man's bodily life is as much a public affair as are the lives of animals and reptiles and even as the careers of trees, crystals, and planets.

But minds are not in space, nor are their operations subject to mechanical laws. The workings of one mind are not witnessable by other observers; its career is private. Only I can take direct cognisance of the states and processes of my own mind. A person therefore lives through two collateral histories, one consisting of what happens in and to his body, the other consisting of what happens in and to his mind. The first is public, the second private. The events in the first history are events in the physical world, those in the second are events in the mental world.

It has been disputed whether a person does or can directly monitor all or only some of the episodes of his own private history; but, according to the official doctrine, of at least some of these episodes he has direct and unchallengeable cognisance. In consciousness, self-consciousness, and introspection he is directly and authentically apprised of the present states and operations of his mind. He may have great or small uncertainties about concurrent and adjacent episodes in the physical world, but he can have none about at least part of what is momentarily occupying his mind.

It is customary to express this bifurcation of his two lives and of his two worlds by saying that the things and events which belong to the physical world, including his own body, are external, while the workings of his own mind are internal. This antithesis of outer and inner is of course meant to be construed as a metaphor, since minds, not being in space, could not be described as being spatially inside anything else, or as having things going on spatially inside themselves. But relapses from this good intention are common and theorists are found speculating how stimuli, the physical sources of which are yards or miles outside a person's skin, can generate mental responses inside his skull, or how decisions framed inside his cranium can set going movements of his extremities.

Even when "inner" and "outer" are construed as metaphors, the problem how a person's mind and body influence one another is notoriously charged with theoretical difficulties. What the mind wills, the legs, arms, and the tongue execute; what affects the ear and the eye has something to do with what the mind perceives; grimaces and smiles betray the mind's moods and bodily castigations lead, it is hoped, to moral improvement. But the actual transactions between the episodes of the private history and those of the public history remain mysterious, since by definition they can belong to neither series. They could not be reported among the happenings described in a person's autobiography of his inner life, but nor could they be reported among those described in some one else's biography of that person's overt career. They can be inspected neither by introspection nor by laboratory experiment. They are theoretical shuttlecocks which are forever being bandied from the physiologist back to the psychologist and from the psychologist back to the physiologist.

Underlying this partly metaphorical representation of the bifurcation of a person's two lives there is a seemingly more profound and philosophical assumption. It is assumed that there are two different kinds of existence or status. What exists or happens may have the status of physical existence, or it may have the status of mental existence. Somewhat as the faces of coins are either heads or tails, or somewhat as living creatures are either male or female, so, it is supposed, some existing is physical existing, other existing is mental existing. It is a necessary feature of what has physical existence that it is in space and time, it is a necessary feature of what has mental existence that it is in time but not in space. What has physical existence is composed of matter, or else is a function of matter; what has mental existence consists of consciousness, or else is a function of consciousness.

There is thus a polar opposition between mind and matter, an opposition which is often brought out as follows. Material objects are situated in a common field, known as "space," and what happens to one body in one part of space is mechanically connected with what happens to other bodies in other parts of space. But mental happenings occur in insulated fields, known as "minds," and there is, apart maybe from telepathy, no direct causal connection between what happens in one mind and what happens in another. Only through the medium of the public physical world can the mind of one person make a difference to the mind of another. The mind is its own place and in his inner life each of us lives the life of a ghostly Robinson Crusoe. People can see, hear and jolt one another's bodies, but they are irremediably blind and deaf to the workings of one another's minds and inoperative upon them.

What sort of knowledge can be secured of the workings of a mind? On the one side, according to the official theory, a person has direct knowledge of the best imaginable kind of the workings of his own mind. Mental states and processes are (or are normally) conscious states and processes, and the consciousness which irradiates them can engender no illusions and leaves the door open for no doubts. A person's present thinkings, feelings and willings, his perceivings, rememberings and imaginings are intrinsically "phosphorescent"; their existence and their nature are inevitably betrayed to their owner. The inner life is a stream of consciousness of such a sort that it would be absurd to suggest that the mind whose life is that stream might be unaware of what is passing down it.

True, the evidence adduced recently by Freud seems to show that there exist channels tributary to this stream, which run hidden from their owner. People are actuated by impulses the existence of which they vigorously disavow; some of their thoughts differ from the thoughts which they acknowledge; and some of the actions which they think they will to perform they do not really will. They are thoroughly gulled by some of their own hypocrisies and they successfully ignore facts about their mental lives which on the official theory ought to be patent to them. Holders of the official theory tend, however, to maintain that anyhow in normal circumstances a person must be directly and authentically seized of the present state and workings of his own mind.

Besides being currently supplied with these alleged immediate data of consciousness, a person is also generally supposed to be able to exercise from time to time a special kind of perception, namely inner perception, or introspection. He can take a (non-optical) "look" at what is passing in his mind. Not only can he view and scrutinize a flower through his sense of sight and listen to and discriminate the notes of a bell through his sense of hearing; he can also reflectively or introspectively watch, without any bodily organ of sense, the current episodes of his inner life. This self-observation is also commonly supposed to be immune from illusion, confusion or doubt. A mind's reports of its own affairs have a certainty superior to the best that is possessed by its reports of matters in the physical world. Sense-perceptions can, but consciousness and introspection cannot, be mistaken or confused.

On the other side, one person has no direct access of any sort to the events of the inner life of another. He cannot do better than make problematic inferences from the observed behaviour of the other person's body to the states of mind which, by analogy from his own conduct, he supposes to be signalised by that behaviour. Direct access to the workings of a mind is the privilege of that mind itself; in default of such privileged access, the workings of one mind are inevitably occult to everyone else. For the supposed arguments from bodily movements similar to their own to mental workings similar to their own would lack any possibility of observational corroboration. Not unnaturally, therefore, an adherent of the official theory finds it difficult to resist this consequence of his premises, that he has no good reason to believe that there do exist minds other than his own. Even if he prefers to believe that to other human bodies there are harnessed minds not unlike his own, he cannot claim to be able to discover their individual characteristics, or the particular things that they undergo and do. Absolute solitude is on this showing the ineluctable destiny of the soul. Only our bodies can meet.

As a necessary corollary of this general scheme there is implicitly prescribed ~~wby ?~~ a special way of construing our ordinary concepts of mental powers and operations. The verbs, nouns and adjectives, with which in ordinary life we describe the wits, characters and higher-grade performances of the people with whom we have do, are required to be construed as signifying special episodes in their secret histories, or else as signifying tendencies for such episodes to occur. When someone is described as knowing, believing or guessing something, as hoping, dreading, intending or shirking something, as designing this or being amused at that, these verbs are supposed to denote the occurrence of specific modifications in his (to us) occult stream of consciousness. Only his own privileged access to this stream in direct awareness and introspection could provide authentic testimony that these mental-conduct verbs were correctly or incorrectly applied. The onlooker, be he teacher, critic, biographer or friend, can never assure himself that his comments have any vestige of truth. Yet it was just because we do in fact all know how to make such comments, make them with general correctness and correct them when they turn out to be confused or mistaken, that philosophers found it necessary to construct their theories of the nature and

place of minds. Finding mental-conduct concepts being regularly and effectively used, they properly sought to fix their logical geography. But the logical
geography officially recommended would entail that there could be no regular or
effective use of these mental-conduct concepts in our descriptions of, and
prescriptions for, other people's minds.

2. THE ABSURDITY
OF THE OFFICIAL DOCTRINE

Such in outline is the official theory. I shall often speak of it, with deliberate
abusiveness, as "the dogma of the Ghost in the Machine." I hope to prove that
it is entirely false, and false not in detail but in principle. It is not merely an as-
semblage of particular mistakes. It is one big mistake and a mistake of a special
kind. It is, namely, a category-mistake. It represents the facts of mental life as if
they belonged to one logical type or category (or range of types or categories),
when they actually belong to another. The dogma is therefore a philosopher's
myth. In attempting to explode the myth I shall probably be taken to be denying
well-known facts about the mental life of human beings, and my plea that I aim
at doing nothing more than rectify the logic of mental-conduct concepts will
probably be disallowed as mere subterfuge.

I must first indicate what is meant by the phrase "Category-mistake." This
I do in a series of illustrations.

A foreigner visiting Oxford or Cambridge for the first time is shown a number
of colleges, libraries, playing fields, museums, scientific departments, and ad-
ministrative offices. He then asks "But where is the University? I have seen
where the members of the Colleges live, where the Registrar works, where the
scientists experiment and the rest. But I have not yet seen the University in
which reside and work the members of your University." It has then to be
explained to him that the University is not another collateral institution, some
ulterior counterpart to the colleges, laboratories and offices which he has seen.
The University is just the way in which all that he has already seen is organized.
When they are seen and when their co-ordination is understood, the University
has been seen. His mistake lay in his innocent assumption that it was correct to
speak of Christ Church, the Bodleian Library, the Ashmolean Museum, *and* the
University, to speak, that is, as if "the University" stood for an extra member of
the class of which these other units are members. He was mistakenly allocating
the University to the same category as that to which the other institutions belong.

The same mistake would be made by a child witnessing the march-past of
a division, who, having had pointed out to him such and such battalions, batteries, squadrons, etc., asked when the division was going to appear. He would
be supposing that a division was a counterpart to the units already seen, partly
similar to them and partly unlike them. He would be shown his mistake by
being told that in watching the battalions, batteries, and squadrons marching
past he had been watching the division marching past. The march-past was
not a parade of battalions, batteries, squadrons, *and* a division; it was a parade
of the battalions, batteries, and squadrons *of* a division.

One more illustration. A foreigner watching his first game of cricket learns what are the functions of the bowlers, the batsmen, the fielders, the umpires, and the scorers. He then says "But there is no one left on the field to contribute the famous element of team-spirit. I see who does the bowling, the batting, and the wicket-keeping; but I do not see whose role it is to exercise *esprit de corps.*" Once more, it would have to be explained that he was looking for the wrong type of thing. Team-spirit is not another cricketing-operation supplementary to all of the other special tasks. It is, roughly, the keenness with which each of the special tasks is performed, and performing a task keenly is not performing two tasks. Certainly exhibiting team-spirit is not the same thing as bowling or catching, but nor is it a third thing such that we can say that the bowler first bowls *and* then exhibits team-spirit or that a fielder is at a given moment *either* catching *or* displaying *esprit de corps.*

These illustrations of category-mistakes have a common feature which must be noticed. The mistakes were made by people who did not know how to wield the concepts *University, division,* and *team-spirit.* Their puzzles arose from inability to use certain items in the English vocabulary.

The theoretically interesting category-mistakes are those made by people who are perfectly competent to apply concepts, at least in the situations with which they are familiar, but are still liable in their abstract thinking to allocate those concepts to logical types to which they do not belong. An instance of a mistake of this sort would be the following story. A student of politics has learned the main differences between the British, the French, and the American Constitutions, and has learned also the differences and connections between the Cabinet, Parliament, the various Ministries, the Judicature, and the Church of England. But he still becomes embarrassed when asked questions about the connections between the Church of England, the Home Office, and the British Constitution. For while the Church and the Home Office are institutions, the British Constitution is not another institution in the same sense of that noun. So inter-institutional relations which can be asserted or denied to hold between the Church and the Home Office cannot be asserted or denied to hold between either of them and the British Constitution. "The British Constitution" is not a term of the same logical type as "the Home Office" and "the Church of England." In a partially similar way, John Doe may be a relative, a friend, an enemy, or a stranger to Richard Roe; but he cannot be any of these things to the Average Taxpayer. He knows how to talk sense in certain sorts of discussions about the Average Taxpayer, but he is baffled to say why he could not come across him in the street as he can come across Richard Roe.

It is pertinent to our main subject to notice that, so long as the student of politics continues to think of the British Constitution as a counterpart to the other institutions, he will tend to describe it as a mysteriously occult institution; and so long as John Doe continues to think of the Average Taxpayer as a fellow-citizen, he will tend to think of him as an elusive insubstantial man, a ghost who is everywhere yet nowhere.

My destructive purpose is to show that a family of radical category-mistakes is the source of the double-life theory. The representation of a person as a ghost mysteriously ensconced in a machine derives from this argument. Because, as is true, a person's thinking, feeling, and purposive doing cannot be described solely in the idioms of physics, chemistry, and physiology, therefore they must be described in counterpart idioms. As the human body is a complex organised unit, so the human mind must be another complex organised unit, though one made of a different sort of stuff and with a different sort of structure. Or, again, as the human body, like any other parcel of matter, is a field of causes and effects, so the mind must be another field of causes and effects, though not (Heaven be praised) mechanical causes and effects.

3. THE ORIGIN OF THE CATEGORY-MISTAKE

One of the chief intellectual origins of what I have yet to prove to be the Cartesian category-mistake seems to be this. When Galileo showed that his methods of scientific discovery were competent to provide a mechanical theory which should cover every occupant of space, Descartes found in himself two conflicting motives. As a man of scientific genius he could not but endorse the claims of mechanics, yet as a religious and moral man he could not accept, as Hobbes accepted, the discouraging rider to those claims, namely that human nature differs only in degree of complexity from clockwork. The mental could not be just a variety of the mechanical.

He and subsequent philosophers naturally but erroneously availed them-selves of the following escape-route. Since mental-conduct words are not to be construed as signifying the occurrence of mechanical processes, they must be construed as signifying the occurrence of non-mechanical processes; since mechanical laws explain movements in space as the effects of other movements in space, other laws must explain some of the non-spatial workings of minds as the effects of other non-spatial workings of minds. The difference between the human behaviours which we describe as intelligent and those which we describe as unintelligent must be a difference in their causation; so, while some move-ments of human tongues and limbs are the effects of mechanical causes, others must be the effects of non-mechanical causes, i.e. some issue from movements of particles of matter, others from workings of the mind.

The differences between the physical and the mental were thus represented as differences inside the common framework of the categories of "thing," "stuff," "attribute," "state," "process," "change," "cause," and "effect." Minds are things, but different sorts of things from bodies; mental processes are causes and effects, but different sorts of causes and effects from bodily movements. And so on. Some-what as the foreigner expected the University to be an extra edifice, rather like a college but also considerably different, so the repudiators of mechanism repre-sented minds as extra centres of causal processes, rather like machines but also considerably different from them. Their theory was a para-mechanical hy-pothesis.

That this assumption was at the heart of the doctrine is shown by the fact that there was from the beginning felt to be a major theoretical difficulty in ex-plaining how minds can influence and be influenced by bodies. How can a mental process, such as will, cause spatial movements like the movements of the tongue? How can a physical change in the optic nerve have among its effects a mind's perception of a flash of light? This notorious crux by itself shows the logical mould into which Descartes pressed his theory of the mind. It was the self-same mould into which he and Galileo set their mechanics. Still unwittingly adhering to the grammar of mechanics, he tried to avert disaster by describing minds in what was merely an obverse vocabulary. The workings of minds had to be described by the mere negatives of the specific descriptions given to bodies; they are not in space, they are not motions, they are not modifications of matter, they are not accessible to public observation. Minds are not bits of clock-work, they are just bits of not-clockwork.

As thus represented, minds are not merely ghosts harnessed to machines, they are themselves just spectral machines. Though the human body is an engine, it is not quite an ordinary engine, since some of its workings are governed by another engine inside it—this interior governor-engine being one of a very special sort. It is invisible, inaudible and it has no size or weight. It cannot be taken to bits and the laws it obeys are not those known to ordinary engineers. Nothing is known of how it governs the bodily engine.

A second major crux points the same moral. Since, according to the doctrine, minds belong to the same category as bodies and since bodies are rigidly governed by mechanical laws, it seemed to many theorists to follow that minds must be similarly governed by rigid non-mechanical laws. The physical world is a deterministic system, so the mental world must be a deterministic system. Bodies cannot help the modifications that they undergo, so minds cannot help pursuing the careers fixed for them. *Responsiblity, choice, merit,* and *demerit* are therefore inapplicable concepts—unless the compromise solution is adopted of saying that the laws governing mental processes, unlike those governing physical processes, have the congenial attribute of being only rather rigid. The problem of the Freedom of the Will was the problem how to reconcile the hypothesis that minds are to be described in terms drawn from the categories of mechanics with the knowledge that higher-grade human conduct is not of a piece with the behaviour of machines.

It is an historical curiosity that it was not noticed that the entire argument was broken-backed. Theorists correctly assumed that any sane man could already recognise the differences between, say, rational and non-rational utterances or between purposive and automatic behaviour. Else there would have been nothing requiring to be salved from mechanism. Yet the explanation given presupposed that one person could in principle never recognise the difference between the rational and the irrational utterances issuing from other human bodies, since he could never get access to the postulated immaterial causes of some of their utterances. Save for the doubtful exception of himself, he could never tell the difference between a man and a Robot. It would have to be conceded, for example, that, for all that we can tell, the inner lives of persons who are classed as idiots or lunatics are as rational as those of anyone else. Perhaps only their overt behaviour is disappointing; that is to say, perhaps "idiots" are not really idiotic, or "lunatics" lunatic. Perhaps, too, some of those who are classed as sane are really idiots. According to the theory, external observers could never know how the overt behaviour of others is correlated with their mental powers and processes and so they could never know or even plausibly conjecture whether their applications of mental-conduct concepts to these other people were correct or incorrect. It would then be hazardous or impossible for a man to claim sanity or logical consistency even for himself, since he would be debarred from comparing his own performances with those of others. In short, our characterisations of persons and their performances as intelligent, prudent, and virtuous or as stupid, hypocritical, and cowardly could never have been made, so the problem of providing a special causal hypothesis to serve as the basis of such diagnoses would never have arisen. The question, "How do persons differ from machines?" arose just because everyone already knew how to apply mental-conduct concepts before the new causal hypothesis was introduced. This causal hypothesis could not therefore be the source of the criteria used in those applications. Nor, of course, has the causal hypothesis in any degree improved our handling of those criteria. We still distinguish good from bad arithmetic, politic from impolitic conduct and fertile from infertile imaginations in the ways in which Descartes himself distinguished them before and after he speculated how the applicability of these criteria was compatible with the principle of mechanical causation.

He had mistaken the logic of his problem. Instead of asking by what criteria intelligent behaviour is actually distinguished from non-intelligent be-haviour, he asked "Given that the principle of mechanical causation does not tell us the difference, what other causal principle will tell it us?" He realised that the problem was not one of mechanics and assumed that it must therefore be one of some counterpart to mechanics. Not unnaturally psychology is often cast for just this role.

When two terms belong to the same category, it is proper to construct con-junctive propositions embodying them. Thus a purchaser may say that he bought a left-hand glove and a right-hand glove, but not that he bought a left-hand glove, a right-hand glove, and a pair of gloves. "She came home in a flood of tears and a sedan-chair" is a well-known joke based on the absurdity of conjoining terms of different types. It would have been equally ridiculous to construct the disjunction "She came home either in a flood of tears or else in a sedan-chair." Now the dogma of the Ghost in the Machine does just this. It maintains that there exist both bodies and minds; that there occur physical processes and mental processes; that there are mechanical causes of corporeal movements and mental causes of corporeal movements. I shall argue that these and other analogous conjunctions are absurd; but, it must be noticed, the argu-ment will not show that either of the illegitimately conjoined propositions is absurd in itself. I am not, for example, denying that there occur mental processes. Doing long division is a mental process and so is making a joke. But I am saying that the phrase "there occur mental processes" does not mean the same sort of thing as "there occur physical processes," and, therefore, that it makes no sense to conjoin or disjoin the two.

If my argument is successful, there will follow some interesting conse-quences. First, the hallowed contrast between Mind and Matter will be dissi-pated, but dissipated not by either of the equally hallowed absorptions of Mind by Matter or of Matter by Mind, but in quite a different way. For the seeming contrast of the two will be shown to be as illegitimate as would be the contrast of "she came home in a flood of tears" and "she came home in a sedan-chair." The belief that there is a polar opposition between Mind and Matter is the belief that they are terms of the same logical type.

It will also follow that both Idealism and Materialism are answers to an improper question. The "reduction" of the material world to mental states and processes, as well as the "reduction" of mental states and processes to physical states and processes, presuppose the legitimacy of the disjunction "Either there exist minds or there exist bodies (but not both)." It would be like saying, "Either she bought a left-hand and a right-hand glove or she bought a pair of gloves (but not both)."

It is perfectly proper to say, in one logical tone of voice, that there exist minds and to say, in another logical tone of voice, that there exist bodies. But these expressions do not indicate two different species of existence, for "existence" is not a generic word like "coloured" or "sexed." They indicate two different senses of "exist," somewhat as "rising" has different senses in "the tide is rising," "hopes are rising," and "the average age of death is rising." A man would be thought to be making a poor joke who said that three things are now rising, namely the tide, hopes, and the average age of death. It would be just as good or bad a joke to say that there exist prime numbers and Wednesdays and public opinions and navies; or that there exist both minds and bodies. In the succeeding chapters I try to prove that the official theory does rest on a batch of category-mistakes by showing that logically absurd corollaries follow from it. The exhibition of these absurdities will have the constructive effect of bringing out part of the correct logic of mental-conduct concepts.

4. HISTORICAL NOTE

It would not be true to say that the official theory derives solely from Descartes' theories, or even from a more widespread anxiety about the implications of seventeenth century mechanics. Scholastic and Reformation theology had schooled the intellects of the scientists as well as of the laymen, philosophers, and clerics of that age. Stoic-Augustinian theories of the will were embedded in the Calvinist doctrines of sin and grace; Platonic and Aristotelian theories of the intellect shaped the orthodox doctrines of the immortality of the soul. Descartes was reformulating already prevalent theological doctrines of the soul in the new syntax of Galileo. The theologian's privacy of conscience became the philosopher's privacy of consciousness, and what had been the bogy of Predestination reappeared as the bogy of Determinism.

It would also not be true to say that the two-worlds myth did no theoretical good. Myths often do a lot of theoretical good, while they are still new. One benefit bestowed by the para-mechanical myth was that it partly superannuated the then prevalent para-political myth. Minds and their Faculties had previously been described by analogies with political superiors and political subordinates. The idioms used were those of ruling, obeying, collaborating, and rebelling. They survived and still survive in many ethical and some epistemological discussion. As, in physics, the new myth of occult Forces was a scientific improvement on the old myth of Final Causes, so, in anthropological and psychological theory, the new myth of hidden operations, impulses, and agencies was an improvement on the old myth of dictations, deferences, and disobediences.

13

part ii

Gilbert Ryle PSYCHOLOGY

Ryle was quite aware that the thesis he was urging in *The Concept of Mind* might be misunderstood and identified with other behaviorisms which came before. In the last chapter of his book, reprinted below, he attempts to summarize what he has done and indicate what he takes the consequences of his view to be for the science of psychology.

1. THE PROGRAMME OF PSYCHOLOGY

In the course of this book I have said very little about the science of psychology. This omission will have appeared particularly perverse, since the entire book could properly be described as an essay, not indeed in scientific but in philosophical psychology. Part of the explanation of the omission is this. I have been examining the logical behaviour of a set of concepts all of which are regularly employed by everyone. The concepts of learning, practice, trying, heeding, pretending, wanting, pondering, arguing, shirking, watching, seeing, and being perturbed are not technical concepts. Everyone has to learn, and does learn, how to use them. Their use by psychologists is not different from their use by novelists, biographers, historians, teachers, magistrates, coastguards, politicians, detectives, or men in the street. But this is not the whole story.

When we think of the science or sciences of psychology, we are apt, and often encouraged, to equate the official programmes of psychology with the researches that psychologists actually carry on, their public promises with their laboratory performances. Now when the word "psychology" was coined, two hundred years ago, it was supposed that the two-worlds legend was true. It was supposed, in consequence, that since Newtonian science explains (it was erroneously thought) everything that exists and occurs in the physical world, there could and should be just one other counterpart science explaining what exists and occurs in the postulated non-physical world. As Newtonian scientists studied the phenomena of the one field, so there ought to be scientists studying

From *The Concept of Mind*, Chap. 10, by Gilbert Ryle (1949) by permission of The Hutchinson Publishing Group.

the phenomena of the other field. "Psychology" was supposed to be the title of the one empirical study of "mental phenomena." Moreover, as Newtonian scientists found and examined their data in visual, auditory, and tactual perception, so psychologists would find and examine their counterpart data by counterpart, non-visual, non-auditory, non-tactual perception.

It was not, of course, denied that there existed and could exist plenty of other systematic and unsystematic studies of specifically human behaviour. Historians had for two thousand years been studying the deeds and words, opinions and projects of men and groups of men. Philologists, literary critics, and scholars had been studying men's speech and writing, their poetry and drama, their religion and philosophy. Even dramatists and novelists, in depicting ways in which the creatures of their fancy acted and reacted, were showing in fable how they thought that real people do or might behave. Economists study the actual and hypothetical dealings and expectations of men in markets; strategists study the actual and possible perplexities and decisions of generals; teachers study the performances of their pupils; detectives and chess-players study the manoeuvres, habits, weaknesses, and strengths of their adversaries. But, according to the para-Newtonian programme, psychologists would study human beings in a completely different way. They would find and examine data inaccessible to teachers, detectives, biographers, or friends; data, too, which could not be represented on the stage or in the pages of novels. These other studies of man were restricted to the inspection of the mere tents and houses in which the real men dwelt. The psychological study of man would use direct access to the residents themselves. Indeed, not until psychologists had found and turned the key, could the other students of human thought and behaviour hope to do more than batter vainly on locked doors. The visible deeds and the audible words of human beings were not themselves exercises of the qualities of their characters or intellects, but only external symptoms or expressions of their real but privy exercises.

Abandonment of the two-worlds legend involves the abandonment of the idea that there is a locked door and a still to be discovered key. Those human actions and reactions, those spoken and unspoken utterances, those tones of voice, facial expressions and gestures, which have always been the data of all the other students of men, have, after all, been the right and the only manifestations to study. They and they alone have merited, but fortunately not received, the grandiose title "mental phenomena."

But though the official programme of psychology promised that the subject matter of its investigations would consist of happenings differing in kind from, and lying "behind," those bits of human conduct which alone were accessible to the other studies of man, the experimental psychologists in their daily practice had perforce to break this promise. A researcher's day cannot be satisfactorily occupied in observing nonentities and describing the mythical. Practising psychologists found themselves examining the actions, grimaces and utterances of lunatics and idiots, of persons under the influence of alcohol, fatigue, terror, and hypnosis, and of the victims of brain injuries. They studied sense perception as ophthalmologists, for example, study sense perception, partly by making and applying physiological experiments and partly by analysing the reactions and verbal responses of the subjects of their experiments. They studied the wits of children by collecting and comparing their failures and successes in various kinds of standardised tests. They counted the blunders made by typists at different stages of their day's work, and they examined people's differing liabilities to forget different kinds of memorised syllables and phrases by recording their successes and failures in recitations after the lapse of different periods of time. They studied the behaviour of animals in mazes and of chickens in incubators. Even the spellbinding, because so promisingly "chemical," principle of the Association of Ideas found its chief practical application in the prompt word-responses voiced aloud by subjects to whom test words were spoken by the experimenter.

There is nothing peculiar in such a disparity between programme and performance. We ought to expect wisdom about questions and methods to come after the event. The descriptions given by philosophers of their own objectives and their own procedures have seldom squared with their actual results or their actual manners of working. They have promised, for example, to give an account of the World as a Whole, and to arrive at this account by some process of synoptic contemplation. In fact they have practised a highly proprietary brand of haggling, and their results, though much more valuable than the promised Darien-panorama could have been, have not been in any obvious respects like such a panorama.

Chemists once tried hard to find out the properties of phlogiston, but, as they never captured any phlogiston, they reconciled themselves to studying instead its influences and outward manifestations. They examined, in fact, the phenomena of combustion and soon abandoned the postulate of an uninspectable heat-stuff. The postulation of it had been a will-o'-the-wisp, the sort of will-o'-the-wisp that encourages the adventurous to explore uncharted thickets and then, ungratefully, to chart the thickets in maps that make no further mention of those false beacons. Psychological research work will not have been wasted, if the postulate of a special mind-stuff goes the same way.

However, the question "What should be the programme of psychology?" has still to be answered. Attempts to answer it would now be faced by the following difficulty. I have argued that the workings of men's minds are studied from the same sorts of data by practising psychologists and by economists, criminologists, anthropologists, political scientists, and sociologists, by teachers, examiners, detectives, biographers, historians, and players of games, by strategists, statesmen, employers, confessors, parents, lovers, and novelists. How then are certain inquiries to be selected, while all the rest are to be rejected, as "psychological"? By what criteria are we to say that statistical results of Schools Examination Boards are not, while the results of intelligence tests are, the products of psychological investigations? Why is the historian's examination of Napoleon's motives, intentions, talents and stupidities not, when that of Sally Beauchamp's is, a psychological study? If we give up the idea that psychology is about something that the other human studies are not about, and if we give up, therewith, the idea that psychologists work on data from which the other studies are debarred, what is the *differentia* between psychology and these other studies?

Part of the answer might be given thus. The country postman knows a district like the back of his hand; he knows all the roads, lanes, streams, hills, and coppices; he can find his way about it in all weathers, lights, and seasons. Yet he is not a geographer. He cannot construct a map of the district, or tell how it links on to adjoining districts; he does not know the exact compass-bearings, distances, or heights above sea-level of any of the places that, in another way, he knows so well. He has no classification of the types of terrain that his district contains, and he can make no inferences from its features to features of neighbouring districts. In discussing the district he mentions all the features that the geographer might mention, but he does not say the same sorts of things about them. He applies no geographical generalisations, uses no geographical methods of mensuration, and employs no general explanatory or predictive theories. Similarly, it might be suggested, the detective, the confessor, the examiner, and the novelist may be thoroughly conversant, in a rule of thumb way, with the kinds of data which the psychologist would collect, but their handling of them would be unscientific, where the psychologist's handling of them would be scientific. Theirs would correspond to the shepherd's weather-lore; his to the meteorologist's science.

But this answer would not establish any difference between psychology and the other scientific or would-be scientific studies of human behaviour, like economics, sociology, anthropology, criminology, and philology. Even public librarians study popular tastes by statistical methods, yet, though tastes in books are indubitably characteristics of minds, this sort of study of them would not be allowed to rank as psychology.

The right answer to the question seems to be that the abandonment of the dream of psychology as a counterpart to Newtonian science, as this was piously misrepresented, involves abandonment of the notion that "psychology" is the name of a unitary inquiry or tree of inquiries. Much as "Medicine" is the name of a somewhat arbitrary consortium of more or less loosely connected inquiries and techniques, a consortium which neither has, nor needs, a logically trim statement of programme, so "psychology" can quite conveniently be used to denote a partly fortuitous federation of inquiries and techniques. After all, not only was the dream of a para-Newtonian science derived from a myth, but it was also an empty dream that there was or would be one unitary, because Newtonian, science of the "external world." The erroneous doctrine that there was a segregated field of "mental phenomena" was based on a principle which also implied that there was no room for the biological sciences. Newtonian physics was proclaimed as the all-embracing science of what exists in space. The Cartesian picture left no place for Mendel or Darwin. The two-worlds legend was also a two-sciences legend, and the recognition that there are many sciences should remove the sting from the suggestion that "psychology" is not the name of a single homogeneous theory. Few of the names of sciences do denote such unitary theories, or show any promise of doing so. Nor is "cards" the name either of a single game, or of a "tree" of games.

The analogy suggested above between psychology and medicine was misleading in one important respect, namely that several of the most progressive and useful psychological researches have themselves been in a broad sense of the adjective, medical researches. Among others, and above all others, the researches of psychology's one man of genius, Freud, must not be classed as belonging to a family of inquiries analogous to the family of medical inquiries; they belong to this family. Indeed, so deservedly profound has been the influence of Freud's teaching and so damagingly popular have its allegories become, that there is now evident a strong tendency to use the word "psychologists" as if it stood only for those who investigate and treat mental disabilities. "Mental" is commonly used, from the same motives, to mean "mentally disordered." Perhaps it would have been a terminological convenience, had the word "psychology" been originally given this restricted sense; but the academic world is now too well accustomed to the more hospitable and undiscriminating use of the word to make such a reform possible or desirable.

Probably some people will be inclined to protest that there does exist some general and formulable distinction between psychological inquiries and all the other inquiries that are concerned with the wits and characters of human beings. Even if psychologists enjoy no proprietary data on which to found their theories, still their theories themselves are different in kind from those of philologists, camouflage-experts, anthropologists, or detectives. Psychological theories provide, or will provide, causal explanations of human conduct. Granted that there are hosts of different ways in which the workings of men's minds are studied, psychology differs from all the other studies in trying to find out the causes of these workings.

The word "cause" and the phrase "causal explanation" are, of course, very solemn expressions. They remind us at once of those unheard impacts of those little invisible billiard-balls which we learned to fancy, erroneously, were the truly scientific explanation of everything that goes on in the world. So when we hear the promise of a new scientific explanation of what we say and do, we expect to hear of some counterparts to these impacts, some forces or agencies of which we should never ourselves have dreamed and which we shall certainly never witness at their subterranean work. But when we are in a less impressionable frame of mind, we find something unplausible in the promise of discoveries yet to be made of the hidden causes of our own actions and reactions. We know quite well what caused the farmer to return from the market with his pigs unsold. He found that the prices were lower than he had expected. We know quite well why John Doe scowled and slammed the door. He had been insulted. We know quite well why the heroine took one of her morning letters to read in solitude, for the novelist gives us the required causal explanation. The heroine recognised her lover's handwriting on the envelope. The schoolboy knows quite well what made him write down the answer "225" when asked for the square of 15. Each of the operations he performed had put him on the track to its successor.

There are, as will be seen in a moment, a lot of other sorts of actions, fidgets, and utterances, the author of which cannot say what made him produce them. But the actions and reactions which their authors can explain are not in need of an ulterior and disparate kind of explanation. Where their causes are well known to the agent and to all of his acquaintances, the promise of surprising news about their real but hidden causes is not merely like the promise, but is a special case of the promise of news about the occult causes of mechanical happenings whose ordinary causes are notorious. The cyclist knows what makes the back wheel of his cycle go round, namely, pressure on the pedals communicated by the tension of the chain. The questions, "What makes the pressure on the pedals make the chain taut?" and, "What makes the tautening of the chain make the back wheel go round?" would strike him as unreal questions. So would the question, "What makes him try to make the back wheel go round by pressing on the pedals?"

In this everyday sense in which we can all give "causal explanations" for many of our actions and reactions, mention of these causes is not the perquisite of psychologists. The economist, in talking of "sellers' strikes," is talking in general terms about such episodes as that of the farmer taking his pigs back to the farm because he found that the prices were too low. The literary critic, in discussing why the poet used a new rhythm in a particular line of his verse, is considering what composition worry was affecting the poet at that particular juncture. Nor does the teacher want to hear about any back-stage incidents, in order to understand what made the boy get to the correct answer of his multiplication problem; for he has himself witnessed the front-stage incidents which got him there.

On the other hand, there are plenty of kinds of behaviour of which we can give no such explanations. I do not know why I was so tongue-tied in the presence of a certain acquaintance; why I dreamed a certain dream last night; why I suddenly saw in my mind's eye an uninteresting street corner of a town that I hardly know; why I chatter more rapidly after the air-raid siren is heard; or how I came to address a friend by the wrong Christian name. We recognise that questions of these kinds are genuine psychological questions. I should, very likely, not even know why gardening is unusually attractive when a piece of disagreeable letter-writing awaits me in my study, if I had not learned a modicum of psychology. The question why the farmer will not sell his pigs at certain prices is not a psychological but an economic question; but the question why he will not sell his pigs at any price to a customer with a certain look in his eye might be a psychological question. Even in the field of sense perception and memory the corresponding thing seems to hold. We cannot, from our own knowledge, tell why a straight line cutting through certain cross-hatchings looks bent, or why conversations in foreign languages seem to be spoken much more rapidly than conversations in our own, and we recognise these for psychological questions. Yet we feel that the wrong sort of promise is being made when we are offered corresponding psychological explanations of our correct estimations of shape, size, illumination, and speed. Let the psychologist tell us why we are deceived; but we can tell ourselves and him why we are not deceived.

The classification and diagnosis of exhibitions of our mental impotences require specialised research methods. The explanation of the exhibitions of our mental competences often requires nothing but ordinary good sense, or it may require the specialised methods of economists, scholars, strategists and examiners. But their explanations are not cheques drawn on the accounts of some yet more fundamental diagnoses. So not all, or even most, causal explanations of human actions and reactions are to be ranked as psychological. But, furthermore, not all psychological researches are searches for causal explanations. Many pyschologists are occupied, with greater or less profit, in devising methods of mensuration and in making collections of the measurements so achieved. Certainly the hope is that their measurements will one day subserve the establishment of precise functional correlations or causal laws, but their own work is at best only preparatory to this ulterior task. So, as it must be styled "psychological research," "psychological research" cannot be defined as the search for causal explanations.

It will now be realised why I have said so little about psychology in the body of this book. Part of the purpose of the book has been to argue against the false notion that psychology is the sole empirical study of people's mental powers, propensities and performances, together with its implied false corollary that "the mind" is what is properly describable only in the technical terms proprietary to psychological research. England cannot be described solely in seismological terms.

2. BEHAVIOURISM

The general trend of this book will undoubtedly, and harmlessly be stigmatised as "behaviourist." So it is pertinent to say something about Behaviourism. Behaviourism was, in the beginning, a theory about the proper methods of scientific psychology. It held that the example of the other progressive sciences ought to be followed, as it had not previously been followed, by psychologists; their theories should be based upon repeatable and publicly checkable observations and experiments. But the reputed deliverances of consciousness and introspection are not publicly checkable. Only people's overt behaviour can be observed by several witnesses, measured and mechanically recorded. The early adherents of this methodological programme seem to have been in two minds whether to assert that the data of consciousness and introspection were myths, or to assert merely that they were insusceptible of scientific examination. It was not clear whether they were espousing a not very sophisticated mechanistic doctrine, like that of Hobbes and Gassendi, or whether they were still cleaving to the Cartesian para-mechanical theory, but restricting their research procedures to those that we have inherited from Galileo; whether, for example, they held that thinking just consists in making certain complex noises and movements or whether they held that though these movements and noises were connected with "inner life" processes, the movements and noises alone were laboratory phenomena.

However it does not matter whether the early Behaviourists accepted a mechanist or a para-mechanist theory. They were in error in either case. The important thing is that the practice of describing specifically human doings according to the recommended methodology quickly made it apparent to psychologists how shadowy were the supposed "inner-life" occurrences which the Behavourists were at first reproached for ignoring or denying. Psychological theories which made no mention of the deliverances of "inner perception" were at first likened to "Hamlet" without the Prince of Denmark. But the extruded hero soon came to seem so bloodless and spineless a being that even the opponents of these theories began to feel shy of imposing heavy theoretical burdens upon his spectral shoulders.

Novelists, dramatists and biographers had always been satisfied to exhibit people's motives, thoughts, perturbations, and habits by describing their doings, sayings, and imaginings, their grimaces, gestures, and tones of voice. In concentrating on what Jane Austen concentrated on, psychologists began to find that these were, after all, the stuff and not the mere trappings of their subject. They have, of course, continued to suffer unnecessary qualms of anxiety, lest this diversion of psychology from the task of describing the ghostly might not commit it to tasks of describing the merely mechanical. But the influence of the bogy of mechanism has for a century been dwindling because, among other reasons, during this period the biological sciences have established their title of "sciences." The Newtonian system is no longer the sole paradigm of natural science. Man need not be degraded to a machine by being denied to be a ghost in a machine. He might, after all, be a sort of animal, namely, a higher mammal. There has yet to be ventured the hazardous leap to the hypothesis that perhaps he is a man.

The Behaviourists' methodological programme has been of revolutionary importance to the programme of psychology. But more, it has been one of the main sources of the philosophical suspicion that the two-worlds story is a myth. It is a matter of relatively slight importance that the champions of this methodological principle have tended to espouse as well a kind of Hobbist theory, and even to imagine that the truth of mechanism is entailed by the truth of their theory of scientific research method in psychology.

It is not for me to say to what extent the concrete research procedures of practising psychologists have been affected by their long adherence to the two-worlds story, or to what extent the Behaviourist revolt has led to modifications of their methods. For all that I know, the ill effects of the myth may, on balance, have been outweighed by the good, and the Behaviourist revolt against it may have led to reforms more nominal than real. Myths are not always detrimental to the progress of theories. Indeed, in their youth they are often of inestimable value. Pioneers are, at the start, fortified by the dream that the New World is, behind its alien appearances, a sort of duplicate of the Old World, and the child is not so much baffled by a strange house if, wherever they may actually lead him, its bannisters feel to his hand like those he knew at home.

But it has not been a part of the object of this book to advance the methodology of psychology or to canvass the special hypotheses of this or that science. Its object has been to show that the two-worlds story is a philosophers' myth, though not a fable, and, by showing this, to begin to repair the damage that this myth has for some time been doing inside philosophy. I have tried to establish this point, not by adducing evidence from the troubles of psychologists, but by arguing that the cardinal mental concepts have been credited by philosophers themselves with the wrong sorts of logical behaviour. If my arguments have any force, then these concepts have been misallocated in the same general way, though in opposing particular ways, by both mechanists and paramechanists, by Hobbes and by Descartes.

If, in conclusion, we try to compare the theoretical fruitfulness of the Hobbes-Gassendi story of the mind with that of the Cartesians, we must undoubtedly grant that the Cartesian story has been the more productive. We might describe their opposition in this picture. One company of a country's defenders instals itself in a fortress. The soldiers of the second company notice that the moat is dry, the gates are missing and the walls are in collapse. Scorning the protection of such a rickety fort, yet still ridden by the idea that only from forts like this can the country be defended, they take up their stand in the most fort-like thing they can see, namely, the shadow of the decrepit fort. Neither position is defensible; and obviously the shadow-stronghold has all the vulnerability of the stone fort, with some extra vulnerabilities of its own. Yet in one respect the occupants of the shadow-fort have shown themselves the better soldiers, since they have seen the weaknesses of the stone fort, even if they are silly to fancy themselves secure in a fort made of no stones at all. The omens are not good for their victory, but they have given some evidence of teachability. They have exercised some vicarious strategic sense; they have realised that a stone fort whose walls are broken is not a stronghold. That the shadow of such a fort is not a stronghold either is the next lesson that they may come to learn.

We may apply this picture to one of our own central issues. Thinking, on the one view, is identical with saying. The holders of the rival view rightly reject this identification, but they make this rejection, naturally but wrongly, in the form that saying is doing one thing and thinking is doing another. Thinking operations are numerically different from verbal operations, and they control these verbal operations from another place than the place in which these verbal operations occur. This, however, will not do either, and for the very same reasons as those which showed the vulnerability of the identification of thinking with mere saying. Just as undisciplined and heedless saying is not thinking but babbling, so, whatever shadow-operations may be postulated as occurring in the other place, these too might go on there in an undisciplined and heedless manner; and then they in their turn would not be thinking. But to offer even an erroneous description of what distinguishes heedless and undisciplined chattering from thinking is to recognise a cardinal distinction. The Cartesian myth does indeed repair the defects of the Hobbist myth only by duplicating it. But even doctrinal homeopathy involves the recognition of disorders.

14

P. F. Strawson ON REFERRING

"On Referring" is the most famous challenge which has been directed against Russell's theory of descriptions. Russell had assumed that since assertions such as "The present king of France is wise" are neither meaningless nor true, they must be false. He attempted in his theory of descriptions to account for their meaningful falsity without postulating odd entities.

Strawson argues that Russell made at least two mistakes: He did not fully realize that a sentence can have a variety of uses, and he mistakenly thought that every meaningful sentence must be either true or false. According to Strawson, a sentence such as "The present king of France is wise," when used today, is neither true nor false, for the question of its truth or falsity does not even arise. Such a sentence presupposes, but does not assert, that there is a king of France, and since this presupposition is false, the question of truth or falsity cannot be an issue. Russell's theory is unnecessary since the problem it was designed to solve does not exist.

This selection should be read in conjunction with selections 1 and 15.

For additional reading on this topic see the bibliographical footnotes in Chapter XVIII of Passmore's *A Hundred Years of Philosophy.*

I

We very commonly use expressions of certain kinds to mention or refer to some individual person or single object or particular event or place or process, in the course of doing what we should normally describe as making a statement about that person, object, place, event, or process. I shall call this way of using expressions the "uniquely referring use." The classes of expressions which are most commonly used in this way are: singular demonstrative pronouns ("this" and "that"); proper names (*e.g.* "Venice," "Napoleon," "John"); singular personal and impersonal pronouns ("he," "she," "I," "you," "it"); and phrases beginning with the definite article followed by a noun, qualified or unqualified, in the singular (*e.g.* "the table," "the old man," "the king of France"). Any

From *Mind,* vol. LIX, no. 235 (July, 1950). Used by permission of the editor and the author.

expression of any of these classes can occur as the subject of what would traditionally be regarded as a singular subject-predicate sentence; and would, so occurring, exemplify the use I wish to discuss.

I do not want to say that expressions belonging to these classes never have any other use than the one I want to discuss. On the contrary, it is obvious that they do. It is obvious that anyone who uttered the sentence, "The whale is a mammal," would be using the expression "the whale" in a way quite different from the way it would be used by anyone who had occasion seriously to utter the sentence, "The whale struck the ship." In the first sentence one is obviously *not* mentioning, and in the second sentence one obviously *is* mentioning, a particular whale. Again if I said, "Napoleon was the greatest French soldier," I should be using the word "Napoleon" to mention a certain individual, but I should not be using the phrase, "the greatest French soldier," to mention an individual, but to say something about an individual I had already mentioned. It would be natural to say that in using this sentence I was talking *about* Napoleon and that what I was *saying* about him was that he was the greatest French soldier. But of course I *could* use the expression, "the greatest French soldier," to mention an individual; for example, by saying: "The greatest French soldier died in exile." So it is obvious that at least some expressions belonging to the classes I mentioned *can* have uses other than the use I am anxious to discuss. Another thing I do not want to say is that in any given sentence there is never more than one expression used in the way I propose to discuss. On the contrary, it is obvious that there may be more than one. For example, it would be natural to say that, in seriously using the sentence, "The whale struck the ship," I was saying something about both a certain whale and a certain ship, that I was using each of the expressions "the whale" and "the ship" to mention a particular object; or, in other words, that I was using each of these expressions in the uniquely referring way. In general, however, I shall confine my attention to cases where an expression used in this way occurs as the grammatical subject of a sentence.

I think it is true to say that Russell's Theory of Descriptions, which is concerned with the last of the four classes of expressions I mentioned above (*i.e.* with expressions of the form "the so-and-so") is still widely accepted among logicians as giving a correct account of the use of such expressions in ordinary language. I want to show, in the first place, that this theory, so regarded, embodies some fundamental mistakes.

What question or questions about phrases of the form "the so-and-so" was the Theory of Descriptions designed to answer? I think that at least one of the questions may be illustrated as follows. Suppose some one were now to utter the sentence, "The king of France is wise." No one would say that the sentence which had been uttered was meaningless. Everyone would agree that it was significant. But everyone knows that there is not at present a king of France. One of the questions the Theory of Descriptions was designed to answer was the question: how can such a sentence as "The king of France is wise" be significant even when there is nothing which answers to the description it contains, *i.e.*, in this case, nothing which answers to the description "The king of France"? And one of the reasons why Russell thought it important to give a

but "stock the mind with puzzles" — how is Strawson going to handle all the other things?

correct answer to this question was that he thought it important to show that another answer which might be given was wrong. The answer that he thought was wrong, and to which he was anxious to supply an alternative, might be exhibited as the conclusion of either of the following two fallacious arguments. Let us call the sentence "The king of France is wise" the sentence S. Then the first argument is as follows:

(1) The phrase, "the king of France," is the subject of the sentence S.

Therefore (2) if S is a significant sentence, S is a sentence *about* the king of France.

But (3) if there in no sense exists a king of France, the sentence is not about anything, and hence not about the king of France.

Therefore (4) since S is significant, there must in some sense (in some world) exist (or subsist) the king of France.

And the second argument is as follows:

(1) If S is significant, it is either true or false.

(2) S is true if the king of France is wise and false if the king of France is not wise.

(3) But the statement that the king of France is wise and the statement that the king of France is not wise are alike true only if there is (in some sense, in some world) something which is the king of France.

Hence (4) since S is significant, there follows the same conclusion as before.

These are fairly obviously bad arguments, and, as we should expect, Russell rejects them. The postulation of a world of strange entities, to which the king of France belongs, offends, he says, against "that feeling for reality which ought to be preserved even in the most abstract studies." The fact that Russell rejects these arguments is, however, less interesting than the extent to which, in rejecting their conclusion, he concedes the more important of their principles. Let me refer to the phrase, "the king of France," as the phrase D. Then I think Russell's reasons for rejecting these two arguments can be summarised as follows. The mistake arises, he says, from thinking that D, which is certainly the *grammatical* subject of S, is also the *logical* subject of S. But D is not the logical subject of S. In fact S, although grammatically it has a singular subject and a predicate, is not logically a subject-predicate sentence at all. The proposition it expresses is a complex kind of *existential* proposition, part of which might be described as a "uniquely existential" proposition. To exhibit the logical form of the proposition, we should re-write the sentence in a logically appropriate grammatical form; in such a way that the deceptive similarity of S to a sentence expressing a subject-predicate proposition would disappear, and we should be safeguarded against arguments such as the bad ones I outlined above. Before recalling the details of Russell's analysis of S, let us notice what his answer, as I have so far given it, seems to imply. His answer seems to imply that in the case of a sentence which is similar to S in that (1) it is grammatically of the subject-predicate form and (2) its grammatical subject does not refer to anything, then the only alternative to its being meaningless is that it should not really (*i.e.* logically) be of the subject-predicate form at all, but of some quite different form. And this in its turn seems to imply that if there are any sentences which are genuinely of the subject-predicate form, then the very fact of their being significant, having a meaning, guarantees that there *is* something referred to by the logical (and grammatical) subject. Moreover, Russell's answer seems to imply that there are such sentences. For if it is true that one may be misled by the grammatical similarity of S to other sentences into thinking that it is logically of the subject-predicate form, then surely there must be other sentences grammatically similar to S, which *are* of the subject-predicate form. To show not only that Russell's answer seems to imply these conclusions, but that he accepted at least the first two of them, it is enough to consider what he says about a class of expressions which he calls "logically proper names" and contrasts with expressions, like D, which he calls "definite descriptions." Of logically proper names Russell says or implies the following things:

1. That they and they alone can occur as subjects of sentences which are genuinely of the subject-predicate form;
2. that an expression intended to be a logically proper name is *meaningless* unless there is some single object for which it stands: for the *meaning* of such an expression just is the individual object which the expression designates. To be a name at all, therefore, it *must* designate something.

It is easy to see that if anyone believes these two propositions, then the only way for him to save the significance of the sentence S is to deny that it is a logically subject-predicate sentence. Generally, we may say that Russell recognises only two ways in which sentences which seem, from their grammatical structure, to be about some particular person or individual object or event, can be significant:

1. The first is that their grammatical form should be misleading as to their logical form, and that they should be analysable, like S, as a special kind of existential sentence;
2. The second is that their grammatical subject should be a logically proper name, of which the meaning is the individual thing it designates.

I think that Russell is unquestionably wrong in this, and that sentences which are significant, and which begin with an expression used in the uniquely referring way fall into neither of these two classes. Expressions used in the uniquely referring way are never either logically proper names or descriptions, if what is meant by calling them "descriptions" is that they are to be analysed in accordance with the model provided by Russell's Theory of Descriptions. There are no logically proper names and there are no descriptions (in this sense).

Let us now consider the details of Russell's analysis. According to Russell, anyone who asserted S would be asserting that:

(1) There is a king of France.
(2) There is not more than one king of France.
(3) There is nothing which is king of France and is not wise.

It is easy to see both how Russell arrived at this analysis, and how it enables him to answer the question with which we began, *viz.* the question: How can the sentence S be significant when there is no king of France? The way in which he arrived at the analysis was clearly by asking himself what would be the circumstances in which we would say that anyone who uttered the sentence S had made a true assertion. And it does seem pretty clear, and I have no wish to dispute, that the sentences (1)–(3) above do describe circumstances which are at least *necessary* conditions of anyone making a true assertion by uttering the sentence S. But, as I hope to show, to say this is not at all the same thing as to say that Russell has given a correct account of the use of the sentence S or even that he has given an account which, though incomplete, is correct as far as it goes; and is certainly not at all the same thing as to say that the model translation provided is a correct model for all (or for any) singular sentences beginning with a phrase of the form "the so-and-so."

It is also easy to see how this analysis enables Russell to answer the question of how the sentence S can be significant, even when there is no king of France. For, if this analysis is correct, anyone who utters the sentence S to-day would be jointly asserting three propositions, one of which (*viz.* that there is a king of France) would be false; and since the conjunction of three propositions, of which one is false, is itself false, the assertion as a whole would be significant, but false. So neither of the bad arguments for subsistent entities would apply to such an assertion.

II

As a step towards showing that Russell's solution of his problem is mistaken, and towards providing the correct solution, I want now to draw certain distinctions. For this purpose I shall, for the remainder of this section, refer to an expression which has a uniquely referring use as "an expression" for short; and to a sentence beginning with such an expression as "a sentence" for short. The distinctions I shall draw are rather rough and ready, and, no doubt, difficult cases could be produced which would call for their refinement. But I think they will serve my purpose. The distinctions are between:

(A1) a sentence,
(A2) a use of a sentence,
(A3) an utterance of a sentence,

and, correspondingly, between:

(B1) an expression,
(B2) a use of an expression,
(B3) an utterance of an expression.

Consider again the sentence, "The king of France is wise." It is easy to imagine that this sentence was uttered at various times from, say, the beginning of the seventeenth century onwards, during the reigns of each successive French monarch; and easy to imagine that it was also uttered during the subsequent periods in which France was not a monarchy. Notice that it was natural for me to speak of "the sentence" or "this sentence" being uttered at various times during this period; or, in other words, that it would be natural and correct to speak of *one and the same* sentence being uttered on all these various occasions. It is in the sense in which it would be correct to speak of one and the same sentence being uttered on all these various occasions that I want to use the expression (A1) "a sentence." There are, however, obvious differences between different *occasions of the use* of this sentence. For instance, if one man uttered it in the reign of Louis XIV and another man uttered it in the reign of Louis XV, it would be natural to say (to assume) that they were respectively talking about different people; and it might be held that the first man, in using the sentence, made a true assertion, while the second man, in using the same sentence, made a false assertion. If on the other hand two different men simultaneously uttered the sentence (*e.g.* if one wrote it and the other spoke it) during the reign of Louis XIV, it would be natural to say (assume) that they were both talking about the same person, and, in that case, in using the sentence, they *must* either both have made a true assertion or both have made a false assertion. And this illustrates what I mean by *a use* of a sentence. The two men who uttered the sentence, one in the reign of Louis XV and one in the reign of Louis XIV, each made a different use of the same sentence; whereas the two men who uttered the sentence simultaneously in the reign of Louis XIV, made the same use [1] of the same sentence. Obviously in the case of this sentence, and equally obviously in the case of many others, we cannot talk of *the sentence* being true or false, but only of its being used to make a true or false assertion, or (if this is preferred) to express a true or a false proposition. And equally obviously we cannot talk of *the sentence* being *about* a particular person, for the same sentence may be used at different times to talk about quite different particular persons, but only of *a use* of the sentence to talk about a particular person. Finally it will make sufficiently clear what I mean by an utterance of a sentence if I say that the two men who simultaneously uttered the sentence in the reign of Louis XIV made two different utterances of the same sentence, though they made the same *use* of the sentence.

If we now consider not the whole sentence, "The king of France is wise," but that part of it which is the expression, "the king of France," it is obvious that we can make analogous, though not identical distinctions between (1) the expression, (2) a use of the expression, and (3) an utterance of the expression. The distinctions will not be identical; we obviously cannot correctly talk of the expression "the king of France" being used to express a true or false propo-

---

[1] This usage of "use" is, of course, different from (*a*) the current usage in which "use" (of a particular word, phrase, sentence) = (roughly) "rules for using" = (roughly) "meaning"; and from (*b*) my own usage in the phrase "uniquely referring use of expressions" in which "use" = (roughly) "way of using."

sition, since in general only sentences can be used truly or falsely; and similarly it is only by using a sentence and not by using an expression alone, that you can talk about a particular person. Instead, we shall say in this case that you *use* the expression to *mention* or *refer to* a particular person in the course of using the sentence to talk about him. But obviously in this case, and a great many others, the *expression* (B1) cannot be said to mention, or refer to, anything, any more than the *sentence* can be said to be true or false. The same expression can have different mentioning-uses, as the same sentence can be used to make statements with different truth-values. "Mentioning," or "referring," is not something an expression does; it is something that some one can use an expression to do. Mentioning, or referring to, something is a characteristic of *a use* of an expression, just as "being about" something, and truth-or-falsity, are characteristics of *a use* of a sentence.

A very different example may help to make these distinctions clearer. Consider another case of an expression which has a uniquely referring use, *viz.* the expression "I"; and consider the sentence, "I am hot." Countless people may use this same sentence; but it is logically impossible for two different people to make *the same use* of this sentence: or, if this is preferred, to use it to express the same proposition. The expression "I" may correctly be used by (and only by) any one of innumerable people to refer to himself. To say this is to say something about the expression "I": it is, in a sense, to give its meaning. This is the sort of thing that can be said about *expressions*. But it makes no sense to say of the *expression* "I" that it refers to a particular person. This is the sort of thing that can be said only of a particular use of the expression.

Let me use "type" as an abbreviation for "sentence or expression." Then I am not saying that there are sentences and expression (types), *and* uses of them, *and* utterances of them, as there are ships *and* shoes *and* sealing-wax. I am saying that we cannot say *the same things* about types, uses of types, and utterances of types. And the fact is that we do talk about types; and that confusion is apt to result from the failure to notice the differences between what we can say about these and what we can say only about the *uses* of types. We are apt to fancy we are talking about sentences and expressions when we are talking about the uses of sentences and expressions.

This is what Russell does. Generally, as against Russell, I shall say this. Meaning (in at least one important sense) is a function of the sentence or expression; mentioning and referring and truth or falsity, are functions of the use of the sentence or expression. To give the meaning of an expression (in the sense in which I am using the word) is to give *general directions* for its use to refer to or mention particular objects or persons; to give the meaning of a sentence is to give *general directions* for its use in making true or false assertions. It is not to talk about any particular occasion of the use of the sentence or expression. The meaning of an expression cannot be identified with the object it is used, on a particular occasion, to refer to. The meaning of a sentence cannot be identified with the assertion it is used, on a particular occasion, to make. For to talk about the meaning of an expression or sentence is not to talk about its use on a particular occasion, but about the rules, habits, conventions governing its correct use, on all occasions, to refer or to assert. So the question of whether a sentence or expression *is significant or not* has nothing whatever to do with the question of whether the sentence, *uttered on a particular occasion*, is, on that occasion, being used to make a true-or-false assertion or not, or of whether the expression is, on that occasion, being used to refer to, or mention, anything at all.

The source of Russell's mistake was that he thought that referring or mentioning, if it occurred at all, must be meaning. He did not distinguish B1 from B2; he confused expressions with their use in a particular context; and so confused meaning with mentioning, with referring. If I talk about my handkerchief, I can, perhaps, produce the object I am referring to out of my pocket. I can't produce the meaning of the expression, "my handkerchief," out of my pocket. Because Russell confused meaning with mentioning, he thought that if there were any expressions having a uniquely referring use, which were what they seemed (*i.e.* logical subjects) and not something else in disguise, their meaning must *be* the particular object which they were used to refer to. Hence the troublesome mythology of the logically proper name. But if some one asks me the meaning of the expression "this"—once Russell's favourite candidate for this status—I do not hand him the object I have just used the expression to refer to, adding at the same time that the meaning of the word changes every time it is used. Nor do I hand him all the objects it ever has been, or might be, used to refer to. I explain and illustrate the conventions governing the use of the expression. This *is* giving the meaning of the expression. It is quite different from giving (in any sense of giving) the object to which it refers; for the expression itself does not refer to anything; though it can be used, on different occasions, to refer to innumerable things. Now as a matter of fact there is, in English, a sense of the word "mean" in which this word does approximate to "indicate, mention, or refer to"; *e.g.* when somebody (unpleasantly) says, "I mean you"; or when I point and say, "That's the one I mean." But *the one I meant* is quite different from *the meaning of the expression* I used to talk of it. In this special sense of "mean," it is people who mean, not expressions. People use expressions to refer to particular things. But the meaning of an expression is not the set of things or the single thing it may correctly be used to refer to: the meaning is the set of rules, habits, conventions for its use in referring.

It is the same with sentences: even more obviously so. Every one knows that the sentence, "The table is covered with books," is significant, and every one knows what it means. But if I ask, "What object is that sentence about?" I am asking an absurd question—a question which cannot be asked about the sentence, but only about some use of the sentence: and in this case the sentence hasn't been used, it has only been taken as an example. In knowing what it means, you are knowing how it could correctly be used to talk about things: so knowing the meaning hasn't anything to do with knowing about any particular use of the sentence to talk about anything. Similarly, if I ask: "Is the sentence true or false?" I am asking an absurd question, which becomes no less absurd if I add, "It must be one or the other since it's significant." The question is absurd, because the *sentence* is neither true nor false any more than it's *about* some object. Of course the fact that it's significant is the same as the fact that it *can* correctly be used to talk about something and that, in so using it, some one will be making a true or false assertion. And I will add *what's This?*

that it will be used to make a true or false assertion *only* if the person using it *is* talking about something. If, when he utters it, he is not talking about anything, then his use is not a genuine one, but a spurious or pseudo-use: he is not making either a true or a false assertion, though he may think he is. And this points the way to the correct answer to the puzzle to which the Theory of Descriptions gives a fatally incorrect answer. The important point is that the question of whether the sentence is significant or not is quite independent of the question that can be raised about a particular use of it, *viz.* the question whether it is a genuine or a spurious use, whether it is being used to talk about something, or in make-believe, or as an example in philosophy. The question whether the sentence is significant or not is the question whether there exist such language habits, conventions or rules that the sentence logically could be used to talk about something; and is hence quite independent of the question whether it is being so used on a particular occasion.

Agree that Russell is wrong about the significance issue; but that the contextual definition is exactly right for non-indexical uses.

III

Consider again the sentence, "The king of France is wise," and the true and false things Russell says about it.

There are at least two true things which Russell would say about the sentence:

1. The first is that it is significant; that if anyone were now to utter it, he would be uttering a significant sentence.

2. The second is that anyone now uttering the sentence would be making a true assertion only if there in fact at present existed one and only one king of France, and if he were wise.

What are the false things which Russell would say about the sentence? They are:

1. That anyone now uttering it would be making a true assertion or a false assertion;

2. That part of what he would be asserting would be that there at present existed one and only one king of France.

I have already given some reasons for thinking that these two statements are incorrect. Now suppose some one were in fact to say to you with a perfectly serious air: "The king of France is wise." Would you say, "That's untrue"? I think it's quite certain that you wouldn't. But suppose he went on to *ask* you whether you thought that what he had just said was true, or was false; whether you agreed or disagreed with what he had just said. I think you would be inclined, with some hesitation, to say that you didn't do either; that the question of whether his statement was true or false simply *didn't arise*, because there was no such person as the king of France.[2] You might, if he were ob-

---

[2] Since this article was written, there has appeared a clear statement of this point by Mr. Geach in *Analysis*, vol. 10, no. 4, March, 1950.

viously serious (had a dazed astray-in-the-centuries look), say something like: "I'm afraid you must be under a misapprehension. France is not a monarchy. There is no king of France." And this brings out the point that if a man seriously uttered the sentence, his uttering it would in some sense be *evidence* that he *believed* that there was a king of France. It would not be evidence for his believing this simply in the way in which a man's reaching for his raincoat is evidence for his believing that it is raining. But nor would it be evidence for his believing this in the way in which a man's saying, "It's raining" is evidence for his believing that it is raining. We might put it as follows. To say, "The king of France is wise" is, in some sense of "imply," to *imply* that there is a king of France. But this is a very special and odd sense of "imply." "Implies" in this sense is certainly not equivalent to "entails" (or "logically implies"). And this comes out from the fact that when, in response to his statement, we say (as we should) "There is no king of France," we should certainly *not* say we were *contradicting* the statement that the king of France is wise. We are certainly not saying that it's false. We are, rather, giving a reason for saying that the question of whether it's true or false simply doesn't arise.

And this is where the distinction I drew earlier can help **us.** The sentence, "The king of France is wise," is certainly significant; but this does not mean that any particular use of it is true or false. We use it truly or falsely when we use it to talk about some one; when, in using the expression, "The king of France," we are in fact mentioning some one. The fact that the sentence and the expression, respectively, are significant just is the fact that the sentence *could* be used, in certain circumstances, to say something true or false, that the expression *could* be used, in certain circumstances to mention a particular person; and to know their meaning is to know what sort of circumstances these are. So when we utter the sentence without in fact mentioning anybody by the use of the phrase, "The king of France," the sentence doesn't cease to be significant: we simply *fail* to say anything true or false because we simply fail to mention anybody by this particular use of that perfectly significant phrase. It is, if you like, a spurious use of the sentence, and a spurious use of the expression; though we may (or may not) mistakenly think it a genuine use.

And such spurious uses are very familiar. Sophisticated romancing, sophisticated fiction,[3] depend upon them. If I began, "The king of France is wise," and went on, "and he lives in a golden castle and has a hundred wives," and so on, a hearer would understand me perfectly well, without supposing *either* that I was talking about a particular person, *or* that I was making a false statement to the effect that there existed such a person as my words described. (It is worth adding that where the use of sentences and expressions is overtly fictional, the sense of the word "about" may change. As Moore said, it is perfectly natural and correct to say that some of the statements in *Pickwick Papers* are *about* Mr. Pickwick. But where the use of sentences and expressions is not overtly fictional, this use of "about" seems less correct; *i.e.* it would not *in general* be correct to say that a statement was about Mr. X or the so-and-so, unless there were such a person or thing. So it is where the romancing is in danger

---

[3] The unsophisticated kind begins: "Once upon time there was. . . ."

of being taken seriously that we might answer the question, "Who is he talking about?" with "He's not talking about anybody"; but, in saying this, we are not saying that what he is saying is either false or nonsense.)

Overtly fictional uses apart, however, I said just now that to use such an expression as "The king of France" at the beginning of a sentence was, in some sense of "imply," to imply that there was a king of France. When a man uses such an expression, he does not *assert*, nor does what he says *entail*, a uniquely existential proposition. But one of the conventional functions of the definite article is to act as a *signal* that a unique reference is being made—a signal, not a disguised assertion. When we begin a sentence with "the such-and-such" the use of "the" shows, but does not state, that we are, or intend to be, referring to one particular individual of the species "such-and-such." *Which* particular individual is a matter to be determined from context, time, place, and any other features of the situation of utterance. Now, whenever a man uses any expression, the presumption is that he thinks he is using it correctly: so when he uses the expression, "the such-and-such," in a uniquely referring way, the presumption is that he thinks both that there is *some* individual of that species, and that the context of use will sufficiently determine which one he has in mind. To use the word "the" in this way is then to imply (in the relevant sense of "imply") that the existential conditions described by Russell are fulfilled. But to use "the" in this way is not to <u>state that those conditions</u> are fulfilled. If I begin a sentence with an expression of the form, "the so-and-so," and then am prevented from saying more, I have made no statement of any kind; but I may have succeeded in mentioning some one or something.

The uniquely existential assertion supposed by Russell to be part of any assertion in which a uniquely referring use is made of an expression of the form "the so-and-so" is, he observes, a compound of two assertions. To say that there is a ϕ is to say something compatible with there being several ϕ's; to say there is not more than one ϕ is to say something compatible with there being none. To say there is one ϕ and one only is to compound these two assertions. I have so far been concerned mostly with the alleged assertion of existence and less with the alleged assertion of uniqueness. An example which throws the emphasis on to the latter will serve to bring out more clearly the sense of "implied" in which a uniquely existential assertion is implied, but not entailed, by the use of expressions in the uniquely referring way. Consider the sentence, "The table is covered with books." It is quite certain that in any normal use of this sentence, the expression "the table" would be used to make a unique reference, *i.e.* to refer to some one table. It is a quite strict use of the definite article, in the sense in which Russell talks on p. 30 of *Principia Mathematica*, of using the article "*strictly*, so as to imply uniqueness." On the same page Russell says that a phrase of the form "the so-and-so," used strictly, "will only have an application in the event of there being one so-and-so and no more." Now it is obviously quite false that the phrase "the table" in the sentence "the table is covered with books," used normally, will "only have an application in the event of there being one table and no more." It is indeed tautologically true that, in such a use, the phrase will have an application only in the event of there being one table and no more *which is being referred to*, and that it will be understood to

[margin handwritten note: But Russell never said these sentence states that 3 conditions are fulfilled]

have an application only in the event of there being one table and no more which it is understood as being used to refer to. To use the sentence is not to assert, but it is (in the special sense discussed) to imply, that there is only one thing which is *both* of the kind specified (*i.e.* a table) *and is being referred to* by the speaker. It is obviously not to assert this. To refer is not to say you are referring. To say there is *some table or other* to which you are referring is not the same as referring to a particular table. We should have no use for such phrases as "the individual I referred to" unless there were something which counted as referring. (It would make no sense to say you had pointed if there were nothing which counted as pointing.) So once more I draw the conclusion that referring to or mentioning a particular thing cannot be dissolved into any kind of assertion. To refer is not to assert, though you refer in order to go on to assert.

Let me now take an example of the uniquely referring use of an expression not of the form, "the so-and-so." Suppose I advance my hands, cautiously cupped, towards someone, saying, as I do so, "This is a fine red one." He, looking into my hands and seeing nothing there, may say: "What is? What are you talking about?" Or perhaps, "But there's nothing in your hands." Of course it would be absurd to say that in saying "But you've got nothing in your hands," he was *denying* or *contradicting* what I said. So "this" is not a disguised description in Russell's sense. Nor is it a logically proper name. For one must know what the sentence means in order to react in that way to the utterance of it. It is precisely because the significance of the word "this" is independent of any particular reference it may be used to make, though not independent of the way it may be used to refer, that I can, as in this example, use it to *pretend* to be referring to something.

The general moral of all this is that communication is much less a matter of explicit or disguised assertion than logicians used to suppose. The particular application of this general moral in which I am interested is its application to the case of making a unique reference. It is a part of the significance of expressions of the kind I am discussing that they can be used, in an immense variety of contexts, to make unique references. It is no part of their significance to assert that they are being so used or that the conditions of their being so used are fulfilled. So the wholly important distinction we are required to draw is between:

1. using an expression to make a unique reference; and
2. asserting that there is one and only one individual which has certain characteristics (*e.g.* is of a certain kind, or stands in a certain relation to the speaker, or both).

This is, in other words, the distinction between

1. sentences containing an expression used to indicate or mention or refer to a particular person or thing; and
2. uniquely existential sentences.

What Russell does is progressively to assimilate more and more sentences of class 1 to sentences of class 2, and consequently to involve himself in insuperable difficulties about logical subjects, and about values for individual variables generally: difficulties which have led him finally to the logically disastrous theory of names developed in the *Enquiry* and in *Human Knowledge*. That view of the meaning of logical-subject-expressions which provides the whole incentive to the Theory of Descriptions at the same time precludes the possibility of Russell's ever finding any satisfactory substitutes for those expressions which, beginning with substantival phrases, he progressively degrades from the status of logical subjects.[4] It is not simply, as is sometimes said, the fascination of the relation between a name and its bearer, that is the root of the trouble. Not even names come up to the impossible standard set. It is rather the combination of two more radical misconceptions: first, the failure to grasp the importance of the distinction (section II above) between what may be said of an expression and what may be said of a particular use of it; second, a failure to recognise the uniquely referring use of expressions for the harmless, necessary thing it is, distinct from, but complementary to, the predicative or ascriptive use of expressions. The expressions which can in fact occur as singular logical subjects are expressions of the class I listed at the outset (demonstratives, substantival phrases, proper names, pronouns): to say this is to say that these expressions, together with context (in the widest sense) are what one uses to make unique references. The point of the conventions governing the uses of such expressions is, along with the situation of utterance, to secure uniqueness of reference. But to do this, enough is enough. We do not, and we cannot, while referring, attain the point of complete explicitness at which the referring function is no longer performed. The actual unique reference made, if any, is a matter of the particular use in the particular context; the significance of the expression used is the set of rules or conventions which permit such references to be made. Hence we can, using significant expressions, pretend to refer, in make-believe or in fiction, or mistakenly think we are referring when we are not referring to anything.

This shows the need for distinguishing two kinds (among many others) of linguistic conventions or rules: rules for referring, and rules for attributing and ascribing; and for an investigation of the former. If we recognise this distinction of use for what it is, we are on the way to solving a number of ancient logical and metaphysical puzzles.

My last two sections are concerned, but only in the barest outline, with these questions.

IV

One of the main purposes for which we use language is the purpose of stating facts about things and persons and events. If we want to fulfil this purpose,

---

[4] And this in spite of the danger-signal of that phrase, "*misleading* grammatical form."

we must have some way of forestalling the question, "What (who, which one) are you talking about?" as well as the question, "What are you saying about it (him, her)?" The task of forestalling the first question is the referring (or identifying) task. The task of forestalling the second is the attributive (or descriptive or classificatory or ascriptive) task. In the conventional English sentence which is used to state, or to claim to state, a fact about an individual thing or person or event, the performance of these two tasks can be roughly and approximately assigned to separable expressions.[5] And in such a sentence, this assigning of expressions to their separate roles corresponds to the conventional grammatical classification of subject and predicate. There is nothing sacrosanct about the employment of separable expressions for these two tasks. Other methods could be, and are, employed. There is, for instance, the method of uttering a single word or attributive phrase in the conspicuous presence of the object referred to; or that analogous method exemplified by, *e.g.* the painting of the words "unsafe for lorries" on a bridge, or the tying of a label reading "first prize" on a vegetable marrow. Or one can imagine an elaborate game in which one never used an expression in the uniquely referring way at all, but uttered only uniquely existential sentences, trying to enable the hearer to identify what was being talked of by means of an accumulation of relative clauses. (This description of the purposes of the game shows in what sense it would be a game: this is not the normal use we make of existential sentences.) Two points require emphasis. The first is that the necessity of performing these two tasks in order to state particular facts requires no transcendental explanation: to call attention to it is partly to elucidate the meaning of the phrase, "stating a fact." The second is that even this elucidation is made in terms derivative from the grammar of the conventional singular sentence; that even the overtly functional, linguistic distinction between the identifying and attributive roles that words may play in language is prompted by the fact that ordinary speech offers us separable expressions to which the different functions may be plausibly and approximately assigned. And this functional distinction has cast long philosophical shadows. The distinctions between particular and universal, between substance and quality, are such pseudomaterial shadows, cast by the grammar of the conventional sentence, in which separable expressions play distinguishable roles.

To use a separate expression to perform the first of these tasks is to use an expression in the uniquely referring way. I want now to say something in general about the conventions of use for expressions used in this way, and to contrast them with conventions of ascriptive use. I then proceed to the brief illustration of these general remarks and to some further applications of them.

What in general is required for making a unique reference is, obviously, some device, or devices, for showing both *that* a unique reference is intended and *what* unique reference it is; some device requiring and enabling the hearer or reader to identify what is being talked about. In securing this result, the context of utterance is of an importance which it is almost impossible to exag-

---

[5] I neglect relational sentences; for these require, not a modification in the principle of what I say, but a complication of the detail.

gerate; and by "context" I mean, at least, the time, the place, the situation, the identity of the speaker, the subjects which form the immediate focus of interest, and the personal histories of both the speaker and those he is addressing. Besides context, there is, of course, convention;—linguistic convention. But, except in the case of genuine proper names, of which I shall have more to say later, the fulfilment of more or less precisely stateable contextual conditions is *conventionally* (or, in a wide sense of the word, *logically*) required for the correct referring use of expressions in a sense in which this is not true of correct ascriptive uses. The requirement for the correct application of an expression in its ascriptive use to a certain thing is simply that the thing should be of a certain kind, have certain characteristics. The requirement for the correct application of an expression in its referring use to a certain thing is something over and above any requirement derived from such ascriptive meaning as the expression may have; it is, namely, the requirement that the thing should be in a certain relation to the speaker and to the context of utterance. Let me call this the contextual requirement. Thus, for example, in the limiting case of the word "I" the contextual requirement is that the thing should be identical with the speaker; but in the case of most expressions which have a referring use this requirement cannot be so precisely specified. A further, and perfectly general, difference between conventions for referring and conventions for describing is one we have already encountered, *viz.* that the fulfilment of the conditions for a correct ascriptive use of an expression is a part of what is stated by such a use; but the fulfilment of the conditions for a correct referring use of an expression is never part of what is stated, though it is (in the relevant sense of "implied") implied by such a use.

Conventions for referring have been neglected or misinterpreted by logicians. The reasons for this neglect are not hard to see, though they are hard to state briefly. Two of them are, roughly: (1) the preoccupation of most logicians with definitions; (2) the preoccupation of some logicians with formal systems. (1) A definition, in the most familiar sense, is a specification of the conditions of the correct ascriptive or classificatory use of an expression. Definitions take no account of contextual requirements. So that in so far as the search for the meaning or the search for the analysis of an expression is conceived as the search for a definition, the neglect or misinterpretation of conventions other than ascriptive is inevitable. Perhaps it would be better to say (for I do not wish to legislate about "meaning" or "analysis") that logicians have failed to notice that problems of use are wider than problems of analysis and meaning. (2) The influence of the preoccupation with mathematics and formal logic is most clearly seen (to take no more recent examples) in the cases of Leibniz and Russell. The constructor of calculuses, not concerned or required to make factual statements, approaches applied logic with a prejudice. It is natural that he should assume that the types of convention with whose adequacy in one field he is familiar should be really adequate, if only one could see how, in a quite different field—that of statements of fact. Thus we have Leibniz striving desperately to make the uniqueness of unique references a matter of logic in the narrow sense, and Russell striving desperately to do the same thing, in a different way, both for the implication of uniqueness and for that of existence.

It should be clear that the distinction I am trying to draw is primarily one between different rôles or parts that expressions may play in language, and not primarily one between different groups of expressions; for some expressions may appear in either rôle. Some of the kinds of words I shall speak of have predominantly, if not exclusively, a referring rôle. This is most obviously true of pronouns and ordinary proper names. Some can occur as wholes or parts of expressions which have a predominantly referring use, and as wholes or parts of expressions which have a predominantly ascriptive or classificatory use. The obvious cases are common nouns; or common nouns preceded by adjectives, including participial adjectives; or, less obviously, adjectives or participial adjectives alone. Expressions capable of having a referring use also differ from one another in at least the three following, not mutually independent, ways:

1. They differ in the extent to which the reference they are used to make is dependent on the context of their utterance. Words like "I" and "it" stand at one end of this scale—the end of maximum dependence—and phrases like "the author of Waverley" and "the eighteenth king of France" at the other.

2. They differ in the degree of "descriptive meaning" they possess: by "descriptive meaning" I intend "conventional limitation, in application, to things of a certain general kind, or possessing certain general characteristics." At one end of this scale stand the proper names we most commonly use in ordinary discourse; men, dogs and motorbicycles may be called "Horace." The pure name has no descriptive meaning (except such as it may acquire *as a result of* some one of its uses as a name). A word like "he" has minimal descriptive meaning, but has some. Substantival phrases like "the round table" have the maximum descriptive meaning. An interesting intermediate position is occupied by "impure" proper names like "The Round Table"—substantival phrases which have grown capital letters.

3. Finally, they may be divided into the following two classes: (i) those of which the correct referring use is regulated by some *general* referring-cum-ascriptive conventions. To this class belong both pronouns, which have the least descriptive meaning, and substantival phrases which have the most; (ii) those of which the correct referring use is regulated by no general conventions, either of the contextual or the ascriptive kind, but by conventions which are *ad hoc* for each particular use (though not for each particular utterance). Roughly speaking, the most familiar kind of proper names belong to this class. Ignorance of a man's name is not ignorance of the language. This is why we do not speak of the meaning of proper names. (But it won't do to say they are meaningless.) Again an intermediate position is occupied by such phrases as "The Old Pretender." Only an old pretender may be so referred to; but to know which old pretender is not to know a general, but an *ad hoc*, convention.

In the case of phrases of the form "the so-and-so" used referringly, the use of "the" together with the position of the phrase in the sentence (*i.e.* at the beginning, or following a transitive verb or preposition) acts as a signal *that* a unique reference is being made; and the following noun, or noun and adjective, together with the context of utterance, shows *what* unique reference is being made. In general the functional difference between common nouns and

False.   He wants the best shop in the world
He will give the most beautiful shop to his daughter

adjectives is that the former are naturally and commonly used referringly, while the latter are not commonly, or so naturally, used in this way, except as qualifying nouns; though they can be and are, so used alone. And of course this functional difference is not independent of the descriptive force peculiar to each word. In general we should expect the descriptive force of nouns to be such that they are more efficient tools for the job of showing what unique reference is intended when such a reference is signalised; and we should also expect the descriptive force of the words we naturally and commonly use to make unique reference to mirror our interest in the salient, relatively permanent and behavioral characteristics of things. These two expectations are not independent of one another; and, if we look at the differences between the commoner sort of common nouns and the commoner sort of adjectives, we find them both fulfilled. These are differences of the kind that Locke quaintly reports, when he speaks of our ideas of substances being *collections* of simple ideas; when he says that "powers make up a great part of our ideas of substances"; and when he goes on to contrast the identity of real and nominal essence in the case of simple ideas with their lack of identity and the shiftingness of the nominal essence in the case of substances. "Substance" itself is the troublesome tribute Locke pays to his dim awareness of the difference in predominant linguistic function that lingered even when the noun had been expanded into a more or less indefinite string of adjectives. Russell repeats Locke's mistake with a difference when, admitting the inference from syntax to reality to the extent of feeling that he can get rid of this metaphysical unknown only if he can purify language of the referring function altogether, he draws up his programme for "abolishing particulars"; a programme, in fact, for abolishing the distinction of logical use which I am here at pains to emphasise.

The contextual requirement for the referring use of pronouns may be stated with the greatest precision in some cases (*e.g.* "I" and "you") and only with the greatest vagueness in others ("it" and "this"). I propose to say nothing further about pronouns, except to point to an additional symptom of the failure to recognise the uniquely referring use for what it is; the fact, namely, that certain logicians have actually sought to elucidate the nature of a variable by offering such *sentences* as "he is sick," "it is green," as examples of something in ordinary speech like a *sentential function*. Now of course it is true that the word "he" may be used on different occasions to refer to different people or different animals: so may the word "John" and the phrase "the cat." What deters such logicians from treating these two expressions as quasi-variables is, in the first case, the lingering superstition that a name is logically tied to a single individual, and, in the second case, the descriptive meaning of the word "cat." But "he," which has a wide range of applications and minimal descriptive force, only acquires a use as a referring word. It is this fact, together with the failure to accord to expressions used referringly, the place in logic which belongs to them (the place held open for the mythical logically proper name), that accounts for the misleading attempt to elucidate the nature of the variable by reference to such words as "he," "she," "it."

Of ordinary proper names it is sometimes said that they are essentially words each of which is used to refer to just one individual. This is obviously false. Many ordinary personal names—names par excellence—are correctly used to refer to numbers of people. An ordinary personal name is, roughly, a word, used referringly, of which the use is *not* dictated by any descriptive meaning the word may have, and is *not* prescribed by any such general rule for use as a referring expression (or a part of a referring expression) as we find in the case of such words as "I," "this," and "the," but is governed by *ad hoc* conventions for each particular set of applications of the word to a given person. The important point is that the correctness of such applications does not follow from any *general* rule or convention for the use of the word as such. (The limit of absurdity and obvious circularity is reached in the attempt to treat names as disguised description in Russell's sense; for what is in the special sense implied, but not entailed, by my now referring to some one by name is simply the existence of some one, *now being referred to*, who is *conventionally referred to* by that name.) Even this feature of names, however, is only a symptom of the purpose for which they are employed. At present our choice of names is partly arbitrary, partly dependent on legal and social observances. It would be perfectly possible to have a thorough-going *system* of names, based *e.g.* on dates of birth, or on a minute classification of physiological and anatomical differences. But the success of any such system would depend entirely on the convenience of the resulting name-allotments for the purpose of making unique references; and this would depend on the multiplicity of the classifications used and the degree to which they cut haphazard across normal social groupings. Given a sufficient degree of both, the selectivity supplied by context would do the rest; just as is the case with our present naming habits. Had we such a system, we could use name-words descriptively (as we do at present, to a limited extent and in a different way, with some famous names) as well as referringly. But it is by criteria derived from consideration of the requirements of the referring task that we should assess the adequacy of any system of naming. From the naming point of view, no kind of classification would be better or worse than any other simply because of the kind of classification—natal or anatomical—that it was.

I have already mentioned the class of quasi-names, of substantival phrases which grow capital letters, and of which such phrases as "the Glorious Revolution," "the Great War," "the Annunciation," "the Round Table" are examples. While the descriptive meaning of the words which follow the definite article is still relevant to their referring role, the capital letters are a sign of that extra-logical selectivity in their referring use, which is characteristic of pure names. Such phrases are found in print or in writing when one member of some class of events or things is of quite outstanding interest in a certain society. These phrases are embryonic names. A phrase may, for obvious reasons, pass into, and out of, this class (*e.g.* "the Great War").

V

I want to conclude by considering, all too briefly, three further problems about referring uses.

(*a*) *Indefinite References.* Not all referring uses of singular expressions forestall the question "What (who, which one) are you talking about?" There are some which either invite this question, or disclaim the intention or ability to answer it. Examples are such sentence-beginnings as "A man told me that . . . ," "Some one told me that. . . ." The orthodox (Russellian) doctrine is that such sentences are existential, but not uniquely existential. This seems wrong in several ways. It is ludicrous to suggest that part of what is asserted is that the class of men or persons is not empty. Certainly this is *implied* in the by now familiar sense of implication; but the implication is also as much an implication of the *uniqueness* of the particular object of reference as when I begin a sentence with such a phrase as "the table." The difference between the use of the definite and indefinite articles is, very roughly, as follows. We use "the" either when a previous reference has been made, and when "the" signalises that the same reference is being made; or when, in the absence of a previous indefinite reference, the context (including the hearer's assumed knowledge) is expected to enable the hearer to tell *what* reference is being made. We use "a" either when these conditions are not fulfilled, or when, although a definite reference *could* be made, we wish to keep dark the identity of the individual to whom, or to which, we are referring. This is the *arch* use of such a phrase as "a certain person" or "some one"; where it could be expanded, not into "some one, but you wouldn't (or I don't) know who" but into "some one, but I'm not telling you who."

(*b*) *Identification Statements.* By this label I intend statements like the following:

(i*a*) That is the man who swam the channel twice on one day.
(ii*a*) Napoleon was the man who ordered the execution of the Duc D'Enghien.

The puzzle about these statements is that their grammatical predicates do not seem to be used in a straightforwardly ascriptive way as are the grammatical predicates of the statements:

(i*b*) That man swam the channel twice in one day.
(ii*b*) Napoleon ordered the execution of the Duc D'Enghien.

But if, in order to avoid blurring the difference between (i*a*) and (i*b*) and (ii*a*) and (ii*b*), one says that the phrases which form the grammatical complements of (i*a*) and (ii*a*) are being used referringly, one becomes puzzled about what is being said in these sentences. We seem then to be referring to the same person twice over and either saying nothing about him and thus making no statement, or identifying him with himself and thus producing a trivial identity.

The bogey of triviality can be dismissed. This only arises for those who think of the object referred to by the use of an expression as its meaning, and thus think of the subject and complement of these sentences as meaning the same because they could be used to refer to the same person.

I think the differences between sentences in the (*a*) group and sentences in the (*b*) group can best be understood by considering the differences between the circumstances in which you would say (i*a*) and the circumstances in which you would say (i*b*). You would say (i*a*) instead of (i*b*) if you knew or believed that your hearer knew or believed that *some one* had swum the channel twice in one day. You say (i*a*) when you take your hearer to be in the position of one who can ask: "Who swam the channel twice in one day?" (And in asking this, he is not saying that anyone did, though his asking it implies—in the relevant sense—that some one did.) Such sentences are like answers to such questions. They are better called "identification-statements" than "identities." Sentence (ia) does not assert more or less than sentence (ib). It is just that you say (ia) to a man whom you take to know certain things that you take to be unknown to the man to whom you say (ib).

This is, in the barest essentials, the solution to Russell's puzzle about "denoting phrases" joining by "is"; one of the puzzles which he claims for the Theory of Descriptions the merit of solving.

(c) *The Logic of Subjects and Predicates.*   Much of what I have said of the uniquely referring use of expressions can be extended, with suitable modifications, to the non-uniquely referring use of expressions; *i.e.* to some uses of expressions consisting of "the" "all the," "all," "some," "some of the," etc. followed by a noun, qualified or unqualified, in the *plural;* to some uses of "they," "them," "those," "these"; and to conjunctions of names. Expressions of the first kind have a special interest. Roughly speaking, orthodox modern criticism, inspired by mathematical logic, of such traditional doctrines as that of the Square of Opposition and of some of the forms of the syllogism traditionally recognised as valid, rests on the familiar failure to recognise the special sense in which existential assertions may be implied by the referring use of expressions. The universal propositions of the fourfold schedule, it is said, must *either* be given a negatively existential interpretation (*e.g.*, for A, "there are no X's which are not Y's") *or* they must be interpreted as conjunctions of negatively and positively existential statements of, *e.g.*, the form (for A) "there are no X's which are not Y's, and there are X's." The I and O forms are normally given a positively existential interpretation. It is then seen that, whichever of the above alternatives is selected, some of the traditional laws have to be abandoned. The dilemma, however, is a bogus one. If we interpret the propositions of the schedule as neither positively, nor negatively, nor positively *and* negatively, existential, but as sentences such that *the question of whether they are being used to make true or false assertions does not arise except when the existential condition is fulfilled for the subject term,* then all the traditional laws hold good together. And this interpretation is far closer to the most common uses of expressions beginning with "all" and "some" than is any Russellian alternative. For these expressions are most commonly used in the referring way. A literal-minded and childless man asked whether all his children are asleep will certainly not answer "Yes" on the ground that he has none; but nor will he answer "No" on this ground. Since he has no children, the question does not arise. To say this is not to say that I may not use the sentence, "All my children are asleep," with the intention of letting some one know that I have children, or of deceiving him into thinking that I have. Nor is it any weakening of my thesis to concede that singular phrases of the form "the so-and-so" may sometimes be used with a similar purpose. Neither Aristotelian nor Russellian rules give the exact logic of any expression of ordinary language; for ordinary language has no exact logic.

Bertrand Russell MR. STRAWSON

ON REFERRING

Russell's reply to Strawson's "On Referring" first appeared in *Mind* in 1957. Strawson has never published a reply to Russell. The dispute between the two men, at least as Russell conceives it, is sharpened by Russell's evaluation of Strawson's thesis. Of special interest is Russell's contrast between his opinion of the use of an appeal to ordinary language in doing philosophy and Strawson's.

This selection should be read after having read Russell's original theory in selection 1 and Strawson's attack upon it in selection 14.

Mr. P. F. Strawson published in *Mind* of 1950 an article called "On Referring." This article is reprinted in *Essays in Conceptual Analysis,* selected and edited by Professor Antony Flew. The references that follow are to this reprint. The main purpose of the article is to refute my theory of descriptions. As I find that some philosophers whom I respect consider that it has achieved its purpose successfully, I have come to the conclusion that a polemical reply is called for. I may say, to begin with, that I am totally unable to see any validity whatever in any of Mr. Strawson's arguments. Whether this inability is due to senility on my part or to some other cause, I must leave readers to judge.

The gist of Mr. Strawson's argument consists in identifying two problems which I have regarded as quite distinct—namely, the problem of descriptions and the problem of egocentricity. I have dealt with both these problems at considerable length, but as I have considered them to be different problems, I have not dealt with the one when I was considering the other. This enables Mr. Strawson to pretend that I have overlooked the problem of egocentricity.

He is helped in this pretence by a careful selection of material. In the article in which I first set forth the theory of descriptions, I dealt specially with

From *My Philosophical Development,* chap. XVIII, part III. Copyright © 1959 by George Allen and Unwin, Ltd. Reprinted by permission of George Allen and Unwin and Simon and Schuster, Inc.

two examples: "The present King of France is bald" and "Scott is the author of *Waverley*." The latter example does not suit Mr. Strawson, and he therefore entirely ignores it except for one quite perfunctory reference. As regards "the present King of France," he fastens upon the egocentric word "present" and does not seem able to grasp that, if for the word "present" I had substituted the words "in 1905," the whole of his argument would have collapsed.

Or perhaps not quite the whole, for reasons which I had set forth before Mr. Strawson wrote. It is, however, not difficult to give other examples of the use of descriptive phrases from which egocentricity is wholly absent. I should like to see him apply his doctrine to such sentences as the following: "the square-root of minus one is half the square-root of minus four," or "the cube of three is the integer immediately preceding the second perfect number." There are no egocentric words in either of these two sentences, but the problem of interpreting the descriptive phrases is exactly the same as if there were.

There is not a word in Mr. Strawson's article to suggest that I ever considered egocentric words, still less that the theory which he advocates in regard to them is the very one which I had set forth at great length and in considerable detail.[1] The gist of what he has to say about such words is the entirely correct statement that what they refer to depends upon when and where they are used. As to this, I need only quote one paragraph from *Human Knowledge* (page 107):

"This" denotes whatever, at the moment when the word is used, occupies the centre of attention. With words which are not egocentric, what is constant is something about the object indicated, but "this" denotes a different object on each occasion of its use: what is constant is not the object denoted, but its relation to the particular use of the word. Whenever the word is used, the person using it is attending to something, and the word indicates this something. When a word is not egocentric, there is no need to distinguish between different occasions when it is used, but we must make this distinction with egocentric words, since what they indicate is something having a given relation to the particular use of the word.

I must refer, also, to the case that I discuss in which I am walking with a friend on a dark night. We lose touch with each other and he calls "Where are you?" and I reply "Here I am!" It is of the essence of a scientific account of the world to reduce to a minimum the egocentric element in an assertion, but success in this attempt is a matter of degree, and is never complete where empirical material is concerned. This is due to the fact that the meanings of all empirical words depend ultimately upon ostensive definitions, that ostensive definitions depend upon experience, and that experience is egocentric. We can, however, by means of egocentric words, *describe* something which is not egocentric; it is this that enables us to use a common language.

All this may be right or wrong, but, whichever it is, Mr. Strawson should

---

[1] Cf. *An Inquiry into Meaning and Truth*, chap. VII, and *Human Knowledge*, part II, chap. IV.

not expound it as if it were a theory that he had invented, whereas, in fact, I had set it forth before he wrote, though perhaps he did not grasp the purport of what I said. I shall say no more about egocentricity since, for the reasons I have already given, I think Mr. Strawson completely mistaken in connecting it with the problem of descriptions.

I am at a loss to understand Mr. Strawson's position on the subject of names. When he is writing about me, he says: "There are no logically proper names and there are no descriptions (in this sense)." But when he is writing about Quine, in *Mind*, October 1956, he takes a quite different line. Quine has a theory that names are unnecessary and can always be replaced by descriptions. This theory shocks Mr. Strawson for reasons which, to me, remain obscure. However, I will leave the defence of Quine to Quine, who is quite capable of looking after himself. What is important for my purpose is to elucidate the meaning of the words "in this sense" which Mr. Strawson puts in brackets. So far as I can discover from the context, what he objects to is the belief that there are words which are only significant because there is something that they mean, and if there were not this something, they would be empty noises, not words. For my part, I think that there must be such words if language is to have any relation to fact. The necessity for such words is made obvious by the process of ostensive definition. How do we know what is meant by such words as "red" and "blue"? We cannot know what these words mean unless we have seen red and seen blue. If there were no red and no blue in our experience, we might, perhaps, invent some elaborate description which we could substitute for the word "red" or for the word "blue." For example, if you were dealing with a blind man, you could hold a red-hot poker near enough for him to feel the heat, and you could tell him that red is what he would see if he could see—but of course for the word "see" you would have to substitute another elaborate description. Any description which the blind man could understand would have to be in terms of words expressing experiences which he had had. Unless fundamental words in the individual's vocabulary had this kind of direct relation to fact, language in general would have no such relation. I defy Mr. Strawson to give the usual meaning to the word "red" unless there is something which the word designates.

This brings me to a further point. "Red" is usually regarded as a predicate and as designating a universal. I prefer for purposes of philosophical analysis a language in which "red" is a subject, and, while I should not say that it is a positive error to call it a universal, I should say that calling it so invites confusion. This is connected with what Mr. Strawson calls my "logically disastrous theory of names." He does not deign to mention why he considers this theory "logically disastrous." I hope that on some future occasion he will enlighten me on this point.

This brings me to a fundamental divergence between myself and many philosophers with whom Mr. Strawson appears to be in general agreement. They are persuaded that common speech is good enough, not only for daily life, but also for philosophy. I, on the contrary, am persuaded that common speech is full of vagueness and inaccuracy, and that any attempt to be precise and accurate requires modification of common speech both as regards vocabulary and as regards syntax. Everybody admits that physics and chemistry and medicine each require a language which is not that of everyday life. I fail to see why philosophy, alone, should be forbidden to make a similar approach towards precision and accuracy. Let us take, in illustration, one of the commonest words of everyday speech: namely, the word "day." The most august use of this word is in the first chapter of Genesis and in the Ten Commandments. The desire to keep holy the Sabbath "day" has led orthodox Jews to give a precision to the word "day" which it does not have in common speech: they have defined it as the period from one sunset to the next. Astronomers, with other reasons for seeking precision, have three sorts of day: the true solar day; the mean solar day; and the sidereal day. These have different uses: the true solar day is relevant if you are considering lighting-up time; the mean solar day is relevant if you are sentenced to fourteen days without the option; and the sidereal day is relevant if you are trying to estimate the influence of the tides in retarding the earth's rotation. All these four kinds of day—decalogical, true, mean, and sidereal—are more precise than the common use of the word "day." If astronomers were subject to the prohibition of precision which some recent philosophers apparently favour, the whole science of astronomy would be impossible.

For technical purposes, technical languages differing from those of daily life are indispensable. I feel that those who object to linguistic novelties, if they had lived a hundred and fifty years ago, would have stuck to feet and ounces, and would have maintained that centimetres and grammes savour of the guillotine.

In philosophy, it is syntax, even more than vocabulary, that needs to be corrected. The subject-predicate logic to which we are accustomed depends for its convenience upon the fact that at the usual temperatures of the earth there are approximately permanent "things." This would not be true at the temperature of the sun, and is only roughly true at the temperatures to which we are accustomed.

My theory of descriptions was never intended as an analysis of the state of mind of those who utter sentences containing descriptions. Mr. Strawson gives the name "S" to the sentence "The King of France is wise," and he says of me "The way in which he arrived at the analysis was clearly by asking himself what would be the circumstances in which we would say that anyone who uttered the sentence S had made a true assertion." This does not seem to me a correct account of what I was doing. Suppose (which God forbid) Mr. Strawson were so rash as to accuse his charlady of thieving: she would reply indignantly, "I ain't never done no harm to no one." Assuming her a pattern of virtue, I should say that she was making a true assertion, although, according to the rules of syntax which Mr. Strawson would adopt in his own speech, what she said should have meant: "there was at least one moment when I was injuring the whole human race." Mr. Strawson would not have supposed that this was what she meant to assert, although he would not have used her words to express the same sentiment. Similarly, I was concerned to find a more accurate and analysed thought to replace the somewhat confused thoughts which most people at most times have in their heads.

Mr. Strawson objects to my saying that "the King of France is wise" is false if there is no King of France. He admits that the sentence is significant and not true, but not that it is false. This is a mere question of verbal convenience. He considers that the word "false" has an unalterable meaning which it would be sinful to regard as adjustable, though he prudently avoids telling us what this meaning is. For my part, I find it more convenient to define the word "false" so that every significant sentence is either true or false. This is a purely verbal question; and although I have no wish to claim the support of common usage, I do not think that he can claim it either. Suppose, for example, that in some country there was a law that no person could hold public office if he considered it false that the Ruler of the Universe is wise. I think an avowed atheist who took advantage of Mr. Strawson's doctrine to say that he did not hold this proposition false, would be regarded as a somewhat shifty character.

It is not only as to names and as to falsehood that Mr. Strawson shows his conviction that there is an unalterably right way of using words and that no change is to be tolerated however convenient it may be. He shows the same feeling as regards universal affirmatives—i.e. sentences of the form "All A is B." Traditionally, such sentences are supposed to imply that there are A's, but it is much more convenient in mathematical logic to drop this implication and to consider that "All A is B" is true if there are no A's. This is wholly and solely a question of convenience. For some purposes the one convention is more convenient, and for others, the other. We shall prefer the one convention or the other according to the purpose we have in view. I agree, however, with Mr. Strawson's statement that ordinary language has no exact logic.

Mr. Strawson, in spite of his very real logical competence, has a curious prejudice against logic. On page 43, he has a sudden dithyrambic outburst, to the effect that life is greater than logic, which he uses to give a quite false interpretation of my doctrines.

Leaving detail aside, I think we may sum up Mr. Strawson's argument and my reply to it as follows:

There are two problems, that of descriptions and that of egocentricity. Mr. Strawson thinks they are one and the same problem, but it is obvious from his discussion that he has not considered as many kinds of descriptive phrases as are relevant to the argument. Having confused the two problems, he asserts dogmatically that it is only the egocentric problem that needs to be solved, and he offers a solution of this problem which he seems to believe to be new, but which in fact was familiar before he wrote. He then thinks that he has offered an adequate theory of descriptions, and announces his supposed achievement with astonishing dogmatic certainty. Perhaps I am doing him an injustice, but I am unable to see in what respect this is the case.

16

H.P. Grice and P. F. Strawson

IN DEFENSE OF A DOGMA

This essay was written by Grice and Strawson as a reply to Quine's thesis in "Two Dogmas of Empiricism." It should be read after having read Quine's essay in selection 9. As the authors admit, their purpose is wholly negative: to show that Quine's arguments do not invalidate the analytic-synthetic distinction as he thought they did.

Further reading suggestions are to be found in the introduction to selection 9.

In his article "Two Dogmas of Empiricism," [1] Professor Quine advances a number of criticisms of the supposed distinction between analytic and synthetic statements, and of other associated notions. It is, he says, a distinction which he rejects.[2] We wish to show that his criticisms of the distinction do not justify his rejection of it.

There are many ways in which a distinction can be criticized, and more than one in which it can be rejected. It can be criticized for not being a sharp distinction (for admitting of cases which do not fall clearly on either side of it); or on the ground that the terms in which it is customarily drawn are ambiguous (have more than one meaning); or on the ground that it is confused (the different meanings being habitually conflated). Such criticisms alone would scarcely amount to a rejection of the distinction. They would, rather, be a prelude to clarification. It is not this sort of criticism which Quine makes.

Again, a distinction can be criticized on the ground that it is not useful. It can be said to be useless for certain purposes, or useless altogether, and, perhaps, pedantic. One who criticizes in this way may indeed be said to reject a distinction, but in a sense which also requires him to acknowledge its existence.

From *The Philosophical Review*, vol. LXV, no. 2 (April, 1956). Used by permission of the editor and the authors.

[1] W. V. O. Quine, *From a Logical Point of View* (Cambridge, Mass., 1953), pp. 20–46. All references are to page numbers in this book.

[2] Page 46.

He simply declares he can get on without it. But Quine's rejection of the analytic-synthetic distinction appears to be more radical than this. He would certainly say he could get on without the distinction, but not in a sense which would commit him to acknowledging its existence.

Or again, one could criticize the way or ways in which a distinction is customarily expounded or explained on the ground that these explanations did not make it really clear. And Quine certainly makes such criticisms in the case of the analytic-synthetic distinction.

But he does, or seems to do, a great deal more. He declares, or seems to declare, not merely that the distinction is useless or inadequately clarified, but also that it is altogether illusory, that the belief in its existence is a philosophical mistake. "That there is such a distinction to be drawn at all," he says, "is an unempirical dogma of empiricists, a metaphysical article of faith."[3] It is the existence of the distinction that he here calls in question; so his rejection of it would seem to amount to a denial of its existence.

Evidently such a position of extreme skepticism about a distinction is not in general justified merely by criticisms, however just in themselves, of philosophical attempts to clarify it. There are doubtless plenty of distinctions, drawn in philosophy and outside it, which still await adequate philosophical elucidation, but which few would want on this account to declare illusory. Quine's article, however, does not consist wholly, though it does consist largely, in criticizing attempts at elucidation. He does try also to diagnose the causes of the belief in the distinction, and he offers some positive doctrine, acceptance of which he represents as incompatible with this belief. If there is any general prior presumption in favor of the existence of the distinction, it seems that Quine's radical rejection of it must rest quite heavily on this part of his article, since the force of any such presumption is not even impaired by philosophical failures to clarify a distinction so supported.

Is there such a presumption in favor of the distinction's existence? Prima facie, it must be admitted that there is. An appeal to philosophical tradition is perhaps unimpressive and is certainly unnecessary. But it is worth pointing out that Quine's objection is not simply to the words "analytic" and "synthetic," but to a distinction which they are supposed to express, and which at different times philosophers have supposed themselves to be expressing by means of such pairs of words or phrases as "necessary" and "contingent," "a priori" and "empirical," "truth of reason" and "truth of fact"; so Quine is certainly at odds with a philosophical tradition which is long and not wholly disreputable. But there is no need to appeal only to tradition; for there is also present practice. We can appeal, that is, to the fact that those who use the terms "analytic" and "synthetic" do to a very considerable extent agree in the applications they make of them. They apply the term "analytic" to more or less the same cases, withhold it from more or less the same cases, and hesitate over more or less the same cases. This agreement extends not only to cases which they have been *taught* so to characterize, but to new cases. In short, "analytic" and "synthetic" have a more or less established philosophical *use;* and this seems to suggest that it is absurd, even

[3] Page 37.

senseless, to say that there is no such distinction. For, in general, if a pair of contrasting expressions are habitually and generally used in application to the same cases, *where these cases do not form a closed list*, this is a sufficient condition for saying that there are *kinds* of cases to which the expressions apply; and nothing more is needed for them to mark a distinction.

In view of the possibility of this kind of argument, one may begin to doubt whether Quine really holds the extreme thesis which his words encourage one to attribute to him. It is for this reason that we made the attribution tentative. For on at least one natural interpretation of this extreme thesis, when we say of something true that it is analytic and of another true thing that it is synthetic, it simply never is the case that we thereby mark a distinction between them. And this view seems terribly difficult to reconcile with the fact of an established philosophical usage (i.e., of general agreement in application in an open class). For this reason, Quine's thesis might be better represented not as the thesis that there is *no difference at all* marked by the use of these expressions, but as the thesis that the nature of, and reasons for, the difference or differences are totally misunderstood by those who use the expressions, that the stories they tell themselves *about* the difference are full of illusion.

We think Quine might be prepared to accept this amendment. If so, it could, in the following way, be made the basis of something like an answer to the argument which prompted it. Philosophers are notoriously subject to illusion, and to mistaken theories. Suppose there were a particular mistaken theory about language or knowledge, such that, seen in the light of this theory, some statements (or propositions or sentences) appeared to have a characteristic which no statements really have, or even, perhaps, which it does not make sense to suppose that any statement has, and which no one who was not consciously or subconsciously influenced by this theory would ascribe to any statement. And suppose that there were other statements which, seen in this light, did not appear to have this characteristic, and others again which presented an uncertain appearance. Then philosophers who were under the influence of this theory would tend to mark the supposed presence or absence of this characteristic by a pair of contrasting expressions, say "analytic" and "synthetic." Now in these circumstances it still could not be said that there was no distinction at all being marked by the use of these expressions, for there would be at least the distinction we have just described (the distinction, namely, between those statements which appeared to have and those which appeared to lack a certain characteristic), and there might well be other assignable differences too, which would account for the difference in appearance; but it certainly could be said that *the* difference these philosophers supposed themselves to be marking by the use of the expressions simply did not exist, and perhaps also (supposing the characteristic in question to be one which it was absurd to ascribe to any statement) that these expressions, as so used, were senseless or without meaning. We should only have to suppose that such a mistaken theory was very plausible and attractive, in order to reconcile the fact of an established philosophical usage for a pair of contrasting terms with the claim that *the* distinction which the terms purported to mark did not exist at all, though not with the claim that there simply did not exist a difference of any kind between the classes of statements so characterized. We think that the former claim would probably be sufficient for Quine's purposes. But to establish such a claim on the sort of grounds we have indicated evidently requires a great deal more argument than is involved in showing that certain explanations of a term do not measure up to certain requirements of adequacy in philosophical clarification—and not only more argument, but argument of a very different kind. For it would surely be too harsh to maintain that the *general* presumption is that philosophical distinctions embody the kind of illusion we have described. On the whole, it seems that philosophers are prone to make too few distinctions rather than too many. It is their assimilations, rather than their distinctions, which tend to be spurious.

So far we have argued as if the prior presumption in favor of the existence of the distinction which Quine questions rested solely on the fact of an agreed *philosophical* usage for the terms "analytic" and "synthetic." A presumption with only this basis could no doubt be countered by a strategy such as we have just outlined. But, in fact, if we are to accept Quine's account of the matter, the presumption in question is not only so based. For among the notions which belong to the analyticity-group is one which Quine calls "cognitive synonymy," and in terms of which he allows that the notion of analyticity could at any rate be formally explained. Unfortunately, he adds, the notion of cognitive synonymy is just as unclarified as that of analyticity. To say that two expressions *x* and *y* are cognitively synonymous seems to correspond, at any rate roughly, to what we should ordinarily express by saying that *x* and *y* have the same meaning or that *x* means the same as *y*. If Quine is to be consistent in his adherence to the extreme thesis, then it appears that he must maintain not only that the distinction we suppose ourselves to be marking by the use of the terms "analytic" and "synthetic" does not exist, but also that the distinction we suppose ourselves to be marking by the use of the expressions "means the same as," "does not mean the same as" does not exist either. At least, he must maintain this insofar as the notion of *meaning the same as,* in its application to predicate-expressions, is supposed to differ from and go beyond the notion of *being true of just the same objects as.* (This latter notion—which we might call that of "coextensionality"— he is prepared to allow to be intelligible, though, as he rightly says, it is not sufficient for the explanation of analyticity.) Now since he cannot claim this time that the pair of expressions in question (viz., "means the same," "does not mean the same") is the special property of philosophers, the strategy outlined above of countering the presumption in favor of their marking a genuine distinction is not available here (or is at least enormously less plausible). Yet the denial that the distinction (taken as different from the distinction between the co-extensional and the non-coextensional) really exists, is extremely paradoxical. It involves saying, for example, that anyone who seriously remarks that "bachelor" means the same as "unmarried man" but that "creature with kidneys" does not mean the same as "creature with a heart"—supposing the last two expressions to be coextensional—*either* is not in fact drawing attention to any distinction at all between the relations between the members of each pair of expressions *or* is making a philosophical mistake about the nature of the distinction between them. In either case, what he says, taken as he intends it to be taken, is senseless or absurd. More generally, it involves saying that it is always senseless or absurd to make a statement of the form "Predicates x and y in fact apply to the same objects, but do not have the same meaning." But the paradox is more violent than this. For we frequently talk of the presence or absence of relations of synonymy between kinds of expressions—e.g., conjunctions, particles of many kinds, whole sentences—where there does not appear to be any obvious substitute for the ordinary notion of synonymy, in the way in which coextensionality is said to be a substitute for synonymy of predicates. Is all such talk meaningless? Is all talk of correct or incorrect *translation* of sentences of one language into sentences of another meaningless? It is hard to believe that it is. But if we do successfully make the effort to believe it, we have still harder renunciations before us. If talk of sentence-synonymy is meaningless, then it seems that talk of sentences having a meaning at all must be meaningless too. For if it made sense to talk of a sentence have a meaning, or meaning something, then presumably it would make sense to ask "What does it mean?" And if it made sense to ask "What does it mean?" of a sentence, then sentence-synonymy could be roughly defined as follows: Two sentences are synonymous if and only if any true answer to the question "What does it mean?" asked of one of them, is a true answer to the same question, asked of the other. We do not, of course, claim any clarifying power for this definition. We want only to point out that if we are to give up the notion of sentence-synonymy as senseless, we must give up the notion of sentence-significance (of a sentence having meaning) as senseless too. But then perhaps we might as well give up the notion of sense.—It seems clear that we have here a typical example of a philosopher's paradox. Instead of examining the actual use that we make of the notion of *meaning the same*, the philosopher measures it by some perhaps inappropriate standard (in this case some standard of clarifiability), and because it falls short of this standard, or seems to do so, denies its reality, declares it illusory.

We have argued so far that there is a strong presumption in favor of the existence of the distinction, or distinctions, which Quine challenges—a presumption resting both on philosophical and on ordinary usage—and that this presumption is not in the least shaken by the fact, if it is a fact, that the distinctions in question have not been, in some sense, adequately clarified. It is perhaps time to look at what Quine's notion of adequate clarification is.

The main theme of his article can be roughly summarized as follows. There is a certain circle or family of expressions, of which "analytic" is one, such that if any one member of the circle could be taken to be satisfactorily understood or explained, then other members of the circle could be verbally, and hence satisfactorily, explained in terms of it. Other members of the family are: "self-contradictory" (in a broad sense), "necessary," "synonymous," "semantical rule," and perhaps (but again in a broad sense) "definition." The list could be added to. Unfortunately each member of the family is in as great need of explanation as any other. We give some sample quotations: "The notion of self-contradictoriness (in the required broad sense of inconsistency) stands in exactly the same need of clarification as does the notion of analyticity itself."* Again, Quine

* Page 20.

speaks of "a notion of synonymy which is in no less need of clarification than analyticity itself."[5] Again, of the adverb "necessarily," as a candidate for use in the explanation of synonymy, he says, "Does the adverb *really make sense?* To suppose that it does is to suppose that we have already *made satisfactory sense* of 'analytic.'"[6] To make "satisfactory sense" of one of these expressions would seem to involve two things. (1) It would seem to involve providing an explanation which does not incorporate any expression belonging to the family-circle. (2) It would seem that the explanation provided must be of the same general character as those rejected explanations which do incorporate members of the family-circle (i.e., it must specify some feature common and peculiar to all cases to which, for example, the word "analytic" is to be applied; it must have the same general form as an explanation beginning, "a statement is analytic if and only if . . ."). It is true that Quine does not explicitly state the second requirement; but since he does not even consider the question whether any other kind of explanation would be relevant, it seems reasonable to attribute it to him. If we take these two conditions together, and generalize the result, it would seem that Quine requires of a satisfactory explanation of an expression that it should take the form of a pretty strict definition but should not make use of any member of a group of interdefinable terms to which the expression belongs. We may well begin to feel that a satisfactory explanation is hard to come by. The other element in Quine's position is one we have already commented on in general, before enquiring what (according to him) is to count as a satisfactory explanation. It is the step from "We have not made satisfactory sense (provided a satisfactory explanation) of *x*" to "*x* does not make sense."

It would seem fairly clearly unreasonable to insist *in general* that the availability of a satisfactory explanation in the sense sketched above is a necessary condition of an expression's making sense. It is perhaps dubious whether *any* such explanations can *ever* be given. (The hope that they can be is, or was, the hope of reductive analysis in general.) Even if such explanations can be given in some cases, it would be pretty generally agreed that there are other cases in which they cannot. One might think, for example, of the group of expressions which includes "morally wrong," "blameworthy," "breach of moral rules," etc.; or of the group which includes the propositional connectives and the words "true" and "false," "statement," "fact," "denial," "assertion." Few people would want to say that the expressions belonging to either of these groups were senseless on the ground that they have not been formally defined (or even on the ground that it was impossible formally to define them) except in terms of members of the same group. It might, however, be said that while the unavailability of a satisfactory explanation in the special sense described was not a *generally* sufficient reason for declaring that a given expression was senseless, it was a sufficient reason in the case of the expressions of the analyticity group. But anyone who said this would have to advance a reason for discriminating in this way against the expressions of this group. The only plausible reason for being

[5] Page 23.
[6] Page 30, our italics.

harder on these expressions than on others is a refinement on a consideration which we have already had before us. It starts from the point that "analytic" and "synthetic" themselves are technical philosophical expressions. To the rejoinder that other expressions of the family concerned, such as "means the same as" or "is inconsistent with," or "self-contradictory," are not at all technical expressions, but are common property, the reply would doubtless be that, to qualify for inclusion in the family circle, these expressions have to be used in specially adjusted and precise senses (or pseudo-senses) which they do not ordinarily possess. It is the fact, then, that all the terms belonging to the circle are *either* technical terms *or* ordinary terms used in specially adjusted senses, that might be held to justify us in being particularly suspicious of the claims of members of the circle to have any sense at all, and hence to justify us in requiring them to pass a test for significance which would admittedly be too stringent if generally applied. This point has some force, though we doubt if the special adjustments spoken of are in every case as considerable as it suggests. (This seems particularly doubtful in the case of the word "inconsistent"—a perfectly good member of the nontechnician's meta-logical vocabulary.) But though the point has some force, it does not have whatever force would be required to justify us in insisting that the expressions concerned should pass exactly that test for significance which is in question. The fact, if it is a fact, that the expressions cannot be explained in precisely the way which Quine seems to require, does not mean that they cannot be explained at all. There is no need to try to pass them off as expressing innate ideas. They can be and are explained, though in other and less formal ways than that which Quine considers. (And the fact that they are so explained fits with the facts, first, that there is a generally agreed philosophical use for them, and second, that this use is technical or specially adjusted.) To illustrate the point briefly for one member of the analyticity family. Let us suppose we are trying to explain to someone the notion of *logical impossibility* (a member of the family which Quine presumably regards as no clearer than any of the others) and we decide to do it by bringing out the contrast between logical and natural (or causal) impossibility. We might take as our examples the logical impossibility of a child of three's being an adult, and the natural impossibility of a child of three's understanding Russell's Theory of Types. We might instruct our pupil to imagine two conversations one of which begins by someone (X) making the claim:

(1) "My neighbor's three-year-old child understands Russell's Theory of Types,"

and the other of which begins by someone (Y) making the claim:

(1′) "My neighbor's three-year-old child is an adult."

It would not be inappropriate to reply to X, taking the remark as a hyperbole:

(2) "You mean the child is a particularly bright lad."

If X were to say:

(3) "No, I mean what I say—he really does understand it,"

one might be inclined to reply:

(4) "I don't believe you—the thing's impossible."

But if the child were then produced, and did (as one knows he would not) expound the theory correctly, answer questions on it, criticize it, and so on, one would in the end be forced to acknowledge that the claim was literally true and that the child was a prodigy. Now consider one's reaction to Y's claim. To begin with, it might be somewhat similar to the previous case. One might say:

(2') "You mean he's uncommonly sensible or very advanced for his age."

If Y replies:

(3') "No, I mean what I say,"

we might reply:

(4') "Perhaps you mean that he won't grow any more, or that he's a sort of freak, that he's already fully developed."

Y replies:

(5') "No, he's not a freak, he's just an adult."

At this stage—or possibly if we are patient, a little later—we shall be inclined to say that we just don't understand what Y is saying, and to suspect that he just does not know the meaning of some of the words he is using. For unless he is prepared to admit that he is using words in a figurative or unusual sense, we shall say, not that we don't believe him, but that his words have *no* sense. And whatever kind of creature is ultimately produced for our inspection, it will not lead us to say that what Y said was literally true, but at most to say that we now see what he meant. As a summary of the difference between the two imaginary conversations, we might say that in both cases we would tend to begin by supposing that the other speaker was using words in a figurative or unusual or restricted way; but in the face of his repeated claim to be speaking literally, it would be appropriate in the first case to say that we did not believe him and in the second case to say that we did not understand him. If, like Pascal, we thought it prudent to prepare against very long chances, we should in the first case know what to prepare for; in the second, we should have no idea.

We give this as an example of just one type of informal explanation which we might have recourse to in the case of one notion of the analyticity group. (We do not wish to suggest it is the only type.) Further examples, with different though connected types of treatment, might be necessary to teach our pupil the use of the notion of logical impossibility in its application to more complicated cases—if indeed he did not pick it up from the one case. Now of course this type of explanation does not yield a formal statement of necessary and sufficient conditions for the application of the notion concerned. So it does not fulfill one of the conditions which Quine seems to require of a satisfactory explanation. On the other hand, it does appear to fulfill the other. It breaks out of the family circle. The distinction in which we ultimately come to rest is that between not believing something and not understanding something; or between incredulity yielding to conviction, and incomprehension yielding to comprehension. It would be rash to maintain that *this* distinction does not need clarification; but it would be absurd to maintain that it does not exist. In the face of the availability of this informal type of explanation for the notions of the analyticity group, the fact that they have not received another type of explanation (which it is dubious whether *any* expressions *ever* receive) seems a wholly inadequate ground for the conclusion that the notions are pseudo-notions, that the expressions which purport to express them have no sense. To say this is not to deny that it would be philosophically desirable, and a proper object of philosophical endeavor, to find a more illuminating general characterization of the notions of this group than any that has been so far given. But the question of how, if at all, this can be done is quite irrelevant to the question of whether or not the expressions which belong to the circle have an intelligible use and mark genuine distinctions.

So far we have tried to show that sections 1 to 4 of Quine's article—the burden of which is that the notions of the analyticity group have not been satisfactorily explained—do not establish the extreme thesis for which he appears to be arguing. It remains to be seen whether sections 5 and 6, in which diagnosis and positive theory are offered, are any more successful. But before we turn to them, there are two further points worth making which arise out of the first two sections.

1. One concerns what Quine says about *definition* and *synonymy*. He remarks that definition does not, as some have supposed, "hold the key to synonymy and analyticity," since "definition—except in the extreme case of the explicitly conventional introduction of new notations—hinges on prior relations of synonymy." [7] But now consider what he says of these extreme cases. He says: "Here the definiendum becomes synonymous with the definiens simply because it has been expressly created for the purpose of being synonymous with the definiens. Here we have a really transparent case of synonymy created by definition; would that all species of synonymy were as intelligible." Now if we are to take these words of Quine seriously, then his position *as a whole* is incoherent. It is like the position of a man to whom we are trying to explain, say, the idea of one thing fitting into another thing, or two things fitting together, and who says: "I can understand what it means to say that one thing fits into another, or that two things fit together, in the case where one was specially made to fit the other; but I cannot understand what it means to say this in any other

[7] Page 27.

case." Perhaps we should not take Quine's words here too seriously. But if not, then we have the right to ask him exactly what state of affairs he thinks *is* brought about by explicit definition, what relation between expressions *is* established by this procedure, and why he thinks it unintelligble to suggest that the same (or a closely analogous) state of affairs, or relation, should exist in the absence of this procedure. For our part, we should be inclined to take Quine's words (or some of them) seriously, and reverse his conclusions; and maintain that the notion of synonymy by explicit convention would be unintelligible if the notion of synonymy by usage were not presupposed. There cannot be law where there is no custom, or rules where there are not practices (though perhaps we can understand better what a practice is by looking at a rule).

2. The second point arises out of a paragraph on page 32 of Quine's book. We quote:

> I do not know whether the statement "Everything green is extended" is analytic. Now does my indecision over this example really betray an incomplete understanding, an incomplete grasp, of the "meanings" of "green" and "extended"? I think not. The trouble is not with "green" or "extended," but with "analytic."

If, as Quine says, the trouble is with "analytic," then the trouble should doubtless disappear when "analytic" is removed. So let us remove it, and replace it with a word which Quine himself has contrasted favorably with "analytic" in respect of perspicuity—the word "true." Does the indecision at once disappear? We think not. The indecision over "analytic" (and equally, in this case, the indecision over "true") arises, of course, from a further indecision: viz., that which we feel when confronted with such questions as "Should we count a *point* of green light as *extended* or not?" As is frequent enough in such cases, the hesitation arises from the fact that the boundaries of application of words are not determined by usage in all possible directions. But the example Quine has chosen is particularly unfortunate for his thesis, in that it is only too evident that our hesitations are not *here* attributable to obscurities in "analytic." It would be possible to choose other examples in which we should hesitate between "analytic" and "synthetic" and have few qualms about "true." But no more in these cases than in the sample case does the hesitation necessarily imply any obscurity in the notion of analyticity; since the hesitation would be sufficiently accounted for by the same or a similar kind of indeterminacy in the relations between the words occurring within the statement about which the question, whether it is analytic or synthetic, is raised.

Let us now consider briefly Quine's positive theory of the relations between the statements we accept as true or reject as false on the one hand and the "experiences" in the light of which we do this accepting and rejecting on the other. This theory is boldly sketched rather than precisely stated.[8] We shall merely extract from it two assertions, one of which Quine clearly takes to be incompatible with acceptance of the distinction between analytic and synthetic

[8] Cf. pages 37–46.

statements, and the other of which he regards as barring one way to an explanation of that distinction. We shall seek to show that the first assertion is not incompatible with acceptance of the distinction, but is, on the contrary, most intelligibly interpreted in a way quite consistent with it, and that the second assertion leaves the way open to just the kind of explanation which Quine thinks it precludes. The two assertions are the following:

1. It is an illusion to suppose that there is any class of accepted statements the members of which are in principle "immune from revision" in the light of experience, i.e., any that we accept as true and must continue to accept as true whatever happens.

2. It is an illusion to suppose that an individual statement, taken in isolation from its fellows, can admit of confirmation or disconfirmation at all. There is no particular statement such that a particular experience or set of experiences decides once for all whether that statement is true or false, independently of our attitudes to all other statements.

The apparent connection between these two doctrines may be summed up as follows. Whatever our experience may be, it is in principle possible to hold on to, or reject, any particular statement we like, so long as we are prepared to make extensive enough revisions elsewhere in our system of beliefs. In practice our choices are governed largely by considerations of convenience: we wish our system to be as simple as possible, but we also wish disturbances to it, as it exists, to be as small as possible.

The apparent relevance of these doctrines to the analytic-synthetic distinction is obvious in the first case, less so in the second.

1. Since it is an illusion to suppose that the characteristic of immunity in principle from revision, come what may, belongs, or could belong, to any statement, it is an illusion to suppose that there is a distinction to be drawn between statements which possess this characteristic and statements which lack it. Yet, Quine suggests, this is precisely the distinction which those who use the terms "analytic" and "synthetic" suppose themselves to be drawing. Quine's view would perhaps also be (though he does not explicitly say this in the article under consideration) that those who believe in the distinction are inclined at least sometimes to mistake the characteristic of strongly resisting revision (which belongs to beliefs very centrally situated in the system) for the mythical characteristic of total immunity from revision.

2. The connection between the second doctrine and the analytic-synthetic distinction runs, according to Quine, through the verification theory of meaning. He says: "If the verification theory can be accepted as an adequate account of statement synonymy, the notion of analyticity is saved after all." [9] For, in the first place, two statements might be said to be synonymous if and only if any experiences which contribute to, or detract from, the confirmation of one contribute to, or detract from, the confirmation of the other, to the same degree; and, in the second place, synonymy could be used to explain analyticity. But, Quine seems to argue, acceptance of any such account of synonymy can only rest on the mistaken belief that individual statements, taken in isolation from their fellows, can admit of confirmation or disconfirmation at all. As soon as we

[9] Page 38.

give up the idea of a set of experiential truth-conditions for each statement taken separately, we must give up the idea of explaining synonymy in terms of identity of such sets.

Now to show that the relations between these doctrines and the analytic-synthetic distinction are not as Quine supposes. Let us take the second doctrine first. It is easy to see that acceptance of the second doctrine would not compel one to abandon, but only to revise, the suggested explanation of synonymy. Quine does not deny that individual statements are regarded as confirmed or disconfirmed, are in fact rejected or accepted, in the light of experience. He denies only that these relations between single statments and experience hold independently of our attitudes to *other* statements. He means that experience can confirm or disconfirm an individual statement, only given certain assumptions about the truth or falsity of other statements. When we are faced with a "recalcitrant experience," he says, we always have a choice of what statements to amend. What we have to renounce is determined by what we are anxious to keep. This view, however, requires only a slight modification of the definition of statement-synonymy in terms of confirmation and disconfirmation. All we have to say now is that two statements are synonymous if and only if any experiences which, *on certain assumptions about the truth-values of other statements,* confirm or disconfirm one of the pair, also, *on the same assumptions,* confirm or disconfirm the other to the same degree. More generally, Quine wishes to substitute for what he conceives to be an oversimple picture of the confirmation-relations between particular statements and particular experiences, the idea of a looser relation which he calls "germaneness" (p. 43). But however loosely "germaneness" is to be understood, it would apparently continue to make sense to speak of two statements as standing in the same germaneness-relation to the same particular experiences. So Quine's views are not only consistent with, but even suggest, an amended account of statement-synonymy along these lines. We are not, of course, concerned to defend such an account, or even to state it with any precision. We are only concerned to show that acceptance of Quine's doctrine of empirical confirmation does not, as he says it does, entail giving up the attempt to define statement-synonymy in terms of confirmation.

Now for the doctrine that there is no statement which is in principle immune from revision, no statement which might not be given up in the face of experience. Acceptance of this doctrine is quite consistent with adherence to the distinction between analytic and synthetic statements. Only, the adherent of *this* distinction must also insist on another; on the distinction between that kind of giving up which consists in merely admitting falsity, and that kind of giving up which involves changing or dropping a concept or set of concepts. Any form of words at one time held to express something true may, no doubt, at another time, come to be held to express something false. But it is not only philosophers who would distinguish between the case where this happens as the result of a change of opinion solely as to matters of fact, and the case where this happens at least partly as a result of a shift in the sense of the words. Where such a shift in the sense of the words is a necessary condition of the change in truth-value, then the adherent of the distinction will say that the form of words in question changes from expressing an analytic statement to expressing a synthetic statement. We are not now concerned, or called upon, to elaborate an adequate theory of conceptual revision, any more than we were called upon, just now, to elaborate an adequate theory of synonymy. If we can make sense of the idea that the same form of words, taken in one way (or bearing one sense), may express something true, and taken in another way (or bearing another sense), may express something false, then we can make sense of the idea of conceptual revision. And if we can make sense of this idea, then we can perfectly well preserve the distinction between the analytic and the synthetic, while conceding to Quine the revisability-in-principle of everything we say. As for the idea that the same form of words, taken in different ways, may bear different senses and perhaps be used to say things with different truth-values, the onus of showing that this is somehow a mistaken or confused idea rests squarely on Quine. The point of substance (or one of them) that Quine is making, by this emphasis on revisability, is that there is no absolute necessity about the adoption or use of any conceptual scheme whatever, or, more narrowly and in terms that he would reject, that there is no analytic proposition such that we *must* have linguistic forms bearing just the sense required to express that proposition. But it is one thing to admit this, and quite another thing to say that there are no necessities within any conceptual scheme we adopt or use, or, more narrowly again, that there are no linguistic forms which do express analytic propositions.

The adherent of the analytic-synthetic distinction may go further and admit that there may be cases (particularly perhaps in the field of science) where it would be pointless to press the question whether a change in the attributed truth-value of a statement represented a conceptual revision or not, and correspondingly pointless to press the analytic-synthetic distinction. We cannot quote such cases, but this inability may well be the result of ignorance of the sciences. In any case, the existence, if they do exist, of statements about which it is pointless to press the question whether they are analytic or synthetic, does not entail the nonexistence of statements which are clearly classifiable in one or other of these ways and of statements our hesitation over which has different sources, such as the possibility of alternative interpretations of the linguistic forms in which they are expressed.

This concludes our examination of Quine's article. It will be evident that our purpose has been wholly negative. We have aimed to show merely that Quine's case against the existence of the analytic-synthetic distinction is not made out. His article has two parts. In one of them, the notions of the analyticity group are criticized on the ground that they have not been adequately explained. In the other, a positive theory of truth is outlined, purporting to be incompatible with views to which believers in the analytic-synthetic distinction either must be, or are likely to be, committed. In fact, we have contended, no single point is established which those who accept the notions of the analyticity group would feel any strain in accommodating in their own system of beliefs. This is not to deny that many of the points raised are of the first importance in connection with the problem of giving a satisfactory general account of analyticity and related concepts. We are here only criticizing the contention that these points justify the rejection, as illusory, of the analytic-synthetic distinction and the notions which belong to the same family.

17

J. L. Austin OTHER MINDS

"Other Minds" was Austin's contribution to a symposium of the Aristotelian Society held in 1946. Taking up Wisdom's question of how we can ever know that another person is having a certain emotion, Austin discusses in great detail the various ways in which we use the word "know." Of special importance is the analogy he draws between "I know" statements and "I promise" statements in ordinary speech.

For further reading on some of the topics discussed in this selection see:

Austin, J.: *How to Do Things with Words.*
Barnes, W.H.F.: "Knowing," *The Philosophical Review*, January, 1963.
Harrison, J.: "Knowing and Promising," *Mind*, October, 1962.

I feel that I agree with much, and especially with the more important parts, of what Mr. Wisdom has written, both in his present paper and in his beneficial series of articles on "Other Minds" and other matters. I feel ruefully sure, also, that one must be at least one sort of fool to rush in over ground so well trodden by the angels. At best I can hope only to make a contribution to one part of the problem, where it seems that a little more industry still might be of service. I could only wish it was a more central part. In fact, however, I did find myself unable to approach the centre while still bogged down on the periphery. And Mr. Wisdom himself may perhaps be sympathetic towards a policy of splitting hairs to save starting them.

Mr. Wisdom, no doubt correctly, takes the "Predicament" to be brought on by such questions as "How do we know that another man is angry?" He also cites other forms of the question—"Do we (ever) know?," "Can we know?," "How can we know?" the thoughts, feelings, sensations, mind, etc., of another creature, and so forth. But it seems likely that each of these further questions is rather different from the first, which alone has been enough to keep me preoccupied, and to which I shall stick.

From *Aristotelian Society Supplementary*, vol. XX (1946). Reprinted by courtesy of the editor of the Aristotelian Society.

Mr. Wisdom's method is to go on to ask: *Is it like the way in which we know* that a kettle is boiling, or that there is a tea-party next door, or the weight of thistledown? But it seemed to me that perhaps, as he went on, he was not giving an altogether accurate account (perhaps only because too cursory a one) of what we should say if asked "How do you know?" these things. For example, in the case of the tea-party, to say we knew of it "by analogy" would at best be a very sophisticated answer (and one to which some sophisticates might prefer the phrase "by induction"), while in addition it seems incorrect because we don't, I think, claim to *know* by analogy, but only to *argue* by analogy. Hence I was led on to consider what sort of thing does actually happen when ordinary people are asked "How do you know?"

Much depends, obviously, on the sort of item it is about which we are being asked "How do you know?" and there are bound to be many kinds of case that I shall not cover at all, or not in detail. The sort of statement which seems simplest, and at the same time not, on the face of it, unlike "He is angry," in such a statement as "That is a goldfinch" ("The kettle is boiling")—a statement of particular, current, empirical fact. This is the sort of statement on making which we are liable to be asked "How do you know?" and the sort that, at least sometimes, we say we don't know, but only believe. It may serve for a stalking-horse as well as another.

When we make an assertion such as "There is a goldfinch in the garden" or "He is angry," there is a sense in which we imply that we are sure of it or know it ("But I took it you *knew*," said reproachfully), though what we imply, in a similar sense and more strictly, is only that we *believe* it. On making such an assertion, therefore, we are directly exposed to the questions (1) "Do you *know* there is?" "Do you *know* he is?" and (2) "*How* do you know?" If in answer to the first question we reply "Yes," we may then be asked the second question, and even the first question alone is commonly taken as an invitation to state not merely *whether* but also *how* we know. But on the other hand, we may well reply "No" in answer to the first question: we may say "No, but I think there is," "No, but I believe he is." For the implication that I know or am sure is not strict: we are not all (terribly or sufficiently) strictly brought up. If we do this, then we are exposed to the question, which might also have been put to us without preliminaries, "Why do you believe that?" (or "What makes you think so?," "What induces you to suppose so?," etc.).

There is a singular difference between the two forms of challenge: "*How* do you know?" and "*Why* do you believe?" We seem never to ask "*Why* do you know?" or "*How* do you believe?" And in this, as well as in other respects to be noticed later, not merely such other words as "suppose," "assume," &c., but also the expressions "be sure" and "be certain," follow the example of "believe," not that of "know."

Either question, "How do you know?" or "Why do you believe?," may well asked only out of respectful curiosity, from a genuine desire to learn. But again, they may both be asked as *pointed* questions, and, when they are so, a further difference comes out. "How do you know?" suggests that perhaps you *don't* know it at all, whereas "Why do you believe?" suggests that perhaps you *oughtn't* to believe it. There is no suggestion [1] that you *ought* not to know or that you *don't* believe it. If the answer to "How do you know?" or to "Why do you believe?" is considered unsatisfactory by the challenger, he proceeds rather differently in the two cases. His next riposte will be, on the one hand, something such as "Then you *don't* know any such thing," or "But that doesn't prove it: in that case you don't really know it at all," and on the other hand, something such as "That's very poor evidence to go on: you oughtn't to believe it on the strength of that alone." [2]

The "existence" of your alleged belief is not challenged, but the "existence" of your alleged knowledge *is* challenged. If we like to say that "I believe," and likewise "I am sure" and "I am certain," are descriptions of subjective mental or cognitive states or attitudes, or what not, then "I know" is not that, or at least not merely that: it functions differently in talking.

"But of course," it will be said, " 'I know' is obviously more than that, more than a description of my own state. If I *know*, I *can't be wrong*. You can always show I don't know by showing I am wrong, or may be wrong, or that I didn't know by showing that I might have been wrong. *That's* the way in which knowing differs even from being as certain as can be." This must be considered in due course, but first we should consider the types of answer that may be given in answer to the question "How do you know?"

Suppose I have said "There's a bittern at the bottom of the garden," and you ask "How do you know?" my reply may take very different forms:

(*a*) I was brought up in the fens
(*b*) I heard it
(*c*) The keeper reported it
(*d*) By its booming
(*e*) From the booming noise
(*f*) Because it is booming.

We may say, roughly, that the first three are answers to the questions "How do you come to know?," "How are you in a position to know?," or "How do *you* know?" understood in different ways: while the other three are answers to "How can you tell?" understood in different ways. That is, I may take you to have been asking:

1. How do I come to be in a position to know about bitterns?
2. How do I come to be in a position to say there's a bittern here and now?
3. How do (can) I tell bitterns?
4. How do (can) I tell the thing here and now as a bittern?

[1] But in special senses and cases, there is—for example, if someone has announced some top secret information, we can ask, "How do *you* know?," nastily.

[2] An interesting variant in the case of knowing would be "You *oughtn't to say* (you've no business to say) you know it at all." But of course this is only superficially similar to "You oughtn't to believe it"; you ought *to say* you believe it, if you do believe it, however poor the evidence.

The implication is that in order to know this is a bittern, I must have:

1. been trained in an environment where I could become familiar with bitterns
2. had a certain opportunity in the current case
3. learned to recognize or tell bitterns
4. succeeded in recognizing or telling this as a bittern.

1 and 2 mean that my experiences must have been of certain kinds, that I must have had certain opportunities: 3 and 4 mean that I must have exerted a certain kind and amount of acumen.[3]

The questions raised in 1 and 3 concern our *past* experiences, our opportunities and our activities in learning to discriminate or discern, and, bound up with both, the correctness or otherwise of the linguistic usages we have acquired. Upon these earlier experiences depends how *well* we know things, just as, in different but cognate cases of "knowing," it is upon earlier experience that it depends how *thoroughly* or how *intimately* we know: we know a person by sight or intimately, a town inside out, a proof backwards, a job in every detail, a poem word for word, a Frenchman when we see one. "He doesn't know what love (real hunger) is" means he hasn't had enough experience to be able to recognize it and to distinguish it from other things slightly like it. According to how well I know an item, and according to the kind of item it is, I can recognize it, describe it, reproduce it, draw it, recite it, apply it, and so forth. Statements like "I know *very well* he isn't angry" or "You know *very well* that isn't calico," though of course about the current case, ascribe the excellence of the knowledge to past experience, as does the general expression "You are old enough to know better."[4]

By contrast, the questions raised in 2 and 4 concern the circumstances of the current case. Here we can ask "How *definitely* do you know?" You may know it for certain, quite positively, officially, on his own authority, from unimpeachable sources, only indirectly, and so forth.

Some of the answers to the question "How do you know?" are, oddly enough, described as "reasons for knowing" or "reasons to know," or even sometimes as "reasons why I know," despite the fact that we do not ask "Why do you know?" But now surely, according to the Dictionary, "reasons" should be given in answer to the question "Why?" just as we do in fact give reasons for believing in answer to the question "Why do you believe?" However there is a distinction

---

[3] "I know, I *know*, I've seen it a hundred times, don't keep on telling me" complains of a superabundance of opportunity: "knowing a hawk from a handsaw" lays down a minimum of acumen in recognition or classification. "As well as I know my own name" is said to typify something I *must* have experienced and *must* have learned to discriminate.

[4] The adverbs that can be inserted in "How . . . do you know?" are few in number and fall into still fewer classes. There is practically no overlap with those that can be inserted in "How . . . do you believe?" (firmly, sincerely, genuinely, etc.).

to be drawn here. "How do you know that IG Farben worked for war?" "I have every reason to know: I served on the investigating commission": here, giving my reasons for knowing is stating how I come to be in a position to know. In the same way we use the expressions "I know *because* I saw him do it" or "I know *because* I looked it up only ten minutes ago": these are similar to "So it is: it *is* plutonium. How did you know?" "I did quite a bit of physics at school before I took up philology," or to "I ought to know: I was standing only a couple of yards away." Reasons for *believing* on the other hand are normally quite a different affair (a recital of symptoms, arguments in support, and so forth), though there are cases where we do give as reasons for believing our having been in a position in which we could get good evidence: "Why do you believe he was lying?" "I was watching him very closely."

Among the cases where we give our reasons for knowing things, a special and important class is formed by those where we cite authorities. If asked "How do you know the election is today?," I am apt to reply "I read it in *The Times*," and if asked "How do you know the Persians were defeated at Marathon?" I am apt to reply "Herodotus expressly states that they were." In these cases "know" is correctly used: we know "at second hand" when we can cite an authority who was in a position to know (possibly himself also only at second hand).[5] The statement of an authority makes me aware of something, enables me to know something, which I shouldn't otherwise have known. It is a source of knowledge. In many cases, we contrast such reasons for knowing with other reasons for believing the very same thing: "Even if we didn't know it, even if he hadn't confessed, the evidence against him would be enough to hang him."

It is evident, of course, that this sort of "knowledge" is "liable to be wrong," owing to the unreliability of human testimony (bias, mistake, lying, exaggeration, etc.). Nevertheless, the occurrence of a piece of human testimony radically alters the situation. We say "We shall never know what Caesar's feelings were on the field of the battle of Philippi," because he did not pen an account of them: if he *had*, then to say "We shall never know" won't do in the same way, even though we may still perhaps find reason to say "It doesn't read very plausibly: we shall never *really* know the *truth*" and so on. Naturally, we are judicious: we don't say we know (at second hand) if there is any special reason to doubt the testimony: but there has to be *some* reason. It is fundamental in talking (as in other matters) that we are entitled to trust others, except in so far as there is some concrete reason to distrust them. Believing persons, accepting testimony, is the, or one main, point of talking. We don't play (competitive) games except in the faith that our opponent is trying to win: if he isn't, it isn't

---

[5] Knowing at second hand, or on authority, is not the same as "knowing indirectly," whatever precisely that difficult and perhaps artificial expression may mean. If a murderer "confesses," then, whatever our opinion of the worth of the "confession," we cannot say that "we (only) know indirectly that he did it," nor can we so speak when a witness, reliable or unreliable, has stated that he saw the man do it. Consequently, it is not correct, either, to say that the murderer himself knows "directly" that he did it, whatever precisely "knowing directly" may mean.

a game, but something different. So we don't talk with people (descriptively) except in the faith that they are trying to convey information.[6]

It is now time to turn to the question "How can you tell?," i.e. to senses 2 and 4 of the question "How do you know?" If you have asked "How do you know it's a goldfinch?" then I may reply "From its behaviour," "By its markings," or, in more detail, "By its red head," "From its eating thistles." That is, I indicate, or to some extent set out with some degree of precision, those features of the situation which enable me to recognize it as one to be described in the way I did describe it. Thereupon you may still object in several ways to my saying it's a goldfinch, without in the least "disputing my facts," which is a further stage to be dealt with later. You may object:

1. But goldfinches *don't* have red heads
1a. But that's not a *goldfinch*. From your own description I can recognize it as a gold*crest*
2. But that's not enough: plenty of other birds have red heads. What you say doesn't prove it. For all you know, it may be a woodpecker.

Objections 1 and 1a claim that, in one way or another, I am evidently unable to recognize goldfinches. It may be 1a—that I have not learned the right (customary, popular, official) name to apply to the creature ("Who taught you to use the word 'goldfinch'?") :[7] or it may be that my powers of discernment, and consequently of classification, have never been brought sharply to bear in these matters, so that I remain confused as to how to tell the various species of small British bird. Or, of course, it may be a bit of both. In making this sort of accusation, you would perhaps tend not so much to use the expression "You don't know" or "You oughtn't to say you know" as, rather, "But that *isn't* a goldfinch (*goldfinch*)," or "Then you're wrong to call it a goldfinch." But still, if asked, you would of course deny the statement that I do know it is a goldfinch.

It is in the case of objection 2 that you would be more inclined to say right out "Then you don't know." Because it doesn't prove it, it's not enough to prove it. Several important points come out here:

(a) If you say "That's not enough," then you must have in mind some more or less definite lack. "To be a goldfinch, besides having a red head it must also have the characteristic eye-markings": or "How do you know it isn't a woodpecker? Woodpeckers have red heads too." If there is no definite lack,

---

[6] Reliance on the authority of others is fundamental, too, in various special matters, for example, for corroboration and for the correctness of our own use of words, which we learn from others.

[7] Misnaming is not a trivial or laughing matter. If I misname I shall mislead others, and I shall also misunderstand information given by others to me. "Of course I knew all about his condition perfectly, but I never realized that was *diabetes*: I thought it was cancer, and all the books agree that's incurable: if I'd only known is was diabetes, I should have thought of insulin at once." Knowing *what a thing is* is, to an important extent, knowing what the name for it, and the right name for it, is.

which you are at least prepared to specify on being pressed, then it's silly (outrageous) just to go on saying "That's not enough."

(*b*) Enough is enough: it doesn't mean everything. Enough means enough to show that (within reason, and for present intents and purposes) it "can't" be anything else, there is no room for an alternative, competing, description of it. It does *not* mean, for example, enough to show it isn't a *stuffed* goldfinch.

(*c*) "*From* its red head," given as an answer to "How do you know?" requires careful consideration: in particular it differs very materially from "*Because* it has a red head," which is also sometimes given as an answer to "How do you know?," and is commonly given as an answer to "Why do you believe?" It is much more akin to such obviously "vague" replies as "From its markings" or "From its behaviour" than at first appears. Our claim, in saying we know (i.e. that we can tell) is to *recognize:* and recognizing, at least in this sort of case, consists in seeing, or otherwise sensing, a feature or features which we are sure are similar to something noted (and usually named) before, on some earlier occasion in our experience. But, this that we see, or otherwise sense, is not necessarily *describable in words,* still less describable in detail, and in non-committal words, and by anybody you please. Nearly everybody can recognize a surly look or the smell of tar, but few can describe them non-committally, i.e. otherwise than as "surly" or "of tar": many can recognize, and "with certainty," ports of different vintages, models by different fashion houses, shades of green, motor-car makes from behind, and so forth, without being able to say "*how* they recognize them," i.e. without being able to "be more specific about it"— they can only say they can tell "by the taste," "from the cut," and so on. So, when I say I can tell the bird "from its red head," or that I know a friend "by his nose," I imply that there is something *peculiar* about the red head or the nose, something peculiar to goldfinches or to him, by which you can (always) tell them or him. In view of the fewness and crudeness of the classificatory words in any language compared with the infinite number of features which are recognized, or which could be picked out and recognized, in our experience, it is small wonder that we often and often fall back on the phrases beginning with "from" and "by," and that we are not able to *say,* further and precisely, *how* we can tell. Often we know things quite well, while scarcely able at all to say "from" what we know them, let alone what there is so very special about them. Any answer beginning "From" or "By" has, intentionally, this saving "vagueness." But on the contrary, an answer beginning "Because" is dangerously definite. When I say I know it's a goldfinch "Because it has a red head," that implies that all I have noted, or needed to note, about it is that its head is red (nothing special or peculiar about the shade, shape, &c. of the patch): so that I imply that there is no other small British bird that has any sort of red head except the goldfinch.

(*d*) Whenever I say I know, I am always liable to be taken to claim that, in a certain sense appropriate to the kind of statement (and to present intents and purposes), I am able to *prove* it. In the present, very common, type of case, "proving" seems to mean stating what are the features of the current case which are enough to constitute it one which is correctly describable in the way we have described it, and not in any other way relevantly variant. Generally speaking, cases where I can "prove" are cases where we use the "because" formula: cases where we "know but can't prove" are cases where we take refuge in the "from" or "by" formula.

I believe that the points so far raised are those most genuinely and normally raised by the question "How do you know?" But there are other, further, questions sometimes raised under the same rubric, and especially by philosophers, which may be thought more important. These are the worries about "reality" and about being "sure and certain."

Up to now, in challenging me with the question "How do you know?," you are not taken to have *queried my credentials as stated*, though you have asked what they were: nor have you *disputed my facts* (the facts on which I am relying to prove it is a goldfinch), though you have asked me to detail them. It is this further sort of challenge that may now be made, a challenge as to the *reliability* of our alleged "credentials" and our alleged "facts." You may ask:

1. But do you know it's a *real* goldfinch? How do you know you're not dreaming? Or after all, mightn't it be a stuffed one? And is the head really red? Couldn't it have been dyed, or isn't there perhaps an odd light reflected on it?

2. But are you certain it's the *right* red for a goldfinch? Are you quite sure it isn't too orange? Isn't it perhaps rather too strident a note for a bittern?

These two sorts of worry are distinct, though very probably they can be combined or confused, or may run into one another: e.g. "Are you sure it's really red?" may mean "Are you sure it isn't orange?" or again "Are you sure it isn't just the peculiar light?"

1. REALITY

If you ask me, "How do you know it's a real stick?" "How do you know it's really bent?" ("Are you sure he's really angry?"), then you are querying my credentials or my facts (it's often uncertain which) in a certain special way. In various *special, recognized* ways, depending essentially upon the nature of the matter which I have announced myself to know, either my current experiencing or the item currently under consideration (or uncertain which) may be abnormal, *phoney*. Either I myself may be dreaming, or in delirium, or under the influence of mescal, etc.: or else the item may be stuffed, painted, dummy, artificial, trick, freak, toy, assumed, feigned, etc.: or else again there's an uncertainty (it's left open) whether *I* am to blame or *it* is—mirages, mirror images, odd lighting effects, etc.

These doubts are all to be allayed by means of recognized procedures (more or less roughly recognized, of course), appropriate to the particular type of case. There are recognized ways of distinguishing between dreaming and waking (how otherwise should we know how to use and to contrast the words?), and of deciding whether a thing is stuffed or live, and so forth. The doubt or question "But is it a *real* one?" has always (*must* have) a special basis, there must be some "reason for suggesting" that it isn't real, in the sense of some specific way, or limited number of specific ways, in which it is suggested that this experience or item may be phoney. Sometimes (usually) the context makes it clear what the suggestion is: the goldfinch might be stuffed but there's no suggestion that it's a mirage, the oasis might be a mirage but there's no suggestion it might be stuffed. If the context doesn't make it clear, then I am entitled to ask "How do you mean? Do you mean it may be stuffed or what? *What are you suggesting?*" The wile of the metaphysician consists in asking "Is it a real table?" (a kind of object which has no obvious way of being phoney) and not specifying or limiting what may be wrong with it, so that I feel at a loss "how to prove" it *is* a real one.[8] It is the use of the word "real" in this manner that leads us on to the supposition that "real" has a single meaning ("the real world" "material objects"), and that a highly profound and puzzling one. Instead, we should insist always on specifying with what "real" is being contrasted—"not what" I shall have to show it is, in order to show it is "real": and then usually we shall find some specific, less fatal, word, appropriate to the particular case, to substitute for "real."

Knowing it's a "real" goldfinch isn't in question in the ordinary case when I say I know it's a goldfinch: reasonable precautions only are taken. But when it *is* called in question, in *special* cases, then I make sure it's a real goldfinch in ways essentially similar to those in which I made sure it was a goldfinch, though corroboration by other witnesses plays a specially important part in some cases. Once again the precautions cannot be more than reasonable, relative to current intents and purposes. And once again, in the special cases just as in the ordinary cases, two further conditions hold good:

(*a*) I don't by any means *always* know whether it's one or not. It may fly away before I have a chance of testing it, or of inspecting it thoroughly enough. This is simple enough: yet some are prone to argue that because I *sometimes* don't know or can't discover, I *never* can.

(*b*) "Being sure it's real" is no more proof against miracles or outrages of nature than anything else is or, *sub specie humanitatis*, can be. If we have made sure it's a goldfinch, and a real goldfinch, and then in the future it does something outrageous (explodes, quotes Mrs. Woolf, or what not), we don't say we were wrong to say it was a goldfinch, *we don't know what to say*. Words literally fail us: "What would you have said?" "What are we to say now?" "What would *you* say?" When I have made sure it's a real goldfinch (not stuffed, corroborated by the disinterested, etc.) then I am *not* "predicting" in saying it's a real goldfinch, and in a very good sense I can't be proved wrong whatever happens. It seems a serious mistake to suppose that language (or most language, language about real things) is "predictive" in such a way that the future can always prove it wrong. What the future *can* always do, is to make us *revise our ideas* about goldfinches or real goldfinches or anything else.

Perhaps the normal procedure of language could be schematized as fol-

---

[8] Conjurers, too, trade on this. "Will some gentleman kindly satisfy himself that this is a perfectly ordinary hat?" This leaves us baffled and uneasy: sheepishly we agree that it seems all right, while conscious that we have not the least idea what to guard against.

iows. First, it is arranged that, on experiencing a complex of features C, then we are to say "This is C" or "This is a C." Then subsequently, the occurrence either of the whole of C or of a significant and characteristic part of it is, on one or many occasions, accompanied or followed in definite circumstances by another special and distinctive feature or complex of features, which makes it seem desirable to revise our ideas: so that we draw a distinction between "This looks like a C, but in fact is only a dummy, etc." and "This is a real C (live, genuine, etc.)." *Henceforward,* we can only ascertain that it's a *real* C by ascertaining that the special feature or complex of features is present in the appropriate circumstances. The old expression "This is a C" will tend as heretofore to fail to draw any distinction between "real, live, etc." and "dummy, stuffed, etc." If the special distinctive feature is one which does not have to manifest itself in *any* definite circumstances (on application of some specific test, after some limited lapse of time, etc.) then it is not a suitable feature on which to base a distinction between "real" and "dummy, imaginary, etc." All we can then do is to say "Some C's are and some aren't, some do and some don't: and it may be very interesting or important whether they are or aren't, whether they do or don't, but they're all C's, real C's, just the same." [9] Now if the special feature is one which must appear in (more or less) definite circumstances, then "This is a real C" is not necessarily predictive: we can, in favourable cases, make sure of it. [10]

2. SURENESS AND CERTAINTY

The other way of querying my credentials and proofs ("Are you sure it's the *right* red?") is quite different. Here we come up against Mr. Wisdom's views on "the peculiarity of a man's knowledge of his own sensations," for which he refers us to "Other Minds VII" (*Mind,* vol. lii, n.s., no. 207), a passage with which I find I disagree.

Mr. Wisdom there says that, excluding from consideration cases like "being in love" and other cases which "involve prediction," and considering statements like "I am in pain" which, in the requisite sense, do *not* involve prediction, then a man *cannot* "be wrong" in making them, in the most favoured sense of being wrong: that is, though it is of course possible for him to *lie* (so that "I am in pain" may be false), and though it is also possible for him to *misname,* i.e. to use the word "pawn," say, instead of "pain," which would be liable to mislead others but would not mislead himself, either because he regularly uses "pawn" for "pain" or because the use was a momentary aberration, as when I call John "Albert" while knowing him quite well to be John—though it is possible for him to be "wrong" in these two senses, it is not possible for him to be wrong in the most favoured sense. He says again that, with this class of statement

[9] The awkwardness about some snarks being boojums.

[10] Sometimes, on the basis of the new special feature, we distinguish, not between "C's" and "real C's," but rather between C's and D's. There is a reason for choosing the one procedure rather than the other: all cases where we use the "real" formula exhibit (complicated and serpentine) likenesses, as do all cases where we use "proper," a word which behaves in many ways like "real," and is no less nor more profound.

(elsewhere called "sense-statements"), to know directly that one is in pain is "to say that one is, and to say it on the basis of being in pain": and again, that the peculiarity of sense-statements lies in the fact that "when they are correct and made by X, then X knows they are correct."

This seems to me mistaken, though it is a view that, in more or less subtle forms, has been the basis of a very great deal of philosophy. It is perhaps the original sin (Berkeley's apple, the tree in the quad) by which the philosopher casts himself out from the garden of the world we live in.

Very clearly detailed, this is the view that, at least and only in a certain favoured type of case, I can "say what I see (or otherwise sense)" almost quite literally. On this view, if I were to say "Here is something red," then I might be held to imply or to state that it is really a red thing, a thing which would appear red in a standard light, or to other people, or tomorrow too, and perhaps even more besides: all of which "involves prediction" (if not also a metaphysical substratum). Even if I were to say "Here is something which looks red," I might still be held to imply or to state that it looks red to others also, and so forth. If, however, I confine myself to stating "Here is something that looks red to me now," then at last I can't be wrong (in the most favoured sense).

However, there is an ambiguity in "something that looks red to me now." Perhaps this can be brought out by italics, though it is not really so much a matter of emphasis as of tone and expression, of confidence and hesitancy. Contrast "Here is something that (definitely) *looks to me* (anyhow) red" with "Here is something that looks to me (something like) *red* (I should say)." In the former case I am quite confident that, however it may look to others, whatever it may "really be," etc., it certainly does look red to me at the moment. In the other case I'm not confident at all: it looks reddish, but I've never seen anything quite like it before, I can't quite describe it—or, I'm not very good at recognizing colours, I never feel quite happy about them, I've constantly been caught out about them. Of course, this sounds silly in the case of "red": red is so *very* obvious, we all know red when we see it, it's unmistakable.[11] Cases where we should not feel happy about red are not easy (though not impossible) to find. But take "magenta": "It looks rather like magenta to me—but then I wouldn't be too sure about distinguishing magenta from mauve or from heliotrope. Of course I know in a way it's purplish, but I don't really know whether to say it's magenta or not: I just can't be sure." Here, I am not interested in ruling out consideration of how it looks to others (looks to *me*) or considerations about what its *real* colour is (*looks*): what I am ruling out is *my being sure or certain* what it looks to me. Take tastes, or take sounds: these are so much better as examples than colours, because we never feel so happy with our other senses as with our eyesight. Any description of a taste or sound or smell (or colour) or of a feeling, involves (is) saying that it is like one or some that we have experienced before: any descriptive word is classificatory, involves recognition and in that sense memory, and only when we use such words (or names or descriptions, which come down to the same) are we knowing anything, or believing anything. But memory and recognition are often uncertain and unreliable.

[11] And yet she always *thought* his shirt was white until she saw it against Tommy's Persil-washed one.

Two rather different ways of being hesitant may be distinguished.

(a) Let us take the case where we are tasting a certain taste. We may say "I simply don't know what it is: I've never tasted anything remotely like it before. ... No, it's no use: the more I think about it the more confused I get: it's perfectly distinct and perfectly distinctive, quite unique in my experience." This illustrates the case where I can find nothing in my past experience with which to compare the current case: I'm certain it's not appreciably like anything I ever tasted before, not sufficiently like anything I know to merit the same description. This case, though distinguishable enough, shades off into the more common type of case where I'm not quite certain, or only fairly certain, or practically certain, that it's the taste of, say, laurel. In all such cases, I am endeavouring to recognize the current item by searching in my past experience for something like it, some likeness in virtue of which it deserves, more or less positively, to be described by the same descriptive word:[12] and I am meeting with varying degrees of success.

(b) The other case is different, though it very naturally combines itself with the first. Here, what I try to do is to *savour* the current experience, to *peer* at it, to sense it vividly. I'm not sure it *is* the taste of pineapple: isn't there perhaps just *something* about it, a tang, a bite, a lack of bite, a cloying sensation, which isn't *quite* right for pineapple? Isn't there perhaps just a peculiar hint of green, which would rule out mauve and would hardly do for heliotrope? Or perhaps it is faintly odd: I must look more intently, scan it over and over: maybe just possibly there is a suggestion of an unnatural shimmer, so that it doesn't look quite like ordinary water. There is a lack of sharpness in what we actually sense, which is to be cured not, or not merely, by thinking, but by acuter discernment, by sensory discrimination (though it is of course true that thinking of other, and more pronounced, cases in our past experience can and does assist our powers of discrimination).[13]

Cases (a) and (b) alike, and perhaps usually together, lead to our being not quite sure or certain what it is, what to say, how to describe it: what our feelings are, whether the tickling is painful exactly, whether I'm really what you'd call angry with him or only something rather like it. The hesitation is of course, in a sense, over misnaming: but I am not so much or merely worried about possibly misleading others as about misleading myself (the most favoured sense of being wrong). I should suggest that the two expressions "being certain" and "being sure," though from the nature of the case they are often used indiscriminately, have a tendency to refer to cases (a) and (b) respectively. "Being certain" tends to indicate confidence in our memories and our past discernment, "being sure" to indicate confidence in the current perception. Perhaps this comes out in our use of the concessives "to be sure" and "certainly," and in our use of such phrases as "certainly not" and "surely not." But it may be unwise to chivvy language beyond the coarser nuances.

[12] Or, of course, related to it in some other way than by "similarity" (in any ordinary sense of "similarity"), which is yet sufficient reason for describing it by the same word.

[13] This appears to cover cases of dull or careless or uninstructed perception, as opposed to cases of diseased or drugged perception.

It may be said that, even when I don't know exactly how to describe it, I nevertheless *know* that I *think* (and roughly how confidently I think) it is mauve So I do know *something*. But this is irrelevant: I *don't* know it's mauve, that it definitely looks to me now mauve. Besides, there are cases where I really don't know what I think: I'm completely baffled by it.

Of course, there are any number of "sense-statements" about which I can be, and am, completely sure. In ordinary cases ordinary men are nearly always certain when a thing looks red (or reddish, or anyhow reddish rather than green-ish), or when they're in pain (except when that's rather difficult to say, as when they're being tickled): in ordinary cases an expert, a dyer or a dress designer, will be quite sure when something looks (to him in the present light) reseda green or nigger brown, though those who are not experts will not be so sure. Nearly always, if not quite always, we can be quite, or pretty, sure if we take refuge in a sufficiently *rough* description of the sensation: roughness and sureness tend to vary inversely. But the less rough descriptions, just as much as the rough, are all "sense-statements."

It is, I think, the problems of sureness and certainty, which philosophers tend (if I am not mistaken) to neglect, that have considerably exercised sci-entists, while the problem of "reality," which philosophers have cultivated, does not exercise them. The whole apparatus of measures and standards seems designed to combat unsureness and uncertainty, and concomitantly to increase the possible precision of language, which, in science, pays. But for the words "real" and "unreal" the scientist tends to substitute wisely, their cash-value sub-stitutes, of which he invents and defines an increasing number, to cover an increasing variety of cases: he doesn't ask "Is it real?" but rather "Is it denatured?" or "Is it an allotropic form?" and so on.

It is not clear to me what the class of sense-statements is, nor what its "peculiarity" is. Some who talk of sense-statements (or sense data) appear to draw a distinction between talking about simple things like red or pain, and talking about complicated things like love or tables. But apparently Mr. Wisdom does not, because he treats "This looks to me now like a man eating poppies" as in the same case with "This looks to me now red." In this he is surely right: a man eating poppies may be more "complex" to recognize, but it is often not appreciably more difficult than the other. But if, again, we say that non-sense-statements are those which involve "prediction," why so? True, if I say, "This is a (real) oasis" without first ascertaining that it's not a mirage, then I do chance my hand: but if I *have* ascertained that it's not, and can recognize for sure that it isn't (as when I am drinking its waters), then surely I'm not chancing my hand any longer. I believe, of course, that it will continue to perform as (real) oases normally do: but if there's a *lusus naturae,* a miracle, and it doesn't, that wouldn't mean I was wrong, previously, to call it a real oasis.

With regard to Mr. Wisdom's own chosen formulae, we have seen already that it can't be right to say that the peculiarity of sense-statements is that "when they are correct, and made by X, then X knows they are correct": for X may *think,* without much confidence, that it tastes to him like Lapsang, and yet be far from certain, and then subsequently become certain, or more certain, that it did or didn't. The other two formulae were: "To know that one is in pain is to say that one is and to say it on the basis of being in pain" and that the only mistake possible with sense-statements is typified by the case where "knowing him to be Jack I call him 'Alfred,' thinking his name is Alfred or not caring a damn what his name is." The snag in both these lies in the phrases "on the basis of being in pain" and "knowing him to be Jack." "Knowing him to be Jack" means that I have recognized him as Jack, a matter over which I may well be hesitant and/or mistaken: it is true that I needn't recognize him *by name* as "Jack" (and hence I may call him "Alfred"), but at least I must be recognizing him correctly as, for instance, the man I last saw in Jerusalem, or else I *shall* be misleading *myself.* Similarly, if "on the basis of being in pain" only means "when I am (what would be correctly described as) in pain," then something more than merely *saying* "I'm in pain" is necessary for knowing I'm in pain: and this something more, as it involves recognition, may be hesitant and/or mistaken, though it is of course unlikely to be so in a case so comparatively obvious as that of pain.

Possibly the tendency to overlook the problems of recognition is fostered by the tendency to use a direct object after the word *know.* Mr. Wisdom, for example, confidently uses such expressions as "knowing the feelings of another (his mind, his sensations, his anger, his pain) in the way that *he* knows them." But, although we do correctly use the expressions "I know your feelings on the matter" or "He knows his own mind" or (archaically) "May I know your mind?," these are rather special expressions, which do not justify any general usage. "Feelings" here has the sense it has in "very strong feelings" in favour of or against something: perhaps it means "views" or "opinions" ("very decided opinions"), just as "mind" in this usage is given by the Dictionary as equivalent to "intention" or "wish." To extend the usage uncritically is somewhat as though, on the strength of the legitimate phrase "knowing someone's tastes," we were to proceed to talk of "knowing someone's sounds" or "knowing someone's taste of pineapple." If, for example, it is a case of *physical* feelings such as fatigue, we do not use the expression "I know your feelings."

When, therefore, Mr. Wisdom speaks generally of "knowing his sensations," he presumably means this to be equivalent to "knowing *what* he is seeing, smelling, &c.," just as "knowing the winner of the Derby" means "knowing *what won* the Derby." But here again, the expression "know what" seems sometimes to be taken, unconsciously and erroneously, to lend support to the practice of putting a direct object after *know:* for "what" is liable to be understood as a relative, = "that which." This is a grammatical mistake: "what" *can* of course be a relative, but in "know what you feel" and "know what won" it is an interrogative (Latin *quid,* not *quod*). In this respect, "I can smell what he is smelling" differs from "I can know what he is smelling." "I know what he is feeling" is not "There is an *x* which both I know and he is feeling," but "I know the answer to the question 'What is he feeling?'" And similarly with "I know what I am feeling": this does *not* mean that there is something which I am *both knowing and feeling.*

Expressions such as "We don't know another man's anger in the way he knows it" or "He knows his pain in a way we can't" seem barbarous. The man doesn't "know his pain": he feels (not knows) what he recognizes as, or what he knows to be, anger (not his anger), and he knows that he is feeling angry. Always assuming that he does recognize the feeling, which in fact, though feeling it acutely, he may not: "Now I know what it was, it was jealousy (or gooseflesh or angina). At the time I did not know at all what it was, I had never felt anything quite like it before: but since then I've got to know it quite well." [14]

Uncritical use of the direct object after *know* seems to be one thing that leads to the view that (or to talking as though) sensa, that is things, colours, noises, and the rest, speak or are labelled by nature, so that I can literally *say* what (that which) I *see*: it pipes up, or I read it off. It is as if sensa were *literally* to "announce themselves" or to "identify themselves," in the way we indicate when we say "It presently identified itself as a particularly fine white rhinoceros." But surely this is only a manner of speaking, a reflexive idiom which the French, for example, indulge more freely than the English: sensa are dumb, and only previous experience enables *us* to identify them. If we choose to say that they "identify themselves" (and certainly "recognizing" is not a highly voluntary activity of ours), then it must be admitted that they share the birthright of all speakers, that of speaking unclearly and untruly.

If I Know I Can't Be Wrong

One final point about "How do you know?," the challenge to the user of the expression "I know," requires still to be brought out by consideration of the saying that "If you know you can't be wrong." Surely, if what has so far been said is correct, then we are often right to say we *know* even in cases where we turn out subsequently to have been mistaken—and indeed we seem always, or practically always, liable to be mistaken.

Now, we are perfectly, and should be candidly, aware of this liability, which does not, however, transpire to be so very onerous in practice. The human intellect and senses are, indeed, inherently fallible and delusive, but not by any means *inveterately* so. Machines are inherently liable to break down, but good machines don't (often). It is futile to embark on a "theory of knowledge" which denies this liability: such theories constantly end up by admitting the liability after all, and denying the existence of "knowledge."

"When you know you can't be wrong" is perfectly good sense. You are prohibited from saying "I know it is so, but I may be wrong," just as you are prohibited from saying "I promise I will, but I may fail." If you are aware you may be mistaken, you ought not to say you know, just as, if you are aware you may break your word, you have no business to promise. But of course, being aware that you may be mistaken doesn't mean merely being aware that you are a fallible human being: it means that you have some concrete reason to suppose that you may be mistaken in this case. Just as "but I may fail" does not mean merely "but I am a weak human being" (in which case it would be no more exciting than adding "D. V."): it means that there is some concrete reason for

---

[14] There are, of course, legitimate uses of the direct object after *know*, and of the possessive pronoun before words for feelings. "He knows the town well," "He has known much suffering," "My old vanity, how well I know it!"—even the pleonastic "Where does he feel his (= the) pain?" and the educative tautology "He feels *his* pain." But none of these really lends support to the metaphysical "He knows his pain (in a way we can't)."

me to suppose that I shall break my word. It is naturally *always* possible ("humanly" possible) that I may be mistaken or may break my word, but that by itself is no bar against using the expressions "I know" and "I promise" as we do in fact use them.

At the risk (long since incurred) of being tedious, the parallel between saying "I know" and saying "I promise" may be elaborated.[15]

When I say "S is P," I imply at least that I believe it, and, if I have been strictly brought up, that I am (quite) sure of it: when I say "I shall do A," I imply at least that I hope to do it, and, if I have been strictly brought up that I (fully) intend to. If I only believe that S is P, I can add "But of course I may (very well) be wrong." If I only hope to do A, I can add "But of course I may (very well) not." When I only believe or only hope, it is recognized that further evidence or further circumstances are liable to make me change my mind. If I say "S is P" when I don't even believe it, I am lying: if I say it when I believe it but am not sure of it, I may be misleading but I am not exactly lying. If I say "I shall do A" when I have not even any hope, not the slightest intention, of doing it, then I am deliberately deceiving: if I say it when I do not fully intend to, I am misleading but I am not deliberately deceiving in the same way.

But now, when I say "I promise," a new plunge is taken: I have not merely announced my intention, but, by using this formula (performing this ritual), I I have bound myself to others, and staked my reputation, in a new way. Similarly, saying "I know" is taking a new plunge. But it is *not* saying "I have performed a specially striking feat of cognition, superior, in the same scale as believing and being sure, even to being merely quite sure": for there is nothing in that scale superior to being quite sure. Just as promising is not something superior, in the same scale as hoping and intending, even to merely fully intending: for there *is* nothing in that scale superior to fully intending. When I say "I know," I *give others my word: I give others my authority for saying* that "S is P."

When I have said only that I am sure, and prove to have been mistaken, I am not liable to be rounded on by others in the same way as when I have said "I know." I am sure for *my part,* you can take it or leave it: accept it if you think I'm an acute and careful person, that's your responsibility. But I don't know "for my part," and when I say "I know" I don't mean you can take it or leave it (though of course you *can* take it or leave it). In the same way, when I say I fully intend to, I do so for my part, and, according as you think highly or poorly of my resolution and chances, you will elect to act on it or not to act on it: but if I say I promise, you are *entitled* to act on it, whether or not you choose to do so. If I have said I know or I promise, you insult me in a special way by

---

[15] It is the use of the expressions "I know" and "I promise" (first person singular, present indicative tense) alone that is being considered. "If I knew, I can't have been wrong" or "if she knows she can't be wrong" are not worrying in the way that "if I ('you') know I ('you') can't be wrong" is worrying. Or again, "I promise" is quite different from "he promises": if I say "I promise," I don't say I *say* I promise, I *promise,* just as if he says he promises, he dosen't say he says he promises, he promises: whereas if I say "he promises," I do (only) say he *says* he promises—in the other "sense" of "promise," the "sense" in which *I say I promise,* only *he* can say he promises. I *describe* his promising, but I *do* my own promising and he must do *his* own.

refusing to accept it. We all *feel* the very great difference between saying even "I'm absolutely sure" and saying "I know": it is like the difference between saying even "I firmly and irrevocably intend" and "I promise." If someone has promised me to do A, then I am entitled to rely on it, and can myself make promises on the strength of it: and so, where someone has said to me "I know," I am entitled to say *I* know too, at second hand. The right to say "I know" is transmissible, in the sort of way that other authority is transmissible. Hence, if I say it lightly, I may be *responsible* for getting *you* into trouble.

If you say you *know* something, the most immediate challenge takes the form of asking "Are you in a position to know?": that is, you must undertake to show, not merely that you are sure of it, but that it is within your cognisance. There is a similar form of challenge in the case of promising: fully intending is not enough—you must also undertake to show that "you are in a position to promise," that is, that it is within your power. Over these points in the two cases parallel series of doubts are apt to infect philosophers, on the ground that I cannot foresee the future. Some begin to hold that I should never, or practically never, say I know anything—perhaps only what I am sensing at this moment: others, that I should never, or practically never, say I promise—perhaps only what is actually within my power at this moment. In both cases there is an obsession: if I know *I can't be wrong*, so I can't have the right to say I know, and if I promise *I can't fail*, so I can't have the right to say I promise. And in both cases this obsession fastens on my inability to make *predictions* as the root of the matter, meaning by predictions claims to know the future. But this is doubly mistaken in both cases. As has been seen, we may be perfectly justified in saying we know or we promise, in spite of the fact that things "may" turn out badly, and it's a more or less serious matter for us if they do. And further, it is overlooked that the conditions which must be satisfied if I am to show that a thing is within my cognisance or within my power are conditions, not about the future, but about *the present and the past*: it is not demanded that I do more than *believe* about the future.[16]

We feel, however, an objection to saying that "I know" performs the same sort of function as "I promise." It is this. Supposing that things turn out badly, then we say, on the one hand "You're proved wrong, so you *didn't* know," but on the other hand "You've failed to perform, although you *did* promise." I believe that this contrast is more apparent than real. The sense in which you "did promise" is that you did *say* you promised (did say "I promise"): and you did *say* you knew. This is the gravamen of the charge against you when you let us down, after we have taken your word. But it may well transpire that you never fully intended to do it, or that you had concrete reason to suppose that you wouldn't be able to do it (it might even be manifestly impossible), and in another "sense" of promise you *can't* then have promised to do it, so that you *didn't* promise.

Consider the use of other phrases analogous to "I know" and "I promise."

[16] If "Figs never grow on thistles" is taken to mean "None ever have and none ever will," then it is implied that I *know* that none ever have, but only that I *believe* that none ever will.

Suppose, instead of "I know," I had said "I swear": in that case, upon the opposite appearing, we should say, exactly as in the promising case, "You *did* swear, but you were wrong." Suppose again that, instead of "I promise," I had said "I guarantee" (e.g. to protect you from attack): in that case, upon my letting you down, you can say, exactly as in the knowing case "You *said* you guaranteed it, but you *didn't* guarantee it." [17] Can the situation perhaps be summed up as follows? In these "ritual" cases, the approved case is one where *in the appropriate circumstances,* I say a certain formula: e.g. "I do" when standing, unmarried or a widower, beside woman, unmarried or a widow and not within the prohibited degrees of relationship, before a clergyman, registrar, etc., or "I give" when it is mine to give, etc., or "I order" when I have the authority to, etc. But now, if the situation transpires to have been in some way not orthodox (I was already married: it wasn't mine to give: I had no authority to order), then we tend to be rather hesitant about how to put it, as heaven was when the saint blessed the penguins. We call the man a bigamist, but his second marriage was not a marriage, is null and void (a useful formula in many cases for avoiding saying either "he did" or "he didn't"): he did "order" me to do it, but, having no authority over me, he *couldn't* "order" me: he did warn me it was going to charge, but it wasn't or anyway I knew much more about it than he did, so in a way he couldn't warn me, didn't warn me.[18] We hesitate between "He didn't order me," "He had no right to order me," "He oughtn't to have said he ordered me," just as we do between "You didn't know," "You can't have known," "You had no right to say you knew" (these perhaps slightly different nuances, according to what precisely it is that has gone wrong). But the essential factors are (*a*) You said you knew: you said you promised (*b*) You were mistaken: you didn't perform. The hesitancy concerns only the precise way in which we are to round on the original "I know" or "I promise."

To suppose that "I know" is a descriptive phrase, is only one example of the *descriptive fallacy,* so common in philosophy. Even if some language is now purely descriptive, language was not in origin so, and much of it is still not so. Utterance of obvious ritual phrases, in the appropriate circumstances, is not *describing* the action we are doing, but *doing* it ("I do"): in other cases it functions, like tone and expression, or again like punctuation and mood, as an intimation that we are employing language in some special way ("I warn," "I ask," "I define"). Such phrases cannot, strictly, *be* lies, though they can "imply" lies, as "I promise" implies that I fully intend, which may be untrue.

If these are the main and multifarious points that arise in familiar cases where we ask "How do you know that this is a case of so-and-so?," they may be

[17] "Swear," "guarantee," "give my word," "promise," all these and similar words cover cases both of "knowing" and of "promising," thus suggesting the two are analogous. Of course they differ subtly from each other; for example, *know* and *promise* are in a certain sense "unlimited" expressions, while when I swear I swear *upon* something, and when I guarantee I guarantee that, upon some adverse and more or less to be expected circumstance arising, I will take *some more or less definite action* to nullify it.

[18] "You can't warn someone of something that isn't going to happen" parallels "You can't know what isn't true."

expected to arise likewise in cases where we say "I know he is angry." And if there are, as no doubt there are, special difficulties in this case, at least we can clear the ground a little of things which are not special difficulties, and get the matter in better perspective.

As a preliminary, it must be said that I shall only discuss the question of feelings and emotions, with special reference to anger. It seems likely that the cases where we know that another man thinks that 2 and 2 make 4, or that he is seeing a rat, and so on, are different in important respects from, though no doubt also similar to, the case of knowing that he is angry or hungry.

In the first place, we certainly do say sometimes that we know another man is angry, and we also distinguish these occasions from others on which we say only that we *believe* he is angry. For of course, we do not for a moment suppose that we *always* know, of *all* men, whether they are angry or not, or that we could discover it. There are many occasions when I realize that I can't possibly tell what he's feeling: and there are many *types* of people, and many individuals too, with whom I (they being what they are, and I being what I am) never can tell. The feelings of royalty, for example, or fakirs or bushmen or Wykehamists or simple eccentrics—these may be very hard to divine: unless you have had a prolonged acquaintance with such persons, and some intimacy with them, you are not in any sort of position to know what their feelings are, especially if, for one reason or another, they can't or don't tell you. Or again, the feelings of some individual whom you have never met before—they might be almost anything: you don't know his character at all or his tastes, you have had no experience of his mannerisms, and so on. His feelings are elusive and personal: people differ so much. It is this sort of thing that leads to the situation where we say "You never know" or "You never can tell."

In short, here even more than in the case of the goldfinch, a great deal depends on how familiar we have been in our past experience with this type of person, and indeed with this individual, in this type of situation. If we have no great familiarity, then we hesitate to say we know: indeed, we can't be expected to say (tell). On the other hand, if we *have* had the necessary experience, then we can, in favourable current circumstances, say we know: we certainly can recognize when some near relative of ours is angrier than we have ever seen him.

Further, we must have had experience also of the emotion or feeling concerned, in this case anger. In order to know what you are feeling, I must also apparently be able to imagine (guess, understand, appreciate) what you're feeling. It seems that more is demanded than that I shall have learned to discriminate displays of anger in others: I must also have been angry myself.[19] Or at any rate, if I have never felt a certain emotion, say ambition, then I certainly feel an *extra*

---

[19] We say we don't know what it must feel like to be a king, whereas we do know what one of our friends must have felt when mortified. In this ordinary (imprecise and evidently not whole-hog) sense of "knowing what it would be like" we do often know what it would be like to be our neighbour drawing his sword, whereas we don't know (can't even guess or imagine), really, what it would feel like to be a cat or a cockroach. But of course we don't ever "know" what in our neighbour accompanies the drawing of his sword in Mr. Wisdom's peculiar sense of "know what" as equivalent to "directly experience that which."

hesitation in saying that his motive is ambition. And this seems to be due to the very special nature (grammar, logic) of feelings, to the special way in which they are related to their occasions and manifestations, which requires further elucidation.

At first sight it may be tempting to follow Mr. Wisdom, and to draw a distinction between (1) the physical symptoms and (2) the feeling. So that when, in the current case, I am asked "How can you tell he's angry?" I should answer "From the physical symptoms," while if *he* is asked how *he* can tell he's angry, he should answer "From the feeling." But this seems to be a dangerous oversimplification.

In the first place, "symptoms" (and also "physical") is being used in a way different from ordinary usage, and one which proves to be misleading.

"Symptoms," a term transferred from medical usage,[20] tends to be used only, or primarily, in cases where that of which there are symptoms is something undesirable (of incipient disease rather than of returning health, of despair rather than of hope, of grief rather than of joy): and hence it is more colourful than "signs" or "indications." This, however, is comparatively trivial. What is important is the fact that we never talk of "symptoms" or "signs" except *by way of implied contrast with inspection of the item itself.* No doubt it would often be awkward to have to say exactly where the signs or symptoms end and the item itself begins to appear: but such a division is always implied to exist. And hence the words "symptom" and "sign" have no use except in cases where the item, as in the case of disease, is liable to be *hidden*, whether it be in the future, in the past, under the skin, or in some other more or less notorious casket: and when the item is itself before us, we no longer talk of signs and symptoms. When we talk of "signs of a storm," we mean signs of an impending storm, or of a past storm, or of a storm beyond the horizon: we do *not* mean a storm on top of us.[21]

The words function like such words as "traces" or "clues." Once you know the murderer, you don't get any more clues, only what were or would have been clues: nor is a confession, or an eye-witness's view of the crime, a particularly good clue—these are something different altogether. When the cheese is not to be found or seen, then there may be traces of it: but not when it's there in front of us (though of course, there aren't, then, "no traces" of it either).

For this reason, it seems misleading to lump together, as a general practice, all the characteristic features of any casual item as "signs" or "symptoms" of it: though it is of course sometimes the case that some things which could in appropriate circumstances be called characteristics or effects or manifestations or

---

[20] Doctors nowadays draw a distinction of their own between "symptoms" and "(physical) signs": but the distinction is not here relevant, and perhaps not very clear.

[21] There are some, more complicated, cases like that of inflation, where the signs of incipient inflation are of the same nature as inflation itself, but of a less intensity or at a slower tempo. Here, especially, it is a matter for decision where the signs or "tendencies" end and where the state itself sets in: moreover, with inflation, as with some diseases, we can in some contexts go on talking of signs or symptoms even when the item itself is quite fairly decidedly present, because it is such as not to be patent to simple observation.

parts or sequelae or what not of certain items may *also* be called signs or symptoms of those items in the appropriate circumstances. It seems to be this which is really wrong with Mr. Wisdom's paradox (Other Minds III) about looking in the larder and finding "all the signs" of bread, when we see the loaf, touch it, taste it and so on. Doing these things is not finding (some) signs of bread at all: the taste or feel of bread is not a sign or symptom of bread at all. What I might be taken to mean if I announced that I had found signs of bread in the larder seems rather doubtful, since bread is not normally casketed (or if in the bin, leaves no traces), and not being a transeunt event (impending bread, etc.), does not have any normally accepted "signs"; and signs, peculiar to the item, have to be more or less normally accepted. I might be taken to mean that I had found traces of bread, such as crumbs, or signs that bread had at one time been stored there, or something of the kind: but what I could *not* be taken to mean is that I had seen, tasted, or touched (something like) bread.

The sort of thing we do actually say, if the look is all right but we haven't yet tasted it, is "Here is something that looks like bread." If it turns out not to be bread after all, we might say "It tasted like bread, but actually it was only bread-substitute," or "It exhibited many of the characteristic features of bread, but differed in important respects: it was only a synthetic imitation." That is, we don't use the words "sign" or "symptom" at all.

Now, if "sign" and "symptom" have this restricted usage, it is evident that to say that we only get at the "signs" or "symptoms" of anything is to imply that we never get at *it* (and this goes for "*all* the signs" too). So that, if we say that I only get at the *symptoms* of his anger, that carries an important implication. But *is* this the way we talk? Surely we do not consider that we are never aware of more than *symptoms* of anger in another man?

"Symptoms" or "signs" of anger tend to mean signs of *rising* or of *suppressed* anger. Once the man has exploded, we talk of something different—of an expression or manifestation or display of anger, of an exhibition of temper, and so forth. A twitch of the eyebrow, pallor, a tremor in the voice, all these may be symptoms of anger; but a violent tirade or a blow in the face are not, they are acts in which the anger is vented. "Symptoms" of anger are not, at least normally, contrasted with the man's own inner personal feeling of anger, but rather with the actual display of anger. Normally at least, where we have only symptoms to go upon, we should say only that we *believe* that the man is angry or getting angry: whereas when he has given himself away we say that we *know*.[22]

The word "physical" also, as used by Mr. Wisdom in contrast to "mental,"

[22] Sometimes, it is said, we use "I know" where we should be prepared to substitute "I believe," as when we say "I know he's in, because his hat is in the hall": thus "know" is used loosely for "believe," so why should we suppose there is a fundamental difference between them? But the question is, what exactly do we mean by "prepared to substitute" and "loosely"? We are "prepared to substitute" *believe* for *know* not as an *equivalent* expression but as a weaker and therefore preferable expression, in view of the seriousness with which, as has become apparent, the matter is to be treated: the presence of the hat, which would serve as a proof of its owner's presence in many circumstances, could only through laxity be adduced as a proof in a court of law.

seems to me abused, though I am not confident as to whether this abuse is misleading in the current case. He evidently does not wish to call a man's feelings, which he cites as a typical example of a "mental" event, *physical*. Yet this is what we ordinarily often do. There are many physical feelings, such as giddiness, hunger, or fatigue: and these are included by some doctors among the physical signs of various complaints. Most feelings we do not speak of as either mental or physical, especially emotions, such as jealousy or anger itself: we do not assign them to the *mind* but to the *heart*. Where we do describe a feeling as mental, it is because we are using a word normally used to describe a physical feeling in a special transferred sense, as when we talk about "mental" discomfort or fatigue.

It is then, clear, that more is involved in being, for example, angry than simply showing the symptoms and feeling the feeling. For there is also the d play or manifestation. And it is to be noted that the feeling is related in a unique sort of way to the display. When we are angry, we have an impulse, felt and/or acted on, to do actions of particular kinds, and, unless we suppress the anger, we do actually proceed to do them. There is a peculiar and intimate relationship between the emotion and the natural manner of venting it, with which, having been angry ourselves, we are acquainted. The ways in which anger is normally manifested are *natural* to anger just as there are tones *naturally* expressive of various emotions (indignation, etc.). There is not normally taken to be [23] such a thing as "being angry" apart from any impulse, however vague, to vent the anger in the natural way.

Moreover, besides the natural expressions of anger, there are also the natural *occasions* of anger, of which we have also had experience, which are similarly connected in an intimate way with the "being angry." It would be as nonsensical to class these as "causes" in some supposedly obvious and "external" sense, as it would be to class the venting of anger as the "effect" of the emotion in a supposedly obvious and "external" sense. Equally it would be nonsensical to say that there are three wholly distinct phenomena, (1) cause or occasion, (2) feeling or emotion, and (3) effect or manifestation, which are related together "by definition" as all necessary to anger, though this would perhaps be less misleading than the other.

It seems fair to say that "being angry" is in many respects like "having mumps." It is a description of a whole pattern of events, including occasion, symptoms, feeling, and manifestation, and possibly other factors besides. It is as silly to ask "What, really, *is* the anger *itself?*" as to attempt to fine down "the disease" to some one chosen item ("the functional disorder"). That the man himself feels something which we don't (in the sense that he feels angry and we don't) is, in the absence of Mr. Wisdom's variety of telepathy,[24] evident enough,

[23] A new language is naturally necessary if we are to admit unconscious feelings, and feelings which express themselves in paradoxical manners, such as the psychoanalysts describe.

[24] There is, it seems to me, something which does actually happen, rather different from Mr. Wisdom's telepathy, which does sometimes contribute towards our knowledge of other people's feelings. We do talk, for example, of "feeling another person's dis-

and incidentally nothing to complain about as a "predicament": but there is no call to say that "that" ("the feeling") [25] is the *anger*. The pattern of events, whatever its precise form, is, fairly clearly, peculiar to the case of "feelings" (emotions)—it is not by any means exactly like the case of diseases: and it seems to be this peculiarity which makes us prone to say that, unless we have had experience of a feeling ourselves, we cannot know when someone else is experiencing it. Moreover, it is our confidence in the general pattern that makes us apt to say we "know" another man is angry when we have only observed parts of the pattern: for the parts of the pattern are related to each other very much more intimately than, for example, newspapermen scurrying in Brighton are related to a fire in Fleet Street. [26]

The man himself, such is the overriding power of the pattern, will sometimes accept corrections from outsiders about his own emotions, i.e. about the correct description of them. He may be got to agree that he was not really angry so much as, rather, indignant or jealous, and even that he was not in pain, but only fancied he was. And this is not surprising, especially in view of the fact that he, like all of us, has primarily learnt to use the expression "I am angry" of himself by (*a*) noting the occasion, symptoms, manifestation, etc., in cases where other persons say "I am angry" of *themselves* (*b*) being told by others, who have noted all that can be observed about *him* on certain occasions, that "You are angry," i.e. that he should say "I am angry." On the whole, "mere" feelings or emotions, if there are such things genuinely detectable, are certainly very hard to be sure about, even harder than, say, tastes, which we already choose to describe, normally, only by their occasions (the taste "of tar," "of pineapple," etc.).

All words for emotions are, besides, on the vague side, in two ways, leading to further hesitations about whether we "know" when he's angry. They tend to cover a rather wide and ill-defined variety of situations: and the patterns they cover tend to be, each of them, rather complex (though common and so not difficult to recognize, very often), so that it is easy for one of the more or less necessary features to be omitted, and thus to give rise to hesitation about what exactly we should say in such an unorthodox case. We realize, well enough, that the challenge to which we are exposed if we say we *know* is to *prove* it, and in this respect vagueness of terminology is a crippling handicap.

So far, enough has perhaps been said to show that most of the difficulties which stand in the way of our saying we know a thing is a goldfinch arise in rather greater strength in the case where we want to say we know another man is angry. But there is still a feeling, and I think a justified feeling, that there is a further and quite *special* difficulty in the latter case.

This difficulty seems to be of the sort that Mr. Wisdom raises at the very

---

pleasure," and say, for example, "his anger could be felt," and there seems to be something genuine about this. But the feeling we feel, though a genuine "feeling," is *not*, in these cases, displeasure or anger, but a special *counterpart* feeling.

[25] The "feelings," i.e. sensations, we can observe in ourselves when angry are such things as a pounding of the heart or tensing of the muscles, which cannot in themselves be justifiably called "the feeling of anger."

[26] It is therefore misleading to ask "How do I get from the scowl to the anger?"

outset of his series of articles on "Other Minds." It is asked, might the man not exhibit all the symptoms (and display and everything else) of anger, even ad infinitum, and yet still *not (really) be* angry? It will be remembered that he there treats it, no doubt provisionally, as a difficulty similar to that which can arise concerning the reality of any "material object." But in fact, it has special features of its own.

There seem to be three distinguishable doubts which may arise:

1. When to all appearances angry, might he not really be labouring under some other emotion, in that, though he normally feels the same emotion as we should on occasions when we, in his position, should feel anger and in making displays such as we make when angry, in this particular case he is acting abnormally?

2. When to all appearances angry, might he not really be labouring under some other emotion, in that he normally feels, on occasions when we in his position should feel anger and when acting as we should act if we felt anger, some feeling which we, if we experienced it, should distinguish from anger?

3. When to all appearances angry, might he not really be feeling no emotion at all?

In everyday life, all these problems arise in special cases, and occasion genuine worry. We may worry (1) as to whether someone is *deceiving* us, by suppressing his emotions, or by feigning emotions which he does not feel: we may worry (2) as to whether we are *misunderstanding* someone (or he us), in wrongly supposing that he does "feel like us," that he does share emotions like ours: or we may worry (3) as to whether some action of another person is really deliberate, or perhaps only involuntary or inadvertent in some manner or other. All three varieties of worry may arise, and often do, in connexion with the actions of persons whom we know very well.[27] Any or all of them may be at the bottom of the passage from Mrs. Woolf:[28] all work together in the feeling of loneliness which affects everybody at times.

None of these three special difficulties about "reality" arises in connexion with goldfinches or bread, any more than the special difficulties about, for example, the oasis arise in connexion with the reality of another person's emotions. The goldfinch cannot be assumed, nor the bread suppressed: we may be deceived by the appearance of an oasis, or misinterpret the signs of the weather, but the oasis cannot lie to us and we cannot misunderstand the storm in the way we misunderstand the man.

Though the difficulties are special, the ways of dealing with them are, initially, similar to those employed in the case of the goldfinch. There are (more or less roughly) established procedures for dealing with suspected cases of deception or of misunderstanding or of inadvertence. By these means we do very

---

[27] There is, too, a special way in which we can doubt the "reality" of our own emotions, can doubt whether we are not "acting to ourselves." Professional actors may reach a state where they never really know what their genuine feelings are.

[28] [Quoted by Wisdom in his contribution to this Symposium. Ed.]

often establish (though we do not expect *always* to establish) that someone is acting, or that we were misunderstanding him, or that he is simply impervious to a certain emotion, or that he was not acting voluntarily. These special cases where doubts arise and require resolving, are contrasted with the normal cases which hold the field [29] *unless* there is some special suggestion that deceit, etc., is involved, and deceit, moreover, of an intelligible kind in the circumstances, that is, of a kind that can be looked into because motive, etc., is specially suggested. There is no suggestion that I *never* know what other people's emotions are, nor yet that in particular cases I might be wrong for no special reason or in no special way.

Extraordinary cases of deceit, misunderstanding, etc. (which are themselves not the normal), do not, *ex vi termini*, ordinarily occur: we have a working knowledge of the occasions for, the temptations to, the practical limits of, and the normal types of deceit and misunderstanding. Nevertheless, they *may* occur, and there may be varieties which are common without our yet having become aware of the fact. If this happens, we are in a certain sense wrong, because our terminology is inadequate to the facts, and we shall have thenceforward to be more wary about saying we know, or shall have to revise our ideas and terminology. This we are constantly ready to do in a field so complex and baffling as that of the emotions.

There remains, however, one further special feature of the case, which also differentiates it radically from the goldfinch case. The goldfinch, the material object, is, as we insisted above, uninscribed and *mute:* but the man *speaks.* In the complex of occurrences which induces us to say we know another man is angry, the complex of symptoms, occasion, display, and the rest, a peculiar place is occupied by the man's own statement as to what his feelings are. In the usual case, we accept this statement without question, and we then say that we know (as it were "at second-hand") what his feelings are: though of course "at second-hand" here could not be used to imply that anybody but he could know "at first-hand," and hence perhaps it is not in fact used. In unusual cases, where his statement conflicts with the description we should otherwise have been inclined to give of the case, we do not feel bound to accept it, though we always feel some uneasiness in rejecting it. If the man is an habitual liar or self-deceiver, or if there are patent reasons why he should be lying or deceiving himself on this occasion, then we feel reasonably happy: but if such a case occurred as the imagined one where a man, having given throughout life every appearance of holding a certain pointless belief, leaves behind a remark in his private diary to the effect that he never did believe it, then we probably should not know what to say.

I should like to make in conclusion some further remarks about this crucial matter of our believing what the man says about his own feelings. Although I know very well that I do not see my way clearly in this, I cannot help feeling sure that it is fundamental to the whole Predicament, and that it has not been given the attention it deserves, possibly just because it is so obvious.

The man's own statement is not (is not treated primarily as) a sign or

---

[29] "You cannot fool all of the people all of the time" is "analytic."

symptom, although it can, secondarily and artificially, be treated as such. A unique place is reserved for it in the summary of the facts of the case. The question then is: "Why believe him?"

There are answers that we can give to this question, which is here to be taken in the general sense of "Why believe him ever?" not simply as "Why believe him this time?" We may say that the man's statements on matters other than his own feelings have constantly been before us in the past, and have been regularly verified by our own observations of the facts he reported: so that we have in fact some basis for an induction about his general reliability. Or we may say that his behaviour is most simply "explained" on the view that he does feel emotions like ours, just as psycho-analysts "explain" erratic behaviour by analogy with normal behaviour when they use the terminology of "unconscious desires."

These answers are, however, dangerous and unhelpful. They are so obvious that they please nobody: while on the other hand they encourage the questioner to push his question to "profounder" depths, encouraging us, in turn, to exaggerate these answers until they become distortions.

The question, pushed further, becomes a challenge to the very possibility of "believing another man," in its ordinarily accepted sense, at all. What "justification" is there for supposing that there is another mind communicating with you at all? How can you know what it would be like for another mind to feel anything, and so how can you understand it? It is then that we are tempted to say that we only mean by "believing him" that we take certain vocal noises as signs of certain impending behaviour, and that "other minds" are no more really real than unconscious desires.

This, however, is distortion. It seems, rather, that believing in other persons, in authority and testimony, is an essential part of the act of communicating, an act which we all constantly perform. It is as much an irreducible part of our experience as, say, giving promises, or playing competitive games, or even sensing coloured patches. We can state certain advantages of such performances, and we can elaborate rules of a kind for their "rational" conduct (as the Law Courts and historians and psychologists work out the rules for accepting testimony). But there is no "justification" for our doing them as such.

Final Note

One speaker at Manchester said roundly that the real crux of the matter remains still that "I ought not to say that I know Tom is angry, because I don't introspect his feelings": and this no doubt is just what many people do boggle at. The gist of what I have been trying to bring out is simply:

1. *Of course* I *don't* introspect Tom's feelings (we should be in a pretty predicament if I did).
2. *Of course* I *do* sometimes know Tom is angry.
Hence
3. to suppose that the question "How do I know that Tom is angry?" is meant to mean "How do I introspect Tom's feelings?" (because, as we know, that's the sort of thing that knowing is or ought to be), is simply barking our way up the wrong gum tree.

18

J. L. *Austin* A PLEA FOR EXCUSES

The following paper is Austin's Presidential Address to the Aristotelian Society in 1956. Its main importance stems from the fact that he here states most clearly his general views concerning the proper role of philosophy and the value of his distinctive kind of analysis of ordinary speech for resolving philosophical problems.

Austin's discussion of philosophizing should be contrasted with Russell's remarks in selection 2, Ayer's in selection 7, and Wittgenstein's in the concluding pages of selection 11.

For further reading on Austin's philosophical method see:

Hampshire, S.: "In Memoriam: J. L. Austin 1911–1960," *Proceedings of the Aristotelian Society*, 1959–1960.
Warnock, G. J., and Urmson, J. O.: "J. L. Austin," *Mind*, 1961.

The July, 1963, issue of *Philosophy* is devoted almost exclusively to articles on Austin.

The subject of this paper, *Excuses*, is one not to be treated, but only to be introduced, within such limits. It is, or might be, the name of a whole branch, even a ramiculated branch, of philosophy, or at least of one fashion of philosophy. I shall try, therefore, first to state *what* the subject is, *why* it is worth studying, and *how* it may be studied, all this at a regrettably lofty level: and then I shall illustrate, in more cogenial but desultory detail, some of the methods to be used, together with their limitations, and some of the unexpected results to be expected and lessons to be learned. Much, of course, of the amusement, and of the instruction, comes in drawing the coverts of the microglot, in hounding down the minutiae, and to this I can do no more here than incite you. But I owe it to the subject to say, that it has long afforded me what philosophy is so often thought, and made, barren of—the fun of discovery, the pleasures of co-operation, and the satisfaction of reaching agreement.

From *Proceedings of the Aristotelian Society*, n.s., vol. LVII (1956–1957). Reprinted by courtesy of the editor of The Aristotelian Society.

What, then, is the subject? I am here using the word "excuses" *for a title,* but it would be unwise to freeze too fast to this one noun and its partner verb: indeed for some time I used to use "extenuation" instead. Still, on the whole "excuses" is probably the most central and embracing term in the field, although this includes others of importance—"plea," "defence," "justification," and so on. When, then, do we "excuse" conduct, our own or somebody else's? When are "excuses" proffered?

In general, the situation is one where someone is *accused* of having done something, or (if that will keep it any cleaner) where someone is *said* to have done something which is bad, wrong, inept, unwelcome, or in some other of the numerous possible ways untoward. Thereupon he, or someone on his behalf, will try to defend his conduct or to get him out of it.

One way of going about this is to admit flatly that he, X, did do that very thing, A, but to argue that it was a good thing, or the right or sensible thing, or a permissible thing to do, either in general or at least in the special circumstances of the occasion. To take this line is to *justify* the action, to give reasons for doing it: not to say, to brazen it out, to glory in it, or the like.

A different way of going about it is to admit that it wasn't a good thing to have done, but to argue that it is not quite fair or correct to say *baldly* "X did A." We may say it isn't fair just to say X did it; perhaps he was under somebody's influence, or was nudged. Or, it isn't fair to say baldly he *did* A; it may have been partly accidental, or an unintentional slip. Or, it isn't fair to say he did simply A—he was really doing something quite different and A was only incidental, or he was looking at the whole thing quite differently. Naturally these arguments can be combined or overlap or run into each other.

In the one defence, briefly, we accept responsibility but deny that it was bad: in the other, we admit that it was bad but don't accept full, or even any, responsibility.

By and large, justifications can be kept distinct from excuses, and I shall not be so anxious to talk about them because they have enjoyed more than their fair share of philosophical attention. But the two certainly can be confused, and can *seem* to go very near to each other, even if they do not perhaps actually do so. You dropped the tea-tray: Certainly, but an emotional storm was about to break out: or, Yes, but there was a wasp. In each case the defence, very soundly, insists on a fuller description of the event in its context; but the first is a justification, the second an excuse. Again, if the objection is to the use of such a dyslogistic verb as "murdered," this may be on the ground that the killing was done in battle (justification) or on the ground that it was only accidental if reckless (excuse). It is arguable that we do not use the terms justification and excuse as carefully as we might; a miscellany of even less clear terms, such as "extenuation," "palliation," "mitigation," hovers uneasily between partial justification and partial excuse; and when we plead, say, provocation, there is genuine uncertainty or ambiguity as to what we mean—is *he* partly responsible, because he roused a violent impulse or passion in me, so that it wasn't truly or merely me acting "of my own accord" (excuse)? Or is it rather that, he having done me such injury, I was entitled to retaliate (justification)? Such doubts merely make it the more urgent to clear up the usage of these various terms. But that the defences I have for convenience labelled "justification" and "excuse" are in principle distinct can scarcely be doubted.

This then is the sort of situation we have to consider under "excuses." I will only further point out how very wide a field it covers. We have, of course, to bring in the opposite numbers of excuses—the expressions that *aggravate*, such as "deliberately," "on purpose," and so on, if only for the reason that an excuse often takes the form of a rebuttal of one of these. But we have also to bring in a large number of expressions which at first blush look not so much like excuses as like accusations— "clumsiness," "tactlessness," "thoughtlessness," and the like. Because it has always to be remembered that few excuses get us out of it *completely*: the average excuse, in a poor situation, gets us only out of the fire into the frying pan—but still, of course, any frying pan in a fire. If I have broken your dish or your romance, maybe the best defence I can find will be clumsiness.

Why, if this is what "excuses" are, should we trouble to investigate them? It might be thought reason enough that their production has always bulked so large among human activities. But to moral philosophy in particular a study of them will contribute in special ways, both positively towards the development of a cautious, latter-day version of conduct, and negatively towards the correction of older and hastier theories.

In ethics we study, I suppose, the good and the bad, the right and the wrong, and this must be for the most part in some connexion with conduct or the doing of actions. Yet before we consider what actions are good or bad, right or wrong, it is proper to consider first what is meant by, and what not, and what is included under, and what not, the expression "doing an action" or "doing something." These are expressions still too little examined on their own account and merits, just as the general notion of "saying something" is still too lightly passed over in logic. There is indeed a vague and comforting idea in the background that, after all, in the last analysis, doing an action must come down to the making of physical movements with parts of the body; but this is about as true as that saying something must, in the last analysis, come down to making movements of the tongue.

The beginning of sense, not to say wisdom, is to realize that "doing an action," as used in philosophy,[1] is a highly abstract expression—it is a stand-in used in the place of any (or almost any?) verb with a personal subject, in the same sort of way that "thing" is a stand-in for any (or when we remember, almost any) noun substantive, and "quality" a stand-in for the adjective. Nobody, to be sure, relies on such dummies quite implicitly quite indefinitely. Yet notoriously it is possible to arrive at, or to derive the idea for, an over-simplified metaphysics from the obsession with "things" and their "qualities." In a similar way, less commonly recognized even in these semi-sophisticated times, we fall for the myth of the verb. We treat the expression "doing an action" no longer as a stand-in for a verb with a personal subject, as which it has no doubt some uses, and might have more if the range of verbs were not left unspecified, but as a self-explanatory, ground-level description, one which brings adequately into the open

---

[1] This use has little to do with the more down-to-earth occurrences of "action" in ordinary speech.

the essential features of everything that comes, by simple inspection, under it. We scarcely notice even the most patent exceptions or difficulties (is to think something, or to say something, or to try to do something, to do an action?), any more than we fret, in the *ivresse des grandes profondeurs,* as to whether flames are things or events. So we come easily to think of our behaviour over any time, and of a life as a whole, as consisting in doing now action A, next action B, then action C, and so on, just as elsewhere we come to think of the world as consisting of this, that and the other substance or material thing, each with its properties. All "actions" are, as actions (meaning what?), equal, composing a quarrel with striking a match, winning a war with sneezing: worse still, we assimilate them one and all to the supposedly most obvious and easy cases, such as posting letters or moving fingers, just as we assimilate all "things" to horses or beds.

If we are to continue to use this expression in sober philosophy, we need to ask such questions as: Is to sneeze to do an action? Or is to breathe, or to see, or to checkmate, or each one of countless others? In short, for what range of verbs, as used on what occasions, is "doing an action" a stand-in? What have they in common, and what do those excluded severally lack? Again we need to ask how we decide what is the correct name for "the" action that somebody did —and what, indeed, are the rules for the use of "the" action, "an" action, "one" action, a "part" or "phase" of an action and the like. Further, we need to realize that even the "simplest" named actions are not so simple—certainly are not the mere makings of physical movements, and to ask what more, then, comes in (intentions? conventions?) and what does not (motives?), and what is the detail of the complicated internal machinery we use in "acting"—the receipt of intelligence, the appreciation of the situation, the invocation of principles, the planning, the control of execution and the rest.

In two main ways the study of excuses can throw light on these fundamental matters. First, to examine excuses is to examine cases where there has been some abnormality or failure: and as so often, the abnormal will throw light on the normal, will help us to penetrate the blinding veil of ease and obviousness that hides the mechanisms of the natural successful act. It rapidly becomes plain that the breakdowns signalized by the various excuses are of radically different kinds, affecting different parts or stages of the machinery, which the excuses consequently pick out and sort out for us. Further, it emerges that not *every* slip-up occurs in connexion with *every*thing that could be called an "action," that not every excuse is apt with every verb—far indeed from it: and this provides us with one means of introducing some classification into the vast miscellany of "actions." If we classify them according to the particular selection of breakdowns to which each is liable, this should assign them their places in some family group or groups of actions, or in some model of the machinery of acting.

In this sort of way, the philosophical study of conduct can get off to a positive fresh start. But by the way, and more negatively, a number of traditional cruces or mistakes in this field can be resolved or removed. First among these comes the problem of Freedom. While it has been the tradition to present this as the "positive" term requiring elucidation, there is little doubt that to say we acted "freely" (in the philosopher's use, which is only faintly related to the everyday use) is to say only that we acted *not* un-freely, in one or another of the many heterogeneous ways of so acting (under duress, or what not). Like "real," "free" is only used to rule out the suggestion of some or all of its recognized antitheses. As "truth" is not a name for a characteristic of assertions, so "freedom" is not a name for a characteristic of actions, but the name of a dimension in which actions are assessed. In examining all the ways in which each action may not be "free," i.e. the cases in which it will not do to say simply "X did A," we may hope to dispose of the problem of Freedom. Aristotle has often been chidden for talking about excuses or pleas and overlooking "the real problem": in my own case, it was when I began to see the injustice of this charge that I first became interested in excuses.

There is much to be said for the view that, philosophical tradition apart, Responsibility would be a better candidate for the role here assigned to Freedom. If ordinary language is to be our guide, it is to evade responsibility, or full responsibility, that we most often make excuses, and I have used the word myself in this way above. But in fact "responsibility" too seems not really apt in all cases: I do not exactly evade responsibility when I plead clumsiness or tactlessness, nor, often, when I plead that I only did it unwillingly or reluctantly, and still less if I plead that I had in the circumstances no choice: here I was constrained and have an excuse (or justification), yet may accept responsibility. It. may be, then, that at least two key terms, Freedom and Responsibility, are needed: the relation between them is not clear, and it may be hoped that the investigation of excuses will contribute towards its clarification.[2]

So much, then, for ways in which the study of excuses may throw light on ethics. But there are also reasons why it is an attractive subject methodologically, at least if we are to proceed from "ordinary language," that is, by examining *what we should say when,* and so why and what we should mean by it. Perhaps this method, at least as *one* philosophical method, scarcely requires justification at present—too evidently, there is gold in them thar hills: more opportune would be a warning about the care and thoroughness needed if it is not to fall into disrepute. I will, however, justify it very briefly.

First, words are our tools, and, as a minimum, we should use clean tools: we should know what we mean and what we do not, and we must forearm ourselves against the traps that language sets us. Secondly, words are not (except in their own little corner) facts or things: we need therefore to prise them off the world, to hold them apart from and against it, so that we can realize their inadequacies and arbitrariness, and can relook at the world without blinkers. Thirdly, and more hopefully, our common stock of words embodies all the distinctions

---

[2] Another well-flogged horse in these same stakes is Blame. At least two things seem confused together under this term. Sometimes when I blame X for doing A, say for breaking the vase, it is a question simply or mainly of my disapproval of A, breaking the vase, which unquestionably X did: but sometimes it is, rather, a question simply or mainly of how far I think X responsible for A, which unquestionably was bad. Hence if somebody says he blames me for something, I may answer by giving a *justification,* so that he will cease to disapprove of what I did, or else by giving an *excuse,* so that **he** will cease to hold me, at least entirely and in every way, responsible for doing it.

men have found worth drawing, and the connexions they have found worth marking, in the lifetimes of many generations: these surely are likely to be more numerous, more sound, since they have stood up to the long test of the survival of the fittest, and more subtle, at least in all ordinary and reasonably practical matters, than any that you or I are likely to think up in our arm-chairs of an after-noon—the most favoured alternative method.

In view of the prevalence of the slogan "ordinary language," and of such names as "linguistic" or "analytic" philosophy or "the analysis of language," one thing needs specially emphasizing to counter misunderstandings. When we examine what we should say when, what words we should use in what situations, we are looking again not *merely* at words (or "meanings," whatever they may be) but also at the realities we use the words to talk about: we are using a sharpened awareness of words to sharpen our perception of, though not as the final arbiter of, the phenomena. For this reason I think it might be better to use, for this way of doing philosophy, some less misleading name than those given above—for instance, "linguistic phenomenology," only that is rather a mouthful.

Using, then, such a method, it is plainly preferable to investigate a field where ordinary language is rich and subtle, as it is in the pressingly practical matter of Excuses, but certainly is not in the matter, say, of Time. At the same time we should prefer a field which is not too much trodden into bogs or tracks by traditional philosophy, for in that case even "ordinary" language will often have become infected with the jargon of extinct theories, and our own prejudices too, as the upholders or imbibers of theoretical views, will be too readily, and often insensibly, engaged. Here too, Excuses form an admirable topic; we can discuss at least clumsiness, or absence of mind, or inconsiderateness, even spon-taneousness, without remembering what Kant thought, and so progress by degrees even to discussing deliberation without for once remembering Aristotle or self-control without Plato. Granted that our subject is, as already claimed for it, neighbouring, analogous, or germane in some way to some notorious centre of philosophical trouble, then, with these two further requirements satisfied, we should be certain of what we are after: a good site for *field work* in philosophy. Here at last we should be able to unfreeze, to loosen up and get going on agreeing about discoveries, however small, and on agreeing about how to reach agreement.[3] How much it is to be wished that similar field work will soon be undertaken in, say, aesthetics; if only we could forget for a while about the beautiful and get down instead to the dainty and the dumpy.

There are, I know, or are supposed to be, snags in "linguistic" philosophy, which those not very familiar with it find, sometimes not without glee or relief, daunting. But with snags, as with nettles, the thing to do is to grasp them—and to climb above them. I will mention two in particular, over which the study of excuses may help to encourage us. The first is the snag of Loose (or Divergent or Alternative) Usage; and the second the crux of the Last Word. Do we all say the same, and only the same, things in the same situations? Don't usages

---

[3] All of which was seen and claimed by Socrates, when he first betook himself to the way of Words.

differ? And, Why should what we all ordinarily say be the only or the best or final way of putting it? Why should it even be true?

Well, people's usages do vary, and we do talk loosely, and we do say different things apparently indifferently. But first, not nearly as much as one would think. When we come down to cases, it transpires in the very great majority that what we had thought was our wanting to say different things of and in *the same* situation was really not so—we had simply imagined the situation *slightly* differently: which is all too easy to do, because of course no situation (and we are dealing with *imagined* situations) is ever "completely" described. The more we imagine the situation in detail, with a background of story—and it is worth employing the most idiosyncratic or, sometimes, boring means to stimulate and to discipline our wretched imaginations—the less we find we disagree about what we should say. Nevertheless, *sometimes* we do ultimately disagree: sometimes we must allow a usage to be, though appalling, yet actual; sometimes we should genuinely use either or both of two different descriptions. But why should this daunt us? All that is happening is entirely explicable. If our usages disagree, then you use "X" where I use "Y," or more probably (and more intriguingly) your conceptual system is different from mine, though very likely it is at least equally consistent and serviceable: in short, we can find *why* we disagree—you choose to classify in one way, I in another. If the usage is loose, we can understand the temptation that leads to it, and the distinctions that it blurs: if there are "alternative" descriptions, then the situation can be described or can be "structured" in two ways, or perhaps it is one where, for current purposes, the two alternatives come down to the same. A disagreement as to what we should say is not to be shied off, but to be pounced upon: for the explanation of it can hardly fail to be illuminating. If we light on an electron that rotates the wrong way, that is a discovery, a portent to be followed up, not a reason for chucking physics: and by the same token, a genuinely loose or eccentric talker is a rare specimen to be prized.

As practice in learning to handle this bogey, in learning the essential *rubrics,* we could scarcely hope for a more promising exercise than the study of excuses. Here, surely, is just the sort of situation where people will say "almost anything," because they are so flurried, or so anxious to get off. "It was a mistake," "It was an accident"—how readily these can *appear* indifferent, and even be used together. Yet, a story or two, and everybody will not merely agree that they are completely different, but even discover for himself what the difference is and what each means.[4]

---

[4] You have a donkey, so have I, and they graze in the same field. The day comes when I conceive a dislike for mine. I go to shoot it, draw a bead on it, fire: the brute falls in its tracks. I inspect the victim, and find to my horror that it is *your* donkey. I appear on your doorstep with the remains and say—what? "I say, old sport, I'm awfully sorry, &c., I've shot your donkey *by accident*"? Or "*by mistake*"? Then again, I go to shoot my donkey as before, draw a bead on it, fire—but as I do so, the beasts move, and to my horror yours falls. Again the scene on the doorstep—what do I say? "By mistake"? Or "by accident"?

Then, for the Last Word. Certainly ordinary language has no claim to be the last word, if there is such a thing. It embodies, indeed, something better than the metaphysics of the Stone Age, namely, as was said, the inherited experience and acumen of many generations of men. But then, that acumen has been concentrated primarily upon the practical business of life. If a distinction works well for practical purposes in ordinary life (no mean feat, for even ordinary life is full of hard cases), then there is sure to be something in it, it will not mark nothing: yet this is likely enough to be not the best way of arranging things if our interests are more extensive or intellectual than the ordinary. And again, that experience has been derived only from the sources available to ordinary men throughout most of civilized history: it has not been fed from the resources of the microscope and its successors. And it must be added too, that superstition and error and fantasy of all kinds do become incorporated in ordinary language and even sometimes stand up to the survival test (only, when they do, why should we not detect it?). Certainly, then, ordinary language is *not* the last word: in principle it can everywhere be supplemented and improved upon and superseded. Only remember, it *is* the *first* word.[5]

For this problem too the field of Excuses is a fruitful one. Here is matter both contentious and practically important for everybody, so that ordinary language is on its toes: yet also, on its back it has long had a bigger flea to bite it, in the shape of the Law, and both again have lately attracted the attentions of yet another, and at least a healthily growing, flea, in the shape of psychology. In the law a constant stream of actual cases, more novel and more tortuous than the mere imagination could contrive, are brought up *for decision*—that is, formulae for docketing them must somehow be found. Hence it is necessary first to be careful with, but also to be brutal with, to torture, to fake and to override, ordinary language: we cannot here evade or forget the whole affair. (In ordinary life we dismiss the puzzles that crop up about time, but we cannot do that indefinitely in physics.) Psychology likewise produces novel cases, but it also produces new methods for bringing phenomena under observation and study: moreover, unlike the law, it has an unbiased interest in the totality of them and is unpressed for decision. Hence its own special and constant need to supplement, to revise and to supersede the classifications of both ordinary life and the law. We have, then, ample material for practice in learning to handle the bogey of the Last Word, however it should be handled.

Suppose, then, that we set out to investigate excuses, what are the methods and resources initially available? Our object is to imagine the varieties of situation in which we make excuses, and to examine the expressions used in making them. If we have a lively imagination, together perhaps with an ample experience of dereliction, we shall go far, only we need system: I do not know how many of you keep a list of the kinds of fool you make of yourselves. It is advisable to use systematic aids, of which there would appear to be three at least. I list them here in order of availability to the layman.

First we may use the dictionary—quite a concise one will do, but the use

---

[5] And forget, for once and for a while, that other curious question "Is it true?" May we?

must be *thorough*. Two methods suggest themselves, both a little tedious, but repaying. One is to read the book through, listing all the words that seem relevant; this does not take as long as many suppose. The other is to start with a widish selection of obviously relevant terms, and to consult the dictionary under each: it will be found that, in the explanations of the various meanings of each, a surprising number of other terms occur, which are germane though of course not often synonymous. We then look up each of *these*, bringing in more for our bag from the "definitions" given in each case; and when we have continued for a little, it will generally be found that the family circle begins to close, until ultimately it is complete and we come only upon repetitions. This method has the advantage of grouping the terms into convenient clusters—but of course a good deal will depend upon the comprehensiveness of our initial selection.

Working the dictionary, it is interesting to find that a high percentage of the terms connected with excuses prove to be *adverbs*, a type of word which has not enjoyed so large a share of the philosophical limelight as the noun, substantive or adjective, and the verb: this is natural because, as was said, the tenor of so many excuses is that I did it but only *in a way*, not just flatly like that—i.e. the verb needs modifying. Besides adverbs, however, there are other words of all kinds, including numerous abstract nouns, "misconception," "accident," "purpose," and the like, and a few verbs too, which often hold key positions for the grouping of excuses into classes at a high level ("couldn't help," "didn't mean to," "didn't realize," or again "intend," and "attempt"). In connexion with the nouns another neglected class of words is prominent, namely, prepositions. Not merely does it matter considerably which preposition, often of several, is being used with a given substantive, but further the prepositions deserve study on their own account. For the question suggests itself, Why are the nouns in one group governed by "under," in another by "on," in yet another by "by" or "through" or "from" or "for" or "with," and so on? It will be disappointing if there prove to be no good reasons for such groupings.

Our second source-book will naturally be the law. This will provide us with an immense miscellany of untoward cases, and also with a useful list of recognized pleas, together with a good deal of acute analysis of both. No one who tries this resource will long be in doubt, I think, that the common law, and in particular the law of tort, is the richest storehouse; crime and contract contribute some special additions of their own, but tort is altogether more comprehensive and more flexible. But even here, and still more with so old and hardened a branch of the law as crime, much caution is needed with the arguments of counsel and the dicta or decisions of judges: acute though these are, it has always to be remembered that, in legal cases—

1. there is the overriding requirement that a decision be reached, and a relatively black or white decision—guilty or not guilty—for the plaintiff or for the defendant;

2. there is the general requirement that the charge or action and the pleadings be brought under one or another of the heads and procedures that have come in the course of history to be accepted by the Courts. These, though fairly numerous, are still few and stereotyped in comparison with the accusations and

defences of daily life. Moreover contentions of many kinds are beneath the law, as too trivial, or outside it, as too purely moral—for example, inconsiderateness;

3. there is the general requirement that we argue from and abide by precedents. The value of this in the law is unquestionable, but it can certainly lead to distortions of ordinary beliefs and expressions.

For such reasons as these, obviously closely connected and stemming from the nature and function of the law, practising lawyers and jurists are by no means so careful as they might be to give to our ordinary expressions their ordinary meanings and applications. There is special pleading and evasion, stretching and strait-jacketing, besides the invention of technical terms, or technical senses for common terms. Nevertheless, it is a perpetual and salutary surprise to discover how much is to be learned from the law; and it is to be added that if a distinction drawn is a sound one, even though not yet recognized in law, a lawyer can be relied upon to take note of it, for it may be dangerous not to—if he does not, his opponent may.

Finally, the third source-book is psychology, with which I include such studies as anthropology and animal behaviour. Here I speak with even more trepidation than about the Law. But this at least is clear, that some varieties of behaviour, some ways of acting or explanations of the doing of actions, are here noticed and classified which have not been observed or named by ordinary men and hallowed by ordinary language, though perhaps they often might have been so if they had been of more practical importance. There is real danger in contempt for the "jargon" of psychology, at least when it sets out to supplement, and at least sometimes when it sets out to supplant, the language of ordinary life.

With these sources, and with the aid of the imagination, it will go hard if we cannot arrive at the meanings of large numbers of expressions and at the understanding and classification of large numbers of "actions." Then we shall comprehend clearly much that, before, we only made use of *ad hoc*. Definition, I would add, explanatory definition, should stand high among our aims: it is not enough to show how clever we are by showing how obscure everything is. Clarity, too, I know, has been said to be not enough: but perhaps it will be time to go into that when we are within measurable distance of achieving clarity on some matter.

So much for the cackle. It remains to make a few remarks, not, I am afraid, in any very coherent order, about the types of significant result to be obtained and the more general lessons to be learned from the study of Excuses.

1. *No Modification without Aberration.* When it is stated that X did A, there is a temptation to suppose that given some, indeed perhaps *any*, expression modifying the verb we shall be entitled to insert either it or its opposite or negation in our statement: that is, we shall be entitled to ask, typically, "Did X do A Mly or not Mly?" (e.g. "Did X murder Y voluntarily or involuntarily?"), and to answer one or the other. Or as a minimum it is supposed that if X did A there must be at least *one* modifying expression that we could, justifiably and informatively, insert with the verb. In the great majority of cases of the use of the great majority of verbs ("murder" perhaps is not one of the majority) such suppositions are quite unjustified. The natural economy of language dictates that for the *standard* case covered by any normal verb—not, perhaps, a verb of omen such as "murder," but a verb like "eat" or "kick" or "croquet"—no modifying expression is required or even permissible. Only if we do the action named in some *special* way or circumstances, different from those in which such an act is naturally done (and of course both the normal and the abnormal differ according to what verb in particular is in question) is a modifying expression called for, or even in order. I sit in my chair, in the usual way—I am not in a daze or influenced by threats or the like: here, it will not do to say either that I sat in it intentionally or that I did not sit in it intentionally,[6] nor yet that I sat in it automatically or from habit or what you will. It is bedtime, I am alone, I yawn: but I do not yawn involuntarily (or voluntarily!), nor yet deliberately. To yawn in any such peculiar way is just not to just yawn.

2. Limitation of Application. Expressions modifying verbs, typically adverbs, have limited ranges of application. That is, given any adverb of excuse, such as "unwittingly" or "spontaneously" or "impulsively," it will not be found that it makes good sense to attach it to any and every verb of "action" in any and every context: indeed, it will often apply only to a comparatively narrow range of such verbs. Something in the lad's upturned face appealed to him, he threw a brick at it—"spontaneously"? The interest then is to discover why some actions can be excused in a particular way but not others, particularly perhaps the latter.[7] This will largely elucidate the meaning of the excuse, and at the same time will illuminate the characteristics typical of the group of "actions" it picks out: very often too it will throw light on some detail of the machinery of "action" in general (see 4), or on our standards of acceptable conduct (see 5). It is specially important in the case of some of the terms most favoured by philosophers or jurists to realize that at least in ordinary speech (disregarding backseepage of jargon) they are not used so universally or so dichotomistically. For example, take "voluntarily" and "involuntarily": we may join the army or make a gift voluntarily, we may hiccough or make a small gesture involuntarily, and the more we consider further actions which we might naturally be said to do in either of these ways, the more circumscribed and unlike each other do the two classes become, until we even doubt whether there is *any* verb with which both adverbs are equally in place. Perhaps there are some such; but at least sometimes when we may think we have found one it is an illusion, an apparent exception that really does prove the rule. I can perhaps "break a cup" voluntarily, *if* that is done, say, as an act of self-impoverishment: and I can perhaps break another involuntarily, *if*, say, I make an involuntary movement which breaks it. Here, plainly, the two acts described each as "breaking a cup" are really very different, and the one is similar to acts typical of the "voluntary" class, the other to acts typical of the "involuntary" class.

3. The Importance of Negations and Opposites. "Voluntarily" and "involuntarily," then, are not opposed in the obvious sort of way that they are

[6] Caveat or hedge: of course we can say "I did *not* sit in it 'intentionally' " as a way simply of repudiating the suggestion that I sat in it intentionally.

[7] For we are sometimes not so good at observing what we *can't* say as what we can, yet the first is pretty regularly the more revealing.

made to be in philosophy or jurisprudence. The "opposite," or rather "opposites," of "voluntarily" might be "under constraint" of some sort, duress or obligation or influence: [8] the opposite of "involuntarily" might be "deliberately" or "on purpose" or the like. Such divergences in opposites indicate that "voluntarily" and "involuntarily," in spite of their apparent connexion, are fish from very different kettles. In general, it will pay us to take nothing for granted or as obvious about negations and opposites. It does not pay to assume that a word must have an opposite, or one opposite, whether it is a "positive" word like "wilfully" or a "negative" word like "inadvertently." Rather, we should be asking ourselves such questions as why there is no use for the adverb "advertently." For above all it will not do to assume that the "positive" word must be around to wear the trousers; commonly enough the "negative" (looking) word marks the (positive) abnormality, while the "positive" word, *if* it exists, merely serves to rule out the suggestion of that abnormality. It is natural enough, in view of what was said in (1) above, for the "positive" word not to be found at all in some cases. I do an Act A_1 (say, crush a snail) *inadvertently* if, in the course of executing by means of movements of my bodily parts some other act A_2 (say, in walking down the public path) I fail to exercise such meticulous supervision over the courses of those movements as would have been needed to ensure that they did not bring about the untoward event (here, the impact on the snail).[9] By claiming that A_1 was inadvertent we place it, where we imply it belongs, on this special level, in a class of incidental happenings which must occur in the doing of any physical act. To lift the act out of this class, we need and possess the expression "not . . . inadvertently": "advertently," if used for this purpose, would suggest that, if the act was not done inadvertently, then it must have been done noticing what I was doing, which is far from necessarily the case (e.g. if I did it absent-mindedly), or at least that there is *something* in common to the ways of doing all acts not done inadvertently, which is not the case. Again, there is no use for "advertently" at the *same* level as "inadvertently": in passing the butter I do not knock over the cream-jug, though I do (inadvertently) knock over the teacup—yet I do not by-pass the cream-jug *advertently:* for at this level, below supervision in detail, *anything* that we do is, if you like, inadvertent, though we only call it so, and indeed only call it something we have done, if there is something untoward about it.

A further point of interest in studying so-called "negative" terms is the manner of their formation. Why are the words in one group formed with *un-* or *in-*, those in another with *-less* ("aimless," "reckless," "heedless," etc.), and those

---

[8] But remember, when I sign a cheque in the normal way, I do *not* do so *either* "voluntarily" *or* "under constraint."

[9] Or analogously: I do an act A_1 (say, divulge my age, or imply you are a liar), *inadvertently* if, in the course of executing by the use of some medium of communication some other act A_2 (say, reminiscing about my war service) I fail to exercise such meticulous supervision over the choice and arrangement of the signs as would have been needed to ensure that. . . . It is interesting to note how such adverbs lead parallel lives, one in connexion with physical actions ("doing") and the other in connexion with acts of communication ("saying"), or sometimes also in connexion with acts of "thinking" ("inadvertently assumed").

in another with *mis-* ("mistake," "misconception," "misjudgement," etc.)? Why *carelessly* but *inattentively*? Perhaps care and attention, so often linked, are rather different. Here are remunerative exercises.

4. The Machinery of Action. Not merely do adverbial expressions pick out classes of actions, they also pick out the internal detail of the machinery of doing actions, or the departments into which the business of doing actions is organized. There is for example the stage at which we have actually to *carry out* some action upon which we embark—perhaps we have to make certain bodily movements or to make a speech. In the course of actually *doing* these things (getting weaving) we have to pay (some) attention to what we are doing and to take (some) care to guard against (likely) dangers: we may need to use judgement or tact: we must exercise sufficient control over our bodily parts: and so on. Inattention, carelessness, errors of judgement, tactlessness, clumsiness, all these and others are ills (with attendant excuses) which affect one specific stage in the machinery of action, the *executive* stage, the stage where we *muff* it. But there are many other departments in the business too, each of which is to be traced and mapped through its cluster of appropriate verbs and adverbs. Obviously there are departments of intelligence and planning, of decision and resolve, and so on: but I shall mention one in particular, too often overlooked, where troubles and excuses abound. It happens to us, in military life, to be in receipt of excellent intelligence, to be also in self-conscious possession of excellent principles (the five golden rules for winning victories), and yet to hit upon a plan of action which leads to disaster. One way in which this can happen is through failure at the stage of *appreciation* of the situation, that is at the stage where we are required to cast our excellent intelligence into such a form, under such heads and with such weights attached, that our equally excellent principles can be brought to bear on it properly, in a way to yield the right answer.[10] So too in real, or rather civilian, life, in moral or practical affairs, we can know the facts and yet look at them mistakenly or perversely, or not fully realize or appreciate something, or even be under a total misconception. Many expressions of excuse indicate failure at this particularly tricky stage: even thoughtlessness, inconsiderateness, lack of imagination, are perhaps less matters of failure in intelligence or planning than might be supposed, and more matters of failure to appreciate the situation. A course of E. M. Forster and we see things differently: yet perhaps we know no more and are no cleverer.

5. Standards of the Unacceptable. It is characteristic of excuses to be "unacceptable": given, I suppose, almost any excuse, there will be cases of such a kind or of such gravity that "we will not accept" it. It is interesting to detect the standards and codes we thus invoke. The extent of the supervision we exercise over the execution of any act can never be quite unlimited, and usually is expected to fall within fairly definite limits ("due care and attention") in the

[10] We know all about how to do quadratics: we know all the needful facts about pipes, cisterns, hours and plumbers: yet we reach the answer "3¾ men." We have failed to cast our facts correctly into mathematical form.

case of acts of some general kind, though of course we set very different limits in different cases. We may plead that we trod on the snail inadvertently: but not on a baby—you ought to look where you are putting your great feet. Of course it *was* (*really*), if you like, inadvertence: but that word constitutes a plea, which is not going to be allowed, because of standards. And if you try it on, you will be subscribing to such dreadful standards that your last state will be worse than your first. Or again, we set different standards, and will accept different excuses, in the case of acts which are rule-governed, like spelling, and which we are expected absolutely to get right, from those we set and accept for less stereotyped actions: a wrong spelling may be a slip, but hardly an accident, a winged beater may be an accident, but hardly a slip.

6. Combination, Dissociation, and Complication.

A belief in opposites and dichotomies encourages, among other things, a blindness to the combinations and dissociations of adverbs that are possible, even to such obvious facts as that we can act at once on impulse and intentionally, or that we can do an action intentionally yet for all that not deliberately, still less on purpose. We walk along the cliff, and I feel a sudden impulse to push you over, which I promptly do: I acted on impulse, yet I certainly intended to push you over, and may even have devised a little ruse to achieve it: yet even then I did not act deliberately, for I did not (stop to) ask myself whether to do it or not.

It is worth bearing in mind, too, the general rule that we must not expect to find simple labels for complicated cases. If a mistake results in an accident, it will not do to ask whether "it" was an accident or a mistake, or to demand some briefer description of "it." Here the natural economy of language operates: if the words already available for simple cases suffice in combination to describe a complicated case, there will be need for special reasons before a special new word is invented for the complication. Besides, however well-equipped our language, it can never be forearmed against all possible cases that may arise and call for description: fact is richer than diction.

7. Regina versus Finney.

Often the complexity and difficulty of a case is considerable. I will quote the case of *Regina* v. *Finney*.[11]

Shrewsbury Assizes.   1874   12 Cox 625
Prisoner was indicted for the manslaughter of Thomas Watkins.
The Prisoner was an attendant at a lunatic asylum. Being in charge of a lunatic, who was bathing, he turned on hot water into the bath, and thereby scalded him to death. The facts appeared to be truly set forth in the statement of the prisoner made before the committing magistrate, as follows: "I had bathed Watkins, and had loosed the bath out. *I intended putting in a clean bath,* and asked Watkins if he would get out. At this

---

[11] A somewhat distressing favourite in the class that Hart used to conduct with me in the years soon after the war. The italics are mine.

time *my attention was drawn* to the next bath by the new attendant, who was asking me a question; and *my attention was taken from the bath* where Watkins was. I put my hand down to turn water on in the bath where Thomas Watkins was. *I did not intend to turn the hot water, and I made a mistake in the tap. I did not know what I had done until* I heard Thomas Watkins shout out; and *I did not find my mistake out till* I saw the steam from the water. You cannot get water in this bath when they are drawing water at the other bath; but at other times it shoots out like a water gun when the other baths are not in use. . . ."

(It was proved that the lunatic had such possession of his faculties as would enable him to understand what was said to him, and to get out of the bath.)

A. Young (for Prisoner). The death *resulted from accident.* There was no such *culpable negligence* on the part of the prisoner as will support this indictment. A *culpable mistake,* or some degree of *culpable negligence,* causing death, will not support a charge of manslaughter; unless the *negligence* be so gross as to be *reckless.* (*R. v. Noakes.*)

Lush, J. To render a person liable for *neglect of duty* there must be such a degree of culpability as to amount to *gross negligence* on his part. If you accept the prisoner's own statement, you find no such amount of *negligence* as would come within this definition. It is not every little *trip or mistake* that will make a man so liable. It was the duty of the attendant not to let hot water into the bath while the patient was therein. According to the prisoner's own account, *he did not believe that* he was letting the hot water in while the deceased remained there. The lunatic was, we have heard, a man capable of getting out by himself and of understanding what was said to him. He was told to get out. A new attendant who had come on this day, was at an adjoining bath and he *took off the prisoner's attention.* Now, if the prisoner, knowing that the man was in the bath, had turned on the tap, and turned on the hot instead of the cold water, I should have said there was gross negligence; for he ought to have looked to see. But from his own account he had told the deceased to get out, and *thought he had got out.* If you think that indicates gross *carelessness,* then you should find the prisoner guilty of manslaughter. But if you think it *inadvertence* not amounting to culpability—i.e., what is properly termed an *accident*—then the prisoner is not liable.

Verdict, Not guilty

In this case there are two morals that I will point:

(i) Both counsel and judge make very free use of a large number of terms of excuse, using several as though they were, and even stating them to be, indifferent or equivalent when they are not, and presenting as alternatives those that are not.

(ii) It is constantly difficult to be sure *what* act it is that counsel or judge is suggesting might be qualified by what expression of excuse.

The learned judge's concluding direction is a paradigm of these faults.[12] Finney, by contrast, stands out as an evident master of the Queen's English. He is explicit as to each of his acts and states, mental and physical: he uses different, and the correct, adverbs in connexion with each: and he makes no attempt to boil down.

8. *Small Distinctions, and Big Too.* It should go without saying that terms of excuse are not equivalent, and that it matters which we use: we need to distinguish inadvertence not merely from (save the mark) such things as mistake and accident, but from such nearer neighbours as, say, aberration and absence of mind. By imagining cases with vividness and fullness we should be able to decide in which precise terms to describe, say, Miss Plimsoll's action in writing, so carefully, "DAIRY" on her fine new book: we should be able to distinguish between sheer, mere, pure, and simple mistake or inadvertence. Yet unfortunately, at least when in the grip of thought, we fail not merely at these stiffer hurdles. We equate even—I have seen it done—"inadvertently" with "automatically": as though to say I trod on your toe inadvertently means to say I trod on it automatically. Or we collapse succumbing to temptation into losing control of ourselves—a bad patch, this, for telescoping.[13]

All this is not so much a *lesson* from the study of excuses as the very object of it.

9. *The Exact Phrase and Its Place in the Sentence.* It is not enough, either, to attend simply to the "key" word: notice must also be taken of the full and exact form of the expression used. In considering mistakes, we have to consider seriatim "by mistake," "owing to a mistake," "mistakenly," "it was a mistake to," "to make a mistake in or over or about," "to be mistaken about," and so on: in considering purpose, we have to consider "on," "with the," "for the," etc., besides "purposeful," "purposeless," and the like. These varying ex-

---

[12] Not but what he probably manages to convey his meaning somehow or other. Judges seem to acquire a knack of conveying meaning, and even carrying conviction, through the use of a pithy Anglo-Saxon which sometimes has literally no meaning at all. Wishing to distinguish the case of shooting at a post in the belief that it was an enemy, as *not* an "attempt," from the case of picking an empty pocket in the belief that money was in it, which *is* an "attempt," the judge explains that in shooting at the post "the man is never on the thing at all."

[13] Plato, I suppose, and after him Aristotle, fastened this confusion upon us, as bad in its day and way as the later, grotesque, confusion of moral weakness with weakness of will. I am very partial to ice cream, and a bombe is served divided into segments corresponding one to one with the persons at High Table: I am tempted to help myself to two segments and do so, thus succumbing to temptation and even conceivably (but why necessarily?) going against my principles. But do I lose control of myself? Do I raven, do I snatch the morsels from the dish and wolf them down, impervious to the consternation of my colleagues? Not a bit of it. We often succumb to temptation with calm and even with finesse.

pressions may function quite differently—and usually do, or why should we burden ourselves with more than one of them?

Care must be taken too to observe the precise position of an adverbial expression in the sentence. This should of course indicate what verb it is being used to modify: but more than that, the position can also affect the *sense* of the expression, i.e. the way in which it modifies that verb. Compare, for example:

a_1 He clumsily trod on the snail.
a_2 Clumsily he trod on the snail.
b_1 He trod clumsily on the snail.
b_2 He trod on the snail clumsily.

Here, in a_1 and a_2 we describe his treading on the creature at all as a piece of clumsiness, incidental, we imply, to his performance of some other action: but with b_1 and b_2 to tread on it is, very likely, his aim or policy, what we criticize in his execution of the feat.[14] Many adverbs, though far from all (not, for example, "purposely") are used in these two typically different ways.

10. *The Style of Performance*. With some adverbs the distinction between the two senses referred to in the last paragraph is carried a stage further. "He ate his soup deliberately" may mean, like "He deliberately ate his soup," that his eating his soup was a deliberate act, one perhaps that he thought would annoy somebody, as it would more commonly if he deliberately ate *my* soup, and which he decided to do: but it will often mean that he went through the performance of eating his soup in a noteworthy manner or *style*—pause after each mouthful, careful choice of point of entry for the spoon, sucking of moustaches, and so on. That is, it will mean that he ate *with* deliberation rather than *after* deliberation. The style of the performance, slow and unhurried, is understandably called "deliberate" because each movement *has the typical look* of a deliberate act: but it is scarcely being said that the making of each motion is a deliberate act or that he is "literally" deliberating. This case, then, is more extreme than that of "clumsily," which does in both uses describe literally a manner of performing.

It is worth watching out for this secondary use when scrutinizing any particular adverbial expression: when it definitely does not exist, the reason is worth inquiring into. Sometimes it is very hard to be sure whether it does exist or does not: it does, one would think, with "carelessly," it does not with "inadvertently," but does it or does it not with "absent-mindedly" or "aimlessly"? In some cases a word akin to but distinct from the primary adverb is used for this special role of describing a style of performance: we use "purposefully" in this way, but never "purposely."

[14] As a matter of fact, most of these examples *can* be understood the other way, especially if we allow ourselves inflexions of the voice, or commas, or contexts. a_2 might be a poetic inversion for b_2: b_1, perhaps with commas round the "clumsily," might be used for a_1: and so on. Still, the two senses are clearly enough distinguishable.

11. *What Modifies What?*   The Judge in *Regina* v. *Finney* does not make clear what event is being excused in what way. "If you think that indicates gross carelessness, then. . . . But if you think it inadvertence not amounting to culpability—i.e. what is properly called an accident—then. . . ." Apparently he means that Finney may have *turned on the hot tap* inadvertently: [15] does he mean also that the tap may have been turned accidentally, or rather that *Watkins may have been scalded* and killed accidentally? And was the carelessness in turning the tap or in thinking Watkins had got out? Many disputes as to what excuse we should properly use arise because we will not trouble to state explicitly *what* is being excused.

To do so is all the more vital because it is in principle always open to us, along various lines, to describe or refer to "what I did" in so many different ways. This is altogether too large a theme to elaborate here. Apart from the more general and obvious problems of the use of "tendentious" descriptive terms, there are many special problems in the particular case of "actions." Should we say, are we saying, that he took her money, or that he robbed her? That he knocked a ball into a hole, or that he sank a putt? That he said "Done," or that he accepted an offer? How far, that is, are motives, intentions and conventions to be part of the description of actions? And more especially here, what is *an* or *one* or *the* action? For we can generally split up what might be named as one action in several distinct ways, into different *stretches* or *phases* or *stages*. Stages have already been mentioned: we can dismantle the machinery of the act, and describe (and excuse) separately the intelligence, the appreciation, the planning, the decision, the execution and so forth. Phases are rather different: we can say that he painted a picture or fought a campaign, or else we can say that first he laid on this stroke of paint and then that, first he fought this action and then that. Stretches are different again: a single term descriptive of what he did may be made to cover either a smaller or a larger stretch of events, those excluded by the narrower description being then called "consequences" or "results" or "effects" or the like of his act. So here we can describe Finney's act *either* as turning on the hot tap, which he did by mistake, with the result that Watkins was scalded, *or* as scalding Watkins, which he did *not* do by mistake.

It is very evident that the problems of excuses and those of the different descriptions of actions are throughout bound up with each other.

[15] What Finney says is different: he says he "made a mistake in the tap." This is the basic use of "mistake," where we simply, and not necessarily accountably, take the wrong one. Finney here attempts to account for his mistake, by saying that his attention was distracted. But suppose the order is "Right turn" and I turn left: no doubt the sergeant will insinuate that my attention was distracted, or that I cannot distinguish my right from my left—but it was not and I can, this was a simple, pure mistake. As often happens. Neither I nor the sergeant will suggest that there was any accident, or any inadvertence either. If Finney had turned the hot tap inadvertently, then it would have been knocked, say, in reaching for the cold tap: a different story.

12. *Trailing Clouds of Etymology.* It is these considerations that bring us up so forcibly against some of the most difficult words in the whole story of Excuses, such words as "result," "effect," and "consequence," or again as "intention," "purpose," and "motive." I will mention two points of method which are, experience has convinced me, indispensable aids at these levels.

One is that a word never—well, hardly ever—shakes off its etymology and its formation. In spite of all changes in and extensions of and additions to its meanings, and indeed rather pervading and governing these, there will still persist the old idea. In an *accident* something befalls: by *mistake* you take the wrong one: in *error* you stray: when you act *deliberately* you act after weighing it up (*not* after thinking out ways and means). It is worth asking ourselves whether we know the etymology of "result" or of "spontaneously," and worth remembering that "unwillingly" and "involuntarily" come from very different sources.

And the second point is connected with this. Going back into the history of a word, very often into Latin, we come back pretty commonly to pictures or *models* of how things happen or are done. These models may be fairly sophisticated and recent, as is perhaps the case with "motive" or "impulse," but one of the commonest and most primitive types of model is one which is apt to baffle us through its very naturalness and simplicity. We take *some very simple action*, like shoving a stone, usually as done by and viewed by oneself, and use *this*, with the features distinguishable in it, as our model in terms of which to talk about other actions and events: and we continue to do so, scarcely realizing it, even when these other actions are pretty remote and perhaps much more interesting to us in their own right than the acts originally used in constructing the model ever were, and even when the model is really distorting the facts rather than helping us to observe them. In primitive cases we may get to see clearly the differences between, say, "results," "effects," and "consequences," and yet discover that these differences are no longer clear, and the terms themselves no longer of real service to us, in the more complicated cases where we had been bandying them about most freely. A model must be recognized for what it is. "Causing," I suppose, was a notion taken from a man's own experience of doing simple actions, and by primitive man every event was construed in terms of this model: every event has a cause, that is, every event is an action done by somebody—if not by a man, then by a quasi-man, a spirit. When, later, events which are *not* actions are realized to be such, we still say that they must be "caused," and the word snares us: we are struggling to ascribe to it a new, unanthropomorphic meaning, yet constantly, in searching for its analysis, we unearth and incorporate the lineaments of the ancient model. As happened even to Hume, and consequently to Kant. Examining such a word historically, we may well find that it has been extended to cases that have by now too tenuous a relation to the model case, that it is a source of confusion and superstition.

There is too another danger in words that invoke models, half-forgotten or not. It must be remembered that there is no necessity whatsoever that the various models used in creating our vocabulary, primitive or recent, should all fit together neatly as parts into one single, total model or scheme of, for instance, the doing of actions. It is possible, and indeed highly likely, that our assortment of models will include some, or many, that are overlapping, conflicting, or more generally simply *disparate*.[16]

13. In spite of the wide and acute observation of the phenomena of action embodied in ordinary speech, modern scientists have been able, it seems to me, to reveal its inadequacy at numerous points, if only because they have had access to more comprehensive data and have studied them with more catholic and dispassionate interest than the ordinary man, or even the lawyer, has had occasion to do. I will conclude with two examples.

Observation of animal behaviour shows that regularly, when an animal is embarked on some recognizable pattern of behaviour but meets in the course of it with an insuperable obstacle, it will betake itself to energetic, but quite unrelated, activity of some wild kind, such as standing on its head. This phenomenon is called "displacement behaviour" and is well identifiable. If now, in the light of this, we look back at ordinary human life, we see that displacement behaviour bulks quite large in it: yet we have apparently no word, or at least no clear and simple word, for it. If, when thwarted, we stand on our heads or wiggle our toes, then we are not exactly *just* standing on our heads, don't you know, in the ordinary way, yet is there any convenient adverbial expression we can insert to do the trick? "In desperation"?

Take, again, "compulsive" behaviour, however exactly psychologists define it, compulsive washing for example. There are of course hints in ordinary speech that we do things in this way—"just feel I have to," "shouldn't feel comfortable unless I did," and the like: but there is no adverbial expression satisfactorily pre-empted for it, as "compulsively" is. This is understandable enough, since compulsive behaviour, like displacement behaviour, is not in general going to be of great practical importance.

Here I leave and commend the subject to you.

[16] This is by way of a general warning in philosophy. It seems to be too readily assumed that if we can only discover the true meanings of each of a cluster of key terms, usually historic terms, that we use in some particular field (as, for example, "right," "good" and the rest in morals), then it must without question transpire that each will fit into place in some single, interlocking, consistent, conceptual scheme. Not only is there no reason to assume this, but all historical probability is against it, especially in the case of a language derived from such various civilizations as ours is. We may cheerfully use, and with weight, terms which are not so much head-on incompatible as simply disparate, which just do not fit in or even on. Just as we cheerfully subscribe to, or have the grace to be torn between, simply disparate ideals—why *must* there be a conceivable amalgam, the Good Life for Man?

BIOGRAPHIES

J. L. AUSTIN Selections 17 and 18

The international reputation of J. L. Austin has been growing steadily since his death. Like Wittgenstein, he published little during his lifetime. The bold originality of his views, however, exerted an enormous influence on his students and colleagues, exciting much interest in the "Austinian" way of philosophizing. Since his death, two sets of lectures and his collected papers have been published.

John Langshaw Austin was born in 1911. He was educated at Shrewsbury School and Oxford. He was a Fellow and Tutor at Oxford from 1935. In 1952 he became White's Professor of Moral Philosophy at Oxford and a Fellow of Corpus Christi College. He died in 1960.

A. J. AYER Selection 7

A(lfred) J(ules) Ayer is undoubtedly the most famous British Logical Positivist. Although he has modified many of his views considerably since his earliest writings, he is still identified by many with the Positivist movement.

Ayer was born in 1910 and educated at Eton and Oxford. During the Second World War he served in the Welsh Guards and in Military Intelligence. He was a Fellow and Dean of Wadham College in 1945–1946. He became Grote Professor at the University of London in 1946 and remained there until 1959, when he became Wykeham Professor of Logic at Oxford. He was a fellow of the British Academy. He died in 1989.

C. D. BROAD Selection 6

C(harlie) D(unbar) Broad was born in 1887. He was educated at Dulwich College and Cambridge. In 1911 he became a Fellow at Cambridge; he was appointed Knightsbridge Professor of Moral Philosophy at Cambridge in 1933, and retired in 1953. From 1920 onward he maintained a deep interest in psychical research. He died in 1971.

Broad's engaging autobiography in *The Philosophy of C. D. Broad*, P. A. Schilpp (ed.), may be consulted for additional information about his life.

RUDOLF CARNAP   Selection 8

Rudolf Carnap is, with the possible exception of Schlick, the most famous of the Logical Positivists. Born in Germany in 1891, he received a degree from Jena and then taught from 1926 to 1935 in Vienna and Prague. One of the early members of the Vienna Circle, he came to the United States in 1935, as the group was disintegrating. He taught for many years at the University of Chicago. In 1954 he accepted the Chair in Philosophy at the University of California at Los Angeles. He died in 1970.

More information concerning his life and intellectual development may be found in *The Philosophy of Rudolf Carnap*, P. A. Schilpp (ed.).

H. P. GRICE   Selection 16

Paul Grice was a fellow and tutor at St. John's College, Oxford, from 1938 to 1967. In 1967 he was appointed Professor of Philosophy at the University of California at Berkeley. He died in Berkeley in 1988 at age 75.

CARL HEMPEL   Selection 10

Carl Gustaf Hempel was born in Germany in 1905. He studied at the Universities of Vienna, Göttingen, and Heidelberg before receiving his Ph.D. in Berlin in 1934. He came to the United States in 1937 and has taught at the University of Chicago, City College of New York, Queens College, and Yale University. He became a naturalized citizen in 1944. Since 1956 he has been Stuart Professor at Princeton University.

G. E. MOORE   Selections 4, 5, and 11

G(eorge) E(dward) Moore has often been characterized as the paradigm contemporary example of a "philosopher's philosopher." Unlike Russell, Moore restricted his writings to philosophy. As a consequent he is not as well known outside philosophical circles as Russell, although within them he has exerted an equally powerful influence.

Born in London in 1873, Moore entered Cambridge in 1892. His first studies and interests were in classics, but he soon was influenced by Russell to enter philosophy. He published his first book, the influential *Principia Ethica*, in 1903. He began teaching at Cambridge in 1911, became a Fellow in 1925, and died at Cambridge in 1958. He was for many years the editor of *Mind*. In 1951 he was awarded the Order of Merit.

The best source available for details of Moore's life and personality is his charming autobiography to be found in *The Philosophy of G. E. Moore*, P. A. Schilpp (ed.).

W. V. QUINE Selection 9

W(illard) V(an) O(rman) Quine was born in Akron, Ohio, in 1908. He was educated at Oberlin College and Harvard University, where he received a Ph.D. in 1932. He became an Instructor at Harvard in 1936. During the Second World War he was a Lieutenant Commander in the USNR. He has been Edgar Pierce Professor at Harvard since 1955. He is a member of the American Academy of Arts and Sciences.

BERTRAND RUSSELL Selections 1, 2, 3, and 15

One of the giants of twentieth-century philosophy, Bertrand Russell was deeply involved in important issues of his time. Toward the end of his life, his defense of nuclear disarmament made him a figure of international controversy.

Born in 1872, Russell studied at Cambridge University, where he also later lectured for a time. His earliest intellectual interests were divided between mathematics and philosophy. He was dismissed from Cambridge in 1916 for pacifist activities and in 1918 was jailed by the government. He wrote prodigiously and published an enormous number of books and articles in fields ranging from philosophy to fiction. His wide spectrum of interests was equalled only by his courageous insistence on expressing his opinion, no matter how unpopular. He died in 1970.

A complete bibliography of Russell's writings up to 1960 may be found in *The Philosophy of Bertrand Russell*, P. A. Schilpp (ed.). For additional details on Russell's life see his "My Mental Development" in the same volume.

GILBERT RYLE Selection 13

Gilbert Ryle was born in 1900 and was educated at Brighton College and Queen's College, Oxford, where he was a Classical Scholar. In 1924 he began teaching at Oxford, where he later became the Waynflete Professor of Metaphysical Philosophy. In 1948 he succeded G. E. Moore as editor of *Mind*. He died in 1976.

P. F. STRAWSON Selections 14 and 16

P(eter) F(rederick) Strawson is one of the best-known of the younger Oxford philosophers. Born in 1919, he was educated at St. John's College, Oxford, and has been a Fellow of University College since 1948. During the Second World War he served as an officer in the British Army. He has visited the United States as a visiting professor several times. He is a Fellow of the British Academy.

JOHN WISDOM Selection 12

Arthur John Terence Dibben Wisdom was born in 1904 and educated at the Aldeburgh Lodge School and at Cambridge University, where he received his M.A. in 1934. He became Professor of Philosophy at Cambridge in 1952.

LUDWIG WITTGENSTEIN   Selection 11 by G. E. Moore

Ludwig Wittgenstein was born in Vienna in 1889. He studied engineering in Germany until 1908, when he went to the University of Manchester in England to continue his studies. His interest in mathematics brought him into contact with Bertrand Russell, who influenced him to enter philosophy. During the First World War, Wittgenstein served with the Austrian army as a volunteer. He taught school for several years in Austria after the war. In 1929 he was persuaded to return to England and philosophy. He was associated with Cambridge University from 1929 until his retirement in 1947. He died at Cambridge in 1951.

For a fuller account of his life and personality see Norman Malcolm's *Ludwig Wittgenstein: A Memoir* (Oxford, New York: Oxford University Press, 1958).

SELECTED BIBLIOGRAPHY

This Bibliography contains only a selection from the extensive body of works which has appeared in and on analytic philosophy during roughly the last half-century. Although it is not intended to be exhaustive, with few exceptions, the works cited below are ones which have been widely read and discussed by philosophers.

More extensive bibliographies of writings in analytic philosophy may be found, among other places, in the following sources:

Passmore, J.: *A Hundred Years of Philosophy* (1957).
Edwards, P., and Pap, A. (eds.): *A Modern Introduction to Philosophy* (1958).
Ayer, A. J. (ed.): *Logical Positivism* (1959).

The bibliography has been divided into three parts. The first part cites a number of books which are primarily introductory or expository in nature and which are recommended for further independent study. The second part lists most of the more important anthologies which have appeared on analytic philosophy. The third part consists of a selective sampling of major writings in analytic philosophy.

PART I   Recommended for Independent Reading
Ayer, A. J., et al.: *The Revolution in Philosophy* (London: Macmillan, 1956).
Carnap, R.: *Philosophy and Logical Syntax* (London: Kegan Paul, 1935).
Copleston, F.: *Contemporary Philosophy* (London: Burns and Oates, 1956).
Hospers, J.: *An Introduction to Philosophical Analysis* (Englewood Cliffs, N.J.: Prentice-Hall, 1953).
Kraft, V.: *The Vienna Circle* (New York: Philosophical Library, 1953).
Nagel, E., and Newman, J. R.: *Gödel's Proof* (New York: New York University Press, 1958).
Pap, A.: *Elements of Analytic Philosophy* (New York: Macmillan, 1949).
Passmore, J.: *A Hundred Years of Philosophy* (London: Duckworth, 1957).
Pears, D. F. (ed.): *The Nature of Metaphysics* (London: Macmillan, 1957).

Russell, B.: *The Problems of Philosophy* (London: Home University Library, 1912).

Toulmin, S.: *Philosophy of Science* (London: Hutchinson, 1953).

Urmson, J. O.: *Philosophical Analysis* (Oxford: Clarendon Press, 1956).

Warnock, G. J.: *English Philosophy since 1900* (London: Oxford University Press, 1958).

Warnock, M.: *Ethics since 1900* (Fair Lawn, N.J.: Oxford University Press, 1960).

PART II   Anthologies and Collections

Ayer, A. J. (ed.): *Logical Positivism* (New York: The Free Press of Glencoe, 1959).

Black, M. (ed).: *Philosophical Analysis* (Ithaca, N.Y.: Cornell University Press, 1950).

Caton, C. (ed.): *Philosophy and Ordinary Language* (Urbana, Ill.: University of Illinois Press, 1963).

Chappel, V. (ed.): *The Philosophy of Mind* (Englewood Cliffs, N.J.: Prentice-Hall, 1962).

———: *Ordinary Language* (Englewood Cliffs, N.J.: Prentice-Hall, 1964).

Edwards, P., and Pap, A. (eds.): *A Modern Introduction to Philosophy* (New York: The Free Press of Glencoe, 1958).

Feigl, H., and Brodbeck, M. (eds.): *Readings in the Philosophy of Science* (New York: Appleton-Century-Crofts, 1953).

——— and Scriven, M. (eds.): *The Foundations of Science and the Concepts of Psychology and Psychoanalysis* (Minneapolis: University of Minnesota Press, 1956).

——— and ———: *Minnesota Studies in the Philosophy of Science*, 3 vols. (Minneapolis: University of Minnesota Press, 1956, 1958, 1962).

——— and Sellars, W. (eds.): *Readings in Philosophical Analysis* (New York: Appleton-Century-Crofts, 1949).

Flew, A. (ed.): *Logic and Language,* 2 series (Oxford: Blackwell, 1951, 1953).

———: *Essays in Conceptual Analysis* (London: Macmillan, 1956).

Lewis, H. D. (ed.): *Contemporary British Philosophy,* third series (London: Allen and Unwin, 1956).

Linsky, L. (ed.): *Semantics and the Philosophy of Language* (Urbana, Ill.: University of Illinois Press, 1952).

Macdonald, M. (ed.): *Philosophy and Analysis* (Oxford: Blackwell, 1954).

Mace, C. A. (ed.): *British Philosophy in the Mid-century* (London: Allen and Unwin; New York: Macmillan, 1957).

Muirhead, J. H. (ed.): *Contemporary British Philosophy,* first and second series (London: Allen and Unwin, 1924, 1925).

Schilpp, P. A. (ed.): *The Philosophy of G. E. Moore* (Evanston: Northwestern University, 1942, 1952).

———: *Albert Einstein: Philosopher-Scientist* (Evanston: The Library of Living Philosophers, 1949).

———: *The Philosophy of Bertrand Russell* (Evanston: Northwestern University, 1954; New York: Evanston; London: Harper and Row, 1963).

————: *The Philosophy of C. D. Broad* (New York: Tudor Publishing Company, 1959).

————: *The Philosophy of Rudolf Carnap* (Chicago, Ill.: Open Court, in preparation).

Sellars, W., and Hospers, J. (eds.): *Readings in Ethical Theory* (New York: Appleton-Century-Crofts, 1952).

Wiener, P. (ed.): *Readings in Philosophy of Science* (New York: Charles Scribner's Sons, 1953).

PART III   Some Important Books

Anscombe, G. E. M.: *Intention* (Oxford: Blackwell, 1957).

Austin, J. L.: *Philosophical Papers* (Oxford: Clarendon Press, 1961).

————: *Sense and Sensibilia* (Oxford: Clarendon Press, 1962).

————: *How to Do Things with Words* (Oxford: Clarendon Press, 1962).

Ayer, A. J.: *Language, Truth and Logic* (London: Gollancz, 1936).

————: *The Foundations of Empirical Knowledge* (London: Macmillan, 1940).

————: *Thinking and Meaning* (London: H. K. Lewis, 1947).

————: *Philosophical Essays* (London: Macmillan, 1954).

————: *The Problem of Knowledge* (London: Macmillan and Penguin Books, 1958).

————: *The Concept of a Person* (New York: St Martin's Press, 1963).

Barnes, W. H. F.: *The Philosophical Predicament* (London: A. and C. Black, 1950).

Bergmann, G.: *The Metaphysics of Logical Positivism* (London: Longmans, Green & Co., Ltd., 1954).

————: *Philosophy of Science* (Madison, Wis.: University of Wisconsin Press, 1957).

————: *Meaning and Existence* (Madison, Wis.: University of Wisconsin Press, 1960).

————: *Logic and Reality* (Madison, Wis.: University of Wisconsin Press, 1964).

Black, M.: *The Nature of Mathematics* (London: Kegan Paul; New York: Harcourt, Brace & World, Inc., 1933).

————: *Language and Philosophy* (Ithaca, N.Y.: Cornell University Press, 1949).

————: *Problems of Analysis* (London: Routledge and Kegan Paul, 1954).

————: *Models and Metaphors* (Ithaca, N.Y.: Cornell University Press, 1962).

Blanshard, B.: *Reason and Analysis* (London: Allen and Unwin, 1962).

Braithwaite, R. B.: *Scientific Explanation* (London: Cambridge University Press, 1953).

Bridgeman, P. W.: *The Logic of Modern Physics* (New York: Macmillan, 1927).

————: *The Nature of Physical Theory* (Princeton, N.J.: Princeton University Press, 1936).

Broad, C. D.: *Perception, Physics and Reality* (London: Cambridge University Press, 1914).

————: *Scientific Thought* (London: Kegan Paul, 1923).

————: *The Mind and Its Place in Nature* (London: Kegan Paul, 1925).

Broad, C. D.: *Five Types of Ethical Theory* (London: Kegan Paul, 1930).
———: *An Examination of McTaggart's Philosophy*, 2 vols. (London: Cambridge University Press, 1933, 1938).
———: *Religion, Philosophy and Psychical Research* (New York: Harcourt, Brace & World, Inc., 1953).
———: *Human Personality and the Possibility of Its Survival* (Berkeley, Calif.: University of California Press, 1955).
———: *Lectures on Psychical Research* (London: Routledge and Kegan Paul, 1962).
Carnap, R.: *Der Logische Augbau der Welt* (Berlin: Weltkreis-Verlag, 1928).
———: *Philosophy and Logical Syntax* (London: Kegan Paul, 1935).
———: *Logical Syntax of Language* (London: Kegan Paul; New York: Harcourt, Brace & World, Inc., 1937).
———: *Foundations of Logic and Mathematics* (Chicago: University of Chicago Press, 1939).
———: *Introduction to Semantics* (Cambridge, Mass.: Harvard University Press, 1942).
———: *Meaning and Necessity* (Chicago: University of Chicago Press, 1947).
———: *Logical Foundations of Probability* (Chicago: University of Chicago Press, 1950).
———: *The Continuum of Inductive Methods* (Chicago: University of Chicago Press, 1952).
———: *Introduction to Symbolic Logic* (New York: Dover, 1958).
Chisholm, R.: *Perceiving: A Philosophical Study* (Ithaca, N.Y.: Cornell University Press, 1957).
Ducasse: C. J.: *Nature, Mind and Death* (LaSalle, Ill.: Open Court, 1951).
Frank, P.: *Philosophy of Science* (Englewood Cliffs, N.J.: Prentice-Hall, 1957).
Gellner, E.: *Words and Things* (London: Gollancz, 1959).
Goodman, N.: *The Structure of Appearance* (Cambridge, Mass.: Harvard University Press, 1951).
———: *Fact, Fiction and Forecast* (London: Athlone Press, 1954; Cambridge, Mass.: Harvard University Press, 1955).
Hampshire, S.: *Thought and Action* (London: Chatto and Windus, 1959).
Hare, R.: *The Language of Morals* (Oxford: Clarendon Press, 1952).
———: *Freedom and Reason* (Oxford: Clarendon Press, 1963).
Hempel, C.: *Fundamentals of Concept Formation in Empirical Science* (Chicago: University of Chicago Press, 1952).
Joad, C. E. M.: *A Critique of Logical Positivism* (London: Gollancz; Chicago: University of Chicago Press, 1950).
Jorgenson, J.: *A Treatise of Formal Logic* (London: Oxford University Press, 1931).
———: *The Development of Logical Empiricism* (Chicago: University of Chicago Press, 1951).
Kneale, W.: *Probability and Induction* (Oxford: Clarendon Press, 1949).
Körner, S.: *Conceptual Thinking: A Logical Enquiry* (London: Cambridge University Press, 1955).
Lazerowitz, M.: *The Structure of Metaphysics* (London: Routledge and Kegan Paul, 1955).

Lean, M.: *Sense Perception and Matter* (London: Routledge and Kegan Paul, 1953).

Lewis, C. I.: *Mind and the World-order* (New York: Charles Scribner's Sons, 1929).

———: *An Analysis of Knowledge and Valuation* (LaSalle, Ill.: Open Court, 1946).

Malcolm, M.: *Dreaming* (London: Routledge and Kegan Paul; New York: Humanities Press, 1959).

———: *Knowledge and Certainty* (Englewood Cliffs, N.J.: Prentice-Hall, 1963).

Moore, G. E.: *Principia Ethica* (London: Cambridge University Press, 1903).

———: *Ethics* (London: Home University Library, 1912).

———: *Philosophical Studies* (London: Routledge and Kegan Paul, 1922; Reprinted for U.S.A. sale by Littlefield: Adams and Co., 1959).

———: *Some Main Problems of Philosophy* (London: Allen and Unwin, 1953; New York: Collier Books, 1962).

———: *Philosophical Papers* (London: Allen and Unwin; New York: Macmillan, 1959).

———: *Commonplace Book: 1919–1953* (London: Allen and Unwin; New York: Macmillan, 1962).

Morris, C.: *Foundations of the Theory of Signs* (Chicago: University of Chicago Press, 1938).

———: *Signs, Language and Behavior* (Englewood Cliffs, N.J.: Prentice-Hall, 1946).

Nagel, E.: *Principles of the Theory of Probability* (Chicago: University of Chicago Press, 1939).

———: *Sovereign Reason* (New York: The Free Press of Glencoe, 1954).

———: *Logic without Metaphysics* (New York: The Free Press of Glencoe, 1956).

———: *The Structure of Sciences* (New York: Harcourt, Brace & World, Inc., 1961).

Neurath, O. et al.: *Encyclopedia and Unified Science* (Chicago: University of Chicago Press, 1938). (Volume 1, Number 1 of The International Encyclopedia of Unified Science.)

———: *Foundations of the Social Sciences* (Chicago: University of Chicago Press, 1944).

Nicod, J.: *Foundations of Geometry and Induction* (London: Kegan Paul, 1930).

Ogden, C. K., and I. A. Richards: *The Meaning of Meaning* (London: Kegan Paul, 1923).

Pap, A.: *The A Priori in Physical Theory* (New York: King's Crown Press, 1946).

———: *Semantics and Necessary Truth* (New Haven, Conn.: Yale University Press, 1958).

Passmore, J.: *Philosophical Reasoning* (New York: Charles Scribner's Sons, 1961).

Popper, K.: *The Open Society and Its Enemies* (London: Routledge, 1945).

Popper, K.: *The Logic of Scientific Discovery*, English translation (London: Hutchinson, 1959).

Price, H. H.: *Perception* (London: Methuen, 1932).

———: *Truth and Corrigibility* (London: Oxford University Press, 1936).

———: *Hume's Theory of the External World* (Oxford: Clarendon Press, 1940).

———: *Thinking and Representation* (Annual Lecture: British Academy Proceedings, 1946).

———: *Thinking and Experience* (London: Hutchinson; Cambridge, Mass.: Harvard University Press, 1953).

Quine, W. V. O.: *A System of Logistic* (Cambridge, Mass.: Harvard University Press, 1934).

———: *Mathematical Logic* (New York: W. W. Norton and Co., 1940).

———: *From a Logical Point of View* (Cambridge, Mass.: Harvard University Press, 1953).

———: *Word and Object* (Cambridge, Mass.: The M.I.T. Press, 1960).

———: *Set Theory and Its Logic* (Cambridge, Mass.: Harvard University Press, 1963).

Ramsey, F. P.: *The Foundations of Mathematics and Other Logical Essays* (London: Kegan Paul, 1931).

Reichenbach, H.: *Experience and Prediction* (Chicago: University of Chicago Press, 1938).

———: *Philosophical Foundations of Quantum Mechanics* (Berkeley and Los Angeles, Calif.: University of California Press, 1944).

———: *The Rise of Scientific Philosophy* (Berkeley and Los Angeles, Calif.: University of California Press, 1951).

———: *The Philosophy of Space and Time*, English translation (New York: Dover Publications, Inc. 1958).

Robinson, R: *Definition* (Oxford: Clarendon Press, 1950).

Russell, B.: *A Critical Exposition of the Philosophy of Leibniz* (London: Cambridge University Press, 1900).

———: *The Principles of Mathematics* (London: Cambridge University Press, 1903).

———: *Philosophical Essays* (London and New York: Longmans, Green & Co., 1910).

———: *Our Knowledge of the External World* (London: Allen and Unwin; Chicago, Ill., and London: Open Court, 1914).

———: *Mysticism and Logic* (New York: Longmans, Green & Co., 1918).

———: *Introduction to Mathematical Philosophy* (London: Allen and Unwin, 1919).

———: *The Analysis of Mind* (London: Allen and Unwin; New York: Macmillan, 1921).

———: *The Analysis of Matter* (London: Kegan Paul, 1927).

———: *An Inquiry into Meaning and Truth* (New York: W. W. Norton and Co.; London: Allen and Unwin, 1940).

———: *Human Knowledge: Its Scope and Limits* (London: Allen and Unwin; New York: Simon and Schuster, 1948).

Russell, B.: *Logic and Knowledge* (R. C. Marsh, ed.) (London: Allen and Unwin, 1956).

——: *My Philosophical Development* (London: Allen and Unwin, 1959).

Ryle, G.: *Philosophical Arguments* (London: Oxford University Press, 1945).

——: *The Concept of Mind* (London: Hutchinson, 1949).

——: *Dilemmas* (London: Cambridge University Press, 1954).

——: *A Rational Animal* (London: Athlone Press, 1962).

Schlick, M.: *Space and Time in Contemporary Physics* (Oxford: Clarendon Press, 1920).

——: *Problems of Ethics* (Englewood Cliffs, N.J.: Prentice-Hall, 1939).

——: *Philosophy of Nature* (New York: Philosophical Library, 1949).

Singer, M. G.: *Generalization in Ethics* (New York: Knopf, 1961).

Stebbings, S.: *Logical Positivism and Analysis* (Annual Lecture: British Academy Proceedings, 1933).

——: *Philosophy and the Physicists* (London: Methuen, 1937).

Stevenson, C. L.: *Ethics and Language* (New Haven, Conn.: Yale University Press, 1945).

Strawson, P. F.: *Introduction to Logical Theory* (London: Methuen, 1952).

——: *Individuals* (London: Methuen, 1959).

Tarski, A.: *Introduction to Logic and to the Methodology of the Deductive Sciences* (London: Oxford University Press, 1941).

——: *Logic, Semantics and Meta-mathematics* (Oxford: Clarendon Press, 1956).

Toulmin, S.: *The Place of Reason in Ethics* (London: Cambridge University Press, 1950).

——: *The Uses of Argument* (London: Cambridge University Press, 1958).

von Mises, R.: *Positivism: A study in Human Understanding* (Cambridge, Mass.: Harvard University Press, 1951).

von Wright, G. H.: *A Treatise on Induction and Probability* (London: Routledge and Kegan Paul, 1951).

——: *The Logical Problem of Induction,* second revised edition (Oxford: Blackwell, 1957).

Waismann, F.: *Introduction to Mathematical Thinking* (London: Hafner, 1951).

Weinberg, J. R.: *An Examination of Logical Positivism* (London: Kegan Paul; New York: Harcourt, Brace & World, Inc., 1936).

White, M.: *Toward Reunion in Philosophy* (Cambridge, Mass.: Harvard University Press, 1956).

Williams, D.: *The Ground of Induction* (Cambridge, Mass.: Harvard University Press, 1947).

Wisdom, J.: *Interpretation and Analysis* (London: Kegan Paul, 1931).

——: *Problems of Mind and Matter* (London: Cambridge University Press, 1934).

——: *Other Minds* (Oxford: Blackwell, 1952).

——: *Philosophy and Psycho-analysis* (Oxford: Blackwell, 1953).

Wisdom, J. O.: *Foundations of Inference in Natural Science* (London: Methuen, 1952).

Wittgenstein, L.: *Tractatus Logico-Philosophicus* (translated by C. K. Ogden) (London: Kegan Paul, 1922). Translated by D. F. Pears and B. F. McGuinness (New York: Humanities Press, 1961).

————: *Philosophical Investigations* (Oxford: Blackwell; New York: Macmillan, 1953).

————: *Remarks on the Foundations of Mathematics* (Oxford: Blackwell, 1956).

————: *The Blue and Brown Books* (Oxford: Blackwell; New York: Harper, 1958).

————: *Notebooks, 1914–1916* (Oxford: Blackwell, 1961).

Woodger, J. H.: *The Axiomatic Method in Biology* (London: Cambridge University Press, 1937).

Ziff, P.: *Semantic Analysis* (Ithaca, N.Y.: Cornell University Press, 1960).

INDEX